S0-BFO-416

DISCARD

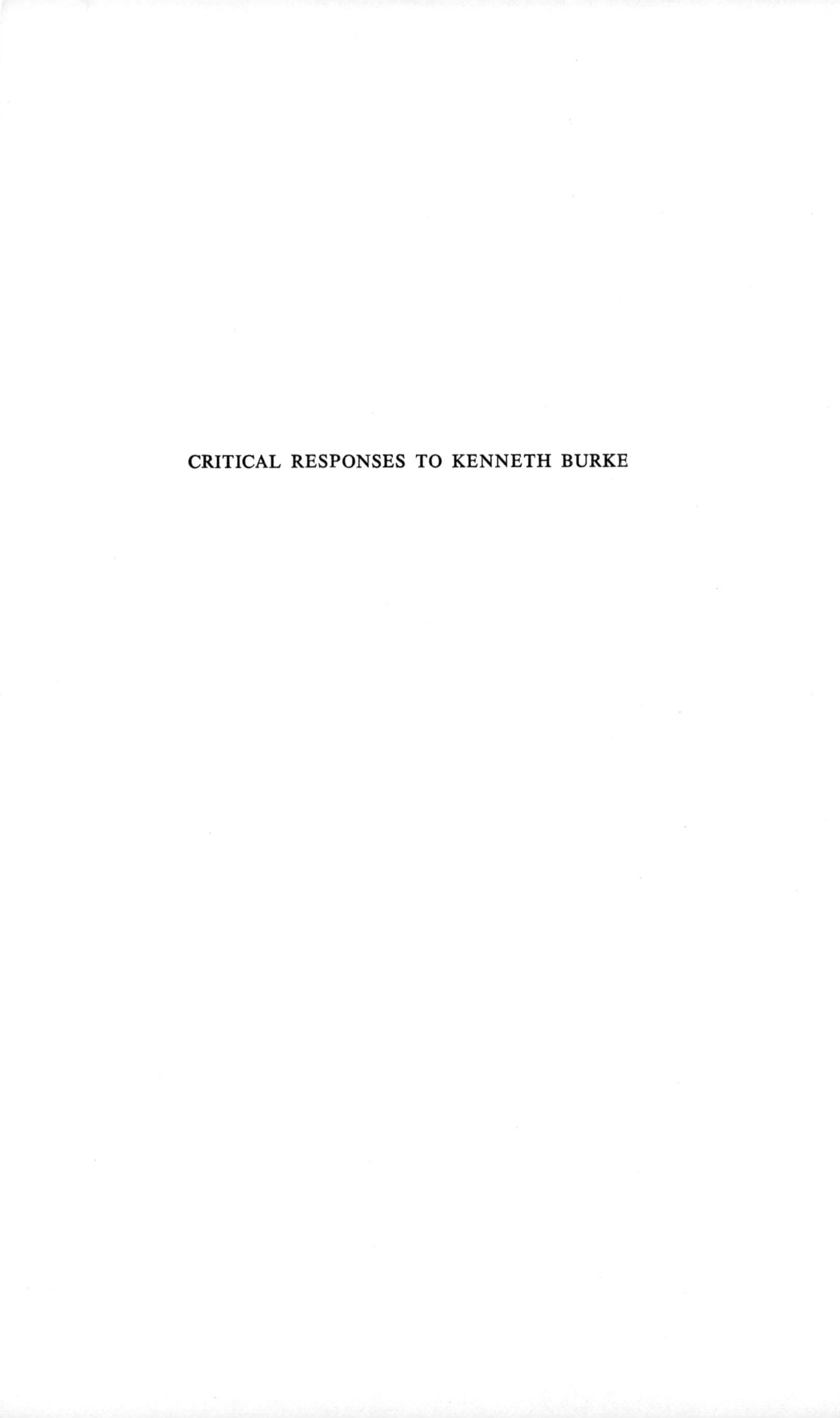

CRITICAL RESPONSES TO KENNETH BURKE

CRITICAL RESPONSES TO

KENNETH BURKE

1924 1966

William H. Rueckert, editor

UNIVERSITY OF MINNESOTA PRESS MINNEAPOLIS

Printed in the United States of America at the North Central Publishing Company, St. Paul. *Library of Congress Catalog Card Number: 71-75973.* Published in Great Britain, India, and Pakistan by the Oxford University Press, London, Bombay, and Karachi, and in Canada by the Copp Clark Publishing Co. Limited, Toronto

for Libbie Burke

PROLOGOS · EPILOGOS

◇◇◇

Preface

THE purpose of this volume is to honor Kenneth Burke for his achievements as an American man of letters by assembling a chronological selection of significant critical responses to his work from 1924 through 1966. In good Burkeian fashion, I have included pieces that are both for and against the man and his works so that the dialectical polarities might be clear and the record accurate. No secret disrespect is intended by this inclusion of the opposition; so tough and skillful a veteran of the dialectical wars as Burke could not feel honored by the exclusion of his adversaries. He knows, as we all do, that the verbal wars will go on and that the peace he makes with history will be the start of another man's fight with it (and him).

This collection is not (in spite of its size) anything like a complete record of the critical responses to Burke through the terminal date indicated above. There are now so many published (and unpublished) responses of various kinds, and Burke's influence is so widespread and devious, that only a selective account can be rendered. What I have tried to create here is a full and representative selection of reviews, essay-reviews, essays, and parts of books which chronicle the responses to Burke as poet, short story writer, editor, critic, novelist, reviewer, theorist, verbal analyst, social commentator, system builder, and man of his time — in short, as that rare and vanishing breed in American life, the all-purpose intellectual and man of letters who, lacking our mid-century habit of caution, will undertake almost anything. With very few exceptions, the responses collected here are part of the published record; and with no exceptions, they all bear directly upon the nature of Burke's work and his achievements over the last forty and more years.

Although it was a temptation to do so — because Burke is a great and powerful person whose life is intrinsically interesting — I did not include any purely biographical essays or undertake the writing of one myself. The life will have to be rendered elsewhere, by some other person: This collection honors the man by discussing his works. As Burke would surely want it, the emphasis is upon his life as a symbol-using animal and upon the extraordinary uses to which he has put the nearly five million words he has published (how many he has actually written and delivered publicly as lectures is something else again).

I have arranged the selections by date of original publication because the collection is meant to provide a historical record; and I have reproduced each piece exactly as it was published, save for the correction of obvious errors, typographical or otherwise. The volume was not put together as a "sampler"; which means that the pieces really ought to be read in chronological order and that the notes which follow each selection have been written to be read in this way. Like any collection which includes works by so many different activated minds, covers so long and vital a period of time, and is devoted to so interesting a figure as Burke, the chronology of responses takes on an integrity of its own which is both of and beyond Burke. Out of the dialogue with Burke there develops a larger dialectic which is central to and continuous in the intellectual and moral life of America in our time. The whole collection has a kind of double structure and inwardness which is partially lost if the chronology is abandoned and the lesson of time ignored.

For someone like Burke, whom everyone feels compelled to mention in charged, often very witty language, it is possible to collect a great many choice terms, wonderfully turned sentences, and stunning short passages of abuse and praise. For example: John Simon, in trying to locate the great American critic, said it could not be Kenneth Burke because he does not write English; someone once spoke of Burke's "peeping thomism"; and Charles Feidelson, Jr., pointed out (in a footnote!) that Burke had reduced logic to literature. One could select and arrange the best of these passages in a timeless and spaceless order to create a stream of commentary from the collective and conscious critical mind. But the whole idea of doing this, even though it has obvious and interesting uses, seemed somehow suspect because it is part of a larger principle which is absolutely suspect: snippit collecting, as a colleague once labeled it. The reduction of critical responses to isolated insights — even brilliant ones — could not possibly render the way in which a thinker of Burke's range and complexity has been received because it tends to strip the responses to mere verbal effects. Bound to the principle of organic wholeness by a lifetime of training and reading (including Burke), I have violated the integrity of a selection only when I could not do otherwise and it was clearly better to have something rather than nothing. Where I have had to cut a piece, I have always tried to present a continuous and coherent section rather than bits and pieces of a whole essay strung together on ellipsis marks. Sometimes it was necessary — for reasons which I need not enumerate here — to omit selections I wanted to use. I regret these omissions, especially Isaac Rosenfeld's essay-review of *A Grammar of Motives*; but I think that even without the missing pieces the volume has a sufficiency and is accurate as a record of the critical responses to Burke.

Each of the selections is followed by a note and each note has a number of functions: I have identified the contributors in a way that seemed useful to an understanding of what they had to say about Burke; I have commented on the content of each selection and, as I went forward, I have tried to write a cumulative running commentary on the responses to Burke. Where it seemed appropriate, I have used a specific note as an occasion for commentary on the critical, historical, and other kinds of contexts which have a bearing upon Burke's reception. I have tried to avoid polemics, but I have freely judged many of the selections in accordance with the way in which I read Burke and see him in relation to our time. My positions are clear in context and do not need to be previewed here. The notes, as as organic part of the structure of the book, were undertaken in lieu of a long introduction at the suggestion of Allen Tate. The idea of writing all these notes *after* I thought I had finished the editing job was not — at first — a particularly welcome one. Now that I am done, I want to thank Mr. Tate for proposing that I do them; and the late Marcia Strout (that patient and exemplary editor at the University of Minnesota Press) for encouraging me (which was the same as allowing me) to be as informal as I was.

I have had a good deal of help from a great many different people and institutions during the rather long period it took me to do this collection (my talents as an editor being something less than extraordinary). To all of the following my gratitude: the Research Board of the University of Illinois, Urbana, for financing all of the Xeroxing I needed done (and to all of the Xerox machines and their human helpers, without which and whom I could not have done this collection at all); the staffs of the University of Illinois and University of Rochester libraries for their help; the Summer Fellowship Committee, College of Arts and Science, University of Rochester, for a grant which enabled me to do some of the work on this collection; the typing pool, University of Rochester, for typing and other kinds of help; all of the people who responded to my many pleas for charity in the matter of fees; Lee Griffin, Bernard Brock, Armin Paul Frank, Mechthild Frank, and Denis Donoghue who wrote all or parts of their selections especially for this volume; Armin Paul Frank and Mechthild Frank for many different kinds of help, including support during sagging periods; Lee Griffin for sending his marvelous essay at exactly the right time; Kenneth Burke for answering whatever questions I put to him about various contributors; Libbie Burke and Kenneth Burke for unspecifiable help; Hugh Duncan, who should have done the book in the first place rather than suggest that I do it; and my wife Betty, for the usual and always correct reasons.

I would also like to acknowledge the assistance I got from the two editors at the University of Minnesota Press with whom I have worked: Marcia Strout, who died, to my great regret, while the volume was in process; and Jeanne Sinnen, who took the job over after Miss Strout's death. No mere acknowledgment could possibly indicate how, between them, these two helped me to get this book put together and published.

The passage by Robert Martin Adams which begins this collection is the concluding paragraph in his review of the second edition of Burke's novel, *Towards a Better Life*. Yes, he is right; and may the rest of the selections so honor Burke.

WILLIAM RUECKERT

Rochester, N.Y.
April 1968

z *Table of Contents*

CRITICAL RESPONSES TO KENNETH BURKE

A WORD HERE, *in celebration of Mr. Kenneth Burke. He has been among us so long in so many capacities, and to such pervasive effect, that it is easy to lose track of how much the literary temper of our time owes to him. In whatever genre, his work has always carried the strong stamp of his individuality; he has never dissolved it into pap for the multitude or codified it into tablets for quick absorption by graduate students. He has never made it with a book club; he has never seemed ashamed of being learned. The subtlety of his critical work has challenged, its perversity has provoked, its original insights have opened up immense corridors of thought. Nobody who is capable of following him at all plodges in his footsteps; he is a critic for the adventurous, you take from him what you can get, and only realize later how much that was. Our sense of how literature can work and be worked upon is immensely richer because of him.*

— ROBERT M. ADAMS

REPRINTED FROM *The New York Review of Books*, 20 OCTOBER 1966

PHOTO BY BETTY RUECKERT

◇◇

2 *Experimental*

BY Matthew Josephson

A COLLECTION of stories, executed in many manners and shifting through diverse moods and forms, composes this first book by Kenneth Burke [*The White Oxen and Other Stories*]. The opening stories are patterned brilliantly after known and respected models. Because of the skill and maturity with which Mr. Burke treats of profoundly American characters, they will have a wide appeal. The long opening work, "The White Oxen," is a piece of social realism in which the mediocre, placid and yet pathetic career of the principal character is illuminated through the symbolism of these domesticated beasts. And, similarly, "Mrs. Maecenas," a story which attracted attention when published some years ago in *The Dial*, is a piece of delicious satire, written with much spirit and wit.

However accomplished these stories within their limits may be, it seems more honest to judge Mr. Burke by what are evidently his own aims as revealed in the latter half of *The White Oxen and Other Stories*. For the book represents "a progression of method," according to the brief Author's Note, and it is really in his later experimental work that he excites me to unstinted admiration. Here a gradual departure takes place from the "realistically convincing and true to life," from the representative manner, and there is a movement toward the more rhetorical properties of prose. As against the eclectic novel, the human document, you arrive at the conception of literature as "rhetoric," as the art of discourse. Given words, given the capacity to portray with words, emotions, people, mountain ranges, storms, ideas — into what form can these things be spilt so that an inner sense of beauty is satisfied? Burke is thinking here of form in the sense of a Bach fugue rather than of a Dickens novel. He is at once revolting against "programmistic" literature, and responding to the hankering for the abstract which is well-nigh universal in modern art.

EDITOR'S NOTE: Reprinted from *The New York Herald Tribune Books*, 16 November 1924, p. 4, by permission of the author.

The later stories, then, "Mrs. Wurtelbach," "In Quest of Olympus," "Prince Llan," provide the highest form of literary entertainment. They are fantasies written in the large and vigorous mood of epics. Because Burke is not confined to, let us say, the drab souls of several oversexed Middle Westerners in a stuffy farmhouse kitchen, he is able to be romantic, heroic, cerebral or dialectical, in turn. There are pages which actually breathe the grand style. Characters, actions, situations are twisted and maneuvered with bold imagination in order to secure a certain tempo, or the shocks of succeeding transitions, and ultimately an artistic resolution of all the business. The interest in sheer literary technique, in the effect, dominates. But Mr. Burke evidently feels at home in this fantastic story medium he has invented and there is many a bold, bad outburst of prose fire.

This is not rebellion against literature. On the contrary, the writer is intensely conscious of all the traditions, the sly tricks. One passage, for instance, in "The Quest of Olympus" is highly Shakespearean. A clown in Shakespeare, according to Burke, is always an unspeakable clown, and a king always an immense and lordly king. Thus Treep, a little peasant who dies while struggling to chop down an oak, is apotheosized, and once among the gods, assumes immediately the proportions of a mountain and the tones of thunder.

It is fascinating to see these theories gaily carried out. The game is all very deliberate, of course, and the sensitive reader is only too aware at times of the author's elaborate struggles with his technique. The reader feels least impeded by technique in the story called "David Wassermann," a hilarious and vulgar satire of the American scene.

Seldom does a new writer appear with the impressive literary equipment, the resourcefulness, the presence of mind — and for that matter, the self-consciousness — of Mr. Burke. Despite Mr. Ernest Boyd's rather muddled misgivings as to the "younger generation" the pages of *The White Oxen* are alive with alternate fulfillment and promise.

You must judge Mr. Burke by other measures than those which might be applied to his contemporaries, Sinclair Lewis, Dreiser, Sherwood Anderson. He is, after all, a complex, sophisticated personality, intensely conscious, as they are in no way, of what is being done in literature elsewhere in the world, of what has been done in the past, and of what may yet be done. In his whole approach to writing he has chosen totally different methods, and "in stressing one aesthetic quality we simply lose others."

The stories in *The White Oxen* are grouped in the chronological order of their completion, and I must hasten to state that my encomium is prompted by the brilliant manner in which Mr. Burke poses the whole problem of literature in his later phase, rather than by his earlier work, which more nearly resembles that of his contemporaries.

For his continual progression, however, from one form to another Mr. Burke pays a price: the loss to the reader of a sense of conviction, since each last story disproves the foregoing one. Upon finishing the last piece of prose, even one who is prompted by the utmost sympathy for literary experiment is startled by the thought that perhaps there is only the pistol left now for the author. What, indeed, will Mr. Burke's next book be like? Will it be "formless" and unbridled like "David Wassermann," or will it be a "conventional" novel?

◇◇

MATTHEW JOSEPHSON was born in Brooklyn, New York, in 1899. He is a member of the National Institute of Arts and Letters, served as editor of such little magazines as *Broom* and *Transition,* and is the author of diverse books: *Galimathias* (poems); *Zola and His Time*; *Portrait of the Artist as American*; *The Robber Barons*; *The President Makers*; *Sidney Hillman: Statesman of American Labor*; *Edison*; and *Life among the Surrealists* – to name some of them.

This review of *The White Oxen* is among the first pieces to be published about Burke's work. Like so many of the selections which follow, it is the work of a friend and fellow man of letters. It recognizes the experimental and essentially radical nature of Burke's early (and later) endeavors in prose fiction, the essential counterthrusting characteristic of this first (and all subsequent) work, and the emphasis on rhetoric which, of course, has been lifelong with Burke. Finally, it also recognizes the search for the appropriate form which was such a powerful motive in the first period (1924–31) of Burke's development.

◇◇

2 Gulliver

BY Malcolm Cowley

THE motives for which men write have changed in emphasis, especially during the last thirty years. Once they became authors to per-

EDITOR'S NOTE: Reprinted from *The Dial,* LXXVII (1924), 520–522, by permission of the author.

petuate their dreams, record their observations and ideas, perhaps more simply out of vanity or empty purses. These reasons will always retain their force, but good writing to-day is regarded more and more as an adventure. We seek those territories of the imagination which lie across the border of the last formula. We are driven forward by a quotidian fever which Kenneth Burke likes to call "a perpetual grailism"; though perhaps a better comparison would be that of travellers, not like Columbus over real seas, but like Gulliver. A book like *The White Oxen* is a voyage of discovery, and its fifteen short stories mark the successive landings.

For this reason its unity cannot be one of attitude or method, which change continually; instead it has unity of direction. "I see these stories," Burke writes in a prefatory note, "as a gradual shifting of stress away from the realistically convincing and true to life; while there is a corresponding increase of stress upon the more rhetorical properties of letters. It is a great privilege to do this in an age when rhetoric is so universally despised." One might add that his progress is even more in the direction of a personal expression.

The volume opens with a novelette in the manner of Flaubert. The characterization is good, the construction without a flaw, but the story as a whole is almost completely anonymous. Flaubertian realism has become a commodity: any trained writer can manufacture it, and any editor, if he desires, buy it across the counter. Burke's reaction must have been something of the sort, for his next long story ("Mrs. Maecenas" appeared some years ago in *The Dial*) is written with an aim of satire which is already beyond the limits of pure realism.

If one can distinguish between the terms, it might be said that the method of the stories which follow "Mrs. Maecenas" has changed from realism to accuratism. Though events are reported with a detail which becomes increasingly exact, the aim is no longer to make an image of life; but rather, through the combination of observed facts, to create another reality corresponding to nothing outside the author's mind. The naturalism of stories like "David Wassermann" is almost a pretence. At a certain point (on page 169, to be exact; near the end of "My Dear Mrs. Wurtelbach") he tires even of this pretence; gathering his puppets, he sweeps them into the wings and declaims from the centre of the stage, in his own voice.

The voice bears some resemblance to Dean Swift's; with the same note of irony, the same bitter understatements, and even little tricks of style in common. Of more significance is their feeling of the unclean and the clean. Swift, the neatest man that ever wrote English prose; the most careful, in his conversation, never to shock the ear, was driven by pure aversion to write pages as foul as any in our literature. He was outraged by the filthiness of human motives. "I hate and detest that animal called man," he wrote to Pope.

He adds, "although I heartily love John, Peter, Thomas, and so forth." Instead Burke's hatreds are directed at these individuals of the species: such "compleat gentlemen" as are described in "Portrait of an Arrived Critic," or literary Don Juans like the Clarence Turner who serves as dubious hero for "The Death of Tragedy." Their pretensions and mean niceties drive him to extremes like those of Swift, and his moral indignation is the same. "Let us erect," he says, "a dirty little monument to these intellectuals."

The resemblance is strongest in "Mrs. Wurtelbach" and the four stories which follow. They are full of travellers, men without character, great recording eyes like Gulliver. These pilgrims wander into all four corners of the imagination. It was Yul who found a square city of grey granite, where people with grey eyes slipped in and out of the oblong holes which served as doors. Christ walked on Broadway; whereas Mr. Dougherty, the financier, was lassoed from a window by Indians in aeroplanes, and carried off to be eaten on an island in the South Seas. None of these impossible adventures seems out of place, for each of them adds a quality demanded, in its particular place, by the structure and movement of the story. This obviously is what the author meant when he referred to a progress away from the realistically convincing and toward "the more rhetorical properties of letters."

There is a stage in the career of every successful writer when he finds a medium which seems exactly suited to his equipment. Such was the fortune of Kenneth Burke in this group of later stories. His aim was to make them a sort of sophisticated lyric, and in this aim his success was complete. Still he remains unsatisfied. He casts about for other qualities: more depth, a clearer logic. Eager for new discoveries he moves on; he destroys his edifice of theory and moves on; "the Prince crashed a rock through their little house, and the three moved on across the face of the earth, across its nose, mouth, cheeks, and hair."

Prince Llan, coming at the end of the volume and described with incredible care, should be the greatest of Burke's characters; indeed he is not the least. He does interesting things, delivers speeches of a fine bluster, but he remains a shadow: somebody moving, in quest of some Olympus, from dreams into a dream. Two hundred pages or seven years before, the hero of Burke's first story, after suffering the depths of tragedy, looked up: he saw the hills beyond the river, the cloud over the last hill, and felt suddenly that his life still lay before him. The end of Prince Llan is to go wandering down corridors in a half-sleep, till having pushed open a last door with the remnant of his forces, he catches the glimpse of another corridor, another door.

It is the close not merely of Prince Llan's adventures, but of a cycle in the life of his author. Burke can write adventure stories or psychological novels; abandon fiction for poetry or metaphysics; go Dada or Gaga, but his grailism makes him incapable of going back. The virtue of *The White Oxen* is to be unique; not even its own author could write it again. Meanwhile the great lump of the country rolls on, "with Howard swiping apples out of the cellar, and a high-school sophomore pimpled with pubescent love, and elderly men dressed up to apply for jobs, and unexecuted rapes . . . half-ambitions . . . fractional insights . . . while as for Clarence Turner, his book—thank God!—had already reached its eighth edition."

◇◇

MALCOLM COWLEY was born in Belsano, Pennsylvania, in 1898. He was a long-time editor—1929–44—of *The New Republic,* has been a literary adviser to the Viking Press, a part-time academician, and, as the list below shows, an active and distinguished man of letters since the late twenties. Mr. Cowley's books include *Blue Juaniata* and *The Dry Seasons,* both collections of poems; *Exile's Return* and *The Literary Situation,* both valuable studies of literary life during Mr. Cowley's time; *The Portable Hemingway, The Portable Faulkner, The Portable Hawthorne, The Stories of F. Scott Fitzgerald, Three Novels of F. Scott Fitzgerald, Leaves of Grass: The First Edition,* and a volume of *Writers at Work: The Paris Review Interviews*—all significant editorial work, usually with modern texts, which often included important and pioneering introductions; and, most recently, *The Faulkner-Cowley File: Letters and Memories 1944–1962,* the title of which is self-explanatory.

Malcolm Cowley has been a lifelong friend of Burke's and a constant, astute commentator on his work. This selection is the first of three by him. Like Josephson and Burke, Cowley was helping to make the literary scene and wrote this review from direct experience of what was happening and, surely, with the benefit of much inside information about the stories. Like Josephson's, Cowley's emphasis is upon the experimental nature of the whole endeavor and upon Burke's drive toward his own organic form.

◇◇

2 Gulliver on the Subway

BY John Peale Bishop

HERE [in *The White Oxen*] is a collection of short tales, composed with labor and thought, and indicating between one tale and the next, as the Elizabethans did between their scenes of the English kings, a considerable lapse of time. The book does show, as the author claims in his Foreword, a "certain progression of method." An appreciable distance has been traversed between the story which opens the book, "The White Oxen," with its illusion of actuality and its rather obvious realistic symbolism, and the subtly disordered "Prince Llan," with its grey and twisted poetry, its rhetorical discussions of inanity and of things which should not be inane but are. But whatever the stage of his progress, Mr. Burke knows exactly what he is doing, what effects he is aiming at, and how he means to go about achieving them. Each of the fifteen stories has been approached as a distinct aesthetic problem; the difficulties have been consciously faced, and an appropriate manner has been found. But, for various reasons, the solution of the problem as often as not leaves us quite cold; we can approve the method and grant the correctness of applying it without in the least being excited over the skill with which it has been used.

I am prepared to admire rhetoric and to applaud anyone who will, as Mr. Burke has lately done, insist that writing is a form of activity to be cultivated for its own sake. I am also, I hope, aware of the advantages which the conscious artist has over the purely spontaneous one. But surely, once the stuff is under the fingers and in the process of being moulded, even the most scrupulous artistic conscience must allow the material to make its own demands. No one could have planned his labor with more care than Henry James; but readers of his prefaces will know how often he complains that his story before it had done had far exceeded his original conception and demanded an elaboration of which he had not dreamed when first it was outlined. And this is what one feels has never happened to Mr. Burke: the story he has written has always been exactly the story he planned. The use of the white oxen as a symbol in the tale of the boy who, still ignorant of his own likeness, goes out into the world vainly seeking to find in others qualities which only exist in his own soul is excellent — to begin with; but the symbol is insisted on until its quality is lost; Mr. Burke has

EDITOR'S NOTE: Reprinted from *The Saturday Review of Literature*, I (3 January 1925), 427.

been so determined that his trick should come off that when it finally does everybody is aware that it was only a trick.

It is when the volume is viewed as a whole, and not as fifteen disparate tales, that "The White Oxen" takes on its proper interest. For if none of these stories is quite satisfactory as a work of art, having its own existence apart from the mind of its creator, taken together they begin to assume another importance. The book has, in spite of the variety of methods employed, a curious unity – monotony, if you will. Mr. Burke has, during his performance, put on many costumes, sack-suits and the sackcloth of the ascetics, princely doublets, and sober gowns of grammarians and clerics; his hands have moved incessantly, sliding through various tricks; but his attitude from start to finish has not changed, his expression throughout is the same, icily irregular, aloof but marked by pain, intelligent, skeptical. In the end we are far more interested in the quality of the author than in anything he has done. He has recorded his sensibility without always having made use of it as an artist. He has given proof of the clarity of his mind, but in a way which is itself obscure.

It is when considered as a whole, that the book may be seen as a kind of Gulliver's Travels on the Subway. One can imagine this new Lemuel Gulliver wandering in the midst of a race of Yahoos, who have displayed a mechanical inventiveness unknown to their ancestors, who have taken over the wildest notions of the Laputans, but who have never in spite of their cunning been able to overcome their repulsive instincts or disguise the offensive odor of their bodies. One can imagine this Lemuel Burke riding daily on the uptown express at the rush hour, contemplating the crowds pressed together, their skins smelling of fatigue and cold sweat, their bodies making, as they are jerked about by the rocking of the train, movements that are in a horrible and grotesque way suggestive of love, making as they sway back and forth, pressed one to another, not the mild beast with two backs but an hundred-backed monster. Swaying with them, himself a part of their carnality, he cannot but be aware of the changes that are taking place in his own mind, which if it retains its clarity has lost all power of orderly thought. Reduced almost to incoherence, he wonders, mounting again to the air, what has happened during this journey underground to all those amazing and orderly structures which in the past the human intellect raised for its own contemplation and delight – to the dogmas of the holy Roman and apostolic church, the mysteries of the saints, the amorous pastorals of Italian poets, to the tragedy of Hamlet, Prince of Denmark. But even these ruminations on the subway stairs are tainted by the close scent of the urinals.

This new Gulliver is very far removed from the old — his peculiar misanthropy could never have been acquired except in America, his nerves could never have been rasped quite as they have been except in a mechanistic civilization. Mr. Burke's sensibility is profoundly interesting, not for its private value whatever that may be, but because it shows a state of mind and nerves which must be, in less extreme form, rather common. It is that sensibility which we like to think first made its appearance with Rousseau, since made more subtle in an hundred ways, and now under the influence of the subways brought to a point which cannot be attenuated without touching madness.

◇◇

JOHN PEALE BISHOP, born in Charles Town, West Virginia, in 1892, was a contemporary of F. Scott Fitzgerald and Edmund Wilson at Princeton and, like the other commentators thus far, was actively involved in the intellectual and literary life of the times. He wrote poems, stories, a novel, and a great many reviews and essays. With Edmund Wilson he wrote *The Undertaker's Garland* in the twenties and later (1942) edited the *American Harvest* with Allen Tate. These two friends collected and edited his poems and essays after his death in 1944.

Now, when we have so much more to work with, one recognizes this as an extraordinarily perceptive review. So true (so accurate and prophetic) a reading of a first work is rather frightening. Mr. Bishop points out that the stories have a double nature: they are rational in the extreme in the deliberately made fictional forms; and they are nonrational, or perhaps counter-rational, in an equally extreme way in the nonrealistic subject matter and in what Mr. Bishop speaks of as the persistent fecal emphasis in the book. A full-length study of Burke could be developed from these three points, especially on the dialectic of doubleness that characterizes all Burke's work in all forms.

◇◇

2 *In and About the Workshop of Kenneth Burke*

BY Gorham B. Munson

[THE first part of Mr. Munson's essay deals with Burke's book of short stories, *The White Oxen*. He attempts to render the book by analyz-

EDITOR'S NOTE: Originally published in 1926. Reprinted from *Destinations: A Canvas of American Literature since 1900* (New York: J. H. Sears and Company, 1928), pp. 146–159, by permission of the author.

ing three of the stories: "Olympians," "The Book of Yul," and "Prince Llan." The stories are used by Munson to illustrate Burke's own statement that the stories are arranged in the order of their composition and that there is in this progression a "gradual shifting of stress away from the realistically convincing and true to life" and toward "the more rhetorical properties of letters." The selection below begins after Mr. Munson has discussed the first two stories; his object is to work out the relation between the "rhetorical properties" of the last story and the theoretical stress on rhetoric in some of the essays which were later to be part of *Counter-Statement.* I have begun the selection here in order to show how Mr. Munson gets from the fiction to the criticism.]

Burke experimented with other stories written under the general esthetic – art to display art – that governed "The Book of Yul," no two of which, however, were occupied with the identical problem, and rounded off his book with a new type of design, "Prince Llan," more static than the progressions he had hitherto written and more influenced by the current conceptions of painting. I am privileged to quote from a letter written by Kenneth Burke while composing "Prince Llan":

"Here is why there is so much searching for a definition of form at the present time. Once the plot always centered around a conflict. The scene was set, the conflict began, the big moment was the drawing together of the threads. This was form. It is the form of all drama. In 'abstract' writing there is no conflict of this nature. The movement is usually a simple straight line or curving line. There is no conflict because *the plot is the hero*; and a plot either does things or does not – it cannot baffle itself, for even baffling itself is a simple plot. Thus, like Joyce, we must turn to the *Odyssey,* or some such, instead of to the tragedy (the psychological novel turned to the tragedy). A challengelike beginning, and a coda end – and in between the main thing is diversity of attack, turning here and then there. With, of course, somewhat of a splurge right before the coda. Then one must devote his time to minor organisms, trying if possible to make each paragraph a microcosm, with its own formal development. But aside from the beginning, end, and coda, there are, it seems to me just now, no other major functions. The rest are simply *relationships between the parts,* such as ending a conversation chapter with some speechless act growing out of it, or following a letter with an image, and so forth. While, of course, the letter or the conversation should have gone through some still smaller curve in themselves." (My italics.)

"Prince Llan," embellished with neat "program notes," is described by the subtitle as "An Ethical Masque in Seven Parts, Including a Prologue and a Coda," the majority of these parts being related by qualities rather than by obvious progression. I shall not go further into its design than this — for after all the approach has been defined, the key given, the story is consummately managed, and the reader has his own gifts for appreciation. However, after glancing at Burke when he is theorizing and criticizing more formally than the extract from the letter shows, I should like to return to "Prince Llan" and inquire why he refers to it as "an Ethical Masque."

Burke appears to be destined to become one of the most formidable of American critics. He has trained himself to formulate exactly and clearly. He is equipped with a sensitive ear that enables him to differentiate subtly the rhythms of his prose. His sensibility throws up images or figures when they are needed — "nosing about the teat of classicism," "just as yeast, flourishing in the fruit mash, multiplies with ebullience and fervor, until, by its own processes, it has generated sufficient alcohol to kill it." These figures invariably enliven or flush the exposition, and, as illustrations, drive vividly into the reader's mind the ideas he has stated. He is in love with ideas. And he is clever: Mencken, he says, "has demonstrated the stupidity of many a stupidity and has invariably shown that it was stupid."

By picking up erudition as he moves along, he is increasing the power of his native endowments and working toward standards of literary excellence — based on Shakespeare, Racine, Goethe, in particular — standards that he may in time be able to objectify. When he is engaged in technical analysis, he is most expert: beyond that, he suffers from the distress caused by not having achieved a comprehensive point of view. Sometimes he is absolutist, sometimes relativistic, often he is merely uncomfortable as he shifts among the classical, neo-classical and romantic attitudes toward life, always avoiding the religious viewpoint. This, I believe, arises from a personal dilemma which can be held up to view when we re-examine "Prince Llan."

But, though a comprehensive point of view has not been settled upon, Burke's esthetic theory is consistent. In his paper on "The Correspondence of Flaubert" (*The Dial,* February, 1922), he maintains brilliantly that Flaubert "was trying by the exercises of processes which were primarily intellectual to write under an esthetic whose processes were primarily intuitive." He argues that Flaubert, if he had been what he wanted *au fond* to be, namely, a thorough disciple of art for art's sake, would, if he were sowing a field in what he considered an arresting manner, have sown not seed but sand, since it was the process and not the result he was stressing. And it was precisely this bold step, which, if Burke be right, Flaubert missed, that the young American has taken in his short stories. In justification of this step or rather leap, Burke offers two essays, "The Poetic Process," (*The Guardian*, May–June, 1925) and "Psychology and Form" (*The Dial*, July, 1925).

These papers are keen, shrewd, subtle, ingenious, and complex: it is delicate work to condense them. If one may be permitted to adopt a textbook procedure and grieve for it, the essential propositions may be listed as follows:

The Function of Art: "It is right that art be called a 'waking dream.' The only difficulty with this definition . . . is that to-day we understand it to mean art as a waking dream for the artist. . . . It is, rather, the audience which dreams, while the artist oversees the conditions which determine this dream."

The Essence of Art: ". . . form would be the psychology of the audience. Or, seen from another angle, form is the creation of an appetite in the mind of the audience, and the adequate satisfying of that appetite. . . . In information, the matter is intrinsically interesting. . . . While it would, furthermore, be absurd to rule intrinsic interest out of literature. I wish simply to have it restored to its properly minor position, seen as merely one out of many possible elements of style. . . . The method most natural to the psychology of form is eloquence . . . we have made three terms synonymous: form, psychology, and eloquence. And eloquence thereby becomes the essence of art, while pity, tragedy, sweetness, humor, in short, all the emotions which we experience in life proper, as non-artists, are simply the material on which eloquence may feed. . . . Eloquence is simply the end of art, and is thus its essence."

The Poetic Process: "We can discuss the basic forms of the human mind under such concepts as *crescendo*, contrast, comparison, and so on. But to experience them emotionally, we must have them singularized into an example, an example which will be chosen by the artist from among his emotional and environmental experiences."

The Artists' Personal Process: "The artists' means are always tending to become ends in themselves. The artist begins with his emotion, he translates this emotion into a mechanism for arousing emotion in others, and thus his interest in his own emotion transcends into his interest in the treatment."

This is, of course, the purest estheticism, and estheticism, equally of course, is one aspect of romanticism. For all its discipline and order, estheticism desires the same result as romanticism: emotional unity or integration achieved at the expense of a possible harmony and synthesis with the practical and intellectual functions of man. Waking dream . . . the adequate satisfying of emotional cravings by form . . . the individuating of the psychological principles governing the human being so that they may have emotive appeal . . . the artist losing his engrossment in his original subject-matter to become engrossed in its treatment which is designed to produce a waking dream: such is the circle of Burke's thought and each segment of it, one sees, touches only the responding emotions of the audience.

Let us grant immediately that he has dealt perspicaciously with one necessity of the literary artist, but are there not two necessities? The esthete really starts with a very precarious assumption: that noble and reasonable and effective living, which depends on profound and accurate self-knowledge, is not the first value. He assumes instead that a good life is the multiplication of those satisfying emotional experiences which contact with works of art produces. In other words, he balances, or rather compensates for, the disorder, the unintelligibility, the tedium of much of his life by, as often as possible, creating or experiencing at least emotional integration in the ordered world of art. It may be, however, that the esthete, disregarding potential development as he does, is merely childishly adjusting to circumstance and environment, quite asleep to the fact that the part of a man would be the effort to master life, beginning logically with a search for methods to achieve mastery. But let these assumptions lie, the second necessity can be established without going into them.

In his criticism of Gertrude Stein (*The Dial,* April, 1923) Burke wrote: "But Milton's line has something more than Miss Stein's. The significant form is backed by subject-matter, and this backing produces a heightened emotion . . . if form is sufficient to produce an emotion, subject-matter is required to heighten it. Art, that is, is a process of individualization; form is general; subject-matter is specific." Then he accuses Miss Stein of ignoring the inherent property of words: "that quality in the literary man's medium which makes him start out with a definiteness that the other Arts do not possess. That is, if the musician plays G-sharp he has prescribed no definitions; but if the literary man writes 'boy,' he has already laid down certain demarcations." This is a crevice in Burke's theory, but it lets in more than the theory can contain.

If words have definiteness, then it is an obligation for the user of them to ensure that his meanings are definite; that is, that his words have meanings that are objective. Many words, as a matter of easily ascertainable fact, refer to nothing. (E.g., "humanity" as used by the social reformer instead of "mankind," which can have real meaning.) Many more words have at present only varying personal or subjective meanings. (E.g., will, soul, "God made Man in His Own Image," love, and so on.) The most that we can do as writers, until some means is found of giving objectivity to our experience, is to formulate as precisely as possible our *subjective* meanings, but these subjective meanings are conditioned by what we individually are. Thus, the writer's bias, temperament, defects, attitudes, preferences, dislikes, exclusions, private psychology creep into his work with almost every word he employs.

But what is more, even an esthete purposes to make his subject-matter heighten the formal effect. In his choice of subject he is limited by the range of his own experience, he is guided by its nature, and he is subject to its defects. Thus, as in the case of Burke's stories, the reader has data, perhaps unwittingly presented, for forming opinions about the author: his attitude toward women, the correctness of his characterizations, the immaturity or maturity of his emotional reactions, the quality and inclusiveness of his understanding, and a thousand more deductions from his behavior as a writer.

So, if the first necessity of the literary artist is objectivity and consciousness concerning form, the second necessity is objectivity and consciousness concerning subject-matter. If the literary artist refuses to recognize the second necessity, the result inevitably will be that, while he is designedly making some effects, he is at the same time unconsciously producing other effects which may vitiate his whole effort to conquer the reader. Consequently, Burke's endeavor to make form the major element in art is simply the endeavor to choose between two necessities, which is impossible, as mathematicians apparently know better than artists.

It is a grave mistake to lean on Aristotle alone. On the other side, there is Socrates, particularly apropos our discussion, the Socrates who speaks on composition in Plato's *Phædrus*. Taken together, they cover both the necessities presiding over literature, whether critical or creative.

To return at last to the Ethical Masque, "Prince Llan," there we discover Burke trying with some measure of desperation to observe the two necessities. For, in its highly fantastic way, this story gives a series of variations on the theme of monism, a series of disruptions by warfare among the head, the heart, and the solar plexus (intellect, emotions and instincts), and a conclusion that upholds an ingenious dualism and cites a "perfect" cycle of human activity based upon this dualism — followed, however, by the gesture of a fictitious suicide of the author at beholding his solution. There is a good deal of this story that is profound or, at least, has the potentiality of being profound, but the dualism at its close does not appear to me to require very serious treatment.

What it amounts to is a theory of balance of parts. Man, in Burke's perfect cycle, simply lives in one part after another, but always as a fragment. That is, he works on his farm, giving his instinctive demands the "right of way"; he reads his books in the evening to satisfy his intellectual curiosities; he enjoys the silhouette of the black hills at night and goes to his wife emotionally alive. This Burke calls "a dualism at one with itself, a dualism not of strife but of mutual completions, a dualism of systole and diastole." The theory, however, reckons without the psychological nature of man who does, indeed, live fragmentarily, but by the same token lives as far as he is concerned without control. And, unless there is control, how can the parts be balanced? To participate in each activity of a day's cycle as a whole man implies on the other hand control, and control means more than a dualism of balanced contestants: it means a harmony of the many regulated by the one.

But will Burke work in the directions we have been indicating? All that can be said now is that he is pulled one way by romantic estheticism and pulled another way by neo-classical yearnings, the yearning for some *consensus omnium bonorum*, some racial faith, some group of commonly accepted assumptions, upon which he might rest untroubled by skepticism. But alas! the authorities that might serve for contemporary neo-classicism do not exist today. The result for Burke is tension of a disagreeable character, for he does not want to be philosophic and he is too intelligent to remain an esthete. And, as yet, his friendship for the views of Oswald Spengler has solved nothing.

But, whatever the outcome of his present conflict, this, at least, can always be said of him: he writes an excellent prose, he has made important laboratory researches and discoveries in the art of composing fiction, and he is a fine resistant type of critic. The last is no mean function to perform in an era of new programs, and the whole is no slight achievement for one who is still under thirty.

◇◇

GORHAM B. MUNSON was born in Amityville, New York, in 1896. He has been a writer, editor, and teacher all his life and is the author of a wide range of books on American and modern literature. He was very active in the literary life of the twenties and did much to record and shape that life as an editor (of *Secession*), commentator, and friend of writers.

This essay was originally published in England in 1926, which makes Mr. Munson the first critic, and one of the few ever, to publish anything on Burke in England. It is also the first long essay on Burke to treat him as a serious new writer of fiction and criticism and to explore, as others were to do later, the sometimes strange relations between

Burke the artist and Burke the critic. Finally, it is an important and representative example of how Burke was received early on and shows how seriously his work was taken and how carefully his development was followed.

◇◇

2 *Kenneth Burke*

BY William Carlos Williams

WRITING is made of words, of nothing else. These have a contour and complexion imposed upon them by the weather, by the shapes of men's lives in places. Their combined effect is not sculptural; by their characters they are joined to produce a meaning. This is termed good writing. By success with the words the success of the composition is first realized.

Writing otherwise resolves itself into trite sentences of occasional grace, the idea becomes predominant, the craft becomes servile. Kenneth Burke is one of the few Americans who know what a success of good writing means – and some of the difficulties in the way of its achievement. His designs are difficult, possibly offensive, at times recondite.

From the shapes of men's lives imparted by the places where they have experience, good writing springs. One does not have to be uninformed, to consort with cows. One has to learn what the meaning of the local is, for universal purposes. The local is the only thing that is universal. *Vide* Juan Gris, "The only way to resemble the classics is to have no part in what we do come of them but to have it our own." The classic is the local fully realized, words marked by a place. With information, with understanding, with a knowledge of French, a knowledge of German, I do not hear Burke calling out: Good-bye New Jersey! No place is important, words.

I know Burke would like to go to Paris if he could afford it. He doesn't have to listen to the dialect of some big Swede or others in order to paste up a novel. Words will come to him just as they come to them, but of a different order. Writing.

This is rather negative in the way of praise, but in a starving coun-

EDITOR'S NOTE: Reprinted from *The Dial*, LXXXVII (1929), 6–8. A shortened version was later published in *Selected Essays* by William Carlos Williams, copyright © 1931, 1954 by William Carlos Williams. Reprinted by permission of the publisher, New Directions Publishing Corporation.

try one might as well at least talk of food. This will be at least important to American Literature, though negatively, if there will ever be an American Literature. And when there is, that will be important to French Literature, English Literature, and so finally to the world. There is no other way. Burke seems to me to be stalled in the right place. But that doesn't finish him.

For me, his life itself is a design, gives me satisfaction enough, always from the viewpoint of an interest in writing. He is one of the rarest things in America: He lives here; he is married, has a family, a house, lives directly by writing without having much sold out.

Any cricket can inherit a million, sit in a library and cook up a complicated or crotchety style. Plenty of Americans who know the importance of the word, if it is French or British, can be taught to do smooth puttying. But damned few know it and know the reward and would rather work with the basic difficulty to what end is not apparent.

Kenneth Burke (and family, very important) found a place out in the country where they *could* live. That's all.

The White Oxen is a varied study, as any book where writing is the matter, must be. American beginnings — in the sense of the work of Gertrude Stein, difficult to understand, as against, say the continuities of a De Maupassant. It is a group of short accounts, stories, more or less. They vary from true short stories to the ridiculousness of all short stories dissected out in readable pieces: writing gets the best of him, in the best of the book: "The Death of Tragedy" and "My Dear Mrs. Wurtelbach." "Then they were all gone. They had all gone ahead, leaving the log behind them, and fresh rips in the ferns growing out of the rotten leaves, Wurtelbach had avoided the cow-flops, as well as the eyes of the girls."

Americans would prefer to be soothed, to have their wronged gentilities cold creamed, their tightened muscles massaged into relaxation after the manner of the professionals, the really understanding. This *is* literature to them.

It is hard not to have time in a rich country.

The recent "Declamations" depart further from the "story" in any form and move closer to writing as a savour of words. Burke, let us say, is now avowedly lost, in a way that is to perform brilliantly. Without question the "Declamations" are his best work. To me they offer the extraordinary rarity of plain sense as an incentive to composition. It leads to the unusual satisfaction that comes of words placed to represent — blocks, as if the lies which amuse us in romances were a conscious effort to avoid touching anything solid. There is, in the

"Declamations," freedom from the effort to please, to condone, to yield to the inertia of a tide of sentences; the thought becomes the deed and stays wilfully upon the word — to have both steady against a shifting, sliding, gravitating quicksand of vulgarity.

I don't care much what he is trying to say so long as he is saying it all the time in every word.

I wish someone would start the American renaissance by publishing brochures to be sold at a low price, where writing like Burke's might be available for those who appreciate it.

◇◇

WILLIAM CARLOS WILLIAMS was born in Rutherford, New Jersey, in 1883 and died in 1963. He is best known as a poet and doctor and is now recognized as one of America's greatest modern poets and most distinguished men of letters. He wrote steadily and profusely from 1909 until his death; his more than forty books include poems, stories, novels, biographies, history, autobiography, translation, reviews, essays, letters, and plays.

Burke and Williams were neighbors (more or less) and friends from the twenties on; they exchanged many letters and wrote about each other's work. In this brief essay, here reprinted in its original form from *The Dial*, Williams comments, in his usual idiosyncratic style, on Burke from the position he worked out so brilliantly in his 1925 collection of essays, *In the American Grain*. He is one of the few ever to point out the importance of place — Burke has lived in the same place since 1922 — and family for Burke and even to suggest that the life style Burke conceived and lived might be related to his work. Always sensitive to radical American forms, Williams, like Cowley, Bishop, and Josephson, also stresses the experimental nature of Burke's early fictional work.

◇◇

2 A Defense of Eloquence

BY Granville Hicks

COUNTER-STATEMENT contains two essays on the principles of literary composition, an essay on the status of art, an essay on Flaubert,

EDITOR'S NOTE: Reprinted from *The New Republic*, LXIX (2 December 1931), 75–76, by permission of *The New Republic*, copyright © 1931, Harrison-Blaine of New Jersey, Inc.

Pater and De Gourmont, an essay on Gide and Mann, an essay called "Program," a "Lexicon Rhetoricae" and an essay on "Applications of the Terminology." The two essays first mentioned are the backbone of the book. The "Lexicon" codifies the principles laid down in these essays and draws certain corollaries from them; "The Status of Art" applies these principles in a defense of art against the attacks that have been made in the past century; "Program" indicates the social and political implications of the principles; "Applications of the Terminology" employs them to solve certain ancient dilemmas of critical discourse; and the discussions of particular writers both illustrate the principles and demonstrate their utility in literary analysis.

The writer begins, says Mr. Burke in the essay on "The Poetic Process," with a mood. This mood is a universal experience, though its pattern will depend on the relationship between the particular organism—*i.e.*, the writer—and its environment. The writer's aim is to find a symbol for this mood, a symbol being "a verbal parallel to a pattern of experience." To illustrate, Mr. Burke imagines a writer who is suffering sullenly and mutely under a feeling of inferiority until "he spontaneously generates a symbol to externalize this suffering"—a story, say, of a king and a peasant. "This means simply," he goes on, "that he has attained articulacy by linking his emotion to a technical form, and it is precisely this junction of emotion and technical form which we designate as 'the germ of a plot,' or 'an idea for a poem.'"

What he means by form Mr. Burke has already indicated in the preceding essay: "Form is the creation of an appetite in the mind of the auditor, and the adequate satisfying of that appetite." Precisely how the discovery of the symbol involves this question of form is never made quite clear; Mr. Burke merely assures us that the symbol is "a principle of logical guidance" because it indicates a relationship whose repetition "in varying details . . . makes for one aspect of technical form." Let us assume that he is right and follow him as he develops his theory. The object of any work of art is to arouse and fulfill desires, he insists, not to impart information or to act as a substitute for life. The inappropriate methods of maintaining interest are surprise and suspense; the proper method is eloquence. Eloquence is, therefore, the essence of art. A work based on eloquence may be read again and again, and each time a desire is aroused and each time fulfilled. A work based on suspense, however, will not bear a second reading. (This distinction throws some light on the question of form in Faulkner's *Sanctuary*.) The literary virtues are: eloquence, thoroughness, power and complexity (of the symbol and of the pattern underlying the symbol), manner (power without monotony) and style (complexity without diffusion).

This summary indicates, of course, merely the bare essentials of Burke's rhetoric. The first question that will occur to the reader is, doubtless, whether literary creation always goes on in this order. May not an author begin, for example, with the desire to treat certain materials and subsequently seek the best point of view – best for him, for his mood – from which to treat them? But the more important question concerns the actual value of this set of principles for critical purposes. On Burke's assumptions, one cannot criticize the author's mood, for it is a mode of a universal experience. One cannot criticize the symbol, for, as he takes pains to point out, its power is determined by factors outside the control of the artist. One cannot criticize the individuation of the symbol, the choice of details to body it forth, except with relation to the symbol itself, for their sole purpose is to give it substance. One can, then, only criticize the form, the arrangement of details. And even here one cannot criticize the desire that the artist seeks to arouse, for all desires are natural, but only the success of the artist in arousing and satisfying that appetite. In short, the only proper concern of the critic is technique.

There is much to be said for this conclusion, and Mr. Burke says it in such a way that he clarifies many related issues. The trouble with the conclusion is that it prohibits the critic from dealing with many questions that may well interest him and will almost certainly interest the reading public. Do some moods lend themselves more effectively to artistic purposes than others? Are some periods better for art than others? In the writing of the novel can eloquence be a substitute for insight into character? Or, to put the question more generally, in the novel is not individuation always the most important matter? If power and complexity are virtues, does it not follow that the writer who has a clear understanding of the needs which his symbol is to meet for his readers and an imaginative power that meets those needs on the highest level is a greater writer than one who succeeds in arousing and fulfilling, however completely, a desire that is related to no fundamental need? Can the whole question of philosophical and social attitudes be disposed of by saying that a man who utilizes one set of principles will appeal to one group and a man who utilizes another set will appeal to another group?

These are only a few of the questions that are outside the scope of Mr. Burke's critical apparatus. He is aware of them, of course; he discusses some of them, if only to try to show that they are irrelevant. But he does not deal with any of them in such a way as to clarify the treatment which other critics might make of them. His nearest approach to a discussion of this kind is in the section on hierarchies. Here he says, "In asking that literature produce one sort of effect rather than another, we should be asking that literature fit one sort of situation rather than another." This is perfectly true, and one expects him, in view of the opinions already outlined, to let the matter go at that, taking it for granted that such a request is ridiculous. But no, he goes on, rather half-heartedly, to explain that there are two general bases of critical exhortation, one a concept of an ideal situation and the other a concept of the contemporary situation. And he proceeds by discussing, and in a way defending, the latter basis. But his heart is not in it; his heart is where, if one may speak in parables, his treasure is; he remains principally concerned with eloquence.

The conclusion to which these objections point is, of course, that there can be no system of esthetics that is not based on an ethic and a philosophy. (Mr. Burke's "Program" outlines social views derived from his critical system, not social views from which his system is derived.) This theme is one which cannot be developed here, but we might consider a kind of test case. We live in a period of transition, as Burke says. People are confused in their thinking and disorganized in their manner of living; the artist cannot assume any community of ideals or of emotional habits. What are writers to do? One writer, believing that his highest aim is to arouse and satisfy an appetite, will seek a symbol that is as far removed as possible from the controversial and important issues of the day, and will sacrifice the force of his symbol and its underlying pattern, to use Burke's terminology, in order to give full sway to his eloquence. Another writer, conceiving his business to be the discovery of a symbol which will interpret a representative and important situation — and Burke admits this is a legitimate basis of appeal in the symbol — will plunge into this contemporary chaos, even though he thereby risks that clarity of outline and intensity of manner and style that arouse and satisfy the reader's desire. Which writer will the critic single out for praise? On Burke's basis, the former; on some other basis, the latter. To explain what that other basis is would require a book at least the size of Burke's; to me it would be a more interesting and a more important book.

◇◇

GRANVILLE HICKS, born in Exeter, New Hampshire, in 1901, has had a varied career, which includes teaching, editing (*The New Masses*), radio work, and acting as literary consultant and contributing editor (*The Saturday Review*). Most consistently he has been a writer and has, since 1933, published more than a dozen books on many different subjects. Among these books are *The Great Tradition, John Reed, I Like America, Small Town, Where We Came Out,* and *Part of the Truth: An Autobiography.*

The early emphasis in Burke was, first, as a fiction writer, on the creation of effects, on verbal manipulation; and second, as a critic, on the systematization and defense of the creation of effects. In both cases, the stress falls on form, on technique, on rhetoric. The value of Mr. Hicks's review, in context, is twofold: after Josephson's, Cowley's, and Bishop's, and like Munson's it connects the fiction to the criticism through rhetoric; and, somewhat ironically in view of Burke's later development in the thirties, it raises what are essentially political and social objections to what Mr. Hicks calls Burke's pure aestheticism. All of which goes to show that people can and do change and that the more they change the more they are the same. Hicks's objections — summarized in his final paragraph — were to return, through other critics, to haunt and plague Burke later. A thinker who never really liked to give up anything, Burke's habit was to carry old attitudes forward into new contexts; and it often took his critics a long time to forget the old or recognize the new. Granville Hicks was the first of many to object to Burke's lack of social and political concern because he failed to see how profoundly motivated Burke has always been by social and political problems.

◇◇

7 A New View of Rhetoric

BY Isidor Schneider

THE almost flippantly modest introduction to this book [*Counter-Statement*] should not deceive the reader. It is a work of revolutionary importance introducing a principle that brings a natural, not a dialectic, clarity into the field of esthetics. It is important (in spite of its title) as statement. What there is in it of counter-statement is of less consequence.

Mr. Burke's new principle is so sane, so sure and useful a standard for esthetic judgment that one wonders how it could have been pos-

EDITOR'S NOTE: Reprinted from *The New York Herald Tribune Books*, 13 December 1931, p. 4, by permission of the author.

sible for the many thoughtful and brilliant writers on the subject to have avoided discovering it. The fact is, of course, that the principle is implicit in the work of all sensitive critics, but has never been released in direct statement and has, therefore, never been available for direct application.

The clue to it, I believe, Mr. Burke found in I. A. Richards's experimental studies in the psychology of reader reactions. Richards, coolly exposing his students to unidentified examples of poetry and tabulating their responses, probably provided Mr. Burke with the original data for his discovery, which is announced and developed in the two remarkable essays, "Psychology and Form" and "The Poetic Process." The subsequent essays, "Lexicon Rhetoricae" and "Applications of Terminology," form a more ambitious but, to my taste, a less necessary and less palatable restatement and elaboration of the idea in the form of a new vocabulary of rhetoric.

It is extremely difficult to find the few exact words that could make an acceptable definition of the principle. Mr. Burke himself has not yet hit upon a generalizing form for it. I therefore urge my readers by no means to be content with my nutshell, but to dwell in the idea, as it requires, in the finely proportioned, logical structure which Mr. Burke has given it in these two essays.

It is, in essence, a new view of rhetoric. This word itself has become so disreputable that to call a book "rhetorical" is to condemn it offhand. It is confused with *bad* rhetoric and is conceived of as a set of professional tricks employed to cheat and confuse the reader. No other word, however, with the same content, has been supplied to take the place of "rhetoric," so that the values which it once expressed have suffered along with the depreciated term.

Mr. Burke says that rhetoric, far from being artifice, is the most natural and constant feature of literature. It is formed to the reader's desires, which it stimulates and fulfills. It is a use of the reader's emotions by a technique that knows how to arouse them, allay them, charge them and discharge them, concentrate them and scatter them by rhythm, by contrasts, by delays, by evasions; in short, by being psychologically the master of the situation. (This was thoroughly appreciated in the past. Indeed, the very admiration for these powerful effects led to their being taken out of their text and isolated in anthologies as "gems," with a consequent misunderstanding of their nature and their purposes. It brought about the conviction that writers who used rhetoric ably composed in order to be anthologised, to be broken up into unrelated passages.)

In the part of the book to which the title *Counter-Statement* may be applied, we change from the serene and broad light of discovery to the flickering lanterns of controversy. Recalling that the content of most classical literature was familiar to its audience and that the writer then obtained his effects by his unhindered play with the prepared mind, Mr. Burke makes a comparison with modern writers dealing with audiences whose minds are unprepared, who can be appealed to chiefly by the shocks of surprise, by a constant supply of new information. Realism is the literature of information; and as opposed to the psychology of form using rhetoric, the psychology of information uses the more primitive, the blunter method of plot surprises.

In this analysis Mr. Burke overlooks, I think, two important considerations. First, that the appetite for information is a strong one and its appeasement can be and is as esthetic as any other. Secondly, that the content of realism is, in its way, as familiar to modern audiences, as the content of the classics was to their audience. *Main Street* delighted its readers by being a salient presentation of the familiar, just as the classics did. It is possible, indeed it is necessary, to apply Mr. Burke's principle to the masterpieces of realism for which it will be found to work as well as for what Mr. Burke considers their antitheses.

More formidable is Mr. Burke's defense of literature against its many detractors. The material is found in the essay "The Status of Art," a profound and adroitly reasoned piece of writing.

In a certain sense writers are the most unfortunate of all the classes of artists. Unlike music and the plastic arts, their medium, letters, is shared by so many other users and turned to so many other purposes that it is constantly being confused with, and judged by, the standards of other activities functioning through the written word. As early as Plato there has been conscious propaganda against the imaginative writer; and in every civilization literature had a long and hard struggle before it freed itself from subordination to religious – therefore propaganda – functions.

The pervading prestige and authority of Pragmatism, whose influence is strong in philosophy and science and strongest in general opinion, flings before the writer a constant challenge. The psycho-analyst finds a perverted use for him as a fascinating semi-lunatic, a psychopath diverting mankind by his tragic conflicts. Historians like Spengler dismiss him by associating him with the charming exuberance of the youth of our culture, but hold that now, in its winter, he is an anachronism. Economists, especially Marxian economists, condemn him for providing mankind with an evasion of its duties. In fact, there is hardly a single self-conscious and vocal section of modern life that does not cry "fool" or "traitor" at the writer. To all of them Mr. Burke gives triumphantly clear and vigorous and conclusive answers. I have read very few things to equal his brilliant exposure of the heads-I-win-tails-you-lose argument of the psycho-analysts who diagnose a "psychosis," then explain away inconsistencies as "sublimations," or "compensations."

But Mr. Burke then proceeds to do the thing his own work has most explicitly forbidden – to provide the writer with a purpose. This is contained in the single essay which I consider a failure, the essay entitled "Program." Here he is, in effect, recommending what is little more than a gesture undignified and uncomfortable for the artist, and unserviceable. The artist, says Mr. Burke, must be an eccentric weathercock, discovering the direction of all the winds of opinion and determinedly pointing the opposite. It is true that Mr. Burke offers this as a prescription for our own times, which he views with distaste. But the writer works best when working from conviction even when it is only a temporary one. It would impose a great and certainly an unnecessary and probably paralyzing burden upon the writer to reject his convictions (as he would be obliged to if Mr. Burke's logic were followed inexorably) and spend his time wavering to and fro. I am aware that Mr. Burke means that in most cases the artist's opposition should take implicit forms. Thus, as he says, in a lyric celebrating the beauties of idling on the banks of the Mississippi a dissent from our urban civilization may be implied. But what sort of lyric would it be were the implication to become deliberate?

Aspects of Mr. Burke's ideas on the psychology of form appear in his essay, "Three Adepts of Pure Literature," dealing with Flaubert, Pater and De Gourmont; interpretations in accordance with his "Program," appear in his essay "Thomas Mann and André Gide." Both essays are first rate. They penetrate and disclose their subjects; but they do so in the special light of his theses. Thus they are, like portraits developed under special rays which screen out unwanted or unmanageable colors, only partial portraits.

There is a final word to be said on the point of style. Mr. Burke has chosen to argue rather than to persuade, and a good deal of the book has the dryness of Dialectics, many of whose favorite words he employs. The result is an occasional grotesque seriousness which becomes unintentionally funny as in such passages as "a locomotive can cause terror if onrushing." On the other hand its consistency is sometimes set in disorder by a capricious humor. Here, for instance, is an example that first confuses the reader, then irritates him, at the same time that it disintegrates the logic of the entire passage in which it occurs: "One cannot awaken a sense of strangeness in the reader by talking of Xanadu if the reader happens to be Kubla Khan" – a bad example because it is an impossible one. These, however, diminish into minor irritations as the style is seen to be, by the steady and serene progress of its arguments, remarkably suited to its purpose.

◇◇◇

ISIDOR SCHNEIDER was born in 1896. He is the author of the following books: *Doctor Transit*; *The Temptation of Anthony*, a novel in verse and poems; *Comrade*, a book of poems; *From the Kingdom of Necessity*; and *The Judas Tree*. He also helped to edit *Proletarian Literature in the U.S.* with Granville Hicks and others, and edited *World of Love* and *Enlightenment*. During the late twenties and early thirties he was a frequent reviewer.

Mr. Schneider wrote two excellent pieces on Burke, of which this is the first. With this review, as seen against that of Granville Hicks, the dialectic which was to develop about Burke as a critic and theoretician begins. In the late 1960's it is somewhat unnerving to realize just how early the predominant emphasis on rhetoric in Burke emerged and set, and just how persistent it has been in Burke's long and complex development. As Mr. Schneider rightly points out, Burke was powerfully influenced by I. A. Richards and he (Burke, and Richards as well) did work toward an essentially new view of rhetoric.

◇◇◇

ζ A Review of "Counter-Statement"

BY Harold Rosenberg

PAUL VALERY's *Introduction to the Method of Leonardo da Vinci* (1894) contains this statement: "Edgar Allan Poe has clearly established his appeal to the reader on the basis of psychology and probable effects. From this angle, every combination of elements made to be perceived and judged depends upon a few general laws, and on a particular adaptation defined in advance for that chosen category of minds to which the whole is specially addressed; and the work of art becomes a machine designed to arouse and combine the individual formations of these minds. This suggestion is quite opposite to the ordinary idea of the sublime, and I foresee the indignation it will arouse. . . ." I do not

EDITOR'S NOTE: Reprinted from *The Symposium*, III (January 1932), 116–120, by permission of the author.

know whether it is possible any longer to arouse indignation, but the position outlined above can be as productive of counter-statements and contradictions today as it was in 1845, in 1894, or in 1908.[1] Both collections of essays before us * are characterised by an antipathy for ordinary ideas not only of the sublime but of the sublunar and subliminal as well. Mr. Burke, advocating Form as the essence of art, impugns the arguments of the economic critics that art is 'caused' by the social context in which it is produced, of the psychologists who hold the 'escape-theory' of art, of Spengler and the historical determinists, of those who believe that the artist is the frenzied utterer of his emotions, of those who condemn poetic diction because it is not 'true to life,' who cannot understand that 'unnatural' is not synonymous with 'untrue,' and who forget that art was never intended to compete with the newspaper, the soap-box, the pulpit, or the microscope. He prefers ceremonial and formal art, in which eloquence is of chief moment, to that biographical and informative material which artists offer who have confused their *genre* with that of the scientist; he insists that the artist, as a deliberate evoker of emotions in a previsioned audience, is boldly, even aggressively, conscious in his approach to experience; he bases true criticism not upon that acceptance of a work which depends upon a personal sympathy with the symbol used, but upon a technical understanding of and admiration for the craftsman-skill with which the artist constructs his symbol. . . . With most of this Mr. Belgion, though he differs strongly on other matters, would seem to concur. He too has a chapter arguing that art cannot be 'true to life,' and he too says: "The specifically aesthetic emotion is delight in the contemplation of technical ability, as manifested in its result." Mr. Belgion here adds that the critic must also "see to what extent the emotion imitated is profound and serious," a qualification omitted by Mr. Burke because he has a theory about 'universal experiences' which makes it possible for all emotions to be 'profound and serious.' On his own side, Mr. Belgion combats the idea that art is revelation, that it ought to be produced out of automatic associations, that it is a spiritual rendering of essences. Each book contains an essay on the poetic process which emphasizes the degree to which artistic expression is a conscious, premeditated 'making.'

Both authors concern themselves for the main part with theories of art; but since these involve other problems as well, they show a willing-

[1] In the November 1908 issue of *Revue Philosophique* Charles Lalo attacked the *Einfühlung* theory of criticism and stressed the importance of an apprehension of the technical excellence of a work of art.

* [EDITOR'S NOTE: Mr. Rosenberg was reviewing *The Human Parrot and Other Essays* by Montgomery Belgion as well as *Counter-Statement*.]

ness to expand their interests. In fact, Mr. Belgion is not attracted to art for its own sake; he states that his essays have as "their common purpose to make plain how it is not in art that we can find, morally, 'an ever surer and surer stay' ": on the other hand, Mr. Burke carries his attitude on art into its political and economic implications in order to discover "what could be the particular practical results of this particular 'aesthetic.' " Which means that both, though they start from different positions, are attempting to reach useful conclusions about life in general in its relation to art.

Mr. Burke's liking for art is greater than Mr. Belgion's. He is more desirous of contributing to its theory; and there are indeed many brilliant insights diffused through his essays. Yet his book, though it aims at a discussion of important problems, fails to become important for at least three reasons.

We may consider first the idea that a work of art is a successfully constructed psychological machine deliberately designed to arouse emotions. Now this idea is no doubt descriptive of what a work which we call successful in effect does, and it is also an excellent hypothesis with which to destroy vague, 'mystical' nonsense. But as a theory of method it is so abstract that it depends for its value on the individual using it. Mr. Valéry, for example, expands it in later works into the perfect technique of a pure consciousness in comparison with which the experience and literary style of a Pascal are 'ambiguous and impure.' To Mr. Burke, however, "we can use the concept of perfection only by making it of no critical value." To him Rhetoric or Form is so completely relative to the audience's appetites that there is almost no point in his theory of it which could not be shown to touch equally upon *Oedipus* and a Broadway hit. In other words, Mr. Burke's version of the idea leads him to neglect the whole problem of poetry without entirely realising that he has done so.

Further (I trust Mr. Burke will forgive me for looking over his head for the moment at Mr. Valéry), the idea as stated is not a true description of poetic method. It implies that the most delicate problems of mass and individual psychology were consciously solved in every adequate line. Yet if there is 'a chosen category of minds' to which

> Hier la chair profonde, hier, la chair maîtresse
> M'a trahie . . .

is addressed, this audience-element is composed in the poet by a critical model, more or less representative, who shares his experience by judging it; the 'category' is not a crowd. Nor is form, as Mr. Burke says, "the result of that desire in the artist to make a work perfect by adapting it in every minute detail to the racial appetites," but of a concurrence of the imagination with this internal critic. Mr. Valéry's line was written in consideration of no one's appetites but his own, or perhaps of Mallarmé's, who was dead; and he himself has more recently remarked in this connection, "Il y avait un Boileau en Racine, ou un image de Boileau."[2] In short, form or technique depends upon rules of judgment and not, as Mr. Burke insists, upon psychology.

Mr. Burke has accepted a too naïve form of the artist as craftsman and communicator idea; and this is related to the even greater ingenuousness with which he treats certain philosophical problems: "For we need but take his [Plato's] universals out of heaven and situate them in the human mind (a process begun by Kant), making them not metaphysical but psychological. Instead of divine forms, we now have 'conditions of appeal.' " It would be unfair to Mr. Burke to quote this absurd passage were it not at the root of his misconception of the poetic problem. His 'psychological universals,' mere descriptive abstractions, like hatred, despair, etc., neither limit nor qualify particular experiences, and their acceptance, far from aiding him to distinguish the value of experiences and works, forces him to speak of them as though they lay in their 'individuated forms' on a dead-level equality to be raised or lowered according to their hold on audiences. But the fact that all men are capable of experiencing despair does not render despair a 'universal experience,' because despair in the abstract is not an experience; and since each man experiences it in his own way, as Mr. Burke knows, there is no actual similarity on that basis. There are, then, no universal feelings; common experiences can arise only out of common judgments. My experience does not resemble another's because I feel the same species of emotion that he feels, but because I judge what I feel as he judges what he feels.

Mr. Burke's theoretical limitations also prevent him from turning up the deeper ground of the fallacies he means to destroy, and it is unlikely that one who has been convinced by them will feel himself undermined.

[The section of the original review which dealt with Belgion's book is omitted here.]

◇◇

HAROLD ROSENBERG is the author of *The Tradition of the New*, and, recently, *The Anxious Object: Art Today and Its Audience*, both of which have come out of a long study of the contemporary scene.

This review continues the argument against Burke's early view of

[2] "Situation de Baudelaire," *Variété II* (Paris, 1930).

form and eloquence and is thus part of a much larger dialectic. It should be seen in relation to Mr. Schneider's review and as the first of many attacks on Burke for philosophical naiveté – for his unorthodox logic and sometimes unrigorous use of and approach to "sacred" texts. Burke has always been a pragmatist about how he used texts and has always followed a rule he later formulated: To use all that is there to use. Formally trained and essentially scholarly minds find his use of texts odd and irritating. No philosopher I know of has ever treated Burke kindly – which tells one something about both Burke and the philosophers.

◇◇

Unwilling Novelist

BY Malcolm Cowley

THE author began this book [*Towards a Better Life*] with the intention of writing a novel; he ended by writing a novel in spite of his most diligent efforts. Between this beginning and this ending there intervened a long process of thought which is partially described in the preface. Three times, Burke says, he sat down to write the opening scene, a conversation in a Greenwich Village speakeasy. Two men conversed "for a fitting period, telling each other a few things which it was very necessary for the reader to know; a bell rang, the waiter's steps could be heard going down the hall, a peephole was opened; next the slinging of a bolt, then the unlatching of the iron grate; the newcomer, after low-voiced words at the door, could be heard striding along the hall; he entered the room where the two men were talking; 'Hello,' he said – and for the third time your author tossed Chapter One into the discard."

For the qualities that distinguish the ordinary novel – for suspense, verisimilitude, headlong action, the feeling of immediate participation in events of an exciting nature – Burke felt himself to be unfitted by temperament. He had no interest whatever in the problem of getting people in and out of situations, in and out of doors. The problem on which he was working was that of rendering emotion. "Lamenta-

EDITOR'S NOTE: Reprinted from *Think Back on Us* by Malcolm Cowley (Carbondale: Southern Illinois University Press, 1967). Originally printed in *The New Republic*, LXX (17 February 1932), 23–24. Reprinted by permission of the author.

tion, rejoicing, beseechment, admonition, sayings, and invective—these seemed to me central matters, while a plot in which they might occur seemed peripheral, little more than a pretext, justifiable not as 'a good story,' but only insofar as it could bring these six characteristics to the fore." In order to focus attention on them, "I reversed the process, emphasizing the essayistic rather than the narrative, the emotional predicaments of my hero rather than the details by which he arrived at them . . . In form the resultant chapters are somewhat like a sonnet sequence, a progression by stages, by a series of halts." And yet these chapters, these eighteen "epistles or declamations," together make a true novel—with plot, movement, suspense, verisimilitude and, at the end, a feeling of participation in a terrifying tragedy.

This novel, however, is of a sort that is almost unknown in English letters and rarely encountered even in France. Its great prototype, the one book to which, in spite of all differences, it bears a striking spiritual resemblance, is *A Rebours*. Huysmans, in his most famous novel, was concerned with the search for refuge of a man incapable of living in society. Despising the people of his time, both the bourgeois and the aristocrats, the skeptical and the devout, this hero devoted the remnants of his ducal fortune to the task of creating an individual paradise, a paradise of the senses. It took the shape of a house on the outskirts of Paris. Here, in the midst of erudite pictures, flesh-eating plants and fantastic Latin authors, the owner lived in the company of his dreams, trying feverishly to enjoy himself in spite of the real and imaginary diseases that made him a slave to the doctors, and hence to society as a whole.

The story of *Towards a Better Life* is essentially the same. John Neal, like Jean des Esseintes, despises the people about him, the successful ones blind to their own abjectness, the tame radicals who can safely be admitted to bankers' houses "like castrated lion whelps." Incapable of living in society, he determines to create an individual refuge, and goes about this task by methods proper to himself. He is too intelligent to believe that he can build a physical paradise by decorating any house whatever with books, paintings and hallucinations; he is in fact wholly indifferent to his physical surroundings. His refuge will be mentally constructed and defended, by two categories of thinking. First, he will transvaluate all values, so that the busy, complacent people about him are shown to be mentally sluggish, morally evasive; while he himself, the ingrate and smell-feast, assumes his true role as an active and courageous prophet. Second, he will protect himself from misfortune by running forward to meet it, or else by imagining worse catastrophes than could ever occur, so that real blows will fall upon him harmlessly.

He is in love with Florence and yet, when a happier man pays court to her, he contrives that his rival shall triumph. Since this rival is rich, Neal squanders his little fortune to give the impression of having a great one. Then, taking flight to an unknown village, he marries and becomes a local dignitary. Florence reënters his life; she is traveling from county seat to county seat with a company of penniless actors and is ready, now, to accept John Neal's advances; but he, on discovering that she has been deserted by his rival, dismisses her also – and thereupon feels that a chapter in his life is definitely ended. He wanders back to New York with a girl named Genevieve, always lamenting, rejoicing, beseeching, admonishing and inveighing, always rich in aphorisms. He says: "God pity the man or the nation wise in proverbs . . . for there is much misery and much error gone into the collecting of such a store."

The end of the story and that of *A Rebours* are similar in implication. Des Esseintes, like most self-centered people, became a hypochondriac; his imaginary disorders were aggravated by real ones. The doctors ordered him back to the world of ordinary people; the waves of human mediocrity were about to engulf his refuge. "O Lord," he prayed, "pity the Christian who doubts, the skeptic who would believe." The choice before him was either the arms of the Church, as a French critic said, or the mouth of a pistol. John Neal is also defeated by himself. He now loves Genevieve all-absorbingly; his passion is returned; but he has ceased to be capable of normal happiness. "Through living under difficulty," he says in explaining why he drove her away, "one learns the mode of thinking, feeling and acting best suited to cope with difficulty. No wonder he prizes a discovery which he has made at so great inconvenience to himself, and will not relinquish it but calls upon it to maintain precisely those adversities which it was at first designed to remedy." Thus, inevitably, he cuts the last tie that bound him to the world. His character begins to disintegrate; he has delusions of persecution and grandeur; he has entered a vicious circle from which he cannot escape. He fancies that there are several choices before him, "madness, travel, drugs, the Faith, death by one's own hand," but in reality there is no choice whatever; John Neal is hopelessly insane.

The book is disturbing, sometimes perplexing, always stimulating. Whatever the author's intentions, his story has a moral, and one that is identical, moreover, with that implied in *A Rebours.* There is no salvation apart from society. The individual paradise – whether we seek to create it on the outskirts of Paris, in Abyssinia or Tahiti, in a mythical Axel's castle, or simply behind the parapets of the mind – proves in the final test to be a fool's paradise. The end of the attempt is written in the beginning. The end, for the creator of Des Esseintes, was to surrender himself to society as represented by the Church. The end for John Neal is to sink through squalor and delusions into a final speechless separation from mankind — "Not only not responding, but even refraining from soliloquy — for if we tell no one, the grave burden accumulates within us. Henceforth silence, that the torrent may be heard descending in all its fulness."

◇◇

See the note on p. 6.

THIS review treats Burke in the third of his early roles as writer and attempts to link the three in an interesting and significant way. Mr. Cowley finds embodied in the protagonist of this novel an idea toward society which he relates to the theoretical aestheticism of *Counter-Statement* and the purely rhetorical emphasis of *The White Oxen.* This change of attitude toward individual isolation is a sign of the time — 1932 — and foreshadows the fundamental change which was then taking place in Burke and later appeared in *Permanence and Change. Towards a Better Life* marks the end of the first period of Burke's development; he was well received during this period as a significant new American writer of fiction and literary criticism, essentially radical and experimental. One cannot say of Burke's beginnings that he was an unknown, unrecognized, laboring in silence. This painful silence was to occur later; the early reception of his work was all promise and mostly praise.

◇◇

2 *Second Person Singular*

BY Robert Cantwell

WE HAVE had novels written in the first and third person singular often enough in the past — novels in which "I" performed certain actions and made various descriptive and analytical comments upon the actions, explaining them, apologizing for them, or merely describing them. The repetition of this process has had the effect of making literature a humble and shamefaced profession; the artist stands before his audience,

EDITOR'S NOTE: Reprinted from *The Nation*, CXXXIV (9 March 1932), 289–290, by permission of the author.

explains what has happened and why it is important, draws character sketches of various people, and suggests the relationship between them, and the involved course of coincidences, resentments, and affections that led to the catastrophe. In *Towards a Better Life* Mr. Burke may be said to have written a novel in the second person singular — instead of "I did this" or "he did this" we have the accusing "you did this." Instead of pleading with his audience, Mr. Burke attacks it. Reading *Towards a Better Life* may be likened to overhearing a quarrel in the street. A character named John Neal is addressing someone we do not know, a man he calls Anthony, and we learn of what has happened in the same way that we build up an imaginative preface to a quarrel we overhear; stray clues may guide us, or a mention of some specific incident, but the quarrel is the important matter, not its cause, and in the end each listener's interpretation of the cause will depend upon his own experiences and upon his memories of them.

It is John Neal's emotion that attracts us first, and his wit. He feels that Anthony has wronged him, and he attacks him with a savage sarcasm, making incidental remarks on the implications of some incident that are concise and unexpected. Neal is a brilliant speaker, but his emotion seems to prevent his developing his arguments logically. His moods change rapidly; he remembers various encounters, people they both knew, a suicide, a trip. We learn that Florence, whom he loved, has been Anthony's mistress, and presently we learn that he has found Florence, learned of her disgrace, and sent her away. Another woman, Genevieve, has entered his life, but he has sent her away as well, and quarreled with his friends. Unlike most apologists, Neal seems determined to present himself in as unfavorable a light as possible, and he succeeds. He lies continually; he is pompous and boastful; he paints himself in an attractive light only to confess that he has been lying. Yet when we grow impatient with him, and turn away from his confused troubles, he wins us again with a brilliant phrase, or a flash of pathetic recollection, or a purely lyric flight — for Anthony has disappeared, the "you" has become the reader, or society, or all mankind. And with Anthony's disappearance Neal grows increasingly eloquent; he no longer speaks in confidence, but addresses a multitude, calling upon the outcasts — "Oh, lepers of mankind, gutter rats, printers of the sewers" — and turns upon the prosperous — "the well-fed and well-intrenched, comfortably summoning the people to rebel." He tries to pray but he cannot believe, and in the end his eloquence has exhausted itself; he can only speak in disjointed whispers, telling himself that he is "humbled . . . that silence cannot be advocated silently."

There is no parallel for *Towards a Better Life*. In form it resembles the sermon, but based on the authority of observation rather than Scripture. Ideally, the comments should treat of experiences common to everyone, rather than an involved and personal story. It is important in that it seeks to restore the original dignity of learning and art, advocating a militant literature of command rather than the persuasive plucking at the sleeve the novelist has been forced to resort to in his attempt to gain attention.

◇◇◇

ROBERT CANTWELL was born in Little Falls (now Vader), Washington, in 1908. He has worked as a consultant and editor for Time-Life, Inc., since 1935. When he wrote this review he was, like Burke (but considerably younger), a beginning novelist. His two early (and only) novels were *Laugh and Lie Down* and *The Land of Plenty*. He is also the author of *Nathaniel Hawthorne* and *Alexander Wilson*.

This short review is chiefly important because it dignifies Burke's efforts as a novelist by recognizing the seriousness of his purpose and the authentic innovative nature of the endeavor. All the early reviews of this remarkable novel should be read along with the later ones written after the second edition in 1966 when, as in 1932, the book was also enthusiastically received, but in a much larger Burkeian and literary context.

◇◇◇

7 A Review of "Towards a Better Life"

BY Isidor Schneider

LATE in 1931 occurred an event that I believe will be accounted one of the surviving assets of that too insolvent year — the publication of Mr. Burke's *Counter-Statement.* The book was more than a rehabilitation of rhetoric; it was a restatement of its nature in terms that could win the respect of modern minds. The shift from a craft problem to a psychological problem was masterly, and as revealing in its way as the shift of history from the battlefield to the market.

EDITOR'S NOTE: Reprinted from *The Bookman,* LXXV (1932), 101–102, by permission of the author.

Mr. Burke's new book may be taken to be a working out of the principles projected in *Counter-Statement,* but it is to be remembered that it is a single experiment and that it would be futile to judge either of the two books by the other; to say, for instance, that the principles in *Counter-Statement* are invalidated by the failure to apply them in *Towards a Better Life,* or that the latter work is a failure because it does not fulfil those principles to the letter.

In his preface to *Towards a Better Life,* Mr. Burke sets down an epitomized counter-statement. He tells us that "Lamentation, rejoicing, beseechment, admonition, sayings, and invective – these seemed to me central matters, while a plot in which they might occur seemed peripheral, little more than a pretext, justifiable not as 'a good story,' but only insofar as it could bring these six characteristics to the fore. These mark, these six mark, in a heightened manner, the significant features of each day in our secular, yet somewhat biblical, lives – and what I most wanted to do was to lament, rejoice, beseech, admonish, aphorize and inveigh."

Thus, it will be seen that Mr. Burke takes the exactly opposite position of the modern realistic novelist. Realism assumes that given the events, the emotions will follow. Mr. Burke assumes that given the emotions the events will follow in retrospect, or will not be required. Each expects too much from the reader. The emotions stirred in the reader by the realistic novel are as crude and unformed as those stirred in him by the events in his own life. They are not guided by the writer since he fails to provide the necessary eloquent expressions for them, into the splendid and heightened forms that are the majestic achievements of our greatest literature. Mr. Burke, on the other hand, provides the reader the expressions without material to apply them. For almost half the book eloquence drains out for lack of a vessel. In the later half of the book, merely because the story has taken form, the lamentations and the rejoicings resound; the beseechings and the admonitions disquiet us; and the sayings and invectives have point.

The outstanding essay in *Counter-Statement* was "Psychology and Form." In it Mr. Burke brilliantly analyzed the ghost scene in *Hamlet,* showing what a command Shakespeare had upon the psychology of the audience, how by the arrangement of the incidents of the plot he prepared his audience for the full outburst of his rhetoric. In other words, then, the writer who makes a fiction must have invention equal to his expression. Without it, he is handicapped in the same way as a philosopher who would argue by conclusions alone without the reasons. Mr. Burke practically admits this in his preface when, in making a plea for a plotless novel, he admits that he is justifying his defects as a novelist.

Yet by the book's evidence we can only conclude that Mr. Burke is a completer novelist than he realizes.

The book itself, as I have intimated, contains the novelist as well as the anti-novelist. We realize at the end that it has plot enough for a trilogy. And in the second half the plot, becoming formed, imparts a sudden power to the book. We are moved; we become obsessed like its heroic Schlemiel with the strength of his deliberate sufferings. Mr. Burke succeeds in making a pathology realistic.

Towards a Better Life takes its place among the major literary experiments of our time and Mr. Burke is certain to give a new direction to his contemporaries. It may be, as he says, that "What I have learned through being in grave extremities, some one, coming after me, will handle with ease." This perhaps will not be true only because Mr. Burke will have made the task easier for his successor, but because he has made the task harder for himself by a somewhat stilted style. It lacks sensuousness above all. Its beauties are those of the agile mind; its excitements are the pleasures of alert and keen perceptions. Its very vocabulary seems to me the vocabulary of dialectics and inhibitory to the sensual. Its rhythms I found harsh, counter-cutting frequently rather than counter-pointing. Its formalism was in some instances grotesque rather than stately. Often I had the feeling that I was reading a translation, the effect of the book being so often alien to the fluency that is, I believe, one of the most general characteristics of English literature. The larger movements, however, are beautifully handled and give the exhilarating effect to the memory of tremendous upheavals and ebbs.

◇◇

See the note on p. 26.

THIS is the second of Mr. Schneider's two pieces on Burke and builds on the first by applying *Counter-Statement* to *Towards a Better Life*. Mr. Schneider points out that Burke's own apologetics are themselves part of an elaborate fictional rhetoric. In addition, Mr. Schneider acknowledges, as others did, the important experimental nature of the work and accurately describes many of the main characteristics of the novel – and of Burke's mind.

◇◇

Z Kenneth Burke: His Mind and Art

BY Austin Warren

[The first two sections of this essay have been omitted here.]

"HEAVEN alone knows what is to become of the novel," Burke wrote in 1920, reviewing John Cournos' *Mask*. "As early as 1884 Huysmans was sick of it, and began his series of compilations with *A Rebours*. But on the whole, although it is so short-lived, it has become astonishingly autocratic [as a *form*]. Keen minds have accepted it as naïvely as the infallibility of a Pope. In spite of the hemorrhage of verse that is splattering about the earth, I suppose there is still one novel published for every poem. Huysmans, Gide, de Gourmont, Joyce, Lewis [presumably Wyndham] – I can think of no others who have showed any interest in even *stretching* the novel . . . Yet if perfection can kill a thing, the novel should have died at the end of the century, since Mann had already written *Buddenbrooks*."

Both Burke's reviews in *The Dial* and his sketches and tales gathered together in *The White Oxen* show his restlessness under any dogmatic, absolutistic theory of the *genres*, his inveterate sympathy with experimentation and the development of new forms, his fondness for the laboratory and the workshop. Writing particularly of de Gourmont's ventures into fiction, Burke has noted: "the nature of his books is never the same in two successive volumes. Like a rough little mountain stream, he cuts a new path after every rain." Precisely the same thing has been said, by Ramon Fernandez, of the whole long series of André Gide's writings; and it is of course this experimentalism with literary *genres* (Gide himself calls but one of his fictions, *Les Fauxmonneyeurs*, a *roman*) as well as with "life" which has won Burke's admiration for the Frenchman.

Burke's latitudinarian theories of the novel are in no sense, then, to be dismissed as special pleading for his own latitudinarian practice.

But he is too conscientious a workman to wish it said that he has essayed the unconventional for want of skill to effect the conventional: in the age of *vers libre* he would surely have published at least a volume in traditional forms to establish his craftsmanship. It is, therefore, not at all surprising to learn, from Munson's review of *Towards a Better Life*, that Burke's first announcements to his friends concerned a novel in more or less conservative idiom: "One gathered that it was to be

EDITOR'S NOTE: Reprinted from *The Sewanee Review*, XLI (1933), 344–354, copyright 1933 by the University of the South, by permission of the author and publisher.

about the rise, flourishing and decay of a religious colony, the Spenglerian cycle exhibited in small. Then his conception altered somewhat: he thought of two characters 'one superficial, but triumphant at finance, ambition, love; the other, keen, philosophical, unsuccessful.' " Attempting conventional treatment of this contrast, he found it inadequate to the ends he proposed.

Burke's preface to his "novel" describes further fruitless attempts at the "customary manner of the objective, realistic novel" with its "plot, settings, incidental characters, and the like," all of which properties he had worked through in outline.

But the important thing is not to write what may be readily classified, whether as novel or as any other recognized *genre*. The important thing is to get oneself on paper, to accomplish the aesthetic ends for the gratification of which alone one set pen to its infinite labor on paper. Why *save* the "novel," and lose one's soul, one's end? Certain sorts of rhetorical expression aroused Burke to creation. A plot mattered merely as giving opportunity for the employment of "lamentation, rejoicing, beseechment, admonition, sayings, and invective": Burke does not trouble to retain the traditional names for his rhetorical forms, except perhaps for sayings – that is to say, aphorisms, *sententiae*. But he makes himself quite clear. He is going to sacrifice the "realistic, objective novel" for the sake of a framework suited to the inserting of "declamations." Instead of emphasizing the *flow* of time he is going to emphasize its arrests: his camera aims not at the cinematic flux but at the posed and artful, artistic, utterly formal studio photograph, the ceremonial portrait. Burke himself supplies, in elucidatory analogy to his chapters, the son net sequence and the pre-Wagnerian opera "in which the stress is laid upon the arias whereas the transition from one aria to the next is secondary," mere recitative.

"Declamation" and "rhetoric": what quaint, archaic words, reminiscent of public speaking courses and silver-tongued orators and early nineteenth-century prose poets – De Quincey and Ruskin, perhaps. What curious and daring taste, to use them in eulogistic sense! Burke is quite conscious, quite aware of the times and current literary vogues; and he avowedly hopes to return to favor both words and things dignified. He protests the current dominance of American fiction by the journalistic idiom, the more because its authors so often affect a carelessness, an avoidance of the right word, the nuance, while actually possessed of the leisure and taste to compose with style and finish. Burke feels no sympathy with Hemingway and the "hard guy" school of literature now on exhibition in the pages of *Contact* and *Pagany*. With his keen analytical powers he can, of course, comprehend the motives which lead the subtle, sophisticated, and effete to admire the wholly extroverted, the normal strong, inarticulate males of street-corner and speakeasy. But he does not sympathize with their attempts at a literature as unliterary as possible, their efforts at subtracting from their equipment as artists. He calls, persuasively, for a return to style, to "more formalized modes of writing. There is no reason why prose should continue to be judged good prose purely because it trails along somewhat like the line left by the passage of a caterpillar. Why should an author spend a year or more on a single book, and end by talking as he would talk on the spur of the moment?" The "arid stretches of monosyllabic words and monosyllabic perceptions which, partially engaging a sluggish corner of the mind, pass today as the major concern of fiction, would seem to justify anything unlike them, even to the extent of that *Zopfstil,* that 'periwig style' . . ." The preface of *Towards a Better Life* concludes with Burke's apology for having progressed so timidly towards the "re-erection of the 'structural' sentence, the 'Johnsonese' if you will, as opposed to the 'conversational' style which enjoys current favour"; proffers his book merely as testifying to his faith in the approaching turn "from the impromptu towards the studied."

Doubtless we are not to take Burke with absolute literalness when he construes *Facit indignatio versus* as "An author may devote his entire energies to rage purely through a preference for long sentences" and when he proceeds to tell us that his hero has been chosen merely as "the most likely vehicle for these outpourings," as one, that is, who can be counted on, with plausibility, to lament, rejoice, beseech, admonish, aphorize, and inveigh. There is too much parallelism between the favorite themes of *Towards a Better Life* and *Counter-Statement,* between the praise of Gide and Mann and the philosophy put upon the lips of the novel's hero. Burke says of his hero: "I can say nothing in his favour except that he is busy, and busy in ways that will not add a single car to our thoroughfares"; and again, "He has an enquiring mind, which he converts into a liability, or at best employs industriously to arrive at zero." The first dictum is a wearily ironic praise of the artist and the philosopher as not idlers but possessed of their own sort of activity; the second attributes to Burke's hero what Burke has said of Mann: "Implicit in his work there is a cult of conflict, a deliberate entertaining of moral vacillation, which could not permit a rigid standard of judgments. He has said that the artist must contain his critic, must recognize the validity of contraries. This attitude would make such simple certainty as moral indignation impossible." Burke's hero (I use the term but for convenience) is in no sense himself; Burke breaks with the Anglo-American tradition of autobiographical novels, and no more writes the story of his own life than he essays the broad sociological canvas of a Balzac, Tolstoi, Sinclair Lewis, or Dos Passos. But like Burke, his hero is a writer and a philosopher pretty much isolated intellectually, a solitary who pursues his own development as an inner necessity, "a very frank, a very earnest, a very conscientious man." Burke warns us, however, that his hero lacks a sense of humor. What Burke has doubtless done is to segregate a portion of his own inner life, a group of his logical insights and rhetorical devices, and to subject it to intensive and rigorous development. Granted the isolation of one sequence of thought and emotion which often besets a man, granted the dropping away of the rest of his intellectual and emotional constitution, granted the logical playing out to the end of this sequence: what would be that end? What Burke has done is, I believe, to effect this segregation of a part of his inner life and to invent for it a *symbol*, or *myth*, in the shape of a fiction, a series of events calculated to give manifestation to this inner life.

John Neal, Burke's hero, goes insane at the end of his course. Can one trace the successive stages of his mania? Yes and no. At no point does the rhetoric break down, and not till the last chapter does the logic, the inner articulation and coherence of Neal's thought, give way to glimpses, images, phrases, fragments. Neal goes *crazy*, not *foolish*. He loses his relation to the world of men, loses his power of seeing them with any degree of objectivity, comes to dwell entirely in himself. But his own universe of discourse, most completely set out before us in the next to the last chapter, is keen, acute, logical. The contrast between this chapter and the chapters immediately preceding and following it is startling. The last chapter stammers its last utterances before silence closes down; the earlier chapter gives clear evidence of Neal's dementia as he walks the city streets, has dealings with men. Why, then, the clarity and intellectual vigor of the mediate chapter? Burke is not purporting more than a very moderate degree of verisimilitude anywhere in his novel: he remains at heart nearer expressionism than realism. But the explanation for this chapter is precisely that Neal's inner world, the world of his self-justification, his own *reading* of his life and of humanity's life, survives, unscarred, the collapse of Neal's relations with the outer world. He remains the philosopher after he ceases to be a man.

The novel chronicles the outer course of his disasters while it swathes the chronicle in Neal's commentary on an equipment which, by its philosophical aptitude for endurance, courted the disasters it deplored.

Neal is an introvert who finds compensation for his ineptness and gaucherie in the "world" by his intellectual subtlety and agileness. The other persons in the chronicle who emerge sufficiently for the author to name them are Anthony, a socially accomplished and wealthy "friend"; Florence, an actress, loved by both Neal and Anthony; and Genevieve, subsequently Neal's mistress.

Neal longs for Florence, yet will not have her through her pity or her want of other opportunity. He suffers at her passion for Anthony, but, steeling himself, throws them in each other's way; and when the alliance has been consummated, and he has run through his money, he leaves the city, buying his railroad ticket for an unknown country village.

Two years elapse between Parts One and Two. During this interval, Neal has been living with Genevieve in the country village, all the while "by many subterfuges of thought and action bargaining to keep insanity logically submerged." He has pretended to Genevieve that he was already married; then he announces to her that he is to marry a woman of the village. She departs; he marries, and by his marriage acquires a farm and two children (neither wife nor children are named or characterized). He writes a play for the pupils of the local school; in return for his success he is given a minor office in the school.

This quasi-prosperity is interrupted by the advent of Florence. She has come to town with a company of hacks who are acting *The Merchant of Venice.* She alleges having married a man of wealth but indulging herself, from time to time, in professional sallies like the present. But in a drab hotel chamber the truth comes bitterly out. Anthony, wearied of her, has cast her off, and she has descended to her present destitution through an intermediate stage of cohabiting with a pugilist.

When Neal hears her story, his desire for her leaves him. "Florence is a hunted thing," he writes, — "so much in need of kindness that to gain a confidant she sacrificed a lover." "We desire the desired" seems the caustic moral.

The Third Part opens with Neal's consciousness that his reason for existence has evaporated. "It was because of Florence that I had gone into this section of the country and attempted to reconstruct a new manner of living . . . She made me live as though there were a score I had to settle and living were a vengeance. My fear of her had been the beacon for me to steer by . . . For even a life of bitterness is desirable as compared with a life without purpose."

He deserts his home, goes in search of Genevieve, corrodes her into accompanying him on a bourneless wandering from city to city. Neal takes to chipping grotesque, obscene shapes out of stone, leaving them behind to tenant the rooms he abandons. He grows neurotically jealous of Genevieve; and after a mad encounter with a mad girl in white, he sends Genevieve out into the streets, telling her to supply their destitution by getting money from any man. She vanishes, never to reappear.

Now the real isolation begins. A period of Neal's life with "Alter Ego," a man of similar tastes but equipped with wealth, is chronicled at some length; but Neal's comment a little later upon the "negligible shred of comfort he has got for himself recently by talking in two voices" would imply that "Alter Ego" was strictly deducible from his name. Neal is utterly alone: "by his very need of companionship he drove people from him." He resorts to dire expedients. "In sitting among audiences, and looking in the same direction with them, one feels not wholly outcast." He is fascinated by a wooden policeman set in front of a cigar store, fascinated by the fear that he will hail the policeman. One day he finds that he has spoken. He draws up a desperate "Memorandum: Rules to Self": "If a person whistles or calls, give no evidence of hearing. The signal was not intended for you. If children begin shouting, do not quicken your pace. The shouting has to do with some game of theirs. You are dressed like every other man that passes along these streets." And then the end: "Testamentum meum"; "Henceforth silence, that the torrent may be heard descending in all its fulness."

I have said that Neal incarnates a sequence of Burke's thought. "If we have spent the best of our years in repairing our defenses, we may find ourselves unequipped for times of peace. Then John Neal, in choosing difficulty, was not acting without purpose?" The hero asks himself in one passage, and some pages away he answers that he is "a man whose purpose never wavered. Through living under difficulty, one learns the mode of thinking, feeling, and acting best suited to cope with difficulty. No wonder he prizes a discovery which he has made at so great inconvenience to himself, and will not relinquish it but calls upon it to maintain precisely those adversities which it was at first designed to remedy." Neal's early sufferings have led him to equip himself for suffering; and then the equipment requires a continuation of the state in which, so admirably, it operates.

His early suffering isolated him from his fellows, his introversion alienated him from the accommodation necessary to successful entry into society. His adjustment to the situation was the development of an attitude crystallized in a vocabulary of caustic and disdainful analysis. With the consequence that toward the end of his book Neal writes: "Thus, since they [his despisals of his fellows] spring forth without the provocations of a personal dilemma, since there is no canker of frustration discoverable in them, they are not a comparison, but of vocation. They occur precisely because my terminology best equips me to discharge them." One's phrases, one's diction, one's style: these harden, rigidify, till they stand alone, till they shape our attitude instead of yielding to and expressing it.

How can such a sequence justify the title, *Towards a Better Life*? Or is it sheer irony. Not the latter, surely. Burke is an earnest person, not given to pulling his reader's leg. One may, of course, say that the title describes Neal's quest as Neal saw it: though he attained insanity he was in search of salvation. But its application is wider. All Burke's writings (in spite of his disclaim of humanitarian impulse) are aimed toward a better life, even though they take up with none of most acclaimed politico-economic panaceas of the day. This novel pursues an inquiry, tests one method. Malcolm Cowley asserts, "Whatever the author's intentions, his story has a moral, and one that is identical, moreover, with that implied in *A Rebours*. There is no salvation apart from society. The individual paradise — whether we seek to create it on the outskirts of Paris, in Abyssinia or Tahiti, in a mythical Axel's castle, or simply [with John Neal] behind the parapets of the mind — proves in the final test to be a fool's paradise." Cowley refrains from attributing this "moral" to Burke, and rightly; Marxians may be left to extract this commonplace; it presumably never occurred to Burke, whose mind is too nuanced for that sort of primer morality.

But we have been long occupied with *story* and *theme* despite Burke's assurance that these have concerned him but, or principally, as vehicle for "lamentation, rejoicing, beseechment, admonition, sayings, and invective." What of its *form* and *forms*?

The book comprises eighteen epistles, addressed to Anthony but, as we learn, never sent. Ten of these epistles were published separately, and without any intimation of their relation to any intended whole, as "Declamations." One might make of this simply that Burke, who is both a slow and, in seventeenth century parlance, *painful* writer and, at the same time, persistently indigent, was in need of turning some of his book into cash before its completion. Such a procedure on such motivation seems, however, thoroughly inconsistent with the rigor of Burke's artistic conscience; and I believe the reason to be rather that he felt the interest of his "epistles" or "declamations" not to depend entirely on their story or their dramatic sequence. Burke himself compares his "declamations" to the successive sonnets in a sonnet sequence, each of which has a certain independence and a certain unity in its crystallization of a mood or a situation, even though each sonnet gains in emotional force when read in its context. Some works of art command our admiration as wholes though the parts, subtracted for special study, lack interest; other works abound in brilliant detail but come to no fusion. *Towards a Better Life* is not a masterpiece of the impressionistic school which makes its effect only upon the spectator who stands at a respectful distance but which, observed at close range, turns into dabs and mounds of pigment. It is "old school" in the sense that its workmanship is patient and detailed, from composition in its architectonic sense to firm, adroit handling of sentence structure. Burke is never a flashy or even a purple writer. But if one may use the word without implying the lack of the complementary interest, the architectonic, Burke *is* a *stylist*; and the principal reason, doubtless, for the separate and serial publication of ten declamations was Burke's quite justifiable feeling that prose-sonnets so compact of wit and finely precise sensibility, so expertly hewn out as to paragraph and sentence, could stand alone till the whole was ready to enclose and bind them.

Burke's novel gains greatly from being read as a whole. Its author has written me of the work which he has now in progress: "In some ways my introductory chapter is not completely representative of the whole, as I attempt to disarm readers by attempting to conceal my ultimate purpose (which, if the book turns out as planned, will not be fully disclosed until the end)." The same purpose prevailed assuredly in the composition of *Towards a Better Life*, which is in a real sense a crescendo (albeit a *crescendo* only from the author's and the reader's point of view. From John Neal's point of view it is all a diminuendo: isolation and frustration more and more set in, and the world ends, not with a bang but with a whimper). The novel is a study in *suspense*. Up till the very end, disclosures which are necessary to the clarification of Neal's past continue to be made; there is a constant return and amplification of themes.

Nevertheless very great interest attaches to the minor forms with which Burke decorates and enriches his principal sequence. I distinguish four chief forms of which he makes use: the episode; the set or series of examples; the *pensée* or meditation; and the aphorism. There are four episodes: meetings and conversations with men who (and which) do not concern the main sequence but possess interest in themselves. The most brilliant of these episodes concerns a scholar who, inhibited by the atmosphere of piety in which he was reared, is unable to hold his sweetheart against a rival of "a certain physical obviousness." Upon it, Burke-Neal comments: "I cherish such meetings, when each man puts his wares upon the table for the other to observe and value.

Even while hearing little beyond his own old soliloquies, he profits by the alterations which a fresh auditor demands of him."

Of the long sets of parallel examples, sequences of crisp, terse vignettes of people, there are three. From the first sequence I choose an admirable example: "There was a woman so assured of others' kindliness that all who knew her conspired in limiting her experiences to this simpler reality. She sat, I believe, in the shade of an arbour, or in equivalent places, learning of the contemporary through the courtesies of her visitors and the filtrations of well-modulated prose."

The *pensées* are too long (though they remain *pensées* and never distend to the dimensions of essay) for quotation in full. Let me cite as suggestive aperçus which are given a degree of development the "thought" that he who "possesses some elect insight" must "make efforts to procure its material replica" and the ingenious counterattack on the business man's contempt for the artist. Quite as plausible as the theory that the artist is an unsuccessful business man is the theory that the business man is an unsuccessful artist. "There is not one of them [the Philistines] but would be an adept at repartee, and withal not one of them fit to apply the sound epithet to a single item of God's universe." Burke gives further development to this *pensée* in *Counter-Statement.*

As for aphorism, there is richness. Burke can be clever: "When people are both discerning and unhappy, they tend to believe that their unhappiness is derived from their discernment." And "Hypocrisy which does not know itself is, in a gracious woman, graciousness . . ." But Burke does not aspire to cleverness, and his aphorisms tend more characteristically to be wise. "We create new ills, I thought, and call it progress when we find the remedies." ". . . When rewards are commensurate with efforts, they find us already too exhausted to enjoy them, and too dispirited through the practise of long patience to feel assured that they will not be taken from us." ". . . The knowledge of living is not something to be learned in advance of the calls made upon it; it accumulates with age, matures as its utility diminishes, and under favourable circumstances dies at ninety."

Burke's preface protests forcefully against journalistic prose. Burke's own style is never in a moment's danger of journalism. His sentence structure is often periodic. Balance and parallelism are yet more characteristic. His diction is everywhere meticulous in its precision. He has a fine feeling for cadence, which gives endorsement, when it is occasionally necessary, to such an inversion as "for this I am to Genevieve permanently grateful" (let the reader try the effect of placing the adverb and adjective directly after the verb). In "The Poetic Process," Burke writes, apropos of Chesterton's monotonous use of paradox, "The exploitation of a few technical forms produces *mannerism*, while the use of many produces *style*." In this sense, Burke himself is without mannerisms, but he has, very definitely, a style and, like Pater and Henry James, a definitely literary one. It is tense and hard rather than soft and relaxed. It suggests an unusually intelligent translation from Burke's favorite Latin, or a felicitous modernization of eighteenth century neo-classical prose. It is not conversational but formal; and it will be appreciated in proportion to the reader's acquaintance with Latin and English prose styles of the ornater sort and the training of his ear to a taste for *schemes*.

[The last ten pages of the essay have been omitted here.]

◇◇

AUSTIN WARREN was born in Waltham, Massachusetts, in 1899. He has been a distinguished teacher of British and American literature at Boston University, the University of Iowa, and the University of Michigan. He has written books on Pope, the elder Henry James, and Crashaw; edited a selection of Hawthorne's work; published two collections of essays on a great variety of subjects; and with René Wellek he wrote the important *Theory of Literature*.

This early and very long essay on Burke – the first major study and even now the only substantial work on Burke's fiction – was (and is) a work of love and devotion. Only one part – the middle section on *Towards a Better Life* – is reprinted here. I see no point in listing the virtues of Mr. Warren's analytic appreciation of Burke and his novel, but wish only to assert that he makes many fine (precise, accurate, just) points about Burke and his fiction in a nonprogrammatic way.

It is difficult to say how much influence an essay such as this one had; its function was double: it allowed Professor Warren to announce his discovery and to express some sort of profound appreciation. The essay does both of these things and lives on as a permanent Burkemark for those who have come after. Even though Professor Warren's attitude toward Burke clearly underwent a significant change as a result of some fundamental changes in both of them during the thirties – see his review of *Permanence and Change* which begins on p. 51 – he continued to testify in Burke's behalf, in and out of the classroom. Here, then, is a proper place to acknowledge the undocumentable but extraordinarily important role of teachers like Professor Warren in the reception of writers like Burke.

◇◇

7 A Critic's Job of Work

BY R. P. Blackmur

[The first pages of this essay are omitted here.]

IT IS the interest and fascination of Mr. [I. A.] Richards' work in reference to different levels of sensibility, including the poetic, that has given him both a wide and a penetrating influence. No literary critic can escape his influence; an influence that stimulates the mind as much as anything by showing the sheer excitement as well as the profundity of the problems of language – many of which he has himself made genuine problems, at least for readers of poetry: an influence, obviously, worth deliberately incorporating by reducing it to one's own size and needs. In T. S. Eliot the influence is conspicuous if slight. Mr. Kenneth Burke is considerably indebted, partly directly to Mr. Richards, partly to the influences which acted upon Mr. Richards (as Bentham's theory of Fictions) and partly to the frame of mind which helped mold them both. But Mr. Burke is clearly a different person – and different from anyone writing today; and the virtues, the defects, and the élan of his criticism are his own.

Some years ago, when Mr. Burke was an animating influence on the staff of *The Dial*, Miss Marianne Moore published a poem in that magazine called "Picking and Choosing" which contained the following lines.

> and Burke is a
> psychologist – of acute and raccoon-
> like curiosity. *Summa diligentia;*
> to the humbug, whose name is so amusing – very young and ve-
> ry rushed, Caesar crossed the Alps on the 'top of a
> *diligence.*' We are not daft about the meaning but this familiarity
> with wrong meanings puzzles one.

In the index of Miss Moore's *Observations*, we find under Burke that the reference is to Edmund, but it is really to Kenneth just the same. There is no acuter curiosity than Mr. Burke's engaged in associating the meanings, right and wrong, of the business of literature with the business of life and vice versa. No one has a greater awareness – not even Mr. Richards – of the important part wrong meanings play in establishing the consistency of right ones. The writer of whom he re-

EDITOR'S NOTE: Originally published in 1935. Reprinted from *Language as Gesture* (New York: Harcourt, Brace and Company, 1952), pp. 291–294, copyright 1952 by Richard P. Blackmur, by permission of Harcourt, Brace & World, Inc.

minds us, for the buoyancy and sheer remarkableness of his speculations, is Charles Santiago Saunders Peirce; one is enlivened by them without any *necessary* reference to their truth; hence they have truth for their own purposes, that is, for their own uses. Into what these purposes or uses are it is our present business to inquire.

As Mr. Richards in fact uses literature as a springboard or source for a scientific method of a philosophy of value, Mr. Burke uses literature, not only as a springboard but also as a resort or home, for a philosophy or psychology of moral possibility. Literature is the hold-all and the persuasive form for the patterns of possibility. In literature we see unique possibilities enacted, actualized, and in the moral and psychological philosophies we see the types of possibility generalized, see their abstracted, convertible forms. In some literature, and in some aspects of most literature of either great magnitude or great possibility, we see, so to speak, the enactment or dramatic representation of the type or patterns. Thus Mr. Burke can make a thrilling intellectual pursuit of the sub-intelligent writing of Erskine Caldwell: where he shows that Caldwell gains a great effect of humanity by putting in *none himself*, appealing to the reader's common stock: i.e., what is called for so desperately by the pattern of the story must needs be generously supplied. Exactly as thrilling is his demonstration of the great emotional role of the outsider as played in the supremely intelligent works of Thomas Mann and André Gide. His common illustrations of the pervasive spread of symbolic pattern are drawn from Shakespeare and from the type of the popular or pulp press. I think that on the whole his method could be applied with equal fruitfulness either to Shakespeare, Dashiell Hammett, or Marie Corelli; as indeed he does apply it with equal force both to the field of anarchic private morals and to the outline of a secular conversion to Communism—as in, respectively, *Towards a Better Life* and *Permanence and Change.*

The real harvest that we barn from Mr. Burke's writings is his presentation of the types of ways the mind works in the written word. He is more interested in the psychological means of the meaning, and how it might mean (and often really does) something else, than in the meaning itself. Like Mr. Richards, but for another purpose, he is engaged largely in the meaning of meaning, and is therefore much bound up with considerations of language, but on the plane of emotional and intellectual patterns rather than on the emotional plane; which is why his essays deal with literature (or other writings) as it dramatizes or unfolds character (a character is a pattern of emotions and notions) rather than with lyric or meditative poetry which is Mr. Richards' field. So we find language containing felt character as well as felt co-ordination. The representation of character, and of aspiration and symbol, must always be rhetorical; and therefore we find that for Mr. Burke the rightly rhetorical is the profoundly hortatory. Thus literature may be seen as an inexhaustible reservoir of moral or character philosophies in action.

It is the technique of such philosophies that Mr. Burke explores, as he pursues it through curiosities of development and conversion and duplicity; it is the technique of the notions that may be put into or taken out of literature, but it is only a part of the technique of literature itself. The final reference is to the psychological and moral possibilities of the mind, and these certainly do not exhaust the technique or the reality of literature. The reality in literature is an object of contemplation and of feeling, like the reality of a picture or a cathedral, not a route of speculation. If we remember this and make the appropriate reductions here as elsewhere, Mr. Burke's essays become as pertinent to literary criticism as they are to the general ethical play of the mind. Otherwise they become too much a methodology for its own sake on the one hand, and too much a philosophy at one remove on the other. A man writes as he can; but those who use his writings have the further responsibility of re-defining their scope, an operation (of which Mr. Burke is a master) which alone uses them to the full.

◇◇◇

R. P. BLACKMUR was born in Springfield, Massachusetts, in 1904 and died in 1965. He was on the editorial board of *The Hound and the Horn* and from 1940 until his death taught English and creative writing at Princeton. He was influential both as a teacher of young writers and as one who helped formulate, apply, and defend the "new criticism." He published several books of poems and four important collections of essays: *The Double Agent, The Expense of Greatness, Language as Gesture,* and *The Lion and the Honeycomb.*

Burke and Blackmur shared an interest in language and verbal analysis, and Burke, at least, was indebted to Blackmur and acknowledged that debt in *Attitudes toward History.* It is somehow appropriate, then, that Blackmur should be the first in this collection to point out just how central language is for Burke, how rhetoric is his real subject, and what the general relation of mind to language is in Burke's *Permanence and Change.* Blackmur also identifies the debt to Richards, the differences between Richards and Burke, and comments in a very famous passage on the democratic (he did not put it so kindly) nature of Burke's methodology. This nondiscriminatory practice of Burke's has rasped on the sensibilities of fellow critics from the beginning—especially the sensibilities of those critics who followed T. S. Eliot through this troubled period.

◇◇

2 *The Sceptic's Progress*

BY Austin Warren

[Mr. Warren begins his review-essay of Burke's *Permanence and Change* with a long, dense philosophical discussion of skepticism and faith or belief; this discussion is developed quite apart from Burke's book for many pages but is clearly going to serve as the intellectual context into which Mr. Warren will put Burke and his book when he gets to them. The selection below begins at the point where Mr. Warren approaches Burke as the skeptic of his title. The two alternatives mentioned are skepticism and its opposite, unquestioning faith or belief. It is helpful in reading this essay-review to remember the problems posed for modern Americans by T. S. Eliot's expatriation and later commitments to orthodox and conservative religious, political, and intellectual positions. Mr. Warren has this modern dilemma in mind when he writes.]

AND indeed, more largely, we may say that to doubt everything is to believe — everything.

One extreme invites the other. The credulous, once the critical abyss opens before him, becomes a complete sceptic; the sceptic, in disaster or despair, becomes a bigot. As we survey the world about us, we discern a widespread flight from scepticism to credulity. The imminence of another world war and the universal precariousness of states and economics have broken in upon all save the most inviolate solipsisms, and men look about for safety, thinking with Hobbes that any dogmatically enforced order is preferable to uncertainty, any "views" sufficiently sweeping more honourable than confessed fallibility. Suddenly looking up from their reveries or their professional projects, men find the furniture about them in flames; instead of applying water or chemicals they evacuate the house and build anew according to a freshly conceived and untried architecture. Hysteria leaves a man prey to all species of "evil spirits"; and the last state of that man is worse than the first.

EDITOR'S NOTE: Reprinted from *The American Review*, VI (1935–36), 199–213, by permission of the author.

In politics and sociology, to *follow reason* is not to construct logical politics and paper systems but to relate and synthesize the findings of human experience. Theories of "total depravity" and "natural goodness" make admirably clear and definite dogmas; their only fault is that they do not tally with introspection and observation; and we may be certain that governments built upon the "logical" theories of idealogues, whether theocratic or materialist, will not endure. At the pain of being dubbed muddled, we are bidden to choose between Rome and Moscow, or again between communism and a *laissez-faire* capitalism, or between anarchy and despotism. These are the promptings of the Absolutist Demon which seeks to convince us that man must be either a god or an animal, and that every *via media* is a compromise.

That character develops only through freedom is an ethical commonplace; but the intellect has its own morality, its own "probation." Were certainty and not probability the guide of life, men would never err, but then they would never think. We have eaten of the "tree of knowledge"; hereafter we are no longer intellectually irresponsible, but we are stewards, men by whom the soil must be tilled.

"To be sure," says Kenneth Burke in his *Counter-Statement*, "so long as we feel the need of certitude, the state of doubt is discomforting, and by its very prolongation can make for our hysterical retreat into belief. . . . [Yet] one need not suffer under insecurity any more than an animal suffers from being constantly on the alert for danger. This state of technical apprehension can be a norm, and certainly an athletic norm."

There are prices too exorbitant for peace, for security, for assurance. There is the peace of the postprandial nap, the ease of the easy chair or the overstuffed sofa supporting the overstuffed matron, the ease of those who are at ease in Zion, the security of the fool. But all save a weary or despairing or senile humanity desires rather the ease of the dancer who preserves equilibrium and grace in movement, the poise of the spiritual athlete who, under constant discipline, knows his body steel, his muscles sinewy, his reach sure, his grasp firm.

But these are times in which the world seems toppling, and many break training, trusting to the fortress rather than their swords on the open field.

Burke's new book, *Permanence and Change*, is brilliant in detail, constantly exhilarating, and no competent reader can fail to find it a whetstone to his wits. To discern its drift is another matter; and one has long to wait before the smoke sufficiently clears to let one discover who has won and why. Weak in structure, despite its elaborate preliminary digest and captions, the book is best read as a sensitive and subtle mind's colloquies with itself. Certain themes fascinate this mind, and it plays with them, turns them about, drops them, returns to them. There are digressions and episodes — *pensées.* But of system-building, which at length it craves, it appears incapable.

Burke's volume traverses a wide territory — language, rhetoric, logic, psychology, ethics (disposed of to his apparent satisfaction in a short chapter), and metaphysics. For the parts of this ambitious undertaking, he is unequally equipped — amateurish at the last two, most professional at the first two, most actively a reader of psychology. The really valuable work is that "On Interpretation," a study which confessedly owes its inception to the work of I. A. Richards, but which, *me judice,* is the work of a mind natively more piercing and more philosophical than Richards', and which uses *The Meaning of Meaning* but as a point of departure. The ancestor of all such studies concerning the interpenetration of language and thought is Book III of Locke's *Essay Concerning Human Understanding,* and Burke's conclusion that arguments addressed to the reason ought to eschew emotionally weighted terms, while poetry must necessarily employ them, is anticipated in bolder outline by Locke ("But yet if we would speak of things as they are, we must allow that all the art of rhetoric, besides order and clearness, all the artificial and figurative application of words eloquence hath invented, are for nothing else but to insinuate wrong ideas, move the passions, and thereby mislead the judgement; and . . . they are certainly, in all discourses that pretend to inform or instruct, wholly to be avoided. . . ."). Burke's mind is at variance with itself, so pulled asunder by the attractions of his uncertain discussion: after, in effect, warning us against language, ethically coloured, he finally stands up to be counted among the poets. Every reader, however, can profit by the *aperçus* of his essay.

The native turn of Burke's mind is clearly and finely apparent in parts of his earlier *Counter-Statement* (1931) — especially the essay "Gide and Mann" and the "Program." Though a mind sceptical about ultimates, it is mildly and mellowly rather than truculently so disposed. It is a mind capable of defending its scepticism, not on any absolute basis, but as an ingredient in the temperamental mixture of any complete community. Society, it maintains, can endure and even profit from a considerable admixture of doubt and doubters. There will always be dogmatists enough, both naïve and learned, to stabilize the world. For one doubting Thomas there are eleven who believe. Thomas too has his vocation, his mission; and we need not fear that the Thomases will too rapidly propagate their kind. Finally, it urges that men's "biological imperatives" will effectively counteract any undue corrosion of the dissolving intellect: the belly and the blood cry out even in the enervated constitution of the "thinker."

Permanence and Change exhibits the sceptic toppling from his posture, less confident of its present usefulness, yet unable to shift its muscles to another equilibrium. Burke cannot live up to his titular prospectus. He now desires a balance of flux and fixity, but he is infinitely more *conscious* of that which moves than of that which abides. The waves really ebb and flow, but the shores remain hypothetical.

Instead of receding, his scepticism has actually advanced. From feeling sympathetic with the sceptics in a world of dogmatists, he now can entertain a sceptical sympathy with contending dogmatists. Yet it is, after all, a naïve kind of doubt which can sweep away the theologies of the world as myths and delusions. The really corrosive acid is the doubt of my doubt. Perhaps after all these Hindu jungles are as real as my neat little Yankee flat. What warrant is there that "modernism" is really *le dernier cri*, that we shall not live to see it palpably as flat and flatulent as deism or utilitarianism, that Bertrand Russell will not prove a vain thing for safety? The old-fashioned sceptic knew that Catholicism was all priest-devised imposture and the superstition of women and children; his modish grandson, feeling no such comfortable certainty, is likely to adopt the patronizing tolerance of a Santayana. Anything *may* be true – the irrational quite as probably as the rational! So speaks the model of 1935.

Burke has reached a high degree of this sceptical comprehensiveness. He can *enter sympathetically* into the magical, the mystical, the Lawrentianly primitivist "views." He can show how self-consistent, how self-sustaining, each "classical" system is. "Frazer seems to think that the belief in the efficacy of magic broke down through the discovery of its errors; yet the rationalization as he describes it was so totally consistent and so well corroborated by 'practical successes,' that I do not see how it could possibly have lost prestige through disproof." And we, in turn, may ask: How can the sceptic *disprove* the Christian belief in the efficacy of prayer? The naïve zealot no doubt finds his prayers answered when they are granted, but the theologian is not so guileless: prayers can be answered in the negative as well as the affirmative; the prayer is not divinely ignored because divinely denied. The gloss on "Give me my daily bread" is "Thy will be done." Calvinism, it will be recalled, broke down, like the one-horse shay, not a piece at a time but *totum simul*.

Mr. Burke's *sympathetic* scepticism has the advantage of liberating him from dogmatic modernism and from its corollary, the belief that Christians and other idealists are all hypocrites or, more charitably viewed, deluded rationalizers. Quite properly he stigmatizes as parochial the psychoanalytic interpretation of religion. "The entire motivation by which Augustine lived and wrote is categorically discarded [by Rebecca West] in favour of a few sexual impulses which can, at best, be shown to have been an ingredient in his motivation. By what authority can one call them the essence of his motivation? Non-sexual interests may be interpreted as the symbolization of sexual interests — but then again, sexual interests may themselves be considered as the symbolization of non-sexual interests." So they may; catch the apologetic who can. Burke does not linger; he throws out the hint "in passing." His *dialectic of motivation* lands him at no terminus of conviction; it is a species of mind-flexing jugglery, an essay in scepticism.

The "classic" systems of thought seem to him disprovable. And in a real sense, this is the case. There are logical gaps, to be sure, in every system; but in the greater philosophies we are impressed with the customary *sequitur* of deductions from "first principles." Philosophers and theologians, however, start, and must start, from some axiom or set of axioms which their critics may dub assumptions but which the propounders accept as the testimony of experience or as self-evident. In his *Creative Sceptics,* T. V. Smith has recently had some harsh words to say about "self-evident" ideas, regarding them indeed as the last and despicable refuge of the rationalizer. It is no doubt true that what seems basic and obvious to one man does not seem so to all — even the *consensus fidelium* can be found only by first defining the *fideles.* If I undertake to apply the Cartesian criterion, "de ne comprendre rien de plus en mes jugements que ce qui se présenterait si clairement et si distinctement à mon esprit que je n'eusse aucune occasion de le mettre en doute," I may succeed in finding such a base for my own thought; but thought propels itself toward the universal: I feel no deep concern to discover ideas unassailably *clear* and *distinct* to my apprehension if they are so for *me* alone; and so soon as I undertake to compare notes with my fellows, contemporary or past, I find a wide divergence as to *what* ideas are clear and distinct.

Human nature is not, however, so variable that the self-evident varies from individual to individual; and in our progress up from solipsism we may take a "rest stop" at the position that there are possible only limited numbers of reasonably self-consistent systems. The student of Greek philosophy is impressed by the fact that all conceivable systems appear represented, in embryo, at least, within its limits. Heraclitus, Democritus, Pythagoras, Plato, Aristotle, Epictetus, Epicurus, Pyrrho, Plotinus: do not these names run the gamut of all our *Weltanschauungen* — monism, pluralism, materialism, idealism, pragmatism, mysticism, ethicism? Of modern systems, Marxism, with its cluster of associated ideas — materialism, determinism, the denial of personality, and the abolition of private property — seems undeniably one. Can we say, with William James, that a philosophy represents a reasoned form of an initial temperamental insight? If so, we can add that the basic temperamental types are few enough so that the developed systems which follow from these initial *aperçus* are also few, but as permanent as are, in human nature, the absolute sceptic, the materialist, the rationalist, and the mystic. It is, then, in their initial insight rather than in their logical method that men differ. They reason honestly enough, but their experience being limited, their initial stock of assumptions is similarly limited, and so is the applicability of their inferences.

To clear the ground of all save five or six basic if rival systems, each accounting for the universe with such order and completeness as reason can supply — this seems encouraging. Our probing may, however, press to the analysis of more restricted and fluid types, which we may call the *professional* views. If I am a dentist, can I avoid scrutiny of the crowns, bridges, and plain apertures in the mouths of my neighbours; if I am a psychologist or a physician, can I help seeing them as "cases" or patients; if I am a business man, as customers or "prospects"; as an English teacher, can I avoid, mentally at least, correcting the grammar of those who board at the same table? "The doctor looks at literature?" To be sure. And so do the economist and the banker and the clergyman, each with a focus of his own. Burke discusses such vocational responses; but at the end of the book he falls into the universal trap, and after having made us conscious of how inevitably *we* look through our own professional *pince-nez*, he dons his own: life is most accurately seen by the literary man; "the ultimate metaphor for discussing the universe and man's relations to it must be the poetic or dramatic metaphor." That the vocabulary of rhetoric may, by analogy, be applied to life no one can deny, and that our thinking, at its most abstract, remains more metaphorical (as well as more anthropomorphic) than we know, I shall not deny; but why is the rhetorician more ultimate in diagnostic than the doctor, with his metaphors of health and disease, or the farmer, with his of seedtime and harvest, of rain, sunshine, and frost, of blight, dry-rot, and ripeness?

Here we have been presented with a half-truth or a third truth. One sort of rebuttal is offered by Coleridge, who, addressing his *Aids to Reflection* to all earnest men, irrespective of vocation, urges that by analysis and mediation "you may draw from the fleeting facts of your wordly trade, art, or profession, a science permanent as your immortal soul": in the universe of thought, that is, no blind alleys exist; this village road enters one upon a system of highways which encircle the world. Start anywhere, ask your way from town to town, and you will end up everywhere. The full implications of "flower in the crannied wall" – or turnip in the garden patch – land us at the destination for which all souls are bound. What serves the indolent traveller as terminal may serve another as junction and yet another as initiation.

This answer postulates, on the part of its candidate, such extraordinary qualifications as belong to but few: earnestness, intellectual eagerness, method. But even the "plain man" has not had justice done him by any caricature which restricts him to his trade. The physician, far from dealing solely in pills and potions, is also a husband, a father, and a Mason; the banker is a son, a brother, an uncle, a Republican, and a Unitarian; the celebrated industrialist plays golf, teaches Sunday School, and patronizes the opera. Even the most arrant specialist is not exhausted by the dimensions of his speciality. And no relationship is exclusively one-sided: while the teacher corrects his students' "themes," his own knowledge of human nature is corrected by what they write; when the "doctor looks at literature," we must not, in remembering who he is, forget at what he looks.

Perhaps all "views" of the universe, though couched in so many series of metaphors, all, equally, afford a guide to its meaning; perhaps they play the same cosmic melody but in many keys, on instruments of various timbre; perhaps, like some giant fugue in multiple voices they enter and re-enter, pitching the theme at the octave, the fifth, the third. . . . But in seeking to "explain" the unified reference of various analogical systems I myself fall into the musician's metaphor!

The scheme is tempting, but it must be rejected if it postulates any equipollence of metaphors. Assuredly it does matter whether I think of the universe under the type of Paley's watch and Adams's dynamo or conceive of it under some more humane and spiritual guise – whether I take my start from matter or from mind, whether man or machine be my center for exploration. Let us at least call a truce. If the prescientific ages saw the physical world anthropomorphically, animistically, we need not counter by mechanistic invasion of the world within, nor turn society into a sociological laboratory. The sciences may adopt the machine as their symbol; the humanities seek a more flexible and creative metaphor.

Does this split the universe asunder, set the "free man" in the context of an alien and incomprehensible environment? Not so, I think. The machine is man's vassal and his tool; "things" are man's "saddle": one metaphor ministers to its master.

Philosophers used to speak with condemnation of argument by analogy. Recently, however, the humane voice of W. P. Montague, the

William James of our day, has been raised in behalf of the thesis that the universe should be regarded as not Reason or Will but Imagination. Have artists, like women and mystics, their "way of knowing"? Is there a "woman's reason"; is there a "*raison du coeur*"; do "we musicians know"? Doubtless all our thinking is more metaphorical, as well as more anthropomorphic, than we recognize; and Burke has done us the service of drawing this mental trait into the open. Doubtless, too, the women, the artists, and the mystics are witnesses to kinds of experience which reason, the coordinator, must take into inclusive account. But whatever future development may await it, the "logic of metaphor" is yet primitive and undisciplined; perhaps by its very nature it cannot be more. Further, metaphorical languages, like national vernaculars, are specialized and divisive; man has felt the need of an intellectual Latin, a universal tongue into which whatever in the "vulgar languages" was capable of abstraction could be translated. The idiom of reason, philosophy, seems to me that abstractive universal language, the common denominator of our technical and personal speech. My metaphors are comprehended only by those of like temperament and vocation with myself: the denuded language of reasoning is our only hope of transcending these conditionings and mounting to the *homo*.

Thirty-three pages from the end, Burke hits upon a metaphor which seems to him to validate our passage from solipsism or vocational conditioning to a more objective truth. It is "recalcitrance" – that is to say, whatever I may *think*, there are always the blunt facts; and sooner or later I stub my intellectual toes against them. This sounds suspiciously like Johnson's refutation of Berkeley; it appears, further, to be an afterthought and not integral to Burke's earlier *modus vivendi*. Has he not earlier shown that neither magic nor mysticism is refutable by an appeal to *facts*? By implication, at least, he holds the view that he who undertakes to refute one philosophy does so by means of a rival philosophy which offers a variant interpretation of the same data.

By "recalcitrance," a backhanded term, Burke doubtless means what is ordinarily called "reality," one aspect of which we can recognize under this name. Five or six systems may, as I have suggested, be worked out, with equal logical consistency, from their initial assumptions. Of philosophies in general we may say that they may fail on either or both of two scores: their premises or their inferences. How are we able to criticize the premises; what can correct a false beginning? We come into conflict either with opposing views held by others, leading us to reconsider and perhaps to enlarge the basis upon which we stand; or our theory of what should happen fails of pragmatic justification: experience does not conform to our laws. When I am checked up short by that of which I had not taken due account, I am corrected by "recalcitrance."

Human error is partly intellectual — we don't reason accurately; partly moral — we don't employ, with proper vigour and persistence, what intellectual powers we possess; partly — perhaps chiefly — our inevitable finiteness. God is, by reason of his omniscience, the only absolutely true philosopher. Since we "see in part," what wonder that we don't see "eye to eye"! But seeing in part is partial *seeing*, and offers no warrant for despair; for it is evident that some men see no further than their noses and other men as far as the horizon. Our progress toward the "truth" is attained partly by the better ordering of what experience, immediate and vicarious, we already possess; but also — and more important — by enlarging that experience which, systematized, forms our "view." Introspection and extraspection: both can be deepened and developed. To be sure, I cannot totally escape my "temperamental self" — and there is no reason why I should wish it, since to my temperament also has been revealed its measure of the whole truth; but I can transcend it by attending to the testimonies of others, not merely among my countrymen and my contemporaries but among the remote and the immortals. I can approach the "universal man."

The final step from scepticism is one of faith. It is impossible to "think" unless we *assume* that the nature of the universe, physical and mental, constitutes a coherent whole, a uni-verse; otherwise we are reduced to voicing our tastes, our "as I like it," our evanescent moods — reduced to speaking alternately, not in dialogue. We cannot argue unless occasionally we can cry out "Illogical"; we cannot reason unless we believe that something "follows" from something else; we cannot even deny the coherence of the cosmos without affirming our possession of that criterion. We must make that act of faith. In practice, no man can persistently limit himself to mere personal testimony. On instinct, we assume that our experiences are at least partially comparable, that our assertions refer to a common ground, that, though our postures and languages differ, we are talking about the same thing.

If any school of philosophers may be called rationalists in the grand style, it is that of the post-Kantian idealists; yet what does Bradley say? "Metaphysics is the finding of bad reasons for what we believe upon instinct, but to find these reasons is no less an instinct." Santayana calls it "animal faith." Catholicism posits but one escape from ultimate scepticism: "an act of faith, faith that man can know, that reason and experience can gain him true knowledge." On this thesis, three very dissimilar witnesses appear to agree. We can have reasons for Reason, but Reason itself can find commencement nowhere else than in faith.

To doubt reasons and reasonings is sound and necessary; to doubt reasoning and reason is intellectual suicide.

◇◇

See the note on page 47.

THIS second of Mr. Warren's pieces on Burke is less accepting than the first. By 1935 and with *Permanence and Change* Burke had undergone a profound change and begun to articulate a position which had wide and disturbing social and political as well as literary and intellectual ramifications. R. P. Blackmur saw very clearly what some of these were; Professor Warren addresses himself to others. From this point on, almost nothing on Burke can really avoid the larger implications of his work – and the implications got larger for the next twenty-five years.

Specifically, Mr. Warren discusses the transient skepticism which marked Burke's development through the thirties and on into the late forties when the dramatistic system set. This skepticism is a form of openness – what William Knickerbocker was later to call Burke's maw – and remains as an essential characteristic even of dramatism, a system which, in a very Emersonian way, remains open by accommodating change to permanence in a remarkable manner. Mr. Warren writes all around *Permanence and Change* and his own title; in so doing he explores the polarities of Burke's title in ways that were to concern Burke until the certainties of his own system earned him rest – and the censure of those coming after who distrusted even such certainties as those.

With these last two selections we enter into the history of the intellectual life of our time in a way that is not true of the previous selections. This involvement remains to the end, because Burke, like all great men, beat out his own rhythms to the music of his own times. And he had an unusually fine ear.

◇◇

7 *Meaning and Communication*

BY Harold Rosenberg

ONE of Burke's conclusions is that "the ultimate metaphor for discussing the universe and man's relations to it must be the poetic or

EDITOR'S NOTE: Reprinted from *Poetry*, XLVII (March 1936), 347–349, by permission of the author and publisher.

dramatic metaphor." *Permanence and Change* includes an examination of the conditions under which such a form of communication could exist; for this belief in the great rôle of poetry as a language implies that poetry works in relation to men's needs and is not an ultimate in itself.

I should call Burke's book a "pre-poem," a poem in a gestatory stage (in the sense that Gide's *Counterfeiters* is a pre-novel and Pirandello's dramas are often pre-plays); it is as if Burke were preparing himself to write an elaborate philosophic poem by analyzing nature, the mind, and the usages of speech, in order to learn their tricks. For nothing in poetry seems arbitrary to Burke: the same devices are to be found everywhere; and no natural illusion is arbitrary or irrelevant to human life, because it is reproduced in man's poetic instrumentalities. Thus Burke's essay of exploration is directed essentially towards poetry, and itself stands on the fringe of poetic composition.

What causes this unfulfilment of form to become itself a form of modern writing? Why does one who feels that poetry is *the* way of speaking, "the ultimate metaphor," find himself forced to communicate in abstract, more or less rationally organized language?

Burke himself suggests the answer to these questions: It is because "the poetic medium of communication is weakened [that] the center of authority must be situated in a philosophy, or psychology, of poetry, rather than in a body of poetry, until the scene itself becomes sufficiently stabilized for linkages [of verbal meaning] to acquire greater spread and permanence throughout the group."

In the discords of modern life, words, no longer capable of evoking and maintaining collective responses, must become, in order to possess general meaning, instruments of scientific instruction; for wherever speech can find no social "togetherness" behind it, it tends, through abstraction, to produce unity by its own means. Science today promotes coöperation and thus turns society towards conditions favorable to poetry, so that the enemies of science are also the enemies of society and of poetry; but scientific language has not the fullness of poetry.

To communicate under the present circumstances, language as gesture must be supported and very often replaced by language of definition. This is the poetic justification of Burke's book as a non-poetic work; but it is also a justification of modernist poetry — a willed confusion through the obliteration of categories. Since all perspectives, including those of science, politics, social tradition, etc., have become along with the weakening of direct social communication, "perspectives by incongruity," the creators of grotesques, poetry too, in compliance with this historic situation, acts grotesquely, in despair of acting so as to be understood. If poetry must cease being poetry in order to be significant, it preserves itself through persisting in its own laws; that is to say, through "organized bad taste" – and thus it comes to mean something after all.

"The ultimate goal of the poetic metaphor would be in a society in which the participant aspect of action attained its maximum of expression."

Meanwhile, competition forces our participating gestures into isolated atomic groups, each with an "incongruous perspective" of its own; and style, becoming, as soon as it attempts to communicate meanings, an instrument of competition, is depleted of its poetic qualities. It may follow from this thesis that only through the establishment of a coöperative society, can poetry reach its proper rôle as the fusing power of collective purpose.

◇◇

See the note on pages 29–30.

EVERY now and then one comes across genuine and accurate prophecy. Harold Rosenberg, like Burke always an acute reader of signs, saw in 1936 that *Permanence and Change* was only the beginning of a very long book which Burke is still writing, and that the whole endeavor was to be a kind of poem, a creative and visionary work on the grand scale. It was a long time before anyone else saw so clearly what Burke was going to do.

◇◇

7 *Mr. Burke and the Historical Environment*

BY Allen Tate

IN THIS brief essay I shall try to raise a few questions suggested by Mr. Kenneth Burke's able paper, "Symbolic War," published in the Summer, 1936, issue of *The Southern Review*. Mr. Burke alone of the extreme left-wing critics seems to me to possess the historical and philosophical learning necessary to the serious treatment of the literary problems of Marxism: before his "conversion" to Communism he had subjected himself to a rigorous critical discipline. Although Mr. Burke is a

EDITOR'S NOTE: Reprinted from *The Southern Review*, II (1936–37), 363–372, by permission of the author and publisher.

political partisan, he approaches the new radical literature in the spirit of inquiry, and for that reason, I suppose, he was subjected to some bitter obloquy by his colleagues at the American Writers' Congress held in New York in April, 1935. (See the volume *American Writers' Congress*, International Publishers, pp. 165ff.) At this congress Mr. Burke was attacked for describing the class-struggle as a myth competing with other myths for supremacy in the modern world: at that stage of the discussion Mr. Burke was compelled to say, "I was speaking technically before a group of literary experts, hence I felt justified in using the word in a special sense. A poet's myths, I tried to make clear, are *real*" – an effort that won only moderate success before an audience of which Mr. Granville Hicks, as a literary expert, was a member.

In "Symbolic War" Mr. Burke begins: "Poetry, I take it, is a matter of welfare – as religion and politics are matters of welfare. And welfare, in this imperfect world, is grounded in material necessities." It is true enough to be a truism, and for that reason the statement is very likely, if it mean anything, to turn out to be as false as it is true. The chief trouble is in the term "matter." The phrase "is a matter of" may mean "depends upon," "is a reflection of," or "is a way of achieving"; but these phrases all mean something different. I am not chopping Mr. Burke's logic. I am pointing out that the ablest logician in the Communist camp, when confronted with the question of the economic base of literature, is driven to subsume so much under so vague a general term that he ends up with the assumption of a "truth" that it is his business to prove. The burden placed upon "welfare" is more than it can be made to bear.

Mr. Burke goes on to say: "The dispossessed man is in a different 'environment' from the man who enjoys the fruits of the society's wealth. He has a different 'relation to the productive forces.' And in so far as this situation sharpens his fears, hopes, and conflicts, it helps to condition his 'morality.'" That is to say, under finance-capitalism we do not have a community of culture because we do not have an ordered society in which every member has an economic stake. Within the general "culture" we get the beginnings of a new "culture" that may or may not replace the old. There is thus the rise of "class-consciousness." But Mr. Burke is aware there is no one-to-one relation, in the individual person, between his economic class and his morality. "We can belong," he says, "in as many classifications as scientists or philosophers care to invent." And this fact is largely due to another fact – that our "economic environment," our specific relation to the "forces of production," is not our total environment. For Mr. Burke insists upon a distinction between the merely historical environment –

an abstraction resulting from the simplification of our personal situation into a historical pattern, Marxism, agrarianism, etc. — and the "human environment"; this latter, Mr. Burke calls the "resources of the body itself" from which rise certain "superstructural counterparts," love, hate, desire for mobility, intelligence. (I cannot see mobility as coördinate with love, hate, and intelligence, but it is worth recording that Mr. Burke is the first Communist critic to come to my notice who seems to allow any autonomy to intelligence apart from the all-engrossing economic environment of the orthodox Marxist.) In some sense the relation of the superstructure of love, hate, intelligence, to the "resources of the body" corresponds to the superstructure of culture that a class erects upon its economic environment. I wish Mr. Burke had pursued this correspondence further and had isolated the dynamic factor at work in each relationship. I think we shall see in a moment that Mr. Burke is here almost a pure determinist, that the economic environment of the class and the human environment, the "resources of the body," respectively condition or perhaps actually effect the rise of their superstructures of general culture and personal experience. And it is this determinism, it seems to me, which cripples Mr. Burke's theory of literature, making it possible for him to take seriously certain modern works that merely illustrate new combinations of economic forces; I refer to such examples of "proletarian" writing as are contained in *Proletarian Literature in the United States* (International Publishers). Apart from the contributions by Edwin Seaver and Robert Cantwell, that volume seems to me to be almost worthless; and so it seems to Mr. Burke, but his own political bias commits him to the respectful consideration of unfavorable analysis which is too often mollified by *but* and *perhaps*. Of a very bad story he writes: "Ben Field's 'Cow' is interesting as a problem in propaganda because of its vigorous attempt to combat anti-Semitism by destroying the stereotype image of the Jew and assembling a different cluster of traits in its stead. Perhaps he approaches his task a little too head on."

Of the conflict between the economic environment and the human environment Mr. Burke says: "Many of the recent literary battles hinge about this issue." Let us see in just what terms Mr. Burke understands the issue as it affects literature.

> The presence of this "human" environment, the "natural" frame of reference that is wider than the "historical," may be discussed as the tendency of the poet to "transcend" the peculiar economic necessities of his times. Not even a fish could be said to live in a totally different environment from man. The "moralities" of man and fish must tend to overlap, destroying the symmetry of complete differentiation, in so far as both "classes" live by respiration

and locomotion. A happy translator might do a fairly reputable job at turning a fish's delight in gills and fins into a glorification of lungs and legs.

I very much fear that in this passage Mr. Burke has committed himself to the metaphorical logic of popular journalese. (His partial awareness of this is in the quotes around "transcend.") If the historical environment is the product of historical and scientific method, it is, on its necessarily quantitative basis, infinitely wider than the human environment; so the poet in achieving the human point of view probably engages in a procedure that can in no wise be conveyed by the verb *to transcend*. He is more likely proceeding to his objective with an entirely different quality of intelligence from that employed in isolating the economic or historical environment, a kind of cognition which differs from the historical not merely in being wider or narrower but in being, apart from physical range, intensive. Mr. Burke is, of course, in the passage about the fish, adumbrating a theory of the universal in art: it is preëminently an eighteenth-century theory couched in a biological analogy dear to the nineteenth. The universal is the general average of observation drawn from the *widest* possible field. It is not a universal of implicit intensiveness, but a universal of scientific formulation. Instead of a proposition like "Man is vile," we get "Man is a vertebrate."

But Mr. Burke is aware that this kind of formula in literature has its dangers, not because it is an inadequate formula but because its adherents may push it too far.

> The oversimplifying advocate of "proletarian" art would stress the historic environment to the exclusion of all else (and would then invent all sorts of subterfuges and epicycles to explain a liking he might have for Dante or Aeschylus, perhaps finally deciding that they were "workers" in their field). And the oversimplifying advocate of the universally human would lay all emphasis upon the continuity of "man's burden" throughout the ages, as he incessantly confronts the critical events of birth, growth, love, union, separation, initiation, sorrow, fear, death, and the like.

I do not know if Mr. Burke is driven into the subterfuges that he seems a little jibingly to attribute to his colleagues; I gather that he is not. Nor is he committed to the catalogue of spurious universals that he finds in the repertoire of the nonproletarian writer. I cannot imagine why Mr. Burke ridicules his own theory, but I should like to guess why: he does not believe in it, but he cannot allow himself to think up any other because he has previously subscribed to a theory of the relation of the human and the economic environments, a theory that misleads him into the belief that the human is wide and abstract, the historical narrow and concrete, and that the latter may be transcended by the former, and indeed must be transcended at least, one supposes, to a certain degree, if the artist is to escape the stigma of mere contemporaneity, a stigma earned by an excessive zeal for propaganda.

The question that arises here, and it is a question that I should like to see Mr. Burke undertake to answer, is the extent to which the artist, *qua* artist, must transcend the mere historical environment. That is to say, in what proportion shall the two environments be mixed? In Mr. Burke's analysis of the artist's situation into these two environments, the question that I have just posed must, I think, be necessarily asked in those terms – the terms, not of fusion, but of mixture. Mr. Burke asks: "Might we not suspect that, unless men were brutes or gods (and Aristotle reminds us that they are not either) they must inevitably exemplify imagination and propaganda both?" That sounds reasonable. But what does "exemplify" mean; and are imagination and propaganda coördinate terms? Upon close examination most of Mr. Burke's propositions about this problem of propaganda turn out to be merely rhetorical logic – when he is not actually ridiculing his own terms. The distinction between imagination and propaganda is rhetorical. When a critic as astute as Burke falls afoul of terms we are entitled to look for a very dark nigger hiding in the rhetorical woodpile.

That nigger, as I dimly see him, looks like this: he is the effort of a profound critic to conceal from himself the true nature of his problem in order to justify the literary practice of his political allies. One more quotation and my exhibit of this tendency in Mr. Burke's essay – a tendency that does not appear in *Permanence and Change* – will be complete:

> One may hypothetically picture the two opposite procedures: that of the "partisan" writer, who begins by discovering a "propaganda situation," and proceeds to exploit it by inventing characters to fit; and in contrast, there is the "imaginative" writer, who might begin with an attachment to some very appealing character, and in the course of depicting him, might show him at work in some propaganda situation, such as the harboring of a labor leader hunted by vigilantes. Ultimately, there need be nothing at odds between the two approaches: an expression that is not truncated will encompass both. But if the partisan factor is emphasized with too much greed, it may lead to schematization of character, with nothing of appeal in so far as the situation itself lacks appeal.

That too looks sensible – but to me the whole passage is meaningless. Is the artist rendering his subject, or is he merely mixing ingredients – is he at liberty to *emphasize* this and to pass over that? (Mr. Burke's verbs will bear watching.) And what is Mr. Burke going to do about the writer who begins "with an attachment to some very appealing character" whose life is so lived that he has never seen a labor leader and never even heard of vigilantes? I personally know dozens of people, of fathomless interest as characters, who are like that. Will Mr. Burke reply with the orthodox Communist reply, that such a writer, dealing with such characters, is outside the Great Tradition, that he is frivolous, irrelevant, and a disguised apologist of capitalism – simply because implicit in this writer's characters there is no "propaganda situation," because the writer ignores the "economic environment" as it is defined by the Marxists? I do not think that Mr. Burke will say this; but I am not sure.

Mr. Burke's aesthetic standards are offended by the propagandist excesses of his colleagues; but the only warning that he issues to them in "Symbolic War" is an appeal for moderation; he asks them *not to go too far*. He asks them not to mix too much of the ingredient of propaganda into the gruel of art. He does not ask them to do some fundamental aesthetic thinking that might eliminate altogether the need for compromise between the different pairs of antinomies that he describes: propaganda and imagination, historical and human environments, etc.

How far is too far? Mr. Burke must obviously be an opportunist in this, since on principle he cannot establish a point at which the poet must eschew propaganda; Mr. Burke will have to decide each case as it appears. And it seems to me that this is due to the underlying significance of his dichotomy between propaganda and imagination, between the historical and the human environments. For, in the long run, from whichever end of the dilemma the artist may begin, he is cut off, under Mr. Burke's theory, from the exercise of the critical intellect.

It is astonishing to observe that political revolutionists evince such timidity in aesthetic theory. Mr. Burke's theory of literature is the standard eighteenth-century belief in the inherent dignity of the subject: some subjects are good, some bad. It is too large a field of discussion to describe here, yet the equivalent for literature of Mr. Burke's "historical environment" is the decorous subject that from the time of Addison dominated criticism until the time of Matthew Arnold. The very use of the term "sincerity" by many Communist critics today is closely related to Arnold's notion that it is the same as high seriousness. On this point Mr. Cleanth Brooks is instructive: "If Arnold states that high seriousness 'comes from absolute sincerity,' one remembers Coleridge's objection to the play of wit because it implied 'a leisure and self-possession incompatible with the steady fervor of a mind possessed and filled with the grandeur of its subject.' Indeed, Arnold's high seriousness amounts to little more than this *steady fervor*." The steady fervor about the Cause—Victorian morality or Marxian doctrine—cannot admit of critical examination; and, under Mr. Burke's theory, least of all can it admit of the exercise of the critical wit which tends to place all "causes" in the whole context of experience. The steady fervor cannot be fused into an integral expression of sincerity and intelligence; they come together in a mixture.

I have indicated that Mr. Burke sees in his "historical environment" the concrete reality, and in the "human environment" the wider abstract medium through which artists transcend the merely local view. Yet it is apparent that the act of transcending carries the artist over into a very thin realm of miscellaneous emotions in which Mr. Burke obviously feels very little conviction; he is aware of a vague duty to do justice to the eternal verities—love, union, hate, and the rest. They are all, of course, only a miscellany of Platonic abstractions, and although Mr. Burke calls them the "human environment" they actually have no environment at all: they were once the decorous subjects of eighteenth-century poetry and criticism. They were susceptible to the application of Coleridge's steady fervor. I need not quote exhibits of the poetic language appropriate to that zeal: criticism in the last twenty years has sufficiently described the state of the poetic vocabulary at the end of the nineteenth century. From the neo-classical belief in decorum there is a direct development of theory and practice through the Romantics and Victorians into a belief in the higher decorum, which makes the poet the "unacknowledged legislator" and, for Arnold, the Teacher.

And that is all that Mr. Burke's theory, it seems to me, allows him to be. The poet may be a purveyor of the eternal verities, and thus I suppose a capitalist poet in the "traditional" culture; or he may be concerned with the historical environment of Marxism—in which case he is still a teacher.

Mr. Burke's scheme of the two general procedures possible to the poet seems to me vulnerable at two points. First, the distinction between the human environment and the historical environment is a distinction without a difference. They are both realms of practical abstractions for the service of the will—the will of the individual prophet-teacher and the will of the radical reformer. And secondly Mr. Burke's scheme offers only a mechanical explanation of the relation of the poet to his material: in making the poet's apprehension of "ideas" explicit and self-conscious he commits himself to a theory closely resembling that of Mr. Paul Elmer More. The anomaly of this association of names disappears when one remembers that there has been no general revolution in criticism since Dryden. For, after the rise of materialism under Hobbes and Locke,* the poet lost confidence in his own special function – the whole and inutile creation of the human experience – and began to compete with the scientist, until at last the poet has begun *to be* a social scientist. The practical abstraction has usurped the whole realm of the poet. Criticism for two hundred years has been based, not upon Shakespeare, for whom the "idea" has no meaning apart from the concrete experience, but upon the weaker side of Milton, upon his professed mission as Teacher and not upon his performance as a poet.

The mechanism of the abstract idea underlying Mr. Burke's theory has dominated our criticism for two centuries. Its dominion over Mr. Burke's intelligence witnesses the absence of revolutionary critical thought in a political movement whose avowed aim is revolution. If among the American Communists there were any radical thinking in literary criticism I think Mr. Burke would be aware of it, or we might expect him to supply it. Mr. Burke's case for the "proletarian" writers is persuasive, but it is not convincing on the special ground of their originality. Some of these writers are interesting, but they are interesting, from the strict critical point of view, not for their zeal in reform, but rather for whatever merit they have achieved as writers. They have most of the merits and most of the defects of other writers living within the mentality of the present age.

The test of the economics of literature is in the long run the test of time. And time here signifies not merely the stability of an economic system but the continuity of a certain way of life. Whether a Communist economic order in America – whatever it may do in Europe – can achieve a continuous pattern of life is debatable; it is debatable equally for and against. Finance-capitalism has developed on the economic side in well-defined and predictable directions; on the social, moral, and religious side there has been steady deterioration. A system of production may be made to work a high efficiency without in the least effecting for society a moral pattern durable enough for men to depend upon; without, moreover, making any sort of pattern necessary or desirable. This is indeed inevitable when men have no moral control over the method of production. And here it is difficult to see any fundamental moral difference between the giant corporation of the present and the giant supercorporation, which is the state, of tomorrow.

Communist literature gives us no clue to such a difference. In Mr. Burke's own analysis of the situation of the American Communist writer, the novelist and the poet must be preoccupied, directly or indirectly, with the "historical environment," a picture of men abstracted

* See Cleanth Brooks, *Three Revolutions in Poetry*, II, "Wit and High Seriousness." *The Southern Review*, Autumn (1935), pp. 328–338.

into two warring classes, capitalist and worker. That is the subject of greatest "reality" to the Communist writer. Yet so far as successful works of literature are concerned the test of their reality is not the historical and political conviction of the authors, but the works themselves. It is probable that political conviction transformed into the reality of experience based upon a definite, and not merely a hoped for, order of life is the matrix of literature. There is no evidence that Shakespeare was aware, in terms of modern historical thinking, of the conflict of dying feudalism and rising capitalism. For him it was an inexhaustible subject— but not in those terms.

◇◇

ALLEN TATE was born in Winchester, Kentucky, in 1899. He is a poet, novelist, biographer, critic, editor, and teacher. From 1951 to 1968 he was a professor of English at the University of Minnesota. He was an editor of *The Fugitive* and *The Sewanee Review*, and one of the contributors to *I'll Take My Stand*. Like Burke, he has been directly and continuously involved in American intellectual, cultural, and creative life since the early twenties. His published works include several volumes of very important critical essays. Like R. P. Blackmur, Cleanth Brooks, John Crowe Ransom, and Robert Penn Warren, Allen Tate was early associated with the "new criticism" and was a major force in the formulation and defense of the theoretical foundations of that critical movement.

Because he has always stubbornly defended an essentially conservative and oddly traditional position, Allen Tate has tended to be somewhat combative in print. This is the role in which one sees him here (as defender of the faith); and perhaps that is why he radically oversimplifies Burke's position and seems to be indulging much of the time in mere term-splitting. Whatever the validity of Tate's attack, his essay has a very great historical interest and importance precisely because of the political and theoretical issues raised. Many of the central critical problems of the thirties reveal themselves here in some form or another. Burke was both one and not one of the "new" critics. He was never someone they openly and warmly accepted, and though they all seem to have borrowed from and used him in one way or another, most of them have been curiously silent about him in print.

◇◇

2 Kenneth Burke: The Critic's Critic

BY Charles I. Glicksberg

I

A SUBTLE and adventurous critic, Kenneth Burke is willing to follow the trail of an idea wherever it may lead, without regard to established sanctities of meaning. In a style that is logical, compact, almost wearisome in its insistence on defining terms and clarifying meanings, he ventures upon the ambitious task of reappraising all hitherto existing critical values. This involves him in a study of linguistics, logic, anthropology, psychology, and methodology. His method — the utilization of the principle of polarity — is simple but daring: he takes a number of commonly accepted truths and values, reduces them to their elementary premises, and then quietly inquires if the converse could not be regarded as equally true. This process he calls achieving perspective through incongruity. In other words, he demonstrates that a statement may be both true and false at the same time. Its "truth" depends on the frame of reference within which it is situated, the point of orientation from which it is viewed. By means of this method he is able to puncture the pretensions of many a vested critical system. His primary object is to secure terminological exactitude by reducing meanings, which are essentially social in origin and purpose, to their component elements.

It is not likely that Kenneth Burke will be widely read or that he will receive generous public recognition. The reason is not far to seek. His books are too technical, packed too solidly with speculative material that requires careful analysis. He is too skeptical, too discriminating and iconoclastic a thinker. His preoccupation with the nature of meaning, his command of a style that is laboriously precise — these alone will cause him to remain the intellectual leader of a small minority. He is the critic's critic par excellence. Not that he is unable to write simply; he does, in fact, write simply; but the material he deals with is often so recondite and complex that no other style seems possible for his scrupulous and exacting intelligence.

In an age of disintegrating faith, when all of man's knowledge and belief is undergoing a searching re-examination, he has taken upon himself the enormously difficult task of tearing down the whole cumbersome critical structure and building anew on a firmer and more lasting foundation. To do so, he was compelled to erect his premises

EDITOR'S NOTE: Reprinted from *The South Atlantic Quarterly*, XXXVI (1937), 74–84, by permission of the author.

and postulates, to formulate a series of consistent concepts and bind them together in a functionally valid body of ideas. Such an undertaking naturally led him to a consideration of our linguistic heritage, the genealogy of words, the function and psychological bearing of language. Once words are stripped of their sacred, emotive qualities, it is possible to proceed to a discussion of fundamentals. It is primarily the technical character of his work, not his style, which has militated against his literary "success." The general public is not interested in questions of form, methods of appeal, the morphology of style, terminological consistency, pure truth. And yet there are few critics writing at the present time who are exerting a more pronounced, though subterranean, influence than Kenneth Burke. If in the future American criticism moves in the direction of increased clarity, precision, and understanding, it will be due in no small measure to the important contributions made by this comparatively young critic.

His reputation, such as it is, rests on two books, *Counter-Statement* and *Permanence and Change,* both of which are concerned with the basic principles of criticism. *Counter-Statement* attempts to present a coherent point of view, which is "somewhat apologetic, negativistic, and even antinomian, as regards everything but art." He does more than construct the scaffolding of a general critical theory; he endeavors to interpret and evaluate a number of significant writers — Thomas Mann, Gide, Pater, and Flaubert — in the light of this theory. In one chapter, entitled "Program," he tries to come to terms with the socio-economic conception of art. Even then he had already arrived at the conclusion that life is conditioned by the social structure, though he had not yet made up his mind as to the nature of the conditioning process or in what manner society should be reformed. He had not yet taken the plunge into the deep and troubled waters of literary Marxism. Highly suggestive, too, is the "Lexicon Rhetoricae," which is a kind of judgment machine he designed "to serve as an instrument for clarifying critical issues, not so much for settling issues as for making the nature of a controversy more definite." This he does by elaborating some key terms for the purpose of nomenclature and analysis.

Permanence and Change covers a vast terrain of thought. It seeks to postulate a philosophy of social values as well as to present a critique of social thought and expression. His method of achieving perspective through incongruity, of hunting for the antithesis of what has been taken for granted in various fields of action and speculation, comes into full play. The instrument of logic is wielded like a surgical knife cutting away diseased or superfluous tissue. Intellectually enterprising and ingenious, he succeeds in introducing a rich varied assortment of provisional ideas and in overhauling our whole critical vocabulary. He owes a great deal to workers in other vineyards — I. A. Richards, Veblen, Dewey, and Freud; indeed, one criticism that might be made of this book is that it is largely derivative in substance. His borrowing, however, is done in no subservient, academic spirit. Fundamentally he is a disciple of Dewey, applying his philosophy of instrumentalism to language, social values, and art. The contributions of Freud are accepted as offering fertile clues, but the intrusion of bias and error in psychoanalysis is sharply exposed. Though his sympathies veer decidedly towards communism, Burke's rationalism prevents him from completely embracing any system of values without a preliminary "scientific" investigation to determine its validity.

II

The problems which Burke takes up are fundamental to an understanding of our age. Science, he feels, has advanced too far and at too fast a rate for us to adjust our spiritual and mental resources to the revolution. Arguing that there is an important distinction between scientific and artistic truth, he maintains that a poet may develop a belief which he knows to be false. The poet writes "as if" what he says is true. All that the artist can do is to endeavor to be consistent and sincere within the framework of the fiction he constructs. "The 'sum total' of art relieves the artist of the need of seeing life steadily and seeing it whole."

In *Permanence and Change*, Burke's attitude towards science has crystallized. Though recognizing the achievements of science, he points out the great harm that scientific thought has done. It has created a closed universe; it has transformed man into a machine conditioned by his material environment; it has stripped him of the illusion of free will, which is at the heart of ethics. Burke distrusts the arbitrary ideology perfected and dictated by science. Something is lacking in the scientific ideal, he insists, which is tremendously important for mankind. Negatively we are given to understand that science leaves out of account a number of moral and religious affirmations without which man cannot create a satisfying metaphor of the universe, a convincing world-orientation.

Since science as an organized body of knowledge rests upon a foundation of first principles, it cannot go far without a concept of the end striven for. To envisage this end, Burke declares, is to set up an aim, and hence a philosophy of science. All this has been said before. Much of it is undoubtedly true. But is it not a mistake to argue that the basic assumptions of science are to be tested by the standards of reason alone — as if these assumptions were syllogistic exercises, the fallacies of which could be discovered by the patient application of logic? On the contrary, these assumptions are rooted in experience, in a special kind of experience — experiments conducted under certain controlled conditions, which can be repeated again and again for the purpose of verification. If the conclusions arrived at do not confirm the original premise, the assumptions are revised and a new hypothesis formed. Reasoning in science is not a thing apart, a self-sufficient entity; it is part of the experience, part of the experiment and is itself subject to verification. Reason is inherent in the empirical process. There is a scientific mode of reasoning and of observing the workings of the mind. Skepticism against science is justified, but it must be a neutral kind of skepticism, freed from emotional or ethical imperatives. Too often skepticism is generated by an underlying impatience with science because it fails to satisfy some spiritual yearning or subjective wish.

Burke's method of rationalizing the revolt against science is extremely interesting. Occasionally he uncovers his trump cards and plays with them face down on the table, without any great pretense of logical justification. The scientific rationalization, he believes, must be corrected by a move "in the direction of the anthropomorphic or poetic." Poetry by taking the place of religion may yet save the world. The philosophic corrective that he envisages would derive support from biology and would also satisfy pragmatic needs. A rationale of art — art in its widest sense as an art of living — would thus supplant an inadequate scientific rationalization. Why should the universe, he asks, be forced to fit into a man-made system of communication, "particularly when there is so strongly a *creative* or poetic quality about its goings-on"? One stops to wonder whether the philosophic corrective he so earnestly recommends is not man-made, too.

Perhaps the weakest, the least convincing part of Burke's work is that which seeks to overthrow the Goliath of science. It has become fashionable among a number of metropolitan critics to attack the scientific spirit. The truth is that science and art have no quarrel with each other. What possible objection can there be against an increase of knowledge? It is sheer sentimentalism to assert that the progress of science is inimical to the growth of culture and art. It may prove inimical to a certain kind of art, which then becomes obsolete, but it compensates by opening new continents of thought for artistic exploration and development. It is a powerful testimony to the influence of science that critics like Krutch and Burke oppose its extension. That the protest against science springs from an emotional source, that it is motivated by the desire to reassert the freedom of the will, is indicated by Burke's sudden leap from a corrective philosophy of science to a militant Marxist gospel.

III

This apostle of linguistic skepticism announces, without apparently perceiving the incongruity involved, that "the only coherent and organized movement making for the subjection of the technological genius to humane ends is that of Communism." The fundamental criteria of communism, he has discovered, have a "highly humanistic or poetic nature." That the process of political conversion was not a painless one may be seen by a consideration of his view on the economic interpretation of art in *Counter-Statement.* Though he then conceded that the economic attack upon art contained a grain of truth, he assailed the economic critics for transforming economics into cause and art into effect. Art was not merely a reflection of political and economic forces.

The pressure of the age has driven many able critics, not in the least fitted for such a task, into the field of socio-economic speculation and analysis. In *Counter-Statement,* Burke is manfully laboring to solve all our economic ills. He engages in an extended discussion of industrialism, the agrarian ideology, capitalism, the dole, technological unemployment, and so on, all of which he associates with his central issue. It is the duty of the artist, he declares, to set himself in opposition to the ominous trend of industrialism. The innovation of the artist must reside in providing a cultural counterpart of our industrial, mechanized régime. If mechanization makes society disastrously complex, then "the aesthetic must serve as anti-mechanization, the corrective of the practical." To illustrate the constructive aspect of his anti-industrial program, he suggests that some efficacious means of redistributing wealth be devised. The wholesale application of the dole, he is convinced, will eliminate the misery of joblessness and guarantee a minimum subsistence. His whole program at this time may be summed up as follows: The machine is powerful enough to survive and prosper of itself; no philosophy of efficiency is required to support the menace of overproduction. The counter principle of inefficiency must therefore be invoked to prevent the machine from becoming too powerful.

Then, in his latest book, he abruptly abandons his "romantic" opposition to the machine. He has suddenly discovered that communism is the way and the light. But the description of that discovery is neither sudden nor brief. Burke goes through a lengthy, elaborate ordeal of verbal contortions to explain the how and why of his political conversion. It is not with him, he assures us, a personal problem but a solution of all critical problems. He is concerned primarily with a philosophy of being, with the development of a norm based on the assumption that there is a universal biological constant. Since a sound system of communication cannot be developed within a society ruled by economic warfare, society must become economically as well as spiritually communistic. A master purpose must be defined and put into practice integrating the conflicting whirl of nationalities and cultures. The future will witness the growth of the "associative, or congregational state."

Deflected by the Marxian outlook and by the philosophy of instrumentalism, Burke struggles to formulate an occupational morality. Action involves choice, it is fundamentally ethical, ethics being conceived instrumentally as the choice of means. Since poetry is also ethical in nature, he maintains that the ethical is integrally linked with the communicative or creative process. Every form of universe-building, he insists, is ethical. Burke at this point forsakes his linguistic skepticism and gives too wide a latitude to the meaning of the term "ethical." What is ethical to one group with a particular psychosis may be anathema to another group with a different and perhaps opposed set of values. To apply the ethical concept to any method of selecting means, regardless of its efficacy or social import, is to strip the word of its concrete, relativistic meaning. Burke, significantly enough, formulates an occupational morality in order to pave the way for his assertion of faith in the poetic metaphor. Man in contemporary society is unable to achieve spiritual co-ordination. Without some master purpose to guide and control his thinking, he cannot achieve a stable and harmonious culture. "In other words, *freedom* must be defined by *purpose*. . . . A Communist movement can provide such a master purpose."

Since all life is based on some fiction, we must proceed to construct a universe of values satisfactory to human needs. Burke emphasizes the thought that the ethical perspective through which one views the universe is itself part of the universe. "To live is to have a vocation, and to have a vocation is to have an ethics or scheme of values." Moreover, as it seeks to communicate itself, our point of view will become increasingly objective. It will have to do so in order to overcome the recalcitrance it encounters. Determinism he condemns on the ground that it is too mechanical. It neglects to point out that a point of view, once in operation, introduces a new causal factor. The ultimate metaphor for discussing the universe and man's place in it "must be the poetic or dramatic metaphor."

Thus Burke gravitates irresistibly towards communism because it seems to be a rationalization in harmony with the poetic metaphor. It offers man a socially healthy and organic vocation. It enables man to accommodate the machine to his fundamental needs. Communism once established as a way of life, "the poetic metaphor would be the best guide (indeed the only conceivable guide) in shaping the new pieties of living." His book, which began with a plea for skepticism, ends on a mystical note.

IV

One may well ask: What has all this to do with literary criticism? In a period of ideological dissension and economic instability, many critics have been driven to the desperate expedient not only of re-examining their critical assumptions and arranging them in some new and more satisfying philosophy, but also of playing the part of social and political engineers. They have experienced the urgent need of proclaiming their political faith, of settling once for all the problems that perplex the world. Obviously such a point of view leads to a circuitous detour, an elaborate system of rationalization — the attempt to translate literary criticism in terms of politics and economics. Not that such intellectual excursions are without their value; they do help the critic to think clearly on certain vital contemporary issues, they expand the limits of his mental horizon, they liberate him from narrow aesthetic preconceptions, from considering art exclusively as a thing-in-itself. But if sociological criticism has its advantages, it also works decided harm when carried to extremes. It transforms criticism into a department of the "dismal science." It converts critical issues into a political debate.

Burke is too honest a thinker to embrace communism directly on emotional grounds; it takes him a long time before he can logically convince himself that Marx provides the only feasible solution. At heart he is a relativist; his essential skepticism will force him to modify his views — at least as far as literature is concerned. When the economic crisis is ended, when the contemporary tension is eased, he will probably return to his first love — literary criticism.

He is most at home in the realm of esthetic criticism. He has consistently sought to evolve a comprehensive philosophy of art. In examining the nature of the creative process, he has rightly taken exception to the current tendency which restricts self-expression to the spontaneous utterance. For the self-expression of the artist consists not in voicing emotions but in arousing them in others — that is to say, in communication.

As a critic, Burke is particularly interested in the problem of communication. The essence of communication lies in socialization. Thought is not only a prelude to action; it is in itself a form of action. Since the artist is a member of a cultural group in which he functions and to which his work is addressed, he too deals with the "occupational psychosis." By building and manipulating the intellectual superstructure, he succeeds in fathering "the appropriate habit-patterns useful to his particular economic system." Marxism and instrumentalism are thus reconciled. This thesis, however, requires considerable modification if it is to stand the test of empirical investigation. Exactly how is the artist involved in this process? Does he consciously manipulate certain cultural elements because he is closely bound up with economic society? If so, what is the precise nature of his relation to society? What habit-patterns does he father by his artistic contribution? Burke speaks of a capitalistic, monetary, agrarian, individualist, proletarian, and technological psychosis. For a critic employed in extracting the meaning of meaning, the use of such abstractions is rather mystifying. The economic interpretation of literature confuses rather than clarifies the central critical issue.

The method which Burke uses with greatest effect is to turn accepted linguistic and conceptual categories upside down and inside out. Regardless of how a process has been labeled or a belief formed, he examines it in a new light. Words are symbols, not concrete fragments of reflected reality. In this way he piles up a miscellaneous assortment of incongruities. This tendency, though it is part of the present confused social order, has been a salutary influence in that it has encouraged a critical interpretative attitude. "The myriad orientations will be tragically wasted, the genius of one of the world's most vigorous centuries will be allowed to go unused, unless we can adopt its very welter of interpretations as skeptical grounding for our own certainties." That this is as yet far removed from a positive affirmation is evident in the adjective "skeptical." He hopes, however, that the deliberate cultivation of planned incongruity will result in a definite gain. Every conventional linkage, he urges, should be broken and reassembled in a new empirical linkage. Opposites, even the seemingly fantastic and absurd, should be magnified. Exploration may lead to momentous discoveries. The mind must be freed from fixed associations, from traditional methods of inquiry. It must start afresh, even to the extent of adopting postulates known to be false. Such a method will no doubt yield novel and perhaps fruitful conclusions, but it may be carried too far and then it culminates in a gargoyle intellectualism. The juggling of concepts may simply result in the canonization of new concepts, equally confusing and inapplicable.

Burke's relation to Pater is too striking to be missed. Stylistically, temperamentally, even aesthetically, the two have much in common. In both are evident the same acute critical faculty, the same love of fine distinctions, of complex ideas neatly resolved, the same passion for the exact phrase. If Pater wrote fiction as though he were writing essays, Burke writes criticism as if he were writing a kind of mathematical, ritualistic poetry. What he says of Pater applies also to his own work – namely, that Pater wrote "as a scholar, interested vitally in the mechanism of his sentences, using words with an almost philological emphasis." And again the parallel holds when he says that Pater manifested "that philosophic – or perhaps, in the truest sense, cultured – turn of mind which finds the specific interesting only through its correlation with the general."

He parts company with Pater in his confident reliance on skepticism as a method and a state of mind. Like Gide, he would approve of humanizing the condition of doubt. He is strongly in sympathy with any movement which is dissociative, experimental, plagued by conflict and contradiction. Before he had allied himself with communism, he could write: "Since the body is dogmatic, a generator of belief, society might be benefited by the corrective of a disintegrating art, which converts each simplicity into a complexity, which ruins the possibility of ready hierarchies, which concerns itself with the problematical, the experimental, and thus by implication works corrosively upon those expansionistic certainties preparing the way for our social cataclysms." This might very well serve as a statement of his critical method. To work by contrarieties and incongruities, to pit opposites one against the other, to throw open the whole question of value – that is his favorite method of attack. In *Counter-Statement* he argued that it was possible to accept the unknown, the contingent without loss of balance or a paralysis of the springs of action. "This state of technical apprehension can be a norm, and certainly an aesthetic norm." That is to say, for him, at one stage of his development, a state of suspended judgment, an attitude of provisional doubt, is not only congenial, but a source of stimulation; it provides a sense of adventure, a feeling that one is living dangerously; it makes possible at the same time a freer and more accurate critical evaluation.

His work, however, suffers – and was bound to suffer – from the defects of its primary virtues. It is too technical and abstract in its operations to reach a wide audience. Every sentence posits a problem, forms a link in a closely-knit logical chain, intrudes a doubt, shatters a privileged truth. So deep-seated, so pervasive is his skepticism as applied to social, philosophic, and linguistic matters, that he erects no constructive system of his own. Despite its communistic conclusions, *Permanence and Change* is the breviary of skepticism. Terms are defined and redefined, placed in novel juxtaposition with remote or related terms, viewed from difficult angles of vision, till they lose their original and familiar connotations. Incongruity becomes a repetitive device, a logical trick which, however effective in exploding certain dogmas, affords no true perspective. He has failed as yet to build the skeptical grounding for that ideological synthesis which is the crying need of our time.

◇◇

CHARLES I. GLICKSBERG was born in Warsaw, Poland, in 1901. He is a professor of English at Brooklyn College and a member of the faculty of the New School for Social Research. He is the author of *Literature and Religion* and *Tragic Vision in Twentieth-Century Literature* and the editor of an anthology of American literary criticism.

This is one of the earliest and best essays in which Burke is treated as a systematic critic. In this sense it is a pioneering study comparable to that of Austin Warren in the way it shows how the working people in the profession received and used Burke. Unlike Allen Tate, who does little but argue and quibble with Burke, Mr. Glicksberg accepts and then questions him. Specifically, he very accurately summarizes Burke's position, identifies some of his sources, discusses his "Marxism," and argues that Burke is *essentially* a literary critic. As a whole, it seems to me that Mr. Glicksberg rightly emphasizes Burke's addiction to perspective by incongruity as intellectual therapy, his skepticism, which is sometimes a form of perspective by incongruity, his contemporaneity, his love of dialectics and polarity, and the "poetic" nature of his endeavor. Retrospectively, it is interesting that Mr. Glicksberg ends his essay lamenting Burke's failure to "build the skeptical grounding for that ideological synthesis which is the crying need of our time." Burke did nothing else — almost — for the next thirty years. The rest of this book charts his progress.

◇◇

7 *Accepting and Rejecting Kenneth Burke*

BY Arthur E. DuBois

IT TAKES courage nowadays to assert that there are civilized persons. Yet I believe that Max Eastman, Heywood Broun, and Norman Thomas,

EDITOR'S NOTE: Reprinted from *The Sewanee Review*, XLV (1937), 343–351, 354–356, copyright 1937 by the University of the South, by permission of Kenneth DuBois and the publisher.

an occasional writer for *The New Yorker* or *The New Republic*, perhaps F. D. Roosevelt, and maybe a thousand others, are civilized. On university faculties, though they probably let it be known as seldom as possible, there are possibly a hundred more. There are you and I and the smiling editor of *The Sewanee Review*. And there is Kenneth Burke, author of "Acceptance and Rejection" in *The Southern Review* and "The Critic's Critic" whom Charles I. Glicksberg discusses in *The South Atlantic Quarterly*.

Mr. Burke suggests one token of the civilized person: he will not call an opponent "villainous"; instead, he will call him "mistaken." Perhaps he will call him "half-right" even oftener than "mistaken." There are other signs of the civilized person. He will not need to say things tentatively, for he will understand the mood of civilized conversations, that all matters worth discussion are still open for it even though he has said his word or two. He will not require all sheep to be black, white, or even spotted. He will know that a great deal of acceptance or rejection must end short of perfection, in Yes-and-no rather than in Yes or than in No. And he will therefore not be like the Russians who could not understand Shaw's refusal to be absolutely for or absolutely against them. The civilized person will proceed to conviction rather than to coercion, and be sensitive enough to human needs in himself or others not to wish to re-make the world exclusively in his own image but, on the other hand, not to resist change or growth because it is change or because it curtails established privileges.

The civilized person will assist the fakir to demonstrate that 2 and 2 equals 3 quite as readily as he will assist the giaour to demonstrate that 2 and 2 equals 5, providing that each acts accordingly. He will have in him something of the spirit of the pioneer or adventurer, including even a large portion of naïveté, a sense of wonder at people, things, and ideas, and a curiosity to see them rightside up and upside down.

The crusader can hardly be civilized and successful as a crusader—he can be civilized only in his "off" moments. Professional people, if they are only doctors or lawyers or clergymen or teachers, likewise can hardly be civilized. Their fixed viewpoint is too rigid, narrow, or smug. The civilized person cannot be typical of only limited groups. He must be, rather, egregious, eccentric, creative. In other words, even to himself he must often seem like a fool. Perhaps this is but to say that he will be typical in so comprehensive a sense as to be human, not superhuman, not sub-human, not humanitarian, and not humanist!

Universities tend to produce uncivilized offsprings, especially persons lost in the rigmaroles, rituals, costumes, immunities, techniques, or jargons of their professional or social class. All institutions, in fact, have this tendency. Even our language, an institution, is studded with words from all sorts of sources to connote disapprobation for the stranger who brings the potter new designs, colors, or molds for the pot. Any deviator from an established powerful class or type or mode is a pagan, peasant, heathen, yokel, bolshevist, villain, barbarian, gentile, cadet, grisette, snob, plebeian, hooligan, vagabond, varlet, vagrant, rascal, wanton, pariah, philistine, blackguard, ryot, landlubber, etc. In fact, this practice of condescension toward the outsider is so established that it is no longer true that sticks and stones will crack the bones but names won't hurt. The regular practice of politicians in and out of session is to damn an opponent by calling him names. One is safe only because one is likely to be called, for better or Hearst, fascist and communist at the same time. The academician damns a writer by the words "unsound scholarship" if for a minute he transgresses beyond footnotabilities or beyond the microscopic field in which he has written a thesis and is supposed to be a specialist.

As a result, persons like Kenneth Burke, repelled by academies and privileged somehow to escape their name-callings, are doing work which the academicians themselves should do, should have done, and possibly could do better. Part of this work is finding out what "names" mean. Similarly, Kenneth Burke is prevented by this work from doing what would seem to be his peculiar job. Meanwhile, the academician is probably a bit ashamed of his degrees, of his journals, even of the fact that registration for courses in literature is steadily dropping off. And then Kenneth Burke is doubtless a little over-proud or ostentatious of his self-made learning. The result is a confusion of tones which ultimately becomes a confusion in terminologies and ideologies and consequently in acceptance and rejection.

Mr. Burke has a quick, assimilative, complicated mind, one not devoted to trivialities but not above them — the kind of mind which we stand to profit most from but which we do most to cramp in colleges. It is essentially a creative mind. Though devoted to criticism it is not less creative than the minds of most of the so-called "creative writers." It is especially creative in its ability to perceive connections between disparate entities. By choice he has worked mainly outside universities, as a critic among living writers rather than as a literary historian or philosopher among dead or classical writers.

Yet even outside universities one feels he has not altogether escaped a confinement of mind too, resulting chiefly perhaps from an exclusive self-stimulation. There is an appearance of a kind of inarticulateness which has nothing to do with want of words or ability to use them but which is associable with his own extensive but curious reading and thinking. It has something to do with the idol of the cave, a status more often forced on one than sought. And there is also, consequentlv, something of the appearance in his work of naïveté or dilettantism.

Mr. Burke is not a dilettante. But as a consequence of a kind of loneliness, I suppose, his awareness of previously-undefined connections between apparently unlike things seems to work overtime: it is as though, having published too little, when he publishes a little more he publishes too much. And so, somehow, he trivializes his own work. Mr. Burke will find few peers with his agility of mind. A giant can only condescend to others than giants: a Lincoln must wait lonely in the park until he sees a Whitman to bow to – otherwise, he must bend. He makes an awkward bow when courtesies between tall persons are finally possible.

Anyway, in the course of about thirty pages Mr. Burke speaks with something like the authoritative voice of a last word on Aquinas, Aristotle, Augustine, Baudelaire, Belloc, Bentham, Bunyan, Blake, Lewis Carroll, Cowley, the Communist Manifesto, Darwin, Defoe, Dewey, Dickens, Dostoevsky, Emerson, Empson, Gay, Gray, Goethe, the Greeks, Hardy, Hegel, Heraclitus, Hobbes, Homer, Wm. James, Joyce, Juvenal, D. H. Lawrence, W. Lewis, Machiavelli, Malraux, Mandeville, Mann, Marinetti, Marx, Meredith, the Niebelungenlied, Nietzsche, New Testament, Piers Plowman, Pound, I. A. Richards, Lola Ridge, *Saturday Evening Post* advertisers, Savonarola, Schopenhauer, Schiller, Shakespeare, Adam Smith, Caroline Spurgeon, Spencer, Spengler, J. J. Sweeney, Swift, A. Tate, Trotzky, Veblen, Virgil, Wagner, Whitman, Yeats. It is not always clear that these references are the most relevant to his line of thought at the moment. Meanwhile he does up proletarian literature, the Agrarians, the Futurists, the feudalists, the Hellenists, *The Tempest*, and some other matters. He serves notice who is the greatest living English critic, pauses to point out a similarity between poems by Wordsworth and Whitman, and in a parenthesis, like a freshman instructor, gives a first lesson in composition, to the effect that beginnings and endings are important. A kind of burlesque of T. S. Eliot climaxes a serious discussion of literary terms. The oxymoronic mingles with good and evil, Latin with italicized phrases. Finally, though not mystical, "Acceptance and Rejection" hardly stops in the grotesque short of being comic.

Despite the rococo manner, "Acceptance and Rejection" is none the less a sinewy paper, in which three themes interweave. First, poetry is motivated as an act by the author's acceptance or rejection of the world he finds himself in. Literature, hence, is either living or equipment for living. Second, literary forms have identities resulting from modes of acceptance or rejection — they are "frames" of reconciliation or repudiation. It is therefore possible "to bring the classical and romantic modes together," the classical being formal, the romantic having been fairly impatient with, or indifferent to, forms in an exclusive concern to take or leave the universe. Third, relativism, a Yes-and-no answer to the riddles of the world, makes comedy a healthy mode of acceptance-rejection nowadays, especially for Mr. Burke and in criticism.

Nobody will be disposed, I imagine, seriously to question the first thesis unless it be those "pure artists" for whom pure form alone is sufficient as stimulation and achievement. Except by these I suppose the thesis never has been questioned: literature is, and always has been, an act of acceptance or rejection. But there is considerable point in reiterating it now, for it re-centers literature in the distinguished person of the author using all the faculties at his disposal to reduce the chaos he soon finds himself in to order. Literature, consequently, is not to be confused with such impersonalities as Marxism, Catholicism, or Protestantism; nor is it to be regarded, as by the usual literary historian, as undistinguished flotsam drifting senselessly in a time-lined current of ideas; nor is it to be identified with techniques or such literary forms as the ode or epic which are only consequences or tools of a reach-and-grasp instinct.

Nor is the second thesis questionable: literary forms are "frames" of acceptance or rejection, and there is not the disparity between the classical and the romantic which we sometimes imagine. But there are confusions involved in Mr. Burke's development of this thesis, in his definitions and incidental conclusions, even in his original hypothesis that the forms lapsed.

We are told, for example, that in the romantic era distinctions between forms (comedy, tragedy, etc.) broke down, and we are advised that this essay will, so to speak, revivify them, identifying the functions behind them with the function ascribed by the romantics to literature generally. But if under the force of the romantic notion that literature is equipment for living the classical forms did lapse and if with Mr. Burke we accept this notion as valid now, then the only purpose of re-distinguishing the literary forms would be to "reject" by means of an escape into an exclusive formalism. If this were Mr. Burke's objective, there would be considerable point in charging him with only a kind of cynical nominalism or formalism as Mr. Glicksberg in his criticism of Mr. Burke in "The Critic's Critic" seems inclined to do. Formalism seems to me a cart-before-the-horse business, *con*formative rather than *in*formative, and not very important. I don't believe Mr. Burke is guilty of it. At least if he is, in spirit if not in letter, his first thesis is in conflict with his second, the distinguished personality of the author being sacrificed for the more accountable literary forms of tradition.

Meanwhile, it is doubtful if the literary forms, defined in terms of function, ever did break down. Some of them became unavailable at various times because the mode of acceptance-rejection behind them for various reasons became insupportable, not because of any real scorn of form. The 19th-century sonnet is equalled only by the Elizabethan, and Victorians and romanticists did notable things with such forms as the ode, elegy, and pastoral. The romanticists wrote tragedy; in fact, it is often held against them that they wrote no comedy.

Their tragedies, however, began to lose such unnatural adjuncts as the "noble" hero or the death-ending because more and more it was realized that the functions of tragedy and comedy are similarly social and effective of an emotional katharsis and that such artificial distinctions as the "high" and "low" character for each is irrelevant and incompetent. In the Victorian era, as the social rather than the personal or individualistic point of view came to predominate optimistically and as the species were observed always to survive the individual (as function survives form in Wordsworth, the song, the nightingale in Keats) – under these conditions tragedy waned and changed, not because of a distrust of form but because acceptance-rejection was principally comic. Except of certain types of drama like the Greek primitive, therefore, it is no longer true that tragedy is cosmic, comedy social in its treatment of man: both are social or cosmic, with emphasis upon the individual in tragedy perhaps, upon the group in comedy.

It is also true that in the Victorian era, often the two forms began to blend into one piece, and audiences were made to laugh and cry at once in tragic comedies as the high character became lower and the low higher, and as we were concerned with the individual and society together. Ultimate results were such plays as *Strife* or *The Hairy Ape*. None the less, tragedy still exists, and is often recommended purely as such, as in J. A. Clark's "The Middle West – There it Lies" in *The Southern Review*. When tragic comedies or tragi-comedies are written, our impression of the separate, though complementary, identities of each is still clear as the very names we use prove. Mr. Burke himself still recognizes what Meredith was sure about, at least, the functional identity of comedy. Both tragedy and comedy involve a hard or soft emotional acceptance or rejection, expressible understandingly in tears or laughter as tokens of such emotions as pity or terror or as love or scorn. The two forms are distinguished still by the kind of emotion played upon (pity versus admiration, terror versus hate) and the kind of emotional response provoked (laughter or tears) for the sake of acceptance or rejection. The lapsing of the literary forms is a myth originating in a loss within the forms of only unnecessary habits.

An additional kind of confusion is fairly wide-reaching in the middle part of "Acceptance and Rejection" because Mr. Burke seems to be talking about literary forms whereas he is actually discussing only the accepting-rejecting function which characterizes all literature, which distinguishes some of the forms, and which never lapsed. There is consequently a *non sequitur* from the definitions of terms through the hypothesis that the forms lapsed to the thesis that the romantic and classical modes are reconcilable. Often, in fact, he discusses functions, varieties or styles, of acceptance or rejection (as behind the grotesque, the sentimental, the burlesque, the satirical, the didactic), which produced no literary forms at all. These discussions further confuse the issue when he discusses such authentic forms as the epic, tragedy, pastoral, elegy, and especially comedy.

One is consequently led to suspect that the conflict between the first and second themes of Mr. Burke's article may be as real as it is apparent. Whatever discrepancy there may have been between classical and romantic modes of acceptance may exist now also in Mr. Burke: are you going to condition acceptance in the writer, subjectively, or in the form, objectively? One reason for the confusion is more or less irrelevant to the argument, a consequence of a kind of over-zealousness, of trying to reconcile too much connotatively behind the terms "acceptance" and "rejection" in a brief space, not only the romantic with the classical (not too closely defined), but also language experimenters (like the group behind *New Directions*) with economic-philosophic experimenters (as the Marxists) with impressionists (perhaps Mr. Burke himself) with traditionalists (like several writers for *The Southern Review* or humanists). In being over-connotative the essay becomes too little denotative, approaching the comic beyond the grotesque. Another reason is that the forms did not lapse but were only modified. And Mr. Burke's argument for reconciling the romantic with the classical seems to serve the purpose only of reviving what was never asleep or dead.

At any rate, the pursuit of names or forms is following a line away from the personality of the writer who accepts or rejects, and results in losses when the vocabulary of names pursued is not exclusive. Pursuing names, the nominalist or formalist, especially, loses track of the poor mortal using his faculties as best he may to account for his universe beautifully or meaningfully, designating (as Mr. Burke suggests) what is good (or evil), true, and beautiful. It would seem that beginning with these faculties and accounting for such frames of acceptance-rejection as the Hebraic, Hellenist, humanist, neo-classic, romantic, realistic, Mr. Burke might more successfully indicate the healthy relationship between the classical and the romantic and at the same time mark significant *Attitudes toward History*. Perhaps he will do so in this promised book, but if he does not I invite any editor to give me the chance with 25 pages and the title "This and That" or "Yes-and-No."

The difficulty is less that Mr. Burke is mistaken in his conclusion that the classicals like the romantics do accept and reject though cherishing literary forms than that the terms of discussion, even the mode, are misleading. And there is consequently a sense of frustration at the end, as of having accomplished little since the approach is not historical, hardly philosophical, and since Mr. Burke does not propose, I hope, beginning to write odes for the sake of odes or even always discuss literary form when he seems to. Throughout most of this chapter of the proposed book, there is the false appearance of having a subjective, not orderly, point of view, but of reaching out for some objective standard in forms as well as of settling a person by calling him names.

[Pages 351–354 of the original essay have been omitted here.]

The most stimulating discussions of terms are those of "the grotesque" and "the sentimental." The former is said to focus in mysticism, but probably it is truer that mysticism focuses in the grotesque but not mystical. The grotesque is useful to the metaphysical poet, like Emerson of "The Sphinx," whose ideas are so complicated or beyond-sense that no single or pure image can represent them. Demonstrating his ideas, the poet has to use several images, a medley or a humbug of imagery. Often in concrete, gargoyles, basilisks, phoenixes, chimeras, hydras, minotaurs, griffins, sagittaries, rocs, unicorns are consequences which might still be useful to an evolutionist, just as strange combinations of disparate images, personifications, allusions, distortions are too. Of course, the mystic is metaphysical. He hears, sees, feels, silences, nothings, white radiances beyond colored domes. He is especially apt to need the humbug or medleyed image because by nature he functions with his faculties beyond the sensation of real butterflies, grasshoppers, and ants, and uses sense-contacts with these realities only in the secondary act of translating his discoveries. But, after all, the grotesque is only a style, not a form or even a function, of acceptance-rejection. The didactic is promotive acceptance-rejection, also a style. Allegory, then, is a kind of grotesque mode of didacticism, a hybrid of styles.

The sentimental would seem to be a negative acceptance of irreconcilable ideas or things, often with tears. The sentimentalist holds over articles of faith from a preceding age as bric-a-brac when it is already apparent to others that these articles are incompatible with each other. When the sentimentalist discovers the conflict as a conflict, if he will relinquish neither article, then like Browning he becomes an ironist. Mr. Burke's illustration is good. "For a whole century we got books where the honest commoner triumphed over the vicious aristocrat." It should be noted, however, that sentimentality is distinguishable from sentimentalism (a form of naturalism) and that the exponent of the former, of whom both Meredith and Mr. Burke have a natural distrust, has to resort to tricks like the strawberry-mark discovery of long-lost parents to prevent a clash between such sentiments as that love conquers all obstacles, marriage is sacred, a man may not marry for money, which may seem to hold a loving bastard and a princess apart. In the instance given by Mr. Burke, of course the commoner and the aristocrat are in conflict but the conflict is avoided in the strawberry-mark manner by the tricky introduction of the vice-versus-virtue device: virtue, not the commoner, wins.

Though one may add to or detract from Mr. Burke's discussion of terms, the fact remains that they do serve to evaluate certain modes of acceptance-rejection and that they do serve to make "acceptance" and "rejection" connotative – this pair should be a useful addition to the vocabulary of criticism.

The best part of Mr. Burke's paper seems to me to be the conclusion, logical from the ambivalent viewpoint of the whole, that criticism should be comic. The comic spirit has well expressed itself in the drama, novel, poetry, music, and painting. It is time critics fell into line. Mr. Burke's peculiar job as comic critic would seem to be that of the editor, the director of theses, or publisher's reader, of the doctor of men of letters rather than of the doctor of letters. With ready sympathy and perception, he would stand by to assist anybody to his course of acceptance or rejection as a result of discovering that 2 and 2 equals 0, 3, 5, 7, 11, 22, or anything else.

Of course we know that 2 plus 2 equals 4. But republicans, democrats, socialists, communists, farmer-laborites, distributionists, social creditors get different results, and they are not all wrong. To understand our "4" we need more of what the Jameses called "intellectual larking," and as this is the adventurous tone or civilized conclusion of "Acceptance and Rejection" it discounts anything unfavorable that may have been said against it. It is courageous, creative, civilized. And it will take more than Nine Old Men to illegalize these three C's.

"Acceptance and Rejection," moreover, seems to be a type of article which it is the peculiar function of the general quarterly to publish, since the learned quarterlies busy themselves usually with only footnotable, fact-fancying articles, with reachings for certainties called "sound scholarship" and therefore with graspings of only little documentabilities which don't matter. *The Southern Review* shares the three C's with Mr. Burke.

◇◇

ARTHUR E. DUBOIS was born in Bethel, New York, in 1904 and died in 1965. He taught English at various universities, including Duquesne and Kent State. He wrote many reviews, articles, and poems.

This long essay-review, a short part of which has been omitted, should be read against Allen Tate's essay; together they represent one set of polarities in the reception of Burke. Mr. Tate (with, later, such people as Marius Bewley) and Mr. DuBois (with, later, such people as William Knickerbocker) can be said to represent the orthodox and the radical, the closed and the open, the Eliot and the Lawrence traditions, or the dogmatic and the discursive of Mr. Knickerbocker's essay. Whatever the label, the dichotomy is a real one and the line-ups against and for Burke tend to follow the dialectics of the dichotomy. It is when one perceives the larger implications of this opposition to and defense of Burke that this collection of critical responses becomes more than just a chronicle of how one thinker was received by his contemporaries.

With Mr. DuBois's essay, we arrive at Burke's fifth book and the point at which more than literary people began to take him up (and put him down). A fundamental principle – in Burke, in the dialectics of his reception, and in the conduct of one's intellectual life – begins to emerge as a basis of praise or blame; Mr. DuBois calls it Burke's "intellectual larking" and characterizes it as the free and sometimes irresponsible and irreverent play of the mind. Many of the essays and reviews that follow for the next few years should really be seen in terms of the acceptance or rejection of this characteristic Burkeian attitude.

◇◇

7 *The Technique of Mystification*

BY Sidney Hook

THE greatest difficulty that confronts the reader of Burke is finding out what he means. His individual sentences seem to be clear, but when

EDITOR'S NOTE: Reprinted from *Partisan Review*, IV (December 1937), 57–62, put together they are obscure, sometimes opaque. To some of his writings Burke distributes guides, just as in the present work he appends a dictionary of basic terms. But these guides, like the racing guides Groucho Marx bought in *A Day at the Races*, themselves need a key. In reading poetry the effort to discover what the poet is trying to say contributes to the process of understanding the structure of the created whole. In reading a critic, even when he writes as suggestively as Burke, the struggle to get at the author's thought is a measure of his failure to communicate. And there is no denying that Burke writes suggestively. Suggestively and, unfortunately, by suggestion. Now and again a neatly turned phrase or an old idea restated as a paradox seems to open up a path for intellectual exploration. But instead of thinking a problem through, Burke follows up by dealing with what its form, its context, even the very sound of the words remind him. It is as if someone were trying to provide an illustration of Mill's defunct psychology of association. The result is that there is neither beginning nor end to his argument. Its course meanders into all fields of knowledge where due to Burke's wide but not very discriminating reading its force is weakened by a lore more quaint than precise.

Nonetheless the reader who grapples with Burke's latest book [*Attitudes toward History*], as well as his previous one, *Permanence and Change*, will find that the author has a position; or more accurately, a position which can be used as a "justification" for taking any position. It is based on the recognition that the mind, or better still, the live creature, brings something to the processes of experience and knowledge. Some perspective of need, interest or organization is necessary not only for the discovery of qualities in a situation but for their very existence. These perspectives are rooted in the physical structure of the organism. The products of this multiform interaction are therefore both relative and objective. If all existence is relational, no description can be intelligent except from some point of view. It is even more obvious that no activity or evaluation can be rational unless guided by some perspective of selection. In any historical period, these basic perspectives of selection function as frames of acceptance and rejection around which the complexities of art, action and experience are organized. There are two generic classes of perspectives – individual and social. Insofar as a culture exhibits an integrated pattern, it imposes (by indoctrination or persuasion) a common frame upon all its habit-bound members. The cultures, "collective poems" Burke calls them, discussed very briefly are Christian evangelism, the mediaeval synthesis, Protestant transition, naive capitalism and emergent collectivism (Russia). Cultures present the materials out of which, and pose the problems in relation to which, individual frames are constructed. The latter are classified in terms of poetic categories; epic, tragic, satiric, didactic, comic, etc. These supply the key metaphors into which all experience is translated. Burke recommends the comic frame as an individual attitude within the social frame of emergent collectivism (Russia).

Before proceeding to an analysis of this position, I wish to indicate some of the peculiar features of the book. Its title is quite deceptive. The individual frames of acceptance or rejection are not attitudes towards history but attitudes towards life – anytime, anywhere – while the common frames are themselves the *stuff* of history. The real problem which the title suggests, viz., how attitudes and purposes affect theories of historical causation and programs of activity, is hardly touched on. The poetic names of the individual frames are recondite metaphors. In every case, Burke's discussion of their nature is open to serious question and his identification of the comic frame with the attitude of humanism is arbitrary. Even for an unsystematic writer, the organization of the book is extremely bad. By the author's own confession, the second volume adds nothing to the argument of the first: it consists of repetitious notes, memoranda and irrelevant autobiographical detail which could not be crammed into the first volume. The excursions into economics are amateurish and second hand, and the psychoanalysis is not so much critical as mythological. Burke's ill-digested reading results in a chop suey of proper names, some of them dragged in, I am sorry to say, apparently for personal reasons only. The undisguised animus against critics of the Communist Party and Russia, I shall consider below.

Burke writes as a critic of life and manners. To his credit, be it said, he has developed independently of technical philosophical thought a kind of home-baked objective relativism. The critical incidence of this philosophy is directed against dogmatic monisms which are unaware of the necessarily partial, limited, and excluding aspects of their central insights. It suggests a method which does not outlaw bias but makes it rational through analysis of its origins and control of its expression. Properly understood it justifies resolute action without the by-products of fanaticism. It relates values to facts without identifying them. Unless carefully safeguarded, however, this position leads to two fundamental errors either one of which is sufficient to make the whole position untenable. They are: (1) The tendency to regard what is revealed in any one perspective of equal validity, in relation to a specific purpose, with what is revealed in any other; and (2) The tendency to espouse some frame of reference or evaluation and then, although admitting theoretically that there *are* other ways of looking at the world, reduce them all to special cases of the first by stretching a metaphor or formula. Burke is consistently guilty of *both* errors and hides their contradictory character from himself by calling the confusion dialectical. This shift from subjectivism to absolutism is basic in all his writing. It reveals much more about Burke's thought and purpose than those obvious logical lapses (which we hereafter shall ignore) where he speaks of "a total vision of reality" correcting the interpretative distortions of class attitudes. On his view, of course, it is nonsense to speak of a total vision of reality, for everything seen is seen from some perspective, no perspective can embrace everything, and not all perspectives can be held at once.

(1) If nothing is valid from every point of view and everything is valid from some point of view, the question naturally arises: why this point of view rather than that? This question is insoluble except where a *problem* is clearly defined and *purposes* openly stated. Only when this is done has the question a meaning, i.e., can conflicting points of view, attitudes, language structures, be tested. Once a point of view is chosen as adequate to a situation, then the consequences of acting out the operations it involves can no longer be called into question by suddenly shifting to another point of view on the ground of the equal validity of all points of view *in the abstract*. Nowhere does Burke state clearly either the problems or purposes which have defined his choice of perspectives. The reader never knows what perspective is relevant to what, whether Burke accepts a perspective because its adequacy is objectively verifiable, or because it appeals to him for some purely private reason. More reprehensible intellectually, are his critiques of perspectives to which he is hostile. Instead of subjecting them to immanent criticism, he jumps out of the orbit in which evidence for the perspective is being considered, to another perspective from which one does not have to consider the evidence offered but can toss it off with a shrug. This is illustrated most focally in his ambivalent attitude towards science – strikingly similar to that of contemporary neo-Thomism – and in his contention that it is only one of a number of metaphorical approaches to the world. From the indisputable truth that a perspective enters into all thinking behavior, Burke goes to the highly dubious proposition that any perspective can be made to fit the deliverances of experience and vice versa. Nowhere is there adequate recognition of the objective compulsions of the realm of fact.

(2) But Burke himself has a definite perspective for which he claims a superior validity over against competing perspectives. It is a "new cooperative frame. . . . Coordinated by 'planners.' Ideal: comic self-consciousness. 'Neo-Catholicizing.' Ideological homogeneity, to be cor-

rected by a *methodology* of latitudinarianism." In another place he describes it as "a return to integrative thought (the over-simplification of which is manifested in adherence to a 'party line')." This ideological homogeneity necessarily demands that the whole of art, science, and politics be interpreted in the exclusive categories of a single perspective. Relativism now becomes only a relativity of *phrasing* for the one true line. The over-simplification of the party-line is to be corrected by latitudinarianism, which Burke admits "is another word for casuistic stretching." That is, everyone must *think* the same things but it is permitted to *say* the same things in different language. The task of the critic is to reaffirm the basic truth of the perspective and by studying the metaphorical migrations of terms, to bring them home to roost in the proper ideological yard. The critic therefore is both a propagandist and a craftsman. But his craftsmanship is really a strategy. It does not justify itself. All justification flows from the pivotal metaphor of the frame of acceptance.

There is a reason for this jockeying back and forth between positions. This will be apparent if we examine some concrete illustrations which exhibit the pattern of Burke's strategy rather than the promise of his philosophy. Some time ago Mr. Burke reviewed Barbusse's *Stalin.** His long review was built around the metaphor of a public monument. Now, of course, the book has many things in common with a public monument. But it also has at least as many things in common with a dung-hill. Why one metaphor rather than another? Unless Burke introduces his special political perspective of allegiance he cannot make his choice explicable. Here, in the realm of values, relativism for him must have limits. Grant him, however, his perspective. His function as a propagandist completed, we expect him to do his duty as a craftsman. The book has at least one major error on every other page; and even some of the photographs — particularly the one showing Lenin with Stalin's head almost on his shoulder — are obviously faked. What do we find in Burke's review? He is simply not interested in investigating the character of the materials which have entered into the public monument, the fitness of the composition, the occasion for the execution. Here, in the realm of *fact*, relativism for him has no limits.

Or examine his reference to the Moscow trials in this book. After some vague speculations on the nature of identity, he writes "such speculations on the nature of identity coupled with our speculations on

* I use this illustration because it exemplifies so eloquently the methodology by which Burke would correct "the over-simplification of the party line." It can be matched with other illustrations from the present work in which they are hastily sketched rather than explicitly worked out.

allegiance to the symbols of authority, might add [sic!] plausibility to the accusations laid against the 'Old Bolsheviks' in the Moscow trials." He then attempts to show by the inevitable reference to Dostoyevsky that it was not psychologically impossible for the defendants to be guilty. As if the question of mere psychological *possibility* has any bearing upon the questions of *evidence.* It is not psychologically impossible that Stalin should have framed his victims nor is it psychologically impossible that Burke should have plotted with them. What follows? The speculation about the psychological guilt of the Moscow defendants functions like a metaphor in Burke's pivotal frame of acceptance. Here he must be an absolutist – blind to other metaphors *despite* the brave relativism with which he starts. But just when we expect him as a craftsman to consider the issues of fact and probability to which his speculations about identity "add" plausibility, he does a disappearing act. His relativism at this point asserts itself so strongly that the logical structure of his perspective etherealizes, and nothing is left except the emotional overtones. The enormity of this outrage against elementary scientific procedure would probably be brought home to Burke himself were someone to tell him that since it was not psychologically impossible for Dreyfus, or Sacco-Vanzetti, or Mooney to be guilty of the crimes they were accused of, this *adds* plausibility to the accusations. There are some kinds of propaganda which are simply not compatible with good craftsmanship.

Or take Burke's discussion of Dewey in the present book. Having pillaged from him to the limits of his understanding, and distorted him in the process, he quite gratuitously attributes views to Dewey in politics and education against which the latter has repeatedly polemicized. To say that Dewey desires a collectivism in which there are only "rights" and "freedoms" and no corresponding duties or restrictions – a glorified anarchism – is so grotesque that even a super-relativistic approach to texts cannot justify it. For Dewey the content of freedom changes with every basic change in social organization: but just as he stresses the continuity between the *technological* economy of capitalism and that of collectivism which grows out of it, he believes that the traditions of critical scientific inquiry and respect for individual difference, which were once part of the ideology of capitalism, can in the same way be taken over and *extended* as part of the heritage from the past. Dewey's emphasis upon critical scientific inquiry is incompatible, of course, with Burke's framework of "ideological homogeneity"; but Burke, fearful of letting the authority of party dogma or metaphor meet the authority of scientific method, must attribute to Dewey views he does not hold. This is always risky where "ideological homogeneity" has not yet found its appropriate totalitarian political frame.

Burke contends that a key metaphor is more important in understanding an author than his arguments. I disagree emphatically. But his assurance (he tells us this in so many words) is based on the evidence drawn from his own case. Let us follow his lead then and see what we find. His key metaphor is "the bureaucratization of the imaginative." The formula applies to everything. It is short-hand for the process by which a possibility in being transformed into an actuality *necessarily* (i) excludes other possibilities, and (ii) falls short of or betrays the pristine ideal. Taken in its own terms, what Burke is saying here is either a truism or an absurdity: a truism, if it follows from the *definitions* of possibility, actuality and ideal; an absurdity if it does not, since ideas and ideals may be framed in such a way that they are not defeated in being realized. However, we are not concerned with this metaphor except as it provides a clue to Mr. Burke's thought. Why does he use it? Because, he tells us, with direct references to Russia "people are thereby kept from being too sensitively exposed to disillusionment as they are affronted by the 'let-down' that necessarily occurs" when the real is confronted with the ideal. Once people think in terms of this metaphor "tendencies toward the negativistic, satanic, sectarian, disintegrative, and 'splintering' fall away." What a revealing juxtaposition of political and moral terms! Learn how to use the formula "the bureaucratization of the imaginative" and you will reconcile yourself to whatever is happening in Russia, you will avoid sectarianism, shun negativistic "splinter groups," and escape the curse of satanism (did not Vyshinsky call the "Trotskyites" the spawn of the devil?)!

Burke is extremely bitter about socialist critics of Russia, accuses them of being Utopians and too prone to use the language of moral indignation. In asserting that critics of Russia are Utopian, Burke must first show that every major aspect of Russian policy from its treatment of peasants, intellectuals, critical workers and communists to its relationships with foreign countries and political parties, is necessary, i.e., unavoidable, given the program and concrete situation. To do this he must argue his case on the basis of evidence. This he consistently refuses to do. He either adopts a relativism in which all facts are etherealized or he invokes his favorite metaphor of bureaucratization to blanket the discussion. He begs every crucial question with a display of rhetorical preciosity. Consequently, "Utopian" in his writing is merely a disparaging epithet which he hurls at honest critics of Russia who refuse to "move in" and "cash in" (the phrases are all Burke's) on the bureaucratic perspective. His own function consists in being an apologist, not after the fact, but *before* the fact, of the latest piece of Stalinist brutality.

It is difficult to name the mode in which Burke writes. It is not comic; nor is it humanistic. But whatever its name, it is in the style in which weak men of minor talent make a bid for acceptance to the side they think will win. Despite his relativism and moral nihilism Burke cannot offer a workable ideology to the political tendency of which he is a fellow-traveller. The stern necessities of totalitarian communism cannot be rationalized in basic metaphors or psychoanalytic myths. Its deeds are too stark and bloody. Burke will find before long that he has chosen a perspective which will obscure his vision. The ideological homogeneity he so warmly embraces will induce a creeping paralysis of the creative centers which means death to the craftsman.

◇◇

Sidney Hook, born in New York City in 1902, has taught philosophy at New York University since 1927. He has written many books — ten or more — and articles on philosophical and political subjects and, since the late thirties, has been an active force in the cultural and intellectual life of New York City.

In some ways the place of publication — *Partisan Review* — of this review is as significant as what Mr. Hook says. This is the first of the *Partisan Review* reviews and all of them, when there have been any, have been militantly partisan and against. This means that a powerful, coherent, and unusually articulate group of American intellectuals has never wanted to have anything to do with Burke. I do not really understand this; it seems strange that a socially and politically oriented journal should occasionally take out after and then otherwise completely ignore one of our most politically and socially oriented critics.

Mr. Hook's objections to Burke are hard to summarize accurately, but they seem to be partly methodological-procedural and ultimately profoundly substantival. As Harold Rosenberg, Charles Glicksberg, and Arthur DuBois pointed out, each in his own way, Burke's procedure is partly poetic and visionary; and despite all of Burke's later disclaimers, his methodology is not scientific and his logic is never classical. As Charles Feidelson, Jr., put it, Burke reduced logic to literature — with astonishing results. Burke proceeds as much by metaphorical as by rational logic and his use of evidence is often more poetic and determined by the needs of his own developing vision than it is scientific and controlled by the facts of the source. This is really very Emersonian and should be recognized as such. I once read a copy of *Attitudes toward History*, for example, in which all of Burke's factual and other kinds of "errors" were carefully noted and corrected in the margin and accompanied by a steadily increasing number of exclamation points and a kind of rising hysteria. It was a compulsive job of negative documentation which filled the margins in a fine hand page after page. But, surely, that careful person missed some essential point about the book and Burke: it was not a historian he was reading, but a visionary, a myth maker and system builder.

I do not offer this as a defense of "logologic" but as an explanation of why people like Professor Hook reacted so powerfully against Burke. Mr. Hook is right in saying that the force of his attack is motivated by the seriousness with which he took Burke, whose procedures surely violate Hook's own deepest commitments. Mr. Hook recognized a true antagonist when he read one. I have included here both Mr. Hook's original review and his response to Burke's reply (see pages 97–101) because he does lay out the case against Burke very thoroughly. The phrasing of the last paragraph of the original review seems to me unfortunate because it states *ad hominum* what is best understood as an attack on a whole mode of thought.

◇◇

Is Mr. Burke Serious?

BY Sidney Hook

IN MY review of his book, I paid Burke the respect of taking his work seriously. His rejoinder* makes me wonder whether he desires me to do so. I cannot understand him except on the assumption that—despite his statement to the contrary—he *does* believe allowance should be made for the fact that his heart is politically in the right place. Now were I evaluating Burke's intentions, as distinct from the validity of his assertions, I certainly would have given him credit for them. Provided, of course, I believed his heart was politically in the right place. In my review, at any rate, I did indicate its location accurately enough. But it so happens that I do not believe it is in the right place. Therefore in a serious attempt to do him justice, I addressed myself

EDITOR'S NOTE: Reprinted from *Partisan Review,* IV (January 1938), 44–47, copyright © 1938 by *Partisan Review,* by permission of the author and publisher.

* EDITOR'S NOTE: Burke's comments on Mr. Hook's original review appeared in *Partisan Review,* IV (January 1938), 40–44.

to what might more legitimately be regarded as the off-spring of his *mind*, i.e., his ideas.

Burke's protest includes other things besides the demand that his intentions and allegiance be evaluated. He also claims (1) that I have completely misrepresented the nature of his book, (2) that my criticism of his relativism is without merit, and (3) that my own position is suspect because I do not approach *his* position from the proper angle. I wish to consider these claims before returning to his intentions and allegiance.

(1) Primarily the function of a critic is to consider, not whether the author says what he means, but the meaning of what has been said. Burke may be the best judge of what he *wanted* to say. But on the meaning of what he *has* said — he is not necessarily more competent than other intelligent readers. Every reader can test the accuracy of my description of Burke's position by reading the book and my review of it. I invite the comparison.

Burke's own evidence that I have misread his book does not establish his claim. I did not "pass over" the material concerned with the psychology of art because I "have never paid attention to such matters." Does Burke really believe that my published work is "ample evidence" of my inattention to such matters? What a wordy world this would be if the only way we could show we were interested in anything was to rush into print about it! Indeed, I wish to assure him that I pay a great deal of attention to such matters. And precisely because I do, I found his psychology of art not worth more than the casual reference I made to it. Were I reviewing Burke's *Counter-Statement* I should have had a great deal to say about his psychology of art, some of it quite appreciative. But in his present book, the detailed discussion of the poetic metaphors, in which the individual frames of reference are expressed, runs out into the thinnest vagaries. More important, these aesthetic discussions are matters of detail. They do not concern, as Burke implies they do, the central theme of his work.

Nor is it apparent what the citation of his prize passage about the "bureaucratization of the imaginative" proves. In my review I gave a brief analysis designed to show that his position here reduces either to a truism or an absurdity.* Then I applied to Burke his *own* principle

* In passing I wish to point out that to speak of science as the bureaucratization of wisdom is not only a misleading but a dangerous metaphor. The methods of science are the only reliable methods by which *new* knowledge (and the wisdom relevant to knowledge) are won. Because it never considers any question as closed, bases its conclusions on verifiable evidence, recognizes no authority except that of experiment and logic, it represents, where it is free, the end of all bureaucratic creedal dogmatism.

that a key metaphor is a better clue to understanding an author than his arguments, and explored the consequences. Although I do not share Burke's principle, the absence of developed argument in his work, justified this approach. I gave some indication of how it was used on several concrete occasions, and then proceeded, on Burke's own recommendation, "to discount" the face value of the phrase, and to note the "interests" it protected. The few *concrete* situations in which practical social conclusions are implied by this metaphor involve Russia. They are directed, not only in the cited passage but in others, against socialist critics. If every venture of the human spirit can be regarded as a bureaucratized compromise – even science and the imagination! – any specific bureaucratic outrage is part of the natural order of things. Criticism can be dismissed as Utopianism. This is a cunning but none the less fallacious linguistic device to attach the emotional associations of authoritative symbols – science, art, invention – to a specific form of political despotism. Employed by commercial advertisers, it is a technique which Burke has castigated elsewhere. Instead of using the hedonic overtones of a sensuous female in a bathtub to sell a bar of soap, Burke uses the poetical overtones of recondite metaphors, whenever his discussion touches concrete issues, to sell the ideas and practices of totalitarian communism under Stalin.

(2) Burke has so completely missed the point of my criticism of his shifts from subjectivism to absolutism that I must repeat it briefly here. An element of arbitrary choice inheres in any perspective or point of view. I can look here or there; accept this set of social ideals or that. But *what can be seen* after I decide to look here or there, *what follows* as a result of actions for or against certain ideals, does not depend upon my choice. I can change my point of view but not the consequences of a point of view. The gravamen of my criticism of Burke is that he gets his relativism and absolutism in the wrong place. When his particular social perspective is confronted by others, he forgets his own theory and tends to regard it as "true," as something assimilable to fact. He absolutizes what cannot be absolutized. But just as soon as anyone holds him to the consequences of his point of view and uses them as evidence of what he is committed to, Burke either denies their relevance or what is still worse, as his airy references to the Moscow trials show, interprets facts and evidence as he pleases. Here he relativizes what cannot be relativized.

Burke asserts that I seek to give the impression that his point of view is that "*of the most restricted kind* of party politics." He must have read my review very hastily. I quoted him as accepting, with direct reference to Russia, a communist frame "of ideological homogeneity, to be corrected by a *methodology* of latitudinarianism." Latitudinarianism, he says, "is another word for casuistic stretching." This works out in practice as follows. Any major policy or action sanctioned by the official interpreters of communist ideological homogeneity must be accepted. But it need not be defended or justified in the official way. Usually the official defense repels intelligent and sensitive people. Burke's "latitudinarianism" in practice amounts to thinking up persuasive rhetorical apologias for conclusions for which there is no *objective evidence.* Burke does not follow a party line to a party conclusion. He follows his own line to a party conclusion. Few know how he will get there, still fewer can understand the amazing ways by which he gets there, but all know he *will* get there — and that's the main thing.

(3) Burke's private bull of excommunication against me because I did not give three socialist cheers in my review of his book, to show where I stood, is amusing. (It's the party line on Hook all right but in Burke's own way.) It is also a little saddening because it verifies in part the prediction I made about the consequences of his political perspective upon his critical powers. His argument is not only *ad hominem* but disingenuous. First, the truth or falsity of my criticisms does not depend upon my socialist opinions. Second, my socialist opinions — good, bad or indifferent — have been expressed in numerous other writings. Third, Burke is acquainted with these writings as his references to them in his own books show. Fourth, for a socialist audience, such as the *Partisan Review* attempts to reach, I regard the exposure of Burke's technique of mystification as necessary in the interests of clarity, truth, and *socialism.*

I now return to Burke's intentions and allegiance which, he insists, must be considered. Very well, I shall oblige him. Nowhere, complains Burke, have I allowed for the fact that his general perspective is prosocialist. A strange complaint! When Burke attacks socialist critics of Stalinism, does *he* call attention to *their* anti-capitalism? He does not! Or when he criticizes Trotsky, or Dewey, or Farrell? He does not! But just as soon as his own position is probed, he makes loud outcry that he is not being given sufficient credit for his socialist intentions. Is Burke really serious?

I cannot give Burke credit for his socialist intentions — not yet. I am prepared to give him credit, if he asks for it, for not taking pennies from a blind man's cup or not scalping his grandmother. But I refuse to give him credit for his "socialism" — *until I know what kind of socialism he believes in!*

Does he believe in a socialism in which judicial and extra-judicial frame-ups are the order of the day? If not, why does he accept and defend the most monstrous frame-ups in all history — the Moscow trials?

Does he believe in a socialism in which the dictatorship of a minority party, subject to the dictatorship of a bureaucracy, subject in turn to the dictatorship of its secretariat, enjoys a monopoly of *all* political power? If not, why his impatience and scorn for those whom he calls Utopians — who affirm that socialism without democracy is not socialism?

Does he believe in a socialism in which all art, science and philosophy are regimented by party-dogmas, imposed by authority and implemented by the threat of force? If not, why has he failed to protest the literary pogroms of the Communist Party, of which he is a leading fellow-traveller, against socialist intellectuals who hold that critical integrity is part of the socialist way of life?

Does he believe in the apotheosis of Stalin to a point which makes every political cult of adoration in the past, including that of Czarism, pale in comparison? If not, why does he write of him as he does? Why does he add his stammering note of spite to the Communist Party abuse of socialists who hold that Stalin's actions must be evaluated by socialist ideals? Why, when I charge him with accepting the political perspective of Stalinism, does he retort that he loves the U.S.S.R.? Are Stalin and the U.S.S.R. one and the same to him? What would he think of an American patriot who would meet a political criticism of Roosevelt with the retort that he loved America?

There are many other questions I would like to have answered before I can give Burke credit for his socialism.

In closing I wish to repeat the conclusion of my review. There are some social and political perspectives to-day which a critic cannot take without doing great harm to his craftsmanship. We have a right to expect more from Burke than from people like Granville Hicks whose intellectual reach, by a divine charity, extends no further than their nearsighted piety. That is why I took Burke seriously.

◇◇

See note on pages 96–97.

◇◇

7 A Review of "Permanence and Change"

BY Louis Wirth

THIS is a book to put some of the authors and publishers of sociological textbooks to shame. It contains more sound substance than any text on social psychology with which the reviewer is familiar. Burke is not a professional sociologist, but he has presented the essentials of what social psychologists profess to treat more clearly and more interestingly than the practitioners have been able to do thus far. He has done it without being obsessed by the jargon that has become the stock in trade — and often the sole intellectual capital — of many of the academically blessed. He has not merely defined his abstract nouns — otherwise known as concepts — but he has predicated something about them. In short, he has said something worth saying and said it well. The book should do something, too, to make us question the American textbook publishing industry, for here is a volume of about three hundred and fifty pages with all the trimmings — good paper, practical binding, chapter headings and subheadings, table of contents, everything but an index, a bibliography, and exercises — for a dollar; and the publishers of the book are not yet bankrupt.

The volume is not an example of popularized science although it is never dull, has a good many witty passages, and throughout exhibits the play of a keen, critical intellect. Still, and despite this advertisement, it probably won't be widely used as a textbook for social psychology courses; in part, because it does not follow the conventional form of organization which these courses have acquired and because it imports too much of what may be regarded as extraneous material from poetry, philosophy, and politics.

Starting with an exposition of the conditioned reflex as a way of altering responses, the author goes on to indicate that the orientation of human beings to their complex cultural structures involves a wider range of problems, which can be met with a greater critical capacity and a larger number of solutions than is the case with dogs or fish. But, although all organisms are critics in the sense that they interpret the signs about them, in his means selecting, man through speech is equipped to go beyond the criticism of experience to a criticism of criticism. He not only interprets the character of events — which animals may also do to some extent — but he also interprets his interpretations.

Burke makes ingenious use of Veblen's notion of "trained incapac-

EDITOR'S NOTE: Reprinted from *The American Journal of Sociology*, XLIII (1937–38), 483–486, by permission of the University of Chicago Press.

ity" (a state of affairs in which one's very abilities can function as blindnesses or hindrances) to avoid the current tendency to employ "avoidance" or "escape" references when discussing orientation, which he finds unsatisfactory because these terms do not serve to explain the action only of some men as is sometimes assumed, but of all men. This leads him into a critique of the loose use of such terms as "scapegoat mechanism," "rationalization," and "illogical behavior" which he finds are question-begging and highly emotive words to be avoided in scientific discourse. There follows a pithy analysis of the relationship of the behavioristic to the *Gestalt* contributions to the understanding of meaning, and a sharp critique of the Freudian psychoanalytic procedure in interpreting motives, the essence of which is contained in the sentence: "To explain one's conduct by the vocabulary of motives current among one's group is about as self-deceptive as giving the area of a field in the accepted terms of measurement."

Motives turn out to be the complex subjective aspect of correspondingly complex situations which invariably reflect the culture. In an integrated, stable, homogeneous society we need no profound reflection to discover our own and our fellows' motives; but, when the culture disintegrates, our motives become confused and uncertain, so that the introspective search for motives reveals something akin to total emptiness. Motives cannot very well be inferred from the isolated acts of the individual, nor induced either from original nature or from an a priori scheme concocted by a psychoanalyst or a psychologist. They are always part of a larger frame of meanings. Thus, Burke, in his search for a valid and workable theory of motivation, arrives approximately at the point to which sociologists like Max Weber carried their analysis of meaningful conduct.

In his treatment of communication Burke furnishes an enlightening account of the role of interest, which carries him into a discussion of John Dewey's concept of "occupational psychosis," referring to the pronounced character of the mind, corresponding to the emphasis which the mode of sustenance of a tribe or group or individual produces in their interests. Dewey's view in this respect is found to be close to that of Marx and that of Veblen. The recognition that what is to a man's interest is not always what he is interested in, Burke shows, is helpful in interpreting some of the most important aspects not only of communication but also of such phenomena as class consciousness and cultural change and "lag."

There follows a penetrating exposition of "style" as a device for communication and the changes style undergoes in a society which, like ours, accents the technological interest. Part I, entitled "Orientation," closes with a statement of the three orders of rationalization: magic, religion, and science; magic being the schema which stresses mainly the control of natural forces; religion, stressing the specifically human forces; and science, the control of the technological order. Burke sees communism, or a rationalization closely akin to it, emerging as "the only coherent and organized movement making for the subjection of the technological genius to humane ends."

While Part I of the book contains most of what will interest social psychologists, Parts II and III are no less meaty and relevant to the perennial problems of sociologists. Part II is essentially an analysis of language and the role of symbols in social life, especially in creating and maintaining loyalties, integrating groups and cultures, facilitating and hindering rationality, and providing perspective. The discordant elements in language and thought corresponding to incongruities in meaning that have occurred in the course of history are judiciously sampled, and the situation of today is shrewdly analyzed and found to be not unlike that of the period of cultural mongrelism where the Christian theology and philosophy first took form as a universalizing attitude. Meaning or symbolism, Burke points out, becomes a central concern precisely at a stage when a given system of meanings is falling into decay. Skepticism or organized doubt is, thus, a symptom of transition between one era of certainty and another.

The search for a sound system of communication adequate to the needs of man is determined by his neurological structure, and the changing social conditions which he encounters must, in the opinion of Burke, be based upon and arise out of the co-operative enterprises of society. A society whose constituent parts are at war with one another cannot give birth to such a system, and the lack of such a system will in turn threaten the structure of rationality itself.

The concluding part of the volume is concerned primarily with a critique of ethics and ethical theory which in this case must be taken to include not merely the realm of morals but the whole scheme of norms involved in aesthetics, science, and action. The discussion is permeated by the insight that "an orientation or *Weltanschauung* tends to become a self-perpetuating structure, creating the measures by which it shall be measured," which the author would have us believe is merely another way of saying that "our thoughts and acts are affected by our interests."

There is much in this treatise that will appear unsystematic and irrelevant to those accustomed to a less personal and poetic mode of discourse. But those sociologists who may be induced to seek new light on their old problems by reading the work of a literary man and critic will agree that a rose under another name smells just as sweet.

◇◇

LOUIS WIRTH was born in Gemunden, Germany, in 1897 and died in 1952. He taught sociology at the University of Chicago and was an editor of *The American Journal of Sociology*. He wrote books on the ghetto and urbanism as a way of life, and numerous essays on city, communal, and social life. He also translated and edited a selection of Karl Mannheim's works.

This late review of *Permanence and Change* is important because it marks the beginning of sociologist's response to and acceptance of Burke. Specifically, Professor Wirth's review seems to me notable for the calm way in which it lays out Burke's main coordinates so as to make them accessible to fellow sociologists; and for the sane way in which his final paragraph describes how Burke must be approached if he is to be used. The discounting of personal foibles — stylistic and otherwise — is a necessitous act for the health of the intellect.

◇◇

7 A Review of "Attitudes toward History"

BY Margaret Schlauch

THERE is both charm and challenge about a book of this sort, which, guilelessly presenting itself as a philosophy of history (or philosophies?), puts on the aspect of a handbook of poetics in the table of contents, enacts a mystical marriage of Freudianism and Marxism in sundry digressions and footnotes, constructs a curve of history resembling an original plot for a five-act drama, and concludes with a "dictionary of pivotal terms" in which linguistic-esthetic-psychological speculation is predominant. The experience of reading *Attitudes toward History* is not unlike adventuring in bespelled *märchen* forests full of shape-shifters. This will appear as no derogatory similitude to Mr. Burke, who attaches profound symbolic import to childhood's reminiscences and dream-life. The reader is, moreover, constantly delighted and stimulated — even when he does not agree — by the dazzling range of topics,

EDITOR'S NOTE: Reprinted from *Science & Society*, II (1937–38), 128–132, by permission of the author and publisher.

the Spenglerian richness of allusion, the incisive eloquence frequently manifest throughout the exposition.

In the course of history Mr. Burke distinguishes two frames of reference which he calls "frames of acceptance and rejection,"[1] and which he exemplifies primarily in poetic categories. "The various poetic categories we have analyzed," he tells us, "illustrate some major psychological devices whereby the mind equips itself to name and confront its situation. They provide in miniature the cues for us to follow when considering the broad course of Western civilization with reference to its 'collective poems,' the total frames of thought and action, roughly classifiable under the heads of primitive evangelism (in the midst of Hellenistic decay), medieval theocracy, Protestantism, capitalism and socialism" (I, 129). Literary forms, philosophical systems and political movements are brought forward and explained in the light of this principle of acceptance and rejection. But one wonders whether the statement "I accept" has any meaning apart from a complementary object, as the grammarians would express it, since the verb is generally understood to be transitive. It is true that William James, whom Mr. Burke particularly admires, once described himself as going about for days feeling completely convinced – though of *what* he did not know. And there are other philosophers and psychologists who appear to talk of acceptance *überhaupt*; but the context of discourse usually gives some hint of their meaning. At times Mr. Burke seems to regard "I accept" as an autonomous expression which, without needing explanation itself, is capable of illuminating the main stresses in the entire course of Western civilization. The patterns of acceptance and rejection appear and reappear in history as he interprets it, migrating from one subject matter to another, living an all but independent life of their own, far too aloof for concern with such desiderata as food and shelter, adequate wages and leisure. He suggests that "insofar as a Communist Society becomes established, hence requiring emphasis on *acceptance,* the attitude of defiance (grounded on defiance of death) will require abatement" (I, 65). Here acceptance and rejection appear, not as natural reactions to historical objects, but as mysterious separate forces which must be dealt with and properly appeased before a communistic society can be established. Burke himself admits the shortcomings of his method. In one passage he disarmingly explains that " 'acceptance' and 'rejection' cannot be sharply differentiated (the 'acceptance' of A involving the

[1] The usefulness of the term "frame" as a tool is somewhat blunted by promiscuous application which neutralizes its metaphoric value. Thus we have "frames" which "melt," "struggle," "contend"; moreover the cultural "crust" (another tool-word in the exposition) is made to perform similar metaphoric feats: "The utterances of the forensic crust, during the period of Hellenistic decay, were mobile" (I, 145).

rejection of non-A) . . ." but he fails to realize the importance of this admission. He does not draw the obvious conclusion that there can therefore be no more acceptance in the epic than in the elegy and no more rejection in communism struggling against capitalism than in capitalism itself. In other words, forms of thought are given a position of primary importance in Burke's scheme of history, despite other passages which seem to disclaim this idealist emphasis.

Similarly, the emphasis is frequently placed upon psychological (rather: psychoanalytical) relationships at the expense of others. Machiavelli, Hobbes, Voltaire, Bentham, Marx and Veblen are designated as "great formulators of economic psychoanalysis" (I, 222). Symbolic castration and like patterns are used to explain, not only the institution of monasticism, but also acceptance of dictatorship and membership in the Communist Party (which is compared, I, 95, and by implication I, 100 n., to a monastic order). Belloc's animadversions on capitalism are thus interpreted: "His plan for the planting of petty-bourgeois seedlings is called a plan of 're-afforestation.' The metaphor suggests symbolic parricide: the author would slay the monopolist patriarch, planting his own little small-enterprise children in its stead" (I, 137). The Christian pattern of guilt and redemption is discovered in contexts where most of us are accustomed to see predominantly economic relations. Marx becomes part of such a pattern: "His attacks upon the established symbols of authority seem likewise to have stimulated some sense of guilt, for he identifies himself in 'pastoral' fashion with the suffering proletariat, who must redeem the world by a blood-sacrifice" (I, 117). It is difficult to engage in clear controversy with such symbolic treatment if it is protected by a claim to accept at the same time an objective economic interpretation of history. But one rebels at statements which must inevitably sound like distortions of fact, no matter how pretty the symbolic pattern formed by them,[2] and no matter how often the author protests to us that they are merely metaphors. The integration of Marxism with Freudianism, if it is to be made at all, will not be accomplished by this method, which in effect divides the world without from the world within. The proletariat *was*, and was being exploited, whether or not Marx suffered from a sense of guilt and made a Paschal lamb of himself and the proletariat.

The quest for symbols turns out to be a very risky game indeed when applied to language. There have been many ingenious attempts since the

[2] *E.g.*: "In Ibsen's case . . . the discovery that he had been a 'Darwinian' dramatist seems to have been a tremendous shock. After this play, he suffered a collapse" (I, 86 n.). Or, "Capitalism shouted to Marx until the annoyance gave him a diseased liver, but it seems to sing a cradle song for men like Ogden Mills" (*ibid.*, 86f.).

Cratylus to establish an essential nexus between the phonetic structure of a word and the thing symbolized by it. In Mr. Burke's exposition, chiefly under the word "cues" in the "Dictionary of Pivotal Terms" (II, 81), we have a sampling of instances from Plato to Sir Richard Paget. We are told that the "essence of *m* is 'acceptance,' because of the physiological similarity between the acts of phonation and of sucking." Thus *mountain, mother, mammal,* and the like, become accepted symbols in essence (assuming, by the way, that the initial phoneme *is* the essence of the word); *p,* a labial explosive, regarded as the opposite of *m,* becomes a sign of rejection, while the interchange of the two becomes "existential" (II, 91). But if *mama* is the essence of acceptance, what of *pap,* which means the same thing? Or is there an existential synthesis involved here? Likewise, if Mr. Burke, frankly leaning on Plato's *Cratylus,* assumes *r* to be the sound of growls and revolution (II, 83), what of *r*epose and *r*esignation, and of the historic instances of the dissimilation of *r* into other sounds? The weakness of these edifying speculations is that they entirely neglect the factor of change. If you isolate a word at any given moment of its history, and declare that precisely then its phonetic pattern conforms to its symbolic structure, you must admit that it not only lacked such harmony in the past, but will lack it again in the future.

Some of the interpretations of words in relation to things suggest the medieval doctrine that *nomina sunt consequentia rerum.* Of course the intent is otherwise; names are merely stimuli acting upon the hearer, or sought unconsciously by the speaker in response to a need. Nevertheless, the theory which sees in the fictitious name "Treep" a symbol of tree plus rejection (noticed *after* the author had unconsciously made the hero thus named cut down a tree) recalls the equally dazzling, if entirely different, methods of Albertus Magnus in operating with *Ave* and *Eva* in the *De Laudibus B. Mariae Virginis.*

The hostility to change implied in these linguistic theories becomes apparent in certain incidental remarks on the noun. Burke indicates the appropriateness of Huysmans' transition from a period of satanism, during which he used unstable prepositional phrases like *A Rebours, En Route* for his titles, to the period of Catholic realism, or stability, when he used nouns. Later, speaking in another connection, he suggests that "if we are ever to recover a world of nouns, going from a philosophy of *processes* to a philosophy of *categories* . . ." a certain analysis of associational clusters will have to be undertaken. Readers of *Science & Society* are not apt to share this nostalgia for a medieval world of stable nouns. They have presumably made themselves at home in a world of verbs and change.

This brilliant essay at a coordination of various poetic-psychological forms with history serves to reveal how much is yet to be done in the general field of Marxism and the humanities. The chief danger in the attempt is that sheer emphasis may make it appear that economic development is subordinate to or dependent upon the history of poetic forms. It must be said in justice to Mr. Burke that this is obviously not his intent; but his literary preoccupations at the expense of economic factors give this impression all too readily.

◇◇

MARGARET SCHLAUCH was born in 1898. She taught English at New York University, was an editor of *Science & Society*, and presently teaches at the University of Warsaw. She is the author or editor of many scholarly books on medieval literature and a book on language (*The Gift of Tongues*).

By the time Burke had finished *Attitudes toward History*, he was (I think) fully committed to a language-centered view of the self and reality similar in its implications to the theory of language Ernst Cassirer had worked out in his monumental *The Philosophy of Symbolic Forms*. Pursued far enough, this commitment leads to a radical – even revolutionary – system of thought. I have written of this at length in my own book on Burke and see no need to repeat here what I said in it. Once the commentators locate this center of Burke, the whole nature of the response to him changes. As with Sidney Hook's review, so with Margaret Schlauch's: the tendencies she locates and discusses are certainly there, inherent in the language-centered view of reality, and they are somewhat confused because Burke had only begun to work them out. The final two paragraphs of Professor Schlauch's review present two continuing objections to Burke, both of which have to do with what appears to be a partially static view of history.

◇◇

7. Kenneth Burke

BY Henry Bamford Parkes

MR. KENNETH BURKE'S *Attitudes toward History* presents, at first sight, a resemblance to a tropical jungle; its fertility is undeniably impressive,

EDITOR'S NOTE: Originally published in 1938. Reprinted from *The Pragmatic Test: Essays on the History of Ideas* (San Francisco: Colt Press, 1941), pp. 202–220, copyright 1941 by Henry Bamford Parkes, by permission of the author.

but it is difficult to decide how much of it has value. A careful study is, however, rewarding not only because Mr. Burke has a singularly active and subtle mind, with a capacity for setting off novel trains of thought and for illuminating old ideas from unfamiliar angles, but also because he is involved in dilemmas which are by no means peculiar to himself but which he shares with almost all his contemporaries.

Men formerly approached political problems with clear ideas of the modes of conduct and the kinds of society which they considered desirable. Political speculations were normally based on religious or philosophical doctrines, from which it was possible to deduce practical values. The individual could thus appraise, and if necessary resist, social processes. In the modern world, however, various factors have combined to destroy faith in the traditional values. They have been undermined by sociological and psychological investigations tending to show that they have no absolute validity but are relative to social environments; they have been discredited by the failure to adapt them to a society dominated by large-scale industry; and they have been rendered futile by the complexity of a world-system which moves forward by a momentum of its own and which individuals can scarcely hope to change. The result is an abdication of the will which ends in tyranny and in international anarchy. By freeing himself from belief in an absolute religion man has become the slave of social processes.

It is easy enough to show that man cannot find in the supremacy of the state or of historic destiny a substitute for moral values. The state is composed of individuals, and the supremacy of the state means, in practice, the supremacy of a dictator or a bureaucracy. To teach submission to historic destiny implies the possibility of interpreting that destiny, and by successfully interpreting it man becomes independent of it. But though such attitudes are intellectually indefensible, there remains the problem of finding a positive alternative. Human beings, for example, formerly professed a faith in individual freedom; but it is doubtful whether the ideal of freedom can be dissociated from a religious belief in the infinite value of the individual soul, and difficult to show how freedom can be preserved in a society where the means of production are owned either by the state or by the banks.

For this dilemma Marxism claims to have a solution. But though in capitalist society Marxism appears to offer a method by which human beings may control their own future, in its ultimate implications it leads to the creation of a new form of tyranny. Marxism attempts to synthesize fatalism and voluntarism in two ways. In the first place it affirms that there is an absolute law of development and that history is leading mankind to a kingdom of freedom. This, however, is a hangover from Christian interpretations of the universe, and if one does not believe in either a divine or a dialectical providence, there is no guarantee that historic destiny is beneficent. In the second place Marxism asserts that the need of human beings for food, clothing, and shelter is an absolute, independent of historic processes, which determines both social environments and individual evaluations. Unfortunately men are not motivated solely by these three needs. They are governed also by emotional drives of other kinds, and their happiness depends on much more than on the satisfaction of their basic economic appetites. Once society has been revolutionized by the triumph of the proletariat, Marxism no longer offers any criteria for political evaluations. Must the individual submit to a proletarian dictator as the instrument of historic destiny? And if there are rival candidates for the position, on what grounds is he to choose between them? If he resists the party in power, must his resistance be based on economic considerations, or are there also noneconomic values which may be asserted?

The case of Mr. Burke is particularly interesting because in different books he has asserted both that individuals should appraise and resist social processes, and also that the individual is himself the creature of those processes. On the one hand he has affirmed a faith in intellectual freedom and has sketched a picture of the kind of society in which he would like to live – a society which would satisfy certain nonhistoric elements in human nature; on the other hand he has advocated the adoption of a general intellectual and political system to which individuals must conform, and has written of history in a manner which implies that it progresses by a logic of its own, independent of human choice, and that capitalism must now develop into Communism. Superficially, it appears that Mr. Burke has been undergoing a gradual conversion from one attitude to the other. For whereas in *Counter-Statement* he wished to encourage individual freedom, in *Permanence and Change* he showed that the evaluations of individuals were relative to their interests and therefore devoid of objective validity, and in *Attitudes toward History* he examines – and approves of – the methods by which individuals achieve conformity with a social system. Yet in spite of the fact that Mr. Burke now considers himself a Communist, he has never genuinely abandoned his earlier beliefs; and there are passages in *Attitudes toward History* in which – in complete contradiction to the main drift of his argument – he continues to praise intellectual freedom and to advocate a society quite different from that envisaged by the Marxists.

Conceivably Mr. Burke may finally succeed in suppressing his non-Marxist convictions. This, however, appears improbable in view of the fact that he rejects as untenable precisely those two features of the Marxist cosmology which give its appearance of optimism and of rationality. He does not believe either in the beneficence of historic destiny or in the economic interpretation of history. The result is that he is unable to present Communism as either a stage in the predestined advance of mankind towards the kingdom of freedom or as a desirable method of satisfying human needs. He can, in fact, within the terms of his argument, offer no very convincing reason why Communism should be adopted at all or why, if men must subordinate themselves to the "curve of history," they should not accept Fascism. It is therefore permitted to hope that Mr. Burke's intellectual development is not yet completed, and that he may proceed to the task of attempting to reconcile the two halves of his intellectual personality.

II

Attitudes toward History may be described as an anatomy of the nonrational factors in social change. Mr. Burke analyzes the psychological processes implicated in the acceptance of different social systems, deriving his evidence both from the works of individual poets and from those "collective poems" which consist of religions and prevalent philosophies of life. This method of approach enables him to coordinate social and aesthetic criticism. By taking the emotional development of the individual as his subject of study, he can show how politics and literature are connected with each other, and at the same time avoid the crudities of the "all-art-is-propaganda" school of criticism.

Mr. Burke begins by discussing the adoption of a "frame of acceptance." By an act of will the individual elects to choose a certain view of life as true – a process which Mr. Burke calls "transcendence" and which is followed by "character-building." A "frame of acceptance" necessarily involves a program of action and an interpretation of human motives; what one wants, or believes oneself to want, is dependent upon what one chooses to believe about the universe. As Mr. Burke explained in *Permanence and Change*, St. Augustine believed that men were "really" motivated by a desire for God; at the present day men prefer to attach "reality" to economic or to sexual needs; and since these conflicting interpretations were deductions from different "frames of acceptance," there is no objective standard by which either can be judged as true or false.

In his first chapter Mr. Burke discusses three examples of an individual "frame of acceptance" – those of Emerson, Whitman, and William James. But his primary concern is with the collective "frames of acceptance" in terms of which a society is organized and of which the most elaborate example is medieval Catholicism. When a society is dominated by a "frame of acceptance," the individual organizes his emotions in accordance with the social norm; and the whole social structure appears to him to be just and rational. Certain individuals, living or mythical, become embodiments of the norm; they function as symbols of authority and are endowed with the insignia of power. The individual identifies himself with the symbol and builds his character by a process of imitation. Such symbols of power function as extensions of the father. In the prepolitical stage of childhood the father is endowed with a magical authority, and the collective symbols with which the adult individual identifies himself are father-substitutes.[1]

A "frame of acceptance," however, carries within itself the seeds of its own destruction. The habits which it encourages eventually reach their "Malthusian limits" and can go no further. It normally involves resignation to certain forms of injustice, and individuals tend to "move in on" that resignation and take advantage of it. The result is that men find it increasingly difficult to regard society as rational, and they begin to suffer from "alienation." Some of them turn against society and denounce the good in it as well as the bad – a negative emphasis which leads to Satanism and to the splintering of opposition parties into sects. Others take refuge in a sensuality which must eventually develop into sadism, or in mysticism and irrationality. Meanwhile the reigning authorities endeavor to cure the situation by the use of force, by "casuistic stretching," through which the "frame of acceptance" is stretched to admit of new developments, and by "secular prayer" (as in the enactment of laws which express aspirations and which cannot be enforced).

There follows a period of confusion. A new "frame of acceptance" is being created, but at first its emphasis is mainly destructive. The true significance of events can be found most clearly in poetry. Poets may endeavor to deny their own meanings, but their real attitudes can be deduced from an analysis of the "clusters" of associated symbols in their work. Poetry is an intellectual stock exchange which registers the rise and fall of "frames of acceptance." During a time of transition poetry will deal with the conflict between symbols of authority and will adopt ambivalent attitudes towards the traditional symbols. Rituals of rebirth, with imagery derived from the prepolitical era of childhood, will be used to symbolize the change in authority (hence, for Mr. Burke, Communism as a house or a "magnetic mountain,"

[1] As Mr. Burke perceives, this implies that dictatorship is the most natural form of government. If this is true, then the British system, which separates magical from real authority, offers the best safeguards against dictatorship.

house and mountain being mother-symbols; hence also the prevalence of homosexual and androgynous symbolisms, since homosexuality results from a conflict in the symbols of prepolitical authority — the father and the mother — and is used as an analogy for the political conflict).

Eventually the new "frame of acceptance" triumphs and becomes orthodox. There ensues a process of compromise and of adjustment to material necessities which Mr. Burke calls the "bureaucratization of the imaginative." In course of time the new frame will probably develop its own inner contradictions and its own possibilities of "alienation" through the "moving in" of a privileged group. The rhythms of cultural death and rebirth are thus likely to be perpetual.

III

This general sketch of social psychology appears to be largely true, and it offers a convenient framework within which one can place specific phenomena. What is open to criticism in Mr. Burke's scheme is not what he says but what he omits to say. What he fails to do is to lay any stress upon the element of rational choice in human affairs. The rise and fall of "frames of acceptance" is apparently determined by factors which are beyond human control. The reasons which have caused Mr. Burke to adopt this attitude are peculiarly significant, since they are derived from the relativism which dominates all contemporary culture.

Mr. Burke has been profoundly influenced by the pragmatist interpretation of epistemology and by the view of the human mind with which it is associated. Our ideas of the world, he believes, are a reflection of our interests. A cosmology is a subjective structure created in accordance with volitional rather than intellectual needs. Thought is subsidiary to action. This attitude has led Mr. Burke to accept the aesthetic doctrine of Mr. I. A. Richards, who declares that the function of art is to organize our emotions, apparently with a view to more effective action; from which it would seem to follow that art is to be judged as good or bad in terms of its practical consequences. Pragmatism has usually assumed that our interests, or our ideas of good and evil, are absolutes, fundamental data which cannot be translated into terms of something else. Mr. Burke, however, knows enough anthropology to be aware of the naïvetés of such an attitude. What we believe to be good is connected with what we believe about the universe; we do not, solely by introspection, even know what we want, for interpretations of human motives vary in different cosmological systems. The result is that he finds himself inside a circle. Interests and "frames of acceptance" determine each other, and there is no appeal to any factor outside the circle.

The only escape from the circle would be by the assertion of some kind of absolute truth: a truth about the universe, such as religions have taught; a truth about the permanent needs of human nature, such as the other half of Mr. Burke's split personality is anxious to find; or a truth about the course of human history and the factors which determine it, such as Marxism — in contradiction to its doctrine of the class determination of intellectual attitudes — professes to have found. But Mr. Burke goes out of his way to deny the possibility of finding truth. He likes to regard even scientific discoveries as symbolic expressions of emotional drives; and he disparages the attempts of science to find a neutral vocabulary which will describe events objectively. In *Permanence and Change* he was inclined to regard science as merely a particular scheme of interpretation, which was not necessarily truer than other schemes. He admitted the existence of certain "recalcitrances" which might necessitate the revision of some of our ideas; but he implied that the role which they played was a small one, and that we could never know very directly what they were.

Such a point of view must necessarily lead to a denial of human freedom and to resignation to historic destiny. Once interests and "frame of acceptance" have become fixed in a given relationship, there is no way by which individuals can afterwards modify them. If they are modified, it can only be by factors outside of human control. The nature of these factors, however, remains somewhat mysterious.

It is doubtful whether the collapse of a "frame of acceptance" can be adequately accounted for by the reasons which Mr. Burke mentions. Why must habits have "Malthusian limits"? What were the "Malthusian limits" of medieval Catholicism? It is not even certain that individualism today has reached any "Malthusian limits." The history of capitalism for the past half century has to a large degree been a history, not of the proliferation of individualism, but of its thwarting and checking by monopoly and state interference. The notion that a ruling class "moves in on" some form of resignation is more intelligible. Finance capitalism has undeniably "moved in on" *laissez-faire* individualism, and the functionaries of the Church "moved in on" medieval Catholicism. But if this were the sole reason for the breakdown of a "frame of acceptance," the obvious remedy would be not to change the frame but to check the process of "moving in." What factors are responsible for the formulation of a new "frame of acceptance"? Why was feudalism followed by capitalism, and why must capitalism be followed by Communism? According to Mr. Burke a new frame is apparently a product not of human volition but of the "curve of history" – a conception from which he deduces that it can be grasped imaginatively by poets before it achieves concrete reality but that conceptual formulation by philosophers does not occur until after it has been realized.[2] The only alternative to this Spenglerian conclusion is to admit an element of rationality into human affairs, to attribute the growth of new "frames of acceptance" to rational attempts to reinterpret man's place in the universe or to changes in the economic system; but this Mr. Burke is unable to do. He admits occasionally the importance of economic changes, but – in spite of his professed Marxism – he cannot consistently explain history in economic terms. For to do so would be to admit that man's desire for worldly goods is an absolute which is independent of all "frames of acceptance."

All these problems come to a head in the most obvious of Mr. Burke's difficulties: the fact that he must ascribe the adoption of a new "frame of acceptance" on the part of an individual to an act of will. This difficulty is not peculiar to Mr. Burke, since we find it also in Mr. Richards, who asserts that after we have grasped the meaning of a poem, we must make a choice – a choice which is apparently based entirely on subjective considerations – as to whether we regard its method of organizing the emotions as good or bad.[3] What determines Mr. Burke's act of will? Is it the result of historic destiny or of rational choice? And by what standards are we to assess the "transcendence" which the act of will produces? Is it better to choose materialism or idealism, Communism or Fascism? To this most important of all ques-

[2] This appears to reverse the true order of events. Conceptual definition may precede the realization of a "frame of acceptance"; aesthetic expression never does. Philosophy may determine conduct in the future; poetry deals primarily with the past. Thus, for example, *The City of God* preceded the medieval synthesis; but *The Divine Comedy* was not written until that synthesis had begun to disintegrate. Poetry at the present day, insofar as it is genuine and not a propagandist poetry of the will, is concerned with the decay of capitalist society, and not with any new social order of the future; its themes are death and disintegration. Mr. Burke's attempts to find some imaginative prophecy of Communism lead him to see in Dostoyevsky's idealization of the Tsar something which was to be realized by Stalin – a defense of Stalin-worship which will delight the Trotskyites. On the other hand he consistently minimizes the importance of conceptual thought in influencing human activities. Yet the ideas of Adam Smith had for three quarters of a century an enormous influence on public policy, and present trends towards the totalitarian state, both on the left and on the right, can very largely be traced back, through various channels, to the philosophy of Hegel.

[3] "The personality stands balanced between the particular experience which is the realized poem and the whole fabric of the past experience and developed habits of mind. What is being settled is whether this new experience can or cannot be taken into the fabric with advantage. Would the fabric afterwards be good or bad?" "There comes a point in all criticism where a sheer choice has to be made without the support of any argument, principles, or general rules." *Practical Criticism*, 302, 303.

tions Mr. Burke is finally driven to confess that he has no answer. The difference between a true "transcendence" and a false one is, he says, an indefinable qualitative *je-ne-sais-quoi* about which nothing can be said.[4]

IV

As a counteractive to this depressing conclusion we may turn to the other Mr. Burke, the Mr. Burke who wrote *Counter-Statement,* and who continues to assert himself periodically in *Permanence and Change* and *Attitudes toward History*.

Throughout *Attitudes toward History* Mr. Burke has much to say in commendation of a "comic frame of reference." The words in themselves mean very little; in fact, Mr. Burke confesses that he has chosen them partly because he likes the sound of the letters "co." What Mr. Burke really means by his "comic frame" is the broadest possible development of consciousness and the maximum independence of all specific philosophies and ideologies. His "comic frame" is similar to Keats's "negative capability" – the capacity of a poet to appreciate all points of view without adopting them. By means of this obscure phraseology Mr. Burke implies that the individual may, after all, achieve moral autonomy and become independent of "frames of acceptance" and historic processes.

By examining Mr. Burke's "comic frame" we may be enabled to recapture certain positions which Mr. Burke has surrendered to the historic determinists. Mr. Burke defines an "I" as a complex of different "collective we's" which meet and sometimes conflict in the same personality. He declares that the function of psychoanalysis is to socialize private impulses; when the analyst "explains" the impulses which are causing a neurosis, he is merely rationalizing them in terms of the prevalent "frame of acceptance"; and when he cures them, he is adapting the individual to society. For Mr. Burke there are apparently two elements in the personality – the "id," which represents private impulse, and the "super-ego," which represents, sometimes in contradictory ways, the morality of society. But according to the psychoanalysts there is also an "ego"; and the aim of the analyst is not to socialize impulses

[4] Under the word "transcendence" Mr. Burke includes phenomena of two quite different kinds. To undergo an emotional experience which leads one to accept the universe as fundamentally good is "transcendence"; to make a choice between idealism and materialism, or between capitalism and Communism, is also "transcendence." Of an emotional experience it is true that one cannot easily determine whether it is true or false. But an intellectual choice must be preceded by a rational consideration of the available evidence. Rejection of capitalism should not be based merely on an act of will but also on a study of economics.

but to strengthen the "ego" and thereby to enable it to dominate both the anarchy of the instincts and the demands, often equally anarchical, of social morality. Mr. Burke blames the psychoanalysts for clinging to individualistic modes of thought. Yet to strengthen the "ego" means, in reality, to encourage Mr. Burke's "comic frame of reference"; it means to promote that true moral growth which consists in the extension of consciousness and of the power of control and which enables the individual not only to accept the obligations and imperatives imposed by society but at the same time to transcend them. The truly moral individual is, as St. Paul explained, not in bondage to the law; and, as Nietzsche declared, in a phrase which Mr. Burke cites but does not fully understand, he is "*beyond* good and evil." Such a person no longer needs to identify himself with paternalistic symbols; and he is capable of rational choice.

By exercising his own faculty of rational choice Mr. Burke has arrived at definite ideas of the kind of society which he would consider desirable. He dislikes mechanization and he dislikes rapid change and excessive mobility. He believes that there ought to be a maximum of physicality; human beings should work with their hands, and—where possible—prefer physical to ideal satisfactions. The sentiments should be cultivated, and passion discouraged. Social life should develop a style, and should satisfy many of those needs which tend today to seek fulfilment in the arts. There should be a spread of immobility, with a few mobile individuals. One might sum up Mr. Burke's ideal by saying that he would like to have lived in Confucian China.

Mr. Burke's dissertations on the good life raise two questions. In the first place, if the argument of *Permanence and Change* and of *Attitudes toward History* is correct, then no political ideal has any absolute validity. A political ideal implies the existence of certain permanent human needs, which are independent of historic societies and ideologies; and since what we believe ourselves to want is dependent upon what we believe about the universe, it involves the adoption as true not only of a morality but also of a cosmology. Even if a society without metaphysical assumptions is theoretically conceivable, it is impossible in practice; for any social system involves certain forms of self-sacrifice, and when men reach a certain level of sophistication self-sacrifice ceases unless it is justified by metaphysical beliefs. By what criteria does Mr. Burke justify his preference for physicality, as against the Catholic belief in the primacy of spiritual forces? Or his dislike of mechanization, as against the Marxist belief in the primacy of the need for material goods? It is improbable that he can find an adequate justification for his political ideals as long as he continues to accept the pragmatist theory of the human mind and to deny the possibility of objective knowledge.

In the second place, how does Mr. Burke expect his political ideals to be realized? His most obvious affiliations would appear to be with the distributivists, who share his dislike of mechanization and his preference for physicality and immobility. Mr. Burke, however, believes that the voice of history has decreed that capitalism must pass into Communism. He accepts the necessity of Communism, and then salves his conscience by attaching to Communism his vision of a nonmechanized stylized society. Once Communism has been established we may hope that men will lose their respect for the machine and return to working with their hands.

What "Communism" means is exceedingly vague. Its negative implications are clear enough, but in its positive sense the word has become a focus for different and often contradictory aspirations to which it is difficult to attach any concrete significance. Nobody has ever formulated a clear and plausible account of how individual freedom can be reconciled with centralized planning, or of how economic efficiency is compatible with the abolition of the free market, and as soon as one attempts to do either one discovers extraordinary difficulties. Mr. Burke appears to believe that the principles of Communist society were laid down by Marx, but this is not true. Marx confined himself to an analysis of capitalism, and offered only the vaguest hints as to what might happen after the revolution. This, incidentally, may serve to elucidate one problem which Mr. Burke has created for himself. If, as he says, a "frame of acceptance" does not achieve conceptual formulation until after it has been established in practice, how then, he asks, was Marx able to conceptualize Communism? The answer is that Marx did no such thing. In 1917 the Bolshevik leaders found themselves with a blank sheet and with no guidance from Marx as to what they were to write on it. What they actually did write on it, after several disastrous false starts, was a species of state capitalism which differed from private capitalism in that profits and losses were assumed by the state instead of by individual entrepreneurs.

If by Communism is meant the system established in Russia, what reasons are there for supposing that it will ever develop into the kind of society which Mr. Burke considers desirable? Whereas Mr. Burke advocates a "comic frame of reference," Communism has been associated with indoctrination into an official philosophy and with a general assault on the moral autonomy of the individual. And whereas Mr. Burke's ideal society is based on the assertion of certain noneconomic values, the primary objective of Communism is to substitute mechanical processes for human labor. It is possible that human beings in a Communist society may finally tire of economic progress, but once the primacy of economic need has been enshrined in a dictatorial state system, presided over by an elaborate bureaucracy, it would probably require a revolution to overthrow it. Before accepting the necessity of Communism and then hoping that some possible revolution in the distant future will transform it into something else, it might be advisable to inquire whether there is not a more direct route to a desirable social order.

V

Mr. Burke's problem is that of reconciling his own humanistic values with what he conceives to be the "curve of history." His solution to it involves contradictions. Yet this is a problem to which any solution, however contradictory, is better than none; for to accept the impossibility of any reconciliation is to succumb to despair. If one clings to values which are negated by the dynamics of history, one can only relapse into pessimism or escape into otherworldly religion. If, on the other hand, one resigns oneself to the "curve of history," it becomes futile to believe in the value of individual integrity or of a "comic frame of reference"; and Mr. Burke's preference for immobility and physicality must be condemned as a form of nostalgic daydreaming. For there is no good reason for supposing that the "curve of history" must eventually lead mankind to a kingdom of freedom. If we allow ourselves to be carried by the drift of social processes, we shall finally arrive – by way of what Mr. Burke calls the "socialization of losses" – at that form of bureaucratic and dictatorial state capitalism which Mr. Belloc called the "servile state." Such has been the end implicit in the strongest tendencies, whether of the left or of the right, which have been at work in Western civilization for the past seventy-five years.

There remains the possibility that Mr. Burke's reading of the "curve of history" is erroneous, and that the future is, in reality, determined not by a Spenglerian destiny but by human choice. Mr. Burke's belief in the necessity of Communism is based not on metaphysical or economic interpretations of history but on the fact that the left-wing movement is the most vital force in contemporary society. He does not, however, inquire what factors have given that movement its vitality, or why it has usually adopted socialist or Communist programs. If these questions are examined rationalistically instead of being left in the obscurities of Marxist mysticism, there appears to be at least a possibility of surmounting the dilemmas in which Mr. Burke finds himself. The revolutionary movement may often profess a belief in determinism, yet actually it is a struggle not to guide history along a predestined path but to divert it in new directions; and its participants may emphasize the primacy of the economic factor, yet actually they are fighting not only for the satisfaction of economic needs but also for noneconomic values, for freedom and human dignity. There appears, therefore, to be a contradiction between the real aims of the left-wing movement and the intellectual formulations in which those aims are expressed; and insofar as the movement is guided by those formulations it will frustrate its own aims. For belief in historic inevitability and in the primacy of economics leads to dictatorship, indoctrination, centralized planning, thoroughgoing mechanization, and the suppression of human freedom. State capitalism is not, however, the only alternative to finance capitalism; it is possible also to conceive of societies which have abolished privately controlled corporations without destroying private property, and which have decentralized power instead of concentrating it; and while such societies may be less efficient than state capitalism in the production of consumable commodities by mechanical processes, they may promote a greater degree of human freedom and of human happiness. This raises a question which cuts deeper than the conflict between Stalinites and Trotskyites, since both alike accept the Marxist creed and the framework of government laid down by Lenin. The question is whether the real desire of those who, throughout the world, struggle against capitalist and Fascist tyranny is for Communism on the Russian model, or whether it is for something closer to the kind of society which appeals to Mr. Burke. It is possible, therefore, that in attempting to stifle his non-Marxist convictions in order to unite himself with the most vital of contemporary movements, Mr. Burke may be making an unnecessary sacrifice. He might perhaps perform a more valuable function if he assisted that movement to achieve a more accurate formulation of its own purposes and of the philosophy of life implicit in them.

◇◇

HENRY BAMFORD PARKES, born in Sheffield, England, in 1904, came to the United States in 1927 and was naturalized in 1940. He has taught history at New York University since 1930, and has written numerous books, among them *Jonathan Edwards*; *Marxism: An Autopsy*; *Recent America*; and *The American Experience.*

This is the last and the longest essay included here on *Attitudes toward History*, the book which marked a turning point in the critical reception of Burke. All the main reviews of *Attitudes toward History* were long and searching and indicated that people in at least four fields (literature, philosophy, history, and sociology) took Burke's accumulated critical-theoretical work seriously. Professor Parkes gives the principal reasons for this in the first two paragraphs of his review and then goes on, as a historian of ideas, to examine in detail the many ways in which the content of *Attitudes toward History* is related to and comes out of the contemporary scene. No better account of Burke as a representative intellectual exists anywhere, and no other account of Burke's odd involvement with Marxism even exists.

The commitment to a language-centered view of reality inevitably pushes a person toward the kind of "relativism" Professor Parkes (along with Professors Hook and Schlauch) objects to in Burke. This is so because verbal action becomes the prime human act and the differences, in kind and value, between verbal acts tend to be forgotten in the emphasis on verbalization as such, on system building, and on language as an act and function of the self. Burke's way out of this dilemma did not really occur to him until the late forties and does not appear until *A Rhetoric of Motives* and the theory of hierarchy formulated there. Professor Parkes examines this dilemma in Section III of his review most perceptively in the peculiarly American context of pragmatism.

◇◇

7 *Wam for Maw: Dogma versus Discursiveness in Criticism*

BY William S. Knickerbocker

FERTILITY of speculation concerning literary processes and products, and an audacity in proposing critical schemata, have characterized literary opinion in the United States since the second decade of this century. The result has been to obliterate recognizable conventions in criticism and has furthered literary anarchy in all literary forms. Encouraging signs of contraction have been evident since the Humanist polemics of a decade ago, chiefly through police measures exercised by some eminent minds of our generation: especially by Messrs. R. P. Blackmur, Allen Tate, Yvor Winters, T. S. Eliot, and I. A. Richards. When Mr. John Crowe Ransom's name is added, one sees the uncertain formation of a new school of critics who have successfully laid the bases

EDITOR'S NOTE: Reprinted from *The Sewanee Review*, XLIX (1941), 520–521, 529–536, copyright 1941 by the University of the South, by permission of the author and publisher.

of a "New Rhetoric": a "new rhetoric" which has its attractions and benefits, to be sure, but which has obviously so far failed to secure a recognizable criterion to discriminate literary quality.

Mr. Ransom's *The New Criticism* and Mr. Burke's *The Philosophy of Literary Form* conspicuously mark discernible poles of literary opinion concerning the nature and purpose of poetry, hereafter impossible to be ignored by venturesome writers of a speculative turn engaged with problems of literary criticism. There may be other points of critical reference, established by other able and suggestive critics, but, for purposes of clarifying a field of aesthetic speculation already confused by pluralistic miscellany, and of securing perspectives in current American literary criticism, these other points may be, for the present, left undiscussed and perhaps unnoticed.

Until now, obsession with criticism has been a mark of "health" in a period of creative fatuity. Clusters of dialecticians here and there have aligned themselves with a "line"; and of these, Mr. Ransom has carried an idea, which the Southern Croceans (sometimes mis-called "Southern Aristotelians") have nobly espoused, to a point of identification which alters the nature and direction of the discussion of poetry. Mr. Burke is a member of no school. As an independent critic, he is particularly arresting. For years he has persisted in his syncretistic forays, enlarging the bounds of the concept of criticism beyond those of the restrictedly aesthetic. His books have serially revealed a cumulative development, fixing coördinates, courageous in exploration, mutations, mutings, and amendments. His *The Philosophy of Literary Form* is, with the exception of the introductory essay which gives the book its title, a collection of his more notable essays in criticism composed during the decade of the 'thirties and manifest the working of his method clearly defined in his relatively little-noticed *Attitudes toward History*, published five years ago. The present attempt to correlate Mr. Ransom's *The New Criticism* and Mr. Burke's *The Philosophy of Literary Form* resolves itself into an effort to move into the newer perspectives of the criticism of poetry, even though the correlation of the two books will indicate that Mr. Burke's book begins where Mr. Ransom's leaves off.

[All of Section I has been omitted here.]

II

Whereas Mr. Ransom considers poetry solely and absolutely as a *product* which "represents ultimately a kind of philosophical temperament that carefully finds the occasion to pursue its science and at the same time to refuse conscientiously to concede that science has a valid world-view, a realistic ontology," Mr. Kenneth Burke in his *The Philosophy of Literary Form* is concerned with poetry as a social and technological *process,* and supplies an organon for the indeterminants in a poem as a gestative act of symbolization.

Both Mr. Ransom and Mr. Burke are agreed on the symbolic significance of a poem: Mr. Ransom's statement that ". . . poems are now the official or approved form of our actions" (page 233 of *The New Criticism*) might have been written by Mr. Burke as the determining idea of his book. But Mr. Burke's mind moves by a process of inclusion, whereas Mr. Ransom's by a process of exclusion. The haunting metaphor which delivers Mr. Burke's "secret" seems to be his obsession with the sea: subsidence in and emergence from liquidity. In his neglected book, *Attitudes toward History,* he called attention to this oceanic attraction and in a revealing footnote of Volume One of that personal confession he supplied a clue to his methodology in his references to the bifocal fish called "anablepsis"; an organism which can simultaneously see in two media – water and air. Mr. Burke undoubtedly is nearer than is Mr. Ransom to Mr. Eliot's statement: "When a poet's mind is perfectly equipped for its work, it is constantly amalgamating disparate experience." The "disparate experience" is undoubtedly the domain of "the forsaken merman" for Mr. Burke. Few living critics are as voracious for knowledge and experience as Mr. Burke: his series of books clearly indicate the most ambitious effort in America to encompass the best of what is being thought and said and to supply clues to the reflective poet for orientation in this vast sea.

Mr. Burke's *The Philosophy of Literary Form* is a contribution to soteriology which should be read as a supplement to, and partial correction of, his *Attitudes toward History.* Perhaps the most comprehensive statement of his view is this: "To an extent, books merely exploit our attitudes – and to an extent they may form our attitudes" (page 235, *Philosophy of Literary Form*). This is a variant of his footnote in Volume II of *Attitudes toward History* (page 113): "We are also suggesting . . . that there is a point at which a man ceases to write a book and the book begins writing the man." Mr. Burke is no Puritan in the commonly-accepted sense of the word, but his high reverence for the printed page is indicated in his belief that poetry is a religious function manifested as "symbolic action." Just so, the Puritan's belief in the plenary inspiration of the Holy Bible. Mr. Burke's creed is appropriately expressed in some unforgettable verses on the last three pages of *The Philosophy of Literary Form*:

Hail to Thee, Logos,
Thou Vast Almighty Title,

William S. Knickerbocker

In Whose Name we conjure—
Our acts the partial representatives
Of Thy whole act.

May we be thy delegates
In parliament assembled,
Parts of Thy wholeness.
And in our conflicts
Correcting one another.
By study of our errors
Gaining Revelation.

May we give true voice
To the statements of our creatures,
May our spoken words speak for them,
With accuracy,
That we know precisely their rejoinders
To our utterances
And so may correct our utterances
In the light of those rejoinders.

Rewarding as "the New Criticism" is, as practised by critics as diverse as Richards, Tate, Ransom, Blackmur, Eliot, and Winters its contraction to rigid rhetoric leaves one gasping for air. By a "transcendental" device Mr. Burke subsumes this "new criticism" but floods it with addenda, enabling his readers to expand intellectually and spiritually. His wide reading, generous reflections on the work of modern thinkers like Thurman Arnold, Stuart Chase, Anton Korzybski, Veblen, Sir Richard Paget, Marx, Freud, James, Dewey, and his responses to significant creative writers from the Greeks to the present richly reward the thoughtful reading of his pages. A radiant blitheness and equanimity of spirit pervade his lines, manifesting a temperament aware of modern complexities and difficulties but resolutely committed to facing them, undiscouraged by the delay of complete and final answers. His sense of the comic is shared by Mr. Ransom: but in this sense of the comic, bravely expounded in his *Attitudes toward History*, is the clue to his "salvation device" or what I, clumsily appropriating his trick, call his "contribution to soteriology." People who prize it in Chaucer, Shakspere, Arnold, and Browning will recognize its presence in Kenneth Burke's style, and miss it in Richards, Winters, and Tate.

The comic sense in Kenneth Burke calls for intelligence, steadied by patience, and a disposition to reach beyond the present schism between the seriousness of matter and lightness of touch in expression. He has what might be called the sense of the levity-gravity principle. "I see no good reason, except perversities arising in response to the complexities of our times," he writes on page 189 of *The Philosophy of Literary Form,* "why one should have to treat the *exposition* of human motives as synonymous with the *debunking* of human motives. And I hold that, if one refuses to accept this equation, one may seek rather such perspectives as interpret human events by making scientific diagnosis and moral exhortation integral aspects of one's program." His own intention is not to *debunk* but to supply techniques of understanding. His method is ingenious: indeed, if it is only considered seriously, it is monstrous, clumsy, and grotesque. But though it may not be lightly dismissed as eternal trifling which breaks the spell, it treats humanly grave problems in a manner quite inviting. It is aërated by Mr. Burke's comic sense.

An illustration of Mr. Burke's comic sense may be seen in his proposal of salvation by consonantal ablaut. (In this effort to illustrate it, I frankly admit my intention to imitate his pleasant ways of expression, and beg my reader to consult *The Philosophy of Literary Form* or *Attitudes toward History* to enjoy and be illuminated by the original.) The Greek word from which we derive "ablaut" means an off-sound but in English the word has been technically limited to the systematic variation of the root vowel in related words, indicating a change of use or meaning. But, if there is no word indicating the systematic variation of the phonetically-determining consonants, Mr. Burke informs us of a passage in Coleridge's *Table Talk* that "the consonants are 'the framework of the word' " and supplements this information, borrowing from Mencken's *The American Language* a suggestion on "forbidden words" in four letters. Upon this basis, Mr. Burke constructs a promising interpretive device which he calls "concealed punning" (*The Philosophy of Literary Form,* pages 51–58).

"Concealed punning," one might suppose, has applications to the names of authors; and by it one may decipher internal tensions in an author's successive acts of writing. Take Keats, for instance. By playing anagrammatically with the five letters of Keats's name, we get the word "steak." By this clue one could correlate the psychosis of Keats in Mr. Burke's manner by proceeding to discourse in this way: Keats, as an apothecary's apprentice, came into close and continuous contact with physicians, themselves continuously exposed to the complexities of flesh in their patients. Apothecaries are notoriously undernourished and therefore are liable to tuberculosis. Keats had t.b. The normative power of his name acted subconsciously upon him, causing "symbolic action" with its suggestion of "steak," and resulting in a passion which could only be fulfilled in his writing poems of an exquisite, sensuous kind:

or which could be satisfied, to use Mr. Burke's convenient phrase, only in "symbolic action."

The possibilities for developing this idea further may be left for others to explore: more pertinent to the present occasion and purpose would be an effort to employ it as an "over-all" instrument, or critical gauge, to Mr. Kenneth Burke. In *Attitudes toward History*, Mr. Burke elucidates his principle of clues as cues. He applies his principle to his own name. ". . . A man writes his name," wrote Mr. Burke, Volume II (pages 85–86), "he says his number. Your correspondent's name and number begins with 'c.' In trying to appropriate the forensic material, he continues to pronounce his name. He says 'you' and 'it' but is secretly saying 'I.' He can do no other. He identifies himself with as much of the corporate, public material (in the contemporary, in history, in philosophy) as he can encompass." Having himself directed our attention to this mode of "decoding" a writer's work by his nomenclature, Mr. Burke alarms me by the suggestiveness of his comments on the letter which begins his family name. "We may further note," he writes in Volume II, page 90 of *Attitudes toward History*, "that 'b' is a modified 'm,' thereby serving to remind us of the mimetic accuracy in Catullus's kiss poem ('kiss' is less accurate mimetically than the archaic 'buss'), where he explains 'da *m*i *b*asia *m*ille,' asking repeatedly for those 'myriad busses' in semialliteration."

Has Mr. Burke been conditioned and directed in his development by his own name? "Kenneth" lends itself reversally to "the neck" which carries the suggestion of a poem which has deeply impressed Mr. Burke – Arnold's "The Neckan," the introductory piece for Arnold's "The Forsaken Merman." Both poems are concerned in reverse order with submergence and emergence: The Neckan emerged from the sea to sing his song about his earth-born wife who had deserted him: the Forsaken Merman, as everyone knows, plunged disconsolately into the depths of the sea, calling his children ("disciples"?) to sink with him to his submarine palaces. Mr. Burke informed us in a footnote of Volume I (pages 19 and 20) of *Attitudes toward History* that his tendency is towards submersion and emergence and says: "I can remember stepping slowly into a lake, until my eyes were even with its surface, the water cutting across the eye-balls," and in that context, specifically cited a couplet from Arnold's "The Forsaken Merman." Revealing as this confession is, the confirmation of it comes from considering "Kenneth" without the anagrammatic distortion: note the given name just as it is. The first syllable obviously equates "know": the second equates "lower" (or "neth-er"): the combination of the two syllables in "Kenneth" resolves into "know what lies under," or "know, by emergence, what is submerged." The whole is comprized by an overall stratagem which discloses the exploratory passion of Kenneth Burke which is strikingly analogous to Matthew Arnold's completion of a similar quest, completed in Arnold's recurrent use of the metaphor of coral islands which "link their arms under the sea." Mr. Burke's paraphrase of this linkage metaphor may be confirmed by referring to page 83 of his Volume II, *Attitudes toward History*, in the passage that plainly says: "But these are merely outstanding peaks of a mimetic mountain range that, for the most part, lies buried beneath the surface of our communicative ocean."

The clan or "cluster" name "Burke," however, subsumes the declensive tendency of "Kenneth," but secures the restoral of equilibrium. "Burke" lends itself, by the soteriological clue of the consonantal ablaut, in three accessible interpretations: "grub," "burg," and "curve." The alteration of "k" into "g" gives the first two: the alteration of "b" to "v" in Burke and the "k" into "c" give the third, or "curve." In "curve," one sees the arc of Mr. Burke's hermeneutics. In brief, the idea would be that "burg" is the symbol of the capitalist order (or bourgeois): but he opposes this in order to compose his mind: what results is the reverse of "burg" (or Burk) into "grub." The hermeneutical act thus illustrated gives this interesting result: the meaning of Kenneth Burke's critical effort is the reconstruction of the burg (or present society) by resorting to grubbing, or delving for roots, motivated by the desire for physical food ("grub") and, at times, he transcends this by his sense of grub as larva with the hope of biological metamorphosis of larva into winged, aerial creatures. All this conforms to Mr. Burke's ingenious "methodology of the pun."[1]

III

This review of Mr. Ransom's *The New Criticism* and Mr. Burke's *The Philosophy of Literary Form* has resulted in an experiment in criticism described by Mr. Burke as "perspectives by incongruity." Perhaps I have made clear the reason why I think the titles of the two books should have been interchanged. Properly, Mr. Burke is writing on "the new criticism" which is *really* new: conversely, Mr. Ransom is

[1] It would be ungracious, if not invidious, for any one to try his hand at Mr. Burke's methodology of the pun by using it other than I have done. It is perhaps unfortunate that, as an historical fact, the word "Burking" may be found in Webster's Dictionary to refer to a Criminal Act passed by the British Parliament in 1828 punishing by death any one who murders a human being with the intention of selling the corpse to medical colleges for dissection purposes. The first man condemned under this Act was named "Burke": hence the word "Burking." In the above illustration of Mr. Burke's methodology of the pun, I have consciously refrained from exploiting this fact.

really not writing about criticism at all, though he *does* employ parts of the work of Messrs. Richards, Empson, Eliot, and Winters to supply the propaedeutic for an epistemological scheme which seeks to establish a Philosophy of Literary Form. Mr. Ransom is primarily a speculative philosopher who is temperamentally committed to the analysis of poetry: he is only incidentally a critic; perhaps more, the satisfying expositor. Mr. Burke is primarily a critic of extraordinary inclusiveness, and only incidentally a philosopher. Mr. Ransom's method proceeds about its analytical business with a strong mission to expel "impurities" which impede the action of literary understanding and assimilation, and is absolutist to the point of discharging psychology, history, or moralism from the cameral view of the poem itself. Mr. Burke's method proceeds syncretistically, markedly contrasting with Mr. Ransom's, finding its power in discursiveness: its hospitality to everything which Mr. Ransom's dogma excludes points the way for the solution of the unresolved paradox which closes Mr. Ransom's book.

Mr. Burke's materials in *The Philosophy of Literary Form* equip the poet for the free activity in a poem which Mr. Ransom's eulogy of the "indeterminants" compels: they supply the "texture" which makes the kind of poem Mr. Ransom likes to analyze. The issue raised by these two books, then, becomes something like an antithesis between criticism-as-dogma and criticism-as-discursiveness; or, to use Mr. Burke's methodology of the pun again, an antithesis between *veracity* and *voracity.* If we think of Mr. Burke's voracity as "maw," we may reverse the letters of that word, creating a new one to describe Mr. Ransom's veracity as "wam."

"Maw" is a wide-open mouth: "wam" is a closing one. Yet both are necessary. For the poet we recommend "maw": for the analyst of his poem we recommend "wam."

◇◇

William S. Knickerbocker was born in New York City in 1892. He taught English for many years at the University of the South and edited *The Sewanee Review* there from 1926 to 1942. He is the editor of *Twentieth Century English* and Matthew Arnold's *Culture and Anarchy*.

The Sewanee Review, beginning with the notable two-part essay by Austin Warren in the early thirties, has always treated Burke at length and with great fairness. Some of the best pieces ever done on Burke have appeared there, and it is one of the few journals from which one can get any accurate and continuous sense of how Burke has been received by his fellow men of letters.

I have included here — regrettably — only two of the three parts of this long and important review-essay. The omitted section on John Crowe Ransom's *The New Criticism* should certainly be read if one is to have any real sense of what some of the true critical and theoretical polarities of our time are. Mr. Knickerbocker's two main images — his whole title, really — identify these polarities and, as I indicated in the note on Allen Tate, are recurrent in the reception of Kenneth Burke.

Mr. Knickerbocker's review does for Burke and literary criticism what Mr. Parkes did for him and the history of ideas. Burke has lived in these two countries of the mind all his published life and it is useful to have these two essays — so different and of such differing kinds of excellence — back to back. By the time of *Attitudes toward History* everybody knew Burke was a major intellect to be reckoned with, and by *The Philosophy of Literary Form* everybody recognized Burke as a major force in practical and theoretical criticism.

Finally, few people have ever tried to write about Burke in his own style and use it as a form of analysis and praise. There is a good deal of foolishness and nonsense in Burke and there is also, in these works of the thirties and early forties, a great deal of semicomic mind-play — intellectual capering and larking, casuistic stretching, juggling of terms and texts, and sheer intellectual improvisation as the expression of a great talent. All this is part of the pleasure of Burke; it seems a pity that so often it offends overly serious or excessively earnest minds. One of the virtues — among many — of Mr. Knickerbocker's serious and delightful review is that he recognizes, discounts, and accepts all at once. His statement of Burke's serious purpose — the last paragraph of Section III — can still stand after all these years. It is reassuring to know that books are read as thoughtfully as Mr. Knickerbocker read this one and, as Emerson said they should be, in the spirit in which they were written.

7 Kenneth Burke's Philosophy of Symbolic Action

BY Harry Slochower

BURKE's latest book, *The Philosophy of Literary Form,* ought to be of particular service to those who find difficulty with his systematic works. The present work is a collection of essays and reviews, written on special

EDITOR'S NOTE: Reprinted from *The University Review,* VIII (Winter 1941), 119–123, copyright 1941 by *The University Review,* by permission of the author and publisher.

occasions, and although it is not an eclectic omnibus of marginal writings, its topical character allows for easier entry into his thought than the more closely knit volumes. This book does not demand the same unrelaxing concentration. Not that Burke writes popularly even here. His style is not "inviting." It makes no compromises, and rarely goes off guard. The argument often omits the intermediate steps which are expected to be made by the reader himself. It is as though Burke were afraid of being "moved in on" too fast. This reminds one somewhat of the character in Burke's *Towards a Better Life* who writes letters, but does not mail them. Once, however, one begins to catch the spirit of the argument, and continues to "watch his steps" (one's own and Burke's), the reward is extraordinarily enriching.

The new book has not only the advantage of discussing topics with which the reader is likely to be acquainted. It is also valuable in being a kind of summary of Burke's catholic scope. Moreover, it introduces his most recent preoccupation which might be termed an attempt to formulate a vocabulary for the scientific charting of laws in the realm of normative judgments, that is, in fields where *attitudes* are manifest, and specifically, in literary and artistic criticism. His position may be characterized as a notable development of Nietzsche's and Veblen's concatenation of social and psychological motivations, or, in terms of more contemporary interests, as a fusion of Marx and Freud.

Seen as a whole, Burke's standpoint is an answer to two extremist camps of our time: the pure substance thinkers (formalists, symbolists, logical positivists), and the pure process thinkers (pragmatists, relativists, actionists). His stand is all the more impressive in that, himself having gone *through* the pit of modern alienations, Burke can properly weight the factors which alternative positions stress. Indeed, his whole attitude and procedure is to interpret "error" as containing "true" reactions. It is this temper and approach which account for the complexity of Burke's stand, as well as for the fact that he is becoming recognized as one of the most seminal minds in American criticism. His "organic" way also contributes to the fact that ingredients of his own early dislocations are carried over into his present formulations.

Burke began in the antithetical mode of esthetic opposition expressed in the volume of short stories *White Oxen* and the novel *Towards a Better Life*. These books are permeated by a deep antinomianism, remindful of Nietzsche's transvaluation of all values and of Gide's absolute doubt. However, Burke would save something from the antithesis. By delving into the perilous and the sinful, we at least become acquainted with the field of the uncharted. But Neal, the hero of Burke's novel, does not resolve his ambivalence and comes to a Nietzschean end.

This antinomianism also pervades Burke's first book of criticism, *Counter-Statement*. In all of these works, Burke leans towards the esthetic solution, the conflict being resolved symbolically, rather than actively or materially. However, *Counter-Statement* already foreshadows the communicative element (which was to be stressed later) in the two essays on "Psychology and Form" and "Lexicon Rhetoricae."

Release from his initial mid-world view is evidenced in *Permanence and Change* — in many respects Burke's strongest book to date. It is effected by the binding link of the social metexis which Burke here calls "the poetic metaphor." It combines a sense of the historic with that of the need for enclosing change within the framework of the eternal. A perspective of Time is arrived at through the incongruities of time. The book attempts to suggest the basis for a philosophy of being, in stressing the fact that human beings are activated by the same underlying motives, and that these motives refer to a common situation. That is, Burke would combine metaphysics and psychology, showing that psychology is a part of the science of Being. And, as he is here primarily concerned with "communication" as a means of *affecting* audiences (in contrast to his earlier "self-expressionist" esthetic), Burke centers his attention on the role of "the word," on the "poetic metaphor." Its ultimate goal "would be a society in which the participant aspect of action attained its maximum expression." Conversely, the fullest expression of this master metaphor in turn requires a society which would allow maximum participation and communication.

Permanence and Change, however, not only corrects but also takes over some of the ambiguities which crossed *Counter-Statement*. The central ambiguity in Burke's work might be stated as a fluid shifting between *what is* and *what ought to be*. At times (and most clearly in *Permanence and Change*) Burke is disturbed by the disparity between what is and what might be, and calls for a bridging of the gap. At other times, he treats both as inevitable and natural expressions of human nature and of human relations. He would have us note the similarity in human desires, motivations, purposes, and gratification, holding that essentially they "will not change." Fundamentally, he writes, "the aims and genius of man have remained the same." The reason lies in the constant of man's neurological structure, "despite the shifts in his environment." That is, Burke bases his philosophy of Being on biology. "It aims less at a *metaphysic* than at a *metabiology*." That this metabiological formula does not achieve the communication needed in our time of alienation is "confessed" indirectly in the eloquent closing of *Permanence and Change*.

This biological constant reappears in the argument of Burke's next book *Attitudes towards History*. Here, the poetic metaphor which in the earlier work allowed one to "open conflict" with those who would uphold the institutions serving an anti-social function is softened into "the comic." The comic frame deals, as did the poetic metaphor, with man in society uniting man in nature with man in heaven. But here, it is more "understanding," and charitable. Here, the "errors" of men are more respected as human "truths." There is a greater sense of our limitations, and of how we naturally tend to "cash in on" our moral assets. It assumes a kind of secular notion of man's original sin, holding that unless one begins with and accepts man's frailties ("guilt"), we arrive at a disintegrative and anti-social philosophy. Burke's comic metaphor is neither wholly debunking nor wholly euphemistic, and provides the attitude "that is required for purposes of persuasion and coöperation." Its human and social value lies "in helping to produce a state of affairs whereby these rigors (of ultimate alienations) may abate." Here again, there is the shift between what is and what ought to be. The emphasis is on acceptance. Yet, towards the end, Burke briefly reverts to his earlier conviction and reminds us that a comic vocabulary of motives "cannot be attained insofar as people are at war, or living under the threat of war."

Attitudes toward History revealed Burke's growing interest in the analysis of literary products (rather than social moments) as rhetorical devices for the affecting of audiences. In the section on the poetic categories, Burke discusses the various ways (the epic, the tragic, etc.) in which audiences are affected. In the long essay "The Philosophy of Literary Form" (which gives the title to the book just published, and is its most important "news" element), Burke shows *how* the effect is produced. His key term is "symbolic action." It unites the poetic with the practical act, thereby pointing to Burke's dual strategy. In noting that art is *symbolic* action, Burke reveals the error made in drawing a one-to-one relationship between art and sociology. The second term, on the other hand, would emphasize that the symbolic ritual is also an *act*. Thus, Burke's term "symbolic action" is pointed against two extreme positions: the so-called "escapist" school which, in times of adverse social pressures, would go back to the study of "art-as-such," of its "grammar," or at most of the psychological processes in literary appreciation, and the environmental school which tends to regard symbols simply as reflections of a basic objectivity.

The rest of the essays and reviews in this book may be viewed as translations of this key term into various fields of study—poetry, theology, metaphysics, diplomacy, historiography—by which reality is stylized in the tactics of symbolic action. The reality is "the situation," the poetic and other stylizations in which the situation is presented is "the strategy." Here, Burke is less concerned with the situation than with the strategy; that is, with the fluctuation in values which, having arisen from the social base, form a new, semi-autonomous "situation" with which the artist and the critic work. Formal works of art, however, are of relevance to "life" in that in their symbolic act, they present a Platonic graph for charting the "informal art of living."

The key-term in these essays (particularly those on "Freud and the Analysis of Poetry," and "Twelve Propositions on the Relation between Economics and Psychology") is "dramatic," which Burke uses to designate the attitudinal features in the more commonly known term "dialectic." It is the category which represents in synecdochic proportions "what goes with what." And Burke employs it as a lever for seeking out *dramatic difference and unity* rather than *dialectic opposition.* It is this temper which distinguishes Burke from those who have *exploited* rather than used the dialectic. With Burke, the dialectic is not the logic of opposition with the function of pulling things apart. (An instance of such misuse of dialectic as a logic of *exclusion* is S. Hook's collection of essays *Reason, Social Myths, and Democracy*). For Burke, the dialectic is a logic of passion which aims to disclose the coöperative elements within clashing attitudes. Hence, he can use it to show the persuasive ingredients in Hitler's *Mein Kampf* which *explain* the Hitler following. Likewise, it places him in a position to demonstrate the unifying constants in the fields of psychology and economics. Finally, he can show that identification with a group (implied in the notion of dramatic interplay) is the only *active* mode of identification.

To be sure, the reservation I mentioned earlier holds for this book as well. Burke's work still lacks a comprehensive frame for encompassing the categories of what is and what ought to be. To put it differently, his dialectic needs a substantive framework, without which it must continue to swerve between regarding the real *as* rational and as *to be made* rational. This oscillation makes it difficult to place Burke's work. At times, it seems to be *a secularization* of scholastics; at other times (and more pronouncedly in his most recent persuasions), he tends towards viewing modern secular frames as aspects of religious patterns, of prayer, rebirth, and transubstantiation. His current projects in which he would equate "motivation" with "structure" is in line with such permanent substantiveness. It should be added that Burke himself is aware of these problems which may be due to the incongruous modes of our time. One of the most impressive aspects of his writing is the confessional tenor of his self-criticism, his open readiness to allow full weight to opposing and differing perspectives. This is an expression of his striving towards unification, a unification to be won *through* diversification. From this angle, Burke's thought belongs with the neo-Spinozistic and neo-Catholic movements of our time. As he once put it in his novel, the attempt aims at summing up the significant features "in our secular, yet somehow biblical lives."

To gauge the general import of Burke's approach, it might be well to contrast it with two alternative trends in our time. Sceptical relativists, such as Stuart Chase and Thurman Arnold, argue that because meaning changes with context, there is no Reality or fundamental objective situation to which the contexts refer. This type of thinking confuses the misuse of symbols for purposes of obfuscating the situation to which they refer with the non-existence of the basic situation itself. To be sure, they cannot even state their very position without themselves postulating some common standards, and Chase finally admits that "abstractions we must use." (Chase's invocation of Einstein to "prove" his criticism of eternal certainties may be an unconscious confession of his own belief in absolutes.) Closely allied with this school of debunking is the movement of experimentalism which has been watering down Dewey's philosophy of criticism. In the case of one of Dewey's followers (S. Hook), certainty is dissolved into a moving platform, and Dewey's tolerant inquiry is turned into criticism *per se*. The result is a "scientific" method which merely attacks and rejects any and all attempts at integration. On the other side is the movement represented by the logical positivists and the semanticists, which would achieve substantive unity by the easy way. The logical positivists would exclude from the realm of meaning anything which has not a *fixed* meaning. Thus, they cannot do justice to fields such as art, ethics, and human relations, where things are not *either* true *or* false. Philosophy, to Carnap, is "the logical syntax of the language of science." But art, literature, and the art of living consist precisely of those border-line problems which cannot be exhausted by the study of language syntax. (In Dewey, there is, at least, the element of continuity and dialectic flexibility which does justice to the *process* of living and acting.) Their universal communication turns out to be a thin, simplified reduction, a *lowest* common denominator. It is its avoidance of an easy relativism of action and the easy universalism of linguistic symbolism that distinguishes Burke's thought among contemporary doctrines.

The present scene is marked by a chaos of standards which is mirrored in our social and esthetic wars. The problem would seem to consist in the attempt to discover in what respects the parts are parts of the whole ("represent" it.) Differences, as Whitehead has suggested, provide an opportunity as well. The opportunity offered by the complex welter of materials is *re*integration on a higher and richer plane. Nietzsche had fought for a perspective through the welding of incongruous elements at a time when there was greater illusion of stability. Today, we have the *advantage* derived from the circumstance that a total crumbling makes possible a rediscovery of the permanent base at the very bottom, a rediscovery which becomes a common, universal necessity. "The age of fundamentals is returning," says one of Malraux's characters. The fundamentals must be reached through the battlefields of alienation.

◇◇

HARRY SLOCHOWER was born in Austria in 1900. He has been a teacher and editor and is the author of many books in which he combines his interests in literature, politics, and psychology. He is a neighbor and friend of Burke's and was clearly influenced by his work of the thirties.

So far as I know, this is one of the few essays on Burke by someone trained (formally or otherwise) in psychology. Erving Goffman was later to make extensive use of Burke in his book *The Presentation of Self in Everyday Life* but he never wrote directly about him. It seems unfortunate, given Burke's really profound debt to Freud, Jung, and psychology in general that we have never had the benefit of work on Burke by experts in this field.

The opening paragraphs of Mr. Slochower's essay are very useful as quick placements or intellectual locations of what Burke was doing; the subsequent paragraphs (four and following) present a useful synopsis of Burke's early development and the dialectic of that development; and the last three paragraphs provide one with a statement of the problems Burke had to solve in *A Grammar* and *A Rhetoric of Motives*. The whole essay is an interesting discussion of Burke's relation to others working toward a solution of the same problems he confronted.

◇◇

7 A Review of "The Philosophy of Literary Form"

BY Helmut Kuhn

IN THE first third of this volume the distinguished critic presents a methodological essay which gives the book its name. For the rest it is

EDITOR'S NOTE: Reprinted from *Philosophy and Phenomenological Research*, II (1941–42), 223–226, by permission of the author and publisher.

a re-publication of articles and reviews which previously appeared in various periodicals. The divers materials, though unequal in value, purpose, and language, have combined into some kind of unity best to be described by the words "While Everything Flows" – the title first contemplated by the author but then rejected. This Heraclitean label was to reflect the character of work done in a changeable decade, the Thirties. As a matter of fact, we seem to witness an energetic swimmer, his eyes riveted to the goal, indefatigably performing uniform movements, while the torrential waters carry him – in their direction.

The author's approach to the methodology of literary criticism is that of an exponent of the "semantic school." Semantics as conceived by Kenneth Burke is derived from three main sources: Marxist-Nietzschean-Freudian psychology is fused with Pragmatism, Neo-positivism furnishing the crucible for this intellectual alchemy. The thinkers of the first group, by dint of their "depth-psychology," undermined the confidence in the current language. Words, they suggested, do not actually mean what they pretend to mean. Seemingly pointing to objects, the linguistic-symbols actually subserve purposes. They are tools or weapons in the service of class interests (Marx), or of a cunningly disguised will to power (Nietzsche) or an all powerful subconscious drive, the libido (Freud). We have to unmask the words and uncover the secret agencies behind the verbal camouflage in order to detect the truth. But how did language fall into the status of servitude? How did the masquerade come about? Pragmatism supplies a convenient answer by asserting that language, just as all other manifestations of the human mind, is essentially an operation through which the human animal keeps alive and adjusts itself to its environment. But once the operational or instrumental character of language is acknowledged as normal, the criticism of language in the Marx-Nietzsche-Freudian manner loses its original meaning. If it is the business of language to do something rather than to tell the truth, no specific language can be accused of lying. Those who still amuse themselves with unmasking ideological terms should be put to the test of their own critical procedure and asked what unavowed destructive desire they subtly gratify. Instrumentalism, pushed to its radical consequences, obliterates any system of reference which might serve as a basis for linguistic criticism. When things are brought to this pass, Neo-positivism offers its saving device. With the scheme of an artificial language, undefiled by traditional bias and purposeful conventions, it invites us to what it considers the safe ground of science. Thus semantics arises. A system of signs is projected, each sign corresponding to an observable "event" and providing the counters for an exact calculus. Our author goes a long way with the semantic language-makers, using their synthetic vocabulary and even enriching it by inventions of his own. His book bristles with terms such as synecdochic, analgesic, monotonic, integrative, attitudinize, familistic consubstantiality, etc. In the author's own words: "The semantic style is bad style except in those who violate its tenets." (159) But so profoundly disquieted is he by the confusion of ordinary speech that he barters his birthright, the intellectual heritage embodied in a living language, for the semblance of scientific exactness. Let us see what he receives in return.

The pragmatic approach chosen by the author assumes "that the poem is designed to 'do something' for the poet and his readers, and that we can make the most relevant observations about its design by considering the poem as an embodiment of this act" (89). The stimulus that prompts the literary or, generally speaking, the artistic action springs from a problem posed by a concrete situation. Its success, therefore, is to be measured by its capacity of solving the problem, or, as the author is fond of saying, of "encompassing the situation." Now the characteristic mode of the artistic act must be distinguished from other classes of acts. The poem is to be described as a "symbolic" action, and this term receives its precise meaning from a scheme of the human situation which comprises and explains all kinds of acts. This scheme presents itself to Mr. Burke as a drama with the human agent as hero. A series of human activities may be set out, with science at one end, mapping out the field for a possible action and strictly refraining, in the execution of its semantic chart, from any kind of tendency or attitude. At the opposite end of the scale we have the action itself, going through the conflict of the drama and hence partial at any moment of its development, working itself out in the dialectical pattern of life. Between these extremes we find the "symbolic act" as the "dancing of an attitude" (9). Instead of remaining outside the zone of conflict like the semantic account it attempts to attain a perspective "atop all the conflicts of attitude" (148). On the other hand, though it is not action, it "contains an implicit program of action" (143). Borrowing from J. C. Ransom, the author splits up the poet's symbolic strategy into two polar types of imagery. The image may unburden an oppressed mind and thus, through confession, achieve catharsis; or again, with the emphasis on internalization rather than externalization, the image gained through mimesis may become a cryptogram of an attitude and impose itself on the hearer's mind through "incantation" (116–119).

There is nothing in this methodological scheme which markedly departs from the best tradition of literary criticism and æsthetic analysis. The somewhat startling terminology merely serves to throw into prominence one special aspect of æsthetic analysis. We generally do not speak of "poetic strategy," "strategic answers" and the like as B. does. But it is true that the traditional terms by which we describe human actions and conditions invariably involve a "directional" element, i.e., they view life as moving toward a goal, mastering problems, achieving a higher or lesser degree of perfection. B., radicalizing the innate pragmatism of the normal language, is more conservative in this respect than it may seem. Moreover, even the radicalization lies merely on the surface and, compared with the semantic substitute, the traditional language is rather more than less pragmatic. It not only tends to show life as directional but to commit itself to a definite goal which it regards as ultimate and the sovereign good. There is no such commitment involved in B.'s semantic scheme, but we may ask whether this absence is not a deficiency rather than an asset. It is good to know that human existence is essentially a drama. But to make the assertion significant we should also be told what the drama is about. Mr. Burke, however, withholds this information. Is the human antagonism to be conceived in terms of the Marxist idea of class struggle? Or in terms of the ritual drama with the symbolism of sacrifice and scapegoat? Or is it psycho-analysis which furnishes the clue to both social and religious antagonisms? Or should we apply to Hegel for a metaphysics of conflict and tragedy? Mr. Burke, in his many-facetted analyses of works of literature, seems to have recourse to one or all of these interpretations as fits the occasion. But is this hospitable indetermination a possible basis for literary criticism? B. senses the danger of a complete relativism and tries to ward it off. Although, in his opinion, the assertion "this is wrong" is merely a stylized variant of the command "Don't do it," he still wishes to distinguish between good and bad commands, between a strategy that "is quite accurate for encompassing the situation" and one that falls short of this requirement (7f.). But it is difficult to see how, in default of a concrete idea of man and human situation, a criterion of failure and success should be obtained. The lack of a metaphysical system of reference in B.'s methodology accounts for the peculiar character of his criticism. Evaluation is largely supplanted with a subtle psychological analysis, and the distinction between poetry and literature is blurred. T. W. Arnold's *The Folklore of Capitalism* and Aeschylus' *Oresteia,* Clifford Odet's *Golden Boy* and the *Ancient Mariner* are all subjected to the same symbolistic-psychological treatment. The discernment for symbolic associations is sharpened in the same measure in which the sense for ranks and hierarchical order is blunted. We are tempted to test this pragmatic criticism pragmatically and to ask what it ultimately is good for.

In one of the finest articles of the collection, entitled "The Rhetoric of Hitler's 'Battle,'" the author convincingly points out how closely Hitler follows a religious pattern of thought. "Did not," he judiciously asks, "much of his lure derive . . . from the *bad* filling of a *good* need?" (218) Very true! But apart from the author's personal good sense, decency, and taste there is nothing in his book in the way of reasoned convictions which entitles him to draw the division-line between good and bad. He has a healthy distaste for the indiscriminate "debunking" dear to many of our contemporaries. But the dams which he himself hopes to erect against the rising flood of active nihilism, his recommendation of a conscientiously cultivated style and similar well-meaning advices, seem a brittle patch-work. Where we desire to find a firmly envisaged goal and the vision of a possible future, we are put off with fantasies about our allegedly "neo-evangelical" era (107). To return to our former metaphor: if the energetic swimmer, with all his sophisticated strokes, does not move any closer to the shore, this is due not to the overpowering might of the current but to a pact which the athlete seems to have made with the current. The present volume testifies to the Thirties as a period not only of a changeable mind, but of one divided in itself.

◇◇

HELMUT KUHN was born in Germany in 1899. He has taught philosophy at the University of North Carolina, at Emory University, and, since 1949, at the Friedrich-Alexander-Universität, Erlangen-Nürnberg, Germany. He is the author of many books in German on aesthetics, Socrates, and Hegel; and of two books in English: *Freedom Forgotten and Remembered* and *Encounter with Nothingness.*

The two focal points of this review are most succinctly stated in paragraphs two and four. The first has to do with what Mr. Kuhn calls Burke's instrumental-operational (phenomenological?) theory of language and methodology; and the second has to do with the absence (as yet) of a coherent vision which would give the powerful methodology some kind of substantival and evaluative center. Professor Kuhn's image of Burke (as the man of energetic action who makes no progress) is only half accurate: the language theory and the methodology were perfected first (in *A Grammar of Motives*) and then, one hesitates to say just how, joined to a vision in *A Rhetoric of Motives.*

But, in all fairness to Mr. Kuhn, one should point out that most of the serious commentators on Burke's work of this period make the same points that he does in slightly different ways and with differing degrees of negative emphasis depending upon their adherence to a fixed reality principle. The larger case against Burke has always been developed along the lines of Mr. Kuhn's review.

◇◇

ζ *An Address to Kenneth Burke*

BY John Crowe Ransom

I HAVE read several times the long title-essay of Kenneth Burke's latest book, *The Philosophy of Literary Form,* and still with the sense of an adventure. It is like following the intrepid explorer who is making a path through the jungle. I indicate the range and density of the speculative field, which is poetic theory, and jungle-like; and also the emancipation of Burke's mind, the explorer's, from common academic restraints – especially from the over-all cast of sobriety which he, in a cold tone, calls "neo-Aristotelian." If he suffers from a restraint, I should think it is a constitutional distaste against regarding poetic problems as philosophic ones. I suppose his feeling would be that poetry is something bright and dangerous, and philosophy is something laborious and arid, and you cannot talk about the one in the terms of the other without a disproportion, and breach of taste. Who would not understand that? Aesthetics has been the fumbling chapter of philosophy. But I believe the philosophers themselves undergo the worst fits of depression, and have to wait for courage to return before they can resume their remote speculations with the right passion.

A kind of discourse which is past the matter-of-fact competence of science to explain, falls to philosophy. I had come to think that poetry must accept this attribution, and philosophy must sharpen its tools.

Nevertheless, there are some streamlined modern "sciences" which might be persuaded to explain poetry without benefit of philosophy. Burke's procedure is to work them for all they are worth, both severally and jointly, and then to supplement them with an ingenious all-out critique of his own. He has a whole arsenal of strategies, like the German general staff, who are said to have whistling-bombs if they like, and whose campaigns rest upon a highly technical and sustained opportunism.

EDITOR'S NOTE: Reprinted from *The Kenyon Review,* IV (Spring 1942), 219–237, copyright 1942 by Kenyon College, by permission of the author and publisher.

He begins by considering the poet as a "medicine man," and the poem as the medicine by which he tries to heal or "encompass" his own difficult practical "situation." We recognize the language of anthropology. The poet is a "primitive," who tries to manage his affairs by religious rite and magic. Burke is wonderfully keen at sniffing out ritualistic vestiges in even a modern poetry — taboo, fetish, name-calling, and so on. I wish he would consider more, though he does consider, the possibility that anthropologists may have put their own bright colors on the forms of primitive religion, and that primitive men are really as various, and therefore as intelligent, as we are. Paul Radin, who spent six years with the Winnebagoes but perhaps is not an orthodox anthropologist, told me that the medicine men were not magicians but philosophers, much as we assume our own best priests to be. But if they really are magicians, how does our own nicer sort of religion originate? The anthropologists do not illuminate this topic, which is discontinuous from theirs. It is striking that Burke does not permit us to confuse *him* with medicine-man mentality: is he then patronizing his poets? He is generous, and after many motions as good as concedes that primitive magic need not have much to do with poetics.

He defines the poem next as being in part a "dream," that is, a work of the unconscious; and there we have the Freudian science. The poem is not what it seems, it is not even what the author thinks it is. Freud announced the following understanding, and so far as I know never recanted from it. A poem is a discreet tract of imagery made laboriously, but without any knowing why, by editing libidinous phantasies that were in substitution for an act forbidden by the censor; the poem as it stands being such an ecstatic innocent — so excited about grey skies and little birds for example — that it is nonsense, it is unmotivated, unless it trails a lurid private history behind it. But what if the innocence is real? And how can you show it is not? There are many images not derived from libidinous phantasies; they happen every few minutes, and why not in poetry? To protract and record an innocent image seems indeed a remarkable action, it seems to be the aesthetic occasion, provoking some sort of philosophy to remark upon it; but if you have no philosophy with which to remark upon it you are being rather arbitrary in remarking that it must be an evidence of secret guilt. Freudians have a most literal and painful version of original sin, and bank fearlessly upon it. But Burke is one of the most intelligent of writers, and has graduated with honors out of so many schools of thought that their testimonies do not tip him over but counterbalance each other. He is not too disposed to lump the guilty poetry and the innocent together, and therefore to think the Freudian strategy will work every time.

Then there is always "social science." With Burke it might be expected that this would have a "Marxist" or "class" complexion, and he is a master of Marxist "dialectic" — an analytic instrument which is acute, and has made incriminating literary discoveries as I know to my discomfiture. But he does not force it, and I wish other Marxists would learn from his moderation. Social science is much wider than Marxism. For Burke the social dimension in the poem embraces such things as "prayer" and its opposite, imprecation, on the understanding, I suppose, that what is not magical in religion is social and addressed to the poet's own community; it has a "confessional" element and an "incantatory" element, terms which are Burke's translations of Aristotle's catharsis and mimesis respectively, and denote the smart way in which the poet manages to shift his own burdens onto the shoulders of society. The social aspect of the poem seems to me inflated under Burke's treatment. But this science too comes to the end of its string.

Burke is within his rights, and puts academic critics in his debt, when he turns these lively sciences upon poetry to see what they will discover. They have their powers of divination, and can find in poetry their own slightly shady materials if they are there. What they find is principally what, according to my feeling, had better not have been there. But Burke's own special approach is quite different, and worth them all put together.

He conceives of poetry as drama, whether completely realized or not. He conceives of drama as the way the poet submits some personal and limited version of the truth about a situation to its ordeal by "unending conversation," to its test of survival against competitor versions. Now some poems, like *Othello*, are actual full-blown dramas; in them you can find the rights of the situation contested by the different characters in turn. You have "dialectic": it is the "social way" of obtaining the truth, or rather, since society can hardly be said to initiate anything, even a search for truth, it is the social way of correcting and refining the truth that a given character has propounded. And the competition is not merely theoretical among the cross-purposes; force, accident, the logic of events, put views to the empirical test, and if the characters do not survive to take this crucial evidence into account the spectators do, and are the wiser. And the best truth furnished by this elaborate testing may not be positive truth at all, but a critical or negative truth; for the practical disposition of the argument may be catastrophe. We may reach a terminus sufficiently "encompassing" or happy for all, or one that is only ironical and indecisive, or one that is tragic and fatal. All this is within the range of the meaning of drama.

I suppose one tends to resist good instruction, and at first I thought that Plato's dialogues, and not dramas in the technical sense, would serve as the perfect type of dialectic for Burke. But I had to observe that they lacked the evidence of the action, and the arbitrament of the event. Then I thought that prose drama would do it, and perhaps do it better than poetic drama, because it would not require that kind of incessant diversion from the argument which is basic in the poetic medium itself, and which I have been privately calling the poetic "texture." I still venture to think so. If the several characters are in earnest about encompassing the situation, each in the simple way that suits his own perspective, and the ways are to prove conflicting, and we are to arrive at the social solution which is the way of ways and the "perspective of perspectives," all that is serious business, and prose is the language for business. But further. Extended units of literature fit Burke's dialectical purpose but not small units: what will he make of the lyric? He considers that a Shakespeare will manage to have every sort of poetry in the plays, somewhere among the speeches. If the lyrical passages have a content not specifically taken up into the argument, and not replied to, I think he would say they could have been replied to, but in fact remain dialectically undeveloped. The independent lyrics that lie outside of formal drama are dramatic to the extent of having a "character" speaker and an imagined "setting" and "business." Lyric becomes then a bit of imperfectly realized drama, and his omnibus conception of poetry as drama has room for it. As it is the less realized, however, it must be inferior. Its truth, he says, is local and relative, and never receives the social correction which would make it "absolute." But I think its localism is exactly what makes it admired, and thought to be poetry in the strictest sense. And he has inverted the usage of relative and absolute. There is an absoluteness in lyric which is primordial, and that is what a poetic theory should make us see.

It is hard to escape the conclusion that Burke does not have a philosophy of poetry, or does not have the right one, or does not have the right one by him always. He and I have exchanged communications recently at a brisk rate about points of doctrine. But I should like to address to him a bigger argument now. I hardly care to say that I propose to "get back to the fundamentals," a locution that sounds smug and religiose, and may be irritating and dangerous; if I lose my fundamentals I lose my case. I prefer his language: for the sake of "perspective" and "drama" I will go back a long way to bring up the argument.

2

Ancient man like modern man had his biological needs; he met them by studying and exploiting his "environment" (the natural and the social) intelligently; and the routines through which he operated were his practical "sciences." As they improved, he prospered. But suddenly and dramatically — for it blazes up with that effect in Greek history — comes a great addition to this common sort of business. After science, or in between sciences, at that comfortable moment when practical life was going very well, came philosophy, the "love of wisdom." I wish the force of the Greek word were still apparent when we speak of philosophy — as when the Phi Beta Kappas convene to talk about the "liberal education" which, like themselves, is so useless, handsome, and philosophical. The "wisdom" in the Greek is not the same word as "science," yet it comes automatically provided with its own motivation. "Philosophy" is indeed a motor term: it is the drive, the passion, for a kind of knowledge which is not practical, and biologically is superfluous. In Greek writings it means that quite fully, and hundreds of times. It would indicate a great indulgence claimed by man by way of diversion from animal constitution, and even the possibility of overdoing it and interfering with animal functioning. But Greeks took their stand on this human right. They were too radical not to be opposed; and for example by those who facetiously styled themselves Sophists, not the lovers of wisdom but the Wise Boys themselves, and contended that there were no motives other than selfish ones, and no wisdom other than practical knowledge. Kenneth Burke, stubbornly researching for the formula by which the poet in his poem would be found "encompassing his own situation," is sophistical; though he could retort that I am playing a "rhetorical" trick in attributing to him a "charged" and pejorative adjective by way of impelling him to make his peace with philosophy, Phi Beta Kappa, and liberal education. But his heresy can be put as simply as that.

Now I would maintain that Greek philosophy represents only, so far as its reputable exponents are concerned, a First Moment of this wisdom, in which the philosophers advance to an impossible extreme in one direction and have to retreat; and that there is a Second Moment, in which philosophy looks boldly in the other direction although — so like the Greeks we are, or so Occidental and like us were the Greeks — its procedure has scarcely yet got a thorough and hearty expression. It is within Philosophy II, not Philosophy I, that we find all that is distinctive in poetry as compared with science, and in "liberal education" as other than the cult of science.

As to the forms of this disinterested wisdom that the Greeks pursued. They found themselves projecting science for its own sake, science as theory rather than practice; projecting it further than need required; then stopping to admire its range, which took it far beyond the senses, and the apodeictic necessity of its conclusions. They defined such extension of science as wisdom, and for such wisdom thanked the faculty of reason. They became fastidious. Practical science, even "natural science" in its whole or extended range, had a certain meanness in that it operated with materials of great concreteness or impurity, so that its conclusions were tainted with corresponding contingency. They proceeded to scorn natural science and seek for a pure science, dealing with proper materials, which would be completely determinate, and whose conclusions would follow by necessity. I am thinking of such figures as Pythagoras, the Eleatics, and Plato, though I am oversimplifying the story. And the forms of knowledge which seemed to answer best to this description were mathematics; logic, an incipient wisdom closely related to mathematics; and ethics. Now for a remark or two.

Logic is a near-relation of mathematics; but ethics, in its philosophical form, is not unrelated. We recall how preeminent among the virtues in glory, for the Greeks, was Justice; it is the most mathematical one. Now ethics seems to deal at best with highly impure and contingent materials. But the ethics of the philosophers differed from the ethics of natural man, first, by forgetting to be selfish – a great shift in motive – and, second, on the theoretical side, by defining Justice, and the other virtues for that matter, in terms of their function in a human society. Ethics becomes what the natural man, like the animals, need not, in matter of fact, possess: a philosophy of society. The mathematical style of this wisdom took hold, for example, when you conceived your own good as being but one unit of human good, and mathematically no better than the unit that might fall to any other man. Many thinkers of sophistical habit have undertaken to demonstrate that the good of the greatest number is your own good in the long run, but the Greek philosophers did not wait upon the demonstration, and in my own experience it is never, upon the critical occasion, coercive. You are just, but it is simply because that is your "philosophy"; you will not find a better reason. And such philosophy is held by "social scientists" as a rule. But, as with other admirable forms of wisdom that come under the First Moment, there is danger in it. Kant, and the Golden Rule, simply envisage any common good, like food or money, and expect us not to care whether it comes to us or to our fellow man. That amounts to justice, the community of goods, and the rule of mathematical indifference. But that may be too elementary for an ambitious philosopher of the First Moment, such as Plato, or Hegel; whereupon he applies himself to building up some specially tidy or "ideal" society, and suits the citizen to the society; then, instead of giving them the common goods as we know them, suits the goods to the citizens.

As for the mathematics, and the logic. These were the wisdoms that seemed to operate upon any materials, and to constitute a knowledge of pure or absolute Being; as if no insubordinacy in the materials could affect them. They deserve this distinction if any wisdoms do. But we may look briefly at some difficulties discovered there by the Greeks. If mathematical and logical existents were Being itself, other existents for dainty philosophers were Non-Being, and they were many. Indeed, all natural objects must rate as Non-Being. For Once-Being was Always-Being, but every natural object was forever undergoing alteration. It had a dimension of time; and Zeno's Paradoxes, including the one about Achilles and the tortoise, do not exactly indicate their intention, but at least they seem to say that some school was contending that calculations involving time were beyond the reach of a cogent mathematics. The natural object was specious Being, or Appearance. At best it was Becoming, something approaching the formal state of Being. The mathematical or logical operation expects that its terms will stay constant long enough to be operated on; but they may or may not; natural objects are given to shifting the very values you assume as your constant. For a long time I was puzzled by the dogmatic refusal of Greek philosophers to admit any grade of existence between Being and Non-Being. But equally I was puzzled by the paramount importance of the tautological Law of Identity, A is A, among philosophers both Greek and modern. I now think the two points of doctrine come to the same thing, and express a scruple of logical method, and also a nervousness at the place where there is most excuse for it. Your A must not change while you are arguing about it; first define it, then watch it to see that the definition sticks; but what happens too easily is that the natural object you define as A, whose residuary property x goes far beyond the A quality of your definition, is going to let its x qualities irrupt to the surface and spoil the A quality; and this can happen even when A refers to the innocent numerical property. (To illustrate. The operation succeeds; but the patient dies. Or, An animal couple has the numerical value of 2; but animals have such energetic substance beneath any single property that presently your 2 has become 3.) The problem of any applied logic comes to this: to find an actual material whose substantival or residuary nature will not interfere with the given or surface quality you are discoursing about. And to keep saying, The least alteration turns our A to Non-A, or, A is A is A is A, is either by way of improving the illusion that you really have and hold your A, or else a mnemonic notice warning you to keep watch on your A lest it revert before you know it to Non-A, which is its other, material, and evil self.

The Eleatics powerfully insist on the Unity and Indivisibility of their so-called Pure Being. The terms meant little to me till I came to the conclusion that Unity and Indivisibility were bad ways of saying: Homogeneity. They refer to the quality of the material, not to the variety of the forms imposed upon it. In mathematics you have an abundance of distinct forms in the most determinate relation to one another, but it is imperative that you have a homogeneous material to support them. Monistic materialism is the objective of Greek or First-Moment philosophy. And, in fact, a scientific construct in any man's actual science is like a little monistic system in that it premises in the material beneath the generic property it is studying, and hopes to find there, a neutrality or inertness on the part of all the other properties which will amount to an effective homogeneity. The famous principle of the "uniformity of nature" is the Eleatic principle of Unity and Indivisibility, and just about as far from being a precise locution. More precise perhaps would be a principle of the "effective homogeneity" of the material. But if this is better language, that does not stop it from representing the scientist's pious hope rather than his objective datum. There is little ground for it in strict theory; which would suggest, on the contrary, that an actual material is substantival in the complete sense, or has an infinite series of properties, and no operation can be safe which does not allow for the whole activity of its material. We must believe therefore that any scientific process or prediction is only a piece of pragmatic knowledge. It is rude, since its calculation cannot be more than superficial, but it will have to do; we will use it as long as it works.

It works, up to some marginal point where it does not pay for itself, in all sorts of situations. Our Occidental mind has been fertile beyond the dreams of our Greek original in finding occasion for its useful or theoretical employment, with the consequence that there are hundreds of going sciences, and others coming on all the time. Their method, whether here or there, is no doubt as good as it can be, and probably through all its technical employments remains logico-mathematical, and is unified and determinate enough. (It might warrant a great international Encyclopedia of Unified Science.) But with respect to their material relations to each other the sciences are haphazard and incommensurable, and their separateness is absolute. Where a group of them deal with the same natural objects, as often happens, it is with different faces of the objects, or different qualitative surfaces, and it is the natural restriction upon a science that it works upon one of the surfaces only. We know that what is "material" to one science is not what is "material" to another though both materials be found in the same objects.

Plato dallied with Eleaticism, and retreated. It required living on principle in a world of such docile materiality as could not be found to exist; the stuff was not there, and if you tried to manage with it you were "not there." He came to terms with the natural world. But within that he could express his kind of preference, and hold to an ideal. He could participate in nature through his senses, while on all possible occasions exercising his reason. He embraced an eschatology, as follows. The rational principle within him was a soul, sent down from the heaven of Pure Being by God to inhabit the sensual body; but it must continue in militant rational activity in order to return to its home after deliverance from the body. I wonder if that seems an amazing doctrine. There is an irony if it sounds too strange for us; what then is to be said about certain dogmas of our own Christianity? In the beginning was the Logos. God is a spirit, and they that worship Him must worship Him in spirit and in truth. The heavenly mansion is a house not built with hands. Earthly treasures are perishable, but neither moth nor rust can corrupt treasures laid up in Heaven. In Heaven is neither marrying nor giving in marriage. The philosophical passion of the Eleatics and Plato, transferred from place to place and generation to generation by many hands, including the one that held the sword of Alexander, came all the way to Jesus and Paul; to mortify the body and the senses in honor of the immortal soul. But there are other and counter dogmas in Christianity. There are Humility and Non-resistance, and there is Love, at the farther pole from Greek ethics. In the hands of the single-minded practitioners, or zealots, these dogmas are likely to realize an anarchy rather than a society; we hear of "philosophical anarchists." Love would seem to defend every kind of natural existence, and to embrace the heterogeneous itself, which for Platonists is the root of evil; and nothing would be more repugnant to it than the attempt to make the beloved objects conform to some standard not their own. The fact is that Christianity is not mere Platonism but has a wealth of doctrine, and there is paradox in its catholicity. And just as the aggregate of all a wise man's many wisdoms though not systematic may be said to "be philosophy," it might be said of Christianity that it "is religion," without much qualification; so inclusive it is.

Aristotle retreated a little further, but always, I think, with a characteristic ambiguity. God remains technically transcendent, and out of nature, but no longer claims a material substance; he is logico-mathematics itself, pure form, and in the sense that this is the ideal toward which the rational processes of man or nature seem to aspire he is the Prime Mover. No eschatology survives to lead to him the souls of the blessed, as if passing from one realm of substance to another. The rational soul has a sort of survival in Aristotle's system, but it is confused with the notion of the soul as entelechy, the principle of organization of the animal body; a principle which tries to keep the heterogeneous substance and the rational form going at the same time. (It is Hegel who makes most of organic form. The animal entelechy is the most brilliant thing in nature, seducing us into the wildest hopes, if we are looking for the power of rational form to dominate natural material on a great and compound scale. But, "by volume" as the chemists say, not much material submits to this fate; and the original materiality still greatly impedes the intelligent animal purposes; and the very best animal dies, as if to intimate that the materials had not been thoroughly converted.) Aristotle's interest is in this world, which under his analysis reveals more powerful determinations and promises than might have been expected by the sceptic. He is kin to the modern naturalists. His bias is towards realistic classification, and the discovery and generation of rational purposes that will actually do work. I am used to regarding this as according to the naturalist program, and naturalism as a kind of critical (or even "realistic") idealism. Perhaps this shows best in Aristotle in the way he likes to look at matter: as a stuff that is meaningless, as good as non-existent, unless regarded as the "potential" of a new determinate existent under a form; and he pictures it as so amenable to the discipline of reason that it desires its own determination, and almost runs to obtain the form that is waiting for it. This view would pass easily into a doctrine of natural evolution and progress, and give us a world pulling itself up by its own bootstraps, which also might be congenial with the sanguine modern naturalists. But he finds this tendency balanced by an equal tendency on the part of the formed objects to disintegrate and revert again to mere matter. His Platonic speculations are bold enough, but he hedges, and saves himself by counter-speculations.

3

This sort of philosophy, ontology, or — religion, if it has anthropomorphic expression, or some animated metaphorical expression — is just as daring in its faith as experience and critical discretion allow. But it means works as well as faith, and suits the temperament that is fond of scientific and social programs. They seem to grow more daring as the faith retreats, the faith and the works coming closer together; the Kingdom of God on Earth, in Christian phrase.

A philosophy of the Second Moment (ambitious locution) if it is going to amount to something should be better than merely this first philosophy in retreat. It should have character of its own, and an attachment for something positive, ontologically "given" and assured. But I will not argue what it should be, for the Second Moment can be presented empirically.

It is the aesthetic philosophy; and as the other philosophy takes its bearings from the data of science, this takes its bearing from the data of art. The art is analogous to the theoretical science, as a sort of creative projection beyond the limits of the practical occasion; for natural man has no more use for art than for such a science. And if determinate form is what the science wants, what the art wants is the stubborn substance against which science breaks its head. Heterogeneous substance was conceded by Greek philosophers in accounting for nature's resistance to scientific process, but in art the heterogeneous substance is embraced. And in aesthetic philosophy, with critical self-consciousness. Though I should not suppose the philosophers would embrace it more warmly than the artists, at least they would draw up its bill of ontological rights, and locate it in the perspective. But it is embarassing to have to think that Schopenhauer, Nietzsche, Bergson, Croce, who have the temperament for it, have not done this so precisely as did Kant and possibly Aristotle, whose sympathies were not fully engaged.

Aristotle says, in the tone of commonplace, that poetry is chiefly an "imitation" or recording of natural objects in their concrete substantiality; or more probably of fictitious objects, provided these are on the order of natural objects and not too much idealized. Plato had said precisely this, but in a scornful tone; accordingly he had almost abandoned poetry as too scandalous for approval. But Aristotle actually adds a redeeming or Platonic qualification: an imitation with a specially devised formal character, namely, phonetic organization or rhythm, as if to furnish a sort of "token" rationality for rational men. But he knows that poetic process is radically different from scientific. In science you "improve on" nature, in that you play up the form and play down the substantival matter, those two elements which, we can scarcely doubt, are equal in the sight of nature and of its ontological "principle." If then, after science, and knowing what science can do as well as what it cannot do, you choose to employ yourself with something described as "imitation," the rendering of the mere backward natural objects, you can only be intending to play up what you have been playing down: the matter. Aristotle remarks that we seem to have a propensity for imitation as well as for rhythm, and that imitation is a means of "learning" something.

Quite independently, Kant makes almost this identical analysis. In art we bridge the feud between those omnipresent faculties, sense and reason. We set up an object in which imagination — that synthetic faculty focussing all the senses at once — finds a complete heterogeneous image, and reason finds a definitive rational form, so that both can take their exercise in the same object. (A big and loose sort of object it should be, with plenty of room in it.) I do not think this understanding of art can be much bettered for introductory purposes. It can be elaborated. From Kant the imitationist, representationist, or "naturalistic" aesthetics, that likes to contemplate the most actual objects, can take its charter; but no more than "formalistic" aesthetics can, with its dogmatic liking for rational patterns. In poetry, the one dwells on the concrete "meaning," the other on the determinate meters.[1]

I will not go much further. But Kenneth Burke, for me, seems to be mostly in what I call the First Moment of philosophy, identifying himself with the scientific movements; which is very well, and any representations of mine against it would be impertinent, and as a matter of fact Kant is somewhere there too, and Burke knows his Kant. Burke has a theory of poetry, however, and Kant has a general aesthetics, and I wish to develop two or three considerations briefly out of Kant and address them to Burke.

And first, I do not think that Kant would go with Burke in his persistent effort to find in a poem the pursuit of some sort of useful or selfish "trust," or even some sort of dialectical or social "truth." Burke knows, we may be sure, that Kant carefully disengaged the artistic motive from "pleasure" in the common sense; then from usefulness, which would involve it in a labor for the sake of pleasure; then from the pursuit of the ethical good and "determinate concepts," which together might be said to be wisdom itself, but wisdom of the First Moment. Art is radically not science, and not affiliated with the idealistic philosophy, and Kant does everything possible to prevent the confusion. The fact that Burke tends to confuse them — and Kant too, later on — might be an evidence that art is not really so "universal" a human activity as science; the "inside knowledge" of it is not so common. I agree that you cannot argue from your inside knowledge. I have been expecting to find somebody writing that Burke seems resolved to read into the poem everything possible along the lines of his own strenuous rationality and very little of the thing that makes the poem poetic; but that would get nowhere; the writer would be pitting his inside knowledge against Burke's. Kant has argued the motive business to the satisfac-

[1] It is more complicated than that, of course. In the matter of the meaning there is the rational structure organizing the surface by which the natural object immediately confronts us, and beyond that the rich concrete texture that discovers itself more gradually. In the matter of the meters there is both the structural regularity and the textural variation. I have written elsewhere of this.

tion of most aestheticians, in cold blood. To extend the Kantian terms a little, I think the trouble with Burke's readings is that his imagination plays too near the rational surface of the poem, and the reason it does not go deeper is that he is no lover of nature. In the last resort we shall not be talking intelligently about art unless we can pronounce with warmth two terms that must have been odious to a proper Greek: Love, and Nature. (I am talking "poetically" now; Burke might say "too poetically.")

Next, we should be on our guard against attributing too much virtue to the "harmonious exercise" in the same poem of imagination and reason. It is splendid of art to have these old fighters making up. But I think it consists in their agreeing to take turn-about with the object, while disagreeing as hopelessly as ever as to what they want the object for. I read respected authors, and I have friends, who seem to me to misplace, and bring up on the wrong occasions, their admiration for harmony, and for such adjunct excellences as reconciliation, resolution, synthesis, unification, and plain unity. They are idealists, and suppose that the artists must share their idealism, it is such a good thing. But in the nature of the case this is impossible. In a scientific process there is harmony in the way the extended parts fit themselves spatially and temporally together, and the way each does its little bit of work for the whole and does nothing on its own account; which is organism, unity, logico-mathematical harmony. But no harmony exists logico-mathematically or organically among the heterogeneous properties of a natural object. You can compose separate apples into a nice total weight or volume or quota or money value or geometrical row or Christmas design of apples, but how can you compose a red and a sweet and a round and a heavy into one apple? To assemble the original properties is the work of nature, and the assemblage, if we think about it, always strikes us as arbitrary and contingent, a pure gift or datum, which reason cannot understand though sense witnesses it indubitably. The image is one thing, and the rational structure is another thing. The difference between the heterogeneous properties is absolute. Absolute also is the difference between the local imagery of the poem and its logical structure. Their being furnished both comfortably in one poem is not a harmony in a very marvelous sense.

Finally, Kant sees the harmony of sense and reason broken in one instance, and reason triumphant most Platonically over sense. The occasion comes when art, or nature itself, manifests sublimity. The natural object exhibits vast magnitude, like the mountain (the mathematically sublime), or stupendous force, like the storm (the dynamically sublime). Both are of supra-sensible dimensions, and imagination cannot take in the object as a whole to form a single image. It trails vainly in the wake of reason, which grasps the object easily. At first the disproportion between the cognitive faculties feels painful, but presently we are supposed to be comforted by the following reflection: The mind must have a supersensible destination; and we should be glad to abandon weak sense in honor of the rationality in store for us. I am obliged to think this comes to a vulgarization of Platonism (I hasten to say I find nothing like it in Burke) since Plato admired the purity or precision of rational form rather than its possible dimensions. In any case the size of the sublime object does not alter the force of the common Greek objection: you could not enter into your supersensible destiny without leaving behind you the sense-property that made your mountain a mountain and your storm a storm. Religions on the cosmic side are perfectly familiar with this crisis, and Kant himself declared, "A concept without a percept is empty." But I am interested in thinking of a possible reversal of the situation, and a "qualitative" or "substantival" sort of sublime. Sense has a fabulous realm to retire to beyond the reach of reason, if it wants to be so bold, a realm in which a chaotic qualitative density obtains. Matter would be its name. But if Form is empty, Matter is blind: "A percept without a concept is blind," as Kant, again, had said. The moral would be that artists can be just as fantastic as rationalists can. Artists have sometimes tried, not exactly to "purify" their art, which might imply the opposite intention, but to "densify" it, to the point where it may achieve emancipation from the bondage of any determinate form. The art feels wonderfully rich and strange to us then and we strain ever so painfully to receive it; an adventure with boundless materiality. There is no passionate lover of his art who has not attempted it. But it eludes us. It is clear that imagination and reason ought to learn from the failures of each other's *tours de force*, and agree to inhabit their common and actual world. We cannot think that Kant found it profitable to sanction a single breach in their easy artistic "harmony."

4

These prolegomena have run beyond bounds, and it embarrasses me to think how many of them must already have been commonplace in Burke's own consciousness. But I can turn back to his view of poetry as "dialectic" with one of the biggest possible perspectives.

There are two kinds of poetry (or at least of "literature") and Burke analyses one kind with great nicety, and honors it, but shows too little interest in the other. The one he honors is the dialectical or critical kind, and the one he neglects is the lyrical or radical kind. But they correlate respectively (a) with the logico-mathematical ontology in retreat, and (b) with the ontology that is positively substantival or aesthetic. If one does not like "ontology" in this connection, then they correlate with two elemental "outlooks" or "world-views," or for that matter with two religions, or two moralities, or even two kinds of politics. And of course they correlate respectively with (a) the temperament that cannot quite abandon its scientific orientation, and (b) the temperament which is capable of taking its art straight.[2]

I concede that the dialectic, which Burke equates with poetry, originates in at least a momentary disaffection with idealistic programs. It originates within a dissident, a critic, a sceptic, anything short of an out-and-out cynic — names which describe a man with a negative attitude. But, in not being quite a cynic, he probably purposes with all his heart after being negative to be positive again; to be helpful. The dialectic entrusted to the characters (and the events) in the drama, who gradually reduce and refine the initial crude "truth" about the situation, till at last they get something workable again, is too much like the consultation of the engineers, who have never really stopped intending to put their project through.

Of course the dialectical work is intelligent. I admire it, and I concede that it is intelligent in the degree that it works with more of the substantival object than the original fond idealist did. What it shows him is, in fact, how the properties which he was in too great a hurry to attend to will assert themselves nevertheless, and will amount to anti-structures throttling his structures.[3] For we do not tell enough if we say that the dialectic simply protests that he is being "too idealistic." So we have in the dialectical literature the familiar "tragic flaw" in the hero's character, which seems to make him the victim of his own virtues; the ironic turn of events that was foreseeable but unforeseen in the very "circumstances" that made the situation look most propitious; and, a still more startling kind of irony, found even within the

[2] If there had been time I think I would have proposed, instead of my rather blank and undescriptive First Moment and Second Moment, two exciting terms taken from politics: *Leftist*, for the logico-mathematical or Platonic or idealistic philosophy, involving the ontology and the religion and the ethics as well as the politics which that term connotes; and *Rightist*, for the substantival or aesthetic ontology, religion, ethics, and politics. These terms would have involved a long discussion. But I believe firmly in the method of philosophical correlations. It might yield us a real definition of temperaments; one more binding than, for example, Jung's introvert and extravert.

[3] I have advocated the view that a poem shows in some fulness both ontological elements: (a) rational structure as its skeleton, and (b) substantival local texture as its body. But I have learned more about structure from Burke, and would change the formula to read: (a) structure and anti-structure, and (b) texture. But I would keep anti-structure under (a), on the ground that it is as distinct from substantival texture as structure is, but is not an ontological element distinct from structure.

restricted range of the lyric and pointed out to us by I. A. Richards, the romantic version of situation which goes to the trouble of accompanying itself with its own "parody," or anti-romantic version of the same situation, in order to anticipate the parody of the stranger-critic. All such turns are worked out in this literature with great specificity and with actual objects for illustration. But the original idealist himself had some image of the object. And the trouble with the dialecticist is that no more than the idealist need he have any patience with the residuary body of the image when he has done with it. The residuary body, with its irrelevance, is what constitutes the "free image." The poet embraces that but not the idealist, naive or critical.

Not, at least, unless the critical idealist who writes plays has within his compound personality, as is quite possible, a poet also. I concede Shakespeare. Naturally I could have no argument with Burke as to Shakespeare's being a great poet as well as a dramatist. But I should try to distinguish the poetic effects from the dialectical ones, and defend the more isolated lyrical passages from any necessity of taking part in the strenuous dialectics. No more comfortable literary type will suggest itself to the Kantian than the big play, with its room for a long and keen work of dialectics or dramatics proper, and also for nearly incessant poetic effects. In general, I feel that the keener and more exacting the dramatics, the less energy there is for the poetry. But I think everybody knows that, and also the corollary proposition, that the imagery tends to be denser and freer in the independent lyric because the logic tends there to be simpler and more commonplace. The conclusion might very well be that the best dialectical or "true" drama comes in prose, the best poetry in the short lyric. And what could that mean but that you simply do not identify the dialectical and the poetical as a single "literary" element?

If there is not a regular and fairly technicalized provision for imagery throughout a body of literature, it should not be estimated as a poetry; and I would go further and raise the question whether it is entitled to be called even a "literature," or whether it is not merely a work of logico-mathematical process, which has every right in the world to use the dialectic in its own business; and I would raise the question at the expense of writings that superficially are fiction, drama, and even verse. I know that men of letters who are most jealous for their art can be very derisive against the notion that some weakly-imagined work should have "literary" rating. They can be fierce, and I like them for it.

I will conclude by citing two technical evidences of substantival or poetic process in literature—without meaning that they are the only evidences. One consists in the "figures" or tropes. If we had an adequate "logic of poetic figure" it would be an anomaly, and would mean: "a logic of logical aberations; applicable to the conventions of poetic language." The tropes make departures from the logico-mathematical level of procedure, normal to prose writing, into substantival imagery, and that is their intention as poetry; at any rate the spectacular tropes do it, and so I have supposed do they all. But there is such a large conventional body of figurative usages, and so much writing in the way of merely halfhearted and verbal borrowing, making use of somebody else's descent into substance, that we have to be on guard against superficial evidence. The test would be one of pure logical analysis, or perhaps "semantics," employed by somebody experienced enough to detect the spurious or echoed old thing from the really new thing.

The other evidence would consist in some variety of "humor." I feel less sure about this evidence, which may require rather subtle interpretation. But I cannot help thinking that laughter is one of the profoundest of human actions, betokening ontological sense, and, specifically, that of the substantival existents as opposed to the better advertised rational forms. I remember being taught that the definition of man as "risible animal" was enough to mark him off from the lower species, and that "risible" came to the same thing as "sapiens" or wise. Bergson's view of laughter is satisfactory enough: we laugh when we are invited to determine a human action by mechanical principles. We should add that the invitation is extended by somebody of logico-mathematical mentality, and that our laughing is at his expense, and at our own to the extent that we were being taken in. So we have satire, where a little touching up, a little more of the same, makes the program of the ingenuous idealist appear too obviously ridiculous; wit, including puns, indicating the inattentive colleague who does not respect the seriousness of the discourse, and broadening out into farce, and obstructive diversion and horseplay; irony, perhaps the subtlest of all, sensing that the simpleton idealist does not know he is handling dynamite and will be hoisted with his own petard. I am putting the grim interpretation upon humor. Like the dialectic, it is critical of programs. But not "constructively," to make them workable; nor does it try to furnish the frail logico-mathematical structure with some decent imagery in order to make it "ontologically" presentable. It sweeps the whole thing away with laughter; which, though wise, is primitive and organic rather than vocal, but, if it could be articulate, would be found reiterating, Substance, Substance. Humor is neither poetic nor anti-poetic but pre-poetic. The ambitious determinant is absurd by the same considerations that mark the substantival poem as beautiful.

However, I strongly advise not to sell Burke's poetics short. For he employs both figures and turns of humor, and his prose has literary distinction. Furthermore, he has written wisely, and in advance of the rest of us, about the logic of the figures, and some other purely poetic usages, to indicate participation in a true aesthetics. But this part of his thinking hardly shows in the work to which he has given the major title of *Philosophy of Literary Form.* He is perspicuous and brilliantly original, and I would venture to quarrel with no positive finding that he makes, but only with his proportions, or his perspective.

◇◇

JOHN CROWE RANSOM was born in Pulaski, Tennessee, in 1888. He was a Rhodes Scholar (1910–13) and later taught English at Vanderbilt University (1914–37) and at Kenyon College (1937–58). He is a distinguished poet, critic, teacher, and editor. He founded and for many years edited *The Kenyon Review* and was certainly one of the major moving forces — perhaps the prime force — in the critical revolution which was to culminate in the "new criticism." He has written and edited many books, among them *God without Thunder, The World's Body,* and *The New Criticism* — the three books in which he worked out and presented his important and influential theory of literature. He is also the author of numerous essays and reviews. Burke and Ransom have been friends and friendly antagonists for many years.

Those familiar with Mr. Ransom's own position — as articulated in the three books noted above — will recognize the extent to which his "Address" to Burke issues from within that position and continues one of the main theoretical arguments of critical discourse in the thirties and forties. Mr. Ransom's way is by indirection; he takes the long route to an issue, through the philosophical arguments, back to the fundamentals and then forward, always subtly, usually somewhat ironically. He has a mind with one of the sharpest cutting edges in modern critical thought and he is, when arguing and defending positions, a formidable stylist and opponent. His essays often have, as this one clearly does, a density of texture which resists summary and forces one to approach them with extreme caution. At one point, I tried to cut this essay but soon discovered that even the remarks apparently most remote (to Burke) have a relevance and are organic to the total "Address."

I make no attempt here to summarize the content of this essay or to reduce Mr. Ransom's long argument (in the philosophical sense) to a synoptic paragraph. The theoretical issues are clear enough. They have to do with the emphasis in Burke on what Mr. Ransom calls, variously, mind, the rational, science, the logico-mathematical, the dialectical, prose, the critical, the utilitarian; and the extent to which these, as part of a larger perspective — a poetics — are essentially (to Mr. Ransom) anti-poetical and hence inadequate as an account of poetry. And worse, they are a threat to, even a denial of, all those things Mr. Ransom so dearly loved: the image, the lyric, poetry, the poetic, the world's body, nature, the organic, the useless and beautiful things. Mr. Ransom's "Address" is to large and fundamental issues; it is searching and brilliantly worked out. It is the kind of address you only make to a worthy adversary. For these reasons, it has always seemed to me a marvelous tribute to the seriousness of Burke's endeavors and to the "brilliantly original" qualities of his mind.

◇◇

2 *Mr. Burke's Dialectic*

BY John Crowe Ransom

THE fascinations of philosophy began for me when a Harvard man told me about his wonderful professor. The course was History of Philosophy, and every week or so, said my informant, a new philosopher came up for notice. So brilliant were the elucidations of the professor that each philosopher was revealed as refuting his predecessor's system by showing how it had developed from certain unproved assumptions, then as going on to expound the perfect system — his own — which did not depend upon them. His triumph was short. The next week the professor would be exhibiting him as refuted by his successor on the ground of assumptions he himself made, though they were not the ones he had condemned. There was no stop in the sequence; philosophy seemed to run on forever, relative always to its initial assumptions, becoming sometimes more expert and technical but never final, never valid. And so it seemed presently to me, as I came to hear the lectures and make the readings in philosophy, and saw how a doctrine may logically be pushed back and back upon its grounds, in the order of their priority, till we come to the grounds which are not grounded but assumed. But the mature reader will imagine what a prig there was then, the superior young man with a sense of the universal relativism, rejecting all the doctrines; how effete, and lacking in common vitality. To be human is to risk assumptions and take decisions.

EDITOR'S NOTE: Reprinted from *The New Republic*, CXIV (18 February 1946), 257–258, by permission of the author and *The New Republic*, copyright © 1946, Harrison-Blaine of New Jersey, Inc.

Kenneth Burke in his writings has not been identifiable with such a young man luxuriating in his disenchantment, nor yet with such a weary professor still inciting the young men to embrace a kind of freedom which, if they could not qualify it, would be like death. Of all our critics Burke is philosophically the subtlest, temperamentally the most ironical. The irony precludes a notable human warmth, and the cool tone repels weak readers as much as the speed and range of the dialectical shifts. Nevertheless if we can read we must acknowledge beneath Burke's sophistication a very real commitment: he is liberal if fastidious in his politics, and elsewhere, and over all, he is a modern humanist.

The new book [*A Grammar of Motives*] is his biggest, like an end-work which assimilates to a new perspective the fragments of one's earlier writings. Burke has a "grammar" in the Aristotelian sense of a set of verbal terms, or categories, or parts of speech, by means of which a discourse can be analyzed, or for that matter performed in the first place. The humanistic bias enters in his choice of categories. Burke's grammar is "dramatistic." Drama occurs for him when the turn of events is as in a play, with purposive acts which are more than the "motions" of science, and moral agents which are more than the "bodies." The dramatistic categories for Burke are five, and constitute his "pentad": Act, Scene, Agent, Agency, Purpose. Soon it occurs to the reader, and is remarked by Burke himself, that the pentad performs pretty much the same work as a certain famous tetrad, which would consist in the Four Causes that Aristotle proposed to distinguish within a turn of events: Material, Efficient, Formal, and Final Causes. Final Cause is Motive; it attributes intelligence to the agent, and humanizes the situation.

Now it is one thing to apply the full pentad, or tetrad, to a situation in which a human being is the cause, and to say that science in reporting the situation in terms of motions and chemico-physical objects misses the factor which is most distinctive. But what if the turn of events is a "natural" one in which no human being participates? Both Aristotle and Burke are ambiguous about this. There are times when they accept the account of science, but there are also times when they take the high ground of philosophical tradition, and the grand manner, and assume the rational or purposive agent. It is a metaphysical assumption. Or, if that is not the name of a real motive, it is a religious assumption. Burke writes frequently as if the natural world were operated universally according to common reason, with operators of the same "familial substance" as rational man; and scarcely has the heart to reproach Plato for the seductive doctrine that the ideas of reason are the father-causes and progenitors of the natural phenomena. But this is to offer on his part the same confusion that he expressly rebukes at one place, where he observes a philosophical pun on the word "prior," leading some thinkers to transform logical priority into temporal priority. It is a charming confusion, and made in a good cause, but still I think the good cause cannot demand confusion, especially from writers with philosophical rather than popular status.

Burke refers disparagingly to a habit of mind which he calls "scientism." And what is that? Science will find chemical and mechanical relations between two objects, and these are rational relations in the sense that the reason of the scientist understands them, but not in the sense that there is rational consciousness in the objects. It would be interesting to see what would become of an Aristotelian ideology if we substituted a category of Human Value for the category of Final Cause. It would put the Aristotelian into the way of some modern pragmatism, where his turn for speculation would undoubtedly suffer some constriction; and I believe that his religious and artistic concerns could not yet find their accounting there. At a thousand points this philosophy reports the technology of natural process as useful to the human species without reporting it as useful by intention. But if this is scientism, it is doubtless the one imperative rule which will promote scientific achievements as we know them. I do not mean to say that Burke thinks otherwise, or that it lies in me to inform him of what he does not know. But he might have found for several modern enterprises a more reputable activity than he seems to concede.

Logical positivism, for instance. This involves the study of human discourse in the syntactical dimension only. Whatever meanings are assigned to the terms, they must not be altered. But the term need not refer to the actual world, and the conclusions need have no practical applications. We might insist that discourse on these conditions is wanting in ordinary motivation, and could not become standard procedure; logical positivists are scarcely authorized to expel the pragmatical implications of discourse. Nevertheless what they contribute to the theory of syntax is valuable for the perfection of any discourse, and most valuable when the pragmatic urgency is greatest and most blinding. And in this way we convert the logical positivists to a human point of view in spite of themselves.

Or take operationalism, Professor Bridgman's rule by which a term is defined as "what it does" within the given discourse. I suppose this means that a scientific term is rigidly held to its functional or technical status, and not allowed to acquire substantiality. Again the question of human concern seems to be waived, but we need not worry. If the result to which the term contributes is not to be picked up and employed within the human economy, there has been a waste of effort, but the operation could hardly have had that intention, and will not be repeated.

And take behaviorism, which undertakes to express a "psychosis" in terms of a "neurosis." Surely it is desirable to carry this project as far as possible. How otherwise will a patient who is warned of his disorder by conscious symptoms obtain the full advantage of materia medica? But on the other hand he may have to obtain his help from psychiatry, unless he is young and obtains it from the psychical "conditioning" process which is accomplished by parents, or an educational establishment. There seems little possibility that either of these normative agencies can be superseded by the other, or that the psycho-physical parallelism can be practically resolved into a monism of either sort. Behaviorists may be boastful, but they are scarcely the enemies of society; probably not theirs nor any other technology can impose itself seriously upon us irrespective of the human value of its performance.

Burke's book is rich in exciting dialectical episodes. I have the feeling that they are there in their aggregate, rather than systematically or serially as they are, for example, in Hegel. Burke is most fertile when he considers the back-and-forth of emphasis which occurs in working a single pair of categories. Thus there is a proper Scene-Act "ratio"; but, if we start with a Scene which is overdetermined on its side, it will dehumanize the Act on the other side; and many consequences have flowed from this principle, both on the stage and in the history of ideas. But in confining himself to a pair at a time among the five categories, Burke is Hegelian, for Hegel's Logic, more than drama, is the classical locus for the dialectic of the pairings. In general, the pentad is not so dramatic in practice as its derivation promised. More often than not, the situation examined is not felt as drama; enactment upon a stage is not imaginable. Why then Burke's dramatism? I think he may have been affected by knowing that the word *drama* meant simply, in its origin, the *doing* of a human agent, and so based his categories upon a Greek and predramatic sense rather than upon our sense of drama as a rounded action upon a stage.

At any rate it seems to be the testimony of history that many events are not suited to drama, for they have gone into fiction. Still other events must not be suited to fiction, for they have gone into poetry. All the time, and everywhere, there is a multitude of events not much suited to any of these arts because they are peculiarly suited to science. And if science does well in not aspiring to be poetry, it does well also in not aspiring to be drama. Perhaps the same thing may be said for philosophy.

◇◇

See the note on pages 158–159.

THERE is a five-year lapse between these two pieces by Mr. Ransom. It was during this period that Burke conceived his *Motives* books and wrote the *Grammar*. This book is both an end and a middle work – as Burke's later development shows. Most reviewers treat it as both by discussing it as the beginning of a long, serious, and complex attempt to confront reality by reducing it to a system. With this review of the *Grammar* we enter a period (which runs through *A Rhetoric of Motives*) when the responses to Burke were the most frequent. These two books were reviewed – or noticed – everywhere as only major books by major figures are received.

In this review, Mr. Ransom continues the argument he had with Burke in 1941. He says that Burke's dialectic is partial, that it does not include enough, that it is partly a trick, and that it is a verbal manipulation which takes one away from nature, from what is human and valuable. Others before Mr. Ransom – notably Mr. Kuhn – said some of these same things; and, as one can discover by reading on, many others after him were to repeat and amplify them.

◇◇

z The Strategy of Kenneth Burke

BY Charles Morris

KENNETH BURKE'S *A Grammar of Motives* is the first work of a trilogy, to be followed by *Rhetoric of Motives* and *Symbolic of Motives*. The series may be regarded as a detailed mining of the territory staked out in the earlier *Permanence and Change*. It is the same Burke with the same quest and the same strategy, as baffling, as inconclusive, as penetrating, as rewarding as ever, working on the largest and most important job of criticism that is being done among us.

The quest is substantiality and the strategy is the criticism of linguistic resources. Substantiality not in the abstract, but in the concrete

EDITOR'S NOTE: Reprinted from *The Nation*, CLXIII (July 1946), 106, copyright 1946 by *The Nation*, by permission of the publisher.

human sense of having an identity, standing for something, being oriented by a goal, answering Shakespeare's "What is your substance?" *Peer Gynt* is searchingly analyzed as a "character in search of his identity"; *A Grammar of Motives* is engaged in the same search. In this sense Burke is after a way of life for himself and modern man. But he differs from the easy prophets who know the answer by a recognition of the arduousness of the task, and in the linguistic means which he employs. His resources are those of the critic; he sometimes seems to believe that salvation can be obtained by semantics.

A Grammar of Motives forces us to assume a succession of points of view from which human motivation has been described, and then dissolves each perspective by showing its partiality in terms of other perspectives. We find ourselves engaged in a dramatic dialectic in which philosophers, political theorists, economists, poets, theologians, and psychologists all have their say, and each mode of saying is shown to need correction by each other mode. The book is experienced as a vast dialogue. The participant reader goes through a complex psychological process in which his initial value-perspective toward human nature is confronted by the multitude of attitudes which other persons have held. One is challenged to find himself by taking the role of others.

Does Burke by this strategy reveal his substance or lead the reader to find his own? Fairness would require that we wait for acts two and three of the critical drama. Yet some preliminary, and perhaps premature, comments are insistent. Burke's hope is surely that in the process of assuming a multiplicity of perspectives toward man something "substantial" will result. Whether this is so is not so clear. In *Permanence and Change* Burke believed that a knowledge of man's biological nature would reveal what is constant in human history, and that communism offered the value-orientation by which contemporary man could attain an ethical identity. In *A Grammar of Motives* Burke does not continue these suggestions; he remains primarily at the level of critic, more detached, more ironic, more uncertain. There are valuable hints that the new self (and the new society) can find its unity only in the dynamic interrelationship of its diversities—that a federated self and a federated society is the answer to the problem of substance and change. But this position is not worked through, and the concluding pages extol a "neo-Stoic" attitude, a rather tame ending for a dramatic inquiry into man conceived as a dramatic animal. We emerge, indeed, with a heightened sense of our linguistic resources, but with no clear indication as to how they are to be employed.

This result is what we should expect. For the work of the critic is not that of the scientist or the philosopher or the prophet. Burke's brilliant exploration of our modes of expression is made in terms of one mode of expression, that of criticism. It cannot give us the full story of our linguistic resources, nor can an analysis of man through his language provide us with a full account of human motives. Burke snaps at science in all his writings, but his literary version of motive and language greatly needs supplementation by the work of psychologists and linguists. His own special orientation to substantiality causes him to ignore important treatments by contemporary philosophers of the problem of substance. And his preoccupation with modes of expression is not the focus from which either poetry or prophecy emerges.

The critic, however, has his own important task, and Burke is performing that task admirably. *A Grammar of Motives* is a significant book. It will be read by those who take seriously the role of words in human life, and by those who are earnestly concerned with the fateful problem of what man is to make of man.

◇◇◇

CHARLES MORRIS was born in Denver, Colorado, in 1901. He taught philosophy at the University of Chicago from 1931 to 1958 and since then has been a research professor of philosophy at the University of Florida. His works includes *Six Theories of Mind*; *Logical Positivism, Pragmatism, and Scientific Empiricism*; *Foundations of the Theory of Signs*; *Paths of Life*; and *Signs, Language, and Behavior*.

In the second paragraph of this brief review one begins to get the kind of awareness that is characteristic of the reception of the *Motives* books. The key phrases here are very significant; as is the precise awareness shown by Mr. Morris in paragraph three of how Burke works and how the reader responds to the way he works. The last paragraphs consider—very accurately—the limitations of the endeavor and the work still to be done before the total vision could be rendered. It seems a pity that Charles Morris, who began, as Burke did, in the thirties to speculate on language, and who, beginning in 1938 with *Foundations of the Theory of Signs,* developed a comprehensive view of language and human behavior, did not write at greater length about Burke's endeavor and place it as only a fellow worker can.

◇◇◇

7 A Review of "A Grammar of Motives"

BY Max Black

DURING the first performance of a modern orchestral work scored for brass, typewriters, and pneumatic drills, a member of the audience elevated a walking stick to which a white handkerchief had been attached and shouted "I surrender." After suffering the prolonged barrage of Mr. Burke's dialectical artillery, I was tempted to confine this review to the same two words. But this would not be fair to the book, or the eminent literary critics whose eulogies decorate the dust cover.

Mr. Burke has set himself the ambitious task of formulating a system of related categories – a "grammar," to use his term – by means of which every human action may be analyzed and evaluated. Every *human* action is characterized by the presence of motives: and every "rounded" statement about motives "must" involve reference to the five elements of Act, Scene, Agent, Agency, and Purpose. Any systematic or philosophical account of motives using all five of the basic terms is "dramatistic" (a eulogistic epithet); and classical philosophies receive severe condemnation for emphasizing one or other of the factors at the expense of the remainder.

The basic terms are highly ambiguous (so much so that at one point in the argument they even dissolve into the four "causes" of Aristotle – p. 228); the general program of the critical undertaking is accordingly to chart "their possibilities of transformation, their range of permutations and combination – and then to see how these resources figure in actual statements about human motives." This leads to the formulation of such notions as that of the "scene-agent ratio" (the imputed relationship between the agent's character and the setting in which his act is performed), the "circumference of the scene" (the range of the background to which explicit or implicit reference is made in mentioning the act) and a few others. It leads also to the attentive scrutiny of a rich variety of "acts," ranging from the dreams of adolescents to the creative activities of Deity, and discussion of such varied artifacts as poems, political constitutions, and metaphysical systems.

Readers of this review will presumably be most interested in the detailed and lengthy discussion of the classical philosophers (Hobbes,

EDITOR'S NOTE: Reprinted from *The Philosophical Review*, LV (July 1946), 487–490, by permission of the author and publisher.

Spinoza, Berkeley, Hume, Leibniz, Kant, Hegel, Santayana, Aristotle, Aquinas, and many more). Mr. Burke's method in such cases consists of exploring the etymology of terms which he regards as central to the philosophy in question (often with the aid of what he likes to call a "representative anecdote" – a paradigm of the linguistic usage considered); he then emerges with a series of distinctions with the aid of which the philosophy can be "placed" (another favorite term), *i.e.*, shown in its relation to its associates and competitors.

Let us see what this all adds up to in the discussion of the critical term "substance" (21–55). We are reminded that the term's etymological origin suggests a support or prop; therefore something outside of, *extrinsic* to, the object supported. Yet when the term is used as roughly synonymous with essence, substance designates something within, *intrinsic* to the object. "Here obviously is a strategic moment, an alchemic moment, wherein momentous miracles of transformation can take place. For here the intrinsic and the extrinsic can change places. To tell what a thing is, you place it in terms of something else" (24). This is "an *inevitable* paradox of definition, an antinomy that must endow the concept of substance with unresolvable ambiguity, and that will be discovered lurking beneath any vocabulary designed to treat of motivation by the deliberate outlawing of the *word* for substance" (Ib.). Spinoza's metaphysics shows this paradox in "full intensity"; for by identifying substance with the totality of all that exists, he puts himself in the position of being unable to define God (discriminate him from anything else that exists), and ends "with a variant of the so-called 'negative theology' which conceived of God as the absence of all qualities" (25). But substance may also be regarded as defined biologically in terms of common ancestry: ". . . the Aristotelian *genus* is originally not a logical, but a biological, concept. We can discern the tribal pattern behind the notion, so characteristic of Greek nationalism, that like causes like or that like recognizes like, as with Democritus' theory of perception. Similarly there was an *ancestral* notion behind the Platonic theory of forms; in fact it was this tribal ingredient that recommended it so strongly to the ages of Western feudalism. Each thing in this world had, as it were, an eponym in heaven, a perfect form from which it was derived – and it shared this derivation with all the other members of its class or genus. And I think we might most quickly understand the mediaeval speculations as to whether universals were 'before the thing, in the thing, or after the thing' if we first tried a dramatist translation of the three formulae respectively thus: 'Does the tribe give birth to its members (universal *ante rem*) or does the tribe exist in its members (universal *in re*) or is the tribe merely a name for the sum of its members (universal *post rem*)?' " (26, 27). We then proceed to discuss "direction substance" and dialectical substance"; but I despair of giving an adequate summary of what is asserted concerning these.

I have quoted some representative passages from Mr. Burke at some length, so that the reader may know what to expect. I shall not stay to consider the correctness of Mr. Burke's headlong etymological excursions; or to wonder what evidence could be produced for Western feudalism's interest in the alleged "tribal ingredient" of the Platonic theory of forms. For my part, I am willing to regard such etymological and sociological exegesis as a working myth, and to concede Mr. Burke the privilege of invoking whatever analogies and speculative resemblances will adorn and illuminate the subject of his criticism. What disquiets me in general (apart from the constant difficulty of reading Mr. Burke's turbid prose) is the lack of resultant illumination. I find it really quite unhelpful to an appreciation of the merits of utilitarianism to be reminded that Bentham was a "crabbed old bachelor" or to be told that he was one who "arriving at the stage of maturity where the dissociation between the maternal woman and the erotic woman must be confronted, developed a philosophy of utility that could deflect erotic purpose into terms (themselves transformed) of maternal agency" (285).

The episode of the "great Bachelors of Capitalist Liberalism" (Ib.) illustrates the general difficulty of determining Mr. Burke's own frame of reference. It is perfectly clear that he is *not* faithful to his recommended ironical and compassionate contemplation of the foibles and embarrassments of human thought: it does not take long to find out that "dramatism" is an alias for neo-aristotelianism, and that materialists, pragmatists, positivists, and naturalists are going to take a beating for neglecting essential aspects of the mystic pentad. But how is this preference for the five-fold description of human motives grounded? What is the evidence for the repeated suggestion that all forms of "reductionism" (failure to pay attention to all five categories) are inadequate and misleading? All I can find in answer to these questions is a series of *obiter dicta*: men's linguistic behavior "reflects real paradoxes in the nature of the world itself" (56); "Our five terms are 'transcendental' rather than formal (and are to this extent Kantian) in being categories which human thought *necessarily exemplifies*" (317) – and so on. The vast rambling edifice of quasi-sociological and quasi-psychoanalytical speculation seems to rest on nothing more solid than a set of unexamined and uncriticized metaphysical assumptions.

◇◇

MAX BLACK was born in Baku, Russia, in 1909, was educated in England, came to this country in 1940, and was naturalized in 1948. He has taught philosophy at Cornell University since 1946. He is the author of many books and articles on language, symbolic logic, and human behavior.

The nature of Burke's work now brought it to the attention of the semanticists, verbal analysts, and philosophers concerned with language theory and language-centered views of reality. Later, *A Rhetoric of Motives* was to bring Burke to the attention of the professional students of classical and modern rhetoric, a group of people who, in general, took to him very readily and used him extensively. The same cannot be said for the group represented by Max Black—or black max, as Burke likes to call him. His response is similar to that of Sidney Hook and yet substantially different. Burke has always been a do-it-yourself sort of philosopher and he suffers, I think, from some of the usual shortcomings of the autodidact. He is not systematic in the way of formal philosophers and, as Mr. Hook pointed out, he does not use his evidence in a way that pleases rigorous and scientifically trained academicians. The last sentence of Mr. Black's review summarizes the nature of his case against Burke. He is not the first, nor will he be the last, to attack Burke on these grounds. He is, though, one of the first to object to Burke's "turbid prose." This prose got turbider before it cleared, which caused many others to repeat Black's complaint.

◇◇

⁊ A Review of "A Grammar of Motives"

BY Abraham Kaplan

NOT the least of the difficulties in the way of a full understanding of Mr. Burke's own motives, and an appraisal of their actualization in

EDITOR'S NOTE: Reprinted from *Journal of Aesthetics and Art Criticism*, V (March 1947), 233–234, copyright 1947 by the American Society for Aesthetics, by permission of the author and publisher.

this book, is the discursiveness of his presentation, and his proclivity to a tangential use of language, to an exploitation of marginal meanings. Such a style has made his book extraordinarily rich and suggestive, coruscating with flashes of insight. But it has also obscured the central issues of his subject, and pushed into the background the logic of his position on these issues.

This rich obscurity begins with the title itself, which contains an important ambiguity running through the book: "grammar" as the elements of an art or science, and "grammar" as a study of the *language* in which the discipline is formulated. Burke explicitly declares his concern to be with the analysis of language, not "reality." But it remains doubtful whether he has in fact clearly distinguished the two and successfully limited himself to the linguistic level.

The subject of the book he describes as an answer to the question, "What is involved, when we say what people are doing and why they are doing it?" He is concerned with the "basic forms of thought . . . exemplified in the attributing of motives." These forms he takes to be generated from five terms necessarily employed in any discourse about motives: *act* (what took place), *scene* (the situation in which it occurred), *agent* (the person or kind of person who performed it), *agency* (means or instruments used), and *purpose*. The "grammar" of motives is the study of the "purely internal relationships" among these five terms, "their possibilities of transformation, their range of permutations and combinations." The resulting twenty combinations (some more important than others, of course), or "ratios" as he calls them, provide Burke with the resources for his subsequent analysis of the attribution of motive in philosophy, literature, and politics.

The different philosophic schools, for example, are to be distinguished, he says, "by the fact that each school features a different one of the five terms, in developing a vocabulary designed to allow this one term full expression (as regards its resources and temptations) with the other terms being comparatively slighted or being placed in the perspective of the featured term." Thus in his analysis realism features "act," materialism "scene," idealism "agent," pragmatism "agency," and mysticism "purpose." Burke's treatment shares the obvious weaknesses of any such schematization; but it does at many points provide a fresh and illuminating perspective.

More important than his specific findings is the rationale of his method, which he calls "dramatism" — the consideration of motives in a perspective developed from the analysis of drama. Underlying this choice of perspective is the conviction that the subject of motivation is a "philosophic one, not ultimately to be solved in terms of empirical science." The physical realm can be dealt with in terms of motion, but the social realm requires treatment in terms of action or drama, which cannot be "scientific."

On behalf of this familiar position Burke adds no new arguments, and, indeed, makes little effort to expound the old ones. An appendix dealing with "poetic realism" characterizes it as emphasizing that in the social realm "mere correlation" is not enough. "Human relations must be *substantial,* related by the copulative, the 'is' of 'being' . . . [and] there can be no 'science' of substance." The issue involved here relates more closely to the conception of science than of interpersonal relations. It is easy to grant that these relations cannot be adequately dealt with in terms of Watsonian behaviorism, but there is surely no reason (or at any rate Burke gives none) to suppose that this exhausts the resources of empirical science when directed to a human subject-matter. There is only the bald assertion that "science is freed of philosophic taints only in so far as it confines itself to terms of motion and arrested motion. . . ." The logical problems involved in the thesis of the "unity of science" are completely ignored in favor of a quotation from a political journal interpreting the slogan as at bottom a plea for jobs for foreign scholars. And Burke's insistence that the book itself "is wholly scientist in its aims" is hardly credible when he indulges in journalistic attacks on animal experimentation as "sadistic" and serving no useful scientific purpose.

This essentially literary approach to scientific problems vitiates, in fact, the whole conception of a "grammar" of motives. It is questionable whether a grammar can be fruitfully abstracted from the non-intellectualistic social and psychological determinants of discourse about motives. The present book is the first of a projected triad, of which the other two are to deal with the "symbolic" and "rhetoric" of motives — the concrete expression and operation in conduct of motivational discourse. In many places of this first book, "rhetorical" and "symbolic" analyses in this sense are given (e.g., the relation between certain theological concepts and the institution of money), and they are on the whole more valuable than the purely "grammatical" analyses. For in fact the so-called internal transformations traced by Burke in motivational discourse are not strictly logical, but socio- and psycho-logical. The patterns of connection lie only in the extra-logical purport, and this must be dealt with in concrete empirical not abstract logical terms. Hence Burke's "grammar" is often instead a thesaurus, displaying a range of meanings but providing no key other than an ambiguous overlap for their derivation from one another. Burke does, to be sure, characterize his analysis as "empiricist in that it must approach experimentally the ultimate problem of the relation between symbolic action and practical conduct. . . ." But this experimental approach is presumably relegated to the later books (to which, it must be said, we are justified in looking forward with great interest). For the present, he contents himself with explaining that "the demands of dramatism [are] the demands of human nature itself," and that he is concerned with "the basic forms of thought which, in accordance with the nature of the world as all men necessarily experience it, are exemplified in the attribution of motives."

The heart of the matter is that for Burke "human nature itself" and "the nature of the world as all men necessarily experience it" can apparently be discovered dialectically. From a *sociology* of literature, metaphysics, and juridicial doctrines, Burke has insensibly moved to an *ontology* of the dramatic. Implicit in his version of "the ways of *homo dialecticus*" is also a version of nature and knowledge ("poetic realism") itself dialectically grounded, and justified by the claim that only in this perspective can motive be made intelligible. This claim is not in turn to be refuted dialectically, but will be met more and more adequately as the sciences of personality and interpersonal relations develop – sciences not in Burke's sense of limitation to physical motions, but in the employment of procedures of observation and experiential control which are applicable to man as to the rest of nature.

Burke's book bears the dedication "Ad bellum purificandum." This avowal of motive crystallizes in a phrase the underlying confusion of logic and psychology, language and fact. "What we now most need," he writes, "is to perfect and simplify the ways of admonition, so that men may cease to persecute one another under the promptings of demonic ambition that arise in turn from distortions and misconceptions of purpose. With a few more terms in his vocabulary of motives, for instance, the rabid advocate of racial intolerance could become a mild one; and the mild one would not feel the need to be thus intolerant at all. And so human thought may be directed towards 'the purification of war' . . . " Changes in our vocabulary of motive may indeed be desirable. But it is dialectics with a vengeance to localise our problem in these changes rather than in the personal and social patterns of which the vocabulary of motive is the instrument and expression.

◇◇

Abraham Kaplan was born in Odessa, Russia, in 1918. He came to the United States in 1923 and was naturalized in 1930. He has taught philosophy at New York University, at the University of California at Los Angeles, and, since 1963, at the University of Michigan. He has been a fellow at the Center for Advanced Study in the Behavioral Sciences, at the Center for Advanced Study at Wesleyan, and both a Guggenheim and a Rockefeller fellow. He has written the following books: *Power and Society* (with Harold Laswell), *The New World of Philosophy, American Ethics and Public Policy,* and *The Conduct of Inquiry.*

This has always seemed to me an exemplary and brilliant review. The management of tone, so difficult in a piece such as this one, is nearly faultless; and the points about Burke – pro and con – are all central and forcefully made. The review is also a model of how the informed and disciplined mind – the hope of the intellectual community – can confront a complex and difficult book. Mr. Kaplan's principal objections to Burke begin in paragraph six and continue to the end of the review. They are in part substantival (to the language-centered view of reality and to the extreme emphasis on dialectics) and in part procedural (to the way Burke uses evidence, to the evidence he never uses at all, and to the resources of empirical science he ignores). Nothing Mr. Kaplan says in his last four paragraphs can be ignored in any serious consideration of Burke's endeavors – however one finally decides to accept or reject his work.

◇◇

7 Kenneth Burke's "Grammar of Motives"

BY Francis Fergusson

THE *Grammar of Motives* is the first part of Mr. Burke's work on the arts of language, to be followed by a *Symbolic* and a *Rhetoric.* Mr. Burke demands, as he tells us, "a fully worked-out version of the ways of *homo dialecticus,*" and what he demands he here provides. The peculiar property of the *Grammar* is that it illuminates many kinds of attempt (sociological, philosophic, psychological) to talk about human motives: it operates Socratically to assist many half-formed theories to become self-conscious and articulate. It continually anticipates what the reader feels he was about to say to himself; or, as Mr. Mark Van Doren puts it, "I have thought much about this, but seldom with the benefit of his sharpness." The reader finds it difficult at last to tell

EDITOR'S NOTE: Originally published in 1946. Reprinted from *The Human Image in Dramatic Literature* (Garden City, N.Y.: Doubleday Anchor, 1957), pp. 193–204, copyright © 1957 by Francis Fergusson, by permission of the author.

just where his thought begins and Mr. Burke's ends. The present review is written from a point of view which Mr. Burke would probably not recognize as "grammatical" at all; yet the *Grammar* has done much to clarify it.

Mr. Burke sets forth his general subject and method as follows: "The book is concerned with the forms of thought which, in accordance with the nature of the world as all men necessarily experience it, are exemplified in the attributing of motives. . . . [These forms of thought] are equally present in systematically elaborated metaphysical structures, in legal judgments, in poetry and fiction, in political and scientific works, in news and in bits of gossip offered at random. We shall use five terms as generating principles of our investigation. They are Act, Scene, Agent, Agency and Purpose. . . . Any complete statement about motives will offer *some kind* of answer to these five questions."

This quotation shows how similar Mr. Burke's point of view is to that of Kant in *The Critique of Pure Reason*. His method is somewhat more empirical: he offers dialectical analyses of various writings which "attribute motives"; but he shows thereby the ineluctable claims of his basic forms of thought or "five terms," as well as the failure of the reason ever to reach finality or completeness in its account of motives.

The *Grammar* may also be compared with a more recent and much-neglected work: Professor Scott Buchanan's *Poetry and Mathematics*. This is a study (suggestive rather than complete) of analogies between the abstract forms of poetry and the abstract forms of mathematics: of the ultimate forms of thought which govern our particular inquiries and our building of metaphysical, scientific and poetic structures.

Both Mr. Burke and Professor Buchanan see the efforts of reason as perpetually doomed to partial failure, and the life of the mind as a never-completed process or succession of acts. It is thus tragic, or comic, and the form of drama is in a sense regarded by both as the most fundamental form of all. Mr. Burke's five terms are, as he says, "dramatistic," and he would probably agree with Professor Buchanan that "drama, at its best, undercuts the scientific and religious habit of mind," and "consequently the best metaphysical criticism of mathematics and poetry is to be found in the drama and the novel." But these authors are both concerned with terms, concepts, forms of *thought*; and (perhaps because of this focus of interest) they tend to *identify* drama and dialectic. One of the questions I wish to raise about the *Grammar* is the relations between Mr. Burke's dialectical method, and the more direct imitation of motivated humans which is "drama at its best."

The other question I wish to raise is closely related to the question of drama versus dramatism. Mr. Burke points out that the project of a *grammar* of motives, the analysis of *terms*, is essentially rationalistic. Yet the key term in his analysis is Act, or Action, or, as he sometimes calls it, Act-Substance; and this term is derived from the Realist philosophies of Aristotle and Aquinas. The attempt to submit it to the authority of the Reason as rationalistically conceived seems to me at best too limiting, at worst very confusing. In what sense, or to what extent, can there be a *grammar* of actions?

"ACT-SUBSTANCE" AND GRAMMAR

The first part of the book is called "Ways of Placement," and it is divided into three sections, Container and Thing Contained, Antinomies of Definition, and Scope and Reduction. In Container and Thing Contained Mr. Burke explains and illustrates from several plays his five terms, especially Act and Scene. He shows how, in the attempt to formulate motives, one is led dialectically from Act to Scene to Agent – how any of the five terms may be "reduced" to one or more of the others. Behaviorism for instance reduces Act to Scene: that is, it interprets human motivation as mechanical response to the physical environment, thereby neglecting essential and inescapable perspectives. "Insofar as men cannot themselves create the universe," Mr. Burke explains, "there must remain something essentially enigmatic about the problem of motives," and "this underlying enigma will manifest itself in inevitable ambiguities and inconsistencies among the terms for motives. Accordingly, what we want is *not terms that avoid ambiguity*, but *terms that clearly reveal the strategic spots at which ambiguities necessarily arise*."

The five terms define the rules or conditions of the reason's attempt to define Act-Substance, which, as I remarked, is the key term for motives. In Antinomies of Definition Mr. Burke runs over the characteristic moves which the reason makes in its efforts to fix its slippery antagonist, trying "contextual definition" and "familial definition" and tangling with the paradoxes of the intrinsic and the extrinsic. From this encounter Act-Substance emerges victorious: undefined but indispensable. Mr. Burke has affirmed its centrality, and our need for it, in any attempt to define motives. He has defended it against several of its most trenchant critics, from Locke to Bertrand Russell. He has had many illuminating things to say about act as this concept figures in Aristotle and Aquinas, pointing out its integral connections with Potency, Form, Matter and Substance. But this is a crucial point in the development of the *Grammar*. "Grammar" must be philosophically neutral, without ontological commitments: it must remain at a level of abstraction higher than that of metaphysics. Act-Substance must be considered as a form of thought or limiting concept only, in complete abstraction from particular Act-Substances, or beings. "One might hypothetically grant that the treatment of motives in terms of 'action' and 'substance' is wholly fallacious," Mr. Burke writes; "yet defend it as central to the placement of *statements* about motives." In short, Mr. Burke requires this concept, yet cannot proceed from it to any of the *things* it signifies, lest he move from thought to experience and the dialectical process come to a pause.

In Scope and Reduction Mr. Burke treats Act-Substance conceptually, showing how the concept *in abstracto* is ultimately inconceivable. He starts, as it would appear, Realistically, with a "Representative Anecdote" which is itself not conceptual or "logical" at all – God's Act of Creation, "We are saying that to study the nature of the term, Act, one must select a prototype or paradigm of action. This prototype we find in the conception of a perfect or total act, such as the 'Act of Creation.'" But we soon see that this "act" is convenient for Mr. Burke's purposes not only because we cannot conceive it, but also because we cannot possibly have any direct experience of it. It is the *term* we are investigating, and in this case terms are all we have. We are, from the first, in the realm of the conceptual only. To call the Creation an *anecdote* ("a narrative, usually brief, of . . . an event of curious interest, told without malice and usually with intent to amuse or please") has also the rhetorical effect of reducing Mediaeval Theology to the logically absurd, and delightful, world of Molièresque comedy. By these strategies "grammar" is saved; but what has become of the notion of Action? Dialectically assaulted, so to speak, at the ultimate level of abstraction, it has completely disappeared.

The theologians of the Middle-Ages were careful to point out that we never could conceive the Act of Creation. Such remote understanding of it as they tried to reach was by analogy only. The theological question is perhaps unimportant in this context, but it seems to me that the nature of the concept of Action is a fundamental puzzle in Mr. Burke's scheme. Action is an analogical concept, and in Scope and Reduction Mr. Burke treats it as though it were univocal. In general, he does not use the notion of analogy in this book, for analogy assumes some direct perception of real things and their relationships, while the *Grammar* is strictly confined to the definition and transformation of our *concepts*.

The Thomistic doctrine of analogy (according to Penido and Maritain) distinguishes it both from univocity and from equivocation. Father Penido explains, in his *De L'Analogie*: "D'une manière très générale, toute analogie suppose deux conditions ontologiques: I⁰ une pluralité réelle d'êtres, et donc entre ces êtres une diversité essentielle — le Monisme est l'ennemi-né de l'Analogie; 2⁰ au sein de cette multiplicité, de cette inégalité, une certaine unité." The analogical concept (unlike the univocal concepts of rationalism, which are clear and distinct in themselves) is not completely abstracted, and hence cannot be understood unless the eye of the mind is kept, so to speak, upon the beings to which the concept refers. "Action" cannot be understood or properly handled abstractly. We can develop our knowledge of it, accumulate a lore, through the study of particular actions. Yet in spite of its dangers and difficulties, the notion of analogy seems to me indispensable for the understanding of human motivation in the widest sense. The *Divine Comedy*, for example, represents poetically and dramatically many acts which are analogous. The *Grammar* would not provide the clue to Dante's composition; and rational or grammatical motivation is a moment only in the hierarchy of human acts which Dante the pilgrim traverses. This moment recurs "by analogy" at many levels of the ascent, and is most completely developed in the central cantos of the *Purgatorio*, when the pilgrim encounters the antinomies of definition which interest Mr. Burke: Action-Passion, Freedom-Determinism, Knowledge-Will, and the like. It is transcended when the soul accepts the limitations of reason, and gets a sense of the analogies between its life and the lives of other creatures:

> Every substantial form, which is distinct from matter and is in
> union with it, has a specific virtue contained within itself
> Which is not perceived save in operation, nor is manifested except
> by its effects, just as life in a plant by the green leaves.

I do not wish to imply that Mr. Burke deifies reason. On the contrary, his dialectic is a continual demonstration of the limitations as well as the resources of reason. Moreover, he often explains very clearly the inherent limitations of a *Grammar* of motives, as for instance when he says that his study of action is limited to action as rational, i.e., to conceptual thought. The second part of his book is called "The Philosophical Schools," and here his method is completely adequate to the vast material. "Our problem in this section is to consider seven primary philosophic languages in terms of the pentad. . . . In treating the various schools as languages, we may define their substantial relationship to one another by deriving them from a common terminological ancestor. . . . Any of the terms may be seen in terms of the others. . . . Dramatistically, the different schools are to be distinguished by the fact that each school features a different one of the five terms." On this basis they are classified as follows:

> For the featuring of scene, the corresponding terminology is materialism.
> For the featuring of agent, the corresponding terminology is idealism.
> For the featuring of agency, the corresponding terminology is pragmatism.
> For the featuring of purpose, the corresponding terminology is mysticism.
> For the featuring of act, the corresponding terminology is realism.

It is clear from this scheme that the adherents of each school will object: I have already indicated my reservations about Mr. Burke's treatment of the realistic concept of "act." But there is nothing to prevent one's enjoying Mr. Burke's treatment of other schools; and what he does with materialism, pragmatism, and idealism seems to me superb. These schools still dominate our intellectual life, not only overt philosophizing, but thinking of all kinds. Mr. Burke's dialectical analysis of their terminologies or basic forms of thought is Aristotelian in spirit. His five terms operate rather like Aristotle's four causes, which enable him to account for the analogous schools of his time without completely dismissing any of them. Mr. Burke enables one to read the modern schools at once sympathetically and critically, and to see them in relation to each other.

The key to his success is in his use of Action. This notion, now limited to the action of the soul as rational, returns to dominate the scene. He is enabled to see the various schools in a wider context than any of them recognizes, by considering "the different kinds of *assertion* which the different schools would exemplify in a hypothetical state of purity." It is the assertion, or action, which his dialectical analysis of their languages reveals. "We believe that an explicit approach to language as a dialectical structure admonishes us both what to look for and what to look out for, as regards the ways of symbolic action (and no statement about motives can be anything other than symbolic action)." Mr. Burke does indeed work dialectically, forewarning us and forearming us against this dangerous art; but so effectively that the substantial world behind it is always clearly implied. He masters dialectic so completely that he points beyond it, to the unwritten drama or comedy of contemporary life.

DIALECTIC AND DRAMA

The last part of the *Grammar* is entitled "On Dialectic." Mr. Burke studies this art first, as is his custom, by means of a Representative Anecdote, "The Dialectic of Constitutions." After an interesting explanation of his choice of this "anecdote," he offers luminous analyses of the languages of constitution-makers, jurists who interpret constitutions, and social theorists who write about them in their historic contexts. His eye is on the efforts of "homo dialecticus," but as usual he sees him so clearly that the reader divines that animal as political also, raising the shaky mental artifact of the Res Publica upon the anomalous "ground" of the diverse and changing ways of life of modern populations. Behind the abstract devising of the American Constitution in the age of the Enlightenment, are the older, half-unavowed religious and moral traditions; behind subsequent efforts to interpret it rationally is the environment which science so rapidly transforms. Mr. Burke's remarkable accomplishment is to throw light upon the real scene and the real protagonists, while austerely limiting himself to his dialectical art, the analysis of rationalizing.

But what exactly is the "stance" which he takes up in order to gain these insights and these perspectives? He is a dialectician who cleans up after himself so well, as he goes along, that both dialectic and dialectician have disappeared when all is over. The only thing which I find disquieting about this magic, is that drama disappears too — as though the substantial development of Tragedy, or of Dante's *via purgativa,* were only another instance of the dialectical transformation of *terms.* It is in the last section of the book, "On Dialectic in General," that Mr. Burke comes close to dealing directly with such questions as I am endeavoring to raise. And here he seems to be saying definitely that drama is only a form of dialectic, dramatic development essentially terminological. He illustrates this view, first, by a long and very illuminating analysis of the *Phaedrus,* with special reference to the transformations of the term Love. He then considers more briefly several works of fiction and drama, including *Death in Venice, Remembrance of Things Past,* and *Peer Gynt.* All these works are quests for a way of life, and hence exhibit transformations; but it is my thesis that neither their content nor their principles of composition can be understood purely dialectically. Behind Mr. Burke's view of the dialectic process there lurks ritual drama, much as Medieval or Aristotelian Realism is lurking behind his account of the action of the rational soul.

The Platonic dialogues are certainly the *locus classicus* for the study of the relation between drama and dialectic. The direct, histrionic sense which we gain of Socrates and Phaedrus themselves, prior to our acquaintance with their thinking, would seem to be dramatic rather than dialectical. But we see them at a particular moment only in the rhythm of human development: they are caught in the act of thinking. Apart from their mild flirtation, their actions are rational only; and though their ideas change, they do not. Socrates is at his spiritual summit when the dialogue opens, and as for Phaedrus, is he not like those contemporary sad young men who "understand" Bach and Plato to no avail? Contrast this with the transformation represented in *Oedipus Rex*. Oedipus's ideas are certainly different at the end of the play from what they were at the beginning, but the change in his ideas appears to result, not from thinking, but from suffering and direct experience – a development of the man himself. This transformation is shown in the whole tragic rhythm of "Purpose to Passion to Perception," or, as Mr. Burke calls it in this book, Poiema-Pathema-Mathema. Plato's drama of thought may have an abstract shape like that of tragedy, but he envisages a different Act-Substance or actualization: the soul as conceptualizing and verbalizing, instead of the creature responding as a whole to a "total situation." In short, if the *Phaedrus* is a drama, it is, as such, a more limited genre than tragedy proper, and the reduction of its transformations to the transformation of terms, whether proper or not, misses the essential property of ritual tragedy. Mr. Burke himself, in his *Philosophy of Literary Form*, proposed to take "ritual drama as the hub," or as he would now put it the Representative Anecdote. It is significant that for the purposes of his *Grammar* he should substitute the Enlightened anecdote of the modern Constitution, for the Realist anecdote of Greek Tragedy.

In the analyses of Proust, Mann and Ibsen, Mr. Burke "substitutes" works of art whose content and principles of composition may be called (with qualifications) subjective-idealist. Aschenbach finds in his dream of Venice (a "circle closed on the outside"), at the end of his quest and its transformations, a narcissistic-homosexual Liebestod which is Wagnerian rather than Platonic or Tragic. Proust finds the pseudo-beatitude of remembered feeling. As for Peer, who is more objectively *represented* than the others, he ends, with a sigh of relief, in the near-nonentity of childhood in Solveig's maternal lap. To say, as Mr. Burke does, that at this moment Peer is "translated to the rôle of the Christ-child, whose conception was an Annunciation," seems to me grotesque. The analogy is much closer to "the rôle" of Mrs. Solness's "nine lovely dolls": the fetish of a woman's thwarted and in-turned love. It is in his account of these works that Mr. Burke's method and attitude produces its least satisfactory results. He is looking at the over-all shape and at the purely abstract formal relations within the work; and from this point of view there are similarities between the Tragic Rhythm, the *via purgativa*, and any process of change whatever. But the crucial questions about works of fiction and drama, which are composed of concrete elements, are missed entirely at this level of abstraction. The crucial questions have to do with the *being* which the artist envisages, and the histrionic, rather than rational, action whereby he imitates or represents it.

Mr. Burke explains that the proper material for revealing the *Grammar* of motives is metaphysics, jurisprudence, and, in general, essentially rational or conceptual arts. In the *Symbolic* and *Rhetoric* which are to follow he will consider primarily poetry, fiction and drama. I hope that in those works he will return to what he has called "Poetic Realism" – a way of the mind's life which is not reducible either to dialectic or to the subjective symbolism and "qualitative progressions" of the idealist tradition.

Meanwhile the *Grammar* is our indispensable guide to the ubiquitous operations of "homo dialecticus" in the actual world of applied science, bureaucracy, money, and abstract principles. It is the sign of Mr. Burke's extraordinary vitality that he is always victoriously engaging the public languages of our time; of his artistic integrity that he does so by the strict practise of dialectic. There are many who share his point of view, but few if any who have worked out such a discipline to effectuate it. And, while confining himself to dialectic, he curiously transcends it. He says in his introduction that he was led to write the *Grammar* through work on a theory of comedy. The comic inspiration is never lost. He shows us the rational mind hopelessly but eternally committed to the definition of human motives, much as Molière shows us Argan, in *The School for Wives*, frantically seeking the logical control of Love. The plight of these heroes is rendered laughable to their audiences, not through tragic or purgatorial transcendence – not because we are invited to occupy a substantially different stance – but through "comic transcendence," through the delightful clarity with which the perpetual-motion machine of their intrigues is presented.

◇◇◇

Francis Fergusson was born in Albuquerque, New Mexico, in 1904. He was an associate director of the American Laboratory Theatre from 1926 to 1930; drama critic for *The Bookman* from 1930 to 1932; a lecturer at the New School for Social Research from 1932 to 1934; professor of humanities and drama at Bennington College from 1934 to 1947; and associated with Princeton from 1947 to 1952. Since 1953 he has been professor of comparative literature at Rutgers University. He has written and edited many books, most notably *The Idea of a Theater*, *Dante's Drama of the Mind*, and *The Human Image in Dramatic Literature*.

Francis Fergusson was a colleague of Burke's at Bennington and belongs to the group of colleague-commentators which also includes Stanley Edgar Hyman, Francis Golffing, and Howard Nemerov. All three of Mr. Fergusson's critical books provide one with wonderful examples of how an acute and original mind has been influenced by Burke. As Robert Martin Adams has pointed out (in the comment serving as an epigraph to this volume), Burke's influence is widespread and essentially beneficent but very hard to trace. It is impossible to tell, for example, how many people (teachers and students alike) have gotten their (or some) Burke from Mr. Fergusson's widely used and extraordinary books on the theater and Dante. Perhaps one cannot do much more than acknowledge, as Mr. Fergusson does in his essay-review, some of the ways in which Burke has entered into the life of the mind in his own time.

His review-essay, one of the best pieces we have on Burke, is a brilliant consideration of the relations between language and action, dialectics and drama (in and out of Burke), and of the tendency in Burke toward purely abstract modes of thought, toward the purified high-level dialectics Mr. Ransom addressed himself to. This is a continuously sane, thoughtful, and penetrating consideration of *A Grammar of Motives.*

◇◇

ζ *Salvation through Semantics*

BY Donald A. Stauffer

KENNETH BURKE has written a book [*A Grammar of Motives*]. He has written it in order to investigate why he has written it, or why in general people act. "What is involved, when we say what people are doing and why they are doing it? An answer to that question is the subject of this book."

The answer, to plunge right away into Mr. Burke's own terminology, is "dramatistic." Five key terms serve as "generating principle" for his investigation: Act, Scene, Agent, Agency, Purpose. This "pentad" is merely a novel means of asking what has always been asked: what? when and where? who? how? why? But it is not so easy as you think. Mr. Burke (Agent) writes this book (Act). Now it becomes harder: the Agency is not so much his typewriter as his intelligence with its bias

EDITOR'S NOTE: Reprinted from *The Virginia Quarterly Review,* XXII (1945–46), 454–460, copyright 1946 by *The Virginia Quarterly Review,* by permission of the publisher.

toward scientific method, or more accurately, toward widely illustrated analytic method. Yet Agency here shades into Scene, for Burke writes this book against the background of the times — the cosmopolitan awareness of discontinuities and complexities, the violent dialectic that grows out of skepticism, the air we breathe compounded of pragmatism, materialism, and self-analysis. Agency also shades into Purpose, which in this instance seems directed "toward the purification of war" through encouraging tolerance by speculation. It is written in "the firm belief that a kind of 'Neo-Stoic resignation' to the needs of industrial expansion is in order." In spite of its basic linguistic skepticism, it shares the utopian hopes of the more extreme followers of Korzybski that semanticism will save the world. In its focus on dialectic speculation it hopes to set up a dispassionate and therefore scientific system, "for it deals with a level of motivation which even wholly rival doctrines of motives must share in common."

Burke's task is Atlantean; few would have dared face it. To attempt to explain systematically the motivation of all acts (and Burke rightly considers acts as primarily mental) while remaining fully aware of the slipperiness of language — what a staggering assignment! To limn the naked Psyche through the shifting and shimmering veils of speech! If I may anagrammatize Coleridge's grammar of motives for Iago, Burke bravely exposes himself to the motiveless malignity of motive-hunting. To some extent he wins out. Readers of this book should thereby be able more clearly to analyze the Act involved in my writing the preceding paragraph. They might decide that the Agency back of that paragraph tended toward instinct and synthesis rather than toward analysis; that the Scene back of that paragraph was more simple, naïve, and traditional than Burke's, less "modern"; that its semantic Scene was closer to Benedetto Croce (whom Burke mentions only once) than to Korzybski; and that its Purpose was to raise a sympathetic eyebrow at such a Quixotic attempt to encompass the world, to give a firm base to our thinking about thinking, and, in a Scene where Kant meets Marx and Aristotle shakes hands with Freud, to explain the meaning of meaning and the motivation of motives.

Kenneth Burke's energy and originality are strong enough, his leadership in modern cultural thought sufficiently established, so that further strictures will not be misunderstood. The flaws and the outpouring of thought may be inseparable. The grasp may fail because the reach exceeds it.

The book is too long. Only the most devoted disciples will read every word of its more than five hundred large pages. The reader is fatigued by the total recall of a powerful mind, set down in a style where exceptions, illustrations, by-plays, new ideas, and sudden speculations burgeon from the main stem of the thought. The reader must still do much thinking that Burke should have done for him. A volume half the length of this one would have possessed twice the impact.

The book is too eclectic. How long can we read with both attention and pleasure when, opening at random, we come on a single page that refers to, or quotes, Horace Gregory, Wallace Stevens, "another writer," Descartes, "the idealist scientist Shelley," Leibnitz, an editor, Pascal, and Rabelais? Ambition here surpasses discrimination.

The book does not escape jargon. Why do so many theorists on language handle words so barbarously? Why do so many set up laboriously their special terms and categories known to their circle alone, only to make some observation which could be expressed *en deux mots*? Too many huge philosophical and semantic derricks are busy hoisting carats of sense. Burke has written and thought enough so that he can be understood by those who will take the trouble. But it is sad to consider how large a number who might profit from his ideas will be frightened away by his terminology: "Ubiquity of the Ratios," "Directional Substance," "Act as Locus of Motives," "Monographic Terms of Placement," "Realist Family and Nominalist Aggregate," "Constitutional Tactics of Coleridge's 'Pantisocracy' Project," "The Four Master Tropes."

Conflict is inevitable between Burke's drive toward tremendous scope and his drive toward philosophic form. The drive toward comprehensiveness is at times bewildering not only because of multiplex references but because his terms necessarily overlap, or shift into new meanings as they react on each other. The reader sometimes feels like Alice in Wonderland, eating or drinking concoctions to grow larger or smaller, meeting people running in order to stand still, and watching kings and queens turn into playing-cards. On the other hand, the striving toward system does not always lead to recognizable consistency. I can see, for example, how Act, Scene, Agent, Agency, and Purpose are needed categories to describe an *action* fully. But in a grammar of *motives* only the last seems directly relevant. A more obviously applicable grammar might be found in Aristotle's seven causes for human actions as quoted by Burke: chance, nature, compulsion, habit, reason, anger, and desire. True, as Burke uses his terms, Scene becomes a kind of social conditioning which will help to explain a motive, and Agent and Agency can likewise be stretched. But in proportion as this is done, the terms lose their usefulness, and the explanation becomes a vague mechanism. Furthermore, if an *act* is needed to explain a *motive*, we are caught in an unprofitable circle, since one might assume our interest in a motive comes from the belief that it will explain an act. If the Act may be considered "as Locus of Motives," why is it considered in their *grammar*? Is this not like saying there are eleven parts of speech by naming among them the teacher, the blackboard, and the chalk?

A Grammar of Motives is only the first of a trilogy, the others being a Rhetoric and a Symbolic. Yet the "grammar" is really the Logic, and the "symbolic" is the Aesthetic or the Psychologic. The Rhetoric will be the rhetoric. Taken together, they are designed to protect us, "once we become aware of the ways in which we are the victims of our own and one another's magic." Burke's idiosyncratic magic, more than once, and not always toward clearer seeing, has woven a circle round us thrice. Macrocosmic in the microcosm, sweeping, passionate, he is a Thomas Wolfe in criticism.

These uncharitable remarks ought to be admitted, though perhaps modified, by Burke's defenders, so that one may get on to his positive qualities. The main service this book performs is to compel the reader to pull together his own bits of knowledge into a single view. Relationships, references, integrations, parallels—here is one writer who is not afraid to attempt the creation, intellectually, of the One World to which so many of us subscribe only in pious principle. Burke opens the casements on many seas, as often when he seems wrong-headed as when prophetic. Anyone who can talk briefly on the thousand thinkers, topics, and sub-topics of the twelve-page index may safely consider himself extraordinarily well-read. (He might also note that such erudition seems beyond the acquaintance of the uncomfortable indexer, who coins such words as "dialectitian," "Nichomachean," and "Nietzche.")

The book is useful for anyone with a strenuous brain who wishes to go pioneering. A lesson in analytics may be experienced by tracing back to the central idea of the book an observation picked up on any page. For example, on page 225 in parentheses Horace Gregory is quoted: "What American poetry needs most is the courage to mature." This quotation casts ironical light on the subject of the paragraph: Wallace Stevens' essay on "young poetry." Stevens' conception of the poetic imagination is used to illustrate "the idealist cluster of terms we have been examining in this section." The section deals with "Agent in General" and argues that idealism, among the philosophies, places most emphasis on Agent among Burke's five key-terms. This occurs in the second part, "The Philosophic Schools," which considers "seven primary philosophic languages in terms of the pentad," thereby giving a perspective of millenniums to Burke's central thesis and establishing its relations, applicability, and emphases historically, as Part One had considered analytically the "Ways of Placement" for his terms. Obviously, this volume is your true practical cogitator. Let anyone avoid it who is not endowed with some philosophic, linguistic, and esthetic training coupled with some power of taut attentiveness.

Most important, in such difficult and dense argument, is Burke's admirable habit of illustrating his points concretely and in many fields of reference. This habit makes comprehensible many utterances otherwise Orphic. Indeed, "anecdote" is one of Burke's weighted words (along with dialectic, liberalism, constitution, Edenic, tactics, synecdoche, metonymy, and irony).

Yet except in plowing up old habits of thought and compelling revaluations, I cannot conceive that this grammar will accomplish much, win many converts, or be of lasting value. Four supplementary essays apply Burke's methods of approach to problems of literary theory and criticism. For the results they achieve, they seem unnecessarily difficult in philosophic structure and terminology. His terms are too specialized. Take an example on which the largest third of the book depends: of the seven philosophic schools of nominalism, rationalism, mysticism, realism, pragmatism, idealism, and materialism, each of five of the schools features, Burke maintains, one of his key terms: Scene, Agent, Agency, Purpose, and Act. The other two philosophies are accounted for indirectly. As a game, let the reader construct the five pairings. I have tried it out on five men of some training and ability; their average was sixteen per cent correct – less than two per cent above the score an automaton could make in a mindless world. Surely a critical vocabulary should have more possibilities for communication! The answers will not be given here, for readers should buy this book and solve this detective story in terminology for themselves.

One further *caveat.* The debunkers, the scientific historians, the psychiatrists, and the semanticists have all warned us to distrust our words and our expressed motives. Burke specifically dissociates himself from the debunkers, although the plan for his Rhetoric might indicate that it will consider the "tactics" by which we fool each other, and for his Symbolic the manner in which we fool ourselves. May not the most tragic form of fooling ourselves lie in the belief that we have attained to the happy state of being well undeceived? Skepticism is certainly not the most pleasant form of life, and not even demonstrably the truest.

Obviously, a book of such range cannot be reviewed adequately in less than ten thousand words. I do not consider this a fair review, and I imagine that most reviews will fall short of justice into adulation or vituperation. For although Burke sends forth this book "ad bellum purificandum," his purpose may not be achieved. He does not wish to do away with war, for dialectic implies opposites, and total war in the modern state may be, in his opinion, the act that comes closest to the representative anecdote for those "matters of substance and enactment as they apply to Constitutions." He wishes us rather to understand, to be able to express dispassionately and to describe, war (or dialectic) and its causes. But his dialectic is more Hegelian than Aristotelian, and far from purifying war, it may precipitate it. He may merely rouse more followers and more antagonists. Burke is bold, original, energetic, fecund, ambitious. Ambition may be a grievous fault. The average reader will find that Burke's style — or his ambition, for they are the same thing — does not purify so much as bewilder.

◇◇

DONALD STAUFFER was born in Denver, Colorado, in 1902 and died in 1952. A Rhodes Scholar, he taught English at Princeton most of his professional life. He is the author or editor of *The Art of Biography*, *The Intent of the Critic*, *The Nature of Poetry*, *The Saint and the Hunchback*, *Shakespeare's World of Images*, *The Golden Nightingale* and *Selected Poetry and Prose of S. T. Coleridge*.

This review-essay sometimes seems to be merely — primarily — an exercise in the style of wit, an occasion, at Burke's expense, for phrase making. And, in fact, it is often just this. But I have included it (1) because it is also a kind of compendium, in an appropriate style, of objections to Burke made (then as now) by formal academicians. Anyone who has discussed Burke with his colleagues has heard these things over and over. And (2) because some of the things Mr. Stauffer says of Burke are true in the sense that they accurately render Burke in fragments, which is one characteristic response to him. The review, then, is true to segments of the "profession" and hence true to the title of this collection.

◇◇

7 *The Agon of Will as Idea: A Note on the Terms of Kenneth Burke*

BY Howard Nemerov

> One should be prepared to chart the genesis, flourishing and decay of a family witticism, precisely as though he were concerned with the broadest processes of cultural change, basic patterns of psychology and

EDITOR'S NOTE: Reprinted from *Furioso*, II (Spring 1947), 29–42, copyright 1947 by Howard Nemerov, by permission of the author.

> history thus being conveniently brought within the scope of the laboratory. One should study one's dog for his *Napoleonic* qualities, or observe mosquitoes for signs of wisdom to which we are forever closed. One should discuss sneezing in the terms heretofore reserved for the analysis of a brilliant invention, as if it were a creative act, a vast synthesis uniting in its simple self a multitude of prior factors.
>
> —*Permanence and Change*, pp. 157–158.*

1. *The Ethics of Order.* This is the situation: we live in an age of utter confusion. This statement (and overwhelming authority for making it) may be found even in newspapers. Superstition, far from having been overcome, has shifted its ground and enlarged the scope and importance of its activities: past times concerned themselves with the superstition of the uneducated, we have now the superstition of the educated to remark upon. The ratio of available knowledge to what may be called 'culture' (the assimilated evaluations of a group, the current 'ways of handling the world') is quite preposterous; that this ratio never actively changes from ratio to paradox may simply be due to our redeeming powers of isolation, our 'aptitude' for schizophrenia, whereby we separate 'business' from 'pleasure,' 'belief' from 'life,' 'profession' from 'practice,' an activity that may be praised as 'orderly' or damned as 'disintegrative' as we please from this moment to that.

Let us first admit it is possible not to care; there remains still the surface, with many lovely objects on it. These, though they have no names (and so give us no power) will glitter, shine, be dull, be hard or soft to the touch, make various sounds when struck, smell sweet or sharp or bitter, and be, each one, absolutely unlike any other. We may walk through the museum, not saying a word, until death. But even here — what constitutes the absolutely unlike? Let us not open our mouths to answer, lest we enter at once (and permanently) the vast confusions of order, and find ourselves helplessly dedicated to cataloguing the number of possible steps between 'like' and 'unlike.'

Say that we liked the museum, but were expelled because we were unable to keep quiet. Now we have little enough to do but talk. We repeat, and our children learn, the legends of the museum; generations, who did not see, discuss. Galleries and wings, perhaps apocryphal, are added in the accounts of what the museum *must* have been *like*. That is, no one pretends that this, here, now, is the museum: but it is certain that the stories refer directly and with great accuracy to the museum, because

* [AUTHOR'S NOTE] Thanks are due to the Princeton library for its copy of *Permanence and Change*, which would otherwise have been unavailable; and to the person unknown who went carefully through that volume noting by the word 'split' in the margin the presence of split infinitives. It is to be hoped that this critic will soon review for us the works of Henry James in this light.

the words composing the stories were 'taken from' the objects to be seen there. We develop a facility for discussing likeness, and this we call metaphor. People are born who study only to regain the museum by turning the words back into the things; and this we call metonymy. Others develop, from metaphor and metonymy, a way of saying that we ourselves are like the museum, the models of the museum, we are the microcosm to its macrocosm; and this we call synecdoche. Still others sadly note that whatever the museum was we were expelled from it; they suggest that had this not happened there could be no museum. We are amazed, and call this irony.

Now we wander in the echoing halls; the labels are affixed to all the glass cases, but the cases are empty. People manufacture articles, and put them in the cases. Are they the real thing? How like are they? Shall we ever know? Children are taught of the museum, but cursorily, perfunctorily. A new idea . . . to build the museum, to stop talking and build it. The children stare at the stuff under glass. We stare. We are . . . comforted, outraged, perplexed. Was it really like this? And if so, should I really have enjoyed it? Is it impious, practical, visionary? Is it a new orthodoxy, an old heresy? How shall we know?

In spare time we trade with the words, we push them back and forth, mysterious entities not things but more powerful than things to make us angry or sad, elated, anxious, confused, to make us mighty in battle, weak in peace, pushovers to our enemies and a holy terror to people we have never met. Words, says one, are born in the gut; they are ourselves, they are emanations from the head or the heart or the solar plexus or the genitals. Words are desires and the armies that desire sends forth.

But of course integrity dictates a protest. If words are these things, if words do these things, they also are not and do not. They are, say, ships which float on the sea. The sea is desire, or will, and without it the ships could not float, but the ships are not the sea. Sometimes they form a navy, and cannonade a single point together; more often they are merchant traders — or pirates. With them we trade, we communicate, we compete, we conflict. Our cooperations are sometimes indistinct from our competitions, we achieve mergers of purpose — as when we produce the major cooperation of a war, or compete in helping one another.

And the words do become, finally, a museum, and faithfully (to the faithful) reflect what we have been doing. They reflect the biologically 'permanent' and the historically changing. One may, even, set up one's own exhibit.

If one does, the problem (at this late day) is: what is the relevance of order to truth? In arranging our own exhibit we group the words in patterns, employing as criteria various devices — of cause and effect, if we are scientists, of resemblances if we are rhetoricians of this or that sort: poets, alchemists, politicians [1] — of relation, of the complexion of things. At last, and not unnaturally, the pattern, the form of relation, becomes the instrument, and particular pieces of 'truth' or 'wisdom' are criticized on the grounds of their relevance to the pattern, on how they 'fit in.' But the fundamental motive for formulating the pattern was, it is supposed (and it is generally claimed), a 'truth,' a 'fact,' or an 'axiom' or 'atom' — a something assumed to be both true and not verbally divisible. Thus scientists, given Mendeljeeff's tables of periodicity, were able accurately to predict the character of an undiscovered element, simply from its place in the system. And thus Kierkegaard was able successfully to mock 'the system' for having obscured the faith on which it was built, and which it expected 'systematically' to describe. And further: "The presupposition of the System that faith is given, resolves itself into a delusion which has deceived itself into thinking that it knew what faith was." [2] Thus it is possible for the truth to be heretical, as it flies in the face of the system which is regarded as the established producer of truth; and scientists, it is pleasant to note, tend to regard Galileo as the first martyr to fall to the regime of the "false and lying gods." Historically, the growth and decay metaphor should quite accustom us to distinguishing a kind of periodicity of alternation between 'primitive simplicity' and 'overweening cultural presumption' preceding the inevitable 'fall.' There is, for instance, always a choice to be made, between the Summa Theologica and what Kierkegaard calls The Scandal of Christianity. And under the heading of a homespun pioneer virtue, 'private enterprise' becomes 'the relation of capital to labor' or the enormous public compound of activity in which unions and the N.A.M. are competitive-cooperative elements. Ethically, it would be possible (and even agreeable) to define the truth as 'that for which one rejects order.' But historically it is equally a necessity to erect an order upon what is supposed the truth. The principle of 'coercive order' then might justly be discussed as the principle of 'coercive destruction of order.'

In the title of this paper, I suggest one expression for a theme that seems to me central to Kenneth Burke's writings. He is Shakesperean, I believe, in his delight in what some philosophers deplore: ambiguity, the range of meanings hidden and evident in, it may be, a single word;

[1] But of course we each participate in all activities, and one of these, at a given time, merely preponderates.

[2] Kierkegaard, *Concluding Unscientific Postscript*, p. 18.

and Shakesperean too, in his willingness to let perspectives criticize one another 'dramatically.' *Agon*, therefore, a dramatic debate; *Of Will As Idea*: of will disguised as idea, wearing its *persona* – and so of will, or purpose, expressing itself dramatically and symbolically throughout language, meeting with the expression of other wills, or with 'material recalcitrance.' And as idea symbolizes will in this trope, so, to Burke, by the shorthand of language, motives symbolize situations.[3]

I suppose his basic assumption to be that all motives and all conflicts of motives express themselves in language; and that these may be got out by devices of stylistic naming that continually shift perspective to focus on new or concealed areas; finally, that language as it stands (or, rather, as it moves) offers 'cues' for all possible programs of action in the future. It would be, perhaps, a delusion to announce that this sort of ordering is especially immune to the ethical questions which affect all orderings; and I should not like either to base my affection for it on any notions of its 'inclusiveness,' however attractive such notions may be. It is possible that I am disarmed by our author's close attention to particulars, his pages full of examples, the sense one has that all is grist to his mill; and that, so disarmed, I distinguish in his writings the flowering-point of order, at which the terms produce analytical certainties without producing dictatorial expectations of certainty. Possible, too, that I shall be chilled to find him bringing out a "logically inevitable proposal for unambiguous right action." But it seems a doubtful possibility.

I am aware of what may seem the impertinence of trying to compass into this brief note the vast complexities and ironies of Burke's writing, especially in terms of a monographic treatment. Yet the essential, in all the complexity, is the terminological simplicity at the root; and I take heart somewhat from considering his own statement, in which he compares his work to "an aerial photograph of two launches, proceeding side by side in a tranquil sea. Their wakes crossed and re-crossed each other in almost an infinity of lines. Yet despite the intricateness of this tracery, the picture gave an impression of great simplicity, because one could quickly perceive the generating principle of its design." (*Grammar of Motives*, p. xvi.)

2. *Perspective by Incongruity*. "A method for gauging situations by verbal 'atom cracking.' That is, a word belongs by custom to a certain category – and by rational planning you wrench it loose and metaphorically apply it to a different category." It is "a methodology of the pun. 'Pun' is here itself metaphorically extended. Literally, a pun links by tonal associations words hitherto unlinked. 'Perspective by in-

[3] *Permanence and Change*, p. 44.

congruity' carries on the same kind of enterprise in linking hitherto unlinked words by rational criteria instead of tonal criteria. It is 'impious' as regards our linguistic categories established by custom."

Further: "The metaphorical extension of perspective by incongruity involves casuistic stretching, since it interprets new situations by removing words from their 'constitutional' setting. It is not 'demoralizing,' however, since it is done by the 'transcendence' of a new start. It is not negative smuggling, but positive cards-on-the-table. It is designed to 'remoralize' by accurately naming a situation already demoralized by inaccuracy."[4] This description immediately and with great propriety summons forth examples from Shakespere (*Romeo and Juliet, Antony and Cleopatra*) and prepares our author to insist that[5] "terms are *characters*, that an essay is an *attenuated play*. The essayist's terms serve to organize a set of interrelated emphases, quite as Othello, Iago and Desdemona are interrelated emphases. There are 'hero' and 'villain' terms, with subsidiary terms attributed about these two poles like iron filings in a magnetic field, and tracing somewhat of a 'graded series' between them. Emphases cannot 'contradict' one another, so far as the 'total plot' is concerned, any more than Iago's function in the play can be said to contradict Othello's."

In discussing this method, or methodology, we might take for a motto Yeats' observation that 'the flowers that bloom in the spring may be over, but cannot be said to have been negated.' Divisive, Socratically 'subversive' as Burke may seem, the attitude that thus shifts perspectives is in fact cooperative and charitable: we do not contradict our opponent in discourse, we compound, instead, our statement with his and, humbly protestant, seek to make with him a catholic unity of much observation and humor. Nor do we always make polar shifts in perspective; more often our revisions towards the whole tend 'insidiously' to disintegrate the simple union of opposites and substitute a more complicated, less 'visual' figure. If, for example, we are told that man 'progresses by adjusting to his environment' we should say 'very true' — and proceed at once to point out the equal justice of saying that 'man progresses by refusing to adjust to his environment; instead he adjusts the environment' or that 'man regresses by adjusting to his environment' as were we to 'resign ourselves' to being cold instead of building a fire; and finally, perhaps, that for the hermit or mystic to so resign himself might indeed be, in his direction, progress. We insist, that is, on the hortatory, the 'wilful' elements present even in supposedly informational speech: will masked as idea. We may even analyze the 'symbolic radiations' in

[4] *Attitudes towards History*, pp. 201–204.

[5] Ibid., p. 208 n.

our opponent's thesis and reveal, in very Freudian manner, how his gratuitous definition covers a wish, in one area, to 'adjust' indeed, that is to resign even at the expense of progress, and sit still; in another, defend a society in which, quite evidently, some people are able to adjust the environment while others must adjust to it.

Two factors condition the method; first, the artistic or 'dramatic' conceit that language reflects or embodies conflicts of volition which may be used as 'cooperations' of volition (Shakespere again; esp. the last plays); second and closely related, the strong insistence on the *moral* nature of language. These factors in combination (or they may be reduced to one) reject the scientific ideal of a power-language which shall be free of ambiguities and shall produce its imperatives in terms of information, disguised. Perspective by incongruity, rather, would substitute some such idea of 'measurement' as that suggested by "Measure for Measure"; that is, "Irony, as approached through either drama or dialectic, moves us into the area of 'law' and 'justice' (the 'necessity' or 'inevitability' of the *lex talionis*) that involves matters of form in art (as form affects anticipation and fulfillment) . . ."[6] or:

> The very mercy of the law cries out
> Most audible, even from his proper tongue,
> "An Angelo for Claudio, death for death!"
> Haste still pays haste, and leisure answers leisure,
> Like doth quit like, and Measure still for Measure.
> (*Measure for Measure*, V. i. 410 & ff.)

It is worth noting, in this light, Burke in his early character of 'dismayed novelist.' In a preface to *Towards a Better Life*, he tells of three unsuccessful attempts to write his first chapter (the novel finally issued as a series of epistles, or declamations) in a conventional manner; and he writes:

> Lamentation, rejoicing, beseechment, admonition, sayings, and invective—these seemed to me central matters, while a plot in which they might occur seemed peripheral, little more than a pretext, justifiable not as a "good story," but only insofar as it could bring these six characteristics to the fore. These mark, these six mark, in a heightened manner, the significant features of each day in our secular, yet somewhat biblical, lives—and what I most wanted to do was to lament, rejoice, beseech, admonish, aphorize and inveigh. . . . a different framework seemed imperative. So I reversed the process, emphasizing the essayistic rather than the narrative, the emotional predicaments of my hero rather than the details by which he arrived at them—the ceremonious, formalized, "declamatory."[7]

[6] *Grammar of Motives*, p. 516.
[7] *Towards a Better Life*, pp. viii–ix.

One can imagine some such statement as this serving as an Elizabethan manifesto.[8] Compare Marston's note "To the General Reader" (prefaced to *Sophonisba*): "Know, that I have not labored in this poeme, to tie my selfe to relate any thing as an historian, but to inlarge every thing as a Poet . . ." So Burke continues the passage quoted above by comparing his chapters "to an old-style opera in which the stress is laid upon the arias whereas the transition from one aria to the next is secondary."

Perspective by incongruity commits our author to a program of planned 'paradox' essentially poetic in origin; he produces oxymorons similar to those of the mystics save that his may be explained, or 'socialized': that is, he creates a piety of impiety, a 'transvaluation of all values' which must never be permitted to stop, to freeze or hypostatize any particular set of 'applications' of value as 'true.' If we speak of the cruelty of the Inquisition he will speak also of its sympathetic, piteous character as it tried by every means to 'include' its victims under the divine mercy. Or he might speak of the 'inquisitional' qualities in trade unions which try, in attenuated variants of the same cruel sympathy, to make particular beliefs official prerequisites to the secular mercy of holding a job. But it is essential to note that these shifting perspectives are not merely instruments of 'debunking'; they do not seek, as does, for example, the Freudian vocabulary, simply to expose the 'altruistic' in terms of the 'egotistic' — a shift which, we may note, demands the later revision and socialization of *all* egotistic motives into a kind of Hegelian higher synthesis whereby they become once again 'acceptable' — e.g. to some extent 'altruistic,' but 'in a new way.' Thus, in the confessional of the analyst, we rid ourselves not of sin, but of the sense of sin.

Rather, Burke's terminology seeks to be syncretistic, moved as much as may be by *all* human activity as expressed in language; and as instrument seeks to become a key, a 'dictionary,'[9] a vocabulary of all vocabularies, finally 'a grammar.' Not, in the formal sense, a 'philosophy,' his writings constitute a method for, perhaps, the amateur philosopher, who seeks to 'delimit the practical' and at the same time to 'unlimit the speculative': catalogues and revisions of catalogues, reductions of A to B, speaking of this in terms of that other, continual emphasis upon the point that metaphor is inescapable — analysis of, say, literature in terms of money, of money in terms of physiology — these form the body of the works, together with the insistence that, to describe a situation, one must include both the actor and what is acted upon, the one who sees as well as the thing seen. The 'subject,' then, the central theme,

[8] For we already noted how the "essayistic," for Burke, becomes the "dramatic."
[9] Vol. II of *Attitudes toward History* takes the form of a dictionary.

is 'attitude' which is on the one hand an 'incipient act' and, on the other, present however furtively and equivocally in all description.

Upon this last point, which brings up again the theme of will as idea, perspective by incongruity makes it possible for Burke to write of education under the heading of 'trained incapacity' (Veblen's term)[10] which has "the great advantage of avoiding the contemporary tendency to discuss matters of orientation by reference to 'avoidance' and 'escape.'" In this sense, one may (without being 'evil,' 'irresponsible' or 'wilful blind') become educated to one's own disaster: "One adopts measures in keeping with his past training—and the very soundness of this training may lead him to adopt the wrong measures. People may be unfitted by being fit in an unfit fitness." Examples of this not very recondite metaphor abound; as when, during the war, certain generals were accused of fighting this war as though it were the previous one, of using tanks as they would have used horses, etc.; the very thoroughness of their strategical groundings betrayed them. But of course the incapacities of training must have also a 'good' sense: when Mrs. Drub goes shopping in her car she should be thankful that her training has presumably incapacitated her for driving like a dirt-track racer.

The method of incongruous perspective has produced, in Burke, two major analytical metaphors for human activity: one may be called the dramatic-dialectic-strategic complex, the three terms having in various parts of the work similar functions; and the other is the metaphor of 'grammar.' The two figures cross and combine in interesting fashions: writing a play, for example, may be compared with the conduct of a battle, as one groups forces of volition, selects a 'field,' skirmishes in subplots and joins the major engagement—if one believed that 'nobody wins' in a 'real' war, this might be expected to influence, in this consideration, the denouement. Or, writing a play might be compared simply to writing a play, and one would discuss the characters as grammatical functions of a meaningful statement, thus: "although *all* the characters in a dramatic or dialectic development are necessary qualifiers of the definition, there is usually some one character that enjoys the role of *primus inter pares*. For whereas any of the characters may be viewed in terms of any other, this one character may be taken as the summarizing vessel, or synecdochic representative, of the development as a whole. . . . This 'most representative' character thus has a dual function: one we might call 'adjectival' and the other 'substantial.' The character is 'adjectival,' as embodying one of the qualifications necessary

[10] See *Permanence and Change*, Chapter I, passim.

to the total definition, but is 'substantial' as embodying the conclusion of the development as a whole."[11]

3. *The Agon.* In the work of an author concerned primarily with 'grammar' and 'drama' it hardly needs prophecy to make us expect some effort on his part to catalogue motives by their expressions, to locate attitudes in their formal equivalents. We have already seen one instance of this in Burke; as in the preface to *Towards a Better Life* he proposed that literature, for him, consisted 'opportunistically' of lamentation, rejoicing, beseechment, admonition, sayings and invective. In volume one of *Attitudes toward History* he considers attitudinal emphases under the heading of Poetic Categories: the epic, tragedy, comedy, elegy, satire, burlesque, grotesque, didactic. The passage on comedy begins by quoting, with agreement, Meredith's statement that comedy is the most civilized form of art. The agreement is enlarged upon as follows:[12]

> Like tragedy, comedy warns against the dangers of pride, but its emphasis shifts from *crime* to *stupidity*. . . . The progress of humane enlightenment can go no further than in picturing people not as *vicious* but as *mistaken*. When you add that people are *necessarily* mistaken, that *all* people are exposed to situations in which they must act as fools, that *every* insight contains its own special kind of blindness,* you complete the comic circle, returning again to the lesson of humility that underlies great tragedy. The audience, from its vantage point, sees the operation of errors that the characters of the play cannot see; thus seeing from two angles at once, it is chastened by dramatic irony; it is admonished to remember that when intelligence means *wisdom* (in contrast to the modern tendency to look upon intelligence merely as a *coefficient of power* for heightening our ability to get things, be they good things or bad), it requires fear, resignation, the sense of limits, as an important ingredient.
>
> Comedy requires the maximum of forensic complexity. In the tragic plot the *deus ex machine* is always lurking, to give events a fatalistic turn in accordance with the old "*participation*" pattern whereby men "anthropomorphize" nature, feeling its force as the taking of sides with them or against them. Comedy must develop logical forensic causality to its highest point, calling not upon astronomical marvels to help shape the plot, but completing the process of internal organization whereby each event is deduced "syllogistically" from the premises of the informing situation. Comedy deals with *man in society*, tragedy with the *cosmic man*.

And correspondingly, in the same work, a 'comic' vocabulary of motives is praised as a 'corrective' to propagandistic and didactic strategy. Comedy is 'charitable.' It may be said to transcend both indignation and

[11] *Grammar of Motives*, p. 516.

[12] *Attitudes toward History*, pp. 51–52.

* The ultimate statement of 'trained incapacity.'

nobility, offering to find its terms in humble and even criminal areas of activity; it would try to respond with its criticisms to the totality of human motives—and it might by some, be felt unkind in its rigorous unwillingness to be deceived into faction for however noble a purpose: "The comic analysis of exploitation prompts us to be on the lookout also for those subtler ways in which the private appropriation of the public domain continues. It admonishes us that social exigencies and 'goodwill' are as *real* a vein to be tapped as any oil deposit in Teapot Dome."[13]

But it seems, as Burke's metaphor developed, it forced upon him a shift in emphasis (prepared by the legislation that tragedy and comedy are 'alike' in warning against the dangers of pride) away from 'the comic' not so much to the tragic as to, simply, the drama or the ritual drama "as the Ur-form, the 'hub,' with all other aspects of *human* action treated as spokes radiating from the hub. That is, the social sphere is considered in terms of situations and acts, in contrast with the physical sphere, which is considered in mechanistic terms, idealized as a flat cause-and-effect or stimulus-and-response relationship. Ritual drama is considered as the culminating form, from this point of view, and any other form is to be considered as the 'efficient' overstressing of one or another of the ingredients found in ritual drama."[14] And immediately following we find a discussion of drama and dialectic, of wisdom as the method or way of the production of wisdom (not, I think, to be confused with the humanistic assertion that the means *is* the end): "Plato's dialectic was appropriately written in the mode of ritual drama. It is concerned with the maieutic, or midwifery, of philosophic assertion, the ways in which an idea is developed by the 'cooperative competition' of the 'parliamentary.' Inimical assertions are invited to collaborate in the perfecting of the assertion."[15]

In the latest work, which bears an increasingly theological, scholastic tone, the figure is given a further development in terms of the 'dramatic' (which enables Burke to discuss situations in terms of 'grammar'): "the dialectical (agonistic) approach to knowledge is through the *act* of assertion, whereby one 'suffers' the kind of knowledge that is the reciprocal of his act."[16] That is, if I interpret correctly, situations are potential dramas (capable, with equal potency, I suppose, of comic or tragic emphases). But an assertion (*hubris*) is required to produce the countering elements resident in the situation; and by these the agent's act is turned into his passion, or his suffering, whereby learning is produced as a 'higher state' than that which prompted the assertion; the tragic

[13] Ibid., p. 218.

[14] *Philosophy of Literary Form*, p. 103.

[15] Ibid., p. 107.

[16] *Grammar of Motives*, p. 38.

hero transcends his assertion by including it in a new, 'suffered' vocabulary of motives. Burke refers here to the 'tragic grammar' of the Greek proverb, "*ta pathemata mathemata,*" the suffered is the learned: to which he prefaces a third term, "*poiemata,*" to describe the initial assertion before it is transformed in suffering. And in the relation of the hero to the audience, in which he becomes scapegoat, his impiety being everyone's impiety, his punishment (and therefore his 'learning') being 'charismatically' everyone's punishment and everyone's lesson, a similar figure is exposed: "(1) an original state of merger, in that the iniquities are shared by both the iniquitous and their chosen vessel; (2) a principle of division, in that the elements shared in common are being ritualistically alienated; (3) a new principle of merger, this time in the unification of those whose purified identity is defined in dialectical opposition to the sacrificial offering." [17]

For dealing with the agon which is his figure for human activity, Burke offers a pentad of terms: scene, act, agent, agency, purpose. ". . . any complete statement about motives will offer *some kind of* answers to these five questions: what was done (act), when or where it was done (scene), who did it (agent), how he did it (agency), and why (purpose)." [18] *A Grammar of Motives* constitutes an inquiry into the internal relationships of these five terms, the ratios of each one to the others: these ratios work both ways – one may speak of acts in terms of their scenes, or of scenes in terms of the acts that take place in them. And at the end of the volume we begin to move in upon the Rhetoric of Motives, as we are given four master tropes: metaphor, metonymy, synecdoche and irony: which may be taken as the reduction of all terms of relation, as the pentad seems to have reduced terms for 'placement,' 'stance' and therefore 'substance.'

Perspective by incongruity seems in this latest work to have recognized most fully a figure for the 'incongruous' that might be called perfecting a methodology of the mistake; just as an Inventor of all inventors might, who had recognized early in life the significance of the many stories current about great discoveries made by accident. He would try to operate so as to insure the greatest number of such 'mistakes.' And so to Burke, perhaps, philosophy is produced by peculiarities, faults, inadequacies of vision quite personal to the philosopher, about which vast orders of 'benign myopia' might erect themselves. Burke's method would stress the exploitation of the recondite, peculiarity-conditioned perspective; and the student in his school might be assigned the task of 'creating' a world from the serious consideration

[17] Ibid., p. 406.
[18] Ibid., Introduction, p. xv.

of, say, Samuel Butler's remark, that a hen is merely an egg's way of producing another egg.

◇◇◇

HOWARD NEMEROV was born in New York City in 1920. He taught literature at Bennington College from 1948 to 1966, when he moved to Brandeis University, and has published profusely in many modes since 1947. His publications include seven books of poems, four books of fiction, a collection of critical essays and reviews, an edition of Longfellow's poems, and *Journal of the Fictive Life,* which I hesitate to classify.

Burke was mostly fortunate in his colleagues at Bennington who chose to write about his work. Nemerov is one of these and, with Stanley Edgar Hyman, one of two who dedicated books to Burke. This essay, long hidden away in an issue of the short-lived *Furioso,* is a good example of how a colleague and friend can receive one's work in a professional way. Mr. Nemerov's essay should be seen against those of Marius Bewley and Donald Stauffer, both of whom reject Burke in some fundamental way and from within what I take to be closed or exclusive systems. Mr. Nemerov's essay is a good illustration of how an approach, a fundamental attitude partially represented by Burke's work, can be accepted without making a total commitment to Burke's system. It is in this way that Burke has often and profitably been used. Mr. Nemerov's essay also illustrates a rare attempt to come at or work into Burke through his metaphors and terminological clusters — which is a way of using Burke on Burke. Nemerov's essay once seemed to me very obscure; now in this present larger context it does not seem obscure at all but a good example of indirect lighting.

◇◇◇

7 *Toward a Grammar of Educational Motives*

BY Kenneth D. Benne

I

KENNETH BURKE's latest book, *A Grammar of Motives,*[1] might properly be described in many ways. For a description of any human action,

EDITOR'S NOTE: Reprinted from *The Educational Forum,* XI (1947), 233–239, copyright 1947 by Kappa Delta Pi, An Honor Society in Education, by permission of Kappa Delta Pi.

[1] Pages cited for quotations in the present essay refer to this book.

of which the writing of a book is an instance, involves the imputation of a "motive" to the actor (author). And no contemporary critic is more aware than Burke of the inherent complexity in the motivations of any author and, correlatively, of the variety of verbal structures, which may be constructed and construed, in the location, charting and evaluation of his motivations. Burke, like the authors he interprets, was no doubt moved to and in his writing by a complex variety of motivations. And an ironic (dialectical) approach to the task of interpreting this book — an approach which Burke seems to favor as a general method of interpretation — would recognize the partiality of each interpretation and move through the opposition generated by this partiality to a more adequate "merger" of motives, ironically aware that each "merger" has within it the seeds of its own destruction.

The present interpretation is frankly an effort to "use" Burke for the author's purposes. It is, therefore important before "using" the author to give some hint of the variety of ways in which his book may be read (and "used"). The book is a rich one for many readers. Readers of this essay should not mistakenly believe that they have exhausted the meaning of the book in this reviewer's favored interpretation of it. Nor should they fail to read the book because they may be repelled by the "central" motivation here imputed to the author.

In the first place, Burke's book may be read as a reaction against "scientistic" attempts to "reduce" the explanation of human conduct to the influence of various conditions and causes — physical, chemical, biological or generally environmental. These attempts Burke sees as, in effect, reducing action to movement determined by selected determinants from the "scene" of human action. Burke recognizes the principle of Occam's razor, "entities should not be multiplied beyond necessity," as "the keystone of scientific terminologies" (p. 81). He evolves a counter principle, "entities should not be *reduced* beyond necessity" (p. 324). The materialist who tells you that "everything is nothing but chemistry" and then proceeds to exhort human chemicals to do this or to do that has fallen into his own reductionist trap. One does not sanely seek to influence the behavior of chemicals by exhortation. His "representative anecdote" out of which he has attempted to chart human motivation has been too narrow. In Burke's words, "We, on the contrary, hold that for the analysis of human relations 'an idiom should be developed by forming itself about some anecdote *summational* in character, some anecdote *wherein human relations grandly converge*' " (p. 324). Though Burke is at that point justifying the choice of the Constitution as a representative anecdote, his more general representative anecdote is that of the play, the human drama. He, therefore, finds an irreducible minimum of terms necessary to the adequate discussion of human motivation from his analysis of dramatic action. These five terms (the pentad) "point" in any human action to an actor, a scene, some agency (means), a purpose, as well as the over-all action in which the other terms are united. Only a "dramatistic" interpretation in which the "independent" claims of each term as well as the complex interrelation of the various terms are recognized is adequate to the explanation of human conduct, the charting and evaluation of human motives. The "scientistic" error consists in reducing its explanations of human conduct to one or another set of "scenic" influences or conditionings.

Another approach to Burke's motivation might seek ironically to explain it in terms of a scenic influence – a trend. Semantic studies have thrived in our society because the "meaning" of our symbols has become a problem to us. Forces of diversification, whether of division of labor, class conflict, or political struggle, have eroded our common meanings, have led to a struggle over our common words of good by various partisan groups, each of which tries to give its own congenial meaning to "freedom," "democracy," "right" or "welfare" and to proselytize "the public" in favor of this or that meaning. "Semantics" has grown up in this context and has tried to establish rules and canons for the "proper" interpretation of meaning. Whatever the various motivations of the semanticists, one may see Burke as a semanticist, seeking to give an interpretation of meaning and its transformation in a "dramatistic" as opposed to the "scientistic" perspective which has prevailed in most semantic studies.

Still another approach to Burke's work would read his title as "A *Grammar* of Motives" instead of "A Grammar of *Motives*." It is a grammar in the sense that it treats the generic terms (the pentad) which are variously used by various philosophers and "philosophists" in the discussion of motives. In focusing on the language of *any* discussion of motives, it is a "grammatical" approach to discourse about motives. On this view, various philosophies become "casuistries" seeking only to apply these grammatical principles in and to "the case" of some actual and given cultural situation. Burke attempts an ingenious "casuistry" of his own, taking major philosophic systems as "cases" and developing their distinctive characters in terms of their variant stress upon one or another of the terms of his pentad in their charting of motives. Thus "materialism" is interpreted as an emphasis upon "scene"; "idealism" as emphasis upon "agent"; "pragmatism" as an emphasis upon "agency"; "mysticism" as emphasis upon "purpose"; and "realism" (of which the Aristotelian and Thomist varieties are the prototypes) as an emphasis upon the whole "action" (or act-potency) in which all the other terms find a "proper" place.[2] This approach highlights "novel" and important meanings in each of the philosophies discussed.

In this same approach to Burke's work the meaning of his book as *grammar* may be seen over against two other works which he is now writing in the general area of linguistic study. The trilogy will constitute an extended comic treatment of human relations, of the "foibles and antics" of "the Human Barnyard." This trilogy will eventually include: a "Rhetoric" concerned with "the basic stratagems which people employ, in endless variations, and consciously or unconsciously, for the outwitting or cajoling of one another"; and a "Symbolic," "concerned with modes of expression and appeal in the fine arts, and with purely psychological or psychoanalytic matters" (p. XVIII).

II

For full appreciation of Burke's book, readers should keep all of these "motives" in mind as they read. The motivation of Burke which I am interested in using directly for my purposes is suggested by his sub-title, "Ad bellum purificandum." All men of good will are interested today in purifying war. It is not, as Burke points out, in discussing the choice of a "representative anecdote" in terms of which to develop and illustrate his dramatistic (dialectic, comic) method, that we wish to represent war as substantially typical of the nature of man. Our "anecdote shaped about war would be designed not so much for stating what mankind *substantially is* as for emphatically pointing out what mankind is in *danger of becoming*" (p. 330). Our sense of war and its threatening imminence may serve an "admonitory" instead of a "constitutive" function in our thinking and talking about human motivation.

I think it is not unfair to one important aspect of Burke's motivation

[2] Burke seems to me least successful, in his interpretations of various philosophies in terms of his pentad, in characterizing the philosophy of John Dewey. Burke rightly points to the relation between the terms of his pentad and Aristotle's four causes; identifying material cause with scene, efficient cause with agent, final cause with purpose and formal cause with act. He then goes on to note that Aristotle "instead of dealing with agency as a special kind of cause (say, an "instrumental cause"), introduces it incidentally to his discussion of "final cause" (p. 228). Now if, in discussing Dewey, he had noted that, in an age of technology in which agencies had multiplied far beyond the means incidentally involved in achieving the endings implicit in "natural" processes (final causes) and that Dewey had recognized the "independent" power of agencies as a factor in human action and the dependence of purposes for their achievement upon the proper use of agencies, Burke would have had little difficulty in showing that Dewey is perhaps better-balanced "dramatist" than either Aristotle or Thomas. At least Dewey's dramatism may be better adapted to the interpretation of human action in a technological age.

to state that his is a humanitarian concern to see how far conflict (war) may be translated practically into linguistic struggle and how such verbal struggle may be made to eventuate in a common enactment short of physical combat. The rational dealing with conflict can be virtually identified with this using of symbolic resources, centrally linguistic, to enact the struggle and to reach a constitutive truce in imagination without joining the opposing forces involved in the conflict in overt physical struggle. Our *rational* resources in mediating, adjusting, synthesizing conflict, whether between competing economic, racial or national groups are ultimately *linguistic* resources. Our waning faith in intelligence and reason "reduces" largely to a loss of faith in talking (thinking) conflicts through together to some common construction. The parliamentary process is talking, verbal combat, whether in the teachers' meeting, the local planning board session, the U.S. Congress or the UN Security Council. Are we justified in hoping that this talking will be able to mediate conflict, to construct common solutions, to reach imaginative mergers of motivation which will direct common action with respect to common enterprises? We have no right in answering this question to forget that the alternative is overt struggle (war) with the forceful imposition of an official "solution" and the suppression of "counter-solutions," preceding, accompanying and following the struggle. Nor have we the right to answer the question negatively until we have explored and revealed the full range and power of linguistic resources which may be employed in the processes of verbal combat and imaginative merger.

Burke's essay toward purifying war may properly be read as such an exploration of linguistic resources. In his concluding statement, "A Neo-Liberal Ideal" (pp. 441–43), he remarks, "our primary purpose has been to express towards language an *attitude* embodied in a *method*." Again, "the Grammar should assist to this end (the purification of war) through encouraging tolerance by speculation." "For better or worse, men are set to complete the development of technology, a development that will require such a vast bureaucracy (in both political and commercial administration) as the world has never before encountered." "To what extent can we confront the global situation with an attitude neither local or imperialistic?" "And as regards our particular project, it would seek delight in meditating upon some of the many ingenuities of speech. Linguistic skepticism, in being quizzical, supplies the surest ground for the discernment and appreciation of linguistic resources."

In this light, Burke's rejection of the "scientistic" attitude toward problems of human conduct and his advocacy of a "dramatistic" attitude, previously noted, take on a new meaning. His attitude toward language is embodied in a method. A "scientistic" approach to language and its uses in human deliberation, based also on a method, is unduly confining; it hides resources of language which may be useful in purification of war. By reducing the "rational" interest in human conduct to a concern with the facts concerning invariant "scenic" factors which condition human action, the "scientistic" approach leaves unrecognized and undisciplined linguistic (mental) processes which do help to shape our motivations and form our actions. The "dramatistic" approach on the other hand puts the search for invariant scenic factors, conditions and means of action (inquiry) in its place within the total act of talking and thinking and illumines those linguistic processes addressed to the clarification of *purpose*, to the expression and objectification of the character of the *agent* and the fusion of these into an acceptable common *action*.

One might wish that, in the interest of better serving this moral motivation, Burke had been more explicit in the formulation of his method. To be methodological one must be normative, preferential. One must venture his prophecy as to how certain denoted processes in thinking and talking can best (or better) be carried on. He can not be content to describe the processes and their interrelations. He must formulate criteria as to the adequate conduct and interrelating of these processes in defensible acts of judgment. Burke, at one point, with disarming self-irony, states that he has produced a "scientistic" account of "dramatism"; he has described the process rather than prescribed norms for its proper discipline. Nevertheless, one can find implicit norms in his description of his method. First of all, his method is called "dialectic." "By dialectics in the most general sense we mean the employment of the possibilities of linguistic transformation." This broad definition obviously includes much of scientific method as well as linguistic transformations more at home in other aspects of "dramatism," as Burke attempts to show (see, e.g., p. 411 and p. 429). Yet, in general, Burke tends to equate dialectic with the method of "dramatism." "A human role . . . may be summed up in certain slogans, or formulae, or epigrams or 'ideas' that characterize the agent's situation or strategy. The role involves properties both intrinsic to the agent and developed with relation to the scene and to other agents . . . where the ideas are in action we have drama; where the agents are in ideation we have dialectic." "Irony generally equated with dialectic arises when one tries, by the interaction of terms upon one another, to produce a development which uses all the terms. Hence, from the standpoint of this total form (this 'perspective of perspectives'), none of the participating 'sub-perspectives' can be treated as either precisely right or precisely wrong They are all voices, or personalities, or positions, integrally affecting one another. When the dialectic is properly formed, they are the number of characters needed to produce the total development" (pp. 511–12).

Now it is clear that a methodology of judgment which squares with Burke's dramatism must be inclusive of the characters of the judgers, the ideas and perspectives with which they are identified, the cherished formulae and epigrams and slogans held to be intrinsic to the agents by the agents. It can not dismiss these as prejudices or hopelessly subjective attitudes as scientific method tends to do and seek to exclude them from the arena of responsible methodological concern. These must be projected interestedly into the arena of conflict which the process of judgment is attempting deliberately to resolve in the interest of restoring or instituting common action. It must, moreover, cultivate a discipline which leads all agents concerned to recognize the partiality of each favored perspective in the conflict, to seek a "perspective of perspectives" in which the values of each partial perspective are in some measure preserved, and to relate the "common" perspective thus achieved, accepted "substantially" by all participants, to the conditions and means through which it may function effectively in the drama of human conduct.

III

It may not be a rude shock at this point to state that the methodology required by Burke's grammar is a methodology of practical judgment – a methodology addressed to the formulation of common decisions, common policies, common principles of conduct in situations broken apart by conflict between rival perspectives, slogans and formulae of action. It may be noted that a book attempting to chart the broad outlines of a methodology in this area of judgment has been published, *The Discipline of Practical Judgment in a Democratic Society.*[3] It seems to the author of this essay that the methodology outlined in this latter book is in keeping with Burke's dramatism. This methodology recognized the operation of three moods of judging in an act of practical judgment – the optative, the imperative and the indicative. In the first mood, the emphasis is on the projection of a desired state of affairs. Out of this projection of competing "purposes" an interplay (dialectic) leads to the clarification of a common *purpose.* In the imperative mood, the necessities and urgencies of the situation, the "musts" represented by the characters of the "agents" dialectically interplay in the formula-

[3] 28th Yearbook, National Society of College Teachers of Education, University of Chicago Press, 1943, Authors: Raup, Benne, Smith and Axtelle.

tion of a common sense of necessity. In the indicative mood, means and conditions of action (agency and scene) are inquired into; the scientific mood here plays its indispensable role in judgment. It is a condition of adequacy that all moods of judging interplay and come to terms with each other if the total judgmental development (act) is to issue in a common persuasion and action. It seems evident that the methodology here outlined attempts to do justice to the meaning of Burke's pentad of dramatistic terms in the act of judgment, though without the employment of his terminology.

The full range of our linguistic resources must be utilized if the construction of common persuasions is to achieve an effective purification of war (conflict). No narrow ideal of accuracy must confine it to the indicative mood of judging. Our language must be responsibly learned with attention to its use in the resolution of conflict, in the purification of war.

This points directly to the educational task involved. The test of intellectual development has long been seen and should today be seen to be "symbolic adequacy." "Symbolic adequacy" can only be developed, mastery of our linguistic resources (which are ultimately our rational resources) can be achieved if acquired in the dramatic perspective of the significant conflicts of our time. We must learn our language as we use it, not alone in acquiring and communicating accurate statements, of fact, though this is immensely important if developed in proper context, but even more crucially in acquiring habits and attitudes of verbal combat, through which a common participant persuasion grows out of conflict to restore common direction and purpose in our conjoint action.

If educators wish to dedicate their efforts ad bellum purificandum, it seems to me that they might well study and ponder the meaning of the two books discussed in this essay — two books which seem fruitfully to supplement each other. Rationality must be reinterpreted today, if it is not to fall prey to a widespread loss of faith in reason as a way of resolving human conflict. And the loss of faith in reason leads wittingly or unwittingly to the adoption of "war" as the "constitutive anecdote" in interpreting human relations. The two books reviewed here make at least a beginning in this task of the reinterpretation of rationality and of contemporary symbolic adequacy. The central motivation of educators must be found in the cultivation of a reinterpreted and inclusive rationality. There is no more pressing task for educators today than this clarification of their central motivation.

I will close this essay with a halfhearted apology to Mr. Burke. It may seem a disservice to him to seek to enlist his *comic* approach to language, in which the actualities of language are related ironically to a free play among unactualized possibilities of language in the tragic cause of judgment as preparation for action. For it is in action that the agent evokes the passion of consequences and learns through the suffering of these. And this is the dialectic of tragedy. Yet the use of the resources of comedy as preparation for the tragedy of action seems to offer the best opportunity to men to learn through their suffering of consequences, if for no other reason than that it seems today to offer the best chance for human beings to survive the consequences of their action. After all, it was at the close of one of our supreme dramatic embodiments of dialectic, Plato's *Symposium* that the master dialectician, Socrates, reached the conclusion that comedy and tragedy were eventually one and the same, a conclusion which unfortunately all of the other revelling dialecticians were too drunk to understand. So perhaps I don't owe Mr. Burke an apology after all.

◇◇

KENNETH BENNE was born in Morrowville, Kansas, in 1908. He has had a varied career, which includes teaching physical and biological sciences in high school, a great many visiting professorships, and numerous administrative jobs in education and human relation councils. Since 1953, he has been Berenson Professor of Education at Boston University. He has written and edited many books since 1943, most of them dealing with the practical and theoretical problems of education in a democratic society.

At some point after *A Grammar of Motives*, Burke's work came to the attention of various influential people in professional education. Kenneth Benne is one of these and his article-review gives one some sense of how Burke was received by these people. Later — in 1955 — Burke was asked to contribute to a volume called *Modern Philosophies and Education*, published by the National Society for the Study of Education, and for that occasion he wrote one of the most complete synopses of his own system available anywhere. How great Burke's influence has been in this field is very hard to say: one hears of Burkeians teaching in the high schools, of Burkeian texts (for example, *Rhetoric and Writing*, 1965, by W. Ross Winterowd) — but no accurate statement about the extent of Burke's influence can be made.

Professor Benne's article marks a kind of turning point in the reception of Burke because it so clearly indicates that he can no longer be regarded as merely a literary critic. Burke spoke to many different disciplines; as a result, one characteristic of his reception has been the variety of uses made of his ideas and methods.

After describing the three Burkes (the motives man, the "grammarian," and the humanist-idealist purifier of war) that he finds in the

Grammar, Mr. Benne takes Burke's idealistic social purpose seriously and considers the relevance of his methodology to that purpose and to education in a democratic society. Mr. Benne is one of the few I know of to take Burke seriously on his own terms and to assess him in relation to the terrible urgencies of our own time. Mr. Benne's own position and his evaluation of Burke can be seen most clearly in the third part of his article. Mr. Benne has surely wonderfully understood the humanist-idealist Burke and owes him no apology at all.

◇◇

7 *Kenneth Burke and the Criticism of Symbolic Action*

BY Stanley Edgar Hyman

[Sections 1 and 2 and part of Section 3 have been omitted here.]

BURKE'S effect on contemporary criticism is, at least in America, fully as pervasive as that of Richards. In addition to R. P. Blackmur (whose relationship to him has been noted above) the men whose work is most closely related to his in this country are Malcolm Cowley, Francis Fergusson, and Harry Slochower. Cowley has not so far published a volume of criticism, but his forthcoming book on American literature, from fragments that have appeared in periodicals, seems to be a major piece of work. In magazine pieces over the past two decades he has utilized many of Burke's concepts, terms, and insights, turning them to his own uses, popularizing them somewhat, and applying them to writers untapped by Burke. His introductory studies of Hemingway and Faulkner for the Viking Portable Library, in particular, are first-rate studies in symbolic action, and almost the first serious examination either writer has received.

Like Cowley, Francis Fergusson is now engaged in writing his first book of criticism after many years of periodical writing. Unlike Cowley, he has been affected by Burke only recently, and then more or less on his own terms. The title "drama critic" has been badly debased until

EDITOR'S NOTE: Originally published in 1948. Reprinted from the revised edition of *The Armed Vision: A Study in the Methods of Modern Literary Criticism* (New York: Knopf Vintage Books, 1955), pp. 354–358, 359–366, 376–381, copyright 1947, 1948, 1955 by Alfred A. Knopf, by permission of the publisher.

it now means a semi-literate reviewer of plays for a newspaper, but for two decades Fergusson has been a drama critic in the proper sense, a critic of both dramatic literature and performance, and probably the best in America. His criticism has three principal strands. The first is a sharp æsthetic morality, a concept of art as disinterested, digested, measured, disciplined, and final, derived in part from the modern classicist, neo-humanist, and traditionalist critics — Maritain, Benda, Fernandez, Babbitt, Eliot — and in part from the classics and writers like Dante, with which concept he has relentlessly punctured the windy and immature, from Eugene O'Neill to Selden Rodman. (This has not kept him, incidentally, although he is generally scornful of the moderns as "spirit-maiming" or "demoralizing," from valuing highly some very unclassical writers like D. H. Lawrence.) At the same time he has applied the comparative technical standard of the rounded and complete Greek ritual drama, as interpreted by Aristotle and best exemplified by Sophocles' *Œdipus the King,* to the study of the serious modern drama, from Ibsen and Chekhov to Lorca and Cocteau.

The third strand is his use of dramatism and the pattern of the Sophoclean ritual drama as a way of reading nondramatic literature; which he stated in *Hound & Horn,* as early as July–September 1933, in a review of Boleslavsky's *Acting: the First Six Lessons,* when he proposed the method as a way of reading lyric poetry; and illustrated in the *Hound & Horn* James number the next year with a reading of "The Drama in *The Golden Bowl.*" It is this third strand which has principally served to unite Fergusson and Burke, and as Burke's method developed into "dramatism" and the "pentad," Fergusson took advantage of many of its conceptual formulations, particularly its "*poiema-pathema-mathema*" formulation, which he converted into "purpose-passion-perception," the three essential stages of the ritual drama, and made the cornerstone of his own work. Fergusson's review of Burke's *Grammar,* the ablest one to appear, announced in terms of high praise their wide area of agreement as well as their limited areas of disagreement (chiefly his objection to Burke's "rationalistic" slighting of medieval realism and "abstractionist" retreat from the earlier concrete "ritual drama as hub").

The man whose books make the most explicit use of Burke is Harry Slochower. Slochower's combination of Marx, Freud, and Gestalt is similar to Burke's socio-psychological integration, although Slochower draws much more heavily on Marxism and on a German philosophic tradition. Some time before the publication of his first book in English, *Three Ways of Modern Man* in 1937 (I have not read his first book, *Richard Dehmel,* written in German), Slochower discovered Burke's terminology, and found it, as did Cowley, Fergusson, and others, an efficient and consistent critical frame for expressing his own ideas. The book appeared with an appreciative Foreword by Burke, and displays a number of Burkian terms, concepts, insights, direct quotes, and even Burke's characteristic quotation marks. At the same time its central emphasis, on novels as expressing formal philosophic "ideologies" (Slochower's three bins are Feudal Socialism, Bourgeois Liberalism, and Socialist Humanism, but in the course of the work they get phrased as Monist, Dualist, Dialectic, even Father, Son, Holy Ghost), is very unlike Burke's personalist "symbolic action" emphasis. Slochower's second book, *Thomas Mann's Joseph Story* (1938) is more like Burke's own work, the lengthy analysis of a single complex work of art in a number of levels, translated into a number of vocabularies, but again with Slochower's distinctive collective-ideology emphasis. His third and most ambitious book, *No Voice is Wholly Lost . . .* (1945) is an attempt to survey almost the whole mass of contemporary literature instead of exploring a few texts in detail.

One of the oddest and most amusing applications Burke has had was by Yvor Winters, surely the last convert anyone would have predicted. Winters's first book, *Primitivism and Decadence*, appeared in 1937 with the introductory Note, in his characteristic churlish tone:

> I have wherever possible employed the terminology of Kenneth Burke, and have acknowledged it, in order to avoid the unnecessary multiplication of terms; my own analysis of rhetorical devices began, however, about as early as his own, and was dropped for a time while his continued, because it did not seem especially fruitful. My own analysis was resumed when I discovered the key to the ethical significance of rhetoric and the possibility of creating an æsthetic on such an analysis; my quarrel with Mr. Burke, which will appear fully in this volume, is precisely that he has failed to do this.

Winters went on in the book to make desultory use of a number of Burke's terms from *Counter-Statement*, particularly one that seems to have charmed him: "qualitative progression," for a type of poetic structure; but the attempt to use a set of terms while quarreling violently with the ideas for which they are shorthand formulas was obviously foredoomed, and after the first book Winters gave it up and created an ethically weighted vocabulary of his own.

In crediting Burke while quarreling with him, Winters was being more generous than a number of other critics, Edmund Wilson and Philip Rahv among them, who have repeatedly drawn on Burke's concepts and insights without credit. (One of the Rahv cases is particularly amusing, in that it appeared in a review in the December 1937 issue of

Partisan Review, on the page following the only formal notice the magazine has ever taken of Burke's work, Sidney Hook's venomous attack.) Several young poets and critics in England, among them Francis Scarfe and Christopher Hill, are either familiar with Burke's work or have independently worked out many of his symbolic-action concepts. In America almost every critic has been influenced by him. Ransom, Tate, Brooks, and Warren have all drawn on Burke somewhat and praised him highly, while generally disagreeing with him; and Burke has in turn drawn on their insights, praised them, and, in the case of Ransom in particular, engaged in elaborate and endless literary polemic with him. Warren's study of "The Ancient Mariner" uses a good deal of Burke's work on the poem as well as the general structure of his method, while quarreling strongly with his "personal" emphasis on Coleridge's drug-addiction and marital troubles. (Burke's review of the book, in *Poetry*, April 1947, replies in kind, praising Warren's reading as having "exceptional merit" and then going on to oppose its central contention with Burke's own detailed reading, even more explicitly "personal" than before in its emphasis, and sweeping over the whole body of Coleridge's other writings for correlations.)

Randall Jarrell has written at least one first-rate Burkian analysis, "Changes of Attitude and Rhetoric in Auden's Poetry," in *The Southern Review*, Autumn 1941, announcing in the opening paragraph: "I have borrowed several terms from an extremely good book – Kenneth Burke's *Attitudes toward History* – and I should like to make acknowledgements for them," and then going on to apply the terms brilliantly in exploring Auden's symbolic and rhetorical action. Delmore Schwartz and a number of other young poets have utilized Burke in their criticism, and Muriel Rukeyser has used his concepts in her poetry, acknowledging material from *Attitudes* in *A Turning Wind*. Herbert Muller relies even more heavily on Burke's concepts and insights in his *Modern Fiction* and *Science and Criticism* than he does on those of Richards, and identifies Burke as "perhaps the most acute critic in America today." Some idea of the spread of Burke's influence in America can be had from noting the wide variety of critics who have at one time or another acknowledged some degree of indebtedness to him. In addition to the ones discussed above, the list would include: Philip Wheelwright, Newton Arvin, Arthur Mizener, David Daiches, John L. Sweeney, Joseph Warren Beach, Ralph Ellison, Morton Dauwen Zabel, and innumerable others.

[A paragraph has been omitted here. Section 4 begins with the next paragraph.]

The reason reviewers and editors have had such trouble fastening on Burke's field is that he has no field, unless it be Burkology. In recent years it has become fashionable to say that he is not actually a literary critic, but a semanticist, social psychologist, or philosopher. A much more accurate statement would be that he is not *only* a literary critic, but a literary critic *plus* those things and others. In his article "The Tactics of Motivation" Burke suggests the general problem of synthesis on a higher level than any single field could handle. He writes:

> But if one offered a synthesis of the fields covered by the various disciplines, which of the disciplines could possibly be competent to evaluate it? Where each specialty gets its worth precisely by moving towards diversity, how could any specialty possibly deal with a project that offered a *unification* among the diversities? Or, otherwise put: if one were to write on the *interrelatedness* among ten specialties, one would be discussing something that lay outside the jurisdiction of them all.

The lifelong aim of Burke's criticism has been precisely this synthesis, the unification of every discipline and body of knowledge that could throw light on literature into one consistent critical frame. Opposing every pious or conventional view that would exclude one critical tool or another as "improper," Burke has insisted: "The main ideal of criticism, as I conceive it, is to use all that is there to use." In another place, defending the use of biographical information on a poet, he writes: "we should use whatever knowledge is available," and explains:

> I grant that such speculations interfere with the symmetry of criticism as a game. (Criticism as a game is best to watch, I guess, when one confines himself to the single unit, and reports on its movements like a radio commentator broadcasting the blow-by-blow description of a prizefight.) But linguistic analysis has opened up new possibilities in the correlating of producer and product—and these concerns have such important bearing upon matters of culture and conduct in general that no sheer conventions or ideals of criticism should be allowed to interfere with their development.

What modern criticism seems to resemble most is pre-Baconian science, as described by Taine in his *History of English Literature:*

> So long as it [science] limited its effort to the satisfying an idle curiosity, opening out speculative vistas, establishing a sort of opera in speculative minds, it could launch out any moment into metaphysical abstractions and distinctions: it was enough for it to skim over experience, it soon quitted it, and came all at once upon great words, quiddities, the principle of individuation, final causes. Half proofs sufficed science; at bottom it did not care to establish a truth, but to get an opinion. . . .

Like Bacon, Burke has set out to do no less than to integrate all man's knowledge into one workable critical frame. In the course of that, he has set out to turn psychology on literature, has discovered that he would first have to synthesize one consistent psychology from the warring schools, has done it; then discovered the same need to integrate sociologies; then work both together as a social psychology; then add linguistics and semantics to the formula; still later add philosophies and theologies; finally, to turn the whole tremendous mass on a poem. His aim, as stated in the conclusion to *Permanence and Change,* has been "to show an integral relationship existing among a great variety of cultural manifestations which are often considered in isolation." The showiest part of Burke's work has been in the vitally necessary task of integrating Marx and Freud, or what he calls "economics" (I would prefer "sociology") and psychology. Thus he offers "a theory of the psychological processes that go with the economic ones," or proposes to unite Marx and Freud on the basic concept of "the symbols of authority," or treats Machiavelli, Hobbes, Voltaire, Bentham, Marx, and Veblen as "great formulators of economic psychoanalysis."

Burke has drawn heavily on Marxism in all his books while at the same time criticizing its mechanical simplifications in *Counter-Statement,* noting its covert "god-function" in *Attitudes,* and so forth; and all his analyses tend to have a sociological dimension, although they are rarely only that (one or two of the shorter articles in *The Philosophy of Literary Form* are exceptions). At the same time Marx himself is one of Burke's heroes, a great "dramatist" or "impresario" in "Twelve Propositions"; the great poet and rhetorician who made *The Communist Manifesto* "a masterpiece" in *A Grammar of Motives.* Burke has also drawn enthusiastically on a wide variety of other social views, from the historical tragic opera of Spengler to the philosophic social psychology of George Herbert Mead.

Similarly, his psychology is integrative and mediative, what Richards would call "centrist" and which Burke has distinguished as "a *phenomenological* science of psychology, rather than the tenuousness of the purely introspective or the impoverishment of the purely behavioristic." Its chief source is psychoanalysis, from which the basic concept of symbolic action is derived, although a psychoanalysis socialized somewhat along the lines of the revisionist Freudians, since "the coordinates of individual psychology invariably place a wrong emphasis upon symbolic acts." Burke has used a tremendous amount of Freudian theory and terminology in his work since *Counter-Statement,* which canonized as permanent parts of a critical vocabulary concepts like "compensation," "transference," and "adjustment." He has written two lengthy evaluations of psychoanalysis, one in *Permanence and Change* under "Secular Conversions," and one, "Freud – and the Analysis of Poetry," in *The Philosophy of Literary Form*, reprinted from *The American Journal of Sociology*. The first attempts to "place" psychoanalytic therapy as a type of "conversion downward by misnomer," the second is a specifically literary application, attempting to suggest "how far the literary critic should go along with Freud and what extra-Freudian material he would have to add." Burke concludes that dream mechanisms like "condensation" and "displacement" are the basic mechanisms of poetry, key terms in poetic analysis, and that psychoanalysis is an approach of great value and subtlety to "poem as dream." Beyond that, "I should say that, for the explicit purposes of literary criticism, we should require more emphasis than the Freudian structure gives (1) to the proportional strategy as against the essentializing one, (2) to matriarchal symbolizations as against the Freudian patriarchal bias, (3) to poem as prayer and chart, as against simply the poem as dream." Burke's discussions of psychoanalysis deal not only with the theories of Freud, but also with those of the chief dissenters: Jung, Adler, McDougall, Rivers, Stekel, and Rank (he quarrels particularly with the last two, preferring Freud's free-association dream readings before Stekel's arbitrary "dream book" symbology was imposed on it, and rejecting Rank's oversimple application of the concept of the "death wish" to art in favor of a fuller "death-and-rebirth" concept). At the same time he sees Freud as he sees Marx, a titanic figure, a great tragic poet who "deserves the eternal respect of mankind because of the profound imaginativeness and methodical skill" by which he brought us face to face with the chthonic and the "cloacal" underlying apparently transcendent concerns.

Next to psychoanalysis Burke's greatest psychological indebtedness has been to the gestaltists, although he tends to see their work as a more usable extension of the experimentation of behaviorists like Watson and Pavlov rather than as a sharp break with the behavioral tradition; and it is in keeping with this that he seems to be more familiar with the laboratory work of men like Köhler and Koffka than with the theoretical work of Wertheimer. Some of Burke's most effective exercises in psychological integration have been translating back and forth among behavioral, Gestalt, and Freudian vocabularies to establish their essential agreement at key points. As much as it can be identified, Burke's own psychology seems to be a Gestalt framework with extensive Freudian additions. At the same time he has drawn on almost every other psychology, and has made particular use of Jaensch's *Eidetic Imagery*, Kretschmer's *Physique and Character*, and the laboratory work of Sherrington with animals and Piaget with children. From the frequency with which he has quoted it, Piaget's study *Language and Thought of the Child* seems to be particularly important to him (this conjecture is borne out in his review in *The New Republic* of Mrs. Colum's *From These Roots,* where he reproaches her specifically — with ignoring Gestalt, Bentham and his successors, Piaget, and critics like Richards and Empson — a distinguished assortment).

Burke has been much more critical of the theoreticians of language, although here too he has found it possible to integrate a number of disparate schools. The theory he has accepted most uncritically is the gesture-origin theory of speech of Sir Richard Paget, which he transforms into a gesture-essence theory.* Burke first used it in *Attitudes toward History,* exploring some significant consonant-sounds in writings, including his own, with the reservation that "most of our vocabulary has come from the accretions of *social* layers that carry us far from biological mimetics." Under attack by Margaret Schlauch and other philologists for holding a theory that is essentially that of the Platonic archetypes and in any case doesn't seem to fit the evidence, Burke defended Paget's theory in "The Philosophy of Literary Form" as not philology but "poetics," philology being the field studying "*the ways in which, if Paget's theory were 100 per cent correct, such linguistic mimesis as he is discussing would become obscured by historical accretions.*" This is ingenious, and it may very well be true, but unfortunately Burke has himself discredited precisely this sort of escape-clause argument in *Counter-Statement:*

> Let us further note the "heads I win, tails you lose" mechanism which the psychoanalysts have at their disposal. Having defined the nature of a man's psychosis, they can fit any act into the scheme. For if the act follows the same pattern as the psychosis, they can explain it as consistent — but if it does not follow this pattern, they can account for it as "sublimated" or "compensatory." With such *vaticinium post eventum* (such explanation by epicycles) at their

* This translation of theories about "origin" into theories about "essence" has become one of the major tactics in Burke's recent work. In "Ideology and Myth" in *Accent,* Summer 1947, he points out that the primitive, having no way to express concepts of "substance," "essence," or logical priority in general, expresses them in terms of temporal priority, as myths of "origin." For a number of years, apparently, Burke has been treating aspects of nineteenth-century evolutionary thinking like Paget's theory of the origins of speech in gesture, Freud's theory of the origin of the Œdipus complex in the slaying of the primal father, the Cambridge theory of the ritual origin of drama, as higher types of this primitive myth-making, and translating them back into statements about the gesture-*nature* of speech, the ritual-*nature* of drama, etc. The process is discussed at some length under "The Temporizing of Essence" in the *Grammar,* pp. 330–40.

command, there is no reason why they should ever be at a loss for explanations in keeping with their tenets.

Modern semantics has had short shrift from Burke. His long essay "Semantic and Poetic Meaning" in *The Philosophy of Literary Form* is an eloquent exploration of the barrenness of the semantic ideal of a "neutral" vocabulary. His own ideal, like theirs, is the "purification of war," but he would achieve it, not through a wild-goose chase after "terms that avoid ambiguity," but by seeking "terms that clearly reveal the strategic spots at which ambiguities necessarily arise." Where the semantic ideal would "eliminate," Burke would "rechannelize," and the most eloquent sentence in *A Grammar of Motives* (which was written all through the war years) is the statement: "And so human thought may be directed towards 'the purification of war,' not perhaps in the hope that war can be eliminated from any organism that, like man, has the motives of combat in his very essence, but in the sense that war can be refined to the point where it would be much more peaceful than the conditions we would now call peace." Nevertheless, while quarreling somewhat with Korzybski and his followers (for nominalism, a "reductive" frame, falling into their own "two-valued orientation" pit, and so on) and Carnap and Morris (for their barren positivist ideal), Burke manages to use a number of concepts and insights from both semantic schools; as distinguished from Ogden and Richards, whom he uses pretty much without attack, and such popularizers as Thurman Arnold and Stuart Chase, whom he attacks without using (although he has credited Arnold with one "serviceable" insight, the distinction between "political government" and "business government").

Into his integration of sociologies, psychologies, linguistics, semantics, and some physical and biological science, Burke has recently added philosophies and theologies. Characteristically, his imagery in *A Grammar of Motives* is of "bargaining with" the philosophers, as where he writes: "It is an important spot to haggle over, however, if you are going to haggle at all. For once you let this point go by unquestioned, you give Kant some important advantages." Burke must have lost his shirt in the deal, because his integrative frame now draws heavily on Aquinas, Augustine, and great numbers of the saints; philosophers from Plato and Aristotle to Nietzsche, Bergson, and Santayana; and he himself has a philosophy or metaphysic, of "substance," which is chiefly defined in terms of the positivism it opposes. Burke even has a curious kind of theology, not of "gods" but of "god-terms," since "gods" are only "names for motives or combinations of motives" common to a group, and every man has the right to worship God "in his own metaphor."

Burke's gods are metaphors, terms, or even words (it is amusing and typical that his reference to "the good book" should be to the dictionary). In "The Tactics of Motivation," he speaks of animals transcending the animal dimension at times "just as complex dialectical operations, developing imagery to conceive beyond imagery, may enable men slightly to transcend the human dimension." In an older theology this would have been to the third realm, the angelic or the divine; it is characteristic of Burke to make it to the "dialectic" or "poetic." (For the record, it might be noted that Burke's angels, in an early story in *The White Oxen,* spend their time in heaven singing their own compositions.)

[The rest of Section 4 has been omitted here. Section 5 begins with the next paragraph.]

Finally, a brief look at Burke's own situation, strategies, attitudes, motives, symbolic actions, purposes, is in order. One factor of great importance is his non-critical writing, of which he has been moderately prolific. He has published two works of fiction, *The White Oxen,* a collection of short stories, in 1924, and *Towards a Better Life,* a novel written as "a Series of Epistles, or Declamations," in 1932. Both works are subtle, ambiguous, fairly obscure, stylized, and highly eloquent: the former progressing from fairly realistic stories to stories bewilderingly symbolic and rhetorical, as a kind of "counter-statement" at a time "when rhetoric is so universally despised"; the latter a gesture of return "to more formalized modes of writing," "from the impromptu to the studied," its concern with plot "peripheral," its central concern with what Burke calls the Six Pivotals: "lamentation, rejoicing, beseechment, admonition, sayings, invective." Both books have been little read or recognized, although they have clearly influenced such writers as Robert M. Coates and Nathanael West, have been praised by William Carlos Williams and attacked as "duller than Thackeray" by Yvor Winters, and *Towards a Better Life* at least seems to me one of the important works of fiction in our time. In relation to his criticism, the only ground for discussing them here, they echo many of the ideas, demonstrate many of the theories in practice, function as the same imaginative "placing" of human motives from a different angle; and while they were written chiefly as rhetorical action, they have given his later criticism endless material for identifying symbolic action.

Wilde, I believe, somewhere remarks that he got his education in public, as a reviewer, and Burke has used his reviewing in a similar fashion. As a comparison of the articles in *The Philosophy of Literary Form* with the reviews printed as an Appendix reveals, the subject of this year's review becomes the subject of next year's references, and by going far afield from imaginative literature in his reviews, he has consistently broadened the horizons of his work. At the same time Burke gets critical ideas directly from problems that arise out of his reviewing ("It was in the attempt to review two books of this sort that we first found ourselves confronting what we consider the typical properties of constitutions"); and in some cases he even writes his reviews in whole or part into his later text. Burke has also written music criticism, including a stint as music critic for *The Nation,* and occasional art criticism, so that his work, particularly *Counter-Statement,* is larded with authoritative musical and plastic references and analogies (although it must be admitted that his art references, unlike his music references, tend to be to rather literary, rarely abstract or modern, works). Burke has also done a great deal of translating from the German, including some of Mann's short stories, and works by Spengler, Schnitzler, von Hoffmannsthal, Emil Ludwig, and others, which then too became grist for his critical mill. Finally, he has published a number of poems, most of them free in form, rhetorical, and emphasizing irony and social protest, which have never been collected in book form.

Burke's social ideas, as expressed most directly in his poetry and in a more complex fashion in his criticism, form a complicated and ambiguous pattern. The chief element is an outspoken dislike for technology and our machine civilization, with its cults of "efficiency," "the higher standard of living," and so on; with a remarkable consistency all of his works from the earliest to the latest have constituted a "counter-statement" to the technological ideal, opposing it with "negativism," "opposition," "interference"; in short: "the æsthetic would seek to discourage the most stimulating values of the practical, would seek — by wit, by fancy, by anathema, by versatility — to throw into confusion the code which underlies commercial enterprise, industrial competition, the 'heroism' of economic warfare; would seek to endanger the basic props of industry." This is from the "Program" in *Counter-Statement,* Burke's early manifesto for æstheticism, but the same themes continue in the Conclusion to *Permanence and Change,* formalized as a poetic communism; and in the section on "Good Life" in *Attitudes toward History,* stated more positively in terms of ideals of active participation and ecological balance. In *The Philosophy of Literary Form* they became more bitter, with references to "our despicable economic structure" making us do "despicable things"; and more pessimistic, with Burke seeing "a dismal political season" in store for us, the only hope temporarily "a campaign base for personal integrity, a kind of beneath-which-not," which is actually Eliot's last-ditch ideal, to "keep something alive." By *A Grammar of Motives*, the social view becomes at once less bitter and less pessimistic. Burke is still antagonistic to our cult of the "gadget," "the higher standard of living," * the "fantastic hardships" that men undergo to have technological "conveniences," but the industrial system and the money motive are now "poignant" rather than "despicable," and he finds an ironic hope: "At a time when the liars, the stupid, and the greedy seem too greatly in control of a society's policies, philosophies of materialistic reduction may bring us much solace in reminding us that *the very nature of the materials* out of which a civilization is constructed, or in which it is grounded, will not permit such *perfection* of lies, stupidity, and greed to prevail as some men might cause to prevail if they could have their way." His conclusion is the proposal of "a kind of 'Neo-Stoic resignation,'" since "For better or worse, men are set to complete the development of technology."

There are two strains in this attitude, which after a time separated. One is an objection to machinery, technology, industrialization per se, in any society, with Burke opposing to them a "maximum of physicality," less button-pressing, less mobility and more action, biological adaptation and "metabiology," and a larger ecological efficiency opposed to the limited "efficiency" of technology. This is the most "reactionary" (in the pure sense of the word) strain in Burke, an agrarian, backward-looking ideal that he shares with Thoreau, the Jeffersonians and Populists, and less savory groups, and which has led Henry Bamford Parkes to write, with a certain accuracy: "he would like to have lived in Confucian China." At its most extreme this is even a dislike of science itself, and there is some truth in a reviewer's charge that Burke, like the old ladies of the anti-vivisection societies, tends to see laboratory scientists as "sadistic rat-torturers." At the other extreme he is prepared to find some good in technology, even defending it against the archæologist Alfred Kidder in his article "Character of Our Culture," finding such real, if negative values as its lessening the ravages of crop failure, pestilence, and other natural disasters. Somewhere in the middle he himself lives ("His life itself is a design," William Carlos Williams wrote in *The Dial*), combining the simple, immobile, and agrarian life with the technology necessary to get him, by car, train, and subway, to the New York Public Library.

The other strain in Burke's social attitude is his objection, not to industrialization per se, but to the specific features of the capitalistic

* By 1947, in an article on "The American Way" in the December *Touchstone*, Burke was describing the whole of American culture as derived from the generalizing principle of "the higher standard of living," used in a non-pejorative sense, with American philosophic and æsthetic concepts either expressions of it or reactions to it.

system. In *Permanence and Change* he embraces Communism (largely of an out-of-the-world variety), proposing a dialectical materialism altered into a "dialectical biologism," and a "poetic" and "stylistic" life achieved through and beyond the Communist society. He argues that Communism is "the only coherent and organized movement making for the subjection of the technological genius to human ends," and that it polarizes such valuable c-words (or "Kenneth-words") as co-operation, communication, communion, collectivism, and communicant. In *Attitudes toward History* he finds collectivism inevitable as the next stage in his curve of history, but presents his collectivist communism with "comic correctives," and the section on the "Good Life" made it clear that his social ideal is actually much more Confucian (if not more confused). Although he still refers approvingly to such orthodox Communist equipment as "dialectical materialism," his later works have veered away from calling his agrarian and decentralized Jeffersonian social ideal "Communism." Fordism is apparently to his mind still Fordism, whether of the American or the Soviet variety.

Burke's ideas on poetry and criticism are inextricably tied up with his ideas on life (he defines art, for example, as "biological adaptation," thus the "good life") and are frequently on a high enough level of abstraction to be both at once. On criticism his keynote is the topic sentence of *Permanence and Change:* "All living things are critics," with the example of the trout, becoming a critic after his jaw is ripped, learning "a nicer discrimination between food and bait." His critic, like Matthew Arnold's, is, in the last analysis, a critic of life; and his job: "to present as many counter-influences as possible," "to integrate technical criticism with social criticism," "to look a gift horse in the mouth." Where the "poet" hypnotizes, it is "the function of criticism to supply the sharp sound that awakens us"; and "whatever poetry may be, criticism had best be comic."

This view is not, however, contemptuous of poetry. The theme that "poetry" (whether as a written lyric, a world-view, or a way of life) is very close to the central value of our existence runs through all of Burke's writing; it is "equipment for living," it "comforts," "protects," and "arms" us. At the same time he insists on the importance of the poetic sensibility, what Blackmur calls "the symbolic imagination," as the ultimate feature of criticism, writing:

> The objection arises when philosophers of science are loath to grant that this very capacity of science demands a compensatory counterpart, variously named "intuition," "imagination," "vision," "revelation," etc. For though one could scientifically break a work of art into many ingredients, and by test arrive at some extremely subtle and perfectly just discriminations about these ingre-

dients, it is when confronting the *synthesis* of the ingredients that the scientific method becomes inadequate.

The other essential ingredient in Burke's scheme is the element in irony, humor, "the comic." He defines humor as the "humanization" that "enables us to accept our dilemmas"; irony as the "humility" that comes from "a sense of fundamental kinship with the enemy"; the comic as a "charitable" attitude containing the paradox of acceptance-rejection, give and take. Essentially all these are aspects of the same thing: an attitude of scrupulosity, reservation, "getting off before the end of the line," counterstating, corrective discounting, "rolling with the punch." Burke's good life would not only be good; it would be comic, ironic, perhaps even funny. In any case it would certainly be undignified. Burke writes in an early essay:

> Dignity? Yes, there seems to be a thirst for personal dignity. There is a trace of the hysterical, the devious, in this need of dignity. Dignity belongs to the conquered; one leaves the room with dignity when he has been routed; the victor can romp. Dignity is a subjective adjustment. It is objectively unpliant; it is unbiological, a dignified man could not run from a lion. One meets facts objectively without dignity. One sacrifices his authority, first asking what mean task the outside thing demands of him. Dignity is Ptolemaic, indignity is Copernican. The development of man in Europe, some one has said, has been a loss of personal dignity in proportion to his mastery of nature.

[The closing pages of the essay have been omitted here.]

◇◇◇

STANLEY EDGAR HYMAN was born in New York City in 1919. He has been on the faculty of Bennington College since 1952. He has been a staff writer for *The New Yorker* since 1940 and was literary critic for *The New Leader* from 1961 to 1965. A prolific writer, he is the author of *The Armed Vision, Poetry and Criticism, The Tangled Bank, Nathanael West, The Promised End,* and *Flannery O'Connor*; and the editor of *The Critical Performance, Kenneth Burke's Perspectives by Incongruity,* and *Kenneth Burke's Terms for Order.*

Mr. Hyman was another of Burke's colleagues at Bennington and is the last to be represented in this collection. Like Howard Nemerov, he also dedicated a book (*The Promised End*) to Burke. The significance of his long chapter on Burke in *The Armed Vision* can hardly be overestimated. It was the first and for many years the only major attempt to systematize Burke's literary theory and critical practice, to see his work whole, and to see Burke in relation to the other major critics of his time. This book, which was widely read in both its hardbound and paperback editions, made Burke available in a new way and must be regarded as some kind of landmark in his reception as a literary critic.

Bernard I. Duffey

It seemed to me likely that most readers of this volume would be familiar with Mr. Hyman's readily available book (in the Vintage edition) and I have therefore made what is essentially a symbolic selection from it. I have tried to use Mr. Hyman to cover points other writers do not discuss and to take advantage of his wide reading. The three selections cover, respectively, people influenced by Burke, influences on Burke, and, finally, Burke's range of endeavors and the relation of his literary to his other ideas.

◇◇

ꙁ *Reality as Language: Kenneth Burke's Theory of Poetry*

BY Bernard I. Duffey

BURKE's central concepts for the interpretation of poetry as "equipment for living" – prayer, chart, and dream – offered clearly to mediate between the naturalistic and anti-naturalistic arguments summarized in "The New Failure of Nerve" controversy and between the hostile criticisms of Ransom and Richards, but the fuller implications of his stand were not made adequately clear until the appearance of his latest book, *The Grammar of Motives.* Though this volume was only the first of a series of three, its importance was considerable. By its means Burke moved to a more direct examination of the debate over naturalism than he had yet made and, by implication at least, moved also toward a relation of poetry to the hostile forces involved. Ransom had claimed for poetry a special cognitive power; Richards attempted to hold it in touch with science. Burke was to mediate by positing it as an operative force, by shifting the grounds of discussion from the ontological to the pragmatic.

As the scientist, or more properly the scientistic philosopher, was by his own deepest instincts doing a just thing in asking the myth-maker to conform to his standards, so the myth-maker could not yield without in turn violating his own craft and his own vision of truth. This was the matter at stake. But if all the bad will between the controversialists had been good will, it would have made little difference. Croce's divi-

EDITOR'S NOTE: Reprinted from *Western Review*, XII (Spring 1948), 132–145, copyright 1948 by *Western Review*, by permission of the author and publisher.

sion between intuition and intellect was not just a matter of convenience. It reflected a real and ubiquitous distinction. While one might know he ought to have all the facts before acting, and might honor such an ideal, he must also confess that he could seldom collect all the facts: that his action would be determined by speculation and hypothesis. The question seemed inseparably bound up with man's ultimate knowledgeability.

For these reasons, Burke's proposals were of climactic importance. He himself advocated the use of the word "dialectic" as synonymous with "dramatistic" in describing his own position and thus suggested the part which his thought could play in solving the dilemma. In Hegelian terms, the naturalistic view might be taken as the thesis, and the anti-naturalistic as the antithesis of the proposition for which dramatism, Burke's scheme, formed the synthesis. As prescribed by Hegel's pattern, Burke's thought was not merely a yoking of opposites in an agreement to disagree, but rather made the effort toward genuine transcendence in which the synthesis posited a new and unifying view of both thesis and antithesis. In this way, naturalism and anti-naturalism could be made to complement each other by indicating in some detail the virtues and limitations of each. They would be seen as incomplete views of the same things rather than as mutually exclusive formulas.

Burke might have run badly afoul of his own purpose at this point by reviving the verbal quibble of which Ransom and Wheelright had made so much – insisting that is upon a designation of the anti-naturalistic disciplines as means toward "knowledge." But this would have added only confusion. There seemed no very conclusive reason why science and rational thought could not be considered the guardians of verifiable and discursive "truth," while the non-scientific disciplines explored a contingent and unpredictable "reality." One was as necessary and as honorable as the other, neither was complete without the other, but neither was complete without translation into human terms of placed and motivated action – and this was the poetic function. Verification was the essence of knowledge as vision was that of insight. But the poem utilized both these: it grounded them and individualized them in terms of a personal symbolic act. Poetry was knowledge, but it was knowledge raised (or lowered) to the point of personal need. It was neither an ontological search nor a scientific search, but a personal discovery and a personal accommodation to reality and truth.

As the first volume of three, *The Grammar of Motives* proposed to examine the basic modes in which speculation itself necessarily moved; to provide, that is, an analysis of philosophy by which one could relate various kinds of thought to each other, or move a step further to see them all as parts of a vast though incomplete whole. In such an endeavor, the grammar would be complemented by a subsequent rhetoric and symbolic. These would, respectively, deal with the problems of communication on the one hand, and with the "modes of expression and appeal in the fine arts . . . with purely psychological or psychoanalytic matters" on the other. In this pattern, the full form toward which Burke's thought had been working since *Counter-Statement,* there was clearly implicit the same threefold division which we have noted in the earlier books. The *Grammar,* that is, was a study in chart – an effort to deal more completely with the problem of truth and reality which the poetic considerations had at first raised. Equally, the *Rhetoric* and *Symbolic* implied a further consideration of prayer and dream. Burke, at least, was taking himself quite literally. As he had suggested this anatomy for the poetic act, an act of understanding, so he was to utilize it for his own thought. The proof of this pudding was to be in the cooking as well as the eating.

Perhaps the fundamental idea in the *Grammar* was that of the act of reduction, the act by which experience was limited and shaped into coherence, together with the problems arising from an over or imperfect reduction. It was in behalf of a more perfect reduction that Burke offered his scheme – the pentad of terms with which he proposed to re-align certain of the great problems of philosophy – act, scene, agent, agency, purpose. He defended it, however, not as the means toward greater "reality" in the ontological sense, but as a means toward a fuller comprehension of human acts. His effort, thus, was not primarily against science as such, but against over-zealous efforts to extend the scientific method to questions where its limited "truth" criterion in practice too often yielded drastic distortions. Like James' radical empiricism, Burke's dramatism made a bid to include extra-naturalistic phenomena within the limits of reality by the simple reason of their mental and motivational existence: "one could, if he wished, maintain that all theology, metaphysics, philosophy, criticism, poetry, drama, fiction, political exhortation, historical interpretation, and personal statements about the lovable and the hateful – one could if he wanted to be as drastically thorough as some of our positivists now seem to want to be – maintain that every bit of this is nonsense. Yet these words of nonsense would themselves be real words, involving real tactics, having real demonstrable relationships, and demonstrably affecting relationships. And as such, a study of their opportunities, necessities, and embarrassments would be central to the study of human motives." This was a recommendation neither for mere semantics nor for the adoption of a simple idea of "as if." It was a bid to shift the real ground of human actions and beliefs from the laboratory to the stage, and to shift poetry from the lists of philosophical dispute to the greater variety of the human scene.

By the dramatistic approach, one might consider a learned, scientific essay not with concern as to whether its contents were "true," though that would be the proper interest of the scientist as such, but rather with an eye to the situation which the paper represented and its implication for the hearer. In this sense, the paper would have a value like that of the dramatic monologue. As Burke had pointed out in his first book, one might substitute for Antony's "Brutus" monologue in *Julius Caesar* "a very competently developed thesis on human conduct, with statistics, intelligence tests, definitions . . . the finest thing ever written." It would then, perhaps, be far "truer" a discussion of motives than is Antony's. The cost of such truth, however, would be a complete alteration, or, more strictly, a cessation of the drama in which the new speech was enclosed, a deadening limitation of effective reality. But if one could thus demonstrate the inadequacy of a purely scientific criterion as applied to a dramatic speech, could one not also demonstrate the limitations of the same criterion as applied to a scientific speech? If such a proposal seemed eccentric or mystogogic, it was only necessary to consider that our scientist was, in fact, a part of a scene which influenced his words; that as an agent he had certain inherent aptitudes and limitations which affected his act of communication (as perhaps the presence or absence of scrupulosity in his temperament); that also what he could say, or even think, depended on the agencies, like language, mathematics, or laboratory equipment, which were available for his use; and that finally, whether it was predetermined or not, his act was in fact shaped by a more or less coherent or complex purpose. Thus one could see that from the new point of view, the speech of the scientist was as dramatic in essence as the speech of Mark Antony, though presumably it differed in being governed by the "psychology of information" rather than the "psychology of form." This difference, however, affected neither discourse as a symbolic act except in its communicability: it was an aspect of prayer rather than chart. If important elements of understanding were lost by regarding Antony's speech with regard only for its truth, only for its scientific quality, in the same way important elements of understanding would be lost in so regarding the scientist's speech. In either case, the understanding was not only of the man, but also of what he had to say. Burke, that is, was not interested in merely adding environmentalism to a scientific concept of truth where, in a Pickwickian sense, one would supplement act on the one hand with scene and actor on the other. The effort here, rather, was to replace such scientific environmentalism with an organic re-fusion of act and scene so that one without the other would be to that extent less coherent in itself.

The fullest and most acceptable act of reduction, in other words, would be that one which took the fullest possible cognizance of the whole pentad and culminated in a concept of act. As the sociologists tended to reduce their problems to a concentration upon scene, so equally their plans suffered from a lack of attention to the other elements. In the same way, psychology might generally be described as an over-reduction to the element of agency. The difficulty, said Burke, is that there are "many naive readers of scientific tracts. And it does not occur to them that a treatment of ethics, sovereignty, power in such terms is by the very logic of its form, a *partial* treatment. A portion of the dialectic having been 'monographically' selected, and made into a monologue that takes up the entire universe of discourse, the reader is prone to take this as a statement covering the essentials of the entire field. That is, instead of reading it as a statement about *ethics considered in terms of material needs,* it is taken as a statement about *the ultimate origin of the ethical.*"

II

All this may seem to have wandered far from the theory of poetry, but actually it remained in very close touch. Burke's effort, in one aspect, may be described as one which intended to find a place for poetic reality without claiming for it a status of absolute hostility to science. He had dedicated the *Grammar* to the purification of war, "*ad bellum purificandum*": and in its argument he had attempted to fix more firmly the concept of knowledge, of "chart," as distinguished from the other two uses of language, those of "prayer" and "dream." The positivistic critic, like Eastman perhaps, would restrict the use of language to a particular version of chart alone, holding that what was not "true" was useless. The realistic critic, of the sort represented by the Richards of the *Principles* as well as the *Coleridge,* would restrict the use of poetry mainly to its elements of prayer, holding that only in so far as poetry achieved a certain fullness and efficacy of communication was it to be valued; idealistic critics, who might in this case be represented by Ransom, would defend poetry as dream, holding that only in the skillful implementation of the poet's free vision did the art find its fulfillment, and, that in so finding, it provided a uniquely valid vision of reality.

For Burke, however, the poem subsumed all three functions in a concept of linguistic act. As the *Grammar* had indicated, the poem as a dramatic entity constituted a grasp of reality, the kind of sizing up of a situation upon which any knowledge depended. It was not in and by itself complete knowledge, but was a valid effort toward it. Consistent with the whole tone of Burke's thought, the poem was a transcending or synthesizing force. It began as a personal imaginative effort of the poet to transcend by "acting out" a problem of his own experience; but, through its embodiment in language and its publication, it became an implement of understanding for whoever could read and ponder. Unless it could, in this circumstance, transcend again the wholly private nature of its origins it must of necessity fail. To dream was not enough for the poet; he must communicate his dream in its fullness and significance, and he must also sufficiently conform to truth, must sufficiently provide a usable chart, so that his reader could find an understandable substance upon which his own freer thought and feeling could build.

But the poem was not merely communication: it was a prototype, a microcosm, of reality itself. It may be said that Burke's general plan was to avoid any strictly ontological discussion by reducing, in his own strict sense of the term, the abstract concept of reality to an effective status by positing the ratio, poetry:act:motive:power:reality, in an ascending order. In so doing, he did not leave anything out. On the contrary, his effort was to get as much in as was possible. Thus, in describing the terms of the pentad, he noted that instead of calling them the necessary forms *of* experience, in a Kantian sense, "we should call them the necessary 'forms of *talk about* experience.' For our concern is primarily with the analysis of *language* rather than with the analysis of 'reality' "; and later, "[Our] method would involve the explicit study of language as the 'critical moment' at which human motives take form, since a linguistic factor at every point in human experience complicates and to some extent transcends the purely biological aspects of motivation." Though its author might balk at the designation, there would be justice in describing his approach to the problem of poetry and reality as a pragmatic one, for it was precisely in so far as he proportioned language, act, and power that his thought gained its consistency and applicability. Where Ransom would designate poetry as an aspect of reality, Burke might argue one of two ways — both of them differing from Ransom's in essentially pragmatic terms. In one case, poetry would be considered as an element of reality on the grounds that it represented, both literally and figuratively, an actualization of human motives. The poem was an act, and according to the new grammar of motives, reality might be considered as a collection of acts. In the second case, Burke might argue, this "reality" about which we are concerned bears a relation to our lives very much like that of Kant's *ding an sich,* which is to say none at all, and in terms of effect and existence, which then become the only possible terms of discussion, the poetic act plays a significant part.

In either case however, and this is the basic point, the poetic act would be restored to a place of honor in a scientific, liberal, and polyglot world. It would not come as a conqueror, as the extreme anti-naturalists might argue that it should, nor would it present itself with mysterious claims of inviolability — with the admonition *noli me tangere* held out to all other constituent parts of that world. Rather it would come as an embodiment, and a superior embodiment, of the same kind of motivation which was to be found in any human act.

The poetic view of reality, as Burke suggested in his essay "Four Master Tropes," was essentially an ironic one, and the essence of irony, in turn, was humility: "True irony, humble irony, is based upon a sense of fundamental kinship with the enemy, as one *needs* him, is *indebted* to him, is not merely outside him as an observer but contains him *within,* being consubstantial with him. This is the irony of Flaubert, when he recognizes that Madame Bovary is himself. One sees it in Thomas Mann — and in what he once called, when applying the term to another, 'Judas Psychology.'" One is reminded briefly of the Leibnizian concept of the best of all possible worlds; evil is necessary to express the fullness of God. And indeed some of the desperateness of Leibniz's conclusion is inherent in Burke's own ethical thinking, or, to speak more properly, in the ethical implications of his thought. But in so far as that thought was ontologically concerned it showed primarily the traits of inclusion and consistency. We have said that Burke regarded the poem as a microcosm of reality; in one aspect, the poem, through its inclusive and humble irony, represented at once a superior ethical state and superior state of cognition. To these conditions, science could lay no claims. It, in contrast with poetry, made a selection rather than a reduction of reality. In consequence it was valid only within the terms which originally governed the selection. One would be justified in *thinking of* water as two parts hydrogen and one part oxygen, but equally it would be useless to try *actually* to slake his thirst with these gasses. Equally, one might well think of people statistically, but one could not act as though they were statistics. In important senses, however, one could act as though they were poems.

III

A criticism of Burke which is both easy and fair is that his thought has failed to provide either a systematic or an original philosophy —

that in effect he adopts conclusions which have already received sufficient exposition and then proceeds to support them with a brilliant but inconclusive and disorderly rationale. Burke himself has described his point of view as a realistic one, and perhaps it is obligation to this ultimately demanding attitude which renders his thought difficult of systematizing. But it is well to lay the principal burden for his lack of pure philosophic validity upon the method of his thought – a method which has caused not only philosophers but ordinary readers of good will to cry out in pain and frustration. Where the philosopher will typically strive for coherence and consistency, Burke seems content with complexity alone. The result, as has frequently been noted, is that of giving acute, isolated insights, the relation and larger purport of which are very difficult to perceive. As one recent critic put it, "Burke's 'grammar' is often instead a thesaurus, displaying a range of meanings but providing no key other than an ambiguous overlap for their derivation from one another."

It is well to admit, then, that Burke has produced a very impure philosophy. But one may also be prepared to discover the virtues as well as the limitations of such a creation. These might be summarized by noting that, in his critical studies, he has formed something like the fullest and most independent theory of literature in existence, and that he has done this in an age which has witnessed almost a plethora of brilliant literary theory. The most significant difference between Burke's thought and that of other critics is just the difference between an approach to the place and function of literature through the complexity and fullness of the literary act itself instead of through the better ordered domains of philosophy (whether aesthetic or ontological), psychology, or even religion. One comes upon a basic proposition here: that literary theory and criticism, though they must make a responsible use of other intellectual disciplines, succeed in so far as they both respect and order the multiple and contingent phenomena which are literature. They are not to be judged primarily by the degree to which they succeed in reducing literature to the demands of another discipline.

Because some such assumption as this seems to underlie Burke's methods and conclusions, his work is singularly free from the constraints of aesthetics, ontology, or mere semantics which have provided uneasy bounds for the views of other critics. If, on the other hand, there is little suggestion of anything like a conventional art-for-art's-sake or pure-poetry attitude in any of Burke's work, it is because he has recognized most fully the fact that literature is an expressive, a symbolic act; that it has existence, cause, and effect; and that a satisfactory theory of literature must take all this fullness into account. Aestheticism, as defined by Pater or Ransom, would see the poet as witness or maker, and his vision as a component of a larger, active whole. While the poetic act itself has an existence apart from philosophy, psychology, or religion, it inevitably gives symbolic expression to matters which may also be found within their limits and is part of a causal chain which may be examined by their means. But any such examination in turn owes its first responsibility to the literary act, the symbolic act itself.

Burke has given a brilliant embodiment to his method in the well known "Symbolic Action in a Poem by Keats," a piece of poetic analysis which excellently illustrates the particular virtues of his method. It would be impossible here to provide any adequate summary of the work: it must suffice to say that in general Burke examines the "Ode on a Grecian Urn" as a type of this poetic act. "To consider [language] as a mode of *action*, is to consider it in terms of 'poetry.' For a poem is an act, the symbolic act of the poet who made it – an act of such a nature that, in surviving as a structure or object, it enables us as readers to re-enact it." In Keats' case, the act is essentially that of creating imaginatively (in the Coleridgean sense) a scene in terms of which the assertion "Beauty is truth, truth beauty," can be successfully made. As such, it compounds aesthetic, ontological, historical, and personal elements into a single meaning which becomes valid throughout the plurality of its contexts.

Burke was by no means the first critic to use analysis, but he brought to it a power which, while not obviating earlier methods, tremendously deepened their possibilities; and it is these new possibilities which are realized in the case of the Ode. Thus Eliot had been among the earliest critics to recommend analysis, but, in his earlier work, he had been constrained always by a sense of poetic autonomy which restricted his insights, despite their brilliance, to matters of poetic technique in almost the strictest sense. Though this was consistent with his concept of poetry as a "superior amusement," and with his limitation of the critical operations to those of analysis and comparison, it nevertheless produced an effect of truncation, a holding-down of poetry to what this particular critic chose to make of it. Perhaps it was this very limitation of critical method which allowed Eliot to produce the sectarian judgments of *After Strange Gods.* But if Eliot's analysis stopped short in this way at what may be called the rhetorical limits of his subject, that of William Empson tended equally to be content with the linguistic limits. These were somewhat broader than Eliot's, but in the same way, they inhibited the critic unnecessarily in his effort toward full understanding. Ambiguity is an undoubted and important agent in poetic language, but it is not the whole of poetic language.

Burke's analysis retains much of the closeness of the earlier methods but views the poem as an act which has an importance to the poet beyond the merely verbal or rhetorical and one which may best be described as a consequence of ritualization. By its means the poet objectifies experience which is in some way a "burden" so as, at best, to transcend the burden. He does not necessarily, as Richards would have him, serve a sort of clinical function – effecting an improvement of his own and his reader's sensibility – but rather accomplishes the kind of understanding which can come only through the interpretation of reality in the dramatistic terms of the pentad. As Ransom had suggested, he does give us at least a segment of the richness which is the world's body; but he gives it to us not passively, as witness, but actively to the limits of symbolic action, as participants.

The essential element in any theory of analysis, Burke's thought might suggest, is its ability to accommodate the unpredictable complexity which any poem may bring to it. To rule "ideas" out of poetry, to institute the metaphysical method as the only valid poetic method, to declare that poetry, whatever else, must contain strong feelings, to restrict it entirely to popularly intelligible sentiments, to insist that the poet give us a "myth," or to declare that he cannot possibly do so – all these suffer from an exclusiveness which Burke's method avoids. Nothing human, and symbolic, is alien to it. Blackmur has criticized Burke's method for failing to provide a way in which to distinguish between the productions of Shakespeare and those of Marie Corelli, but the exaggeration of the charge reveals its weakness; the difficulty may be put in another way. As the theory for which Blackmur speaks can find little sustenance except in one selection of seventeenth century poetry and another of two or three decades of the twentieth, the burden of proof as to undue *narrowness* would seem to lie too heavily upon Blackmur to make his criticism of Burke conclusive. In Burke's view, the "essential matter" in any poem is its "intense linguistic activity," but this activity is both essential and intense because it is symbolic, because it has a significance beyond its narrowly aesthetic one. At the same time, the symbol which is the poem could have had neither an immediate nor an ultimate importance had it not first the particular being which the particular poem itself assumed.

The disorderliness of Burke's approach, vitiating as it is to the purely discursive or philosophic problem, is seen as a positive merit when the question is one specifically of literature. Burke can see *more* in a poem, both close up and far off, than can the disciple of a more orderly but straighter discipline. At the same time, his basic assumptions and techniques are always close enough at hand so that the reader may query his critic's conclusions or originate his own speculations within a consistent whole.

IV

The final statement of Burke's suggestions as to the place and function of poetry is governed especially by what must be called his realism: his strong sense of the manifest. One cannot very well dispute his claim to realistic thinking by answering that his method shows equally positive traits of pragmatism. As he himself has noted, the term pragmatism was, before it became a school-designation, in perfectly good standing as a generic term. One might in this way speak of the "pragmatics of idealism"; in a similar fashion, one could designate Burke's chief interest as the "pragmatics of realism."

It has been characteristic of the new realism to accept the manifest world as the real world, although a division in the ranks has occurred over other points. Thus there has arisen a view which might be designated as "naive" realism, tending on the whole to accept the scientific doctrine of man and the universe and to put its faith in the further development of science. On the other hand, "critical" realism, in part at least, has attempted to push its speculative limits beyond the scientific. If John Locke is the Adam of naive realism, Leibniz is the forebear of the critical realists. Both questioned the complete adequacy of human knowledge beyond the experiential range, but over and above such questioning Locke recommended an extension of the scientific method of inquiry while Leibniz suggested a turning back of knowledge upon itself — the creation of a critical method.

We have noted that Burke suffers from a lack of philosophic method, but there is no questioning his critical zeal. It is, indeed, the power of this latter, when turned upon the naively realistic doctrine of motives represented by science, which gives the characteristic tone to his work and which at times brings it close to the tone of phenomenological or existential research. But Burke is neither Phenomenologist nor Existentialist. Where each of these is concerned with what might be called the idealistics of realism, Burke as we have noted is occupied chiefly with pragmatics. He is interested in symbolic *acts,* their causes and consequences, and beyond such interest he posits the reality of symbolic action to the extent that it can be shown to have cause and consequence.

It is thus that Burke arrives finally at a kind of pan-realism, an acceptance of both concept and percept as real because both constitute effective motives. In turn, the bridge between concept and percept, and the bridge between both of them and the level of human actions, is provided by language: hence it is that language-as-act (poetry) may be regarded not only as an aspect of reality, nor as a reference to reality, but as a reduction of reality itself. In the proposition, poetry:act:motive: power:reality, the relationship "is proportional to" between each of the terms may be taken quite literally. Language is a microcosm. Microcosm is not equal to macrocosm, but it must be wholly consonant with it.

Burke's ethical doctrine, the "neo-liberal ideal," advanced pan-realism definitely into the realm of the pragmatic. As in theory the most perfect "talk about reality" would be that which most nearly caught the proportional nature of reality, so in practice the most perfect thought and action would be that which was most faithful to the humbly ironic and inclusive nature of reality.

> Not that we should avoid the problems of [universal] order. On the contrary, we must turn precisely in the direction of a neo-Stoic cosmopolitanism, with ideals of tolerance and resignation to the bureaucratic requirements implicit in the structure of modern industry and commerce. The only alternatives are fanaticism and dissipation. By fanaticism I mean the effort to impose one doctrine of motives abruptly upon a world composed of many different motivational situations. By dissipation I mean the isolationist tendency to surrender, as one finds the issues of world adjustment so complex that he merely turns to the satisfactions nearest at hand, living morally and intellectually from hand to mouth, buying as much as one can buy with as much as one can earn, or selling as much as one can sell, or in general taking whatever opportunities of gratification or advancement happen to present themselves and letting all else take care of itself.

The common ethical consequences of scientistic philosophies were just those which might be expected to turn easily into dissipation – into the kind of moral relativism which science had so universally spawned. But on the other hand fanaticism or dogmatism was commonly the moral attitude of anti-scientific thought. Each was destructive. Neither was capable of establishing the sort of moral ideal which a world as fragmented as our own required. Our hope must be a double edged one. It necessitates both tolerance and criticism. As a result:

> This work (which would have as its motto *Ad Bellum Purificandum*, or Towards the Purification of War) is constructed on the belief that, whereas an *attitude* of humanistic contemplation is in itself more important by far than any *method*, only by method could it be given the body necessary for its existence even as an attitude. We would thus hold at least that an elaborate analysis of linguistic foibles is justified "in principle." Indeed, the study

of linguistic action is but beginning. And we must be on our guard lest the great need for an *attitude* of linguistic skepticism allow us to be content with too hasty a "policy" as regards the nature of language itself. This is too serious a matter for such "dissipatory" approaches to the subject as we find among the contemporary "debunkers." And even serious approaches are invalidated when formed in keeping with the ideals of an uncriticized scientism, which is *too evasive of the dramatistic to make even an adequate preparatory description* of linguistic forms. To contemplate our subject, we must have a terministic equipment that lends itself to such contemplation. Otherwise one has a *principle of aversion* implicit in the very nature of his investigations, as if one hoped to see accurately by partially averting one's gaze. There may be true and false transcendences in language. Or for the sake of argument, if you will, they are all false. But in any case they *are transcendences.* And we must begin by taking some delight in the contemplation of them as such. By the use of dialectical resources, we shape the versions of human motives that have so greatly much to do with our individual actions and our relations to one another.

We might phrase Burke's conclusion now as "Poetry has a place in human affairs to the extent that reality has." It can provide materials which the thinker needs to create a proper understanding of his world. But more, as act, poetry provides a means for symbolic *participation* in the neo-liberal ethical condition. It is such participation that we at times call the aesthetic state. But the aesthetes must not fob us off with their special pleading. If poetry is indeed reality, it is not the dead end of life, but a very center of it.

◇◇

BERNARD DUFFEY was born in Cincinnati, Ohio, in 1917. He has taught English at the University of Minnesota, Michigan State University, and Duke University. His specialty is modern literature, especially American. He is the author of a book on *The Chicago Renaissance in American Letters* and numerous reviews and articles.

This is surely — still — one of the best analyses we have of Burke's theory of literature, its place in modern literary theory, and the relation of both to some of the larger intellectual and philosophical developments of our time. Mr. Duffey saw early on, with a kind of brilliant finality, how poetry, language, and reality were interrelated by Burke, how this provided him with one of the most extraordinary "justifications" for the study of poetry in modern criticism, and later, by extension (or reduction) for the whole dramatistic study of language.

I mention here only Mr. Duffey's main points. The essay as a whole provides continuous and continuing illumination of Burke. The nature of Mr. Duffey's consideration of Burke — as a major modern literary theorist – is similar to Mr. Hyman's and, looking ahead, to Marius Bewley's. These three provide one with a fairly thorough (for and against) consideration of Burke as a practical and theoretical critic through *A Grammar of Motives.*

7 *Kenneth Burke as Literary Critic*

BY Marius Bewley

IN WRITING of Burke as a literary critic one is up against a difficulty at the very outset. Many have doubted whether he is really a literary critic at all. In the book already named [*The Armed Vision*] we find Mr. Hyman settling this problem with characteristic generosity: 'The reason reviewers and editors have had such trouble fastening on Burke's field is that he has no field, unless it be Burkology. In recent years it has become fashionable to say that he is not actually a literary critic, but a semanticist, social psychologist, or philosopher. A much more accurate statement would be that he is not *only* a literary critic, but a literary critic *plus* those things and others.' I remember Burke's having expressed somewhere a certain dislike for Leonardo, and so he may have found the above passage disagreeable enough. However, whatever injustice is involved, it is *only* as a literary critic that I wish to consider him here, and his volumes as a whole give one reasonable grounds for supposing that he considers himself most fully defined in this term. Towards arriving at some sense of his critical tone I wish to review his criticism briefly here under three headings: (1) the central proposition of his critical theory and what it means; (2) his idea of the function of a critic; and (3) the principal ground of weakness in his criticism.

1. In the Foreword to his book, *The Philosophy of Literary Form*, 1941, Burke remarks that 'the reader who wants the specific criticism of books might be more disappointed [with *The Philosophy*] than the reader who wants a theory of the criticism of books.' Even though one may not like the kind of separation between theory and practice im-

EDITOR'S NOTE: Originally published in 1948. Reprinted from *The Complex Fate* (London: Chatto & Windus Ltd., 1952), pp. 215–226, copyright © by Chatto & Windus, by permission of the publisher. The selection here includes only Part II of the original essay.

plicit in such a statement it is justifiable if there is a constant and intelligent communication between the two levels, neither level tyrannizing over the other, each increasing its effectiveness under disciplines suggested by the other. The passage indicates clearly enough the direction of Burke's bent away from the practical, and one feels that such a quick recognition of a natural predisposition *should* act as a safeguard against the abuses of theory; for the latter can be useful only as long as it works toward the elucidation of particular poems.

Burke's theory of criticism covers many points, but the heart of it may be summed up in this brief statement: 'To consider language as a mode of *action* is to consider it in terms of "poetry." For a poem is an act, the symbolic act of the poet who made it – an act of such a nature that, in surviving as a structure or object, it enables us as readers to re-enact it.' I have already said that with Burke's ideas in themselves one seldom quarrels, and here it is an agreeable task to point to the virtues of the theory itself. Poetry becomes, not a segregated experience, but an experience at one with all human action. Literature is, in such a view, brought into an arena of the widest significance, and theoretically its participation in life is complete – or rather, literature *is* life in an entirely realistic way. Poetry is therefore seen to be ethical, and of the deepest influence in shaping 'our structures of orientation.' Such a view, so far from being new, will be substantially familiar to everyone, but Burke does manage to give it a centrality and completeness of statement that is admirable. And at this point, in the face of the dark hints that have been made here about Burke's critical practices, and before offering substantiations, I should like to say that few critics have been more sensitively aware of the relationship between language and practical action than Burke has been, or have spoken with greater dramatic effectiveness of the problems of communication in contemporary society. *Permanence and Change* is filled with such pointed observations as: 'Speech takes its shape from the fact that it is used by people acting together. It is an adjunct of action – and thus naturally contains the elements of exhortation and threat which stimulate action and give it direction.' But at this time the theory of Symbolic Action was not fully evolved, and Burke was chiefly concerned with the operation of the word in its social context – a field in which he has considerable skill. But he has a proportionate lack of perception in literary matters, and when, in his next book, *Attitudes toward History*, 1937, he turned back to literary criticism again and developed his theory of Poetry as Symbolic Action with great explicitness it became clear that, whatever the virtues of such a view *could* be, Burke lacked the requisite critical tact and awareness to use it as anything other than an implement finally murderous. It was in this book that Burke began in real earnestness to shuttle back and forth from literature to sociology to economics to psychology to magic and religion [1] with a sometimes attractive but decidedly alarming air of irresponsibility as to which station he happened to be in at any given moment, and the situation became genuinely frightening when one gathered, from remarks dropped here and there along the way, that he was never quite certain that *any* station was *not* literary criticism, to which platform his mind *still* frequently reverts as 'home.' Even with such a slender definition of the theory as has been given above it must be obvious that only a very exacting literary critical control could prevent such a theory from sooner or later encountering catastrophe, could have the strength of will to turn down idle invitations often extended to rounds of dissipation during which the integrity of any poem would surely lose its health and die. But it may be that this extension of the influence of literary criticism over the adjacent sciences is partly due to Burke's Marxism. Burke is such a pastoral sort of Marxist (H. B. Parkes' excellent essay on Burke in *The Pragmatic Test* stresses certain political unorthodoxies in his Marxism), that one is likely to underestimate at first the influence of his political thought on his criticism, though Burke himself is terribly explicit about it in every volume. Mr. Hyman, however, suspiciously omits any reference whatever to Burke's politics.

2. But this theme moves the argument from Burke's theory to his idea of the function of the literary critic. In *Attitudes toward History* we find a full definition of his conception of himself in this role:

Our own program, as literary critic, is to integrate technical criticism with social criticism (propaganda and didactic) by taking the allegiance to the

[1] It is again necessary to repeat that I am speaking of Burke's critical practice, which is the only thing that matters, and not of his critical theory. As regards the latter, he seems to have, at least in his last book, *A Grammar of Motives*, a more exacting conscience about the integrity of separate sciences than previously. For example, he quotes as 'the principle of specification' the following remark from Kant: 'Rather than enlarging the sciences, we merely disfigure them when we lose sight of their respective limits.' Burke proceeds to comment: 'The principle of specification is particularly applicable . . . to terminologies of motives that attempt to treat of ethical issues in exclusively non-ethical terms, or of verbal action in terms of non-verbal motion, or of human motives generally in terms of non-human entities, such as the learning processes of lower animals, or the physiology of endocrine secretions, and the like. In brief, we violate the principle of specification when our terms for the examination of one field are got by simple importation from some other field.' However, I remember Burke's having, in an earlier book, discussed the various fields of research as an arbitrary parcelling out of lands at specific dates and in the dominant framework of a prevailing orientation, itself constituting a deflection from purity. In any case, he has always treated literary criticism with considerably more latitude, and his critical practice has never much taken cognizance of this 'principle.'

symbol of authority as our subject. We take this as our starting point, and 'radiate' from it. Since the symbols of authority are radically linked with property relationships, this point of departure automatically involves us in socio-economic criticism. Since works of art, as 'equipment for living,' are formed with authoritative structures as their basis of reference, we also move automatically into the field of technical criticism (the 'tactics' of writers). And since the whole purpose of a 'revolutionary' critic is to contribute to a change in allegiance to the symbols of authority, we maintain our role as 'propagandist' by keeping this subject forever uppermost in our concerns. The approach, incidentally, gives one an 'organic' view of literature, sparing him the discomforts of discussing the 'social' and the 'technical' as though they were on two different levels. He spontaneously avoids a dualism of 'form' and 'content,' 'beauty' and 'use,' the 'practical' vs. the 'esthetic,' etc. He gets a unitary approach to the matter of dialectical interaction.

Here one can see how easily, without an exacting critical conscience, Burke's theory moves through art to propaganda, how easily the literary merges into the revolutionary critic. It is not merely that one may not like what Burke is propagandizing ('Communism is a co-operative rationalization, or perspective, which fulfils the requirement suggested by the poetic metaphor,' he wrote in *Permanence and Change*); it is not that one wholly disagrees with the idea of art *as propaganda,* but the cold-blooded sacrifice of art *to* propaganda that is implicit here is repellent. (Burke always keeps his way out free, however, and anyone wishing to read his reservations on this position should look at *Attitudes toward History*, Volume 2, page 110, and there is also a relevant essay in *The Philosophy*.) And it might be noticed that even in what is commonly considered his best essay, 'Symbolic Action in an Ode by Keats,' which will be analysed later, there is a good deal more of the Marxist critic than appears at first. The 'organic' view of literature recommended above involves an analysis of the work from the viewpoint of political purpose, and ironically enough, not the artist's but the critic's purpose. It also seems debatable whether the compression of motives that would result from interpreting a work towards such an end, so far from sparing the integrity of the work of art, would not result in a distortion far greater than the inevitable violations imposed by any given set of critical terms. And there would still be the 'dialectical inter-action' between two purposes — the poet's and the critic's — that would be resolved at last in an appropriately 'coached' estimate. But one feels how futile it is to discuss these things in Burke's writings at all. The reality he deals with comes increasingly to seem less the reality of the objective world (despite the 'pan-realism' attributed to him) than its image artfully mirrored in a great shiny vocabulary; and if that vocabulary follows the movements of the real world with some skill, it is independently capable of internal readjustments that, at a second's warning, can carry Burke by the grace of a shifting stress fairly off to dialectical safety.

The above passage, which is representative of his style, exhibits his technique at its usual level. Those words of which he hopes, sooner or later, to make special use, he appropriates for his strategies by enclosing in inverted commas. The various key-words in this passage mean in Burke pretty much what they mean anywhere else. Yet to anyone who reads this paragraph with Burke's writings as a whole in memory they will seem to have a great specialness about them. For Burke has endlessly discussed and defined them through his books. Thus: tactics, equipment for living, authoritative structures, basis of reference, symbols of authority, revolutionary, linkages, etc., have all been up for protracted analysis somewhere, and sometimes on a number of different occasions. Burke has seemed to attach quite new and precise meanings to such words, and he has frequently made striking and original comments on them; but in the end the performance exceeds the reality, and we are left very much as we were before. But if Burke has not significantly enlarged or narrowed the meanings of his words, he has in the meantime gained control of the reader's responses to them – he has given his reader great faith in them, and in those intervals when Burke himself is content not to be at grips with meaning, these highly trained words are capable of carrying on like so many theatrical wrestlers who know how to thrill an audience without much pain to themselves. But to return to the above passage more particularly: it is interesting to note his taste for the adverb 'automatically.' (Burke's criticism is especially American in a certain flair it has for the mechanical.) As one draws to the close of the paragraph, however, it is surprising to note that the third point at which he might have been expected to use 'automatically' he uses 'spontaneously' instead, an adverb characteristically applied to life rather than to mechanical processes. It is precisely Burke's tendency to think of literary criticism as, in the end, something automatic; to speak of something living in mechanical terms, that would be a chief complaint against him. I realize, certainly, that when Burke says 'Poetry is Act' he is not referring to mechanical motion, and that he is as far from the merely automatic as he could get in such a phrase. But I am concerned here with the processes (still to be examined) by which Burke converts poetry into a supposedly equivalent act. I remarked in the beginning of this paper that although Burke hated technology and disliked science, at least insofar as it has provided a context for life, the critical "methodology' he has evolved seems designed in tone to betray him into the hands of his enemies. And in a similar manner, he desires to emphasize the human act, to insist on the dramatistic aspect of literature (as opposed, for instance, to a behaviouristic criticism); but for that purpose he is willing to convert a poem into a graph (he analyses poems in terms of Chart, Prayer and Dream in *The Philosophy of Literary Form*), count image clusters to discover the neuroses of a poet, and interpret all art from the viewpoint of Symbols of Authority, which can mean little else in his case than to submit it to an evaluation ultimately Marxist. Or he likes to ring the changes on a rhetorical device by showing how it is at the heart of a variety of complex literary passages. Thus in *Counter-Statement* with great irrelevance he reduces scenes from Racine's *Iphigénie* and Wilde's *Salome,* and verses from 'We are Seven,' together with other specimens, to the trick of 'talking at cross-purposes.' And in his later work he has pointed to the ancient device of what he calls (under a new name in an intricately worked out schema) the 'Act-Scene ratio' as if its mere presence in a poem or play were enough to explain the range of the work's complexities. (The Act-Scene ratio is that tendency of an act and a scene in which it occurs to share a common imagery towards mutual enforcement of a common mood.) And he has a tendency to consider later works of a writer as successive rewritings of some earlier work: thus, *Mario the Magician* is a rewriting of *Death in Venice.* Too much cannot be made of any one of these things, but together they provide Burke's criticism with an aspect I would call 'mechanical,' for Burke uses these methods, not with any sensitive care for the life of the poem, but with the hope of getting beyond the poem entirely into a realm of loosely disciplined symbolism in which he can seek another kind of life and other kinds of satisfactions.

3. This glance at Burke's theory of Poetry as Act and at his conception of the critic's function does not go far in explaining that restlessness and energy that is characteristic of all his writing, and it leaves unnoticed one of the most insistent defects in his work: a monotonous absence of shade and highlight that reduces all of Burke's ideas to a monochrome significance. A book by Burke teems with local activity. Ideas scurry everywhere, and one watches them with something of the fascination with which one studies the combination of aimlessness and purpose that characterizes life in an ant hill. Just how exalted Burke's final purpose really is one realizes only gradually; but how he has laboured the means of reaching it is evident from the first. The greatest point of internal strain in Burke's ideological structure — and the strain is, after all, one of the chief results of all that labour — occurs in an area where two such passages as are quoted below, attempting to collaborate in a final vision of Burke's design, end up by mutually frustrating each other.

First, as illustrating the essential seriousness of his intentions, one could point to this passage from a recent essay:

> But if one offered a synthesis of the fields covered by the various disciplines, which of the disciplines could possibly be competent to evaluate it? Where each specialty gets its worth precisely by moving towards diversity, how could any specialty possibly deal with a project that offered a *unification* among the diversities? Or, otherwise put: if one were to write on the interrelatedness among ten specialties, one would be discussing something that lay outside the jurisdiction of them all.

It might be noted from the tone of this passage that theology would seem to be the only ground in which the desired unification might occur, although we know that such a unification for Burke would be achieved ultimately in a society 'in which the participant aspect of action attained its maximum expression,' a society which he naturally visualizes as Marxist. The passage is further noteworthy as indicating the incapacity of his conception of literary criticism to act as a central discipline – but perhaps it is unfair to stress that point here since the passage ends on an inflection suggesting the desire is for an ontological reality different in nature from a mere evaluating discipline. The seriousness of tone is hardly short of religious. In another place, distressed by the confusion caused today by overlapping 'interpretative frames' in our society, Burke has asked 'What arises as a totality?' And he continues: 'The myriad orientations will be tragically wasted, the genius of one of the world's most vigorous centuries will be allowed to go unused, unless we can adapt its very welter of interpretations as sceptical grounding for our certainties.' The nervousness one feels in the fabric of Burke's writing, then, springs from his necessity of basing his certainties on uncertainties; and the fact that he is religiously solemn about the first, and lacks both the humour and the critical tact to dismiss the second with any assurance does not relieve the tension. But if Burke's readers suffer as a result, certainly Burke suffers more.

As contrasted with the first passage, the one below from *Permanence and Change* exhibits Burke bringing the uncertainties under control. Although it springs from the highly serious purpose just commented upon it demonstrates why so much of Burke's writing seems to end in frivolity, and to express a defective sensibility. The passage is an explanation of a phrase Burke frequently employs, 'perspective by incongruity.' Burke traces the phrase to Nietzsche, and he may also be indebted to Remy de Gourmont's dissociation of conceptual words which he discusses in *Counter-Statement*. 'Perspective by incongruity' is in itself a highly useful device. It operates in something of the manner of a metaphysical image that by collocating unexpected items is capable of providing new and unusual insights; or, by division on the same principle, may reveal unsuspected weaknesses in accepted formulations. Here is the passage:

> . . . we might say that planned incongruity should be deliberately cultivated for the purpose of experimentally wrenching apart all those molecular combinations of adjective and noun, substantive and verb, which still remain with us. It should subject language to the same 'cracking' process that chemists now use in their refining of oil. . . . An idea which commonly carries with it diminutive modifiers, for instance, should be treated by magnification, as were one to discuss the heinousness of an extra slice of beef, or the brain storm that rules when one has stumped one's toe. One should be prepared to chart the genesis, flourishing, and decay of a family witticism, precisely as though he were concerned with the broadest aspects of cultural change, basic patterns of psychology and history thus being conveniently brought within the scope of the laboratory. One should study one's dog for his Napoleonic qualities, or observe mosquitoes for signs of wisdom to which we are forever closed. One should discuss sneezing in terms heretofore reserved for the analysis of a brilliant invention, as if it were a creative act, a vast synthesis uniting in its simple self a multitude of prior factors. Conversely, when the accepted linkages have been of an imposing sort, one should establish perspective by looking through the reserve end of his glass, converting mastodons into microbes, or human beings into vermin upon the face of the earth. Or perhaps writing a history of medicine by a careful study of the quacks, one should, by the principle of the *lex continui,* extend his observations until they threw light upon the processes of Pasteur. Or do a history of poetry by going among the odds and ends of Bohemia, asking oneself why some monkey jumper wore a flowing tie, and letting the answer serve as an explanation of Yeats or Valéry.

The kind of reversal being considered here only degrades the idea of 'perspective by incongruity.' The passage has a faded whimsicality that, so far from being original, has been exploited for many generations by middlebrow essayists who, in little after dinner gems of literature, have waxed solemn about their opera hats or frivolous about their great-aunts' funerals. So far from these distortions effecting new insights there is something about the tone in which Burke marshals them forward that rigidifies the sensibility in an old response at the very moment it should be most receptive to something new. But more important, the impersonal scientific metaphor with which the paragraph opens is unjustifiable. Any 'perspective by incongruity' would be a highly personal thing, since only *certain* terms would be chosen by any one person to be broken down in a *certain* way. The sensibility and wishes of the subject forming such a perspective would be an important factor, and inevitably his perspective would converge at some point previously proposed in some level of his consciousness. It is clear that such a method has great possibilities for a Marxist critic undertaking an interpretation of literature in relation to Symbols of Authority, and here one realizes with a start that the only shocking item in the above list – the last item – is the one by which Burke would be least shocked. The Bohemian's flowing tie as a romantic symbol of caste and function in a capitalist society would undoubtedly perform services similar to the ones Yeats' 'aristocratic' attitudes and imagery performed for him, and such services, we shall see, Burke considers one of the chief functions of literature. It is even a little odd that Burke should consider such an item as his last one a 'perspective by incongruity' at all.

By juxtaposing these two passages one sees Burke deeply concerned with certainties that he is both eager to realize himself and to propagate. One knows that the only tangible certainty he admits is a political one, but this, in all its ramifications, constitutes the 'good life.' He has a strong religious nostalgia, and it confers a solemn authority of tone on his ultimate goal. And as the religious sensibility is particularly sensitive to scepticism one sees him 'transcending' this weakness by behaving like a sceptic himself: and he toils away in the second passage among the contemporary uncertainties, using a neutral critical device, but in the somewhat weighted way that theologians sometimes make their appeals to secular subjects. In the end, his 'perspective by incongruity' converges on a Heavenly City that is not very new considering the circuitous approach he has chosen; and the deep earnestness of that final end, blunting a multitude of intermediary perceptions, is happy to tolerate frequent collapses of literary criticism into the lower regions of polemic. But I must apologize at this point for so largely presuming on the question of the religious inflection. I can only point ahead to a further stage when I shall attempt to isolate this tone more carefully.

◇◇

Marius Bewley is a professor of English at Fordham University. He is the author of *The Complex Fate* and *The Eccentric Design*, both studies of American literature, and of many essays and reviews.

Whether Mr. Bewley studied with F. R. Leavis is not known to me; but he writes from within a kind of Leavis framework, and that does not seem to include any part of Kenneth Burke. Mr. Bewley's review-essay was originally published in *Scrutiny* and did much to set the attitude toward Burke which, it seems, has prevailed in England to the present. Burke, like William Carlos Williams, is perhaps too American for the British; or perhaps the long and still standing British distrust of systems is what has kept them away from a critic and theorist who has much to say to them and could do something for their own languishing critical scene. Until Denis Donoghue and the 8 June 1967 review of Burke's *Language as Symbolic Action*, and of new editions of *The Philosophy of Literary Form* and *Towards a Better Life*, in the *Times Literary Supplement*, the British have greeted Burke with hackles up, once or twice, and otherwise with silence. I do not believe that *A Rhetoric of Motives* was ever reviewed in England, or, for that matter, *The Rhetoric of Religion*. Going backwards from Mr. Bewley's piece the record is too slight to be worth discussing. The feature *TLS* review in 1967, therefore, was something quite extraordinary. It was partly occasioned by the fact that Burke's new publisher – the University of California Press – arranged to have his books published in England by the Cambridge University Press, and that the Louisiana State University Press, which reissued *The Philosophy of Literary Form*, also arranged to have this book released in England.

I do not wish to engage in polemics with Mr. Bewley, who is a real master of that art, and will confine myself to a discussion of his article within the context of this collection. In most ways, his is the most violent, extended, and serious attack made on Burke by anyone in this volume because so much is involved in the disagreement. It is like the differences between T. S. Eliot and D. H. Lawrence, or, more recently and somewhat ironically, like those between Burke and N. O. Brown. Two whole and antagonistic value systems are engaged and they include social values, attitudes toward the self and experience, and, finally, most other significant matters. The literary theory is merely the point of attack; the whole system, all the implications of it, and the assumptions behind it are also being questioned.

Up to a certain point in his own development and in accordance with what seems to be a kind of historical (or perhaps psychological) truism, Burke was always essentially radical, revolutionary, open: he was the great acceptor and synthesizer, the "maw" of Mr. Knickerbocker's essay who (which) was committed to change (change or perish, he once said) without the loss of what was permanent and valuable. His own dramatistic system may be seen as a vision shaped to and by his own needs and the rhythms of his own time. In a cruel historical irony, when the vision finally set – around the mid 1950's – the radical drive that produced it began turning conservative to defend its own. The "maw" was closing; the truth had been revealed; the energies were now expended on applications and defense.

What Mr. Bewley has done here is approach the "maw" from the "wam" position – or, in more appropriate language, he sent the forces of "wam" to attack the "maw" while it was still open. Mr. Bewley is the very type (here) of the excluding, prescriptive, embattled mind defending "poetry" and "criticism" against the enemies of purity. Mr.

Bewley writes as if the old (that is, purely rational) categories still held, as if there really were such definable and unchanging entities as poetry, criticism, the novel, a poem — as if the whole pluralistic tendency in the intellectual life of our time had not (or, is it, should not have) happened. This is really the basis of his — and others' — attack on Burke, and as is often the case, the attack derives from fundamentally different conceptions of mind and reality. As Burke has pointed out, everything has implications beyond itself, and these are what exercised Mr. Bewley. As it has turned out, the kind of critical pluralism Burke developed and defended in *Attitudes toward History* and after has become the prevailing mode; here, then, as in so many other areas of thought, Burke was working close to the radical centers of his own time. It was a mark of his genius to be able to do this while he was also committed in the most profound, almost perverse, and certainly characteristically modern way to many old timey things (like an outhouse, kerosense lamps, local heating, water drawn by pump, and the various analogues for all of these in his thought).

The Lion and the Honeycomb

BY R. P. Blackmur

MR. RANSOM, MR. EMPSON, and MR. BROOKS may object to being called rhetoricians; they have not conspicuously used the term of themselves; but Kenneth Burke must have found it his first cradle-word, and I think he would rather be called Rhetor, as honorific and as description, than anything else. I suspect that like Cicero in *De Finibus* * he regards poetry, philosophy, and religion as matters subordinate to rhetoric in the beginning and in the end to be transformed into rhetoric. His great work is interesting (I am still pursuing my analogy) in the titles of the three volumes. The first was called *A Grammar of Motives,*

EDITOR'S NOTE: Originally published in 1950. Reprinted from Mr. Blackmur's volume *The Lion and the Honeycomb* (New York: Harcourt, Brace and Company, 1955), pp. 193–195, copyright 1950 by Richard P. Blackmur, by permission of Harcourt, Brace & World, Inc.

* This may be a little rough on Cicero. But in *De Finibus* (V, 3) Cicero says in praise of the Old Academy: "They have produced orators, generals and statesmen. To come to the less distinguished professions, this factory of experts in all the sciences has turned out mathematicians, poets, musicians and physicians" (Loeb translation). I am indebted to Erich Auerbach for this quotation.

the second is called *The Rhetoric of Motives,* and for the third there is no certain title (as the book is not written) but he has twice referred to it as The Symbolic. If we remember that one of Mr. Burke's favorite key devices is contained in the remark that language is either *symbolic* action or symbolic *action,* I think we may hazard it that rhetoric will be doing the work in the symbolic. In Mr. Burke rhetoric always does all the work, and in order to do so it has to acquire two specific characters. It has to become very abstract — so abstract that Kant's categories become immediate sensations; and with its abstractness it also has to become neutral. The feeling of spate, of copiousness, you get in Burke is because of this abstract neutrality; he has no need to stop and there is nothing to arrest him: there are no obstacles he cannot transform into abstract or reduce to neutral terms in his rhetoric. He is a very superior example indeed of the mind in which the articulate organization has absorbed the material organized. The rhetoric is so good for any purpose that it very nearly engorges purpose. The methodology is a wonderful machine that creates its own image out of everything fed into it: nobody means what he says but only the contribution of what he says to the methodology.

Now I would suppose that Mr. Burke's rhetoric is a true rhetoric despite its abstractness and neutrality. I would suppose that his rhetoric is a heightened, elaborated, exemplary form of a stage every mind must pass through in taking up mutual relations with dialectic and poetic (or psychology and philosophy), but I am certain that this rhetoric is no place to stay. Nor will it help me to consider that this rhetoric is an act of unification and that the other modes of the mind are to be found organized into it; indeed that is my objection, for, unified, bound together, the modes of the mind lose both their own distinction and the distinct aspects of things they were intended to handle; and furthermore, so closely organized, there is no room for the mind to contain anything besides itself. I would not have Mr. Burke other than he is; he is an exemplary monument; but I would use him, and I hope I do use him, quite other than he is.

Here, of course, I use him somewhat unfairly, as the last step in my effort to show the ultimately rhetorical character of the processes of the "new criticism." It is unfair because Mr. Burke is only a literary critic in unguarded moments, when rhetoric nods. As a regular thing Mr. Burke does not give an account of literature; he substitutes his account for the literature, with a general air that the account does well what the literature did badly and that the only sound use of literature is to furnish rhetoric with one of its incentives. I draw the inference that the characteristic risk of the "new criticism" is that its special skills of analysis may become an omnicompetent methodology and that the risk is underlined by the rhetorical nature of the skills. To put it another way, it is a natural sequence to move from art for art's sake to criticism for criticism's sake. But I do not wish to be misunderstood; I do not suppose there is one of the "new critics" who would not assent to these strictures, and I also suppose that these strictures may with point be applied to myself.

◇◇◇

See the note on pages 50–51.

IN THIS brief later comment — one of the few any of the "new" critics has ever bothered to write about Burke — Mr. Blackmur makes three important points: he notes the central position of rhetoric in Burke's dramatistic system; he comments on the extreme inwardness of Burke's mind, which is seen in Burke's tendency to reduce everything to himself, himself being embodied in the system; and, finally, his assessment combines a characteristic mixture of admiration (Burke is "an exemplary monument"), distrust (mostly of the system and its inwardness), and disinclination to use Burke as he is. These are all significant and characteristic points in the reception of Burke from *A Grammar of Motives* on. Burke's development during these years was inward toward the centralities — the withinness of the within — of his own vision. The four pieces that follow all treat this development in different ways.

◇◇◇

7 *Prolegomena to Kenneth Burke*

BY Malcolm Cowley

IT IS hard for me to write about *A Rhetoric of Motives* because the author is my oldest friend. I first met Kenneth Burke when I was three years old and he was four. At that time my father was the Burkes' family physician and he took my mother and me along with him on one of his visits. Mother used to tell me that I went around the parlor touching everything in my reach while Kenneth followed apprehensively repeating, "Don't touch. Mustn't." One is always tempted to read mean-

EDITOR'S NOTE: Reprinted from *The New Republic*, CXXII (5 June 1950), 18–19, by permission of the author and *The New Republic*, copyright © 1950, Harrison-Blaine of New Jersey, Inc.

ings and patterns into those childhood stories and it is true that in our high-school days I was more venturesome than Kenneth, getting into more scrapes, but afterwards our relations were reversed. As a critic he has been the one who went touching everything from floor to chandelier, while at times I have scolded him by letter for not observing the critical rules handed down by the Elders.

By touching and asking questions and taking nothing for granted he has come to be one of the few truly speculative thinkers of our time. It is not a time that encourages speculation; we have begun to speak wistfully of the past; there is a general longing for certainty or security and meanwhile our few explorations, whether intellectual or geographical, are usually made by organized groups. Even dissent, so far as it is related to Communism or anti-Communism, has become an organized and bureaucratized activity. Burke belongs to an older line, that of the individual seekers after truth; one thinks of William James and his father, too; of C. S. Peirce, John Jay Chapman, and perhaps of Thorstein Veblen more than the others.

I speak of Veblen because he had the same concern with hidden social motives, but I doubt that Burke would like to be compared with him. "Veblen," he says in the *Rhetoric,* "treads cumbrously. And his terminology of motives is far too limited in scope; hence, at every step in his exploration, important modifiers would be needed, before we could have a version of human motives equal to the depths at which the ways of persuasion . . . must really operate." Burke's terminology is wider in scope and permits a deeper reading of human motives. Where Veblen tends to simplify or cheapen a situation, Burke likes to reveal the complexity of motives lying behind it. Where Veblen is critical and even corrosive, Burke is more often admiring. "See how vastly ingenious men are in hiding their follies," he seems to be saying; and he accepts the follies as a condition of the social environment.

Yet he has in common with Veblen a bent of mind that is revealed in his use of a special vocabulary. Veblen had a special vocabulary, too; it was different from Burke's, but it was invented for the same general purposes, one of which was to cast new light on a subject by describing it in terms borrowed from a strikingly different subject; thus, he discussed the American leisure class as if he were an ethnologist writing about the Polynesians. Burke often uses the same method; he calls it "perspective by incongruity."

Veblen began his career as a student of philosophy, but his interest in human relations soon led him into sociology and economics. Burke started from literary criticism and always circles back to it; his critical essays are as fruitful — or one might rather call them seedful — as any written in our time; but I think it is an error to approach him as a critic primarily. In his latest books one finds that his interest in human relations is leading him more and more toward general philosophy, where Veblen began.

A Rhetoric of Motives, the very latest, is the second volume of a trilogy which will be devoted to the strategies of human expression and communication. In the first volume — *A Grammar of Motives* (1945) — he had offered a general statement of principles (the "grammar" of the title was used in the sense of "elements," as one might say "a grammar of painting"). Burke held that there were five elements involved in any statement about human motives; they were act, scene, agent, agency and purpose. His theory was that every philosophical school had laid a special emphasis on one of the five; thus, materialism emphasized the *scene*; idealism, the *agent*; pragmatism, the *agency* or instrument; and mysticism, the ultimate *purpose.* Burke himself showed more sympathy with Aquinas, who, he said, was "dramatistic" in his method and who conceived of existence as an *act.*

Having defined his terms in the first volume, Burke goes forward in the second to discuss language as the medium of human relations. "Rhetoric" in Burke's sense is a very broad term; he seems to define it — though never in exactly these words — as the study of the linguistic and symbolic means by which human beings try to influence one another. Thus, it includes the traditional rhetoric, to which he devotes some interesting chapters, but it also includes topics that are usually regarded as lying in the province of the anthropologists or the economists or the Freudian psychologists. At one point he criticizes the Freudians for "concealing the nature of exclusive social relations behind inclusive terms for sexual relations." He promises that in the last volume of the trilogy, which will be *A Symbolic of Motives,* he will analyze Freud's work to show "how many logical and dialectical principles are, by his own account, involved in the operations of the dream."

In books like the *Grammar* and the *Rhetoric* we begin to see the outlines of a philosophical system on the grand scale, something that Veblen never attempted. The system starts with the definition that *man is a symbol-using animal,* and from this it exfoliates in all directions. In the sense that it is a humanistic or man-centered system it must always remain partial; it does not attempt to deal with the extra-human world of matter and energy. In another sense and within its fixed limits, the system promises to be complete. Already it has its own methodology (called "dramatism"), its own esthetics (based on the principle that works of art are symbolic actions), its logic and dialectics, its ethics (or picture of the good life) and even its metaphysics, which Burke prefers to describe as a meta-rhetoric.

Burke has a reputation for being difficult to read and one must admit that it is partly deserved — while adding the proviso that most Americans, including our college graduates, have been so corrupted by skimming through their newspapers and half-listening to the radio that they find any reading difficult if it deals, even in the simplest fashion, with general ideas. In so far as the difficulty can be ascribed to the author's presentation of a subject, and not to the subject itself or to the audience, I think it is largely a matter of Burke's special vocabulary, which has to be learned like a new language.

He is looking for terms that will cast new light on old situations and he finds them in unexpected places. Sometimes they are colloquial phrases like "moving in on," "slipping out from under," "cashing in" or "being driven into a corner," to which he gives a philosophical meaning. Sometimes they are technical terms that he borrows from anthropology or sociology or semantics. Sometimes they are the words of Greek philosophers or theologians carried over into English; in the present volume I noted, among others, "eristic," "chiliastic," "charismatic," "heuristic," "eschatology," "noetic." It is a good idea to have a big dictionary at hand when reading him for the first time.

Besides a special terminology, Burke also has the habits of thought that make him hard to follow. He is a dialectician who is always trying to reconcile opposites by finding that they have a common source. Give him two apparently hostile terms like poetry and propaganda, art and economics, speech and action, and immediately he looks beneath them for the common ground on which they stand. Where the Marxian dialectic moves forward in time from the conflict of thesis and antithesis to their subsequent resolution or synthesis — and always emphasizes the conflict — the Burkean dialectic moves backwards from conflicting effects to harmonious causes. It is a dialectic of reconciliation or peacemaking and not of war. At the same time it gives a backward or spiral movement to his current of thought, so that sometimes the beginning of a book is its logical ending and we have to read the last chapter before fully understanding the first.

The point I want to make is that, with a little attention, we finally understand all the chapters. Burke is one of the authors who write to be read twice, and if we give his work that second reading most of our difficulties are cleared away. A second reading is like a second journey through a recently discovered mountain pass; the trail is marked now and we no longer get lost in ravines that end at the base of a cliff. There are, it is true, a few sentences that have to be walked around like boulders in the path; but most of the second journey is easy and we make it with a sense of exhilaration, as if we had suddenly learned to be at home in a strange country. What Burke teaches us on the journey is how to interpret human experience, including literary experience, as a series of ritual dramas: initiations, penances, rebirths and castings out of scapegoats. We learn his lesson and, when we come down out of the mountains, we discern a new richness in our favorite books and a new eventfulness in the landscape of our familiar lives.

◇◇

See the notes on pages 6 and 33.

THIS is the last piece by Mr. Cowley to be included in this volume. Few others have had the benefit of Mr. Cowley's long friendship with Burke and few others have read and meditated on his works and development so thoughtfully. For me, this review has always marked a great turning point in Burke's development and in the way his work was received. Mr. Cowley was among the first to recognize what Burke was really about and to identify the whole endeavor accurately. He says that Burke "has come to be one of the few truly speculative thinkers of our time"; that his subject is the drama of human relations; and that he is developing a language-centered system — he calls it a "philosophical system on the grand scale." His last paragraph on what we can learn from Burke is a good antidote to the kind of things Mr. Bewley says.

◇◇

Rhetoric of Rhetoric

BY Richard Chase

THIS [*A Rhetoric of Motives*] is the second volume of Mr. Burke's proposed trilogy on the meaning of meaning, an ambitious and recondite inquiry purporting to examine the relationship of words to human motives. The first volume, *A Grammar of Motives,* appeared in 1945, the third, *A Symbolic of Motives,* is forthcoming. This trilogy already exerts a good deal of influence in our intellectual life. The *Rhetoric*

EDITOR'S NOTE: Reprinted from *Partisan Review,* XVII (1950), 736–739, copyright 1950 by *Partisan Review,* by permission of Frances W. Chase and the publisher.

indicates that the trilogy will be a prime handbook for those who now join in the abandonment of our naturalist and humanist inheritance in favor of the charismatic glamor of ultimate politics and ultimate metaphysics.

If we mean by "semantics" a discipline for investigating the relation of words to non-verbal reality with a minimum of metaphysical bias and with the intent of clarifying our scrutiny of the function of words, then Mr. Burke is hardly a semanticist at all, or, to put it another way, he is so much more than a semanticist that his semantic becomes hopelessly obscured in the wilderness of its own uncontrolled extensions. *A Grammar of Motives,* as Mr. Isaac Rosenfeld said in a brilliant account of the book (*The Kenyon Review,* Spring 1946), was not a Grammar at all but, among other things, "another bit of philosophy, a substance metaphysics." *A Rhetoric of Motives* is less a Rhetoric than what might be called a substance metapolitics. It is a vast and centerless farrago which, besides categorizing linguistics in the five terms of Scene, Act, Agent, Agency, and Purpose, draws attitudes of linguistic analysis from Marx, Bentham, Carlyle, Veblen, and Empson, and, from the whole, attempts to evolve a universal "purification" of language with the help of the "ultimate vocabulary" of Marxist dialectic and of the anagogic method of the medieval writers.

One will be disappointed if one expects from Mr. Burke as rhetorician a firm and adequate idea of politics — and such an idea surely must be implied by (though not confused with) any responsible investigation of rhetoric. The book carries a very heavy charge of political implication, but the author, like so many of his admirers and so much of the modern world, is beyond politics. He has no idea of man as a social animal, no idea of the state, no idea of democratic, socialist, or even aristocratic institutions, and no idea, in any concrete form, of either the philosophy or the rhetoric of politics. He has "purified" politics and political man out of existence.

A small example, or "anecdote," as Mr. Burke would say, may get us to the central issues. Our author discusses at some length the meaning of the story of Abraham and Isaac. He rejects the interpretation of psychoanalysis as not ultimate enough. Mr. Burke throws up his hands at the brutality of psychoanalysis, which, he believes, unwittingly sanctions parricide and infanticide. Psychoanalysis would impute to Abraham a covert desire to kill Isaac. But such an interpretation is unacceptable; it leaves us in the slaughterous "Barnyard" of the bourgeois world, which Mr. Burke is accustomed to identify as the "parliamentary wrangle" and whose motive is competitive murder. Father and son being "consubstantial," says Burke, we see that Abraham's motive was not to kill Isaac but to perform the "dramatistic" ritual of vicariously killing *himself*. "For the so-called 'desire to kill' a certain person is much more properly analysable as a desire to *transform the principle* which that person *represents*." Every aggressive act, in short, may best be seen as beginning in ideology or in man's incorrigible delight in creating symbols and becomes reflexive, in the sense that as an aggressor you are really only using your victim as a device for purging or transforming a principle or "trait" within yourself. Thus, on Mr. Burke's own implicit assumption that the extensions of linguistic method *are* reality, are human events translated into a ghostly dumb show.

From any conceivable naturalistic point of view one would begin with the fact of intended murder and its motives, and one would regard the mythical and ritual components of the Abraham-Isaac story in ascending order as "rationalization," as tragic artistic treatments of the human fact of infanticide, and finally as attempts to grasp philosophically the meaning of the act. But with Mr. Burke the play's the thing. Nobody has ever taken so literally the idea that all the world's a stage. Behind every human event there lurks man's natural desire to perform symbolic acts. The most delightful of symbolic acts is sacrifice—that is, self-sacrifice. And nothing is so striking in this book as the assumption that man is a self-immolating creature and that the great dramatic act of the individual is self-immolation in the name of a transcendent hierarchy.

We arrive at an "ultimate" rhetoric by discerning, first, that a "positive" order of language is too reductive and can deal only with tangible things, and, second, that a "dialectic" order, while more general, winds up in the "parliamentary wrangle" and that instead of a confused clash of conflicting principles, we need principles of principles. To those who still refer to "parliaments" with emotions other than contempt or pity, this might mean that we need to clarify our thinking and seek for common grounds, or at worst, act from mere superior power while at the same time trying not to annihilate the whole possibility of "parliaments." But to Mr. Burke, it means taking a "leap" to the "universal ground of human motives." This ground is mystically felt when we look "socioanagogically" at history, social stratification, or literature, wherein we discern dramatistically bodied forth the ultimate mystery of life, the mystery of "hierarchy." Thus in the perfection of the "ultimate design . . . each tiny act shares in the meaning of the total act." And thus we achieve the ultimate language which may help us toward universal clarity and the "purification of war."

One may remark that for a writer so given to ultimate vocabularies, Mr. Burke is extraordinarily sensitive to the vicissitudes of ideology.

In *A Grammar of Motives,* written during the war years, he accepted war as of man's essence (man "has the motives of combat in his very essence"), and he spoke of the enormous unwieldiness of war "as an anecdote" due to its being "more of a *confusion* than a form." Yet in *A Rhetoric of Motives,* which makes its commitment to the Wallace movement, he writes that war is a "perversion" of peace. He finds less confusion in the phenomenon of war now that the perceptions of rhetorical method show that the United States is the perverter of an otherwise potentially peaceful world. In the *Grammar* he spoke of the "great dialectic interchange still to be completed." In the *Rhetoric* the dialectic interchange is being sabotaged by the Marshall Plan, which – though it does not presume to understand Russian policy – the rhetorical method easily perceives to be nothing but the "sinister" stratagem of capitalist imperialism. In this age of Communist rhetoric such a procedure is indefensible.

Mr. Burke repeatedly disavows any didactic intent. He tells us that this is a linguistic study and should not be taken as indicative of his views in other areas. But these disclaimers are preposterous. No linguistic study can be made to bear one tenth the weight of Mr. Burke's ideology and metaphysics and still remain intelligible as a linguistic study. Equally unconvincing is Mr. Burke's departure from the reductive biases of "scientism," since the alternative – "dramatism" – becomes his warrant for abandoning the admonishments of scientific method on the one hand and accepting on the other that most frivolous and dangerous of modern myths, the myth of total rationalization. As for "scientism" the reader will find its essence in Mr. Burke's proposal to "hire a batch of poets," give them the task of imagining the various modes of the final extinction of life, and then categorize the citizenry as personality types according to their responses to the different modes. This is what Mr. Burke calls "our 'neotragic' school of ethnic classification" and is apparently offered as a joke.

And also unconvincing are Mr. Burke's attacks on technology and bureaucratization, since his thought so plainly issues from the intellectual mystique of these phenomena – a mystique which in our time has evolved into a secular religion philosophically supported by the rags and tatters of western thought thrown together in an obscure jargoning dissonance entirely bereft of emotional innerness, rational tact, and humane purpose.

◇◇◇

RICHARD CHASE was born in Lakeport, New Hampshire, in 1914 and died in 1962. He taught American literature at Columbia University most of his academic life and wrote profusely on that same subject. His published works include *Herman Melville, Emily Dickinson, Walt Whitman Reconsidered, The American Novel and Its Tradition, The Democratic Vista,* and *Walt Whitman.*

As Mr. Chase's books (especially the one on the novel and *The Democratic Vista*) make clear, he was a liberal-radical thinker, and it seems strange at first that he should be so opposed to Burke. At first one thinks that he has not understood Burke, but this is not true at all. Mr. Chase's objections to Burke (somewhat overstated here) are complex and are partly shared by other radical thinkers today. There are two powerful and sometimes contradictory drives in Burke's theoretical and systematic works: the abstracting, idealizing, purely verbal tendency (the rhetoric of rhetoric of Mr. Chase's title, the "ultimate" of everything he speaks of). This is the realm of purely verbal manipulation and problem solving — of purely symbolic action in Burke's sense of this phrase. Mr. Chase objects to this on the grounds that it is essentially conservative and anti-revolutionary because it substitutes verbal for real solutions and hence encourages the maintenance of the status quo. This is like G. B. Shaw's objections to the Salvation Army as he works them out in *Major Barbara.* Others besides Chase (see Benjamin De Mott's piece) have objected to Burke on these grounds and there can be no question that this tendency does exist, powerfully, in Burke and that it supports the motto — toward the purification of war — of *A Grammar of Motives.*

As I pointed out in another note, this tendency is part of a much larger (than Burke) shift to a language-centered view of reality and the extraordinary emphasis that goes with it on purely verbal analysis and on the study of verbal system building as an end in itself. This development tends to encourage intellectual detachment and a curious kind of stoical withdrawal into an ironic contemplation of human affairs — in Burke as well as in someone like Northrop Frye. Mr. Chase, then, is objecting to Burke for exactly the opposite reason that Mr. Bewley does, which seems rather odd until one realizes that this language-centered view of reality always tends toward the mixing, the pluralism, the breaking down of the old categories that Mr. Bewley found so distressing. In its extreme form, this tendency leads to a book such as N. O. Brown's *Love's Body* and his assertions that "it" is all one book, that it is all one language. Perhaps the best thing to say here is that many branches grow from the same trunk and that one has to walk all around a big tree to get a complete view of it.

◇◇

7 A Review of "A Rhetoric of Motives"

BY Hugh Dalziel Duncan

IN THE previous volume of this trilogy on motives (of which two have now appeared: *A Grammar of Motives* [1945], *A Rhetoric of Motives* [1950], while the third, *A Symbolic of Motives,* is now being prepared for the press) Burke holds that the best theoretical construct for understanding motivation will be one that treats language and thought as modes of action. The mode Burke considers is the symbolic and is referred to throughout his work as "symbolic action." For Burke the symbolic is a phase of action, incipient or consummatory as the case may be, but never substitutive. It is, in Mead's terms (Burke makes much use of Mead), a *phase* of the act. Vocal gestures arouse in ourselves the attitudes they arouse in others and thus allow us to adopt the attitude of the other in the formation of our social consciousness. Relations become social in so far as the individual learns to anticipate the attitudes of others toward him. He becomes aware of himself in terms of the "other." His attitudes, being shaped by the attitudes of others as aroused in him by spoken (or other) symbols in infancy and by written symbols in later years, modify his ways of action.

But all this is going on through symbols which have been organized into various symbol systems such as language and its institutionalized form, literature. Language exists prior to the individual, and the individual must learn how to use language, for, without it, no socialization can take place. Through the use of this prime social instrument man is able to learn the traditions of his society and at the same time modify them (as in slang or in the creation of new symbols) when they are no longer of any use for satisfying his needs. That man internalizes traditions mainly through symbols is not a new idea; what is new is that Burke makes it a point of departure, not of arrival. In earlier works such as *Permanence and Change* (1935) and *Attitudes toward History* (1937) Burke stresses that motives cannot be explained without reference to their linguistic expression, since motives arise *in* and *through* language. If this is so, we must then conceive of language as a basic, not a residual, sociological category. We must study it by abstracting it from society and by examining the qualities of experience peculiar to the symbolic

EDITOR'S NOTE: Reprinted from *The American Journal of Sociology,* LVI (1950–51), 592–594, by permission of the University of Chicago Press.

phases of action, as well as by considering language residual to a "context of the situation" within which language is being used.

Where Mead, Cooley, Piaget, and Malinowski analyze verbal communication as it takes place within the primary group, Burke analyzes linguistic communication as it takes place in the larger society. His conception of the structure of communicative acts of this type will be found in what he calls "dramatism."

> In a rounded statement about motives, you must have some word that names the *act* (names what took place, in thought or deed), and another that names the *scene* (the background of the act, the situation in which it occurred); also, you must indicate what person or kind of person (*agent*) performed the act, what means or instruments he used (*agency*), and the *purpose*. Men may violently disagree about the purposes behind a given act, or about the character of the person who did it, or how he did it, or in what kind of situation he acted; or they may even insist upon totally different words to name the act itself. But be that as it may, any complete statement about motives will offer *some kind* of answers to these five questions: what was done (act), when or where it was done (scene), who did it (agent), how he did it (agency), and why (purpose) [*A Grammar of Motives* (New York: Prentice-Hall, Inc., 1945), p. xv (Burke's italics)].

Such a construct makes it possible to avoid monistic approaches to language in terms of sex, class, beauty, magic, fantasy, play, and the like. Burke's method is not an "either . . . or" but a "both . . . and" procedure. We are asked to consider what *proportion* of the act may be analyzed by which theory of symbolic action as these have been developed in philosophy, theology, psychology, anthropology, and sociology.

The problem in every theory of symbolic usage, sociological as well as any other, is that of making clear what is *specific* to symbolic experience. For if we assert that symbolic experience (as in art) is a basic form of experience like evaluation and cognition, we must offer a theory of art which makes clear what is true of symbolic experience in art that is not true of such experience in systems of evaluation and cognition. Burke meets this difficulty by asking us to consider what symbols are used for in a society. His question is: Who is using what kind of symbols in what situations for what purposes? In the present volume Burke attempts to analyze the ways in which men use symbols to arouse co-operative attitudes in others who must be appealed to in various kinds of social situations.

After reviewing traditional treatments of rhetoric and dialectic, Burke points out that, while rhetoric may be considered as a formal or conscious act of persuasion, there is another kind of experience in rhetoric which cannot be explained in these terms – the process of identification. He describes the latter as ranging "from the politician who, addressing an audience of farmers, says 'I was a farm boy myself,' through the mysteries of social status, to the mystic's devout identification with the source of all being" (p. xiv). Identification is essentially an integrating device, a way of overcoming the divisiveness intrinsic in every relationship. Symbols used for purposes of identification must be analyzed in terms of their use by various status groups within a society. We cannot understand even erotic symbols unless we accept the fact that vocabularies of sexual and social courtship are interchangeable, not because one is a mere substitute for the other, but because sexual courtship is intrinsically fused with the motives of social hierarchy. Burke contends also that specific kinds of symbolic appeal are related to specific social structures. In a primitive society magic is the basis of symbolic appeal, in feudal society pageantry and pantomime as in formal etiquette are the dominant forms of communicating status to others. In bourgeois society what Marx calls the "mystifications" and Carlyle the "mysteries" of ownership (as expressed in consumption in clothes) are the chief means of identification, while in a socialist structure where there is a presumed beautiful or holy relation between classes, "pastoral" forms of symbolic appeal are characteristic. (See William Empson, *English Pastoral Poetry* [New York, 1938], for the theory of proletarian literature drawn up by Burke.)

The first section of *A Rhetoric of Motives* considers ways in which symbolic identification may occur in rhetoric. Burke's theory of rhetoric has much in common with the general sociological approach to meaning. He stresses (particularly in this book) the function of language as *addressed*, as a "direct or roundabout appeal to real or ideal audiences, without or within," as this goes on in a society where the form of linguistic expression may be dialectical as well as ritual (that is, where there are *competing* voices, not only a tribal voice).

In the next section Burke considers various conditions of symbolic appeals such as those going on between sexes, age groups, persons, status groups, classes, political, religious and aesthetic groups, in terms of how such social placement affects the use of language and other symbols. We are shown how symbols are used to induce co-operation among beings who are "apart" from one another yet who must exist in terms of each other.

The final section deals with the principles of order, or hierarchy, as these are manifest in symbolic process. The key term here is "courtship," not simply as erotic but as a general process of legitimation. Burke shares

Weber's concern with the problem of legitimation, but his interests are not so much in the structures within which various kinds of legitimation occur as in the symbolic processes going on within these structures. Burke's typology of courtship is a valuable supplement to Weber's typology of legitimation. When Burke uses terms such as "tradition," "charisma," and "authority," he tries to show *how* they develop thorough symbolic appeals in so far as these are based in the process of identification.

The basic unit in Burke's technique of symbolic analysis is the image as it is found in the symbolic work under consideration. The first step is to note what images predominate in a given work. Following this, images are then classified qualitatively. This involves codifying the images which are used at intense and crucial moments of symbolic action. Interrelationships among images are then worked out by asking what image goes with what image in various kinds of action. Burke insists over and over again that what is said of the relations among images must be pointed out in the work itself for it is only when we know what associational clusters exist among images that we know what specific images refer to in the symbolic work. This procedure makes it possible to use various approaches to symbolic analysis so long as we point out specifically in the symbolic content precisely how such an approach *is* manifest. A symbolic work has a structure, a configuration, which must be understood if we are to understand the function of its symbolic units. And it is also being used in a larger set of relationships. Burke does not ask us to stay "within" or "without" the symbolic work in our analysis. He does ask that we make explicit by quotation from the work itself whatever we assume to be the reasons for form and content. (For a specific discussion on method, as well as for other specific examples of his analysis, see the section "On Methodology" in *The Philosophy of Literary Form* [Baton Rouge: Louisiana State University Press, 1941], pp. 66–89.)

Sociologists who are interested in communication will find this a very valuable work. Of all his works, the *Rhetoric* is of most specific interest to sociologists, for here Burke is stressing the *social* components of verbal action. He shows *how* language is related to society (not simply that it *is*) and offers us conceptual and methodological tools for further analysis. In doing so, he carries on the tradition of Dewey, Mead, Cooley, Sapir, Richards, and Malinowski. As matters now stand, it is unwise to talk about communication without some understanding of Burke, for he has assumed the burden of constructing hypotheses on the social effects of communication in terms of the process of identification as this takes place through the use of symbols. We can, and should, go on with our particularistic studies in the field of communication research, but there is a great need for some kind of theoretical framework within which to develop new approaches to the problems arising out of attempts to understand what goes on in symbolic experience. Whatever one's taste in the pursuit of such understanding may be, one must realize that Burke is asking the important question which is not only who reads what but how those who read are affected by what they read.

◇◇

HUGH DALZIEL DUNCAN was born in Bo'ness, Scotland, in 1909. For many years he lived and wrote outside Chicago, occasionally teaching in the city. Since 1964, he has been a professor of sociology at Southern Illinois University, Carbondale. He is the author of *Language and Literature in Society, Communication and Social Order, The Rise of Chicago as a Literary Center, Culture and Democracy,* and other works.

Once Mr. Duncan discovered Burke (when he was lecturing at the University of Chicago) he became a convert and true disciple. He has written more about Burke, used him more completely, and absorbed him more profoundly than anyone else I know of. All of his many books have been about or have been applications of Burke and have been parts of a lifelong attempt to develop a methodology and working model (in the scientific sense of theoretical construct) from Burke for the study of society.

The sheer amount of material available to choose from has made the problem of adequate and proper selection from Mr. Duncan's works nearly impossible. What I have done is to select three pieces, of which this is the first, that give one some sense of why Mr. Duncan found Burke so useful. Hugh Duncan was among the first—with Malcolm Cowley—to perceive and write about the dramatistic system Burke was building as his major contribution to the intellectual life of his time. This review of *A Rhetoric of Motives* shows how Mr. Duncan apprehends that system; and the other two selections show how, over the years, he has used it. The extent of his use can best be seen in his own aptly entitled *Communication and Social Order.*

◇◇

z Burke, Burke, the Lurk

BY Kermit Lansner

I HAVE often wondered at the intemperate reactions to Mr. Kenneth Burke's work. *A Rhetoric of Motives,* to cite the latest instance, has aroused responses ranging from ill-humored scorn, through sheer amusement, to excessive enthusiasm. Of course, Burke has been writing now for almost thirty years and he has devoted the last twenty to the gradual elaboration of a system of theories which embraces many crucial problems. He writes as aesthetician, literary critic, political theorist, political commentator and metaphysician. His subjects are involved with people's loyalties and passions, and he has made friends and enemies who, though they may not really care to find out what Burke is up to, can catch him at his weakest and strongest moments and distort the rest by omission. The fault is not wholly theirs, however. Burke, with his extraordinary preoccupation with opposition and antitheses, would understand me when I say that his writing is such a strange mixture of sense and nonsense that it is almost impossible to give a coherent discursive account of what he really means. This frustration is probably one of the main reasons for all the immoderate criticisms of his latest book.

Sense and nonsense are matters of content. But Burke is equally perplexing in his style, the tone of his analysis and address. Since he lurks patiently in the offing waiting to pounce, I gain no advantage by being coy about my rhetorical strategies. It is necessary to set oneself against Burke's mode of analysis at every turn. He says somewhere that the topics the poet uses are charismatic, for they glow. This is a good appreciation, if the word bears that meaning; it may be that poetry is the proper residence of charisma. The experience of our time has led us to distrust it in men. Now Burke glows through his system and his style. It is relevant to instance his lectures as well as his books. Those who have heard him speak of Joyce or Shakespeare or Coleridge find it difficult to resist his power as he sweeps together art and life, pouring forth a stream of commentary and insight which continues until the body cannot remain and the mind is amazed at the wonder of it all. Here is "systematic intellect" at work – adventurous, unlimited. No realm is closed to it and all are merged in it. Burke characterizes his mind by his description of the method he uses: "So we must keep trying anything

EDITOR'S NOTE: Reprinted from *The Kenyon Review,* XIII (1951), 324–335, copyright 1951 by Kenyon College, by permission of the author and publisher.

and everything, improvising, borrowing from others, developing from others, dialectically using one text as comment upon another, schematizing; using the incentive to new wanderings, returning from these excursions to schematize again, being oversubtle where the straining seems to promise some further glimpse, and making amends by reduction to very simple anecdotes." A strange combination of system and no system. Nothing could seem more unsystematic than this random method, but Burke, as I shall show, is adept at merging opposites; it is the key to his system. We are tempted to his devices though we have no need for them. For — and this is our opposition to Burke himself — to learn from him and to criticize him we must set ourselves against his glow. When Burke flits and darts in scattered paths to reach his end dialectically, we must proceed firmly and dully on the ground with endless "buts" and circumspections; where he plays fast and loose with terms, we must demand definition and consistency; where he glows red and hot, we must remain sober and cold. Burke's master term (he tells us again and again) is "identification"; ours must be division. Nor must this antithesis be dissolved by a Burkean sleight of hand into a synthesis between "identification" and division.

It is essential to suggest some hypothesis which will point to the source of Burke's glow, the passion that even shines through his technical jargon, an unwitting concession, I suppose, to the dominance of the scientific mode of procedure in our time. I should hesitate to say what Burke is *essentially,* but there is no doubt that he is driven by a great enthusiasm for social reform, or even more extremely by the belief that in some way man can find salvation on this earth. Despite his remarkable acuteness to the rhetorical strategies of all the other Utopians who have believed in a similar possibility he is at one with them. "Eulogistically" we can say that Burke is an evangelical Utopian; "dyslogistically" he is a crackpot with a panacea, or at least an explanation, for the world's ills. I find it enlightening to compare him to the sociologist, Ptirim Sorokin, another "mystical" scholar and writer, who now concentrates his attention on the study of Altruism (Burke's identification). Both Sorokin and Burke are passionate and intense, both are strange combinations of sophistication and naiveté, knowledge and ignorance, insight and obtuseness. Both are appalled by the moral oppositions of our "sensate" culture (what Burke calls the Scramble, the Wrangling of the Market Place, the Human Barnyard) and yearn for the free play of Altruism and Love.

A Rhetoric of Motives — one can Burke the title into *The Motives of Rhetoric* and find equal sense — is the second volume of the proposed trilogy which Burke will have completed soon. It stands between *A*

Grammar of Motives, which elaborates the properties of the remarkable pentad, Act, Scene, Agent, Agency and Purpose, the indispensable machinery for the analysis of all forms of human expression, and *A Symbolic* (of Motives?) which, I presume, will bring the full weight of this machinery to bear upon literature alone. In the *Grammar* Burke demonstrates his devotion to the analysis of linguistic manipulations by analysing a number of the great philosophical systems which mark the history of human thought. He seems unconcerned with the pretensions of these philosophies to give some true account of the nature of things, unconcerned, too, with their solutions of the many small problems, some new, some inherited, which each tried to solve. Rather his analysis was one of those strategies, tactics, slants, angles, tricks and shifts which the thinkers used in their endless reshuffling and reformulation of a limited number of views which one can take toward the universe. The *Grammar,* in effect, was an exercise in the application of the ratios which could be drawn from the pentad without any concern for the comparative validity or progress of the materials to which they were applied. Underlying this enterprise was Burke's movement toward a philosophy of his own which reaches a partial statement in the *Rhetoric.*

The first part of the *Rhetoric* gives a general definition of rhetoric and sets forth the principle of identification upon which rhetoric rests; the second part traces the history of rhetoric and analyses, in a fashion remarkably original, the rhetorical preoccupations of many writers whom we honor for different reasons; the third section leads us into the ubiquitous ground of order and hierarchy with its correlates, secrecy, mystery and the kill. Here literature and society meet. Identification! I have suggested that it takes on the meaning of Love in the context of Burke's zeal for reform. It is important to trace some of the other sources from which a principle of such great importance springs. Could its power derive from Burke's sensitivity to puns and from his studies into the multiplicity of meanings a single word can carry? Whereas Mr. Empson has made much of this natural quality of words, but restricted his task to the patient explanation of literary works, Burke has joined it with the vague machinery of the dialectic to arrive at a metaphysic. The source may seem disproportionately trivial to the magnitude of the result, but just as one procedure in science derives a generalization from an examination of a great number of particulars, a Burkean treatise can rise from one small instance fed into the operation of the dialectic.

Mr. Burke, I think, calls himself a literary man, a writer. Not teacher, nor scholar, nor even philosopher, but writer. The general name for his system he calls dramatism. Poetry, drama and rhetoric may be the great abode of identification, for there are the worlds of figure and trope moving to a logic of their own; there language and symbol flourish most powerfully. Yet who else but Burke has taken literature so seriously that it could become the ground which underlies all human activity? The analysis of tropes, which he performs with great fecundity and insight, becomes, by his peculiar transformation, the foundation for the analysis of human motivation and the means for its redirection.

Not only literature, but language generally, assumes a disproportionate importance among human activities. Semiotics is a discipline which, in various guises, is as old as philosophy itself. Recently, in its most acceptable form, it has become an extremely technical and meticulous mode of analysis which has done much to clear up the obscurities and confusions we are prey to in our use of signs and symbols. But around a core of careful workers whose results are important, but very limited, is a fringe of enthusiasts and reformers who see in the operations of language and the possibility of their manipulation the promise for the reform of social life in general. Burke belongs in one of his many roles to this group. He does not consider the many uses of language and symbol, but tends to assimilate them all to the rhetorical, which is most suited to his enterprise. His position is this: "For rhetoric as such is not rooted in any past condition of human society. It is rooted in an essential function of language itself, a function that is wholly realistic and is continually born anew; the use of language as a symbolic means of inducing cooperation in beings that by nature respond to symbols." It would be unjust, and far too simple, to say that Burke is unequivocal about this extreme form of an idealism of rhetoric, but it is certainly one of the main strands of his thought and reappears in many different contexts.

Burke is at one with Aristotle in defining rhetoric as the art of persuasion. Aristotle bulks very large in Burke's theory, but when persuasion is taken to mean identification we can see the unique relation between them. The semanticists of the self-styled non-Aristotelian variety have always harbored a particular animus toward the Law of Identity. Burke is a heavy borrower from the Stagirite but a remarkably selective one. Whereas the hierarchical structure of the *Metaphysics* and its medieval elaborations lies at the source of his discussion of order and the stuff of the *Rhetoric* and the *Topics* is the final standard against which he must always measure his own *Rhetoric*, the empirical side of the biological treatises and the careful exploration of logic in the *Organon* are scarcely mentioned by Burke. He proceeds in deliberate opposition to the traditional logic, building his system upon the very fallacies which contemporary philosophers have exposed as the unwitting errors of the metaphysicians of the past who struggled to give some total coherent account of the universe.

Consider at some length how the concept of identification is introduced. Burke offers a reading of *Samson Agonistes.* At the moment it would be irrelevant to suggest that this is one of several possible readings; they would all but reinforce the density of the identification. Thus:

> We considered, among those "uses" to which *Samson Agonistes* was put, the poet's identification with a blind giant who slew himself in slaying enemies of the Lord; and we saw identification between Puritans and Israelites, Royalists and Philistines, identification allowing for a ritualistic kind of historiography. . . . Then we came upon a more complicated kind of identification; here the poet presents a motive in an essentially magnified or perfected form, in some way tragically purified or transcended; the imagery of death reduces the motive to *ultimate* terms, dramatic equivalent for an "entelechial" pattern of thought whereby a thing's nature would be classed according to the fruition, maturing or ideal fulfillment, proper to its kind.
>
> As seen from this point of view, then, the imagery of slaying (slaying of either the self or another) is to be considered merely as a special case of identification in general. Or otherwise put: the imagery of slaying is a special case of transformation, and transformation involves the ideas and imagery of *identification.* That is: the killing of something is the *changing* of it and the statement of a thing's nature before and after the change is an *identifying* of it.

This lengthy passage is central to Burke's thought and a good example of his method. He uses here the term identification and its variants in at least three senses, merging the amalgamative, assimilative sense of identify with the separative, definitive sense of the term. A moment later, in a passage which immediately follows this, he performs a shift between the symbolic and natural worlds of motivation by denying that poets are "essentially killers" as one (who?) might deduce, but rather "essentially identifiers." This transition is an example of Burke's constant urge to merge terms of narrower scope, such as those of killing, to terms of wider scope, those of identification. The tactic is justified by even another definition: ". . . the word for the autonomous activity's place in this wider context." Combine all these different senses of identification, tie them to Burke's rhetorical and political interests, and you arrive at the remarkable statement which should never be quoted in isolation from its derivation: ". . . we can treat 'war' as a *special case of peace* . . . not as a primary motive in itself, not as *essentially* real, but purely as a *derivative* condition, a *perversion.*" How italics and quotation marks work wonders!

The last meaning given to identification leads Burke into a double attack against science. One assault unfolds against science as an autonomous activity, a method free of all moral value; the other against science as a final good and absolute, serving the function of a God. At this stage it seems gratuitous for Burke to exacerbate the moral anguish which the Bomb has made all too common. But he pursues his point relentlessly, exposing with his usual blend of insight and blindness, the dangers of a "perverse" science which would reflect the moral perversion of the society in which it operates. The autonomy of science is particularly reprehensible to Burke since he equates autonomy with liberalism and liberalism with dispersion, a state of Babel. Burke is no liberal; that much we know. I cannot guess which among existing societies he would choose, but even among Utopias the only one that seems really congenial to his system would be a "coherent" society merged in its parts through the process of identification; something akin to the historical fictions of Sorokin.

The tensions which make up Burke's mind are explicitly illustrated by the two poles around which his book is organized. I have just treated the first section which centers around the concept of identification; the third part is built around the ideas of order and hierarchy. If one were to follow Burke's method of wandering, he might speculate very amusingly about the social and psychological roots of Burke's ceaseless concern with hierarchy. It seems more reasonable, however, to assume that this concern derives, too, from his peculiar misplacement of literature. For again, only in literature, whatever its form may be, can we find the clearly isolable locus of order where the writer can transform the flow and contradictions of life into an ascending movement towards an ultimate moral summit from which the lower stages may be contemplated and judged. The order of literature sometimes seems to be taken as one among many by Burke, but fundamentally, I think, he takes it as the prototype of all order and certainly the most precious of all orders of discourse — what would be called an ultimate order. Burke distinguishes, with cavalier disregard for the careful efforts the philosophers have accorded this problem, three kinds of terms: positive, dialectical and ultimate. The positive terms name things of experience, "a visible and tangible thing that can be located in time and space." Evasive of all the obvious objections, he slips the body of scientific knowledge into this positive vocabulary. As the positive terms deal with motion and perception, the dialectical terms treat of essence and principle, or what seems to be the same thing, idea and action. The dialectical vocabulary, however, leaves its voices competing in "a jangling relation with one another." The ultimate order transcends this discord by placing them in a "hierarchy or sequence or evaluative series" from the viewpoint of a "guiding idea" or "unitary principle." As example of this Burke cites Plato's description of the four types of imperfect government, arranged developmentally in an ascending order which can be judged from the ultimate standard of aristocracy.

Now this analysis of terms is infuriatingly perfunctory although it purports to be part of the theoretical groundwork upon which the literary criticism rests. Burke may be amusing when he speaks of the social implications of science or the manners of scientists, but when he deals with the method and language of science itself he is simply annoying. It is an expression of ignorance to wage war now against a simple positivism or a naive behaviorism, while the attempt to classify scientific discourse and order it on the lowest rung of his hierarchy is simply malicious. Actually Burke's power lies in his analysis of dialectical terms, but his hopes, a confusion of artistic and political hopes, rest with the ultimate order of language. It is one thing to use an ultimate scheme in a work of analysis or in a piece of poetry or narrative; even in the discordant arena of parliamentary debate, when the basic principles of cohesion and existence are unquestioned, there is some hope of ordering conflicting voices. But when interests are really irreconcilable an ultimate ordering is actually impossible except insofar as one voice completely dominates another. There are situations which cannot be affected by "courtship," the rhetorical term that denotes the use of a suasive device for the transcending of social estrangement. How casually Burke treats the idea of interest. "True," he says, "there is much that no vocabulary can do in these matters. Where there are so many intense conflicts of an extraverbal sort, no merely verbal manipulations can remove them. But verbal manipulations may offer a more orderly approach to them, permitting them to be contemplated with less agitation. And where this is the case, verbal manipulations are the very opposite of 'evasive.' "

Burke's stress upon an ultimate ordering allows him to indulge one of the most obvious qualities of his mind. His is an omnibus mind, loath to suppress or forget anything that it has learned — even in the interest of clarity. But Burke makes capital of his failings, for the force of his theories is generated by a tension between all the powerful abstractions about man and literature that he knows. By ordering them he can scorn them without depriving himself of the benefit of their use. Even when he attacks a theory he is reluctant to abandon it. Thus while he denigrates the Freudian analysis of motivation and its application to literature as sex-ridden, he employs it with considerable flexibility and sophistication by resorting to the simplest rhetorical devices. Conversely, while he employs a Marxian mode of analysis of a very high order, he subjects it to so many questionings and inversions that we find ourselves dizzy after being turned upside down once too often. All this might be interpreted as honest reserve in the face of the shortcomings of most theories. But I think not. Burke wants his work of analysis to be one of art. Since he seems unconcerned with the factor of validity, he wants all the contradictions and oppositions of analytic thought, the welter of theories, insights and casual statements which flourish and die as new knowledge and techniques are available, to exist simultaneously in his words and sentences. He says: "The veil of Maya is woven of the strands of hierarchy — and the poet's topics glow through that mist." Burke's method of literary criticism is directed toward the search for the implicit identifications in a work of art, but his own work is not one of art, but one of analysis. The attempt to construct a series of analytic statements through which his topics will glow is responsible for so much of his confusion. Freud, Marx, Carlyle, Bentham, Empson, etc., can be used in a selective conjunction, but not in an identified suspension. Nor can the repeated use of the terms transcendence and dialectic, terms never clearly defined, bring matters into a clear focus.

We are never quite certain whether Burke's literary criticism is determined by his general theories or these theories by his practice of criticism. Ordinarily, I see little reason to push every critic back to his "philosophical" assumptions, for many critics have none at all or improvise makeshift theories to suit the particular problem at hand. However, Burke is always so theoretical, so insistent upon the "philosophy" underlying his reading of a work, that he constantly turns attention away from the stuff of his criticism towards questions of a more theoretical kind. For example, he submits *Venus and Adonis* and *The Castle* to a "socioanagogic" interpretation — the name he has chosen for his type of criticism. Although we may object to the general tendency which marks this book to overstress the rhetorical aspect of the poem or story we cannot deny the intense illumination which Burke sheds upon these works. They emerge from his reading with new and pertinent meanings. And yet it is the notion of "socioanagogic" which is most intriguing. "Socioanagogic" refers to the search for the implicit identifications in the work of art. The search is demanded in principle although the statement of particulars may be far wrong. Burke has taken over the medieval categories of interpretation and infused them with a modern content. Thus the allegorical might refer to a reading in psychoanalytic terms; the tropological to a reading in ritual terms which would clarify the manner in which a reader is involved in a purification or reforming. Burke is aware that on these two levels of interpretation the work of art is reduced to something that it is not: on the one hand, it is oversimplified to an explicit statement of its sources; on the other, to a pragmatic account of what it does. And since Burke is, above all, a modern critic who understands the independence and internal complexity of a work, he must argue strongly against this reductivist bias though it is really very strong in him. The term "socioanagogic" reflects his perplexity: the double passion, to exhaust a work by indicating its every possible meaning and function, and also to bestow upon it an ineffable autonomy. He wants to retain the mystery, the enigma of poetry. One so much concerned with language itself could not do otherwise. Yet at this half-way point toward a pure symbolic, Burke realizes that a poem must do something. Thus the reading of *Venus and Adonis* as a revolutionary challenge directed against the existing social hierarchy. In effect, Burke's method is open to the same objection he makes to other kinds of interpretation. A reading in terms of social class is as much allegorical as a reading in terms of sexual symbolism. Burke tries to forestall this criticism by two means: he concentrates on the mysteries which stem from social stratification and parallels them to the mysteries of a celestial hierarchy, thus attempting a divorce between a materialistic criticism and his "socioanagogic" kind; and then he theorizes about an indeterminate, dialectical ground of artistic motivation — an ultimate ground anterior to the sexual or social. These ultimate motives are only directed and intensified by the social hierarchy which, in some way, parallels them. Since hierarchy is taken as a universal quality of existence there seems little reason why social hierarchy or class should be chosen as the main ground for the analysis of literature. In the loose sense in which Burke conceives of hierarchy, anything — the ages of men, the heights of mountains, the sounds of guns — could be ordered in an ascending series which would generate its own mystery. Of course, sex and class are two most fruitful grounds for the interpretation of literature. But by his insistence on the relevance of an ultimate level, Burke deprives himself of the warrant for some of his most brilliant criticism.

It is too much to expect that a few words of praise can redress these pages of complaint against Mr. Burke's bad philosophy. Yet I must insist that every page of *A Rhetoric of Motives* contains observations about literature, society and politics which are important and enlightening. Yes, even about politics. For some time now certain critics have been in mourning for the loss of the "political sense" in our time. As I understand it, they feel that no one with a simplistic view of human nature or a Utopian view of human destiny can say anything relevant about that activity which they call political. Well, Mr. Burke does.

◇◇

KERMIT I. LANSNER was born in New York City in 1922. He taught philosophy briefly (1948–50) at Kenyon College, was an associate editor of *Art News Magazine* for two years, and is presently managing editor of *Newsweek*.

Like all serious and thoughtful reviewers of *A Rhetoric of Motives*, Mr. Lansner recognizes the presence of a large system in that book and discusses it and Burke in terms of the system. This review-essay has always seemed to me one of the very few and among the most brilliant pieces of intellectual characterization ever written about Burke. Few people have been able to locate and accurately render the strange mixture of "tensions which make up Burke's mind"; and fewer still have been able to assess that mixture properly. The reception of Burke has been complicated by his idiosyncratic, eccentric, and sometimes perverse style and vision. Both have required a certain amount of discounting and both have always made assessment of him extremely difficult. Mr. Lansner here tells us, as some others have tried to do, what we have to discount and how we may assess the man's mind and work.

◇◇

7 Kenneth Burke and the "New Rhetoric"

BY Marie Hochmuth Nichols

"WE DO not flatter ourselves that any one book can contribute much to counteract the torrents of ill will into which so many of our contemporaries have so avidly and sanctimoniously plunged," observes Kenneth Burke in introducing his latest book, *A Rhetoric of Motives*, but

EDITOR'S NOTE: Reprinted from *The Quarterly Journal of Speech*, XXXVIII (1952), 133–144, copyright 1952 by the Speech Association of America, by permission of the author and publisher.

"the more strident our journalists, politicians, and alas! even many of our churchmen become, the more convinced we are that books should be written for tolerance and contemplation."[1] Burke has offered all his writings to these ends.

Burke's first work, *Counter-Statement,* published in 1931, was hailed as a work of "revolutionary importance," presenting "in essence, a new view of rhetoric."[2] Since that time, he has written a succession of books either centrally or peripherally concerned with rhetoric: *Permanence and Change,* 1935; *Attitudes toward History,* 1937; *The Philosophy of Literary Form,* 1941; *A Grammar of Motives,* 1945; and his latest, *A Rhetoric of Motives,* 1950. An unfinished work entitled *A Symbolic of Motives* further indicates his concern with the problem of language.

Sometimes thought to be "one of the few truly speculative thinkers of our time,"[3] and "unquestionably the most brilliant and suggestive critic now writing in America,"[4] Burke deserves to be related to the great tradition of rhetoric.

Although we propose to examine particularly *A Rhetoric of Motives* we shall range freely over all his works in order to discover his principles. We propose to find first the point of departure and orientation from which he approaches rhetoric; next to examine his general concept of rhetoric; then to seek his method for the analysis of motivation; and finally, to discover his application of principles to specific literary works.

In 1931, in *Counter-Statement,* Burke noted, "The reader of modern prose is ever on guard against 'rhetoric,' yet the word, by lexicographer's definition, refers but to 'the use of language in such a way as to produce a desired impression upon the reader or hearer.'"[5] Hence, accepting the lexicographer's definition, he concluded that "effective literature could be nothing else but rhetoric."[6] In truth, "Eloquence is simply the end of art, and is thus its essence."[7]

As a literary critic, representing a minority view, Burke has persisted in his concern with rhetoric, believing that "rhetorical analysis throws light on literary texts and human relations generally."[8] Although Burke is primarily concerned with literature "as art,"[9] he gives no narrow interpretation to the conception of literature. He means simply works "designed for the express purpose of arousing emotions,"[10] going so far as to say, "But sometimes literature so designed fails to arouse emotions — and words said purely by way of explanation may have an unintended emotional effect of considerable magnitude."[11] Thus a discussion of "effectiveness" in literature "should be able to include unintended effects as well as intended ones."[12] "By literature we mean written or spoken words."[13]

As has been observed, the breadth of Burke's concepts results "in a similar embracing of trash of every description. . . . For purposes of analysis or illustration Burke draws as readily on a popular movie, a radio quiz program, a *Herald Tribune* news item about the National Association of Manufacturers, or a Carter Glass speech on gold as on Sophocles or Shakespeare. Those things are a kind of poetry too, full of symbolic and rhetorical ingredients, and if they are bad poetry, it is a bad poetry of vital significance in our lives."[14]

Sometimes calling himself a pragmatist, sometimes a sociological critic, Burke believes that literature is designed to "do something"[15] for the writer and the reader or hearer. "Art is a means of communication. As such it is certainly designed to elicit a 'response' of some sort."[16] The most relevant observations are to be made about literature when it is considered as the embodiment of an "act,"[17] or as "symbolic action."[18] Words must be thought of as "acts upon a scene,"[19] and a "symbolic act" is the "*dancing of an attitude,*"[20] or incipient action. Critical and imaginative works are "answers to questions posed by the situation in which they arose." Not merely "answers," they are "*strategic answers,*" or "*stylized* answers."[21] Hence, a literary work is essentially a "*strategy for encompassing a situation.*"[22] And, as Burke observes, another name for strategies might be "*attitudes.*"[23] The United States Constitution, e.g., must be thought of as the "*answer*" or "*rejoinder*" to "assertions current in the situation in which it arose."[24]

Although Burke distinguishes between literature "for the express purpose of arousing emotions" and "literature for use," the distinction is flexible enough to permit him to see even in such a poem as Milton's *Samson Agonistes,* "moralistic prophecy" and thus to class it as "also a kind of 'literature for use,' use at one remove. . . ."[25]

In further support of his comprehensive notion of art is his conception that since "pure art makes for acceptance," it tends to "become a social menace in so far as it assists us in tolerating the intolerable."[26] Therefore, "under conditions of competitive capitalism there must necessarily be a large *corrective* or *propaganda* element in art."[27] Art must have a "hortatory function, an element of suasion or inducement of the educational variety; it must be partially *forensic.*"[28]

Burke thus approaches the subject of rhetoric through a comprehensive view of art in general. And it is this indirect approach that enables him to present what he believes to be a "New Rhetoric."[29] In part, he has as his object only to "rediscover rhetorical elements that had become obscured when rhetoric as a term fell into disuse, and other specialized disciplines such as esthetics, anthropology, psychoanalysis, and sociology came to the fore (so that esthetics sought to outlaw rhetoric, while the other sciences . . . took over, each in its own terms, the rich rhetorical elements that esthetics would ban)."[30]

II

Sometimes thought to be "intuitive" and "idiosyncratic"[31] in his general theories, Burke might be expected to be so in his theory of rhetoric. "Strongly influenced by anthropological inquiries,"[32] and finding Freud "suggestive almost to the point of bewilderment,"[33] Burke, essentially a classicist in his theory of rhetoric, has given the subject its most searching analysis in modern times.

According to Burke, "Rhetoric [comprises] both the *use* of persuasive resources (*rhetorica utens,* as with the philippics of Demosthenes) and the *study* of them (*rhetorica docens,* as with Aristotle's treatise on the 'art' of Rhetoric)."[34] The "basic function of rhetoric" is the "use of words by human agents to form attitudes or to induce actions in other human agents. . . ."[35] It is "*rooted in an essential function of language itself, a function that is wholly realistic, and is continually born anew; the use of language as a symbolic means of inducing cooperation in beings that by nature respond to symbols.*"[36] The basis of rhetoric lies in "generic divisiveness which, being common to all men, is a universal fact about them, prior to any divisiveness caused by social classes." "Out of this emerge the motives for linguistic persuasion. Then, *secondarily,* we get the motives peculiar to particular economic situations. In parturition begins the centrality of the nervous system. The different nervous systems, through language and the ways of production, erect various communities of interests and insights, social communities varying in nature and scope. And out of the division and the community arises the 'universal' rhetorical situation."[37]

Burke devotes 131 pages to a discussion of traditional principles of rhetoric, reviewing Aristotle, Cicero, Quintilian, St. Augustine, the Mediaevalists, and such more recent writers as De Quincey, De Gourmont, Bentham, Marx, Veblen, Freud, Mannheim, Mead, Richards, and others,[38] noting the "wide range of meanings already associated with rhetoric, in ancient texts. . . ."[39] Thus he comes upon the concept of rhetoric as "persuasion"; the nature of rhetoric as "addressed" to an audience for a particular purpose; rhetoric as the art of "proving opposites"; rhetoric as an "appeal to emotions and prejudices"; rhetoric as "agonistic"; rhetoric as an art of gaining "advantage"; rhetoric as "demonstration"; rhetoric as the verbal "counterpart" of dialectic; rhetoric, in the Stoic usage, as opposed to dialectic; rhetoric in the Marxist sense of persuasion "grounded in dialectic." Whereas he finds that these meanings are "often not consistent with one another, or even flatly at odds,"[40] he believes that they can all be derived from "persuasion" as the "Edenic" term, from which they have all "Babylonically" split, while persuasion, in turn, "involves communication by the signs of consubstantiality, the appeal of *identification*."[41] As the "simplest case of persuasion," he notes that "You persuade a man only insofar as you can talk his language by speech, gesture, tonality, order, image, attitude, idea, *identifying* your ways with his."[42]

In using *identification* as his key term, Burke notes, "Traditionally, the key term for rhetoric is not 'identification,' but 'persuasion.' . . . Our treatment, in terms of identification, is decidedly not meant as a substitute for the sound traditional approach. Rather, . . . it is but an accessory to the standard lore."[43] He had noted that "when we come upon such aspects of persuasion as are found in 'mystification,' courtship, and the 'magic' of class relationships, the reader will see why the classical notion of clear persuasive intent is not an accurate fit, for describing the ways in which the members of a group promote social cohesion by acting rhetorically upon themselves and one another."[44] Burke is completely aware that he is not introducing a totally new concept, observing that Aristotle had long ago commented, "It is not hard . . . to praise Athenians among Athenians,"[45] and that one persuades by "identifying" one's ways with those of his audience.[46] In an observation of W. C. Blum, Burke found additional support for his emphasis on *identification* as a key concept. "In identification lies the source of dedications and enslavements, in fact of cooperation."[47] As for the precise relationship between identification and persuasion as ends of rhetoric, Burke concludes, "we might well keep it in mind that a speaker persuades an audience by the use of stylistic identifications; his act of persuasion may be for the purpose of causing the audience to identify itself with the speaker's interests; and the speaker draws on identification of interests to establish rapport between himself and his audience. So, there is no chance of our keeping apart the meanings of persuasion, identification ('consubstantiality') and communication (the nature of rhetoric as 'addressed'). But, in given instances, one or another of these elements may serve best for extending a line of analysis in some particular direction."[48] "All told, persuasion ranges from the bluntest quest of advantage, as in sales promotion or propaganda, through courtship, social etiquette, education, and the sermon, to a 'pure' form that delights in the process of appeal for itself alone, without ulterior purpose. And identification ranges from the politician who, addressing an audience of farmers, says, 'I was a farm boy myself,' through the mysteries of social status, to the mystic's devout identification with the source of all being."[49] The difference between the "old" rhetoric and the "new" rhetoric may be summed up in this manner: whereas the key term for the "old" rhetoric was *persuasion* and its stress was upon deliberate design, the key term for the "new" rhetoric is *identification* and this may include partially "unconscious" factors in its appeal. Identification, at its simplest level, may be a deliberate device, or a means, as when a speaker identifies his interests with those of his audience. But *identification* can also be an "end," as "when people earnestly yearn to identify themselves with some group or other." They are thus not necessarily acted upon by a conscious external agent, but may act upon themselves to this end. Identification "includes the realm of transcendence."[50]

Burke affirms the significance of *identification* as a key concept because men are at odds with one another, or because there is "division." "Identification is compensatory to division. If men were not apart from one another, there would be no need for the rhetorician to proclaim their unity. If men were wholly and truly of one substance, absolute communication would be of man's very essence."[51] "In pure identification there would be no strife. Likewise, there would be no strife in absolute separateness, since opponents can join battle only through a mediatory ground that makes their communication possible, thus providing the first condition necessary for their interchange of blows. But put identification and division ambiguously together . . . and you have the characteristic invitation to rhetoric. Here is a major reason why rhetoric, according to Aristotle, 'proves opposites.' "[52]

As a philosopher and metaphysician Burke is impelled to give a philosophic treatment to the concept of unity or identity by an analysis of the nature of *substance* in general. In this respect he makes his most basic contribution to a philosophy of rhetoric. "Metaphysically, a thing is identified by its *properties*,"[53] he observes. "To call a man a friend or brother is to proclaim him consubstantial with oneself, one's values or purposes. To call a man a bastard is to attack him by attacking his whole line, his 'authorship,' his 'principle' or 'motive' (as expressed in terms of the familial). An epithet assigns substance doubly, for in stating the character of the object it . . . contains an implicit program of action with regard to the object, thus serving as motive."[54]

According to Burke, language of all things "is most public, most collective, in its substance."[55] Aware that modern thinkers have been skeptical about the utility of a doctrine of substance,[56] he nevertheless recalls that "substance, in the old philosophies, was an *act;* and a way of life is an *acting-together;* and in acting together, men have common sensations, concepts, images, ideas, attitudes that make them *consubstantial.*"[57] "A doctrine of *consubstantiality* . . . may be necessary to any way of life."[58] Like Kant, Burke regards substance as a "necessary form of the mind." Instead of trying to exclude a doctrine of substance, he restores it to a central position and throws critical light upon it.

In so far as rhetoric is concerned, the "ambiguity of substance" affords a major resource. "What handier linguistic resource could a rhetorician want than an ambiguity whereby he can say 'The state of affairs is substantially such-and-such,' instead of having to say 'The state of affairs *is* and/or *is not* such-and-such"?[59]

The "commonplaces" or "topics" of Aristotle's *Rhetoric* are a "quick survey of opinion" of "things that people generally consider persuasive." As such, they are means of proclaiming *substantial* unity with an audience and are clearly instances of identification.[60] In truth, *identification* is "hardly other than a name for the function of sociality."[61] Likewise, the many tropes and figures, and rhetorical form in the large as treated by the ancients are to be considered as modes of identification.[62] They are the "signs" by which the speaker identifies himself with the reader or hearer. "In its simplest manifestation, style is ingratiation."[63] It is an attempt to "gain favor by the hypnotic or suggestive process of 'saying the right thing.'"[64] Burke discusses form in general as "the psychology of the *audience*,"[65] the "arousing and fulfillment of desires."[66] The exordium of a Greek oration is an instance of "conventional"[67] form, a form which is expected by the audience and therefore satisfies it. Other recognizable types of form are "syllogistic progression," "repetitive" form, and "minor or incidental" forms which include such devices as the metaphor, apostrophe, series, reversal, etc.[68] The proliferation and the variety of formal devices make a work eloquent.[69]

Reviewing *A Rhetoric of Motives,* Thomas W. Copeland observed, "It gradually appears that there is no form of action of men upon each other (or of individuals on themselves) which is really outside of rhetoric. But if so, we should certainly ask whether rhetoric *as a term* has any defining value."[70] The observation is probably not fair, for Burke does give rhetoric a defining value in terms of persuasion, identification, and address or communication to an audience of some sort, despite his observation, "Wherever there is persuasion, there is rhetoric. And wherever there is 'meaning' there is 'persuasion.'"[71]

It is true that in his effort to show "how a rhetorical motive is often present where it is not usually recognized, or thought to belong,"[72] Burke either points out linkages which have not been commonly stressed, or widens the scope of rhetoric. A twentieth-century orientation in social-psychological theory thus enables him to note that we may with "more accuracy speak of persuasion 'to attitude,' rather than persuasion to out-and-out action." For persuasion "involves choice, will; it is directed to a man only insofar as he is *free*." In so far as men "*must* do something, rhetoric is unnecessary, its work being done by the nature of things, though often these necessities are not of natural origin, but come from necessities imposed by man-made conditions,"[73] such as dictatorships or near-dictatorships. His notion of persuasion to "attitude" does not alter his generally classical view of rhetoric, for as he points out, in "Cicero and Augustine there is a shift between the words 'move' (*movere*) and 'bend' (*flectere*) to name the ultimate function of rhetoric." And he merely finds that this shift "corresponds to a distinction between act and attitude (attitude being an incipient act, a leaning or inclination)."[74] His notion of persuasion to "attitude" enables him to point out a linkage with poetry: "Thus the notion of persuasion to *attitude* would permit the application of rhetorical terms to purely *poetic* structures; the study of lyrical devices might be classed under the head of rhetoric, when these devices are considered for their power to induce or communicate states of mind to readers, even though the kinds of assent evoked have no overt, practical outcome."[75]

In his reading of classical texts, he had noted a stress "upon *teaching* as an 'office' of rhetoric." Such an observation enables him to link the fields of rhetoric and semantics. He concludes that "once you treat instruction as an aim of rhetoric you introduce a principle that can widen the scope of rhetoric beyond persuasion. It is on the way to include also works on the theory and practice of exposition, description, *communication* in general. Thus, finally, out of this principle, you can derive contemporary 'semantics' as an aspect of rhetoric."[76]

As he persists in "tracking down" the function of the term *rhetoric*, Burke notes an ingredient of rhetoric "lurking in such anthropologist's terms as 'magic' and 'witchcraft,'"[77] and concludes that one "comes closer to the true state of affairs if one treats the socializing aspects of magic as a 'primitive rhetoric' than if one sees modern rhetoric simply as a 'survival of primitive magic.'"[78] Whereas he does not believe that the term *rhetoric* is a "substitute" for such terms as *magic, witchcraft, socialization,* or *communication,* the term *rhetoric* "designates a *function* . . . present in the areas variously covered by those other terms."[79] Thus, one can place within the scope of rhetoric "all those statements by anthropologists, ethnologists, individual and social psychologists, and the like, that bear upon the *persuasive* aspects of language, the function of language as *addressed,* as direct or roundabout appeal to real or ideal audiences, without or within."[80] All these disciplines have made "good contributions to the New Rhetoric."[81]

In "individual psychology," particularly the Freudian concern with the neuroses of individual patients, "there is a strongly rhetorical ingredient."[82] Burke asks the question, "Indeed, what could be more profoundly rhetorical than Freud's notion of a dream that attains expression by stylistic subterfuges designed to evade the inhibitions of a moralistic censor? What is this but the exact analogue of the rhetorical devices of literature under political or theocratic censorship? The *ego* with its *id* confronts the *super-ego* much as an orator would confront a somewhat alien audience, whose susceptibilities he must flatter as a necessary step towards persuasion. The Freudian psyche is quite a parliament, with conflicting interests expressed in ways variously designed to take the claims of rival factions into account."[83]

By considering the individual self as "audience" Burke brings morals and ethics into the realm of rhetoric. He notes that "a modern 'post-Christian' rhetoric must also concern itself with the thought that, under the heading of appeal to audiences, would also be included any ideas or images privately addressed to the individual self for moralistic or incantatory purposes. For you become your own audience, in some respects a very lax one, in some respects very exacting, when you become involved in psychologically stylistic subterfuges for presenting your own case to yourself in sympathetic terms (and even terms that seem harsh can often be found on closer scrutiny to be flattering, as with neurotics who visit sufferings upon themselves in the name of very high-powered motives which, whatever their discomfiture, feed pride." Therefore, the "individual person, striving to form himself in accordance with the communicative norms that match the cooperative ways of his society, is by the same token concerned with the rhetoric of identification."[84]

By considering style as essentially a mode of "ingratiation" or as a technique by which one gives the signs of identification and consubstantiality, Burke finds a rhetorical motive in clothes, pastoral, courtship, and the like.[85]

Burke links dialectics with rhetoric through a definition of dialectics in "its most general sense" as "linguistic transformation"[86] and through an analysis of three different levels of language, or linguistic terminology.[87] Grammatically, he discusses the subject from the point of view of linguistic merger and division, polarity, and transcendence, being aware that there are "other definitions of dialectics":[88] "reasoning from opinion"; "the discovery of truth by the give and take of converse and redefinition"; "the art of disputation"; "the processes of 'interaction' between the verbal and the non-verbal"; "the competition of coöperation or the coöperation of competition"; "the spinning of terms out of terms"; "the internal dialogue of thought"; "any development . . . got by the interplay of various factors that mutually modify one another, and may be thought of as voices in a dialogue or roles in a play, with each voice or role in its partiality contributing to the development of the whole"; "the placement of one thought or thing in terms of its opposite"; "the progressive or successive development and reconciliation of opposites"; and "so putting questions to nature that nature can give unequivocal answer."[89] He considers all of these definitions as "variants or special applications of the functions"[90] of linguistic transformation conceived in terms of "Merger and division," "The three Major Pairs: action-passion, mind-body, being-nothing," and "Transcendence."[91]

Burke devotes 150 pages to the treatment of the dialectics of persuasion in the *Rhetoric*,[92] in addition to extensive treatment of it on the grammatical level.[93] Linguistic terminology is considered variously persuasive in its Positive, Dialectical, and Ultimate levels or orders.[94] "A positive term is most unambiguously itself when it names a visible and tangible thing which can be located in time and place."[95] Dialectical terms "have no such strict location."[96] Thus terms like "Elizabethanism" or "capitalism" having no positive referent may be called "dialectical."[97] Often called "polar" terms,[98] they require an "opposite"[99] to define them and are on the level of "action," "principles," "ideas."[100] In an "ultimate order" of terminology, there is a "guiding idea" or "unitary principle."[101]

From the point of view of rhetoric, Burke believes that the "difference between a merely 'dialectical' confronting of parliamentary conflict and an 'ultimate' treatment of it would reside in this: The 'dialectical' order would leave the competing voices in a jangling relation with one another (a conflict solved *faute de mieux* by 'horse-trading'); but the 'ultimate' order would place these competing voices themselves in a *hierarchy*, or *sequence*, or *evaluative series*, so that, in some way, we went by a fixed and reasoned progression from one of these to another, the members of the entire group being arranged *developmentally* with relation to one another."[102] To Burke "much of the *rhetorical* strength in the Marxist dialectic comes from the fact that it is 'ultimate' in its order,"[103] for a "spokesman for the proletariat can think of himself as representing not only the interests of that class alone, but the grand design of the entire historical sequence. . . ."[104]

In his concept of a "pure persuasion," Burke seems to be extending the area of rhetoric beyond its usual scope. As a metaphysician he attempts to carry the process of rhetorical appeal to its ultimate limits. He admits that what he means by "pure persuasion" in the "absolute sense" exists nowhere, but believes that it can be present as a motivational ingredient in any rhetoric, no matter how "advantage-seeking such a rhetoric may be."[105] "Pure persuasion involves the saying of something, not for an extraverbal advantage to be got by the saying, but because of a satisfaction intrinsic to the saying. It summons because it likes the feel of a summons. It would be nonplused if the summons were answered. It attacks because it revels in the sheer syllables of vituperation. It would be horrified if, each time it finds a way of saying, 'Be damned,' it really did send a soul to rot in hell. It intuitively says, 'This is so,' purely and simply because this is so."[106] With such a concept Burke finds himself at the "borders of metaphysics, or perhaps better 'meta-rhetoric.' . . ."[107]

III

Of great significance to the rhetorician is Burke's consideration of the general problem of motivation. Concerned with the problem of motivation in literary strategy,[108] he nevertheless intends that his observations be considered pertinent to the social sphere in general.[109] He had observed that people's conduct has been explained by an "endless variety of theories: ethnological, geographical, sociological, physiological, historical, endocrinological, economic, anatomical, mystical, pathological, and so on."[110] The assigning of motives, he concludes, is a "matter of *appeal*,"[111] and this depends upon one's general orientation. "A motive is not some fixed thing, like a table, which one can go to and look at. It is a term of interpretation, and being such it will naturally take its place within the framework of our *Weltanschauung* as a whole."[112] "To explain one's conduct by the vocabulary of motives current among one's group is about as self-deceptive as giving the area of a field in the accepted terms of measurement. One is simply interpreting with the only vocabulary he knows. One is stating his orientation, which involves a vocabulary of ought and ought-not, with attendant vocabulary of praiseworthy and blameworthy."[113] "We discern situational patterns by means of the particular vocabulary of the cultural group into which we are born."[114] Motives are "distinctly linguistic products."[115]

To Burke, the subject of motivation is a "philosophic one, not ultimately to be solved in terms of empirical science."[116] A motive is a "shorthand" term for "situation."[117] One may discuss motives on three levels, rhetorical, symbolic, and grammatical.[118] One is on the "grammatical" level when he concerns himself with the problem of the "intrinsic," or the problem of "substance."[119] "Men's conception of motive . . . is integrally related to their conception of substance. Hence, to deal with problems of motive is to deal with problems of substance."[120]

On the "grammatical" level Burke gives his most profound treatment of the problem of motivation. Strongly allied with the classicists throughout all his works in both his ideas and his methodology, Burke shows indebtedness to Aristotle for his treatment of motivation. Taking a clue from Aristotle's consideration of the "circumstances" of an action,[121] Burke concludes that "In a rounded statement about motives, you must have some word that names the *act* (names what took place, in thought or deed), and another that names the *scene* (the background of the act, the situation in which it occurred); also, you must indicate what person or kind of person (*agent*) performed the act, what means or instruments he used (*agency*), and the *purpose*."[122] Act, Scene, Agent, Agency, Purpose become the "pentad" for pondering the problem of human motivation.[123] Among these various terms grammatical "ratios" prevail which have rhetorical implications. One might illustrate by saying that, for instance, between *scene* and *act* a logic prevails which indicates that a certain quality of scene calls for an analogous quality of act. Hence, if a situation is said to be of a certain nature, a corresponding attitude toward it is implied. Burke explains by pointing to such an instance as that employed by a speaker who, in discussing Roosevelt's war-time power exhorted that Roosevelt should be granted "unusual powers" because the country was in an "unusual international situation." The scene-act "ratio" may be applied in two ways. "It can be applied deterministically in statements that a certain policy *had* to be adopted in a certain situation, or it may be applied in hortatory statements to the effect that a certain policy *should be* adopted in conformity with the situation."[124] These ratios are "principles of determination."[125] The pentad would allow for ten such ratios: scene-act, scene-agent, scene-agency, scene-purpose, act-purpose, act-agent, act-agency, agent-purpose, agent-agency, and agency-purpose.[126] Political commentators now generally use *situation* as their synonym for *scene*, "though often without any clear concept of its function as a statement about motives."[127]

Burke draws his key terms for the study of motivation from the analysis of drama. Being developed from the analysis of drama, his pentad "treats language and thought primarily as modes of action."[128] His method for handling motivation is designed to contrast with the methodology of the physical sciences which considers the subject of motivation in mechanistic terms of "flat cause-and-effect or stimulus-and-response."[129] Physicalist terminologies are proper to non-verbalizing entities, but man as a species should be approached through his specific trait, his use of symbols. Burke opposes the reduction of the human realm to terms that lack sufficient "coordinates"; he does not, however, question the fitness of physicalist terminologies for treating the physical realm. According to Burke, "Philosophy, like common sense, must think of human motivation dramatistically, in terms of action and its ends."[130] "Language being essentially human, we should view human relations in terms of the linguistic instrument."[131] His "vocabulary" or "set of coordinates" serves "for the integration of all phenomena studied by the *social* sciences."[132] It also serves as a "perspective for the analysis of history which is a 'dramatic' process. . . ."[133]

One may wonder with Charles Morris whether "an analysis of man through his language provides us with a full account of human motives."[134] One strongly feels the absence of insights into motivation deriving from the psychologists and scientists.

IV

Burke is not only philosopher and theorist; he has applied his critical principles practically to a great number of literary works. Of these, three are of particular interest to the rhetorician. In two instances, Burke attempts to explain the communicative relationship between the writer and his audience. Taking the speech of Antony from Shakespeare's *Julius Caesar,*[135] Burke examines the speech from "the standpoint of the rhetorician, who is concerned with a work's processes of appeal."[136] A similar operation is performed on a scene from *Twelfth Night.*[137]

Undoubtedly one of his most straightforward attempts at analysis of a work of "literature for use," occurs in an essay on "The Rhetoric of Hitler's 'Battle.'"[138] "The main ideal of criticism, as I conceive it," Burke has observed, "is to use all that there is to use."[139] "If there is any slogan that should reign among critical precepts, it is that 'circumstances alter occasions.'"[140] Considering *Mein Kampf* as "the well of Nazi magic,"[141] Burke brings his knowledge of sociology and anthropology to bear in order to "discover what kind of 'medicine' this medicine-man has concocted, that we may know, with greater accuracy, exactly what to guard against, if we are to forestall the concocting of similar medicine in America."[142] He considers Hitler's "centralizing hub of *ideas*"[143] and his selection of Munich as a "mecca geographically located"[144] as methods of recruiting followers "from among many discordant and divergent bands. . . ."[145] He examines the symbol of the "international Jew"[146] as that "of a *common enemy,*"[147] the "'medicinal' appeal of the Jew as scapegoat. . . ."[148]

His knowledge of psychoanalysis is useful in the analysis of the "sexual symbolism" that runs through the book: "Germany in dispersion is the 'dehorned Siegfried.' The masses are 'feminine.' As such, they desire to be led by a dominating male. This male, as orator, woos them – and, when he has won them, he commands them. The rival male, the villainous Jew, would on the contrary 'seduce' them. If he succeeds, he poisons their blood by intermingling with them. Whereupon, by purely associative connections of ideas, we are moved into attacks upon syphilis, prostitution, incest, and other similar misfortunes, which are introduced as a kind of 'musical' argument when he is on the subject of 'blood poisoning' by intermarriage or, in its 'spiritual' equivalent, by the infection of 'Jewish' ideas. . . ."[149]

His knowledge of history and religion is employed to show that the "*materialization*" of a religious pattern is "one terrifically effective weapon . . . in a period where religion has been progressively weakened by many centuries of capitalist materialism."[150]

Conventional rhetorical knowledge leads him to call attention to the "power of endless repetition";[151] the appeal of a sense of "community";[152] the appeal of security resulting from "a world view" for a people who had previously seen the world only "piecemeal";[153] and the appeal of Hitler's "inner voice"[154] which served as a technique of leader-people "identification."[155]

Burke's analysis is comprehensive and penetrating. It stands as a superb example of the fruitfulness of a method of comprehensive rhetorical analysis which goes far beyond conventional patterns.

CONCLUSION

Burke is difficult and often confusing. He cannot be understood by casual reading of his various volumes. In part the difficulty arises from the numerous vocabularies he employs. His words in isolation are usually simple enough, but he often uses them in new contexts. To read one of his volumes independently, without regard to the chronology of publication, makes the problem of comprehension even more difficult because of the specialized meanings attaching to various words and phrases.

Burke is often criticized for "obscurity" in his writings. The charge may be justified. However, some of the difficulty of comprehension arises from the compactness of his writing, the uniqueness of his organizational patterns, the penetration of his thought, and the breadth of his endeavor. "In books like the *Grammar* and the *Rhetoric*," observed Malcolm Cowley, "we begin to see the outlines of a philosophical system on the grand scale. . . . Already it has its own methodology (called 'dramatism'), its own esthetics (based on the principle that works of art are symbolic actions), its logic and dialectics, its ethics (or picture of the good life) and even its metaphysics, which Burke prefers to describe as a meta-rhetoric."[156]

One cannot possibly compress the whole of Burke's thought into an article. The most that one can achieve is to signify his importance as a theorist and critic and to suggest the broad outlines of his work. Years of study and contemplation of the general idea of effectiveness in language have equipped him to deal competently with the subject of rhetoric from its beginning as a specialized discipline to the present time. To his thorough knowledge of classical tradition he has added rich insights gained from serious study of anthropology, sociology, history, psychology, philosophy, and the whole body of humane letters. With such equipment, he has become the most profound student of rhetoric now writing in America.

FOOTNOTES, PAGES 270 TO 284

[1] Kenneth Burke, *A Rhetoric of Motives* (New York: Prentice-Hall, Inc., 1950), p. xv.

[2] Isidor Schneider, "A New View of Rhetoric," *New York Herald Tribune Books*, VIII (December 13, 1931), 4.

[3] Malcolm Cowley, "Prolegomena to Kenneth Burke," *The New Republic*, CXXII (June 5, 1950), 18, 19.

[4] W. H. Auden, "A Grammar of Assent," *The New Republic*, CV (July 14, 1941), 59.

[5] *Counter-Statement* (New York, 1931), p. 265.

[6] *Ibid.*, p. 265. [7] *Ibid.*, p. 53.

[8] *A Rhetoric of Motives*, pp. xiv, xv.

[9] *Counter-Statement*, p. 156.

[10] *Ibid.* [11] *Ibid.* [12] *Ibid.* [13] *Ibid.*

[14] Stanley Edgar Hyman, *The Armed Vision* (New York, 1948), pp. 386, 387.

[15] *The Philosophy of Literary Form* (Louisiana, 1941), p. 89.

[16] *Ibid.*, pp. 235, 236. [17] *Ibid.*, p. 89. [18] *Ibid.*, p. 8. [19] *Ibid.*, p. vii.

[20] *Ibid.*, p. 9. [21] *Ibid.*, p. 1. [22] *Ibid.*, p. 109. [23] *Ibid.*, p. 297. [24] *Ibid.*, p. 109.

[25] *A Rhetoric of Motives*, p. 5.

[26] *The Philosophy of Literary Form*, p. 321.

[27] *Ibid.* [28] *Ibid.*

[29] *A Rhetoric of Motives*, p. 40.

[30] *Ibid.*, pp. xiii, 40.

[31] *The Philosophy of Literary Form*, p. 68.

[32] *A Rhetoric of Motives*, p. 40.

[33] *The Philosophy of Literary Form*, p. 258.

[34] *A Rhetoric of Motives*, p. 36.

[35] *Ibid.*, p. 41. [36] *Ibid.*, p. 43.

[37] *Ibid.*, p. 146. [38] *Ibid.*, pp. 49–180. [39] *Ibid.*, p. 61. [40] *Ibid.*, pp. 61, 62.

[41] *Ibid.*, p. 62. [42] *Ibid.*, p. 55.

[43] *Ibid.*, p. xiv.

[44] *Ibid.* [45] *Ibid.*, p. 55. [46] *Ibid.*

[47] *Ibid.*, p. xiv.

[48] *Ibid.*, p. 46. [49] *Ibid.*, p. xiv.

[50] Kenneth Burke, "Rhetoric — Old and New," *The Journal of General Education*, V (April 1951), 203.

[51] *A Rhetoric of Motives*, p. 22.

[52] *Ibid.*, p. 25. [53] *Ibid.*, p. 23.

[54] *A Grammar of Motives* (New York, 1945), p. 57. For discussion of *substance* as a concept, see, *ibid.*, pp. 21–58; Aristotle, *Categoriae*, tr. by E. M. Edghill, *The Works of Aristotle*, ed. by W. D. Ross, I, Ch. 5; Aristotle, *Metaphysics*, tr. by W. D. Ross, Book △, 8, 1017b, 10; Spinoza, *The Ethics*, in *The Chief Works of Benedict De Spinoza*, tr. by R. H. M. Elwes (London, 1901), Rev. ed., II, 45ff; John Locke, *An Essay Concerning Human Understanding* (London, 1760), 15th ed., I, Bk. II, Chs. XXIII, XXIV.

[55] *The Philosophy of Literary Form*, p. 44.

[56] *A Rhetoric of Motives*, p. 21.

[57] *Ibid.* [58] *Ibid.*

[59] *A Grammar of Motives*, pp. 51, 52.

[60] *A Rhetoric of Motives*, pp. 56, 57.

[61] *Attitudes toward History* (New York, 1937), II, 144.

[62] *A Rhetoric of Motives*, p. 59.

[63] *Permanence and Change* (New York, 1935), p. 71.

[64] *Ibid.*

[65] *Counter-Statement*, pp. 38–57.

[66] *Ibid.*, p. 157. [67] *Ibid.*, p. 159.

[68] *Ibid.*, pp. 157–161. [69] *Ibid.*, pp. 209–211.

[70] Thomas W. Copeland, "Critics at Work," *The Yale Review*, XL (Autumn 1950), 167–169.

[71] *A Rhetoric of Motives*, p. 172.

[72] *Ibid.*, p. xiii.

[73] *Ibid.*, p. 50. [74] *Ibid.* [75] *Ibid.*

[76] *Ibid.*, p. 77. [77] *Ibid.*, p. 44. [78] *Ibid.*, p. 43. [79] *Ibid.*, p. 44.

[80] *Ibid.*, pp. 43–44. [81] *Ibid.*, p. 40.

[82] *Ibid.*, p. 37. [83] *Ibid.*, pp. 37, 38.

[84] *Ibid.*, pp. 38, 39.

[85] *Ibid.*, pp. 115–127; see, also, p. xiv.

[86] *A Grammar of Motives*, p. 402.

[87] *A Rhetoric of Motives*, p. 183.

[88] *A Grammar of Motives*, pp. 402, 403.

[89] *Ibid.*, p. 403. [90] *Ibid.*

[91] *Ibid.*, p. 402.

[92] *A Rhetoric of Motives*, pp. 183–333.

[93] *A Grammar of Motives*, pp. 323–443.

[94] *A Rhetoric of Motives*, p. 183.

[95] *Ibid.* [96] *Ibid.*, p. 184. [97] *Ibid.* [98] *Ibid.*

[99] *The Philosophy of Literary Form*, n. 26, p. 109.

[100] *A Rhetoric of Motives*, p. 184.

[101] *Ibid.*, p. 187.

[102] *Ibid.*

[103] *Ibid.*, p. 190.

[104] *Ibid.*, pp. 190, 191.

[105] *Ibid.*, p. 269.

[106] *Ibid.* [107] *Ibid.*, p. 267.

[108] *The Philosophy of Literary Form*, p. 78.

[109] *Ibid.*, p. 105.

[110] *Permanence and Change*, p. 47.

[111] *Ibid.*, p. 38.

[112] *Ibid.*

[113] *Ibid.*, p. 33. [114] *Ibid.*, p. 52. [115] *Ibid.*

[116] *A Grammar of Motives*, p. xxiii.

[117] *Permanence and Change*, p. 44.

[118] *A Grammar of Motives*, p. 465.

[119] *Ibid.*

[120] *Ibid.*, p. 337.

[121] *Ethica Nicomachea*, tr. by W. D. Ross, III, i, 16.

[122] *A Grammar of Motives*, p. xv.

[123] *Ibid.*

[124] *Ibid.*, p. 13. [125] *Ibid.*, p. 15. [126] *Ibid.*

[127] *Ibid.*, p. 13. [128] *Ibid.*, p. xxii.

[129] *The Philosophy of Literary Form*, pp. 103, 106.

[130] *A Grammar of Motives*, pp. 55, 56.

[131] *Ibid.*, p. 317.

[132] *The Philosophy of Literary Form*, p. 105.

[133] *Ibid.*, p. 317.

[134] Charles Morris, "The Strategy of Kenneth Burke," *The Nation*, CLXIII (July 27, 1946), 106.

[135] "Antony in Behalf of the Play," *Philosophy of Literary Form*, pp. 329–343.

[136] *Ibid.*, p. 330.

[137] "Trial Translation (from *Twelfth Night*)," *ibid.*, pp. 344–349.

[138] *Ibid.*, pp. 191–220. [139] *Ibid.*, p. 23. [140] *Ibid.* [141] *Ibid.*, p. 192.

[142] *Ibid.*, p. 191. [143] *Ibid.*, p. 192. [144] *Ibid.*

[145] *Ibid.* [146] *Ibid.*, p. 194. [147] *Ibid.*, p. 193. [148] *Ibid.*, p. 195.

[149] *Ibid.* [150] *Ibid.*, p. 194. [151] *Ibid.*, p. 217. [152] *Ibid.*

[153] *Ibid.*, p. 218. [154] *Ibid.*, p. 207. [155] *Ibid.*

[156] Malcolm Cowley, "Prolegomena to Kenneth Burke," *The New Republic*, CXXII (June 5, 1950), 18, 19.

◇◇

MARIE HOCHMUTH NICHOLS was born in Dunbar, Pennsylvania, in 1908. She was an editor of *The Quarterly Journal of Speech* and is presently a professor of speech at the University of Illinois, Urbana. She is the author or editor of *American Speeches, A History and Criticism of American Public Address*, and *Rhetoric and Criticism*.

When this article was published, it was the first comprehensive treatment of Burke as a systematic thinker and remained for many years the definitive account of what Burke had achieved. And, of equal importance, it was the first significant piece on Burke in this influential journal by a specialist in modern rhetoric. Many others in this same field, some of them very good, subsequently studied, wrote about, and applied Burke; and Burke was soon to publish one of his most ambitious essays — "A Dramatistic View of the Origins of Speech" — in this journal. Burke's two major spheres of influence up to this point had been among the literary critics and sociologists; Marie Hochmuth Nichols' essay marks the beginning of a long and essentially healthy relationship between Burke and students of modern rhetoric. This group, most of whom are represented in this volume, includes L. Virginia Holland, who studied at the University of Illinois, John Kirk, Father Fogarty, Leland Griffin, Bernard Brock, who studied with Professor Griffin at Northwestern, and Ross Winterowd, who has done a Burkeian rhetoric (*Rhetoric and Writing*, 1965). I do not mean to suggest that Marie Hochmuth Nichols was responsible for all of this. Such a process is always cumulative and some of it can never be accounted for in terms of anyone's direct influence. However, she was certainly very influential. Finally, her essay on Burke is representative of the way people in modern rhetoric (speech) have responded to Burke: through his theory of rhetoric, naturally, but in terms of it as *the* central part of the larger dramatistic system. This means that, unlike many literary critics, they have always tended to see Burke as systematic and whole (which seems to me the proper way to see him).

◇◇

Kenneth Burke and Robert Penn Warren: Criticism by Obsessive Metaphor

BY Newell F. Ford

NOT long ago the writer had occasion to point out certain corruptions in Wordsworth's text initiated by Mr. Empson and perpetuated by Mr. Ransom, then used by both of these critics to condemn Wordsworth for "muddled" thinking and bad poetry (*Philological Quarterly*, January 1950). Now it appears that the sharing of discoveries (distortions?) by the so-called New Critics is not an uncommon procedure. Mr. Robert Penn Warren, for example, in analyzing "The Rime of the Ancient Mariner," is willing to inherit a metaphor from Mr. Kenneth Burke and like Mr. Burke to use this metaphor in place of evidence for establishing an eccentric thesis. Though Mr. Warren is usually scrupulous in citing his sources, he is either unaware of his debt to Mr. Burke or has neglected to acknowledge it. And Mr. Burke himself, one finds, is quite unaware of the extent to which he allows a metaphor (an outworn one at that) to conduct his argument for him. Perhaps the metaphor ("under the aegis of . . .") is "dead" to these critics' conscious minds; perhaps its very deadness explains their unconsciousness of the role it plays in their arguments. Yet it is striking that critics who are known widely as proponents of *fresh* metaphor should fall victim to so patent a cliché.

In Mr. Burke's *Philosophy of Literary Form* (1941) the cliché occurs almost every time "The Ancient Mariner" is mentioned. Since both

EDITOR'S NOTE: Reprinted from *Journal of English and Germanic Philology*, LIII (1954), 172–177, copyright © 1954 by the University of Illinois Press, by permission of the author and the editors of the *Journal*.

Mr. Burke and Mr. Warren wish to prove that all the events of the poem are controlled by the "maleficent" Sun and the "beneficent" Moon (a thesis that can only be maintained in defiance of the evidence), it is significant that almost every time either of them mentions the sun or the moon, the cliché "under the aegis of" appears like a conditioned reflex. Here is the record from *The Philosophy of Literary Form* (the quotations are numbered for easy reference):

1. We would note that the Mariner suffered his punishments *under the aegis of the Sun,* and that his cure was effected *under the aegis of the Moon* (p. 24).

2. . . . as we move from suffering *under the aegis of the Sun* to release *under the aegis of the Moon* (p. 25).

3. . . . with the Mariner returning to shore *under the aegis of* the praying Hermit . . . (p. 72).

4. [in reference to the poem, "The Aeolian Harp"] The marital problem . . . We note that the poet's apologies to the wife, for instance, are offered *under the aegis of noon.* We have the deflection from the marriage-feast in 'The Ancient Mariner' *at high noon* (p. 94).

5. For instance, we find that the Sun in 'The Ancient Mariner' breeds rot. At the end we find the Hermit (*under whose aegis* the Mariner is absolved) praying on a seat of moss covering a rotted old oak stump (p. 95).

6. . . . the Pilot's boy in 'The Ancient Mariner' acts as the vessel that takes upon itself the most malign features of a cure effected *under the aegis of moonlight.* . . . [That is, the Pilot's boy "doth crazy go" because he drains off, like a good scapegoat, the "loon-acy" of the "greybeard loon." Nothing is said of the contradiction in a "beneficent" moon that both cures from and inspires lunacy.] (p. 101).

7. . . . the 'greybeard loon' whose cure had been effected *under the dubious aegis of moonlight* (p. 287).

8. The structure itself becomes more apparent: the 'loon'-atic Mariner begins his cure from drought *under the aegis of a moon* that causes a silly rain, thence by synecdoche to silly buckets . . . (p. 288).

9. Since the poem is constructed about an opposition between punishment *under the aegis of the sun* and cure *under the aegis of the moon,* one could proceed in other works [further books of criticism] to disclose the two sets of equations clustered about these two principles. Indeed, even in "The Ancient Mariner" itself we get a momentous cue [clue?], as the sun is explicitly said to be "like God's own head." (p. 288)

It is a bit startling in the third quotation to observe the "aegis" shifting suddenly and causelessly from cosmic bodies to a hermit in the act of prayer! But the mobility of this aegis does not cease here: in the fourth quotation it leaves all bodies behind — cosmic or hermitic — and attaches itself to a mere *sound:* the "oon"-sound appears to have spellbound the critic (like "noises in a swound," perhaps?) so that he finds great symbolical meanings not only in "moon" and "noon" but even in "greybeard *loon*" (see quotations 6, 7, and 8 above.)

In the fifth excerpt, the aegis is hung again on the hermit, and the natural oxidation (rotting) of a tree stump is perceived to be highly meaningful. Why? Because the word "rot" occurred once previously in the poem, describing becalmed tropic seas.

In the seventh quotation the aegis becomes "dubious." Is there a possible projection here from the critic to his metaphor; does "dubious" reveal a moment of doubt as to the validity of the stated symbolism? As for the eighth quotation, Mr. Burke's "silly rain" is not found in the poem-text. Whatever the Mariner may mean by his reference to "silly buckets," he does not mean: "I hereby invite critics to convert these buckets into manifold significance by waving the wand of Synecdoche." As for the ninth quotation, we have only to turn to the poem to demonstrate that in its context the sun that appears "like God's own head" is neither "explicit" nor "momentous," and hardly calls for "other works" of critical exegesis. The figure is appropriate to the nightmarish state of mind of the crew, and vividly points up their medieval, superstitious, and anthropomorphic notions of godhead.

If every image in a poem is a symbol, and if every symbol is a kind of mental boat, what is to prevent readers from floating freely down myriads of associational streams to whatever chance island they happen to ground upon? Criticism will become an associational brook that, like Tennyson's, rambles on forever.

As we follow Mr. Warren on his cruise of symbolism, it is unjust to imply that he floats on a mere stream of association. Everywhere in his grave and austere essay (cf. *The Rime of the Ancient Mariner, with an Essay by Robert Penn Warren*, 1946) he gives evidence of industry and wide reading, freighting his argument with an imposing mass of learned and expatiatory footnotes. Yet one cannot but conclude that the massed footnotes have a primarily polemical function: to win acceptance for the critic's two main theses, both of which are products of an arbitrary symbolism.[1] The primary thesis is a theological one, finding the Mariner and his two-hundred-man crew guilty of Original Sin, of "corruption of the will," of "pride" and "self-idolatry" (pp. 81, 82, 130, 131). With this ominous and irrelevant resurrection of medieval scholasticism we are not concerned at present (nothing in the poem or in Coleridge's statements about the poem will support such a thesis), but

[1] Professor E. E. Stoll has exhibited many of the vagaries of symbolist criticism as applied to Coleridge ("Symbolism in Coleridge," *PMLA*, March 1948). He has not, however, commented on the points raised in the present paper.

the critic's secondary thesis deserves our attention, for it is here that the "aegis" metaphor of Mr. Burke passes bodily into the language of Mr. Warren, and forthwith conducts the argument in a way that textual evidence could not hope to do. Mr. Warren's secondary thesis is the same as Mr. Burke's thesis about a maleficent Sun and beneficent Moon, though his references to Mr. Burke give barely a hint of this (see notes 95 and 112). Let us see how Mr. Burke's "aegis" plays again its extralogical role in Mr. Warren's argument:

1\. . . . in the poem the good events take place *under the aegis of the moon,* the bad events *under that of the sun* (p. 87).

2\. The voyage begins merrily *under the aegis of the sun* (p. 90).

3\. . . . to the man living in the world of comfortable familiarity, complacent in himself and *under the aegis of the sun . . .* (p. 90).

4\. The fact of these unhappy events *under the aegis of the supposedly beneficent moon* creates a question: Does this violate the symbolism of the moon? (p. 94).

5\. . . . *presided over by* the moon . . . ["presided" here does the work of "aegis"] (p. 96).

6\. The sun, *under whose aegis* the bad events of the poem occur, here appears in a "good" association (p. 97).

7\. . . . the role of the moon — the adored, the guiding, the *presiding* power [Again the translation of "aegis" into "presiding power"] (p. 98).

8\. Then we have the recognition of their [the water-snakes'] beauty *under the aegis of the moon . . .* (p. 104).

9\. Two quotations from Mr. Burke in which the "aegis" metaphor is used — tucked away in the midst of an extended footnote which calls no attention to the "aegis" but which agrees that Mr. Burke "is quite properly struck by the suggestive force of the phrase 'silly buckets.'" (This is the 112th of 168 such massive footnotes!)

As to the first quotation above, the general reader (for whom Coleridge's ballad was presumably intended) may be forgiven if he discerns nothing cosmically significant in the fact that a medieval sailing vessel leaves harbor in the daytime rather than in darkness or moonlight. Is there any causal connection between the "merry" mood of the crew and the fact that the sun rather than the moon is shining? (see quotation #2) . As for the third excerpt, the critic does not appear to notice that his assertedly maleficent sun is here acting in a rather benevolent capacity. The fourth quotation comes face to face with the disconcerting episode, so little in keeping with a "beneficent" moon, in which two hundred mariners dramatically fall dead in the light of the rising moon. Casuistry rescues the arbitrary thesis, however; the two-hundred moon-smitten mariners — and any other failures of evidence to accord with thesis — constitute what Mr. Warren ingeniously calls a "symbolic lag" in the poem (p. 98)! A reader with a sporting sense would like to smile at the cunningness of this maneuver. Mr. Warren never smiles, however.

In quotation #6 the critic again has to admit that his thesis is controverted by the evidence of the poem, but "symbolic lag" will take care of such failures on the part of the poet to anticipate the critic's thesis. The eighth quotation declares the moon's interest in sea-snakes: the snakes are not simply revealed in the light of the moon, they are "under the aegis of the moon." Probably the critic does not intend that we should visualize a lunar shield or protective emblem or a moon-goddess making a sign, but his metaphor encourages something of the sort.

It is hardly necessary to gather evidence to controvert the thesis that the sun and moon are malign and benign agents in the poem. The most striking disproof of the thesis is the death of the two-hundred-man crew beneath the rising moon. This disproof would be final could it be shown that either the moon or the sun are causal agents in the poem. Actually the moon and the sun are nowhere represented as causes or agents in the action. They are mentioned only when Coleridge wishes to indicate the weather, make vivid the setting, or reveal that the vessel is sailing southward toward the antarctic or northward from Cape Horn ("The sun came up upon the left,/ . . . and on the right/ Went down into the sea" — ll. 25–28. "The Sun now rose upon the right:/ . . . and on the left/ Went down into the sea" — ll. 83–86). Coleridge rightly judged that the goings and comings of sun and moon would be eagerly noted on a monotonous sea journey. Demonic and angelic spirits are agents in the action, but sun and moon are neutral.

There is of course no hint of the "aegis" idea in the poem. One is impelled to ask why Mr. Burke and Mr. Warren so iterantly insist on the metaphor. Would it not be simpler to speak of events that happen "under the sun or the moon" rather than under their "aegis"? And what does it mean to hook an aegis not only onto the sun and moon but also onto an Old Hermit and onto the (unbodied) hour of "noon"?

Perhaps we should look for the answer in the *function* of the aegis, not its structure — a distinction that Mr. Burke insists on as basic to aesthetic judgment (pp. 73–74 et seq.). What then is the function of the "aegis" metaphor, assuming that it is not a mere conditioned reflex beneath the threshold of consciousness? The function is presumably rhetorical: instead of logic or evidence, prestige is lent to the thesis from vague heroic associations. The implication is that Coleridge himself was controlled by the aegis-idea even though his poem manifestly contradicts any such assumption.

What is interesting, and not a little dangerous, is the method of "argument" used by both Mr. Burke and Mr. Warren. Beginning with a "hunch," as Mr. Burke sportingly calls it (p. 79), they hop from image to image, touching with a magic wand every image that can be linked by some train of association with this "hunch." The wand automatically converts the image into a "symbol," and from here on the way is easy. Where the evidence controverts the thesis, "Synecdoche" or "symbolic lag" resolves the difficulty.

To say this is not to deny that poetry is often – perhaps always – symbolical. It is simply to remind ourselves that some poems obviously make liberal use of symbolism and some make very scanty use of it. The method applicable to *Prometheus Unbound* is not applicable to ballads. It is not at all, or only very slightly, applicable to "The Ancient Mariner," the meaning and purpose of which are defined not only by the poem-text, but by Coleridge's gloss (added later), his statement to Mrs. Barbauld on the "moral" (*Table Talk*, May 31, 1830), his statement in the *Biographia Literaria* (ch. xiv), Wordsworth's account of the genesis of the poem (in his note to "We are seven"), and the vogue of the supernatural ballad at the time. In short, no interpretation is valid that ignores these controls, and if medieval theology or psychoanalysis are to be intruded, they must be made to harmonize with these controls and they must be justified by them. Otherwise they are "importations," as I. A. Richards well described such irrelevances (*Practical Criticism*). "Contraband," we might frankly label them.

Let it be acknowledged that both Mr. Burke and Mr. Warren furnish quite irreproachable descriptions of method, Mr. Burke in the beginning of his book and Mr. Warren in the conclusion of his. Mr. Burke is always stimulating even when he is absurd; he has a lively and agile mind, and a touch of the circus-rider in him. Since Mr. Warren's achievements as critic and creative writer are numerous and distinguished, it would be particularly unfortunate if his prestige lent authority to the symbolical method as he has applied it to Coleridge's ballad, where he not only engages in an austerely scholastic wrestling-match with Original Sin, but converts the innocuous sun into a malign force equatable with "the reflective faculty" (p. 93), "the light of practical convenience" (p. 93), "the light in which pride preens itself" (p. 93), "the understanding" (p. 93), "the Enlightenment" (p. 93), the "Age of Reason" (p. 93), "the sun of death" (p. 93), "the death-bark" (p. 94), and the "blood bath" of the French Revolution (p. 93); where he converts a simple old Hermit into "a priest of God" (p. 99), "a priest of Nature" (p. 99), "a priest of Society" (p. 100), and "a priest of imagination" (p. 104); and where he requires the Old Navigator himself to become not a seaman but a "poète maudit" (p. 106 et seq.), à la Verlaine. Such a procedure could conceivably, as Mr. Warren hopes, "reconcile . . . the internecine malices" (p. 117) writhing within (some of) us, but for others it will only increase the writhing—and gnashing of teeth.

◇◇◇

NEWELL F. FORD was born in Portland, Oregon, in 1912. He is a professor of English at Stanford University and the author of *The Prefigurative Imagination of John Keats.*

Very few essays on or reviews of Burke have ever appeared in the so-called scholarly journals—which is a clear indication of the kind of academic mind which does not take to or bother with people like Burke. This has been true, also, of the more scholarly students of modern criticism. The most notorious (and shocking) example is Wimsatt and Brooks's *Literary Criticism: A Short History,* which is apparently too short to include any coverage of Burke beyond a footnote and a quotation without commentary to illustrate some point or other.

Some of the reasons for this antipathy may be seen in this polite and wittily conducted but essentially (by intent) devastating attack on Burke's and Warren's critical assumptions, theories, and procedures. Professor Ford's attack issues, I think, from the same sort of assumptions which support Mr. Bewley's arguments, and his essay shares a style with Mr. Stauffer. Mr. Ford's principal objections are stated very clearly in the last three paragraphs of his essay. As Northrop Frye has incisively pointed out in the "Polemical Introduction" to his *Anatomy of Criticism,* such arguments as Professor Ford here advances seem now naive in the extreme.

◇◇◇

z *The Enemy of Bureaucracy*

BY Gerard Previn Meyer

THOSE students of modern poetry who know the work of Kenneth Burke for its difficulty, mainly, will be relieved to discover in his latest book—his first collection of poems, by the way—an eminent readability. In

EDITOR'S NOTE: Reprinted from *Saturday Review,* XXXVIII (3 September 1955), 28–29, copyright © 1955 by Saturday Review, Inc., by permission of the author and publisher.

fact, *Book of Moments,* though a Hermes Publication, is by no means *hermetically* sealed, either in diction or in purport. On the contrary: as a poet (if not, he suggests, "a professional poet") Mr. Burke is by no means hard to get at. He reveals himself in these "excerpts from a sporadic personal diary" as disarmingly open-faced, a Wilsonian in verse, in favor of "open covenants, openly arrived at." The absence of pose throughout, the omnipresence of honesty and directness are pleasantly reminiscent of another poet who may or may not be "professional" — Dr. William Carlos Williams.

There is the same romanticism, too. After all, the theory of moments (Kenneth Burke would not be himself if he did not have a theory!) is in direct opposition to the rigidly enforced balances of the neo-classicists: "Lyrics are 'moments' (says the Foreword) insofar as they pause to sum up a motive. . . . In one's moments one is absolute. . . . Ideally, perhaps, one should break down a motive into many different kinds of moment. . . . The ideal lyrist would probably speak through as many shifting personalities as the ideal dramatist." Does one catch a hint here of Burke's famous "dramatism"? In any case, Burke plumps for "momentary poems" and against those who "find either too much drought/ or too much rain." As delvers into Burke's prose well know, this man is accustomed to provide his audiences with an *embarras de richesse* — "too much drought" perhaps standing for his employment of a tremendous variety of abstract terms, "too much rain" for his concomitant serving-forth of a rich feast of concrete examples. Indeed, it seems a characteristic of this "unclassifiable man" that he can produce drought and rain simultaneously!

The tone of these "moments" is more often than not conversational, frequently dialectical with a satiric flavor. For purposes of immediacy (also recalling Dr. Williams) Burke when he chooses can achieve impact with an in-fact of immediate-see, immediate-be. In "Star-Fire," for example, he experiments with a sort of primitive, Igloo-type language — "Fly-things sing-sit/ On grow-things" — outgrowth of his interest in anthropology, no doubt — which at least for the *moment* strips away verbal bandages to restore a purity of vision. Nor, as in "Two Conceits, Anent Love," is he slow to call upon stream of consciousness and free association to convey the very sound, sight, taste, feel, of a man feeling, thinking, living. The same immediacy is sought after and found in "Pyre," and in such quick, new observations as this (from "Incipiently, By the Sea"): "He never saw the sea/ So Jammed with water."

Burke's wit — his eye for incongruities, illogicalities, and hypocrisies, especially in the field of politics — shows often; here, *e.g.*, is a metaphor: "Making much noise in the name of silence/ Like those that fight wars/ In the name of peace." And a shameless pun: "You said, 'Let's help Democracy in Spain.'/ Well, lad, I think you'd better say again./ Such attitudes are now deemed vile and ranko,/ To be quite Franco." He is capable, as in "Temporary Wellbeing," of a Don Marquis cunning:

> The pond is plenteous
> The land is lush,
> And having turned off the news
> I am for the moment mellow.
>
> With my book in one hand
> And my drink in the other
> What more could I want
>
> But fame,
> Better health,
> And ten million dollars?

—and of play in poetry *à la* e. e. cummings (with perhaps a dash of Hashimura Togo?):

> Whomsoever there are—
> Whether enemies, than which
> there is several,
> Or friends, than which there is
> few—
> Hear me of what I am speak of . . .

Is it unfair to suggest that Burke may be the prime example of the sophisticated mind ready, even eager, to embrace the naive for its value as renewal? "Mark the city as a place where no/ Wrens sing . . ." This culture-type continues, long after the Industrial Revolution, to be repelled by the city's artifacts: he turns away from "A city of five million mucous excitements," proposes "Buildings should not be tall," and suggests that our lapse from an agrarian economy has brought down on us "the prey and combat of the Jungle state." This jump from sophistication to naivete, coupled with a deeply-felt experience of the Depression, would account for a view of society that echoes the old socialist diatribes. One hears Burke the Old Bolshevik sounding off in such socio-politico-poetical moments as "For a Modernist Sermon," "Plea of the People, 1933," and the two "Exercises for Year's End." But truly, if his social protests posit any sort of political alignment, it's more a Thoreau-going party of one than the one-party state. Burke is an inveterate enemy of bureaucracy, as much as George Orwell ultimately was, and his note on a recent un-American phenomenon can be applied equally well to any police state, including the Muscovite: "It is as though, to guard against the suspicion of dangerous thoughts, the people were learning to have no thoughts at all."

He is aware, of course, of his anomalous position as "a Child Not of This Century":

> Think how with all of whom I'm
>   out of step with,
> Think how of all the sleepless
>   nights I've slep with!
> How many bats are need to fill a
>   steeple?
> What makes me be such very aw-
>   ful people?

What indeed? — except, maybe, that Kenneth Burke is more the Old Bohemian than the Old Bolshevik — the last of the Bohemians, possibly, with a humor wry enough to go with his awry feeling: "Running around in circles, in flight from the wheels of technology. Confessing confusion at fission and fusion. (O fatal acrostic: nuclear, unclear. And in the custody of killers?)" In "Second Exercise for Year's End" he does, in fact, come out with it: "Bohemianism, the only *remedy* for Bureaucratism. (We say *remedy*, since there is no known *cure*.) Hard-pressed, crowded into one odd corner of the mind — Walt Whitman with a crying jag."

He remembers: "I had those take-me-way-down-back-down-somewhere-or-other blues." But, despite the pessimistic moments of the cornered romantic — "Dewy, perplexing, wide-eyed moon,/ The traffic mumbles that you are not Artemis" — Burke Bounces Back; the man is not only "endlessly fertile" but endlessly resilient as well. On the last page of his latest "moment" he writes: "Even now, at midnight, I await the beckoning morneth, when the sun cometh uppeth . . ."

The beckoning, Burke-oning, burgeoning morneth cometh!

◇◇

GERARD PREVIN MEYER was born in New York City in 1909. He has taught English in high school and at Columbia, Brooklyn Polytechnic, Hofstra, and Queens College of the City of New York. He has written two books about poetry, two volumes of poems, and *Pioneers of the Press* and has edited the *New Quarterly of Poetry*.

In 1945 Burke announced the trilogy of *Motives* books and spoke of *A Rhetoric of Motives* and *A Symbolic of Motives* as forthcoming. The *Rhetoric* was published in 1951 and by 1955 the *Symbolic* was largely written and much of it published in essay form. However, after 1951 no new critical-theoretical work was published by Burke for the next ten years until *The Rhetoric of Religion*. Even though *Language as Symbolic Action* (1966) includes some of the material one thinks of as belonging to *A Symbolic of Motives*, that book, which was to have been Burke's systematic treatment of poetics, has not yet been published. During this ten-year hiatus, and while many waited for what they had every right to expect would be a monumental work of systematic theoretical and practical criticism, Burke published the book of poems Mr. Meyer here reviews and, with the same small publisher (Hermes which, to my knowledge, has never brought us messages from anyone but Burke), second editions of *Counter-Statement, Permanence and Change*, and *Attitudes toward History*. None of these editions, understandably, greatly exercised the critics, who were waiting for the later mature work on poetics. The effect was to turn Burke off and to bring to an almost complete stop the massive public reception which had begun with *A Grammar of Motives*. So nearly complete was this cessation that when, after ten years, Burke again published a new critical-theoretical book, it was hardly reviewed at all and only his most devoted followers even knew about it and reviewed it for him. The cruelty and injustice (if such a word can be used here) of this does not bear thinking on. Burke, or, more accurately, Burke as an active force in the ongoing intellectual life of his time, has not yet really recovered from his ten years of silence.

What one sees in this review of Burke's poems — to get back to Mr. Meyer — is the reception of what I have elsewhere called the other Burke; and, where the reviewer is able to connect the two Burkes, one sees odd kinds of relations between these two — or more — Burkes. Mr. Meyer's fifth and sixth paragraphs make such connections.

◇◇◇

z *The Critic in Love*

BY John Ciardi

KENNETH BURKE has made his reputation as the master parser and pigeonholer of modern criticism. In moments of the last forty years he has also been moved to poetry, a kind of "sporadic personal diary," as he calls it, and these ninety pages of impromptus [*Book of Moments*] are the generally happy result. Burke certainly has wit, feeling, immediacy, and a sometimes happily haunted sense of the voices of poetry.

EDITOR'S NOTE: Reprinted from *The Nation*, CLXXXI (8 October 1955), 307–308, copyright © 1955 by *The Nation*, by permission of the publisher.

Quite obviously, however, he has wasted no significant amount of time in revision. The strength of these poems is in their verve, their neatness (at best), and in the honesty with which they earn their sentiment. Their principal weaknesses are in their air of being too often simply intellectual exercises, and in their willingness to tolerate a number of lines that could certainly have been improved by the application of some of Mr. Burke's own critical guides. In a good poem titled "Three Seasons of Love," for example, Burke writes (italics mine):

> But when the chill leaps up,
> And the leaves with a *beautiful*
> *melancholy*
> Get out their silks to die in,
> Like *great* lifeless Vikings sent out
> upon the sea,
> *Majestic in their blazing, wealth-*
> *laden galleys* . . .

The base image here strikes me as powerfully right and usable, but has the poet's imagination really worked the passage? Lines three and four are certainly the center and substance of the poetic idea. But what function has the italicized wording? What need is there to tell us that a Viking funeral is beautiful, melancholy, both great and majestic, and that it is staged on a blazing and wealth-laden galley, when all these assertions are already implicit (and therefore more alive) in the image itself?

But Burke's gift as a poet is also real. His word play is in true mortal-fun, and his ear for a rhythm is rich and right. He does especially well in ending a poem on a kind of dissolving rhythm. Not with a bang but a whimper, perhaps, but the whimper sings. Above all, the poems, when put together, generate the sense of a real person — learned, bourbony, getting on to mortality as a bit of a hard case but still, and always, sweet on life. I like both the cantankerousness and the sweetness; one flavors the other. No one should have trouble believing that Kenneth Burke's despairs are humanly real.

And certainly, along with a sprinkling of perfect and near-perfect passages scattered through the uneven poems, "Sonnet to California" and "Industrialist's Prayer" seem unimprovable of their kind. I like, too, the second stanza (a better poem in itself than the whole poem, I think) of "Uneasy Thought of Peace":

> In our street
> We lie in our hovels

And hear it having snowed
By the scraping of shovels.

For a visit to the indescribable, no one should miss the five, so-called, Flowerishes. Many of the individual aphorisms Burke has built into them could surely be improved, but the total idea is a thing to be stunned by.

◇◇

JOHN CIARDI was born in Boston, Massachusetts, in 1916. He is a poet, translator, educator, lecturer and editor (to name a few of the things he does). He taught English for some years at Rutgers; he has been poetry editor of *Saturday Review* since 1956; and since 1940 he has written, edited, or translated enough books to fill sixteen lines in the current *Who's Who.*

This brief review does Burke the courtesy and honor (as Mr. Meyer's also did) of taking his poems seriously as poems — which is the way Burke takes them. It is also nice to have someone comment on the Flowerishes — collaborative creations of Burke and his wife (he writes them and she, a painter, arranges them) — which are among Burke's most original poetic creations.

◇◇

Kenneth Burke's Dramatistic Approach in Speech Criticism

BY L. Virginia Holland

TRADITIONALLY, the rhetorical critic has served as a social critic evaluating a speech in terms of how it meets the social needs and problems of the audience which the speaker faces; and the critic's method, whatever it may be, considers (1) *what* the speaker said, (2) *why* he spoke as he did, and (3) *how* he said it.

The major question with which this paper is concerned may be phrased thus: In the light of the traditional function and objectives of the rhetorical critic, what judgments can we make in evaluating the

EDITOR'S NOTE: Reprinted from *The Quarterly Journal of Speech*, XLI (1955), 352–358, copyright © 1955 by the Speech Association of America, by permission of the author and publisher.

dramatistic strategy, or approach to criticism, advocated by Kenneth Burke?

The first part of this paper will be concerned with showing what Burke's dramatistic approach is, and how it might be used by the critic of speeches. The second part will be concerned with evaluating the effectiveness of this approach for the speech critic.

Before I attempt to explain Burke's dramatistic approach, several things should first be made clear. Burke takes the classical view that the function or ultimate end of the rhetorical critic is to promote social cohesion and to perfect society. His method considers the traditional objectives of what was said, why it was said as it was, and how it was said. His rhetorical view, however, is not strictly classical in one sense: he contends that the aim or main ideal of criticism is to use *all* that there is to use.[1] That is, he is concerned with *all* language instruments — with poems, plays, novels, and written language as well as with spoken language. For him a rhetorical critic does not *confine* his analysis to the spoken words of a speech. A speech is simply *one* of many kinds of language instruments which a rhetorical critic may very properly analyze.

Burke contends that the rhetorical critic must understand the substance of man, what he is, what his problems are, why he acts as he does, and how he molds the thoughts and concepts of others. Burke believes that man's substance may best be described through the dramatistic metaphor of Man as an Actor.[2] He is an actor acting out his life with the purpose in view of achieving the Ultimate Good.[3] Since man is specifically a symbol-using animal who expresses himself symbolically primarily through linguistic structures, the main way that he acts is verbally, or through the medium of language.[4] Through his verbal "naming" or describing of things and situations he acts in speeches he makes and in documents he writes. Thus a man hates war, but he cannot end it literally or physically with his own hands, so he tries to end it through the use of the word-symbol. He tries to get mankind not to wage war by writing a novel, a speech, a play, a poem, in which he describes the brutalities and terror of war. Consequently, his verbal acts (speeches, play, poem) are his symbolic acts.[5] They are his strategies

[1] Kenneth Burke, *The Philosophy of Literary Form* (Baton Rouge: Louisiana State University Press, 1941), p. 23.

[2] For a discussion of *substance* as a concept, see Kenneth Burke's *A Grammar of Motives* (New York, 1945), pp. 21–58, especially pp. 24, 33.

[3] For a further clarification, see Burke's *Attitudes toward History* (New York, 1937), I, 139, 140, 213–226, and *Permanence and Change* (New York, 1936), pp. 300–301.

[4] Kenneth Burke, *Counter-Statement* (Los Altos, California, 1953), pp. 218, 219.

[5] *The Philosophy of Literary Form*, p. 8.

for meeting and overcoming a situation, or possibly learning to bear it if it cannot be overcome.

Burke believes that all literature grows directly out of a social situation and is a man's response to a condition in human affairs. He says: "All critical and imaginative works are answers to questions posed by the situation in which they arose"; "they are not merely answers, they are *strategic* answers, *stylized* answers." [6]

Thus, from Burke's point of view, a speech is *one* kind of strategic answer to a situation. It is the answer of a man who speaks and who stylizes and fits his answer to the needs of a speaking situation, of an audience, and of himself.

Now the rhetorical critic who is especially concerned with the criticism of speeches and speakers must of course use all that there is to use in relation to the speech situation. And Burke believes that he, like the rhetorical critic concerned with written language, will achieve the most valid critical estimate if he uses the dramatistic strategy, or applies what Burke calls the pentad to the speech.

The strategy of the pentad considers man's action from all of the perspectives which anything can have — from five interrelated motivational or causal points of view. The pentad considers the *Act* (that is, it names *what* took place in thought or deed), the *Scene* (the background of the Act, the situation in which it occurred), the *Agent* (the actor, or kind of person who performed the act), the *Agency* (what means or instruments he used), and the *Purpose* (motive or cause which lay behind a given act).[7] In this pentadic approach man is an actor who *purposively* acts through certain *means* (symbolical or linguistic methods as well as physical), and he carries out his action against the backdrop of the historical *scene* — the time and place in which he lives.

If we were to use this dramatistic method in speech criticism, for example, we would ask ourselves, "What did the speech say (act)? Who was the speaker (actor)? What means, or symbolical linguistic devices did he use to accomplish his purpose (agency)? What was the speaker trying to accomplish through his speech (purpose)? What was the background or situation within which the speech was generated and given (scene)?

From Burke's point of view we can never arrive at a valid, realistic description or naming of the nature or substance of the speech until we consider it from all of these interrelated aspects. Hence Burke believes that the substance of ideal criticism is something more than historical, biographical, sociological, or psychological criticism. This something more, from Burke's point of view, is the "whatness" that emerges from

[6] *Ibid.*, p. 1.

[7] *Grammar of Motives*, pp. xv, xxii.

a consideration of the overlap and interrelationship of all of these approaches.

According to Burke, the critic of speeches must realize that a speech is just as much a creative strategy for solving a social problem as building a bridge is a strategy for solving a physical problem. The critic must realize that there are just as many strategies which a speaker may use to solve a situation as there are ways which the speaker has of reacting or responding to a situation. For example, in a situation filled with intolerance, suspicion, and fear, a social critic acting in the role of a speaker might respond with a speech of exhortation in which he tried to incite the audience to adopt certain remedies. On the other hand, he might believe no action should be taken and respond with a speech of satire in which he belittled the fears and suspicions of the audience. In the first case, his over-all strategy to encompass the situation is the strategy of exhortation, in the second case, the strategy of irony.

The speech critic must be aware that there are many ways to conduct an over-all strategy. For example, the speaker using the strategy of exhortation might use such specific devices as these: satirizing, flag-waving, whitewashing, debunking, tear-jerking, getting-on-the-band-wagon, and so on. The *name* which we would give to specific, individual strategies would depend upon our analysis of what the language in the speech was *doing in each part of the speech,* and upon our careful selection of a word which we thought *best described* what the language was doing in each part. Thus the over-all strategy of exhortation is a composite of specific strategies designed to exhort.

Finally, the speech critic must consider what Burke would designate as the strategy of form. According to Burke, "*Form* in literature is an arousing and fulfillment of desires. A work has form in so far as one part of it leads a reader to anticipate another part, to be gratified by the sequence." [8] This concept of form as applied to speechmaking can thus be seen to embrace the concepts of disposition and of style as treated by the classical rhetoricians.[9] Burke subdivides the strategy of form into five strategies: syllogistic progression, qualitative progression, repetitive form, conventional form, and incidental or minor form.[10]

[8] *Counter-Statement,* p. 124.

[9] I am considering disposition here in its general twofold meaning, as embracing both the concept of arrangement, of orderly planning and movement of the whole idea of the speech, as well as the development of the specific divisions of the speech such as the exordium, narration, proof, peroration, or any of the other parts into which certain of the classical rhetoricians divided a speech. I am considering style also in the classical sense of referring specifically to word choice and the way in which words are arranged in the language of a speech.

[10] *Counter-Statement,* pp. 124–128.

Thus each of these subdivisions of the over-all strategy of form shows *how* the language of a speech is doing what it is doing.

From the point of view of the speech critic, speakers use syllogistic progression when they conduct an argument, advancing step by step demonstratively from A to E through steps B, C, and D. On the other hand, a speaker who uses a series of illustrations, each of which is charged with dramatic quality, anticipates the quality of his conclusion, and may be said to be using qualitative progression. A speaker uses repetitive form when he restates a theme by the use of new details. The conventional form of a speech is the appeal which a speech has simply because it is cast in the usual form which a speech takes. When a speaker steps to the platform to present a public address, we do not expect his ideas to be presented to us in sonnet form, or in the dramatistic form of the dialogue of a play. We have certain preconceived notions of the disposition and style of a speech. The conventional form of a speech, then, is the appeal of its form *as form*. Finally, the minor or incidental forms of a speech are those individual strategies within the speech which may be analyzed and enjoyed not because of their use but because of themselves: metaphor, apostrophe, paradox.

We have attempted in the foregoing pages to explain what Burke's dramatistic approach to criticism is, and to show how it might be utilized by the critic of speeches. We have attempted to show that a speech, for Burke, is a strategy which is itself a composite of strategies. The second major question which now confronts us is that of evaluation. How effective for the critic of public address is Burke's dramatistic approach? Would it be advantageous to use it?

I wish to make it perfectly clear that the statements of evaluation which follow are in no sense evangelical. I do not feel that Burke has given us all of the answers or the only answers to the problems of speech criticism. Nevertheless, I do feel that Burke's approach is suggestive for the speech critic, and it is in this light that I wish to treat it. Let us consider what the possible gain might be.

I have already suggested that the use of the dramatistic strategy of the pentad might remind the critic of *all* the factors present in any speech situation. It might help the critic avoid emphasizing the biographical element, or a concern with the speaker only as Actor. It might prevent the critic from emphasizing literary criticism, and stressing the speaker's speech as Act, and the Agency or linguistic devices within the speech, without considering these factors in terms of the speaker's purpose and audience. It might prevent criticism from becoming history by emphasizing the scene or background within which the speech was generated and given.

But would the application of the pentad be a nominal or an actual gain for the speech critic? After all, speech criticism has traditionally been concerned with the speaker, the speech, the occasion, and the audience, or with an approach made up of biographical, literary-rhetorical, historical, and psychological entities. Is there any advantage in giving new names to the old familiar things? What is the advantage of calling the speaker an actor? The speech an act? The linguistic devices within the speech an agency? The occasion and the audience the scene?

If there is an answer to these questions, it would seem to lie in the record of our research. As Wichelns wrote in 1925 in his essay, "The Literary Criticism of Oratory": "Histories of criticism, in whole or in part, we now have, and histories of orators. But that section of the history of criticism which deals with the judging of orators is still unwritten."[11] And despite the appearance in 1943 of *A History and Criticism of American Public Address,* which went a long way towards providing us with criticism of orators, we have only to examine individual studies within that work to find criticisms which are not rhetorical in the complete sense of the word, but may be more accurately described as biographical, literary, or historical studies.

If there is an advantage in applying Burke's dramatistic approach to speech criticism, it would seem to be a psychological one, and to lie in the dynamic stress upon the speech as the "action" of an actor in a scene. The imaginative quality of the metaphor might generate a more balanced consideration of all the speech factors entering into speech criticism. Although we might still find ourselves in the predicament of writing rhetorical criticism which placed too much stress upon the actor, or the scene, or any one part of the pentad, there would seem to be a chance that *thinking* of speech criticism in these dramatistic terms might avoid want of balance and result in a more ideal criticism.

For example, the records seem to indicate that when the speech critic *thinks* in terms of the old frames of reference of speaker, speech, audience, and occasion, he falls rather easily into the snare of thinking of the speaker and presenting biographical criticism, or in thinking of the speech and presenting literary criticism, or in thinking of the audience and presenting psychological criticism. In short, he does these things rather than think of the interrelationships of these factors and thus present a rhetorical criticism. Any method emphasizing the organic nature of the speech is so much gain.

While thinking of the speaker as a speaker allows one to criticize

[11] *Studies in Rhetoric and Public Speaking in Honor of James Albert Winans* (New York, 1925), pp. 181–216. My quotation is from p. 181.

him in terms of his personality, thinking of him as an actor focuses attention upon criticizing him in terms of his actions as an actor.[12] Further, it is almost impossible to think of criticizing an actor without at the same time thinking of the part he is playing, what his acts are, what his dialogue is, the scene against which his action is played, and the meaning or purpose of his part in relation to the play as a whole. Since the dramatistic approach of Burke's pentad begins with a stress upon "action," or upon an "acting," the scene is always merely the backdrop or background of the actor. With such an emphasis, the critic is less apt to think that he is criticizing an actor's acting, if he becomes involved in a minute description and analysis of the scene.

There is still a final question of evaluation which cannot be ignored. Would Burke's concept of a speech as a composite of strategies aid us in analyzing the language of a speech? In classifying speeches and speakers? In analyzing the audience and the times?

Traditionally, when we have analyzed a speaker's language from the point of view of content, we have broken it down into the categories of logical, pathetic, and ethical usage. There is the possibility that, if we analyzed the language of a speech in order to discover and "name" the strategies of which it is composed, we might discover a more descriptive way of telling *what language was doing* when we categorized it as being used logically, or pathetically, or ethically. We might even discover that certain specific strategies *more often than not* appeared when language was used logically, while others appeared when it was used ethically, and still others when it was used pathetically.

Traditionally, when we have analyzed language use from the point of view of form, we have considered the plan or arrangement of the

[12] There is the *Drama of Creation*. God built the stage, designed the scenery, and wrote the script around the actions of the sole actress in the play, Mother Nature. Within this *Drama of Creation* there are many dramas. One such is the Social Drama, or what Burke would call the *Human Comedy*. Each succeeding generation might be said to provide a new cast for this *Human Comedy*. Each new cast must write the script for its play anew. Although the purpose of the play will always be to show how Man may be preserved as a species, the script of the play will vary, and the plot or course of action will change to show how the social needs and problems of each new generation can be met and resolved. Each human being upon this earth can only act within the physiological limitations *determined* for him by Mother Nature. Yet within these limitations, he *can* determine *how* he acts in his role as individual man and what kind of contribution he wants to make in helping write the script anew for the Social Drama or *Human Comedy* of his generation. One of the most important acting roles which a man can take is that of a philosopher-critic who is sensitive to the shifting social scenery against which he acts out his life role. If that peaceful white cloud in the scenic background shows signs of shaping itself into a gigantic mushroom, he notes it and warns his fellow actors they must write new lines into the social script. One such philosopher-critic is the *speaker*. In the ideal sense he is a man who acts (speaks) in such a way as to cause the writing of better social scripts.

speech as a whole, as well as the word choice and manner in which the words are arranged in the speech. We have categorized our word arrangements or stylistic devices by such descriptive names as the simile, metaphor, apostrophe, personification, asyndeton, and so on. We have labeled a speaker's style in a general way as grand, plain or medium. There is a possibility that the use of Burke's strategies of form might be one way of more descriptively explaining *how* the words are saying what they are saying stylistically. We might discover, for example, that the grand style more often makes use of qualitative progression than the plain style does. Any kind of method that might give us additional meaningful ways of talking about speech style, or telling how language is behaving, should be so much to the good. For example, there is a possibility that the statement, "This speaker is using the strategy of exhortation which he is carrying out primarily by using the strategies of flag-waving and invective, expressed stylistically through the strategy of syllogistic progression," *says more, descriptively,* than the statement, "This speaker is persuading through the use of emotional appeal."

Further, Burke's strategy concept might be used as one way of descriptively and dynamically classifying speeches. The ancient rhetoricians categorized speeches as deliberative, forensic, and epideictic. Post-Renaissance tradition has classified them as informative, persuasive, and entertaining. The strategy concept might give us a system for classifying the *kinds* of informative, persuasive, or entertaining speeches. For example, we might classify a persuasive speech as one of exhortation, or sanctification, or defilement. Eventually, we might be able to determine the kinds of strategic language use (or strategies) most often present in persuasive, informative, and entertaining speeches. If we could determine these kinds, we might have a way of attaining a greater understanding of the true nature, or substance, of persuasive, entertaining and informative language per se.

The strategy concept might also provide a descriptive method for classifying the kinds of speakers. For example, speakers might be classified on the basis of the master strategies which they used most consistently, and thus they might be called sanctifiers, defilers, satirists, and so on. It is conceivable that such an approach could give us criteria that would indicate a correlation between a speaker's profession or his beliefs, and the strategies he uses. Eventually, we might be able to predict with reasonable accuracy the strategies we *might expect* to find in the language of groups classified as communists, socialists, democrats, republicans, protestants, catholics, etc.; the strategies we might expect from groups more generally classified as economic and social emancipators; and the strategies we might expect from groups still more generally classified as idealists and materialists. Such knowledge, however we gained it, ought to bring us a heightened critical awareness, and be educationally instructive.

Finally, there is the possibility that the strategy concept might suggest a method of analysis which would give greater insights into the sociological and psychological factors that influence speakers, and into sociology and psychology per se. We might determine the answer to this question, or to questions like this: in what kind of a *situation* does a speaker more often use the master strategy of crusading or of exploitation? Conversely, what are the specific strategies which most often appear in the language of a speech using either of these master strategies? We might eventually find ourselves in a position where we could, with reasonable accuracy, answer these questions: *Given a certain situation,* what kind of strategies might we anticipate that a speaker will use? *Given certain strategies in a speech,* what kind of a situation does it appear the speaker *believed* he faced?

Such an approach might educate us to become better analysts of the social scene, more cognizant of what the problems of society are thought to be, and more critical of the solutions given to those problems by the social critics operating as speakers and writers.

I should like to conclude by suggesting that if the questions we ask determine the answers we receive, it may be that Kenneth Burke is giving us one method for obtaining rewarding answers. The question of what a speaker's strategies are is inherent in Burke's dramatistic approach to criticism, and it may provide us with one means of obtaining a rhetorical criticism that more nearly approaches the ideal. It may be a means of developing a rhetorical critic who is a more expert judge as a social critic, and who, as a consequence, is himself better qualified to make valid social judgments of his own, and better qualified as an acting rhetorician to popularize them through the language strategies of his own rhetoric.

◇◇◇

LAURA VIRGINIA HOLLAND was born in Lincoln, Illinois, in 1915. She has taught English and speech at various high schools and colleges and is at present teaching at Roosevelt High School in St. Louis. She is the author of *Counterpoint: Kenneth Burke and Aristotle's Theories of Rhetoric* (1959). This book, one of three on Burke so far published, explores an important subject in what is finally and, for us, unfortunately, a rather routine way. Very few people with the requisite knowledge have ever been willing or inclined to write about Burke and his sources or influences. Miss Holland was one of the few ever to undertake any part of this large and important task, and we must be grateful for whatever she was able to discover about how Burke was like and not like Aristotle. If others would undertake this with Freud, Marx, Coleridge, and Nietzsche – to name a few – we would certainly be able to understand and see Burke in new and significant ways.

This essay – to get back to the subject at hand – is another example of how modern students of rhetoric have readily accepted, explicated, and applied Burke. They saw almost at once that Burke's system was a system, that it was centered around rhetoric, and that it could provide them with a powerful and socially meaningful theory and methodology for the analysis and evaluation of speech-acts. Miss Holland's exposition and discussion of Burke should be seen in relation to the two later expositions and/or applications of Burke by Professors Griffin and Brock.

◇◇

z A Poetry of Perspectives

BY W. C. Blum

MR. BURKE's collection of lyrics, epigrams, satires, and night thoughts [*Book of Moments*] covers so many years in such a variety of styles, none of them fully exploited, that the easiest thing will be to treat it as history, stopping to inspect landmarks and make comments. The earliest landmark, selected by gamblers' methods from a half dozen items equally unusual, is entitled "*Ver Renatus Orbis Est*" and weaves its vernal spell out of teasingly discontinuous thoughts. The scene is a room on the heights of Weehawken, overlooking the North River:

> No, I shall not go and look out of the window;
> A city of five million mucous excitements;
> I know of a pond now in Ohio
> Where before bed some students are sitting;
> Spring! calling us to the major cycle of conception.

Note that each "thought" in the first stanza is matched and developed by a corresponding one in the second:

EDITOR'S NOTE: Reprinted from *Poetry*, LXXXVII (March 1956), 362–366, copyright © 1956 by W. C. Blum, by permission of the author and publisher.

Timor mortis versus taedium vitae;
Noises from the distance without clarified meaning;
Hot flesh massed dissatisfied in the movies
    Accepting the used-up breath in silence.

From here on, things become dithyrambic. But I have quoted enough of this modern version of the "*Pervigilium Veneris*" to show that the author, at twenty, already distrusted Venus and was capable of unfilial variations on a theme inherited from Pater.

By far the most poetically competitive effort in the book is a six page romantic sequence, "*From Outside,*" written at about the same time as the author's novel, *Towards a Better Life.* The poem is a fascinating succession of recitatives and muted aria-episodes, and I wish there were room to quote from it effectively. Of the same vintage is the sonnet *à clef*, "Atlantis," about "an island of Antiquity –"

Well favored with an *equatorial* sky –
Where Babylonic galleys used to lie
And *inland* music sounded *cumbrously.*

Though long accustomed to such clemency
It felt *obscure disturbances,* whereby
Emitting a huge *geologic* sigh
It lurched, and gently sank beneath the sea.

Its marbles now, in pale aquatic hues
Stand aimless, posturing on heavy floors . . .

I stop here because the next line is a dead give-away, and, besides, nearly all of the important clues (italicized) are now in the hands of the reader – just as they were in 1928 when "Atlantis" was written. Yet no one came forward to point out the "detestable" symbolic content, until, so the story goes, enlightenment suddenly burst on the author a couple of years later, and the rather tame-looking sonnet was revealed as a travesty of Aristotle's cathartic principle.

As though it had magically closed an era by symbolizing what was shortly to happen to the securities market, "Atlantis" is followed in the book by an ominous silence, broken after five years by poems of social protest. These include a moving "Plea of the People," an ironic suggestion "For a Modernist Sermon," and a sonnet, "Buildings Should Not Be Tall," which places the guilt for New York's irresponsible building sprees exactly where it belongs. Even more compelling is this cameo of unemployed despair in a city where the municipal functions go on as usual:

In our street
We lie late in bed
On dull winter mornings
And think of the dead.

In our street
We lie in our hovels
And hear it having snowed
By the scraping of shovels.

An ambitious "Project for a Poem on Roosevelt" was never completed; but the outline for it, consisting of notes on Roosevelt psychology and politics, is to be found in the Appendix. "Admittedly," says the author, "even a Lucretius would have had trouble making this project sing." Maybe so; but there is reason to think that what interfered with the celebration of this relatively benign figure of authority was not so much the disorderliness of the New Deal as the poet's aversion to potentates.

The notes on Roosevelt give more than a hint of the immense expansion and re-organization that were taking place at this time in Mr. Burke's philosophy of criticism, and that were to culminate in a scheme of formidable comprehensiveness – nothing less in fact than a "fully worked-out version of the ways of *homo dialecticus*." Of the scheme's ethics, the "Dialectician's Prayer" is a sort of verse preview, made up, like most prayers, of two parts: a hymn or salutation to the genius of language, and, embedded in it, a prayer for truth-telling, of which the following is a key stanza:

May we compete with one another
To speak of Thy Creation with more justice –
Coöperating in this competition
Until our naming
Gives voice correctly,
And how things are
And how we say things are
Are one.

The "prayer part" is honest and wise enough to have pleased St. Chrysostom; but the "hymn part" is another matter. It begins:

Hail to Thee, Logos,
Thou Vast Almighty Title
In Whose name we conjure –

and ends:

Thy name a Great Synecdoche
Thy works a Grand Tautology.

While the two parts together fulfill the author's purpose to define dialectic "by use of the optative style," one can't help noting ungratefully that the remarkable *tour de force* isn't very songful.

Near the end of the nocturnal complaint, "Archai," the sleepless poet, having paid his respects to the "prisoner in solitary" and the "horned toad in a cornerstone," pauses to ask grandly:

> And what of Thersites,
> Despised of all his tribe . . .
> Loathed by the bard that made him,
> Ultimate filth, speaking against epic war?
> What of Thersites?
>
> Salute —
> To Saint Thersites.

The reference to this much-maligned early pacifist and critic of heroes quite obviously points to Mr. Burke's own program "For the Purification of War," and to his frequent out-of-season snipings at the warlike, of which there are some dandies in the *Book of Moments.* And further parallels present themselves. For example, just as Shakespeare's Thersites managed to exasperate both Greeks and Trojans by the universality of his jibes, so too does Mr. Burke in "The Conspirators," a satire about a young married couple that makes collectivist cant and finance matrimony appear equally hilarious:

> Going into the market, they got tables,
> Chairs, and other properties from the public
> Stock-pile, taking absolute possession
> For them alone. These things, all no one else's,
> They thought, plotting further to increase
> Their store. To have, to hold, to love — theirs only.

The poem is a masterpiece of phrasing, with an easily foreseen but none the less startling conclusion.

We have now arrived at comparatively modern times, and can look at the verse of the last dozen years or so without worrying about landmarks. We note that Mr. Burke is writing verse oftener, especially light verse, not to mention doggerel for subjects unsavory enough to deserve it:

> Were you adaptive during the depression?
> You're now a captive, with or sans confession.
> The situation then? Forget it brother.
> The situation has become another.

There are poems of much rueful charm about late nasturtiums, nesting wrens, and an alcoholic literary lion; about the spirit of alcohol and the spirit of negative theology, and about

California, noble travelogue,
Half endless vistas, half unending smog.

The songfulness that previously wouldn't operate for a political hero or a god-term now appears in lyrics that disarm censorship by inverting the social hierarchy. Thus "Night Piece," a prayer for rhythmic instruction, is addressed, not to the Muse, but to Her choir of crickets:

O pulsant autumnal jungle
Restore me to thy rhythm
Teach me the knack.

I have stood on the edge of the jumping-off place
Waiting.

Have looked down
To see still stars at the bottom of a lake;
Looked out
Upon dark riddle within . . .

Similarly, a hymn of universal praise in pidgin English takes the form of a debate among songsters apparently not very high in the evolutionary scale ("Fly-things sing-sit/ On grow-things.") as to what is to be sung ("Say first/ Not know just why, what.") from which finally emerges a joyous round, the separate voices set apart by quotation marks:

"Tinkle, tinkle, Morn-fire!"
"Stinkle, stinkle, Think-fire!"
"Crinkle, crinkle, Lay Fire!"

In this mood, which gives every sign of continuing, the poet is very nearly irresistible. And although his straightforward verse is a long way from the puzzles of metaphor to which we are accustomed, I think that much of it deserves to be called poetry by virtue of fertile invention – of surprises and insights that are neither images in the ordinary sense, nor conceits, nor even jokes, but might be described as "perspectives."

For utilitarians, who like their wit unrhymed and unmetered, the Appendix offers, in addition to the notes on Roosevelt, two perspective-laden poems in prose, and over six score informal epigrams on life and letters, ranging from tips for writers ("If a critic attacks you stupidly, give him a chance to forget it.") to aphorisms of universal bearing

("Instinct: all or none. Reason: compromise." "It's hard to remember, but often all we need do is nothing."). And, as though to make sure that the *Book of Moments* will be recognized for the high comedy it largely is, the epigrams are printed together in typographical "flowerishes," so baffling that a magnifying glass is needed to unscramble them.

◇◇

W. C. BLUM is a pseudonym; Mr. Blum prefers to remain anonymous. He is a long-time friend of Burke's. I present this descriptive, laudatory review of Burke's poems without comment—beyond the remark that this is the way friends ought to receive one's poems.

◇◇

⁊ *A Grammarian of Motives*

BY Marianne Moore

KENNETH BURKE is a philosopher and a satirist—a humorist of the somatic kind, whose self-styled "flat tire of satire" has been indispensable to the lingual, political, moral, and poetic apparatus which has carried him to an enviable destination—the expert's. He feels that "eye, hand, and mental keenness" should be "busied for the good of the many" ("Plea of the People" [*Book of Moments*], page 58). "We would be men of good will," he says.

> To be strong in hate or to rot in wretchedness—
> Do not force us to this choice that is no choice.

In his "Neo-Hippocratic Oath," although he "cannot offer cures for stony hearts," he "swears that he will try not to belittle the work of those who would," and if he "comes upon unsavory private matters," he "will keep them to himself except insofar as he noises them abroad to everyone/ as observations about everyone" ("Moments," page 8). In his technique of persuasion, he is a philosopher of opposites. He is not "launching an attack; nor does he suffer a sense of defeat." "Each principle advocated is matched by an opposite principle." "The connoisseur will be will-less ("Counter-Statement"). The artist "must recog-

EDITOR'S NOTE: Originally published in 1956. Reprinted from *A Marianne Moore Reader* by Marianne Moore (New York: Viking Press, 1961), pp. 233–237, copyright © 1956 by Marianne Moore, by permission of the Viking Press, Inc.

nize the validity of contraries," he says. On the title page of his *Moments* he quotes Emerson's statement, "Our moods do not believe in each other." He is in agreement with Thomas Mann that "the problematical is the proper sphere of art." Concur and one "will find moral indignation impossible."

His "Moments" "treat of love, politics, and kindred conundrums," he says, and as if to match the philosophy of opposites he says they "are somewhat irresponsible in their way of cancelling out one another." Whatever else they do, they illustrate Plato's antithesis that if we think in universals, we feel in particulars. They are records of experience—"Delight, Promise, Victory, Regret, Apprehension, Arrival, Crossing, Departure, Loneliness, Sorrow, Despair, etc." and are reinforced at the back of the book by several pages of "Flowerishes"—dicta "which emerge these days somewhat dizzily," Mr. Burke says, and as print, flower in circles, serpentines, comet-tails, dotted lines, back to back and turning corners; some in light and some in dark-face. Here are two: "Must it always be wishful thinking? Can't it sometimes be thoughtful wishing?" "Draw out the time—and one part of an eddy going downstream might seem all your life to be going upstream."

In *Counter-Statement* (1931), discussing form "emotional and technical," "a work has form," Mr. Burke said, "insofar as one part leads a reader to anticipate another part and be gratified by the sequence." "Neglect organic progression and our emotions remain static." Alluding to virtues and diseases of form, he mentioned hypertrophy of information as a disease of form, said of Proust that whereas "a single page is astonishing, he becomes wearisome after extended reading"; noted also that "Shakespeare's style approaches mannerism insofar as it over-emphasizes metaphor." Eloquence, he said, consists in "matching the important with the important" and "by innovation is not meant something new but an emphasis to which the public is not accustomed." "A rhythm," he said, "is a promise which the poet makes the reader and in proportion as the reader comes to rely upon this promise, he falls into a state of general surrender which makes him more likely to accept, without resistance, the rest of the poet's material." His to me master-maxim is this: "Truth in art is not discovery of facts or addition to knowledge, it is the exercise of propriety."

With the foregoing aids to composition in mind, how does Mr. Burke come off poetically? He has in his "Problem of Moments"—if I am reliable—a masterpiece:

> I knew a man who would be wonder-wise,
> Having been born with both myopic eyes
> Scratched in again.

"Than tyrannous moments, what more absolute,"
He asked, "except the motionless pursuit
Of us by pain?"

Note squirrel on log, how pert, now in, now out—
But classicists find either too much drought
Or too much rain.

(Wise, eyes, again
Absolute, pursuit, pain
Out drought, rain)

Here we have balance, compression, crescendo, and neatly articulated, impeccably accelerated rhyme, with each stanza punctuated by a rhymeword, the same words grouped in the same order, as climax of the final stanza. "Star-Fire" is expert counterpoint: "Fly-things sing-sit/ On grow-things. . . . Halló-la héllo-ló!" There are many phases of Joyce inter-crossings: "As I lurk look from Look-Out." Mr. Burke is a master of the mellow-sardonic enforced by alliteration, as in his salute to alcohol, "Alky, Me Love": "Always there was something or other/ Just couldn't stand it"; not of the mellow-sardonic only but of the mellow: as "Dozing" then "awaking to the cosmic roar"

Of the sea
(The onrushing, perpetual sea),

He never saw the sea
So jammed with water.

Is not this "exposition," this picture of "Jack's Bandbox"?

The cover of this box is made secure
By a small catch of wire which, when released,
Permits the lid to open with a snap

And this an intrinsic pearl?

Beat the devil, beat the devil, beat the devil,
Beat the devil, beat the devil, beat the . . .

(Hear the train
Drive steadily on
Towards nowhere)

Alert to the practice of others, moreover, Mr. Burke reveals a strong liking for William Carlos Williams, ("The Wrens Are Back"); pleasure in E. E. Cummings ("Frigate Jones") "With hands like feet, and feet in turn like legs/ It was his job to lightly step on eggs"; in Wallace Stevens ("From Outside"):

> He could have called this place a bog; quaking
> With life, made cheap by multitude . . .

and in the rhetoric of the Bible.

Complaints? With Rabelais and Joyce to brother him, Mr. Burke is sometimes coarse. Might he not recall that "the reader has certain categorical expectations that crave propriety?" that "self-expression of the artist is not distinguished by the uttering of emotion but by the evocation of emotion"? The theology in Mr. Burke's suggestions for a "Modernist Sermon," as in his "Lines in the Spirit of Negative Theology," is certainly negative. Led to expect some kind of counter-statement, we find "prayer" a mere figure of speech ("Invective and Prayer," "Dialectician's Prayer," "Industrialist's Prayer"). Looking elsewhere, we can say that solemnity and humility dominate "Night Piece," in which Mr. Burke says:

> I have stood on the edge of the jumping-off place
> Waiting.
>
> Have looked down
> To see still stars at the bottom of a lake;
> Looked out
> Upon a dark riddle within;

and in "Faustkunde," nowhere implies a somewhere – a constancy at least:

> In bed, one thinks of fearsome things.

"When up, one laughs and calls himself a devil." Here, one seems to have both shells of the clam, the seeker for truth, the self-misled – and something alive within. Eternity is made the focus of these reflections,

> Während in dem Wogen, der Ewigkeit er wiegt.

Well; if it is not faith, it is poetry: "in dem wogen er wiegt."

"A capacity is a command to act in a certain way," Mr. Burke says; and, fortunately for us, he has been impelled to think and to teach. A philosopher, a grammarian of motives, a methodologist and precisionist, an authority on language who "uses logic not merely to convince but because he loves logic," he has "felt as opportunity what others feel as a menace" and "taken a professional interest in his difficulties"; is an artist. His "new precisions offer new possibilities of development" and his original theorems do not stale. A poet in what he says and in knowing how what is said has been said, he has – Coleridge-fashion –

doubled roles and planted two harvests, so that in each we have the best strengths of both.

◇◇◇

MARIANNE MOORE was born in St. Louis, Missouri, in 1887. She was an editor of *The Dial* during the great days of that journal in the twenties; she is an essayist, translator, and, most notably, a poet. Her awards, honorary degrees, and other kinds of recognition are too numerous to list here. Her *Collected Poems* has long been recognized as one of the major achievements in modern American poetry.

Marianne Moore has been a friend of Burke's since *The Dial* days. Burke wrote a long essay on her *Collected Poems* and later reviewed a collection of her reviews and essays. Miss Moore returns those compliments in this piece of graceful praise of Burke's poems and other works.

◇◇◇

z Postscript: Bureaucratization of the Imaginative

BY George Knox

AS TEACHER-CRITIC, Burke has given us some tentative illustrations of the uses of criticism. But, along with our newly acquired insect-eye kind of awareness of the endless versatility of our terms, we must somehow maintain a sense of moral responsibility. This, our passion, action, and burden as critics, means earning the complexity, uniqueness, and integrity of a work of art by equally complex and unique acts of reconstruction. Dramatistically, this would be called "re-enaction." We must not overintellectualize art, alienate it from context, reduce or dissolve symbolic unity into conceptual disunity, atomize wholes into disparate particulars. We must walk the fine Burkean line between obfuscation and clarification.

Burke warns us that we have inherited an enormous body of analysis, becoming rich without having earned our wealth. But, looking at this sadly, we see ourselves bent under a pack of ideologies and critiques which grows heavier as we shift and adjust to it. If we dump on a work of art all the accumulated critical lore that Burke might possibly

EDITOR'S NOTE: Reprinted from *Critical Moments: Kenneth Burke's Categories and Critiques* by George Knox (Seattle: University of Washington Press, 1957), pp. 106–112, by permission of the author and the University of Washington Press.

dredge up, might we not become victims of his own bogeyman: "bureaucratization of the imaginative"? In the modern mood, criticism has to be rationalized and fortified, with formidable ideologies, organized and formulated into systems. And we must all the time be conscious of our systematizing, and conscious of the consciousness, and so forth. To read a poem means justifying the poem and everything we say about it. This type of fetish for pseudorational statement has attained such "bureaucratic embodiment" in method and methodology, in quasiphilosophy and quasipsychology, that criticism becomes more and more inaccessible to the reasonably intelligent but uninitiated reader. One is reminded of the obsession with high-fidelity radio sets and record players. The expert becomes less interested in hearing the piece of music and more interested in its oddities. After being subjected to very much of this specialist music, he is ready to plump for "low fidelity."

Burke's own trained incapacity results from this overweening sense of responsibility to shovel around a growing heap of apparently uncorrelated documentation. Critical "re-enaction" becomes impossibly complex, and we wonder whether the slipping away of this detritus would be so tragic, and whether "re-earning" it is only a delusion. Do we not inevitably fall into the "desiccations of psittacism," the occupational disease of academic critics, fast on our several ways to even more dangerous forms of "alienation"? After we try to encompass Burke himself, to make him part of our critical heritage and consciousness, we are perhaps appalled by his turning of insights into methods, methods into methodologies, methodologies into ideologies and theologies. The critic's passion becomes his hypochondriasis, for good or bad, as he acts and turns to scrutinize his act, trying to rationalize his act in relation to the countless acts of "collective lore" and the "collective revelation," a pyramiding process with radical Burkean connotations.

Perhaps Burke's virtue and fault both lie in his attempt to evolve his critical nomenclature for paralleling in analytic terms what the work itself performs imaginatively and creatively. Certainly, he claims to look beyond his terms and to realize that the greater part of his job is overcoming the latent ambiguity of our critical jargons. He has also tried to keep distinct the function of naming and classification from the more subtle acts of intuition and response. But the question is whether his personal needs have not alienated us from the work he analyzes. Critics vary in the ability to discover the literary work's fusing of private and public meanings, but Burke has striven in the solution of particular problems to relate his critical chore to life and the universe generally. He has tried to develop a vocabulary as instrument, a weapon that will "strike and retreat, compliment and insult, challenge and grovel, sing, curse, and whimper, subside and recover." And he would lash his vocabulary down with a rationale at each turn.

He is a procedural critic, offering theoretical arguments and defining the nature of a particular method in each case and establishing a ground or scene for that method. He offers critical illustration and some demonstration as he pitches his method, finally claiming medicinal qualities over and above its value as a special heuristic device. Although he contends that the greater the range, depth, and explicitness the critic can develop, the fuller the critic, he himself lies scattered and fragmentary. To us who might come to him for diagnosis and help, perhaps the best he offers is a limitless range of possibilities for purging off the critical psychosis. So much has been said about extrinsic matters that Burke self-consciously and defensively defines the scenic limitations of his critique each time he wants to make a sociological or historical point. And his tentativeness breaks down further into considerations of poet-plus and poet-minus, citizen-plus and citizen-minus, as he allows for physiological as well as "mystic" criteria. That is, Burke wants to be both a materialist and a transcendentalist.

Although he would have us recognize the poem as an authoritative unit setting up demands uniquely its own, he seems afraid to carry out any analysis. He has fears of living from one critical moment to another, of multiplying particularized insights into a totality of parts, of converting a few pages of text into a chapter of analysis; perhaps his "Ode on a Grecian Urn" exegesis comes close to this. And so he too often stands too fearsomely (in spite of the boldness of his approach) at the cavernous depths opened magically before him by his terminological wand, the poem glimmering, shimmering ("charismatically") enigmatically out of reach. Here, in lyric stasis, running but standing still like the impassioned lover on the Urn, Burke beckons us on.

At the worst we might have to conclude that the literary work is unknowable in our time, that Burke's critical equipment allows at best a partial vision of flitting features of actions on a partial scene. But is this not as much as we should hope for? As critic of criticism, he is, however, caught in a paradox of his own weaving: he must serve fragmentary analyses illustrating policies on wholes. His final goal seems to be somewhere in the realm of linguistics, of linguistic action beyond the sphere of the more pedantic terminologists, grammarians, and philosophical psychologists. His heaven can be reached only by adopting a motto: our end is always a beginning. As a theologian of critical moments, as one who lives off and for esthetic ideas, Burke has built an increasingly sufficient self out of his own image. His freedom has become his burden.

Think how with all of whom I'm out of step with,
Think how of all the sleepless nights I've slep with!
How many bats are need to fill a steeple?
What makes me be such very awful people?
Out of star-born into war-worn,
Into the flat-tire of satire . . .[1]

This is the opposite of his intention. Insofar as he is a political and a social critic, he struggles to relate art with the structures of power and authority, with problems of living from day to day, and with living as a long-term investment.

Nevertheless, beneath the imposing erudition and the magic we detect a note of hopelessness, a frustrated search for symbols of allegiance and stability. Burke has, however, built for himself a critical-esthetic-political form, a principle of value in form: hierarchy. Esthetically, this principle of dominance among parts and elements becomes a kind of correlative, analogue, or archetype of order in the human consciousness. What he will do with hierarchy is yet uncertain. But for better or worse it is with us, and whatever our persuasions, whether we try to locate the substance of human beings in particular roles, verbal or practical, or whether we try to locate them in larger configurations by means of some subtly organized metaphysic, "we must keep trying anything and everything, improvising, borrowing from others, developing from others, dialectically using one text as comment upon another, schematizing; using the incentive to new wanderings, returning from these excursions to schematize again, being over-subtle where the straining seems to promise some further glimpse, and making amends by reduction to very simple anecdotes."[2]

I have chosen to name this work *Critical Moments,* taking the cue from Burke's recently published volume of poems. His critical work as a whole is a collection of "moments," of diverse statements on diverse matters. As a motto in justification of his courageous attempts to systematize diversity, we might cite some lines from his poem, "Dialectician's Prayer":

And may we have neither the mania of the One
Nor the delirium of the Many—
But both the Union and the Diversity—[3]

Anticipating the dangers of his abstract moments: "(And that brings us to critics-who-write-critiques-of-critical-criticism.)"[4]

[1] *Book of Moments: Poems 1915–1954* (Los Altos, Calif.: Hermes Publications, 1955), p. 94.
[2] *A Rhetoric of Motives,* p. 265.
[3] *Book of Moments,* p. 41. [4] *Ibid.,* p. 5.

Perhaps the key to Burke's critical habits and contribution can be found in the Foreword to his *Book of Moments.* As poet and critic he is much the same man. As lyrist he is concerned with "moments" which "sum up a motive." A critic and a poet may have many identities. Above all he is diverse, the great Bohemian seeking organization and system outside bureaucracy. He implicitly supports Emerson's attitude about "a foolish consistency." Thus:

Ideally, perhaps, one should break down a motive into many kinds of moment. For instance, a poet might make it a rule that whatever he happened to vilify in one lyric, he would glorify in another, that whatever he wept about this time he would laugh about the next, etc. The ideal lyrist would probably speak through as many shifting personalities as the ideal dramatist.

But in practice, regardless of the many moods a person experiences in a day, only some of them lend themselves to his particular ways of expression. He skimps on the multiplication and diversification of moments, if only through inability to do otherwise.

Day after day, year after year, he may have a fairly fixed attitude towards something, and may in fact build the whole logic of his life in accordance with this attitude—yet of a sudden, for a spell, he may be invaded by some quite different attitude, and this irruption may be the element that, for him, falls into the pattern of a momentary poem.[5]

Again, we might transplant a remark about his poetic moments to apply to his critical moments. Burke thinks of himself as remaining dramatically whole. He has acted his parts, diverse as they may appear, as a unified act. He may have past moments, and his career may be a record of dead selves, but he keeps ranging on, striving to be completely himself. "Fortunately, some of the writer's more apprehensive moments have already been 'disproved,' except insofar as no moment can be disproved (since it will forever go on having been exactly what it was, thereby possessing at least a sheerly *grammatical* kind of 'perfection')."[6] Burke began as a poet, and, insofar as he failed in that vocation, he would agree with Dryden that "the corruption of a poet is the generation of a critic."

◇◇

George Knox was born in Everett, Washington, in 1918. He is the author of *Critical Moments: Kenneth Burke's Categories and Critiques* (1957) and co-author of *Treaty Trip* (1960). He teaches English at the University of California, Riverside.

Almost nobody has written about Burke as an American; yet he is what Austin Warren once called a Yankee Crank, an authentic native

[5] *Ibid.*, pp. ix–x. [6] *Ibid.*, p. x.

product like William Carlos Williams, Walt Whitman, Edmund Wilson, and Ralph Waldo Emerson. In addition to his participation in at least two major modern endeavors (the development of a language-centered view of reality and the development of a modern literary theory and methodology) Burke is also part of a native endeavor: of the attempt by the American consciousness to shape its own vision. This endeavor has been continuous since the American Renaissance and Burke should be seen in this home context. George Knox is one of the few even to suggest some of the similarities between Burke and his spiritual ancestors – notably Emerson.

Because it was the first book on Burke, George Knox's study has a special place in the reception of Burke. Knox argues, in this selection and in the book as a whole, that Burke is, and is at his best as, a non-systematic thinker, and that his major contributions have been such things as terms, isolated concepts, an attitude, some practical criticism. This is a widely held view of Burke. As his title suggests and as his whole study tries to demonstrate, Mr. Knox really believes that Burke "lies scattered and fragmentary." This view is the opposite of the one which can be found in Hugh Duncan, Mrs. Nichols, Malcolm Cowley, Leland Griffin, and my own book; and it is a view which now seems to be clearly controverted by the facts of everything Burke has published since 1957. Burke's work is clearly systematic and coherent now; in spite of this, many, including Mr. Knox, I think, still feel that his major achievement – his dramatistic system – is a grand but essentially useless structure and that Burke's great value for our time is to be found in his critical moments, in his categories, in his critiques. By the 1960's – to avoid trying to settle the matter here – Burke was being widely used in both of these ways: as he had been used from the very beginning, in bits and pieces through his terms, his concepts, his methods; and, as Hugh Duncan and Leland Griffin have done, as a system builder, as a mind which has provided one with a whole usable model of reality.

◇◇

z Kenneth Burke's Theory

BY Daniel Fogarty, S.J.

TO UNDERSTAND the rhetoric theory of Kenneth Burke, it is essential to point to its roots in sociology and psychology. According to Burke,

EDITOR'S NOTE: Reprinted with permission of the author and publisher from Daniel Fogarty's *Roots for a New Rhetoric* (New York: Teachers College Press, 1959), pp. 56–72, copyright © 1959, Teachers College, Columbia University.

man pours all his energies into establishing and maintaining his personal world of hierarchic order. His survival depends on it. And rhetoric is his specific means of seeking or keeping that order. Not only in intrapersonal relations, where man uses his rhetoric on himself, where he holds inner parliament as both speaker and hearer, but, in all his interpersonal, intergroup, and interclass relations, he is striving for status in an accepted order, for survival by social balance with his inner self and with his world.[1] Rhetoric, then, is the instrument of strife, because it is the means of defending and competing for this order. But it is also the means of accomplishing order, because, for Burke, entreaty, overture, politeness, and diplomacy are all forms of a rhetoric of courtship that promotes union for the sake of order: "The *Rhetoric* must lead us through the Scramble, the Wrangle of the Market Place, the flurries and flare-ups of the Human Barnyard, the Give and Take . . ."[2] Yet, on the other hand: "Rhetoric also includes resources of appeal . . ."[3] "It too has its peaceful moments: at times its endless competition can add up to the transcending of itself. In ways of its own, it can move from factional to universal."[4] Out of the frequent and lengthy conversations between Burke and the present writer,[5] this rhetoric of peace and union emerges as a kind of central theme. He seems to have dedicated his work to the fashioning of peace. His theory of rhetoric pervades all his work. It is directed toward the achievement of peace, as the highest end for which he could have been born.

Burke differs from Aristotle and Richards in some ways. His work is an extension of Aristotelian rhetoric rather than a conflicting theory.[6] The extension, however, is so vast, both in the new broadness of his concept of rhetoric and in its applicability to modern life, that he calls it a "new"[7] rhetoric. Beyond the evident difference between the psychobiological approach of Richards and the sociopsychological approach of Burke, the essential points of comparison between them might be found by contrasting Richards' central interest in a scientific method of interpretation with Burke's preoccupation with dramatistic motiva-

[1] Kenneth Burke, *A Rhetoric of Motives* (New York: George Braziller, Inc., 1955), p. 39.

[2] *Ibid.*, p. 23. [3] *Ibid.*, p. 19. [4] *Ibid.*, p. 23.

[5] Mr. Burke was kind enough to take an enthusiastic interest in this chapter, giving his time frequently and at great length to explain his position, and to read and comment extensively upon a first outline and two subsequent drafts. Interviews and letters as well as his lengthy notes on this summary of his theory will be quoted from time to time.

[6] Burke, *A Rhetoric of Motives*, Introduction, p. x.

[7] Kenneth Burke, "Rhetoric Old and New," *The Journal of General Education*, V (April, 1951), p. 203.

tion.[8] While Burke was interested enough in interpretation to give that name to the first published version of the opening section of *Permanence and Change* (1935)[9] he was much more interested in attitude than in comprehension. At the same time, even though Richards' studies lean more toward the scientific aspects of meaning than toward motivational meaning, still motive is at the heart of his instruments of interpretation. Many additional points of comparison will occur to the reader in the subsequent study of Burke's philosophy of rhetoric. But explicit attention to them will be reserved for Chapter 5 [of *Roots for a New Rhetoric*], where all three emergent theories will be extended to proposals for a modern teaching rhetoric.

We turn now to the six aspects of Burke's rhetoric: his background and approach to rhetoric; his pentad format; his theory of abstraction and the negative; his theory of definition and identification; his philosophy of literary form; and the instrumental applications of his theory.

THE BACKGROUND AND APPROACH TO RHETORIC

For many younger scholars and teachers in composition and communication courses, *The Philosophy of Literary Form* (1941) provided a first acquaintance with Burke's ideas. But there was already a substantial bibliography, beginning with *Counter-Statement* (1931, revised in 1953), *Permanence and Change* (1935, revised in 1954), and *Attitudes toward History* (1937). His interest in the psychology and sociology of motivation grew as he edited publications for the Bureau of Social Hygiene and made sustained contributions to *The Dial, The Nation,* and *The New Republic.* In the meantime he lectured on literary criticism at the University of Chicago in 1938 and again in 1949, and at Bennington College since 1939. Publications and lectures alike showed a man obviously at home in the fields of sociology, psychology, philosophy, and linguistics. Since the appearance of *The Philosophy of Literary Form* (1941), Burke has published two volumes of a planned four-volume series on the language of motivation. *A Grammar of Motives* (1945) discusses the grammatical-logical dimension of language, and *A Rhetoric of Motives* (1950) explains the rhetorical dimension. The two volumes yet unpublished, *A Symbolic of Motives* and *On Human Relations,* will treat the poetic and ethical dimensions of language respectively.[10]

[8] From Burke's comments on the first draft of this summary, Andover, New Jersey, December 22, 1956.

[9] *Ibid.*

[10] Kenneth Burke, *Counter-Statement* (2nd ed. rev.; Los Altos, Calif.: Hermes Publications, 1953), pp. 217–218.

The troubled socioeconomic environment of Burke's maturing years had as much influence upon his later theory as the books he was reading at that time. Life in New York City during the Great Depression and the social and psychological phenomena to be observed there during two world wars were as much a part of his young manhood as Aristotle, Kant, Bentham, and Veblen.[11] Through the economic, social, and ideological strife of those years he was reading Bergson on the negative and de Gourmont on dissociation. "In fact," he says, "Remy de Gourmont was almost a 'traumatic' experience in my development."[12] Both from conversational reassurances to the writer and the opening remarks of "Curriculum Criticum"[13] in *Counter-Statement,* it is evident that the industrial-cultural conflicts of a large city were somewhat similarly traumatic for him. As soon as he was able to do so, he left New York and sought geographic and intellectual peace in a relatively untouched part of New Jersey.

All these readings and experiences led Burke to make an essential connection between language and the nature of man. Man is not just a rational animal. He is a "symbol-using animal,"[14] because his use of symbols is what makes him specifically different from other animals. Also, it is in the use of symbols that a man differentiates himself from other men as he puts his personally projected world in the kind of order he can live with. Further, it is through symbols that he relates himself with others so that, in his organized system of interdependency, he may satisfy his needs. The simplest visceral urgency within him, he translates, with the help of his symbol-making power, into a gesture or phrase that modifies the visceral urgency, or explains it away, but always in terms of the order he is building for himself. For Burke, the whole range of this activity, from a man's inner, subconscious conflicts to the highest kind of conscious abstraction, is rhetoric.[15]

Realizing that this human search for internal and external order provided the motivation for the exercise of rhetoric, Burke began to look for some method or pattern of inquiry with which to discern the meaningful motives behind rhetorical language.

THE PENTAD FORMAT

At some time during the preparation of *A Grammar of Motives,* Burke devised what he calls his pentad format. It served him as a

[11] Interview with Kenneth Burke, Andover, New Jersey, January 3, 1957.

[12] From Burke's comments on the first draft of this summary, Andover, New Jersey, December 22, 1956.

[13] Burke, *Counter-Statement,* pp. 213–214.

[14] Letter from Kenneth Burke, Andover, New Jersey, September 20, 1956.

[15] Burke, *A Rhetoric of Motives,* p. 41.

method of inquiry; but it also developed, as we shall see, into a practical instrument for the application of his theory to a teaching rhetoric. There were developmental stages before the mature format evolved. It seems to have begun with a dialectical, many-angled examination of a problem. Inside his own thinking process, he would state his case, refute his statement, and then formulate a compromise or a neutral, residual statement.[16] Later, realizing that this gave him only two viewpoints at most, he began to exercise his aptitudes for etymological analysis, and acquired at least another dimension for the same problem. He justifies this kind of dialectical horseplay by asking: "Is not the intention always to keep oneself reminded of the linguistic element that necessarily interposes itself between the symbol-using animal and the nonsymbolic reality?"[17] And further on in the same context, realizing that puns are in the same etymological class of split meanings, he says: "Puns involve a sensory element, but are certainly not confined to this, particularly the abstruse kinds that seem to figure in metaphysics, or in theological analogies such as word-Word."[18] Thus the varieties of senses gathered from etymological roots and accepted usages of terms provide Burke with the multiple aspects he can use to examine a problem.

The next step is from the dialectical to the symposium type of inner personal discussion. It is as though Burke were a five- or six-man discussion group, taking all the speaking parts himself until he has sifted the best resultant formulation of the idea in question. All this seems necessary to Burke, even in his thinking, because, early in his career, he convinced himself that any one statement or point of view was necessarily only a part of the attainable truth. It was a kind of part statement, a synecdochic half-meaning at best. So he resolved to keep going back and looking again from a different point of view, until the common, consistent, undeniable meaning stood out unmistakably. Describing this symposium kind of dialectic, Burke says: "Ideally, all the various 'voices' are partisan rhetoricians whose partial voices 'competitively cooperate' to form the position of the dialogue as a whole (a position that transcends all the partial views of the participants, though there may be a Socratic voice that is *primus inter pares*)."[19]

Finally, however, still questing for the best organized method of making repeated beginnings, he saw that the principles or bases from which the repeated starts were to be made must be so fundamental that

[16] Interview with Kenneth Burke, Andover, New Jersey, January 3, 1957.

[17] From Burke's comments on the first draft of this summary, Andover, New Jersey, December 22, 1956.

[18] *Ibid.* [19] *Ibid.*

they would apply to any problem or topic to be looked at.[20] It was at this point that he hit upon what he calls his "pentad" of aspects. This involves what Burke feels is a fivefold viewpoint of anything whatever that a man can discuss. For any action (human, symbol-using act), as opposed to motion (mere animal, nonsymbol-using act), there are always these five points of view: *scene,* the environmental point of view; *act,* the thing itself as represented in an idea; *agent,* the derivational or efficient cause aspect of the thing; *agency,* the "how" and "with what assistance"[21] of the thing or act; and *purpose,* the agent's motivation. Burke now has five questions to ask about any topic or problem, five ways to express fullness of meaning, five ways for the receiver of the communication to test it for deeper motivational meaning behind the symbols. He can not only repeatedly begin his examination, but he can know he is asking the basic and most important and exhaustive questions each time he returns to begin again. In fact, by permutations of pairs of the five questions, he really has ten questions to ask, ten points from which to repeat a beginning: act–scene, act–agent, act–agency, act–purpose, scene–agent, scene–agency, scene–purpose, agent–agency, agent–purpose, and agency–purpose.[22] These are the bases of the repeated-beginnings method of Burke. This, with its terms culled from critical analysis of the drama, is what he calls his dramatistic[23] approach to language and to rhetoric. A term, then, or a symbol, and with it its idea and its referent too, must be looked at much in the same manner as a unit of dramatic action upon a stage. To be understood it must be viewed as an *act,* as the act of *whom,* as *how,* as *where,* and as *why.* The interesting similarity between these pentad forms and the "four ultimate causes" of Aristotle only reassured Burke of their basic nature.[24] The similarity with the alternate questions that Scholastic philosophers asked themselves is also striking: *Quis? Quid? Quibus auxiliis? Ubi? Cur? Quomodo? Quando?* (Who? What? With what assistance? Where? Why? How? When?).[25] The fundamental rule of thumb that used to be taught to journalism students as a way of covering all the pertinent details of a news event indicates how functionally useful is this meta-

[20] Kenneth Burke, *A Grammar of Motives* (copyright, 1945, by Prentice-Hall, Inc., Englewood Cliffs, N.J.), Introduction, p. xvi.

[21] *Ibid.,* pp. xv–xvii. [22] *Ibid.,* pp. xix–xxi. [23] *Ibid.,* p. xxii.

[24] Interview with Kenneth Burke, Andover, New Jersey, January 3, 1957, confirmed this basic similarity. See Aristotle, "Metaphysica," in *The Basic Works of Aristotle,* ed. Richard McKeon, trans. Rhys Roberts *et al.* (New York: Random House, Inc., 1941; originally published by Oxford University Press in 1928), i, ii, and iii, pp. 689–731 (980*a*–1003*a*).

[25] Burke, *Counter-Statement,* p. 141.

physical classification.[26] Sociological research, also, has provided a communication model based on studies in control, content, audience, situation, and effect — really extensions in application of the Lasswell "formula."[27]

With this method of inquiry Burke expects to be able to ferret out the motivational meaning of symbols and symbol clusters that we all use in the organization and protection of the order we need for survival. A second perusal of Burke's important books and writings, based upon a thorough understanding of this method, can prove rewarding. It might also be helpful to the reader who is searching for familiar order in Burke's writings. The train of thought is really dialectical. While his works are not explicit dialogues, he admits that he often thinks and writes in dialogue — or better still, in "pantalogue" — form to embrace all possible facets of any topic under discussion.[28]

Although the pentad format began as a methodology, and proved itself, soon after, as an efficient instrument in the discernment of motivation,[29] its further use as a format for the practice of Burke's rhetoric of peace and union does not become clear until it is considered in connection with the projections and extensions of a modern discussion rhetoric in Chapter 5.

We can now turn to the several aspects of Burke's philosophy of rhetoric: abstraction and the negative; definition and identification; and philosophy of literary form.

THE THEORY OF ABSTRACTION AND THE NEGATIVE

Abstraction and the negative are so intimately related in Burke's philosophy that clarity is the only possible excuse for the separate treatment they are given here.

THEORY OF ABSTRACTION

Abstraction is, for Burke, almost everything it was for Aristotle. The rational mind's power to separate and classify and collect on a choice basis is part of Burke's theory of abstraction, though he has not always

[26] George F. Mott *et al.*, *An Outline Survey of Journalism* (rev. ed.; New York: Barnes and Noble, Inc., 1943), pp. 62–63.

[27] Lyman Bryson, ed., *The Communication of Ideas* (New York: Harper & Brothers, 1948), pp. 37–38.

[28] Interview with Kenneth Burke, Andover, New Jersey, January 3, 1957.

[29] From Burke's notes commenting on the first draft of this summary, Andover, New Jersey, December 22, 1956.

come to it by the same route nor in the same terminology.[30] Furthermore, even the word-thought-thing relationships, which are of course basic to abstraction, are realist in the epistemological theory of Burke. The thought is real with that metaphysical reality that realists give to ideas that represent real things conceptually.[31]

With such an introduction, Burke can be considered as having two things to say about abstraction. First, it is the characteristically human ability that makes a rational man specifically rational. Not only is this abstracting power, which Burke calls "generalization," the specific element of his essence as a man, but it lifts his nature, in kind as well as in degree, above that of other animals. Burke arrives at this conclusion by comparing the nonconceptual sorting and selecting that animals experience with the rational kind of abstracting or generalizing. This is how he sums up:

> When we call attention to the rudiments of generalization, specification, classification, and abstraction in the conditioning and adaptations of nonlinguistic organisms, we do not mean to derive 'rational' human language by a simple 'graded series' from the 'behavioristic pre-language' of sensation and gesture. On the contrary, we subscribe to the view that there is a 'qualitative leap' between the motives of pre-language and those of language. . . .
> Hence to say that the principles of abstraction, classification, generalization, and specification (or division) are present in pre-linguistic behavior is not the same as saying that their linguistic analogues are 'nothing but' more complicated variants of the pre-linguistic.[32]

ON THE NEGATIVE

The second thing Burke has to say about abstraction connects with his theory of the negative and illustrates what he calls the highest kind of symbol-using activity of which man is capable, symbol-using about symbols themselves (as opposed to symbol-using about things), the conscious use of words to talk about words. The theory of the negative comes up here because it is his way of pointing out man's essential difference from nonabstracting animals. If the abstracting process could be shown to be essentially different from the elemental animal sorting, then the essential difference of kind between man and other animals would be clear. Burke considered the Empiricists' theory of ideas. Their approach to the whole idea problem was to reduce the idea to an image and thus materialize it. With every idea reducible to the material, there would be no need to postulate any special kind of meta-

[30] Kenneth Burke, "A Dramatistic View of the Origins of Language," Part I, *The Quarterly Journal of Speech*, XXXVIII (October, 1952), pp. 256–259.
[31] *Ibid.*, p. 259. [32] *Ibid.*, p. 257.

physical reality for ideas at all.[33] Burke proposed, on the other hand, an idea that cannot be so reduced to image and thus materialized. That idea was the idea of *no* or *not*, or, in other words, the negative.[34] It is Burke's contention that *not* can be conceived, in an idea, and yet one can have no image of it. All the images one has in connection with it are not really its image but images of the real things of which it is the negation. As he says, "Though idea and image have become merged in the development of language, the negative provides the instrument for splitting them apart. *For the negative is an idea;* there can be no image of it. *But in imagery there is no negative.*"[35] The negative, then, is the sole example of an idea that cannot be empirically reduced to material. In the capacity to symbolize this negative lies the specific feature of man's linguistic function that is impossible to animals. Burke sums it up: "The essential distinction between the verbal and the nonverbal is in the fact that language adds the peculiar possibility of the negative."[36]

It is pertinent to note that it is in his theory of the negative that Burke traces the origins and development of language. With the most primitive operation of this negative in early language, men first began to show the ability to symbolize. "No's" and cautionary expletives and warnings and protests were not, even then, the mere *positive* turning away of the animal's mouth from what was unpleasant food, but a real head shaking.[37] The growth of the negative was, by and large, the evolution of language. He traces the evolution of the negative from the negative command to the positive attitude *not* to break that command, and on to the propositional or declarative negative.[38] And all the while his great objective is to show his readers that everything is imbued with the negative because it usually implies, at least when the selecting and generalizing are in operation, a limiting and shifting and sorting that, in themselves, mean continually saying no. Choosing will immediately imply saying no, at least to all the things one is ruling out when he is being selective, or exact, or even when he is being general and abstract, because he is classifying.[39]

[33] *Ibid.*, pp. 259–260.

[34] Burke took Bergson's "nothing," changed it to "not" and "no," and insisted upon the hortatory negative (thou shalt not) rather than the propositional negative (it is not) of Bergson. For Burke, it is here in the hortatory negative — "no" and "not" — that we can find the deepest root of language as specifically and essentially human in its symbol-using function. From an interview with Kenneth Burke, New York, May 29, 1957.

[35] Burke, "A Dramatistic View of the Origins of Language," p. 260.

[36] *Ibid.*, Part III, XXXIX (February, 1953), p. 79.

[37] *Ibid.*, Part I, XXXVIII (October, 1952), p. 257.

[38] *Ibid.*, pp. 252 and 262. [39] *Ibid.*, pp. 256–257.

The importance of this abstracting and of what it tends to make us include and exclude in our habitual symbolizing processes will become clearer as we move on to the study of definition and identification.

THE THEORY OF DEFINITION AND IDENTIFICATION

This section will deal with a definition theory and several ambiguities of defining and naming. Then it will introduce motivation in the Burkeian sense before proceeding to a discussion of identification and hierarchy.

DEFINITION

Burke has no specific quarrel with the classic theory of genus and species definition.[40] But he does concentrate on a more usable kind of defining that identifies not only genera and species, but individuals as well. It is a kind of defining that brings modern rhetoric very close to linguistics.

A sentence or proposition points out its subject very clearly, even in the definitional sense, if its order of words allows for a gradual transition from the abstract to the concrete. Burke's example will serve best to illustrate this: "This good man runs very swiftly."[41] Now, this statement makes a predication about a good man. It says he is one who runs swiftly. Burke explains that in the first three words, *this good man*, the idea man, which is as abstract as that reference can be made, is gradually delimited and narrowed down until the other kinds of men (not good) are all ruled out, and finally delimited again until every other man, good or not, except *this* one, is ruled out. The subject, then, has been exactly defined, pinpointed inescapably. Similarly, the general action in *runs* is delimited by its two modifiers, *swiftly* and *very*, until it is nearly as well defined. Then by combination with the substantive half of the sentence, even this action part of it comes to be more accurately defined, and so the whole sentence has its subject and his action exactly defined by this grammatical combination of functions, supplementing the order of words. The more abstract ideas, with which the process is begun, are the genera. The more accurate and concrete ideas, after the process of reduction, are the species and individuals that are defined.[42]

In addition to this double way of defining, illustrated in the one example above, namely by order of words and by grammatical func-

[40] Burke, *A Grammar of Motives*, pp. 409–410.

[41] Burke, "A Dramatistic View of the Origins of Language," Part III, XXXIX (February, 1953), pp. 88–89.

[42] *Ibid.*, pp. 88–92.

tion, Burke cites a third way: by growth of vocabulary. Growth of vocabulary refers to the use of more and more accurate words that pinpoint and demonstrate the subject or action.[43] Such pinpointing amounts to defining because it delimits and points at the object.

But in spite of a clear theory of definition, there is still great possibility of misdirection and inaccuracy in defining. Burke has singled out four general kinds of defining that are sources of ambiguity.

Contextual definition defines, not by describing the thing itself, but by relating it to some other thing in its context.[44] This is clearly not the same thing as the context definition implied in Richards' theory of context. Richards wants the richness of pertinent surroundings and connectives to help us see a Gestalt view of the thing to be defined. Burke wants to be sure we do not emphasize the context at the expense of the subject itself. To try to define a class of people by describing their environment without any description of the people would be giving their class a contextual definition in Burke's sense.[45] Definers who do this lay themselves open to the charge that they are failing to discuss the class of people in themselves.[46] Of course, this kind of defining is one extreme whose converse is just as faulty. To try to define a class without any reference to their contextual surroundings of environment would omit as much of the true sense as would contextual defining.

Derivational definition defines the thing by its sources. Sources, however, are often so highly abstract in a definitional statement that they allow many different meanings. Burke examines the terms *general, generic,* and *genitive* etymologically and finds ambiguity. He points out that, though all these three terms have a common etymological root pointing to familial derivation, they have vastly different meanings. According to *The American College Dictionary, general* means: "pertaining to, affecting, including, or participated in by all members of a class or group; not partial or particular."[47] According to the same source, *generic* seems to have the Peripatetic–Scholastic meaning as its first and most usual one, "pertaining to a genus." *Genitive,* still in the same source, carries the grammatical sense as its first meaning: "denoting the case of nouns generally used to modify other nouns, often

[43] *Ibid.*, pp. 88–89.

[44] Burke, *A Grammar of Motives*, p. 24.

[45] From Burke's notes commenting on the first draft of this summary, Andover, New Jersey, December 22, 1956.

[46] Burke, *A Grammar of Motives*, p. 26.

[47] *The American College Dictionary*, ed. Clarence L. Barnhart (New York: Random House, Inc., copyright 1947), p. 505.

indicating possession, but used also in expressions of measure, origin, characteristic."[48]

Circumference shifting refers to the tendency any one person may have to shift the area of context of his term, agreed upon at the start, to a slightly new context which now has much that it had before but has dropped off some of the context from one edge of the rim and picked up new elements on the other edge. "Now, it seems undeniable, by the very nature of the case, that in definition, or systematic placement, one must see things 'in terms of . . .' And implicit in the terms chosen, there are 'circumferences' of varying scope."[49] If the totality of the context, for instance, of the term "street" were agreed upon by two discussants in Springfield, Illinois, they might both mean an average city street with a tree or two, some ordinary buildings, traffic, and so on. But if one of them is from Manhattan and the other from a village in Vermont, it will be understandable how the New Englander may soon slip off to where he has more shady trees and less traffic on his "street," and the Manhattanite may have begun to introduce a huge electric sign, or traffic jams, or increased noise. The two discussants would have moved away from one another and would soon have two different definitions for "street." They would, in effect, no longer be talking about the same thing.

The ambiguity source of *scope–reduction–deflection* is somewhat similar but refers to the relative sizes and directions of the circumference of an idea that two discussants might have.[50] As usual, Burke looks at it in terms of act, scene, and the like:

> A given act is in effect a different act, *depending upon the scope of the scene in terms of which it is located, or defined.* Define the act in terms of a scene comprising a whole pantheon of warring deities, and it is of one sort; define it in terms of a single God, and it is another sort; define it in terms of godless "nature," and it is another sort; define it in such terms as "The West," or "Victorianism," or "capitalism," or "an apartment in Soho, July 12, 1887," and it is of correspondingly other sorts. Yet there is no set rule for such a choice of scope ("in terms of" which it is to be defined).[51]

The reduction factor is the sloughing off of some or any of the elements of the context so that the context becomes smaller or more concrete than it was when the discussions started, thus affording two different

[48] *Ibid.*, p. 506.
[49] Burke, *A Grammar of Motives*, p. 77.
[50] *Ibid.*, pp. 77–85.
[51] From Burke's notes commenting on the first draft of this summary, Andover, New Jersey, December 22, 1956.

definitions and consequent ambiguity.[52] The factor of deflection in this ambiguity source entails reduction toward a smaller context that leaves out the pertinent elements upon which the discussion depends. The New Englander and the Manhattanite might get into this kind of difficulty if one of them began to talk about "street" as though its essential element were either the village hotel porch with its dozing octogenarians, or, perhaps, the newsstand near the subway entrance.

It is important to remember that, in Burke's thinking, the four kinds of definitional ambiguity just described are not only notable because their ambiguity makes for unclear communication and reception, but, even more especially, because they are the symbol-user's conscious or unconscious ways of getting away from the kind of meaning that does not fit his motivations.[53] It is part of the fortunate richness of language that makes it possible for people to adjust themselves to reality. Personally and subjectively, it allows them to be blind to reality in one spot and not in another. The great point about this kind of ambiguity, as about every kind of motivational manipulation of symbols, is that it must be understood thoroughly by those who wish to receive and communicate real meaning – motivational meaning. "Hence, instead of considering it our task to 'dispose of' any ambiguity by merely disclosing the fact that it is an ambiguity, we rather consider it our task to study and clarify the *resources* of ambiguity."[54]

To point momentarily at where Burke hopes rhetoric of this kind will eventually lead, it is sufficient to visualize a group of discussants with subjective blind spots due to diverse motivations. They might, in a kind of dialectical give and take, light up one another's blind spots, fill out contexts, unify circumferences, and generally come to some residual and mutual agreement both in understanding and action.[55]

[The closing pages of the chapter have been omitted here.]

◇◇◇

DANIEL FOGARTY, S. J., was born in Montreal, Canada, in 1912. He has taught English at Saint Mary's University, Halifax, Canada, and has also served there as dean of the School of Education and, since 1967, as academic vice-president. He is the author of *Roots for a New Rhetoric*, the book from which this selection comes.

Father Fogarty wrote this study of Burke's theory of rhetoric after many long consultations with Burke and at a time when Burke was

[52] Burke, *A Grammar of Motives*, p. 96.
[53] *Ibid.*, Introduction, p. xviii. [54] *Ibid.*, p. xix.
[55] From Burke's notes commenting on the first draft of this summary, Andover, New Jersey, December 22, 1956.

working out some of the final developments of dramatism and was messianically convinced that a lifetime of study and writing had earned him a partial solution to some of the world's most troublesome problems. It is hard to render the conviction of Burke's work during this period. Some sense of it is suggested by Father Fogarty's notes acknowledging the kind of reception and help Burke gave him. Such public reception as Burke received during this period was almost entirely of the kind found here and in the surrounding selections: in books and as part of larger studies of rhetoric or literary criticism or sociology. This might be characterized as the period of exposition, with occasional acts of placement and evaluation. The exposition was made necessary by the widespread realization that Burke had now produced a body of systematic work which required and justified such treatment. This marks a significant change in Burke's reception. The next phases, which have hardly yet begun and will have to use the results of this long expository period, are those of placement and evaluation.

◇◇

2 *Kenneth Burke's Terminological Medium of Exchange*

BY Louis Fraiberg

KENNETH BURKE is in process of synthesizing a number of disparate disciplines into what he hopes will be a workable tool for the analysis of poetry. Believing that literary criticism ought to make use of all available knowledge from relevant sources, he has undertaken the difficult task of mastering the several fields, integrating them and using the product to study literary works. In a sense, it is impossible to understand any single portion of the intricate fabric which he has woven, even in its present incomplete form, without knowing the whole, for if he continues in the manner that he has followed thus far its essence will inevitably turn out to be its totality. However, an examination of one important strand can be instructive not only for its own design but also for what it reveals about the pattern of the rest. Accordingly, this chapter will look at the way Burke has used one of the contributing disciplines, psychoanalysis.

EDITOR'S NOTE: Reprinted from *Psychoanalysis and American Literary Criticism* by Louis Fraiberg (Detroit: Wayne State University Press, 1960), pp. 183–190, 199–201,

In order to do this it is best to begin with his first major treatment of the subject, which occurs in a chapter entitled "Secular Conversions."[1] The title is very instructive. In two words it condenses his entire approach to the problem of human motives circa 1935, summarizing both his ideas and his method. Briefly, he regards motives as religious, or at least as analogous to religious ones, "religious" being used here not in the literal but in a metaphoric sense. In Burke's figure it does not necessarily signify adherence to a theological doctrine but rather to any set of beliefs (which may also include theological ones) that constitute the individual's view of the universe. The word consequently refers to the assumptions upon which men act. These "pieties," as Burke calls them, are for the most part tacitly – i.e., unthinkingly or even unconsciously – held. They provide both the impetus for acts and the means of judging their appropriateness. In Burke's view, all people grow up within a framework of such ideas which gradually harden until they control all actions. It then takes an extraordinary effort to break out of the mold.

Such efforts together with their effects he speaks of as "conversions." A conversion is the adoption of an entirely new set of assumptions, that is, a new set of values. What was permitted the pagan is forbidden the Christian; what the child may do the adult may not; and what causes joy or fear in one setting may evoke the reverse in another. A given act, therefore, may either calm the individual or upset him, depending upon the way he looks at it. An inescapable corollary is that conduct need not be altered provided that the manner of judging it is suitably modified. Upon this line of reasoning Burke approaches psychoanalysis.

He develops this view in a section labeled "The Fundamentals of Psychoanalysis," which is remarkable both for the ingenuity with which he makes an analogy between it and religion and for the almost complete absence of any reference to the fact that it is a scientific discipline. Certainly the resemblance of the psychoanalytic patient's experience to a religious conversion is clear – at least from a special and limited standpoint such as Burke's – but it might with equal justice be compared to a re-education process, and many psychoanalysts do so regard it. Other interpretations are also possible, but Burke ignores them. "From our standpoint," he says, "psychoanalysis can be treated as a simple technique of non-religious conversion." Since it is a great deal more than this, we must inquire further into the standpoint from which he takes his view.

[1] Kenneth Burke, *Permanence and Change* (New York: New Republic, Inc., 1936), pp. 164–193.

As we know from his later books, Burke is striving for an ideological synthesis. But even in his earlier work he seems to have encountered semantic difficulties, at least in his treatment of psychoanalysis. He does not regard it as an outgrowth and branch of biology but as a purely verbal formula very much like an ethical system derived from speculative philosophy instead of from observation of nature. Or rather he does not regard its scientific orientation as of much importance since the terms which it uses "are wholly incongruous with the unscientific nature of the distress." This ignoring or minimizing of perhaps the most important fact about psychoanalysis – its intention of being as objective as it can be about human nature – skews his subsequent treatment so that thereafter we are presented only with isolated fragments of it, in each instance from a special point of view. Burke's system, then, loses whatever benefit it might gain from the derivation of psychoanalytic theory from observed behavior, a considerable handicap for an attempt to deal with motives.

A question of relative values arises here. If conversion takes place, is the patient better or worse off than he was under his previous system of "pieties"? Burke occupies himself so thoroughly with the technique of conversions that he seems to slight their worth or the worth of the "solutions" to which they lead. As a result we are left with the impression that such shiftings of moral ground may follow one another indefinitely and that it does not particularly matter whether the patient ultimately lands among, say, the rationalists or among the true believers. All that Burke seems interested in is the pressure which drives him to seek a change and the means by which he achieves it. He is concerned exclusively with the therapeutic aspect of psychoanalysis; the vast potential which it holds for a larger understanding of motives necessarily lies beyond his horizon.[2]

Even within his self-imposed limitations, however, it is questionable how sound his grasp of psychoanalysis really is, for he persists in treating it merely as a system of verbal symbols whose chief functions are, first, to give a new, and "incongruous," name to the patient's problem and, second, to supply other, and more favorable, names for the things which he must do anyway. Freudian theory and "the various schools of thought that have descended from it"[3] share these features: "the *conversion downwards* of the patient's distress by means of an unfit, incongruous terminology – and the positive development of a substitute terminol-

[2] This was Freud's chief concern in his later years. See Chapter I of this book [*Psychoanalysis and American Literary Criticism*].

[3] Burke does not specify these, a serious omission in the light of the controversy about what is psychoanalysis and what is not.

ogy until it has provided the patient with a brand-new rationalization of motives."[4] *Conversion downwards,* in Burke's special vocabulary, means "the opposite of magnification . . . reduction of scale." It is clear that he is talking about orientation to words alone, not to deeds, and that he means words, quite literally: "By selecting a vocabulary which specifically violates the dictates of style and taboo, it [psychoanalysis] changes the entire nature of his problem, rephrasing it in a form for which there is a solution." This is itself a conversion downwards of the transvaluation of psychic values which has taken place in the neurosis and which is restored to a proper balance in a successful psychoanalysis. What Burke seems to have missed is the psychoanalytic understanding of the relation that a verbal symbol has to a psychic state. An emotional re-education therefore appears to him as simply an exercise in the juggling of logical terms, abetted (if not corrupted) by some of the tricks of propaganda. This makes it possible for him to say of psychoanalysis that, "insofar as it is curative, its effects seem due to the fact that it exorcises the painful influences of a vestigial religious orientation by appeal to the prestige of the newer scientific orientation."[5] Verbal symbols constitute for him a kind of universal medium of exchange, like money but with added magical properties.

It seems to me that he has reasoned fallaciously from the analogy which a financial system bears to his symbol system. The medium of exchange has no necessary organic relationship to the commodities for which it is traded but an arbitrary and shifting one. At the very least Burke is guilty here of inadequately defining his terms, and few things are more unsettling than attempting to follow an exposition in which the meanings of key words are vague. Burke speaks, for instance, of the patient's "basic psychosis" when the context makes it perfectly clear that he is referring to neurosis (and perhaps to something else as well). Since he has used the word neurosis correctly elsewhere, we are at a loss to know why he uses "basic psychosis" here, and he does not tell us. The suggestion has been made that he adopted the term from Dewey who used it to mean something like the outlook a person has on the world when it is colored by his occupational bias, but nowhere does Burke say so. And yet there is a crucial difference between psychosis and neurosis as the terms are used in psychoanalysis. It is a common practice of Burke's to use a familiar word in a special way which he indicates by enclosing it in quotation marks or italicizing it. His pages are freckled with such usages. His long-range plan was to issue a glossary in which all of them would be explained, but they multiplied until

[4] *Permanence and Change*, p. 168.

[5] *Ibid.*, p. 165.

nobody knows their number, and when the glossary finally appeared he sadly admitted that it was hopelessly incomplete. There does not appear to be much chance that he will catch up with his own verbal innovations in time to make them clear to his readers. This casts considerable doubt on the validity of the very means by which he hopes to achieve his great synthesis as well as on his understanding of psychoanalytic concepts.

An illustration of the difficulties encountered occurs when Burke presents what he calls "Freud's doctrine of the six abnormal tendencies in everyone: autoeroticism, homosexuality, sadism, masochism, incest, and exhibitionism." But unless both elements of the phrase "abnormal tendencies" are carefully defined it is impossible to be sure how they are being used, and Burke does not define them at all. Instead he goes on to praise Freud for having promulgated the doctrine since (a) "it is hard to imagine a single manifestation of human interests which could not be reduced to one of these six terms," and therefore (b) "if the six abnormals applied to everybody, it followed that everybody was abnormal, hence it followed that it was normal to be abnormal."[6] Burke is employing verbal tricks here and imputing them to psychoanalysis which, to his mind, evidently "said that *everyman* was in essence a pervert." He is not the only one to have interpreted the findings of psychoanalysis in this way, but this does not make the interpretation valid. Neither does it justify him in charging that psychoanalysis seeks to reduce all conduct to morally repugnant terms. In his difficulties with the concept of normality he has confused neurosis with perversion and psychic tendency with overt behavior. Moreover, he does not see the psychoanalytic view of their respective roles in society.[7]

In all this Burke neglects to consider whether a "reduction downwards" actually does take place in psychoanalytic cures. He offers no proof beyond his assertion that the new context so provided for moral judgments is less complex than the one that has been discarded. He does not examine the relation of each of them to the kind of reality with which it attempts to deal. And he does not propose any measure of efficacy, that is, of psychological, social or moral value, or even appropriateness. The difference between a scientific orientation and a personal, idiosyncratic one is never mentioned. Burke apparently regards psychoanalysis as merely another cult, subject to the vagaries of popular taste and not susceptible to measurement by any objective

[6] *Ibid.*, pp. 166–167.

[7] Later in this chapter we shall see his ready acceptance of McDougall's suggestion that political life supplies the patterns for motivation. In this way the alleged deficiency in psychoanalytic theory is repaired and the importance of sexuality, so difficult for many people to consent to, is diminished.

criteria: "The pansexuality of Freud's formulae seems to have been especially effective because sexual emphases were already outstanding in the orientation of the day, hence a sexual symptom could most easily recommend itself as the *core* of the entire situation, with all else as mere incidental by-products." [8] This disregards the scientific intention and basis of psychoanalysis, and places it in the same category as, say, the latest theory of social causation or decay. And it ignores the fact that Freud was not very much interested in what either the general populace or the intelligentsia — to say nothing of the medical profession! — thought of him or his findings. What counts in psychoanalysis is not what the world thinks of it but the psychoanalyst's understanding of what happens both in the clinic and in the world.

These considerations provide a perspective in which to place Burke's mention of McDougall's theory that important aspects of motivation for the citizens of a given country are patterned after its political structure. Burke admires this conception because he feels that McDougall, "in rebuilding the 'master personality' along the lines of the nation's political pattern . . . is socializing the patient's new mental structure by anchoring it to an obvious feature of the *group psychosis* [sic]." [9] This presumably affords an added source of strength. There are some important implications here for the role of national character (if there really is such a thing) in motivation and for the behavior of large masses of people under totalitarian dictatorships, but it is not clear whether Burke is prepared to trace them. All that he says in this connection which concerns psychoanalysis is that "Freud wrote for a people who had, for many centuries, accommodated themselves to imperial decay — perhaps he wrote for something which we might call the 'psychosis [sic] of the Strauss waltz.' Hence his devices for reorientation would be differently formed [from those of McDougall], to correspond with differences in the local orientation of his group." [10] This is a somewhat more sophisticated version of the earlier objection to psychoanalysis, which asserted that it need not be taken seriously since it merely reflected the notorious sexual looseness of the Viennese and was obviously not applicable to people who lived in other cities. Burke has added to it the weight of a psychological theory. By this maneuver the wind is taken out of Freud's sails, a shift in emphasis is made from the psychic to the social component in motivation, and several obstacles are removed from the path of the forthcoming synthesis.

In Burke's view, then, a traumatic fear — by which he apparently means what psychoanalysts call a neurosis — can be cured by giving it

[8] *Permanence and Change,* p. 168.

[9] *Ibid.,* pp. 173–174.

[10] *Ibid.,* pp. 174–175.

a label which does not carry the original injurious connotations, that is, by misnaming it. The patient can then abandon his "piety" toward the object or situation which aroused the fear and no longer see it in its harmful context. All of the former dangerous associations are broken by the magical act of misnaming, and an entirely new cluster of harmless ones is implied, or at least made possible. In Burke's words, the feared object has thus been exorcised by "the impious devices of incongruity," and its meaning in the patient's system of motives altered, presumably for the better.

Such conversion can take place either upwards or downwards, depending upon which point is selected as the *essence* [the italics are Burke's] of the entire scale. "One's choice usually flows from other aspects of his orientation, or from the particular purpose which his series is designed to fulfill." [11] What this process leaves unsettled is the issue raised before, namely, the relevance of the attempted solution to something beyond itself, to such aspects of reality as we can know, scientifically or otherwise, or to which we can react morally. Burke does not make this clear in *Permanence and Change* but leaves the impression that he adopts a relativistic position. In his view people react to the realities of words whose relationships to their referents are constantly being redefined. What matters to them is not the intrinsic significance of the thing or the situation but the name which is given to it. Connections with reality which have no verbal component apparently do not count. He seems to be trying to extend into a universal principle of human action the tendency of some people to place a high value on their verbal experiences and the inability of others to distinguish clearly between words and things.

[Nine pages are omitted here.]

In his later books (*A Grammar of Motives, A Rhetoric of Motives* and the projected *A Symbolic of Motives*) Burke has built upon the foundation of the earlier ones. The method he devised is brought to a higher degree of development, but the basic principles remain the same. Of that method it would be proper in a comprehensive study to ask several questions. Since it partakes of the nature of philosophy, how valid are its assumptions and its applications of logic? Within its entire framework, so far as it has been presented to us, is the place assigned to psychoanalysis consonant with its character? How much does Burke actually know about this character? How much of what he knows does he use? How much does he omit? Why?

It is not my purpose to conduct a full examination of Burke as a critic

[11] *Ibid.*, p. 191.

but merely to describe and evaluate his use of psychoanalytic ideas in his criticism. Consequently, complete answers to these questions cannot be supplied here. One of the basic problems which they pose, however, is relevant to this study. He is setting out to produce a synthesis of disciplines some of which are at such odds with others as to be mutually contradictory. Can Freudian and Marxian ideas, for instance, be integrated into a meaningful whole without destroying what is essential for one, or both? It seems to me that, for these two, peaceful coexistence is impossible; the only integration which could conceivably be managed is the integration of the lamb with the wolf. The same question can be asked about all the other elements in his projected synthesis. How can he combine the several psychologies, sociologies, philosophies and theologies and still retain the essence of each?

If I understand his intention correctly, it is to find among these disparate entities some point, or area, at which they can be seen to intersect. He seems to ignore the fact that some do not intersect at all, but even for those that do, has he the right to assume that the coincidence occurs precisely at the point where the central significance of each happens to be the strongest? And if this meeting place is off the ideological center, is there not the danger that what is most important in the discipline being so manipulated will be distorted or forgotten? What price synthesis?

It is possible to argue for the consistency of Burke's system, but not at the same time to claim that it embodies the essential values of all its components. In the case of psychoanalysis it seems that such consistency as it possesses has been ignored by Burke. He has fragmented it and tenderly picked a few surviving morsels out of the rubble. But he has not kept even these intact. They have been reshaped and forced into a new context where there is serious doubt that they can perform any useful function having a significant relation to their former state. It is as though a golden statue had been melted down and cast into blocks which were then used to build a wall. In this way they might well acquire a new, architectural value – but in the meantime what would have become of the statue?

Throughout his writings Burke seems to have effected a neat "conversion downwards" of phenomena into terms. His system is, it seems to me, essentially a verbal one which treats words at what is often a great distance from the reality of things and people. It would be interesting (though not within the province of this chapter) to study Burke semantically and to examine, among other things, the fluctuations in verbal level which he employs. His theory of poetic performance leads through the ascending order: poetry, act, motive, power, reality. This scale might well be applied to his critical system. Were this to be done, I have the impression that we would find it to be as much a poetic as a critical performance. If this is indeed the case — and I think there is strong evidence for this quality of mind in Burke — then scientific and logical objections are beside the point, and the proper approach to his work is the kind that a literary critic takes toward a poem. But he has published it as serious literary criticism relying in part on psychoanalytic ideas and has thereby left himself open to censure for his lapses in handling those ideas. A clinically based scientific discipline cannot be dealt with as though its essence were verbal, despite the metaphoric quality of some psychoanalytic terminology. Psychoanalysis cannot exist without words, but this does not mean that words are the only things in it that matter. Burke has been guilty of taking the part for the whole, and this has thrown his entire critical view out of focus.

◇◇◇

LOUIS FRAIBERG was born in Detroit, Michigan, in 1913. He is professor of English and chairman of that department at the University of Toledo. He is the author of *Psychoanalysis and American Literary Criticism* (1960).

Louis Fraiberg and I were fellow students at the University of Michigan and studied and wrote dissertations in criticism under the same man: Norman E. Nelson. Here is an appropriate place to acknowledge his help and to point out that it was such students of modern criticism as Professor Nelson who did much to encourage and further the reception of Kenneth Burke in the graduate schools.

The selection above is part of a longer essay which in turn is a part of a longer study, the subject of which is identified by Mr. Fraiberg's title. With no disrespect to Mr. Fraiberg — he will surely agree with me — I think one should add that he has barely touched upon the extent to which Burke has been influenced by Freud and psychoanalysis in general. Perhaps only a trained psychologist who had also undertaken a study of Burke could properly treat this subject. Freud and his fellow workers and the larger forces behind their own endeavors revolutionized — one wants to say altered — the concept of self and mind in our time and with it the whole nature of literary criticism. After Freud, how could one go back, save perversely, to the old view of the self and, in criticism, to the old ways of reading? History, as Lawrence realized, is inexorable and moves forward — whether one moves with it or not.

This note perhaps seems remote from Mr. Fraiberg's essay; but, again, I mean only to comment on his general subject. His specific remarks on Burke's use of Freud are made within a very limited and rigorously circumscribed definition of what constitutes psychoanalysis (and reality). The first part of his chapter is devoted to showing how, in accordance with his marvelous title, Burke systematically converts everything to a verbal medium and then manipulates it at will until the terms as Burke uses them bear little relation to either (a) reality or (b) their original meaning in someone else's work. Fraiberg attacks Burke for this, as many others did before him, on the ground that it is unscientific, that it is fallacious, that it will not stand up under any sort of examination in accordance with the rules of classical logic. True. It won't, and Burke knows this. As he once pointed out, somewhat wryly, you don't have to use terms the way the Pope uses them. The last part of Mr. Fraiberg's chapter — the last paragraph of this selection — then suggests that Burke's work is as much "poetic" as "critical" and that scientific and logical objections are perhaps beside the point. Glicksberg and Rosenberg made this same point in the thirties. Now, as then, one wants to say "Yes" to this. Burke's beginnings and late returnings — as fiction writer, as poet — should never be forgotten. He has used whatever came to him (he almost never reviewed a book he did not in some way use); like modern philosophy departments, some of which do not even teach it any more, he no longer subscribes to classical logic. The modern view, thanks in part to Freud, is not of a rational universe or self, any more than the modern view of language or imagery could be held to any kind of naive correspondence theory. One power of language lies in its abstracting and fiction making capacity; this has been Burke's main subject and a chief characteristic of his own larger work. In the alembic of verbal analysis, all linguistic acts tend to be reduced to vision. Up ahead, for example, see Benjamin De Mott on Burke, Hyman, and perspectivism.

◇◇

z Kenneth Burke and Identification

BY John Kirk

IN THE October, 1960, issue of *Quarterly Journal of Speech,* Mr. Dennis Day made an effort to throw some light on Kenneth Burke's contributions to our field in an article entitled, "Persuasion and the Concept of Identification." Quoting Marie Hochmuth Nichols' statement that "Burke deserves to be related to the great tradition of rhetoric," Mr. Day proceeded to support this position in his discussion. If this state-

EDITOR'S NOTE: Reprinted from *The Quarterly Journal of Speech,* XLVII (1961), 414–415, copyright © 1961 by the Speech Association of America, by permission of the author and publisher.

ment means, as Mr. Day's paper seems to indicate, that Burke is basically traditional in his approach, then in my opinion Burke "deserves" something more than to be pigeonholed with Aristotle. In order to make full use of Burke's contributions, we need to dwell on what is *new* in Burke.

Mr. Day tells us: "We shall discover that Burke's concept of identification is an extension of traditional rhetorical theory, that it is based upon his philosophical concept of 'substance,' and that the concept of identification itself is expressed implicitly in the writings of A. E. Phillips and explicitly in James Winans' book, *Public Speaking*." My investigation suggests that this description is so superficial that it tends to be grossly misleading, and that it is more profitable and more appropriate to take the position that the term *identification* used by Burke is an essentially new term, with properties that are not found in the traditional use of the term. I should like further to suggest that Burke's whole discussion of rhetoric ought to be viewed by scholars in our field as a new approach to the subject which can no longer profitably be grouped with classical tradition.

The key to Burke's concept of identification is not that it is like the identification of Winans and Phillips. Burke's identification certainly encompasses the concept of Winans and Phillips, but it functions not only as a *process* whereby separate entities are brought together, but also as a *structure* – a hierarchial structure in which the entire process of rhetorical conflict is organized. Identification is then not only a process which operates in rhetoric; it is also the structure which gives it order.

Although Mr. Day is right as far as he goes in saying that "identification at its simplest" can be put "in terms of the joining of interests," he overlooks or ignores the hierarchial function of Burke's identification concept. Mr. Day supports his statement by quoting Burke out of context: "For example, the politician says to the farm group, 'I was a farm boy myself.'" The complete quotation from Burke is: "Identification ranges from the politician who, addressing an audience of farmers, says, 'I was a farm boy myself,' through the mysteries of social status, to the mystic's devout identification with the source of all being." Although Burke admits the traditional rhetorical definition of identification into his definition, he places the greater emphasis in this work on spinning out the implications of the latter part of the statement – the functioning of the hierarchy of identification in the context of social action.

Mr. Day tells us: "Burke generally conceives of rhetoric in traditional terms. Almost one half of *A Rhetoric of Motives* is devoted to what he titles 'traditional principles of rhetoric.'" To characterize the first part of *A Rhetoric of Motives* as a traditional treatment of rhetoric, regardless of what Burke calls it, is a dangerous oversimplification of the facts. Viewing as he does the whole realm of traditional rhetoric from the standpoint of his identification concept, Burke discusses the traditional rhetoric in a far from traditional way. For instance, in summing up his discussion of Aristotle, Burke tells us, "Thus, all told, besides the *extension* of rhetoric through the concept of identification, we have noted . . . purely traditional evidences of the rhetorical motive." He also uses his discussion of Aristotle to introduce ideas of "semi-verbal, semi-organizational," tactics which Burke calls a "Rhetoric of Bureaucracy." In this discussion, Burke is illustrating the workings of the identification hierarchy in the social structure. He points to the devices in Machiavelli's *The Prince* as an example. Surely these ideas cannot properly be called Aristotelian.

I would like to suggest that Mr. Day and other writers in the field who have made such an effort to relate Burke to the rhetorical tradition now take a look at the other side of the coin and examine more closely what is unique in his position.

Identification in its function as a structure is an order based on the resolution of conflicts by finding their common source. A conflict is "resolved" by discovering a larger generalization which will encompass both sides of the conflict. In this structure, "truth" is arrived at not by eliminating one side of a conflict and allowing the other to stand, but by finding a "name" which will describe the state of the conflict at any given time. A result of this approach is a uniquely modern statement of "truth" not in absolute terms but in terms of an ordered *contingency*. This new kind of rhetorical statement is fundamentally akin to Heisenberg's *uncertainty principle,* Weiner's *physics of contingency,* and other contemporary scientific statements about the nature of the universe.

The implications of this new rhetorical statement have yet to be considered by scholars in our field. Aristotle met Plato's challenge in fashioning a rhetoric to deal with the Platonic notion of truth as an absolute. Is it not possible that Burke is fashioning a rhetoric to deal with the modern notion of truth as a contingency? We can answer this question by examining closely Burke's "hierarchy of identification," being careful to avoid over-simplifications and too-easy categorizations of this difficult but exciting concept.

◇◇

JOHN W. KIRK was born in Sewickley, Pennsylvania, in 1932. He has taught speech and theater at the University of Florida, Kearney State

College, and Illinois State University at Normal. He has written numerous articles on rhetoric and the theater.

This brief note is reprinted without benefit of the short article by Mr. Day to which it is a reply because the issues are clear from Mr. Kirk's note. Very often, the reception of Burke has been complicated by the tendency to attack him before one has bothered to understand what he is about. This is Mr. Kirk's first point. And, very often, people have failed to see that what Burke is about is essentially radical in the sense both that it is part of a larger effort to redefine reality and that it is unique — adds something new to the universe of ideas. This is Mr. Kirk's second point. Both seem to me well worth making, especially if one is to understand Burke in his own time and against his predecessors.

◇◇

z *Burke's Verbal Drama*

BY William H. Rueckert

SOME years ago a rumor escaped from Bennington that Kenneth Burke thought he was God. The rumor was current after *A Rhetoric of Motives* (1950) and during the period when Burke was publishing portions of the projected last two volumes of his tetralogy of motives in essay form, reissuing earlier works under the imprint of Hermes Publications, and making pronouncements in a strange sheet called the *Hermes Scroll.* In one of these, Burke said: "In any case, the *Hermes Scrolls* hope in time to wear you down, until you see just how tremendous are the implications of the fact that man is the typically word-using, or symbol-using animal. . . ." Everything written during the early fifties had in common this obsession with symbol-using and nearly all of it was delivered from a high place by a man still the victim of a colossal synthesizing vision. Since that time Burke has come down out of Heaven and expanded the vision into a coherent system built on the proposition that language is the ultimate reduction.

The present book [*The Rhetoric of Religion*] ends with a felicitous and witty "Dialogue in Heaven" before the fall of Lucifer in which Burke — as TL. (The Lord), with S. (Satan) for straight man — bur-

EDITOR'S NOTE: Reprinted from *The Nation*, CXCIV (17 February 1962), 150, copyright © 1962 by *The Nation,* by permission of the publisher.

lesques his rumored delusion, while offering a "logological" explanation of man and the human drama. The book begins with a short piece on analogies between "Words and The Word" which introduces the general subject of all the essays. It is followed by two long, high-powered studies in "logology" and "logologic," one on "Verbal Action in St. Augustine's *Confessions,*" and the other on "The First Three Chapters of Genesis." Logology (the study of words) and logologic (the logic inherent in language) are a division of, and finally inseparable from, "dramatism." This whole system is built on the premise that since man is the symbol-using animal, the essence of man and the drama of human relations may be discovered through a study of language and the uses to which man puts it.

All these matters are most clearly explained and thoroughly applied in "The First Three Chapters of Genesis," where Burke investigates the "cycle of terms implicit in the idea of 'order.' " This 100-page essay is a condensed version of nearly everything Burke has been trying to say since 1945, for in it he develops and applies logologic — a refinement of the logic he had worked out in *A Grammar of Motives* — in a way that allows him to present his own version of the drama of human relations as an extended illustration. In order to do this, Burke offers a logological ("naturalistic and empirical," he calls it) explanation of the Christian drama of creation, disobedience, fall, expulsion, expiation and redemption which, from a theological point of view, is an extended reversed analogy since he moves from "words" to "The Word"; or from the natural, verbal and socio-political to the supernatural as an analogical extension of the first three. Such an approach treats God as the "Idea of Order" and leads to a consideration of the first three chapters of Genesis and the whole Christian drama as a rhetorical wonder — a verbal construct of great formal beauty with extraordinarily persuasive moral power.

Burke's argument, here and elsewhere, is that this moral drama can be accounted for in terms of words rather than The Word because it is implicit in the nature of language and symbol-using. Abstraction and the Negative are the twin essences of language, and the ability to manipulate them is the essence of symbol-using. With these verbal tools man builds his socio-political and supernatural hierarchies, imitating the grammar of ascent inherent in abstraction and embedding the Negative — various thou-shalt-nots — as a principle in all of them.

At this point, man begins trying to make himself over in the image of his distinctive trait, but is never able completely to transcend the limitations of his split (animal-verbal) essence and match the perfection of his abstract symbol-systems. Hence, the "fall" or "original sin" is inherent in symbol-using, and guilt is a central fact of man's existence. Catharsis (purgation and redemption) then becomes a permanent need which is dealt with by a great variety of constructive and destructive physical and verbal acts of mortification, victimage and sacrifice. Since, Burke says, language makes action (as opposed to motion) possible, every key moment in this drama is derived directly or indirectly from it; furthermore, the methodology consists primarily of timeless verbal principles, the main texts are symbolic acts, and the goal (the purification of war) is to be achieved with language. By making language the ultimate reduction, Burke has been able to create his own rhetorical wonder, symmetrical and, in its own way, persuasive.

It is not possible here to summarize Burke's own summary in such a way as to do justice to the subtlety, complexity and power of the essays in this book and the system and method which they develop and apply. One can, however, point out that Burke's approach (logology), the core of his method (logologic), the coherent system (dramatism), his view of human relations (as essentially a purgative-redemptive drama which arises because of and takes place in a perpetual verbal fog) and his attitude (humane, non-dogmatic and comic) represent the findings of a truly speculative man who has thought and written his way through the last forty-one years. The irony of Burke's own dream (that he could purify war) goaded him on till he built above the wreckage of his own century a verbal pyramid to rest in and be remembered by. One may disagree with some of the words, but it is difficult to find fault with a man for that kind of achievement, especially when so much of it is so useful to those who must live amongst the same ruins.

◇◇◇

William H. Rueckert was born in Cleveland, Ohio, in 1926. He is a professor of English at the University of Rochester and the author of *Kenneth Burke and the Drama of Human Relations* and *Glenway Wescott.*

This short review of *The Rhetoric of Religion* was (is), shockingly, one of the few published of that extraordinary book. The review, like my longer study published a year later, is part of the expository phase of the reception of Burke. The main achievement of this phase is to have apprehended and rendered Burke's work through the fifties as coherent and systematic, and to have seen, as I suggest here and later, the monumental nature of Burke's achievement.

◇◇◇

7 A Sociological Model of Social Interaction as Determined by Communication

BY Hugh Dalziel Duncan

THE NATURE OF SYMBOLIC ACTION IN ART AND SOCIETY

WE HAVE argued that social hierarchy infuses all symbolic expression and that the kind of symbols available to us determine social hierarchy. Names, we have argued further, are not signs, but goads to action. The symbolic expression of social sentiments and attitudes keeps them alive in the mind and spirit of the individual actor. The social function of symbolism in great community dramas is to maintain and transmit social bonds from one generation to another, and to create and sustain the emotional dispositions on which society depends for its existence. To be so transmitted, emotions, like ideas, must be given forms, for it is only through form of some kind that transmission of a culture can take place. Such cultural transmission is an enactment, a drama in which the community is born and will be born again.

A group is obviously dependent on physical objects, on inherited systems of signs, and on the biological characteristics of individuals acting within the group, but these do not in themselves constitute the group. Only when signs are invested with meaning and emotion can they be used to develop attitudes. The group as an object of reason, faith, or emotion is created and sustained in the communication of attitudes, but these attitudes must be objectified in concrete symbols before we can act together. We love our country through the flag, our church through the cross, our neighborhood through a landmark.

We use proverbs (as we use all symbolic expression) to sum up situations. The proverb is public; it means what it does, not because an individual artist uses it or because it is indigenous to any individual group, but because it has been accepted by many groups over long periods of time. Unlike the image of the dream or the slogan of an institution, it belongs to no one because it belongs to everyone. When we invoke a proverb we invoke the experience of the group itself. "Everybody's guilt is no one's guilt." The folk do not create proverbs any more than Chicagoans created George Ade's *Fables in Slang*. But

EDITOR'S NOTE: Originally published in 1962. Reprinted from *Communication and Social Order* (New York: Oxford University Press, Galaxy Edition, 1968), pp. 431–438, copyright © 1962 by Bedminster Press, by permission of the author and Bedminster Press.

the people use a proverb so generally, and so often, that what once seemed highly artificial becomes common. We make the sayings of aphorists into maxims of conduct because the forms they impose on experience enable us to act with greater confidence.

An art work exists in its own right. I do not create *Hamlet* and then use it (like a case history is used) to "prove" the hypotheses which inspired me to gather the material for the case history. The "context of situation" for students who use art works begins with the symbolic context. What Freud or Jones says about Hamlet can be examined in the text of *Hamlet*. There is also a body of rich critical thought (from varying points of view) gathered about *Hamlet*. The text of *Hamlet* is a cultural "fact," produced independently of the observer. It is not created by him, and then used as "proof" of what he set out to investigate. Art works, like all symbolic expressions, are *facts*, not inferences. We infer what the Trobriander "did" in his fishing and gardening by citing "factually" a text that tells us what he did.

We get our view of deeds as facts from our sense of words as facts. Thus, even when we refer to nonsymbolic "contexts of situation," we must turn back to the expression of this context for "proof." This does not mean that no inferences or interpretations are smuggled into the text, but that in so far as there is a record, there is an underlying structure of factuality to which we can repeatedly refer in hopes of hermeneutic improvement. The lack of carefully prepared texts, which many workers can use, is one great flaw in all social study. Students of art are at least talking about an object, the art work, which is open to all for inspection. Very few sociological case histories have been prepared for use by students other than those prepared and distributed among sociologists. Often we are told the content of case histories but are not allowed to judge for ourselves whether or not such statements are true — or even plausible.

Proof[1] in symbolic interpretation will contain two elements. First, while grounding itself in reference to the textual facts, it must seek to make clear all elements of inference or interpretation it adds to these facts; and it must offer a rationale for its selections and interpretations. This is very different from symbolic analysis in terms of analogy. If the word "tree" appears in two contexts, we cannot begin by asking what "symbolic" meanings a tree might have in religion or psycho-

[1] Kenneth Burke's treatment of "fact, inference, and proof in the analysis of literary symbolism," as published in *Symbols and Values: An Initial Study* (Thirteenth Symposium of the Conference on Science, Philosophy and Religion), edited by Lyman Bryson, Louis Finkelstein, R. M. McIver, and Richard McKeon (New York and London: Harper and Brothers, 1954), is followed here. Burke's discussion of method deals with specific literary texts which can be readily consulted.

analysis. We begin with the literal fact that the term bridges the two contexts. Or, even where we might begin with a pat meaning for "tree" over and above its meaning as a positive concept, the fact would still remain that the term had one particular set of associates in some particular work. It is easy enough for the anthropologists to say, "It's not just a 'tree' but a tribal symbol." But such symbolic or analogical meanings, even when correct, still leave the question of how the term "tree" is related to other terms in the text. It is the interconnectedness of an identical term as it recurs in changing contexts within the art work itself that we must search out. This is very different from confining interpretations to equivalences or analogies already established before one looks at the text.

THE STRUCTURE OF THE SYMBOLIC ACT

We have argued, following Burke, that analysis of structure of social action as a symbolic act involves definition of structure in terms of dramatic action. There are five elements in the structure of a social act. These are the time and place of the act, the types of characters who perform the act, the kind of act it is, the means by which the act is performed, and its purpose. In Burke's terminology these are called: scene, agent, act, agency, and purpose. For the purposes of developing a sociological model of communicative action we have adapted them as follows:

Scene is the *symbolization of time and place,* the setting of the act which creates the conditions for social action. The environment of man is symbolic. Even nature is symbolized in spatial or temporal imagery. Social time is always present time because we select the kind of pasts and futures we need to act in a present. Futures and pasts are symbolized in terms of what we want to do *now,* of solutions to problems which must be solved in order for action to go on. Thus, conservatives invoke past traditions, radicals future utopias, to legitimize their acts. In science we invoke a past to explain a present, as in genetic theory. Or, we invoke a future, "the goal toward which the organism presses." In psychology we say that the "child is the father of the man."

Agent is the name for the kind of actor groups select to carry out specified social functions.[2] Who is chosen, who is barred, and who is not eligible to enact certain roles (for whatever reason) tell us much about a society. Roles and the kind of actors held necessary to community survival are honored in all kinds of community presentations. In such presentations we observe what roles are honored, in what style

[2] My interpretation of Burke's "dramatism" is biased in terms of a sociological view of human relationships. There is much more to Burke than this necessarily limited view indicates.

such roles are played, how individuals are trained for such roles, and who controls them.

Act is best understood (from a social view) by watching for acts depicting moments of community origin. Such moments are the creative moment, the moment of social birth. These are the great transcendent absolutes, the final "mystery" of society which are valued because they sanctify social bonds. These may be military, religious, intellectual, or familial. A society may be born in war, created by religious prophets, formed in thought by rational discussion, or conceived by divine parents. We are taught that America was born in debate, and the principles of American union purified in debate over slavery. Our founding fathers are not priests, warriors, teachers, or artists, but politicians who debated to form a constitution. Our sacred act is a parliamentary act.

Agency denotes means or ways of acting. We legitimize power through appeals to belief in certain *ways* of establishing and sustaining authority. In America the way to freedom is through money. A free market guarantees a free society. Justice in our courts is reached through a *method* of trial. Science reaches truth through *methods* of investigation. Magic is effective only when the spell is expressed in rigidly prescribed forms. Manners determine society, for the *ways* we meet, greet, and talk create and sustain the "social graces."

Purpose is belief in certain values as necessary to community survival. If we educate more people and intensify the education of our elites, America will survive; if we are more religious, brotherhood will increase – such "ifs" assume ends, purposes, or goals. Even critical intelligence itself must rest on belief that wisdom, as open and informed discussion, is good for society. Ends, values, and purposes may be described either as pasts or futures. Man lives under immanent symbols, the symbols of promise of things to come. Even rationalists assume an "ideal" rational act to be an ultimate social good. None of these ideal ends can be proved, but their immanence invests action with meanings because they organize the act in a present. Ideal pasts are invoked, not to return to the past, for this is impossible, but to press on into a future. History (in the sociological view taken here) is a goal. Pasts are recaptured only to help us to act in a present.

Scene, agent, actor, agency, and purpose seldom stand alone in symbolic phases of the act. Relationships between two, or stress on various combinations of two or more elements, are common. Burke distinguishes ten dominant types of such relationships which are of specific interest to students of society. Paraphrased for our purposes here, these are:

1. *Scene–act* – All statements which ground social motives in conditions, backgrounds, environments, natural laws, objective situations,

existential conditions, historical necessity, equilibrium, time, the body, etc. Whenever space and time become "trends," species "evolve," empires "take the course of destiny," or certain kinds of human relationships are said "to make virtue inevitable," we ground society in scene. All such explanations of social order are both deterministic *and* hortatory, with exhortation smuggled in under the guise of determinism. Thus, to say that only when Negroes can earn and spend as they desire do we have freedom is to say that we ought to let them do so – if we desire a free society based on money.

2. *Scene–agent* – Social conditions here are said to call for actors in keeping with the scene, and the scene, in turn, is depicted as in keeping with the actor. Thus, we hear of politicians who are "prisoners of the situation," former Nazis who explain their crimes as the result of the "leadership principle," or the motivation to motion in a scene where men do not *act* but are *moved to action.*

3. *Scene–agency* – Whenever *ways* of doing something are considered necessary conditions of social action, as when we tell a child that "our family doesn't do that sort of thing." All appeals to customs, usage, traditions, and means, as the condition of ends, enter here.

4. *Scene–purpose* – When the purpose of action is made part of the conditions under which we act. Money determines the "laws of supply and demand," so it is "natural" for men to work for money. Or, as we say, animals and men alike experience the living God because God is in all nature.

5. *Act–purpose* – When a soldier tells us war is necessary to purify the race, the scientist that science alone can save the community, or we are told any kind of act will, in itself, insure community survival, and will do so "inevitably." Here purpose, or the end of action, and action itself are congruent.

6. *Act–agent* – When we explain an action by the character of the agent, or the glory of the role which the agent enacts. Religious "charisma" (the "gift of grace") of the holy man who rules through purely personal qualifications or the office (such as the priesthood), whose glory and mystery transcends the individual who holds it, are examples.

7. *Act–agency* – When we make means into ends, such as the discovery of the cause of motivation in the "tendency" of the "organism" toward equilibrium. Here motion itself *creates* motion.

8. *Agent–purpose* – When the act of the leader becomes the purpose of the community. When Christ said "I am the way" and Louis XIV told the Parliament of Paris "I am the state" their individual wills became the will of the group.

9. *Agent-agency* — When the instincts, drives, states of mind, character (individual or national) of the actor are said to motivate relationships.

10. *Agency–purpose* — When instruments or techniques become ends, as when we are told that operations determine concepts, that is, how we record temperature *is* our concept of temperature, or, in social actions, when we say: "Manners make the man."

THE FUNCTION OF THE SYMBOLIC ACT

The function of this structure, the content of the drama of society, we argued, is a drama of hierarchy in which superiors, inferiors, and equals communicate by symbols which they believe will create and sustain social order. Our first illustration for this drama was taken from Burke's "dramatistic" adaptation of religious ritual considered as a drama of redemption which is the enactment of guilt and redemption through victimage. These are the great moments in the linguistic experience of man in society. But they are also great social moments, for they are the stages we pass through to create what we call the "social bond." In our view, this bond, in so far as it is determined by symbols, is reached through identification which occurs in the enactment of guilt redeemed through victimage, in social order expressed through hierarchy.

All hierarchy, we argued, is based on a final moment of "mystery," a sacred moment in which social hierarchy ends — and begins. We discussed three basic attitudes toward these ends, namely, acceptance, doubt, and rejection. We then codified hierarchal ultimates, in terms of a dramatistic view of the act based on the work of Mead and Burke. We argued that we ground social motives in scene when we invoke laws of nature to explain hierarchy; in the act, or the nature of the action itself, when we say that a certain kind of act constitutes the social bond; in the actor when we say that a certain kind of person, or a specific role has the charismatic power to identify people with each other; in the agency, or means, when we say that how we do something will determine the efficacy of what we do in creating and sustaining social bonds; and in purpose when we say that ends or values determine our motives.

While we recognized that communication has many functions, we argued that its specific sociological function is that of hierarchal address. The rhetoric of hierarchy was described as a rhetoric of courtship, and courtship in turn involved appeals to general audiences, community guardians, significant others (as in dialogue when the "I" addresses its "Me"), the self (as in all forms of soliloquy), and to some great transcendent principle which is believed to create and sustain social order and is expressed through the glory and majesty of hierarchy. We illustrated one of these principles, the principle of money, by showing some of the steps by which money became a symbol of community and thus transcended its immediate function in trade or exchange.

We declared in favor of democracy as the best form of hierarchy, because it minimized the power of priestly mystification which so often arises when authority is grounded in some kind of supernatural power. We admitted to a mystification of our own, namely, that of reason in society. This, we argued, can be kept under control only when there is open, free, and informed discussion of action in society. Comedy was selected as a "representative case" of such discussion, for in comedy ambiguity, doubt, difference, and all forms of social disorganization are exposed, not cloaked, as in tragedy. The comic hero, the clown, offers hopes for the development of a scapegoat who need not be tortured and killed in ritual murder like the scapegoat whose actual sacrifice begins in the symbolic sacrifice of tragedy. For, we argued, in comedy we confront openly many things we must hide and repress when we are "serious."

Reason in society depends, we said, on equality, and equality in turn can become a form of authority only when experience in creating and obeying rules is made possible. For rules represent the will of equals, and even though rules can also become ritual, there is far less danger of malign mystification under the authority of rules since such authority does not rest on supernatural powers "beyond reason." We do not believe rules "even though they are absurd," but because they work, and when they do not we are prepared to change them so that they will work. We noted how little is really known of the authority of rules, and how small is our social psychology of equality, compared to the great amount of work done on superiority and inferiority as a form of hierarchy. We argued that art, as well as religion, supplied forms of symbolic action which might serve for models for thinking about social integration. But art, we proposed in conclusion, should be studied in its comic, not tragic, forms, for the tragic is too close to religion. *The sociology of art, and especially a sociology of comic art, is a general, as well as a specialized, study of society, in so far as society is determined by the communication of significant symbols.*

Much uneasiness, even despair, pervades our search for a way of thinking about how society arises in, and continues to exist through, communication. This is caused by the spectacle of Hitler and the wide gap between what we know as social scientists about human motivation and what such monsters as Hitler can put into practice. They seem to grasp intuitively that social relations are determined by identification, which is reached through *staging* human relationships in community dramas modeled after horrible perversions of religious drama. What drama of reason can we create to match these terrible dramas of unreason? Can we develop theory and method in symbolic analysis which will tell us *how* to do what we *ought* to do, as citizens of a free world? And can we do it soon enough? Throughout this book we have argued that until the wide gap between humanistic and scientific understanding is closed, there is small reason for optimism. We must return the study of man in society to a study of communication, for how we communicate determines how we relate as human beings.

◇◇◇

See the note on page 260.

THIS selection is the conclusion to the revised edition of Mr. Duncan's *Communication and Social Order*, which is the end result of his attempts to absorb and use Burke to his own sociological ends. Anyone who has read his Burke and this book knows how difficult and futile it is to separate the Burke from the Duncan. Hugh Duncan has simply ingested Burke and taken him into his own system, organically. He illustrates a kind of total and beneficent reception of Burke that would be hard to find elsewhere.

◇◇◇

7 *The Little Red Discount House*

BY Benjamin De Mott

EARLY last summer the American Council of Learned Societies and Educational Services Incorporated began circulating a sheaf of mimeographing entitled, "Preliminary Draft of a Proposal for the Support of a Curriculum Development Program in the Humanities and Social Sciences." The aim of the agencies was to win support for a new project for the reform of elementary and secondary school teaching. The reformers were, to a man, reputable academics — social scientists, historians, and teachers of literature — and their "Preliminary Draft" con-

EDITOR'S NOTE: Reprinted from *The Hudson Review*, XV (1962–63), 551–564, copyright © 1963 by the Hudson Review, Inc., by permission of the author.

tained matter of interest to a wide variety of observers. For Foundation men there were enticing work schedules and modest budgetary estimates. For scientists there was pleasing testimony that the people in the other culture were docilely following the patterns developed by mathematicians and physicists in improving instruction in their fields (first a summer meeting of professionals to frame new approaches to old subjects; next a joint effort by university, secondary, and elementary teachers to produce textbooks embodying the fresh ideas; thereafter experimental testing of the texts in classrooms, a summer of intensive revision, national publication of the texts, and finally the institution of retraining programs for teachers committed to the use of the new books). And for the idle gossip there were a few amusingly discussible appendices – a self-teasing glossary of terms favored by the reformers at their meetings ("INTERDISCIPLINARY – a state devoid of discipline in which it is permissible to interrupt whoever is speaking"), a page or two on the best way of teaching reading and writing which concluded, with winning embarrassment, that "reading and writing is best self-taught" (the banger of this soft drum was Professor Mark Harris).

As the appendices suggest, the reformers were at pains to avoid the ordinary styles of educational crusade. Eschewing the rhetoric of light-bringing, they presented themselves simply as people engaged in creating "specific units" that might be "spotted through the elementary curriculum or that might be considered as forming a network as they are tested and more are added": they offered no rationalization of their programs, and seemed mainly bent upon establishing themselves as easy riders. But despite all the engaging self-deprecation, a revolution plainly was implicit in their work. Examination of the "units" offered as samples disclosed that their primary goal was nothing less than a direct encounter between the childish mind and intellectual themes at once powerful and unfamiliar to the elementary or secondary classroom – items that could not have been settled upon merely in hope of stimulating the teacher's ingenuity. The themes in question – the relation between a person's interest and his perspective, the necessity of understanding a point of view as an agent of deflection – retain, to be sure, little grandeur or elegance when adapted to the requirements of Innocence. (One unit called for the teacher to introduce "tape record narratives of the same football game by a television announcer, a sophomore girl, the winning coach, the losing coach, the left guard's mother, and an eight year old brother of one of the players. Tie these in [the instructions went on] with movies or photographs . . . to further illustrate what each person is seeing at specific points throughout the game. This illustrates 'selective perception' – the idea that a person's point of view or 'role' influences what he sees.") But the homeliness of the material did not alter the fact: the apparent center of the ACLS-ESI program was the conviction that the time has come for the ground themes of modernity to be sounded in every glassy corner of the American public school.

That representatives of disciplines not usually pleased with each other were able to arrive at this decision without vicious quarrel is less mysterious than might be supposed. Historians as well as social scientists have caught glimpses of Marx, Frazer, Freud, and the other giants who forced the growth of awareness that beliefs and ideas are gestures of competing interests, that the god-term itself is culture-bound, that no man's unprobed word is to be trusted. And while only a few of the great literary heroes of the century have been notable discounters, great hordes of MLA members nevertheless stopped buying books – i.e., points of view – at list long before Korvette's picked Mrs. Lindbergh as a loss leader. The principles behind the reverse price-fixing among litry folk were tricky and exacting. (So much off the overt argument of any book for roles and points of view, as a matter of course – but then beyond this, so much off for rationalization, repression, the lessons of the symbols, imaginative designs, private vocabularies, a dozen similar cues to interest.) But the principles were well-regarded. The case is, indeed, that contemporary academics in virtually every field became habituated long ago to the idea of selective perception – which is to say that the success in recovering a sense of the notion fresh enough to breathe humor into schoolbooks qualifies as an act of historical imagination.

There are, however, other acts to be performed before the entry of the notion into red schoolhouses and junior highs can rouse more than guarded satisfaction. It is clear that perspectivism is a splendid resource of the mind – a strong defense against ideology and fanaticism, a first-rate incentive to subtlety, complication, and (possibly) acceptance of otherness. It is no less clear that training people up from toddlerdom in this way of thought is altogether feasible. And it is likely (given the perpetual crises of Cold War) that most of the old humanist charges against the discounters – as for example that in multiplying viewpoints they obscure values – will soon strike Old Humanists themselves as lacking in pertinence to the age. (In the past the charges were most popular, in any event, among observers who, when asked straight off where they took *their* stand, preferred not to commit themselves "at this time.") But when these concessions are made, it remains true that perspectivism is itself a mode of expression, and, as such, an agent of interest, an instrument of repression, a potion best cut with a cautionary word. The thinker who seizes on the new mode of thought as his mode (whether in the name of the giants, or merely in the name of wit as defined by Mr. Eliot) needs to study it negatively for a moment – in order to find out precisely what happens when the stuff of his *own* particular learning is no longer bought at full price. Failure to do this means advocating a "sensible scaling-down" of all intellectual claims, while consciously or unconsciously exempting one's own claims from sacrifice. And that way lies megalomania.

In the discipline of literature the best current laboratory for scrutiny of the effects of "discounting for viewpoints" is found, as everyone knows, in the writings of the school of Kenneth Burke. No literary theorist of the century has done more than Burke to acquaint students of imaginative writing with the implications of the perspectivist revolution.[1] In his early books (*Counter-Statement, Attitudes toward History, Permanence and Change*), as well as in the treatises on Motives, the now retired sage of Bennington argued with endless inventiveness for the necessity of Seeing Around the spoken or written word, the announced intention, the "successful" enterprise in persuasion – in order to register the extent of the wordman's probable deflection from the X that is not words. The argument was never simple in its assumptions. It neither grovelled in the slough of logical positivism nor aspired to faith in a truth Out There, waiting to be discovered by the steely mind stripped of all deflectors. It held firm instead to a spiky set of contrarieties: language deflects and interest determines (in part) the nature of the deflection: every definition creates a situation; my definition, hence my situation, may or may not be yours; another vocabulary can always be imagined; there is virtue in "perspective by incongruity" and danger in "temporalization of essence"; society as a community of meanings, a catalogue of created scene-act ratios, continues to exist. Always, though, the theorist's eye (no flatterer) was on the limits of the strategies composed and the positions upheld. You must track down the symbols in order to find the meaningful – *tic* ("The poet . . . squints or jerks when some words are spoken, otherwise not. You disclose the 'symbolic organization' of his tic when you have found the class of words that provokes it"). You must discount not only for the form of the expression but for the moment of biographical and historical time ("Often you cannot take a sentence at face value [you do not 'understand the meaning' until you know the biographical or historic context sub-

[1] Other students as well. *Permanence and Change*, for example, is often recommended as a work indispensable for beginners in social sciences. See C. Wright Mills's *The Sociological Imagination.*

sumed by the speaker when he spoke it"]). And you cannot allow an unmixed motive to stand ("a 'comic' term for the essence of motivation . . . expects an act to be moral, and it expects the actor to 'cash in on' his moral assets"; "in keeping with our distrust of both 'perfectionist' and 'invertedly perfectionist' motivations, we should feel justified in never taking at its face value any motivational reduction to a 'simple' ").

The body of writing Burke has built up on these principles is prized on several grounds. It is first of all the work of that rarest of men, a good humored original genius. It is equal to the age, conversant with ranges of intellection unheard-of by most litterateurs, impatient with elegant, self-indulgent ignorance. It is free of fairy aestheticism, fully responsive to the continuum of human activity, quick to perceive ventures in ordermaking wherever they occur, disinclined to profundum about the separateness of life and art. And finally, unlike most criticism, it is generous to its reader: it tells him he has an active mind, is agile and quick, relishes complication, is scornful of emotional posturing and human enough to enjoy being silly now and then. As the chief critical end-product of perspectivism it is, in short, superb testimony that the influence of the idea can be humane.

But of course — to round on virtues in the desiderated manner — the theories and the theorist have limits of their own. As should be admitted, attempts to name these limits in political or literary terms have usually come off badly. The best-remembered of them are those of Sidney Hook and R. P. Blackmur. The former made his complaint in a famous *Partisan Review* episode of the late thirties; he condemned Burke as "an apologist . . . of the latest piece of Stalinist brutality" (the Moscow trials), claiming that *Attitudes toward History* sought to rationalize in "basic metaphors and psychoanalytic myths" deeds and necessities of the totalitarian state that were "too stark and bloody" to be rationalized. The latter made his complaint in "The Critic's Job of Work"; its point was that the perspectivist's method broke down all distinctions and could be applied "with equal fruitfulness to Shakespeare, Dashiell Hammett, or Marie Corelli." Both charges imply that Burke is an insensitive man — oblivious at once to brutality in life and excellence in art — and the implication is false. But, to the extent that Burke's accusers were not merely repeating mechanical formulae, they were responding to a central quality of his writing — the quality of imperviousness. And it is this quality, this set of the perspectivist being, that rouses distrust even in sympathetic observers aware of the pivotal place of resistance in the ruling strategy of the whole.

As goes almost without saying, the modes of imperviousness — the term means: rigid disbelief in the possibility of direct encounter, obstinate standing off of any and all "descriptions," refusal to accept the other man's metaphor, tone, or joke — are as various as the subjects Burke has attacked. One mode is teacherly:

> Once when I was analyzing the symbolism of sun and moon in Coleridge's poem, "The Ancient Mariner," a student raised this objection: "I'm tired of hearing about the symbolic sun in poems, I want a poem that has the *real* sun in it."
>
> Answer: If anybody ever turns up with a poem that has the real sun in it, you'd better be about ninety-three million miles away. We were having a hot summer as it was, and I certainly didn't want anyone bringing the real sun into the classroom.

Another is Prussian militarist cum Dr. Bovary. It appears in the few essays that address themselves (with an iron inattention to tone) to masterworks — the essay on "The Grecian Urn," for example, of which the following is the final paragraph:

> We may contrast this discussion with explanations such as a materialist of the Kretschmer school might offer. I refer to accounts of motivation that might treat disease as cause and poem as effect. In such accounts, the disease would not be "passive," but wholly active; and what we have called the mental action would be wholly passive, hardly more than an epiphenomenon, a mere symptom of the disease quite as are the fever and the chill themselves. Such accounts would give us no conception of the essential matter here, the intense linguistic activity.

Another is perky-boyish-stubborn, as in Burke's replies to complainants like Hook and Blackmur. He will not "answer" these chiding parental voices: no concession that a brutal deed was done, only a reiteration that historical events are first of all changes in the way human beings choose to define themselves (innumerable choices are possible); no avowal that Miss Corelli is not Shakespeare, only an excursion on the inertness of the classifications of "good taste."

There have been occasions, true, on which this extraordinary contention against "natural" response, or openheartedness, is given over — the essay on "The Rhetoric of Hitler's 'Battle' " is a notable one. But by and large the critic is unrelentingly hostile to Normalcy. And in his latest and most self-regarding book, *The Rhetoric of Religion: Studies in Logology,*[2] Burke remains fiercely unsubmissive to the other writer's voice. The book opens, in the theorist's characteristic fashion, with trumpetry on the theme that words are not things ("Language, to

[2] *The Rhetoric of Religion: Studies in Logology,* by Kenneth Burke, Beacon Press. $6.95.

be used properly, must be 'discounted' . . ."; "all words for the non-verbal must, by the very nature of the case, discuss the realm of the non-verbal in terms of what it is not"). Activizing as ever, it establishes that religion is a form of behavior, redefines behavior as verbal gesture, advances the proposition that "what we say about God will bear a likeness to what we say about words" – and justifies it with a swift clutch of analogies (God is to Christ as thought is to utterance; the succession of words in a sentence is to the meaning of a sentence as time is to Eternity). Thereafter the reader is offered an intense, lengthy, speculative Seeing Around of Augustine's *Confessions* and the opening chapters of Genesis, sections that conclude – on the basis of the grammar of the Biblical verses – that it is in the nature of language itself to construct "providence" or "divine foreknowledge" in principle: ". . . language is just made that way. And in its will is (our definition of) peace." The book ends with a dialogue that shoots off a thousand paradoxes on The Word, words, and conceptions of mystery, and there is enough brilliance in these pages, and twice as much wit, to support a thousand-acre seminary. But the unhearingness *is* muscularly resolute.

To repeat: the resoluteness is the key to the method. The critic never asked to be thought of as a man concerned with works of art "for themselves" or as "experiences" to be lovingly recreated; he never answered eloquence with eloquence.[3] He invariably asserts at the cruces – sometimes in ecstacy – the primacy of his interest ("Then comes what is, for our purposes, the most astoundingly perfect passage conceivable" – this about a moment in the *Confessions* that is, naturally, astounding and perfect for many purposes beside those of the 'comic' perspectivist). Everything in his almost hostile manner of address to the work announces that because it is a confession, a description, a vocabulary, a set of terms, it must necessarily and inevitably be a deceit. Moreover: grounds for forgiveness other than the man's frankness lie ready at hand. Who, after all, would argue that Augustine's tale of his conversion ought to convert a modern reader? Can it really be said that the exasperation occasioned by Burke's harping on Augustine the rhetorician ("an inveterate wordman" and "former word-merchant" occur on page after page) is a major irritant? And is it not true that the hunt for cues and buried symbols does eventually come out at a trove? (The word-

[3] Burke possesses a high eloquence, but here as elsewhere it is released not by the other voice, but instead by one or another psycho-linguistic quirk that attracts his eye and tickles him into poetry – as in the following snippet: "Intimacy with a woman must always argue special intimacy with some word or words like or nearly like the sound of her name. So probably they [the names of Augustine's "toys"] are there [in the *Confessions*] shining out like unseen stars, ambiguously split between terms in the constellation of the divine and terms for the problematic body."

merchant's magnificent passage on the union with God as unutterable silence is shown convincingly to "tie in psychologically with motives vestigially 'infantile.' ").

The questions are not easy to dismiss. But, confronting Burke in the context of general education, the reader does tend to turn away from them – in the direction of the obvious deeper problem. Taken to its end, bureaucratized, brought the full way down into the arena of day-to-day, might not the method easily be put in service of the cause of moral laziness? You cannot *teach* caritas, sympathy, respect for the other – but will these be strengthened if you teach their opposites? Discount the ideal and the labor of *recognition*, and how much of "the humanities" remains?

The possibility exists, needless to say, that intense imperviousness is simply part of the personal configuration called Kenneth Burke, rather than a telling mark and sign (among literary men) of the perspectivist disposition of mind. But examination of other writers of the school lends little backing to this theory. The most substantial recent work produced by a leading member is Stanley Edgar Hyman's *The Tangled Bank.*[4] The literary community owes many debts to this writer. His reviews in *The New Leader* are sharp, forceful, usually unsmutched by schmerz or phony brio. *The Armed Vision* has been a kind of sacred book for two generations of graduate students in English, strengthening their will to believe in the profession at just the moment when the latter presents itself most forcibly in the likeness of a poolshow. And in the new book mentioned, an important bureaucratization of the (Burkean) Imaginative, he has assembled invaluable materials for a perspectivist account of the development of the modern mind. But there is not much in the volume to suggest that imperviousness is a personal tic of the original (Burkean) genius.

As indicated by the subtitle – *Darwin, Marx, Frazer and Freud as Imaginative Writers* – Hyman is assessing the heroes of perspectivism: at last the revolution catches up, as it were, with the revolutionaries. To speak of him as a bureaucratizer of Burke is only to say that each of his chapters on the thinkers in question takes roughly the form of an attempt to specify, from a series of viewpoints, the proper rates of discount to be applied to their versions and visions of experience. The movement of the chapters is from biography through history into formal analysis. The characteristic gesture is of knitting contexts:

> In reality, of course, Darwin's teleology is as sacred and supernatural as Paley's, but with all-seeing Mother Nature substituted for God the Father.

[4] *The Tangled Bank,* by Stanley Edgar Hyman. Atheneum. $10.00.

It was a fit covert religious revolution for Victorian England, but it also had a particular fitness for Darwin, whose deep identification with his dead mother and submission to his overwhelming father suggests a classic Oedipal situation.

His [Darwin's] final moral imperative is curiously akin to Freud's concept of civilization as the taming of the instinctual life: 'The highest possible stage in moral culture is when we recognize that we ought to control our thoughts, and "not even in inmost thought to think again the sins that made the past so pleasant to us."' The quotation is from *The Idylls of the King.* It shows as well as anything could . . . that *The Descent of Man,* this bold attack on Victorian orthodoxy, was the salvation of Victorian orthodoxy in the only terms, imaginative and poetic, in which it could still be saved.

The most obvious repression is of the instinct for reductive explanation; deflecting agents are ceaselessly renamed in multiplying contexts. (The tendency of Freud's work to "temporalize" belief in a "primal cause" into an origin myth must be placed not only in the context of Freud's guilt about his attachment to Fliess, but in the context of his imaginative fascination with the mode of Conan Doyle. Frazer's unclarity about the relations between history and myth, Christ the man and Christ the Saviour, must be placed in the context of contemporary religious argument – "he feels caught in the middle, a Straussite Unitarian fending off the Trinitarian worshippers in one direction and the Bauerite atheists on the other"; and also in the context of the uncertainty of his design – "perhaps the vastness of the book [*The Golden Bough*] really does break down").[5] And the most interesting crisis traceable to the grand strategy takes the form of an Evaluative Situation, wherein the writer reprices back to list the object he has discounted – and then attempts to buy it off himself with a flourish.

An uneasy flourish, necessarily, because the discounter – using perspective by incongruity, analogical form, and a dozen other ploys – has driven hard bargains throughout. The "dramatic and tragic vision of life" in *The Descent of Man* "comes from Darwin, rather than from his subject matter." Frazer's "imaginative reconstruction of the performance of the mysteries in describing the great hall of Initiation of Eleusis seems to have more in common with the Radio City Music Hall than with anything that could have transpired at Eleusis. . . ."

[5] Hyman intends the word "temporalize" to bring Burke to mind here; in point of fact the observation about Freud's explaining present conditions by inventing a mythic past comes directly from *The Grammar of Motives* and *The Rhetoric of Religion.* On Hyman's "Acknowledgements" page Burke's name is placed third in a list of main influences (after the Cambridge School of anthropologists and Empson), and it appears only six times in the text. Burke's vocabulary, however, is used repeatedly, and his injunctions to commentators, historians, and critics are faithfully heeded; plainly but for him this book could not have been written.

Freud's "fullest account of the bedevilled ego is a blare of metaphor." Neither Marx's nor anyone else's economic theories are "true or false in any determinable sense." And *Capital* is best seen as:

. . . a melodrama called something like *The Mortgage on Labor-Power Foreclosed*. In the first act the villain mistreats the virtuous wife and injures her poor little child; in the second act the young laboring hero himself is maimed and sits paralyzed in a wheelchair while the child dies; in the third act they are thrown out into the snow and take refuge in a miserable hovel; in the fourth act the discovery is made that the villain stole the mortgage originally and has no legal or moral rights over our heroes. It needs a fifth act in which the working-class family is rescued and restored to its happy home, but only the proletarian revolution could produce that final curtain, and Marx could not finish *Capital* without it.

But a return to Fair Trade is attempted, once the pricewearing is finished. The strategist begins his final chapter with abuse of those who have refused to take in the meaning (discounted? undiscounted?) of the writers he has been assessing:

It is not that there has been a religious revival so much as an obscurantism revival, a disinterest in knowledge as a good in itself, perhaps a new failure of nerve. . . . The entrenched enemy that Darwin, Marx, Frazer and Freud each battled in his own fashion, the bigoted ignorance and superstition that masks as religion, has survived their onslaughts and is apparently stronger than ever.

He then sheds a seemingly disingenuous tear:

Apart from the influence of religious obscurantism, our century generally seems less interested in ideas than the last, seems to care about them less and to take them less seriously. Some of this is an unfortunate effect of the discounting Marx and Freud have taught us; it is so easy now to dismiss any idea as an ideology or a rationalization.

And thereafter, restoring metaphor as a value in an admirably bold stroke ("perhaps all science is ultimately metaphor, as Freud suggested in his open letter to Einstein"), he ends with a single powerful sentence of approbation: "These great enlightenings are humanist; philanthropic in the root sense, for the love of man."

The strategy of this closing is not without awkwardness, as the summary implies. But what is of interest is that the awkwardness plainly is traceable to the tendencies of mind under discussion here — ferocious resistance, stony imperviousness. Evidence in support of this point can be found in every section of Hyman's book, but particularly in the chapters on Marx and Engels. The latter pages are filled with observations on Marx's imaginative design, dramatic stance, and key metaphors (many of these are likely to seem puzzling to readers with a clear memory of *Capital* itself). But they are also dense with terms of another order — numbers, summaries of statistical tables, quotations from the reports of "firsthand observers" (of non-Marxist deflection) of the conditions of the working class. The reader is given information (originally supplied by Marx but not quarrelled with by Hyman) about towns in which a quarter of the babies born die within a year of birth, about steel-pen and tile plants that employ children four and five years old, about class differences in life expectancy in cities like Liverpool and Manchester (15 years for workers, 35 years for the upper middle class), about tuberculosis rates (an increase of from one in 45 to one in 8 in a decade of lace-making), and about living space (18 people to a room in Newcastle). Only a page before the account of *Capital* as melodrama the writer repeats Marx's quotation from "a magistrate of the lace trade" on child labor:

> Children of nine or ten years are dragged from their squalid beds at two, three, or four o'clock in the morning and compelled to work for a bare subsistence until ten, eleven, or twelve at night, their limbs wearing away, their frames dwindling, their faces whitening, and their humanity absolutely sinking into a stonelike torpor, utterly horrible to contemplate.

Against this language Hyman's heavy irony about a first act portraying a "villain [who] mistreats the virtuous wife and injures her poor little child" clanks incommensurately. The iron will to unresponsiveness has produced, on schedule, yet another analogical form — melodrama — but in meeting the schedule the author has revealed little except his terror of sounding like a bleeding-heart. Embarrassed, the reader withdraws, distrusting any cause that requires him to see sweated children as metaphors.

If this tic, or tactlessness, appeared only once, concern about it could reasonably be belittled as finkery. But in truth it is never out of sight. A chapter or so after the cited passages, Hyman writes about the descriptions offered in Engels' *The Condition of the Working Class in England in 1844* — and distances them in similar fashion. He quotes Engels on the life of a working woman in Manchester:

> M. H., twenty years old, has two children, the youngest a baby, that is tended by the other, a little older. The mother goes to the mill shortly after five o'clock in the morning, and comes home at eight at night; all day the milk pours from her breasts, so that her clothing drips with it —

and an account of the life of Sheffield laborers:

> The cottages are old, dirty, and of the smallest sort, the streets uneven, fallen into ruts and in part without drains or pavement; masses of refuse, offal and sickening filth lie among standing pools in all directions, the atmosphere is poisoned by the effluvia from all these, and laden and darkened by the smoke of a dozen tall factory chimneys. A horde of ragged women and children swarm about here, as filthy as the swine that thrive upon the garbage heaps and in the puddles.

Then, faced with this sentence of his author:

> Yet one is left in doubt whether even this terribly torturing death is not a blessing for the children in rescuing them from a long life of toil and wretchedness, rich in suffering and poor in enjoyment,

he remarks: "When Engels falls into sentimentality, which is not infrequently, we may think of Dickens . . . Engels [redoes] the death of Little Nell."

The question of moment is: what in the quoted sentence is sentimental? Where in the sentence are there feelings in excess of the value of the object? Why is the modern tongue incapable of saying that a sweated child is better off dead, is blessed in extinction? Admittedly the man who raises the question is obliged to suspect his own "interest": I am an opportunist eager to prove that the critic is a hardrock and I am sweet? I am a wailer big with hysterical cries? – as: The world is not words! the Jews were not burnt in dictionaries! the past is not fiction! Frazer is not Cecil B. DeMille! Something somewhere by someone *can* be taken straight! – But after all the "necessary" self-laceration the problem and the sensible conclusion still stand forth in full sight. The problem is, simply, that the last proud sentence of *The Tangled Bank* – ". . . philanthropic in the root sense, for the love of man" – establishes that the author has fine feelings, but establishes it later than might have been hoped. (Or, saying it again, the hooks and eyes that connect the sentence – it occurs 450 pages deep in an oversized ten dollar book – with what has gone before have crept down under the facing and are hard to reach.) And the conclusion is that the literary perspectivist, for all his whirling shifting agility, is finally a man who does hate being moved.

In itself this conclusion is hardly an adequate basis for an assessment of a complete teaching program – the program that features the viewpoints of Losing Coaches and Eight Year Old Brothers. But from this it doesn't follow that reading the school of Burke in the context of educational reform, scrutinizing it for hints as to the nature of future gains and losses under the regime of the perspectivists, is an altogether improper act. (Such a reading does acknowledge the school's significance, after all, even as it claims – in good Burkean fashion – that pedagogical revolutions themselves must not always be taken on their own terms.) As for the losses; the thought of them will turn no reasonable man into a counter-revolutionary – for there are few alternatives to the regime. Linguistic fundamentalism, as represented by the Rosicrucians and Boehme and the John Webster who didn't write plays, is a pretty artifact, but vapid in its nostalgia for the old language of the old nature of the old Adam wherein every verbal sound contained the nature of the thing and no gap existed between verbal expression and reality. Linguistic progressivism from Leibnitz to the psycholinguists has its brisk utopian note, but also a constant overtone of kookieness. And the toughminded objectivism of the shorthaired ladies (Ayn Rand) and sternbrowed men (Norman Mailer) is mainly dumb. You have only to shift your gaze from these items to the beautifully complicated human landscape of Burke, or to the often admirably inclusive "history" of Hyman to discover why the perspectivists are a modern center of hope.

The word to be said, in sum, *is* merely cautionary – meaning the word to be spoken to the humanist-perspectivist who is about to bring his vision out of the library and into the world of men, or of children. This enthusiast must tell himself that the future will be a place in which more will be seen or encompassed – every manifold stretching and stretching – every schoolboy peering over, through, around, underneath: for this is the way Causes are made. But, even as he warms to the prospect, he needs to remind himself that the dilation of vision anticipated is more dependent upon the development of new perspectives, new languages, than upon the rigorous eschewal of the old; only if he does this will his Cause escape reduction to Technics. He must hear every word of the Burkemen: no perspective exempt from scrutiny, only multiplicity can be The Rock, the comic view is essential. And then as he repeats the lesson to youth he must corrupt it with gentleness: by choosing a tone expressive of the possibility that some acts of Seeing Around are more painful to witnesses than other acts, by implying that if imperviousness is the means, sympathy is the end, by contradicting those who think comic means A Joke, and by remembering, finally, that neither in mortuaries nor elsewhere is it demonstrable that wisdom and silence are the same.

◇◇

BENJAMIN DE MOTT was born on Long Island, New York, in 1924. He has taught English at Amherst College since 1951. He is the author of

The Body's Cage, Hells and Benefits, You Don't Say, and a great many reviews and essays.

Like Burke, Mr. De Mott's interests are never merely literary, and like Burke, he has a formidable verbal and intellectual talent. Mr. De Mott insisted that I use all or none of this essay, so it is all here. Behind, beneath, within all this wit, verbal play, and display Mr. De Mott, as usual, has some important points to make about Burke, Hyman, and perspectivism. As I have pointed out, the ultimate reduction of perspectivism is the treatment of all verbal discourse as essentially the same and as forms of system building. The verbal analyst tends to be concerned with the structure of visions rather than with the value of a specific vision and to regard his analyses as a self-justifying intellectual activity. There is certainly this tendency in Burke, in Stanley Edgar Hyman's *The Tangled Bank,* and in many other verbal analysts and perspectivists. As Mr. De Mott points out, the whole tendency exerts a powerful influence in many intellectual fields. His argument is directed against the over-intellectualized and under-emotionalized (he calls them dehumanized) responses of all the perspectivists. Once one recognizes the validity of Mr. De Mott's argument, it becomes and remains a powerful and disturbing objection to some of the things many of us have learned from Burke. The divided minds of most modern American intellectuals, including Mr. De Mott's, are trained to the highly sophisticated and useful modes of perspectivist analysis; Mr. De Mott does not really tell us how to use this resourceful analytic grammar, but he does caution us about the self-deluding gratifications of a powerful methodology.

◇◇

z Selections from "Modern American Criticism"

BY Walter Sutton

SELECTION FROM "LIBERAL AND MARXIST CRITICISM"

KENNETH BURKE's first volume of criticism, *Counter-Statement* (1931), published during the early depression, presents a "program" demonstrating the political and social implications of his critical theory. In a "Curriculum Criticum" appended to the second edition (1953), Burke

EDITOR'S NOTE: Reprinted from *Modern American Criticism* (Englewood Cliffs, N.J.: Prentice-Hall, Inc., 1963), pp. 79–84, 182–184, 205–211, copyright © 1963 by the Trustees of Princeton University, by permission of the publisher.

looks back over his work and recognizes a shift at that time from an individualistic "Aestheticist" period to a concern for the "interdependent, social, or collective" aspects of literature. Like all of Burke's writing, *Counter-Statement* moves toward a synthesis of shifting critical methods. "Psychology and Form," which had first appeared in *The Dial* in 1925, defines form, in terms of a "psychology of the audience," as "an arousing and fulfillment of desires." Burke thus locates the formal matrix of the work in the collective social consciousness of the audience rather than the private consciousness of the writer.

Burke opposes the Marxist position in his hostility to science and technology, which he considers responsible for much of the derangement of taste in modern society, and in his distinction between the truth of science, which is based on a revelation of facts, and aesthetic truth, which emerges when the revelation of science is "ritualized," or converted into a symbolic process which expresses metaphorical truth. His ideas are more characteristic of the romantic idealist than of the dialectical materialist, and his reference to the ritualization of art points to the later myth interpretation that he himself employed in his rebirth-ritual analysis of Keats's "Ode on a Grecian Urn."

Burke sees art as necessarily implicated in the social process. The program he recommends would oppose the bourgeois-practical world, not with a proletarian revolutionary attitude, but with a bohemian or aesthetic negativism. Against the totalitarian or fascist tendency of industrialized society, he urges not a revolutionary Marxism but a negativist democracy, with a system of checks and balances, the inefficiency of which would be a guard against the centralization of power. Burke's plan, for which he hopes to find support among the farmers, is remarkable not so much for its radicalism as for its likenesses to the conservative agrarianism of the Southern writers. A "Lexicon Rhetoricae" included in *Counter-Statement* extends Burke's discussion of form as stimulating and controlling the desires of the audience through devices which appeal to recurrent patterns of experience. It also shows his concern for the language of criticism: he discusses the five aspects of form under such headings as "progressive form (subdivided into syllogistic and qualitative progression), repetitive form, conventional form, and minor or incidental forms." Burke's terminology is more elaborate than that of either the Humanist or the Marxist critics. Poetics and rhetoric are the principal source of his vocabulary here. The words that he is at pains to define precisely include — besides *form* — *rhythm, rhyme, eloquence, symbol, manner,* and *style.* His penchant for categorization is a trait he shares with the Aristotelian genre critic.

In his subsequent criticism of the 1930's Burke professed a commitment to Marxism, but it was a commitment curiously qualified and perhaps neutralized. In *Permanence and Change: An Anatomy of Purpose* (1935), he insists that only communism, under one name or another, can provide the solution for existing social maladjustment. He plays throughout on the words *communism, communicant,* and *communication,* to indicate the interrelationship of political, religious, and aesthetic processes. In the interest of promoting social reorganization he employs the strategy of deliberately scrambling "magical, religious, poetic, theological, philosophical, mystic, and scientific lore." The constant for these various rationalizations of human existence is not the historical development of the means of production but man's neurological structure, which has supplied a permanent basis that underlies changes and differences in environment (hence the title *Permanence and Change*).

Burke's "communism" has a distinctly un-Marxian foundation. In a section entitled "Towards a Philosophy of Being," Burke rejects Hegel and Marx, the promoters of a *historical* approach to human problems through philosophies of *becoming,* and turns "through symbolism to a philosophy of *being,* the Spinozistic concern with man *sub specie aeternitatis.*" The metaphor of progress he would replace by the metaphor of a *norm,* the basis of which is the notion that "at bottom the aims and genius of man have remained the same."

Although this view is heretical in its denial of the upward progress of the forms of social organization and its neglect of environmental factors, Burke continued to profess a commitment to Marxism and to think of criticism as a revolutionary activity. In *Attitudes toward History* (1937), he speaks of the critic as a "propagandist and craftsman" and of his own program as the integration of "technical criticism with social criticism (propaganda, the didactic)": "Since works of art, as 'equipment for living,' are formed with authoritative structures as their basis of reference, we also move automatically into the field of technical criticism (the 'tactics' of writers). And since the whole purpose of a 'revolutionary' critic is to contribute to a change in allegiance to the symbols of authority, we maintain our role as 'propagandist' by keeping this subject forever uppermost in our concerns." The transference of allegiance is from capitalistic and patriarchal symbols to communal and matriarchal ones. Since these identifications are bound up with traditional religious attitudes, as well as with psychological processes, Burke insists that "such matters as 'authority symbols,' 'identification,' 'acceptance and rejection,' 'rituals of purification and rebirth,' 'transcendence upward,' 'transcendence downward,' 'character-building by secular prayer,' 'the collective poems of socio-economic organization,' 'bureaucratization of the imaginative,' 'alienation,' and 'repossession' are at the very basis of both esthetic and moralistic strategy." Discussions of these terms — together with such others as *clusters, communion, imagery, perspective by incongruity, secular prayer, symbolic mergers,* and *transcendence* — are included in the "Dictionary of Pivotal Terms" with which Burke ends *Attitudes toward History.* At one point in the dictionary, under "Lexicological," Burke describes his intention to develop a "tripartite vocabulary" of interrelated religious, capitalist, and aesthetic elements.

Burke's interest in drama is everywhere evident. In the *Philosophy of Literary Form* (1941) he combines dramatic with religious and psychological terms to analyze verbal art as a "symbolic action," the hub of which is "ritual drama," the *ur*-form in any dramatic theory. For Burke, drama supplies a perspective for the analysis of social processes since its dynamic depends upon oppositions comparable to the dialectic of history. Glancing back at the earlier *Attitudes,* the reader can see that the rebirth ritual is a central feature of drama because it deals with a *conversion* of social attitudes involving a *transference* of allegiance from one *authority symbol* to another (capitalism to communism). At one point Burke describes the difference between symbolic drama and the drama of real living as a difference between "imaginary obstacles and real obstacles." But, he goes on to say, "the imaginary obstacles of symbolic drama must, to have the relevance necessary for the producing of effects upon audiences, reflect the real obstacles of living drama."

Having been reading with admiration Caroline Spurgeon's *Shakespeare's Imagery and What It Tells Us* (1935), Burke introduces the technique of analyzing image clusters in his discussion of Clifford Odets' *Golden Boy,* in which the complex of values associated with the *violin* is opposed to that surrounding the *prizefight.* Burke's use of dramatic techniques and image patterns — together with his concern for ritual and myth — places him closer to the emerging formalism and myth than to Marxist criticism. But in *Philosophy of Literary Form* Burke calls his approach to art " 'sociological,' in that it can usefully employ coördinates bearing upon social acts in general." He does not consider it sociological in the sense that "one treats a book as a kind of unmethodical report on a given subject matter."

Although Burke thought of his work as a contribution to the revolutionary Marxist movement, it is difficult to judge it in this light. His theory encouraged analytical criticism sensitive to the social values of literature. But the remoteness of most of his vocabulary from the language of politics tends to obscure its revolutionary implications. This indirection is a mark, not of duplicity in the critic, but of an awareness of the multiplicity of literary meanings. It is also, however, in keeping with Burke's conscious "strategy," for in *Attitudes toward History* he speaks of the critic's receiving guidance from his audience through "the kind of resistance and acceptance that his terms encounter." The critic, that is, will "convert" the language of politics to that of religion or psychology partly in the interest of "converting" his reader. This technique may have made Burke's ideas more palatable. But he may also have alienated readers by discussing revolutionary themes in the language of rebirth rituals rather than more directly. Aside from this problem, which cannot easily be settled, there remains the question of whether Burke's criticism, despite its intelligence and sensitivity, may not be self-defeating in distracting attention from literature to the developing theoretical apparatus of the critic, a mechanism that has come to have a kind of autonomy of its own. This possibility does not lessen his importance as a seminal theorist who has contributed to the vocabularies and influenced the practice of many other critics.

SELECTION FROM "PSYCHOLOGICAL AND MYTH CRITICISM"

Archetype criticism has often characterized the poet or artist as a hero who dies in his work but gains an aesthetic immortality through it. The idea of immortality through art is not new, as Shakespeare's sonnets remind us. It is one that has been particularly attractive to modern poets like Yeats, whose "Sailing to Byzantium" is a familiar example. Kenneth Burke's "Symbolic Action in a Poem by Keats," first published in an appendix to *A Grammar of Motives* (1945), is a sophisticated archetypal interpretation of a romantic poem. Burke analyzes the "Ode on a Grecian Urn" "dramatistically," in accordance with his scheme for interpreting "symbolic action," and finds the poem to be a "viaticum" or sacrament through which the artist achieves immortality as the transitory passions of the living man are transmuted into the fixed and concretized "Cold Pastoral" of art.

The process of immortality, thus conceived, is itself a metaphor, one among many of which the critic may avail himself in interpreting literature. And the sophisticated reader, it is to be assumed, assents to the criticism on these terms.

But a question remains. While most modern critics do not accept the idea of spiritual rebirth in an orthodox religious sense, their use of the language of the rite, without adequate qualification or translation into contemporary language, implies at least a *wish* to accept the religious formula on its own terms. As a result such criticism propagates, somewhat irresponsibly, a mystique of literature that has received all too much support during the past twenty years.

The appeal of this mystique is understandable. It provides a sanction for contemporary interest in the religious patterns of meaning in literature. It also claims a place for literature as a substitute sacrament. But it does so at great cost because it formulates the values of literature in terms that provide too cheaply the luxury of a religious commitment as a "pure" aesthetic gesture, without the responsibility of defending or living a religious conviction or the struggle to express this conviction as a twentieth century experience. For this reason it would seem desirable that myth critics, and literary critics in general, make use of a language and a frame of reference that would give their work meaning in contemporary terms, whether religious or secular.

Most myth and archetype critics have failed to do so. In some cases their avoidance of a reference to contemporary experience may be the result of a historicist desire to treat a work in relation to the milieu of its composition. But it is often difficult to determine the extent to which the critic's treatment is partisan or disinterested.

SELECTION FROM "PSYCHOLOGICAL AND MYTH CRITICISM"

Some eclectic critics have combined Freudian and Jungian ideas, or occasionally psychological concepts and those of other disciplines. Kenneth Burke, whose developing dramatistic theory has absorbed terms and concepts from various sources, has considered the possibility of synthesizing Freudian and Marxist theory.

In *Permanence and Change* (1935), Burke describes psychoanalysis as a "secular conversion" which "effects its cures by providing a new perspective that dissolves the system of pieties lying at the root of the patient's sorrows or bewilderments." He objects, however, to its reductiveness, calling it a "*conversion downwards* of the patient's distress by means of an unfit, incongruous terminology," in which his problems are explained as "autoeroticism, homosexuality, sadism, masochism, incest, and exhibitionism." Although Burke believes that any set of motives is translatable into another and that "Freudianism could 'explain' Marxists psychologically and that Marxism could 'explain' Freudians sociologically," he makes a qualitative distinction between the two systems when he calls one, the Freudian, "impious" and the other a "humanistic and poetic rationalization." And when, in his conclusion, he speaks of poetic metaphor as a guide to radical social changes, he is thinking of the communist rationalization as the inspiration of the society of the future.

The Philosophy of Literary Form (1941) treats psychoanalysis more sympathetically. In "Twelve Propositions on the Relation between Economics and Psychology" Burke notes that both Freudianism and Marxism are interested in shifts in identity or in allegiance to authority symbols and that they both work toward this end dramatistically: "Marx's concept of the 'classless' state following a maximum intensification of class conflict is precisely in line with the Aristotelian recipe for the process of dramatic 'catharsis.' The shock value of Freudian analysis exemplified the same process in tiny 'closet dramas' of private life (the facing and burning out of conflict)." The approach is " 'diagnostic' in that it invites us to note the psychological and material factors *furthering* communication (the coöperative act)."

The essay most concerned with the relation of psychology to literature is "Freud and the Analysis of Poetry," in which Burke defines his subject as "the bearing of Freud's theories upon literary criticism." While acknowledging Freud's function as a pioneer and liberator in revealing a new dimension of human motives, hitherto denied recognition, Burke finds certain limitations in his theory and insists that a distinction must be observed between neurotic and poetic acts. As a correction of the Freudian tendency to interpret literature as wish fulfillment and to regard art as self-expression, Burke considers the motive of communication to be the basic category of literary criticism.

Accordingly, in considering the usefulness of Freudian ideas to the three modes of analysis introduced in *The Philosophy of Literary Form* (dream, prayer, and chart), Burke finds them most illuminating when the work is considered as dream, in terms of its unconscious factors. Here Freud's concepts of "condensation" and "displacement" are invaluable to the critic. But in the analysis of "prayer" (the communicative function) and of "chart" ("the realistic sizing-up of situations that is sometimes explicit, sometimes implicit, in poetic strategies") Freud provides very little assistance.

What is needed is an extension of Freud's theory in dramatistic terms that would point up the communicative and social functions of literature. Such a development would permit the reconciliation of Freudianism and Marxism: "Both Freudians and Marxists are wrong in so far as they cannot put their theories together, by an over-all theory of drama itself (as they should be able to do, since Freud gives us the material of the closet drama, and Marx the material of the problem play, the one treated in terms of personal conflicts, the other in terms of public conflicts)." To make Freud more useful to the critic, a bridge is needed from the familial to the cultural implications of the theory, and for Burke the bridge would be art as symbolic action in a community.

Louis Fraiberg, in *Psychoanalysis and American Literary Criticism* (1960), believes Burke deluded in thinking that the two systems of Freud and Marx can be integrated. Fraiberg contends that the idea of the conversion of terms is the weakest feature of Burke's argument because it denies the status of psychoanalysis as a science grounded in experience. By regarding psychoanalysis as merely a set of words, interchangeable with any other, phenomena are "converted downward" into terms, and any contact between Burke's psychological criticism and experience is severed.

Fraiberg's objection raises a very important question about Burke's idea of the function of language and of literary criticism. If all sets of terms are simply interchangeable and without verifiable reference to reality, how can criticism relate literature to experience and affect social attitudes, as Burke wishes it to do?

Insufficient light is thrown upon this question by *A Grammar of Motives* (1945), in which Burke develops further his theory of symbolic action by introducing the five "key terms" of dramatism through which literature and human behavior can be analyzed: *Act, Scene, Agent, Agency, Purpose.* These represent necessary categories of thought found to be "equally present in systematically elaborated metaphysical structures, in legal judgments, in poetry and fiction, in political and scientific works, in news and in bits of gossip offered at random."

Although any set of terms is translatable into another, the terms for motives will inevitably be ambiguous because of the enigmatic nature of the universe. This is a pleasing thought to Burke, who considers it his task to "study and clarify the *resources* of ambiguity" and to deal in many kinds of transformation since all terms are formally interrelated as "attributes of a common ground or substance": "At every point where the field covered by any one of these terms overlaps upon the field covered by any other, there is an alchemic opportunity, whereby we can put one philosophy or doctrine of motivation into the alembic, make the appropriate passes, and take out another." Burke thinks of his method as necessarily dialectical and metaphysical (defining dialectics as "the employment of the possibilities of linguistic transformation"): "Our speculations as we interpret them should show that the subject of motivation is a philosophic one, not ultimately to be solved in terms of empirical science."

Burke considers these transformations not as "illusions" but as "citable realities." Although positivists might classify all metaphysics, literature, political thought, and personal statements as nonsense, "these words of nonsense would," Burke argues, "be real works, involving real tactics, having real demonstrable relationships, and demonstrably affecting relationships." Burke apparently is assuming that the terms of his analysis have reference to a *reality* identified with whatever system or strategy he may be considering. Later, however, following a discussion of Kant under "Agent in General," Burke remarks that the test of a philosopher is what he can say about nothing and hastens to add that his own five terms are "all about nothing, since they designate not this scene, or that agent, etc. but scene, agent, etc. in general."

Burke may not himself know and it is not possible for the reader to determine to what extent he believes that language can have reference to reality and to what extent he believes that he must assume a verbal universe in which knowledge is purely metaphysical. He concludes that the attitude embodied in his method is one of "linguistic skepticism," in keeping with "linguistic appreciation" since "an attitude of methodical quizzicality towards language may best equip us to perceive the full scope of its resourcefulness."

But some of Burke's ideas are inconsistent with an attitude of skepticism: Self, which is "under the sign of Agent . . . has the same universalized quality [as transcendental idealism], making it a super-self or non-self, that we noticed in the mystic paradox whereby absolute purpose becomes transformed into necessity." He illustrates the idea by the anonymous wanderer in the poems of Shelley: "The kind of super person thus envisaged *beyond* language but *through* language may be *generically* human rather than *individually* human insofar as language is a *collective* product and the capacity of complex symbolic action is distinctive of the human race. Hence the Self we encounter at the outer limits of language would be a *transcendent* Self, an individual 'collectively redeemed' by being apprehended through a medium itself essentially collective."

The idea of a generalized or "universalized" character is reasonable, in view of the collective nature of language and the necessarily abstract nature of both language and art. But when Burke speaks of a capitalized "*transcendent* Self" to be encountered at the "outer limits of language," it sounds as though he is very close to the myth critic's view of art as an object to be transcended rather than as a bond to the world of experience in which the reader lives and has his being.

A Grammar of Motives is the volume to which Burke's analysis of Keats's "Ode on a Grecian Urn" as a rebirth archetype is appended. Burke had commented in *The Philosophy of Literary Form* on the profusion of rebirth rituals in the literature of transitional eras, and his concern for them has a social emphasis, since he is interested in promoting a conversion from patriarchal-competitive to matriarchal-cooperative values. His discussion of Keats's poem and of Shelley's wanderer, however, resists containment by a social and experiential view of literature. Although he has depended heavily on Freud for his ideas and terminology, as his logology has developed he has left behind the empirical attitude of psychoanalysis, and his conception of the function of poetic language is closer to that of the Jungian archetype critic than to that of either the Marxist or Freudian critic.

Rewarding as much of Burke's criticism is, he is so involved in the terminological system he has created that it is difficult to ascertain what his commitment is or how his criticism is grounded in common experience. Not that the critic need establish any simple one-to-one relationship between the work and "reality." But literature, like all art, is concerned with the evocation and evaluation of experience. Critics tend to discuss the values of literature (they can be defined variously) from a selective point of view that represents their own experiential sense of reality. To this extent, at least, criticism has an empirical basis. Burke, however, is less concerned with the individuality of a work and its evaluation of experience than with its resources for the maintenance and development of his theoretical system, which despite his distrust of technology can perhaps best be thought of as a kind of autonomous machine, especially remarkable for the interchangeability of its parts.

◇◇

WALTER SUTTON was born in Milwaukee, Wisconsin, in 1916. He teaches American literature and literary criticism at Syracuse University, where he has been since 1948. He is the editor (with Richard Foster and Vivian Sutton) of two excellent anthologies of literary criticism and of the *Twentieth Century Views* collection on Ezra Pound, and the author of *The Western Book Trade* and *Modern American Criticism.*

The book from which these excerpts come is one of the few and certainly one of the best critical surveys of modern American literary criticism. No isolated selections can possibly do justice to the exciting and complex interpretation of modern criticism which Mr. Sutton develops in his book. What I have tried to suggest by means of these three selections are some of the ways in which Burke can be treated in systematic studies of modern criticism. Mr. Sutton's remarks on Burke, like his book as a whole, are characterized by sanity, astuteness of observation and judgment, and accuracy of placement in a large critical and intellectual context. Finally, Mr. Sutton is, I believe, only the second person to undertake an extended treatment of Burke as a major modern (or modern American) critic.

◇◇

2 *Tragedy as the Representative Anecdote*

BY William H. Rueckert

PROBABLY nowhere in Burke are all of these ideas and methods so clearly seen and brilliantly applied as in the theories of tragedy and catharsis developed since the early forties. All of Burke's thinking about literature as poetic, grammatical, rhetorical, and ethical-personal verbal action culminates in the theories of tragedy and catharsis and the method developed to apply them. This is so because Burke considers tragedy the "ideal" or "perfect" poetic verbal act, the paradigmatic form; he makes tragedy the "essence" of poetry and approaches "poetics" in terms of tragedy. His procedure is to isolate the essential characteristics of tragedy and then, having established the "paradigm" or "pure" form, to look at other poetic verbal acts in terms of or under the aegis of tragedy and to find in other poetic verbal acts what he found in tragedy. The essence of tragedy, Burke says, is the cathartic function which it performs, the purging of the audience's bodily, personal, civic, and religious irresolutions. By this route, Burke goes from poetry to drama to tragedy to catharsis (the term around which the dramatistic theory of literature is built) and back to poetry. Catharsis is also one of the key terms around which his whole system is built, for though it belongs to the poetry-drama-tragedy cluster, it also belongs to the order-cluster discussed in Chapter IV [of *Kenneth Burke and the Drama of Human Relations*]. This means that in any discussion of catharsis Burke will logologically "radiate out" and consider the negative, victimage, mortification, hierarchy, redemption, and categorical guilt. By his logic, all are implicit in the term "catharsis" and, by implication, in the terms "poetry," "drama," and "tragedy," since catharsis links the two clusters.

EDITOR'S NOTE: Reprinted from *Kenneth Burke and the Drama of Human Relations* (Minneapolis: University of Minnesota Press, 1963), pp. 208–226,

A great lover of paradigms, of "pure" or "ideal" forms arrived at through dialectical ascent to ever higher levels of abstraction, and an equally great lover of the paradigmatic embodiment of the "pure" or "ideal" form — the "representative anecdote," the archetypal myth, the perfect imitation of the pure essence — Burke attempts to read into (or is it out of?) tragedy a whole poetics as well as a whole system. One might say that tragedy is Burke's representative anecdote, if one remembers that he selects the *Oresteia* as the ideal tragedy and that this trilogy, in spite of the many differences, is similar in many respects to Dante's *Divine Comedy* in so far as the progression in both is from "hell" through "purgatory" to "heaven." Both follow the purgative-redemptive form discussed in Chapter III and both embody the paradigm of catharsis, though one is called a tragedy and the other a comedy. "The paradigm of catharsis," Burke says, "must contain ideas and images for at least these major elements: unclean, clean, cleansing, cleanser (personal or impersonal), cleansed." As Burke points out, "the cleansing process" does not always "go simply from unclean to cleansed, since the cleanser in some way takes over the uncleanness, which in turn must be disposed of" (*The Kenyon Review*, XXI,367). Like the two works mentioned above, the Burkean drama of human relations and the "myth" he selects to illustrate the drama — the Eden-Christ "myth" — also embody the paradigm of catharsis. If one takes this paradigm as Burke describes it, one can move effortlessly back and forth from it to the seven moments in the Burkean drama: one might be "unclean" because of categorical guilt, the hierarchic psychosis, or the violation of any moral negative; one gets clean through mortification or victimage of some kind, or the clean person may be used as sacrificial victim; cleansing is got by purgation (catharsis) or mortification; the cleanser may be either a sacrificial victim or various acts of mortification; the cleansed is the redeemed person. In other words, all those things discussed in Chapter IV in relation to the order-cluster and the drama of human relations figure in any discussion of catharsis and tragedy. The better one knows Burke the more obvious it becomes that his theory of tragedy and catharsis, ostensibly a theory of poetry — a poetics, as he calls it — is really a theory of human relations as a moral drama in which the "fall" is inevitable and the driving need purgative-redemptive. Unclean, clean, cleansing, cleanser, cleansed; hierarchy, categorical guilt, negative, victimage, mortification, catharsis, redemption; symbols, form, symbolic action, symbol systems: over these terms and their relationships Burke has brooded all his life. In the poetry, drama, tragedy, catharsis, drama of human relations cluster Burke achieves a masterful synthesis in which key concepts from every phase of his long and productive career come together to form a final, coherent system.

Within the framework of his dramatistic theory of literature Burke develops his theories of tragedy and catharsis. This means that tragedy will be defined as the imitation of some essence and will be characterized by identifications (images), oppositions (an agon, or its analogue), progressions (plot, or its analogue), and transformations (dialectic, or its analogue). According to Burke, tragedy is the imitation (or exploitation) of the perfect essence of a tension (or psychosis) in dramatic form where the action (or "plot") of the play as a whole follows, and the tragic protagonist undergoes the tragic rhythm (the progression from action through suffering to knowledge and redemption); the tragic imitation having as its purpose the purging and resolving of the audience's bodily, personal, civic, and religious irresolutions (or tensions). This brief definition is a concocted one because, though Burke has written more about tragedy than any other form, he has never bothered to write a formal definition. I mention this because there is a certain amount of confusion as to exactly what Burke means by a number of crucial terms. Take tension, for example: in writing about tragedy, Burke speaks most often about the particular tension which a given tragedy imitates; but, as is his practice, he usually uses tension in combination with a number of other terms, all of which seem to be synonyms: the most important of these are psychosis, pollution, civic disorders, civic pollutions, disorders within the polis, civic guilt, class conflicts, temporal tensions, and mysteries. The more one studies these terms the more apparent it becomes that by tension Burke means any kind of hierarchic psychosis. As I pointed out, the hierarchic psychosis is produced by the hierarchic motive and causes all kinds of "categorical guilt." So by tension, Burke seems to mean this cluster of hierarchic terms; and in his remarks on tragedy, he seems to suggest that this is what tragic playwrights imitate. There is also a certain amount of confusion as to what Burke means by imitate, for again he uses this term in combination with a number of others, all of which seem to be synonyms. The two most frequently used are symbolize and exploit; the second is probably the most revealing for Burke suggests that tragic playwrights deliberately exploit a tension through complex symbolic manipulations for cathartic purposes. That is, they use (or exploit) the resources of the tension (the perfect essence of which they have come to know either through intensive or extensive experience and study) as well as the resources of their medium (symbolic action) in order deliberately to contrive a cathartic drama which releases the specific civic tensions, as well as various other bodily, personal, and religious tensions which the playwrights have exploited.

Burke establishes as a pre-existing and permanent condition what he calls the extra-aesthetic tensions which a tragedy imitates; the "civic 'pollution' " which tragedies "are designed to ritually cleanse" is "intrinsic to the nature of the state" (*Poetics,**225).). "A state of social tension," Burke says, "just *is*" (*Poetics,*273); it is "static and ineradicable to human societies in the large" (*Poetics,*226) and is like a "stagnant miasmatic" swamp, "trackless" and "aimless" (*Poetics,*273). Tragedy, or any poetic verbal act, does not, could not, bring either permanent relief or permanently remove the ineradicable cause of the tensions, but it can bring temporary relief – to use Burke's own metaphor – by leading one out of the miasmatic swamp for a while. According to Burke, tragedies are purgative journeys which lead one "*from* there [the swamp], *through* here [the work], *to* that place yonder [the state beyond catharsis]" (*Poetics,*226). It is well to remember that a good deal – most of – what Burke writes about poetry starts from this belief in the pre-existing and permanent state of trackless, aimless, miasmatic tension-pollution-guilt which is man's "natural" condition as symbol-user; since all men are in this state most of the time, purgation is a permanent need which can be partly satisfied through symbolic action.

When Burke says that tragedy imitates and exploits the perfect essence of a tension or psychosis he means two things: that every tension has a particular character or personality which constitutes its essential nature; and that there exists in every tension the entelechial possibility of perfect actualization. Tragedy, then, imitates not just the essence of a tension, but the perfect essence, which is Burke's way of saying that tragedy deals with "excessive engrossment," the conditions under which the potential completely actualizes itself. Burke says, for example, that Shakespeare's *Othello* imitates the perfect essence of the "possession" or "ownership" tension. This particular tension is a "triune" one, having as its essential characteristics the three abstract principles of possession: the possessor, possession and what is possessed, and estrangement or threat of loss. The essence of the tension is a paradoxical dialectic; the perfect essence of the tension is a tragic dialectic in which the threat of loss inherent in any ownership situation actualizes itself and becomes partial or total estrangement. Usually it is the latter, for the excessive engrossment, the attempt at absolute possession, leads to the opposite reflexive state of absolute loneliness. Furthermore, the route from absolute possession to absolute loneliness is littered

* *Poetics* refers to an early unpublished version of *A Symbolic of Motives.*

with the victims of the possessor's excessive engrossment; and by the time the possessor has traveled that route, he has himself become the guilt-laden victim of his own excessive engrossment.

It is this tragic dialectic of the possession tension which Shakespeare imitates in *Othello.* The tension, one of Burke's timeless universal clusters that just is, can obviously manifest itself in many ways; in as many ways, in fact, as one can possess a person, place, idea, thing, or means; and in as many ways as there are motives for ownership. In literature the following works imitate some particular manifestation of this always potentially tragic tension, though not all are tragedies and some are not even tragic: *Antigone, The Jew of Malta, Macbeth, Manfred,* Goethe's *Faust, The Spoils of Poynton, 1984,* and *All the King's Men.* The particular manifestation of the tension which Shakespeare imitates and exploits in *Othello* is "the disequilibrium of monogamistic [romantic] love," or, as Burke variously describes it in his essay on *Othello*: "property in human affections"; "sexual love as property and ennoblement"; "the analogue, in the realm of human affinity," to "the enclosure acts, whereby the common lands were made private"; "an act of spiritual enclosure," whereby "love, universal love," is "made private"; and sexual and spiritual ownership, as they are fused in romantic love and marriage. (*The Hudson Review*,IV,166–170.) Here, then, is the particular tension which Shakespeare imitates and exploits. Whatever the actual steps in the creative process, Burke says that ideally the dramatic poet imitates by first "translating" the tension into progressive form, which in a play would be "plot" or "action"; and then by "translating" the tension into the "equivalent terms of personality" by "dramatic dissociation into interrelated roles." Characters, or, as Burke likes to call them, "character recipes," are contrived or built "in accord with the demands of the action"; and the "logic of the action as a whole" is contrived or built in accord with the demands of the tension being imitated; and the play as a whole is contrived or built in accord with the demands of the specific purpose of tragedy, which is to release or purge tensions through symbolic action.

Given the tension and its dialectic, a particular kind of plot progression immediately suggests itself, for the initial and terminal events (possession, estrangement) are themselves part of the triune tension. The specific details of the "intrigue" (another of Burke's words for plot) will connect these two principal events by leading up to and away from the act of possession; from the act through the various complications that result from any attempt at absolute possession (the excessive engrossment necessary for tragedy); to the estrangement (psychic and physical, and usually total) which is the tragic consequence of the excessive engrossment. Often the plot will end here (with total aloneness), but more often, for cathartic purposes, the intrigue will lead away from this state toward some unifying event. The translation of the tension into narrative terms gives the imitation its "rational" structure or form; but, Burke says, all tragedies have a double structure, for "there is a kind of ritualistic form lurking behind" the "intrigue"; "the mythic or ritual pattern (with the work as a viaticum for guiding us through a dark and dangerous passage) lurks behind the 'rational' intrigue." Aside from the rational structure which presents "the natural development in terms of probability and necessity," there is a mythic or ritual structure which follows the form of a cathartic journey. (*The Hudson Review*,IV,175–176). This cathartic journey is actually the tragic rhythm or progression which the play as a whole follows, the progression from initial act through suffering to knowledge and redemption. Sometimes Burke calls this mythic or ritual structure a "persecutional" form because the playwright persecutes the audience in order that it may be purged; due to the marvelous illusions of art and the wonderful skill of the playwright, the audience re-enacts the persecutional and purgative "ritual of riddance."

The mythic or ritual structure is as much a part of the imitation as the rational intrigue for both are ways of translating the tension into progressive form; the mythic pattern is not, Burke says, what is being imitated, but a method of imitation – one of the playwright's resources – and one of the principal means of effecting the catharsis that is the purpose of the play. Considered as a "viaticum" the first part of a tragedy is the "way in"; "it states the primary conditions in terms of which the journey is to be localized or specified this time." And "though the ritual must always follow the same general succession of stages regardless of the intrigue, this course is repeated each time in the details proper to a particular intrigue." This, then, is what gives the play its double structure. In terms of the cathartic journey, the first part of the play is really preparation for that journey; the next part, within the journey metaphor, is "the definite pushing-off from shore" and the certainty of being "under way" on a particular journey. Depending upon the play and the specific rational intrigue, one can be "under way" for varying lengths of time; eventually, however, one has to arrive at "the withinness-of-withinness," "the principle of internality" where, quoting Plato, Burke says "there abides the very being with which true knowledge is concerned; the colorless, formless, intangible essence, visible only to mind, the pilot of the soul." In less abstract terms, one arrives at knowledge of the perfect essence of the tension being imitated. In *Othello* this is the moment of reversal, the peripety, when absolute possession becomes estrangement. "From this point on," wherever it happens to occur in the play, "we are returning. We shall get back to the starting point, though with a difference" for "there is presumably to be some kind of splitting, a 'separating out.' Something is to be dropped away, something retained, the whole [journey] thereby becoming a purification of a sort." The last part of the play would complete the journey and the "separating out" process. "All told, the rite is complete when one has become willing to abandon the figures who vicariously represent his own tension," and when the passion (persecution and suffering) has been transformed into an assertion. (*The Hudson Review*,IV,176–178.) In *Othello*, for example, the passion is transformed into an assertion when Othello, after coming to knowledge, reaffirms the values he denied in murdering Desdemona, and redeems himself (and those values) by sacrificial suicide. The final event in the rational intrigue both completes the cathartic journey (mythic structure) and resolves the tension by completing it. The tragic dialectic inherent in any attempt at absolute possession has been worked out when we arrive at Othello's absolute estrangement, epitomized in his reflexive act of suicide.

When Burke says that the characters or "character recipes" are built in accord with the demands of the logic of the action as a whole, the specific tension being imitated, and the cathartic purpose of the play, he means that, like the plot and mythic structure, they are methods of imitation; that each character is best analyzed as a symbolic construct, a cluster of terms circling round a name, a mass of identifications concocted by the playwright "for producing a desired result." Dialectic, Burke says, is ideas in action; but drama is people in action: to make a play, a poet must do more than translate the tension into progressive form (plot and mythic structure); he must also translate the tension into the "equivalent terms of personality" by "dramatic dissociation into interrelated roles." The "tragic trinity of ownership," particularized in *Othello* in terms of "the disequilibrium of monogamistic love," requires at least three principal interrelated characters to symbolize the possessor (including the act of possession), what is possessed, and estrangement. The three parts of the "triune tension" or psychosis are represented in the play by the following major character recipes: Othello, Desdemona, and Iago. The minor characters also represent some "fragment of the tension" translated into the equivalent terms of personality; these Burke likes to call satellite characters because usually they tend to group around one or another of the three major characters. Aside from their function of "reflecting" some fragment of the tension, the minor characters also perform valuable and necessary plot or intrigue functions in so far as they "help the three major persons dramatically communicate with one another." Actually, then, all of the characters, no matter what their plot function, are symbolic of some part of the tension which is the generating subject of the imitation. (*The Hudson Review*,IV,180.)

In translating the tension into the equivalent terms of personality the playwright must invent a set of major and minor characters who can work out the perfect essence of the tension dramatically, "*in action or through action*" (*The Hudson Review*,IV,187). What Burke means here is that in drama, anyway, the poet is intent upon "making a play, not people" (*The Hudson Review*,IV,187); his problem as a dramatist is to "break down the psychosis" being imitated "into a usable spectrum of differentiated roles," to split it into as many "voices" as are "needed to provide a sufficient range of 'analogies' (with the over-all tension being variously represented in each of them)" (*The Hudson Review*, IV,179). Once he has done this, the poet then translates the "roles" or "voices" into actions, for in drama, it is the agent-act ratio that must be exploited. Burke insists upon the fact that the demands of the tragic imitation control the invention and dramatic presentation of the characters, and that the sense we often have in Shakespeare's plays of "well-rounded" living characters is purely illusory. "The stupidest and crudest person who ever lived," Burke says, "is richer in motivation than all of Shakespeare's characters put together – and it would be either a stupidity or a sacrilege to say otherwise. It is as an artist, not as God, that he invents 'characters.' And to see him [or any other playwright] fully as an artist, we must not too fully adopt the Coleridgean view of art as the 'dim analogue of creation.'" (*The Hudson Review*,IV,187–188.) Drama requires characters in action; a particular play imitating some tension requires certain specific actions; characters are invented to contribute the needed action, each one being given only those "traits that suit [him] for the action needed of [him]" (*The Hudson Review*,IV,179).

Someone once said that much of the play's power comes from the audience's realization that without Iago Othello and Desdemona could enjoy the continuous achieved perfection of romantic love. The power, in other words, comes from the terrible sense of what might have been. The implication, of course, is that the threat is external and that left alone they would have lived "beyond evil." Their destruction did not come from within but from without, from evil which, in the person of Iago, is always bent on destroying good. According to Burke, much of the play's power comes from the exact opposite of this, from the fact that the destruction is internally caused: with or without Iago, the continuous achieved perfection of romantic love is impossible. The tension which the play imitates is the perfect essence of the "disequilibrium of monogamistic [or romantic] love"; this disequilibrium exists with or without Iago as cause: it just is. Given the tragic protagonist's excessive engrossment in monogamistic love – in this particular case an attempt at absolute or perfect possession – the destructive motives (suspicion, threat of loss, estrangement) arise from within and are but externalized or symbolized in Iago. Iago is to be treated as one of the character recipes invented by Shakespeare to perform some of the actions needed in the tragic imitation of the tension. As such, he functions rather than is, and to treat him as a real character rather than a symbol is, Burke says, either a "stupidity or a sacrilege." One of Iago's more obvious functions is to "goad" or "torture" the plot forward, "for the audience's villainous entertainment and filthy purgation" (*The Hudson Review*,IV,170). Another function, of course, is to act as the personal embodiment of the estrangement part of the tension. And the third function is to be one of the three principal "victims" or sacrificial agents, the other two being Desdemona and Othello. As *katharma,* he performs a major cathartic function; he is from the beginning the unclean or polluted agent to whom the audience's own pollutions can be symbolically transferred and thence carried away. As starkly as Burke intends it, Iago performs a sewer-like function: as *katharma,* he represents "that which is thrown away in cleansing . . . the off-scourings, refuse"; as the play proceeds, the audience adds to the refuse pile and at the end of the play that pile, in the person of Iago, is taken away, by the proper authorities, to be disposed of in an appropriate place and way (*The Hudson Review*,IV,166).

In general terms, Desdemona symbolizes the private property in which Othello over-invests, to the point of becoming "himself possessed by his very engrossment" in the idea of "single-mine-own-ness" (*The Hudson Review*,IV,167). Iago symbolizes the "result" of such over-investment; and Othello symbolizes the single-mine-own-ness of possession itself. The act of possession is the initiating act: it begins the tragic rhythm which, Burke says, the tragic protagonist must undergo and the play must follow. In the equivalent terms of personality used in the play, the act is the love marriage between Othello and Desdemona. To possess in the way and for the reasons that Othello marries Desdemona is to involve oneself in the tragic tension and to set the tragic rhythm moving towards its terrible reflexive culmination. This requires of Othello an absolute commitment to Desdemona, a total spiritual and sexual investment in her, and the elimination of even the possibility of such a commitment and such an investment for either of them in anyone else. This is what Burke means when he says the play deals with an "act of spiritual enclosure" where "love, universal love" has "been made private." According to Burke, this is a form of pride (excess, *hubris*), an almost unique human motive, "natural" to man, who, following the tendency towards abstraction inherent in language, is always trying to make himself and others over in the image of his distinctive trait. Pride — Ethan Brand's unpardonable sin — is essentially reflexive; but no tragic protagonist ever seems to realize or really believe this and must learn it — always too late — through suffering the terrible consequences of his ignorance or disbelief. Though the consequences vary, they always involve at least two and usually all three kinds of victimage, and the reduction to absolute loneliness of the tragic protagonist — the tragic irony of achieving the opposite of what is intended. In tragedy, it is always knowledge that transforms the passionate suffering into an assertion, the knowledge having been induced by the suffering and having come at the very nadir of the reductive pattern where absolute loneliness (the self confronting the guilt-ridden self) approaches paralysis and nothingness. The knowledge, which is usually factual, moral, and philosophical, transforms the self-corroding passionate suffering into an assertion because it enables the tragic protagonist to perform a new act which is in some way redemptive, both for himself and the social hierarchy of which he is a part.

Great Pride — excessive engrossment — constitutes the tragic flaw, and always involves ignorance, for pride is a kind of blindness. Tragedy translates into human terms the terrible consequences of pride by dramatizing an excessive engrossment in what all men are to varying degrees engrossed: themselves, various kinds of single-mine-own-ness. This is why all tragic protagonists move from ignorance to knowledge and why tragedies follow the mythic structure. Although not all men are capable of acts of great pride, the temptation is inherent in all social structures in the form of the hierarchic motive, and in fact is embedded in language itself. Tragedy dramatizes this motive in its pure form; it dramatizes the essence of tension itself, for all tensions result directly or indirectly from the hierarchic motive, itself simultaneously a good and a goad. Considered abstractly, great pride is little more than an idea; but translated into and dramatized in tragic terms, it becomes the basis for a powerful, moving experience, capable of arousing great pity and fear, and capable, finally, of effecting a catharsis more thorough and profound than can be brought about by any other kind of poetic symbolic action. For this reason, tragedy is one of the most vital and useful of poetic symbolic acts: tragedy presents over and over again the very essence of the drama of human relations, entertaining, edifying, and purging — all at the same time. Tragedy entertains through the beauty of its form; that form takes the spectator on a purgative journey; and the purgative journey has a number of epiphanal moments in it when, like the protagonist, who is caught in the rhythm of his own tragedy, the spectator sees into himself, the drama of his own life, and the larger drama of human relations.

Tragedy both imitates a specific tension and exploits all kinds of tensions in order to effect as complete a catharsis as possible. "To be complete," Burke says, "catharsis must involve the entire realm of privacy, along with personal and social relationships" (*Poetics*,76). What Burke means here is that through analogical imagery the tragic playwright radiates out until he has identified the specific tension with bodily, personal, familial, and religious tensions; with *other* social tensions; and with both "nature" and "supernature." Burke calls this process "cosmologizing" or "universalizing" and points out that from this process comes the hierarchic or allusive structure found in all tragedies (*The Sewanee Review*,LX,380). Certain workings of this process are obvious and need not be discussed here at any length, for they represent standard poetic "tactics" for giving a work scope and depth; sometimes, of course, they are more than just poetic tactics for they are manifestations of a profound belief in some "underlying principle of oneness" in the universe as a whole. I refer, of course, to the use of "nature" and "supernature" as points of reference, to such things as the storm in Act III of *King Lear,* the plague and blighted crops in *Oedipus Rex,* the apotheosis of Oedipus in *Oedipus at Colonus,* the Ghost in *Hamlet,* the witches in *Macbeth,* and the many signs of supernatural displeasure in the *Oresteia* as a whole. Nature and supernature represent the two extreme limits of the hierarchy; the implication of their use, whether real or illusory, is that any disorders within the social hierarchy have "cosmological" consequences and that punishment will be visited upon the wrongdoer, not only by society and the agent himself, but by nature and the forces of supernature. Again, whether real or just poetic tactics, such cosmologizing stresses the universal consequences of individual acts of pride and, with a vengeance, man's personal responsibility for such actions. Both kinds of stress have much to do with the quantity and quality of pity, fear, and pride, which, Burke says, tragedy arouses and purges.

One of the central ideas in Burke's theory of tragedy is that the tragic play persecutes the audience in order that it may be purged; that the tragic play, through imitation, actually arouses various tensions in the audience, individually and collectively, *in order* to release them. The persecution is in part accomplished by the two forms of cosmologizing discussed above, both of which create the illusion that the vastness of nature on the one hand and the mysteries of the supernatural on the other are *actively* involved in the persecution, either because they are affected by the initiating act or because they actually administer part of the punishment. Actually, these two forms indicate the main intent of cosmologizing, which is to involve the whole in the actions of the part, to achieve what Burke calls a "*tremendous thoroughness*" (*Poetics*,284). Aside from the use of nature and supernature as points of reference, the tragic playwright also uses the bodily, personal, familial, religious, and social as points of reference; that is, he persecutes by showing how one kind of social disorder or tension spreads, like a contagious and sometimes fatal disease, until it has infected the whole person, physically as well as psychically, and affected his personal, familial, social, and religious relationships; and spreads until it has infected the other characters in the play in the same way; and spreads, finally, outward, until it has symbolically infected the whole audience and everyone is in his "very essence persecuted." There are, for example, what Burke calls the "Great Persecutional Words," the great "civic," or "social," or "moral," or "philosophic" abstractions (*Poetics*,283–284; *The Sewanee Review*,LX,380). Among the most important of these are Law, Right, Fate, Justice, Necessity, Vengeance, and Ruin. These constitute the "civic" order of terms and belong to what Burke elsewhere calls the great moral negatives, the thou-shalt-nots which man as symbol-using animal "adds to nature." They belong to the "civic" order of terms because they are "abstractions" rather than metaphysical realities. Burke's point is that through identification with the great persecutional words the specifically human concerns with which the tragedy deals are "heroically transmogrified," the result being a kind of "terrifying thoroughness" of conviction that the moral "proprieties" will be observed: "justice" will be done, punishment will be meted out for the act of pride, vengeance will be exacted, and the law will triumph (*Poetics*, 283–284). All the great persecutional words contain this element of categorical expectancy about the inevitability of punishment and persecution for any kind of wrongdoing; they suggest that a certain kind of act will initiate the tragic rhythm which, once underway, has the irreversible finality of the formal progression in a completed poetic act.

An act of great pride, the specifically human action which initiates the tragic rhythm, and the whole of the tragic rhythm itself, seems naturally to arouse what Burke calls the specifically "personal emotions as such": pity, fear, anger, and the like. That is, the tragic act, the tragic rhythm, and tragedy are "ideal" cathartics; by means of them the poet can effect the most thorough purgation; the more thorough the purge, the greater, Burke says, the healing or regenerating effect for the audience individually and collectively; the greater the regenerative effect, the better able is literature to fulfill one of its primary functions, which is to fight individual and social "illness" by means of symbolic purges. One of literature's primary purposes is to function as an instrument of individual and social "health." "Pollution," Burke says, is "the subject of catharsis"; and catharsis is the subject of poetry (*The Hudson Review*,IV,198). In tragedy, pollution – tensions, irresolutions, psychoses, guilt, discord – is exploited for cathartic purposes. All manner of "personal" tensions are exploited in the tragic imitation to heighten the cathartic effect. The members of the audience make a direct personal identification with these tensions and react to them in the most profound personal way; their reactions are *self*-directed, even though it is Hamlet, Oedipus, and Othello whom they pity and fear. Burke's point seems to be that each of these characters is really a symbolic mirror in which each member of the audience sees some part of himself, some motive by which he has been goaded, some actual or potential action or passion. The external drama then becomes an intense internal and personal one for each member of the audience; this is what Burke means when he says that each member of the audience is in "his essence" persecuted by the tragic imitation.

Tragedy always has a double allusive or hierarchic structure and it persecutes the audience by means of outward and inward progressions: outward from the social tension to the vastness of nature and the mystery of supernature; and inward from the social tension to the familial to the personal to the private until, by means of the double progression, everything has been effected by the single cause and until, for each member of the audience, all possible relationships have been involved and he is persecuted from all sides. The last stage of the inward persecutional progression is reached when the "entire realm of privacy" has been involved (*Poetics*,76). By "private" or "privacy" Burke means the bodily, including the cells and the biological functions. More specifically, he means the privy parts – the "three 'cloacally' interconnected" parts and their functions (*The Kenyon Review*,XXI,356). These he calls the Demonic Trinity; in the *Poetics* he discusses their "literary" function in a long chapter called "The Thinking of the Body."

As with all of the tensions or pollutions exploited by the poet in the tragic imitation, the object is to make the audience suffer the tensions. In this instance, it would be sexual, urinal, and fecal anxieties experienced as such – what Burke calls the "irresolutions of the body" – and these same anxieties as they affect and are affected by personal, familial, civic, and religious motives. By means of scatological puns (Burke calls them "body puns"), overt and covert references to the privy parts and their functions, and all kinds of natural images which are really disguised sexual, urinal, and fecal images, the poet exploits the Demonic Trinity and in this way involves the "entire realm of privacy" in the cathartic drama. "No purification is complete," Burke says, "until the fecal motive has been expressed and redeemed." By a route too devious and tedious to reconstruct here, Burke attempts to demonstrate in his chapter on "The Thinking of the Body" that the personal and specifically tragic emotions of pity, fear, and pride have their bodily or "private" counterparts in the Demonic Trinity. Pity has its counterpart in the sexual; fear in the urinal and diuretic; and pride in the fecal. The Demonic Trinity includes not only the privy parts and their functions, but also their products. This means that the Demonic Trinity can be used as a source of pollution images to express the "fecal motive" and that by shifting the emphasis to the three processes of bodily unburdening, it can also be used as one of the "primary sources of 'cathartic' imagery" (*The Kenyon Review*,XXI,356). The Demonic Trinity, then, can be used both to express and redeem the "fecal motive." When Burke argues that pity, fear, and pride have their bodily counterparts in the sexual, urinal, and fecal, he means on the one hand that excess pity tends toward sexual release, excess fear toward urinal release, and excess pride toward fecal release (in the sense of defecating upon someone below); and on the other that because of these relations, pity, fear, and pride can be expressed and hence evoked by sexual, urinal, and fecal images. Though somewhat strained because of Burke's compulsion to make the correspondence absolute — to always find the sewers from heaven to hell — and finally rather tedious in the way that all obsessions are, there is a good deal of truth in what Burke says here which it would be foolish — or, perhaps, fecal — for us to deny.

The specific civic tensions which tragedy imitates, and the various tensions which it exploits for cathartic purposes, exist outside the play as "brute realities." Given language, the "fall" is automatic and permanent: hierarchic psychoses just *are*; categorical guilt just *is* — they are "brute realities," the "stagnant miasmatic swamps" in which all symbol-users must live (*Poetics*,273). Tragedy — or any other poetic work, for that matter — cannot remove the causes of tension, but it can help to control their destructive effects. Since the general cause can never be removed — unless by total nuclear extinction — periodic symbolic purges are necessary for the health of the individual and society.

The health of the individual and society has been Burke's primary concern since the early thirties when he laid the foundations for his dramatistic system. Since 1945 he has been building that therapeutic system into a vast verbal pyramid, dedicated, somewhat ironically, to the purification of war in a century already littered, like a tragedy, with corpses and threatened with the prospect of nothing but corpses. The verbal pyramid, of course, is Burke's own therapeutic *symbolic* action — the huge verbal construct of a small man; an oversized verbal tomb and memorial for a man who, by his own admission, has been afraid of death all his life; a vast verbal dungheap, the leavings of a man who wrote his way through more than half a ruined century; and, conversely, a verbal heaven, closed and protective in the manner of all beautifully symmetrical systems. But to contemplate the personal therapeutic function of the system for Burke is only to come on the central idea of dramatism by a different route and to discover the comic center of a system which has tragedy as its representative anecdote.

Like all profound thinkers, Burke has multiple vision. Man, he has recently said, is "ROTTEN WITH PERFECTION." And, as he well knows, his own dream — that he can purify war — is rotten with irony. This capacity for comic perception is like the satyr-play which followed a group of three tragedies or a tragic trilogy and — if Euripides' *The Cyclops* is typical — mocked all the serious themes of tragedy by reducing them to the motivational level of the satyrs. In fact, Burke's most recent book — *The Rhetoric of Religion*, 1961 — is the dramatistic equivalent of a tragic trilogy followed — and mocked — by a satyr-play. The book consists of three "tragic" essays on language and the Burkean drama of human relations, followed by a "satyr-essay" entitled "Prologue in Heaven," which is a dialogue between TL (The Lord, Burke) and S (Satan, his straight man) in which Burke burlesques himself in seriocomic fashion. The dialogue concludes with this exchange between TL and S:

TL. But, to the quick summation, and the perfect symmetry: In their societies, they will seek to keep order. If order, then a need to repress the tendencies to disorder. If repression, then responsibility for imposing, accepting, or resisting the repression. If responsibility, then guilt. If guilt, then the need for redemption, which involves sacrifice, which in turn allows for substitution. At this point, the logic of perfection enters. Man can be viewed as perfectly depraved by a formative "first" offense against the foremost authority, an offense in which one man sinned for all. The cycle of life and death intrinsic to the nature of time can now be seen in terms that treat natural death as the result of this "original" sin. And the principle of perfection can be matched on the hopeful side by the idea of a perfect victim. The symmetry can be logologically rounded out by the idea of this victim as also the creative Word by which time was caused to be, the intermediary Word binding time with eternity, and the end towards which all words of the true doctrine are directed. As one of their saints will put it: "The way to heaven must be heaven, for He said: I am the way."

(TL *rises.* S *also rises immediately after.*)

TL (*continuing*). The way to heaven (the means to the end, the agency for the attainment of purpose) must be heaven (scene), for He (agent) said (act as words): I am the way (act as The Word). Here is the ultimate of logological symmetry!

S. Formally, it is perfect. It is perfectly beautiful!

TL. It is truly culminative!

S. Words could do no more!

(*Pause*).

S (*pensively*). In some ways they will be dismal, in some ways they will have a feeling for the grandeurs of form. But when these Word-People are gone, won't the life of words be gone?

TL. Unfortunately, yes.

S. Then, what of us, the two voices in this dialogue? When words go, won't we, too, be gone?

TL. Unfortunately, yes.

S. Then of this there will be nothing?

TL. Yes . . . nothing . . . but it's more complica —

Sudden blackness. . . . (*The Rhetoric of Religion*, 314–315.)

The concluding scene moves from tragedy to symmetry to comedy and ends with resonant dramatistic puns and the fragmentation of the term which has goaded Burke on from the beginning.

This has always been the characteristic movement in Burke; and it has been recurrent, for he has always gone on to complete the term, finish the phrase, and start through the cycle again. Burke's ideal has always been to purify war — the ineradicable brute reality. And his contribution to the health of the individual and society has been — like that of tragedy — to help purify war by means of the same verbal alchemy he has studied all his life. As Burke well knows, there are two kinds of verbal alchemists: those of hell who use words to transform gold into dross, and those of heaven who use words to transform dross into gold. The first make war and the second purify it. Like TL, Burke is one of the heavenly alchemists: he has divided his efforts between the real business of such a person — purifying war — and the comic contemplation of its ironic implications: the work of his brothers in hell who make war (sometimes on and out of him) faster than he can purify it. Yet, as his last book reminds us, the therapeutic pyramid is still abuilding. Even incomplete, it has transcended Burke and stands as a splendid monument.

See the note on page 349.

THIS is the third and concluding part of the fifth and last chapter of my book on Burke. I chose this selection because it seemed to me that it best demonstrates the power and complexity of Burke's later work and because it shows how, in any given area, Burke brings the force of his whole system to bear on that specific point. It seemed to me, also, that much of what I had to say about Burke was somehow in this selection.

My book on Burke is the third (after Knox and Holland) to be published. Other matters aside, its importance in the history of Burke's reception is that it is the first systematic exposition of Burke's work as a whole (excluding his fiction and poetry) and the most complete account of his literary theory and critical practice yet written.

The Mark of a Poet: Marianne Moore

BY William Wasserstrom

FROM the moment when *The Dial* appeared until it ceased to exist, both kinds of influence, Eliot's and Williams', were admired and nurtured. During its last years, however, early in our modern age of criticism, it was Kenneth Burke who embodied its purpose. His first notable essay, "Psychology and Form," had been designed to resolve "the quarrel between the aesthetes and the geneticists," "the only major tempest now raging in the critical teapot." Submitting this, he imagined it would be "the first of a series of three or four essays in which I hope to round out an attitude toward art." He added that he was "tremendously indebted to The Dial" for having accepted it: "Had you refused it, I should not even have tried to place it elsewhere." These remarks, addressed to Alyse Gregory [managing editor of *The Dial* from 1923 to 1925], occur in letters written during the fall of 1924. Since that

EDITOR'S NOTE: Reprinted from *The Time of the Dial* (Syracuse: Syracuse University Press, 1963), pp. 125–129, copyright © 1963 by Syracuse University Press, by permission of the author and publisher.

time, Burke has sought to round out an abiding attitude. Furthermore, the appearance of "Psychology and Form" marks an association which has continued beyond the life of the journal and led to a lifelong friendship among Miss Moore [Marianne Moore, editor of *The Dial* from 1926 to 1929], Burke, and Watson [James Sibley Watson, publisher of *The Dial* from 1920 to 1929].

In March, 1924, Burke had replaced Sophia Wittenberg as editorial assistant. Miss Wittenberg had resigned after her marriage to Lewis Mumford. Watson urged his associates to hire Burke. ("Please bind him with hoops if possible.") That summer, Burke served as Thayer's [Scofield Thayer, editor of *The Dial* from 1920 to 1926 and with Watson financial supporter from 1920 to 1929] private secretary and lived in Thayer's cottage on Martha's Vineyard. But until 1927 his service was spasmodic. During that year he replaced Paul Rosenfeld as *The Dial's* music critic and became a regular contributor. By July, 1928, his career and reputation were identified with those of *The Dial.*

During that month, Watson, asking Miss Moore to help him decide who should receive *The Dial* Award, proposed Wallace Stevens as a prime candidate. Miss Moore concurred but reminded Watson, "It is impossible to get anything from Wallace Stevens." Her predecessor too had hoped to elicit verse, but years earlier Stevens had replied, "My spasms are not chronic." * In 1927, responding to Miss Moore's importunity, he explained, "The extreme irregularity of my life makes poetry out of the question, for the present, except in momentary instances. But when things grow quieter and I have time to do what I want to do, I shall . . . submit something to you." † Replying to Watson, Miss Moore remarked on the range of Burke's performance and the distinction of his genius, on his "faithfulness, discipline and literary susceptibility." Despairing of Stevens, she said Burke was her candidate even though he is "our critic." ‡ Watson agreed. In January, 1929, Burke received the last award.

Burke was literally "our critic," but he was *The Dial's* official critic in ways that Miss Moore may have suspected but did not define. For Burke's thought stems from those Europeans whom *The Dial* had long cherished, from Russell and Mann and Croce, men who never abandoned faith in the efficacies of mind. As Mann wrote of his own aspirations in the German Letter in 1927, so Burke and *The Dial,* "imbued with the social experience of the times," hoped to reconcile "at a stroke"

* Letter, Stevens to Seldes, February 9, 1922. In response to Seldes' request for autobiography, Stevens (May 5, 1922) said, "I am a lawyer and live in Hartford. But such facts are neither gay nor instructive."

† Letter, Stevens to Marianne Moore, September 3, 1927.

‡ Letter, Miss Moore to Watson, July 18, 1928.

what Mann called "art and conscience," that "phase of contemporary literature . . . which is richest and soundest." Just as Croce, in an essay written for this magazine during the same year, visualized a "new type of philosophical student," so Burke chose to inform himself "in the investigations of history and of science, and in the work and life of his own times." His method was derived from another European, Spengler, who, though "ungainly," Burke wrote to Miss Moore in 1926, was "unquestionably a brilliant writer" and a historian whose "methodology . . . is powerful and imaginative." * Later that year, reviewing Spengler's "stupendous piece of work," calling it "formidable, lugubrious, passionate," Burke distinguished between Spengler's method and his conclusion: although men may not be blessed, Burke decided, they are not accursed. Adapting Mann's faith to Spengler's method, then, Burke laid out his task and set his course: he would become what Croce called "a passionately interested observer" who would study all realms of human experience in order to help determine what it is to be "a man in the full sense of the word."

If we regard Miss Moore's familiar tricorn hat as an emblem of its wearer, an emblem symbolic of the motives which thirty years ago animated a woman who planned to fulfill a trio of duties, then we may regard Burke's plan for a trilogy, *The Grammar, Rhetoric and Symbolic of Motives*, as a fulfillment of the whole idea of criticism and of art which animated *The Dial* itself. † The goal of this eclectic miscellany, the instruction of its American readers and writers in the highest intensities of the creative and moral life on earth, is Burke's goal too. "Art being a criticism," he said in an essay on William Carlos Williams, also is "in some sense a corrective." He saw in Williams' verse a kind of poetics in which rhyme connoted "the regimentations of contemporary life" and "anti-rhyme" implied moral freedom. "Artistic truth," he noted in "Psychology and Form," the essay with

* Letter, Burke to Marianne Moore, April 26, 1926.

† "A member of *The Dial* circle since the 1920's, Mr. Burke" has undertaken to "explore human motives in life and literature, and to relate the two." But "if we feel anything for literature at all we cannot read Mr. Burke without distrust, and very often, nausea. . . . And yet we cannot help being impressed by the vast, if shapeless and uncoordinated, labours of this mind which, for the past thirty years, has been labouring at what is no less than an attempt to explore and to order the whole of human nature. If only Mr. Burke had never heard of Freud, or better still of literature!" This mishmash of accurate history and muddled opinion appeared in the section called "Literary Criticism," *The Times Literary Supplement*, September 17, 1954, viii–ix. As Thayer chose Miss Moore, so Watson and Miss Moore selected Burke as a guardian of their purposes in *The Dial*. And Burke is not simply exploring motives but is instead, as Blackmur says of I. A. Richards, intent on "saving man by poetry." R. P. Blackmur, "San Giovanni in Venere," *The Sewanee Review*, LXVII (Winter, 1959), 618.

which he launched himself, is the "externalization of taste." And because the end of art is "the conversion, a transcendence, of emotion into eloquence," then "technique and psychology" are one. How shall I write about music, he wondered in 1927 when he assumed Rosenfeld's task. Is it an "orgy" of the spirit, a substitute for religion? Or is it a "mechanism"? Music, he decided, submits "literal representation" – orgy – "to a purely musical destiny" – mechanism. For "music is a vocabulary," a form of human eloquence, and it is *eloquence* which defines "the essence of art."

Since 1925 Burke has sought to reconcile the Eliot influence and the Williams influence in a theory of eloquence, of human language, which is simultaneously a theory of organic life. The humanism of Mann and Croce, the zeal of a whole generation of organicists who inspired and supported Watson and Thayer are at least comprehended in Burke's effort to compose a theory of language which is also a theory of behavior. "All living things are critics," he said in 1935 in *Permanence and Change*. "All organisms are critics in the sense that they interpret the signs about them." Because speech is accessible to reason, it is viable; human beings alone possess speech and can therefore "go beyond the criticism of experience to the criticism of criticism." Proceeding so, arguing that language is the mark of men in action, Burke has used Spengler's method to weave an organic synthesis of history, philosophy, art, and criticism in a unified field theory of human motive as embodied in human speech.

Once we recognize "our own lives as a kind of rough first draft that lends itself at least somewhat to revision," he remarked ten years later in *The Grammar of Motives*, we in America will confront "the global situation with an attitude neither local nor imperialistic." For Burke's system represents the last frontier of the American imagination, the last best abstraction of utopia, the last resort and final stage of a major enterprise in modern letters. Blending Harvard aestheticism and apocalyptic zeal, Watson and Thayer had shaped a program which synthesized ideas drawn from those persons and magazines that had established the new spirit in letters, from Santayana's *Harvard Monthly* and Bourne's *Seven Arts*, Stieglitz's *Camera Work* and Coady's *Soil*. By the time Miss Moore was appointed editor, *The Dial* had become the best available model of its own doctrine. No mere "Miscellany," it was itself a creation of the highest order of intensity, composed as artfully as the most intricate poem.

Then during Miss Moore's tenure, *The Dial* lost zeal but acquired a taste for discrimination, for technical systems which would expand and refine the arts of criticism so that all men would learn to write and live better. The very tone of Miss Moore's art and the style of her mind were embodied in a journal that displayed the virtues of variety and constraint, of picking and choosing, compunction and conviction, experiment and discipline, daring and scruple. But because Miss Moore was after all a person with roots in the Resurgence, with a taste for Whitman, in her turn as editor she achieved one splendid feat.* She recognized Kenneth Burke as the critic who might well map a path along a middle road to the heavenly kingdom. Proposing that *The Dial*'s award should go to Burke, she did not celebrate his arrival there. Rather she hoped to dramatize the ways in which Burke exercised the highest care and accuracy and diligence in pursuit of the life of letters. In her view, he was the one American critic who possessed technique and sensibility enough to reconcile art and culture, science and imagination in a single theory of literary value which is simultaneously a theory of human virtue in a comprehensive but probably not final sense of that bloody word. †

◇◇

WILLIAM WASSERSTROM was born in Brooklyn, New York, in 1922. He has taught English at Adelphi, Swarthmore, and the University of Rochester and is presently a professor of English at Syracuse University. He is the author of *The Heiress of All the Ages, The Time of the Dial,* and *Van Wyck Brooks.*

Burke was associated with *The Dial* as a literary critic, music critic, reviewer, translator, and editor all through the twenties. It was there that he knew James Sibley Watson, Marianne Moore, and most of the other people involved in the literary and intellectual life of the twenties in New York. This selection deals, somewhat tardily, with Burke's reception during the twenties and, more important, with the relation of Burke's later work to a large tradition in American intellectual life which Mr. Wasserstrom identifies with *The Dial.* To see Burke as "completing" the work of *The Dial,* where *The Dial* represents a vital and significant native American tradition, is to see Burke in a new and quite astounding way.

◇◇

* Miss Moore lives in Brooklyn, on the very street where Whitman "worked as a journeyman carpenter and probably helped build the family house." Malcolm Cowley, "Walt Whitman, Champion of America," *The New York Times Book Review,* February 6, 1955, 1.

† "Miss Moore was too exceptional a poet to make the ideal editor; and high among her faults was the fact that she was so exceptionally conscientious. Another of her notable faults was that she was quite kind to me." Letter, Burke to Wasserstrom, May 6, 1959.

7 *Symbols and Civilization*

BY Joseph Frank

KENNETH BURKE'S *The Rhetoric of Religion,* like everything else that Mr. Burke has written, is highly original, brilliantly stimulating, infinitely suggestive, and ultimately baffling. Mr. Burke is so thoroughly *sui generis* that it is difficult to fit him into any contemporary philosophical pigeon-hole; but if he belongs anywhere, it is certainly with those who have restored the symbolic imagination to a central place in modern thought. Mr. Burke's attention has always centered on the emotive, psychic, and ethical-moral needs of the human spirit, and on the "symbolic actions" by which these needs are expressed. Much of the paradoxical originality of his thinking comes from applying concepts taken from the study of magic or religion and employing them to characterize completely secular historical and cultural phenomena. If a good deal of modern thought has been engaged in debunking, or, to be more formal, in "demythification" – that is, the interpretation of one or another "sacred" ideology in terms of "profane" categories – then Kenneth Burke might be said to have adopted the opposite tack of "remythification." Not, to be sure, that Mr. Burke accepts the vocabularies of magic or religion as objectively valid; but he thinks they express certain permanent emotive needs that crop up in every aspect of cultural life.

Ever since the publication of his *The Grammar of Motives* (1945), Mr. Burke's interest has been focused on language. Language, according to Mr. Burke, is the most important medium through which these emotive needs of mankind are symbolically expressed, and he has devoted himself to a remarkably thorough and ingenious study of the dialectical relations between various vocabularies derived from the most widespread sources. The result has been his system of "dramatism," whose achievements have been well summarized recently by William H. Rueckert in a very useful book called *Kenneth Burke and the Drama of Human Relations.* What Mr. Burke has done, says Mr. Rueckert, "is to systematize a naturalistic, linguistically oriented, secular variant of Christianity. Burke has retained the principal ideas of Christianity and worked out dramatistic equivalents for them with astonishing thoroughness." In practice, this means that "Burke has reduced God to an idea

EDITOR'S NOTE: Reprinted from *The Sewanee Review,* LXXII (1964), 484–489, copyright © 1964 by the University of the South, by permission of the author and publisher.

(or term), Heaven and Hell to psychological states, Purgatory to symbolic action, Christ to the dialectics of redemption, and the grammar of Christianity to a rhetoric of rebirth, with the whole transformation culminating in the reduction of theology (discourse about God) to logology (discourse about discourse)." As we can see, the Existentialists have not been the only thinkers to offer us secular variants of Christianity.

The Rhetoric of Religion is thus a part of Mr. Burke's continuing effort to integrate *all* types of vocabulary into his dramatistic framework. In this book he tackles the vocabulary of theology to show that the fundamental terms used about God and Creation, as well as about the dialectical relations between the two, can equally well be seen as the internal relations of discourse itself. The first section of the book, called "On words and The Word," attempts to establish six analogies between language and theology. For example: just as the idea of literal creation is linked with "The Word," so the creation of meaning is linked with "words"; the relation of words to the nonverbal realm is equivalent to that between Spirit and Matter since the word "transcends" what it names; language "negates" what it refers to since a word is "not" its object, and the original establishment of the ethical by God also involves negation ("Thou shalt not"), etc. This should be enough to show the sort of thing that Mr. Burke is up to, though it can hardly give any sense of the inexhaustible adroitness with which he goes about working out his parallels. All these analogies, to be sure, involve a good deal of skating on pretty thin ice; but one is quite willing to go along for the extreme pleasure of Mr. Burke's intellectual company. One wonders, though, whether Mr. Burke really believes, as he states in his sixth analogy, that "there is some form of *conformity* or *communion* between the symbolized and the symbol," just as there is love — the perfect communion — between the persons of the Holy Trinity. If so, then all language would possess the virtues of the *lingua Adamica* that existed before the Tower of Babel and which, instead of being composed of conventional signs, expressed the very essence of reality.

The second section consists of a long and difficult study entitled "Verbal Action in St. Augustine's *Confessions*." This is a large-scale example of Burkean close reading, and will no doubt prove of great interest to all students of Augustine's work. For the non-specialist, though, even if he has a large supply of interest and good-will, it is likely to constitute a pretty formidable stretch of prose. Mr. Burke becomes so involved in translating Augustine into logology (or Burkese) that the reader is hard put to find any general thesis emerging from the welter of detail (which includes a table of various kinds of *in*-prefixes in Augustine's Latin and, more amusingly, a section written in the style of a medieval *quaestio*). So far as there is any general point, perhaps it lies in the relation between time and eternity in Augustine's thought. This relation, Mr. Burke contends, is reflected in the structure of the *Confessions,* which is narrative (temporal) up through the first nine sections and then becomes dialectical (non-temporal) in the last four where Augustine turns to the problem of the knowledge of God. For Mr. Burke this relation of time and eternity has an empirical equivalent "in the relations between the words of a sentence and its 'meaning.' The syllables of the word are 'born' and 'die.' But the *meaning* of the syllables 'transcends' their sheer nature as temporal motions." This does not imply, of course, that the meaning of the sentence is literally "eternal"; but "the relation between the sentence as a sequence of 'transitory' syllables and the sentence as a 'fixed' unit of meaning provides the makings for a formal distinction that can serve to suggest an ontological distinction between time and eternity."

All this is a preparation for the next and richest section, "The First Three Chapters of Genesis." Here Mr. Burke undertakes to show that if you start with the idea of Creation and the establishment of an Order, all the ethical-moral precepts of Christianity are implicitly contained in the necessary dialectical implications of the latter term. How? Let Mr. Burke explain in a charming little verse:

Order leads to Guilt
(for who can keep commandments!)
Guilt needs Redemption
(for who would not be cleansed!)
Redemption needs Redeemer
(which is to say, a victim!) . . .

These dialectical implications are expressed sequentially in Genesis as history or myth; but this is merely what Mr. Burke calls "the temporizing of essence," that is, the presentation in narrative form of a non-temporal dialectical pattern. Finally, the book concludes with a delightful dialogue between The Lord and Satan, who get along splendidly in view of the dialectical unity of Being and Non-Being and who discuss the odd antics of the Earth-People with amused sympathy because the latter regrettably cannot avoid temporizing their essence as a result of the nature of language.

No one can work through *The Rhetoric of Religion* without being constantly impressed by Mr. Burke's intellectual virtuosity and speculative audacity, and without learning a good deal about the way in which the language of theology both draws on and influences other areas of discourse. It is unlikely, however, that any reader will be entirely persuaded by Mr. Burke's capricious analogies and conceptual acrobatics. One is constantly troubled by the total lack of any attempt to *ground* all these speculations in some theory of language and its relation to thought, or to explore the actual historical relations between language and religion. Mr. Burke cannot of course be expected to do everything; but it is impossible not to wonder whether the dialectic patterns that he finds in English really do hold good, as he seems to think, for *all* other languages. His insouciance on such fundamental matters leads one to read him, so to speak, with a willing suspension of disbelief, rather than as a thinker with whom one wishes seriously to agree or disagree. It would be overly pedantic and beyond my powers to attempt any criticism of *The Rhetoric of Religion* in detail; but there is one crucial problem whose discussion may help to reveal some of the underlying assumptions of Mr. Burke's thought.

This problem concerns the very important issue of freedom in the Burkean system. From his earliest work Mr. Burke has been a staunch opponent of any attempt to view human motivation as determined in any scientific sense. "Behavioristic terminologies of motives," he reiterates in the present volume, "would reduce 'action' to 'motion,' whereas Dramatism holds that 'action' is a more inclusive realm, not capable of adequate description in terms of 'motion' only." But Mr. Burke, a thinker of exemplary honesty, has begun to suspect that his own view of language involves him in a similar determinism; and he objectifies this suspicion by allowing Satan to bring it up in the dialogue. Human behavior, after all, has turned out to be nothing but a temporal unrolling of the pattern of dialectical relations "eternally" present in language. And this leads Satan to inquire whether the Earth-People, who think they are free, really have any grounds for this conviction. It is easy enough for The Lord to show that *formally* the idea of freedom is implicit in the definition of man as a symbol-using animal capable of language. "Further," he remarks, "inasmuch as they can give names to one another, they will be able to conceive of themselves as *Persons*. And a Person is, by definition, a being that can *act*."

All this is very neat, but it does not answer the question of whether man has any freedom not only *formally* but also *factually*. The Lord points out that "in dealing with ideas one at a time (or, as they will put it, 'discursively') they can do many things which can't be done when, like us, all ideas are seen at once, and thus necessarily corrected by one another." From which Satan draws the proper logical inference that human freedom is then only the freedom to become involved in all the errors caused by man's symbolic activity, i.e., language. The Lord contends, however, that "the ability to be wrong within limits will also argue the ability to be right within limits. And insofar as these creatures are right, they will share in that higher freedom which we equate with necessity, an identity's inevitable necessity of being, in all its parts, the simple self-consistency that it must be, in order to be precisely what it is." Mr. Burke's flight of eloquence here is suspiciously evasive. What man *is*, according to his definition, is the symbol-using animal that invented language; and if the temporal form of language necessarily leads only to error, then there is no positive conception of freedom (or "rightness") that one can find in Burkean logology.

Mr. Burke lands in this dilemma because of a crucial divergence between his view of language and that of the philosophers of symbolism, despite the seeming agreement between them implied by his definition of man as "the symbol-using animal." For Mr. Burke, to put it crudely, thinks that language is a kind of excrescence that merely complicates the "real" needs of the human species; and the same is true of the whole long history of human culture that language has created. "The purposes that arise through the tangles made possible by language," he writes, "are not merely the old bodily appetites in a new form. They are appetites differing not just in degree but in kind. And the two kinds differ so greatly that, *as tested by the wishes of the body**, the purposes supplied by language (by doctrine) can amount even to a kind of built-in *frustration*." The phrase with the asterisk is not italicized in the text; but it has been singled out to show that, despite his overt opposition to Behaviorism and scientism, Mr. Burke still assumes a mechanistic (i.e., purely natural or physical) standard by which to measure the vagaries of language and to declare their results superfluous.

In other words, the "real" needs of man are quite simple physical wants; and the complications introduced by man's symbolic activity, which express his emotive and ethical-moral "needs," do not have the same bedrock importance. Mr. Burke is careful not to reduce language to being only the expression of these "real" needs, nor to deny the significance of the emotive ones; but he persistently regards these latter as "physically" mistaken and continually stresses the deleterious cultural role of language in stimulating them. There is something very old-fashionedly American about all this; and while Kenneth Burke and Henry Ford certainly make strange bedfellows, they both seem to be agreeing that history is bunk (or, for Mr. Burke, mostly bunk).

To put it another way, Mr. Burke seems caught half-way between the semanticists who strive totally to eliminate "the tyranny of words" and the philosophers of symbolism who view all types of symbolic activity as the foundations of human culture and who see culture not as an error but as an achievement. As the art-critic Meyer Schapiro pointed out to me in conversation, Kenneth Burke's position in *The Rhetoric of Religion* is very similar to that of Max Müller in the nineteenth century, who believed that myth was an inevitable disease of language because human speech was inherently metaphorical. This view has been abandoned by thinkers like Cassirer and Suzanne Langer on the ground that no essential *human* function can be adequately interpreted only in a negative sense as a disadvantage to the species. It would of course be foolish to deny that language can be (and often has been) a source of confusion and error; but it certainly seems excessive to consider the entire edifice of human culture as just one big mistake for this reason. No doubt the ultimate simplicity of this latter view explains why Mr. Burke still continues to believe that the real problems of the modern world can be solved (or at least alleviated) by translating them into his logology.

◇◇

JOSEPH FRANK was born in New York City in 1918. He teaches comparative literature at Rutgers University. He is the author of *Widening Gyre: Crisis and Mastery in Modern Literature* and the editor of *A Primer of Ignorance*, a posthumous collection of pieces by R. P. Blackmur.

This review of *The Rhetoric of Religion* is one of only four serious considerations of that book to be written when it was published. Like two of the others, it treats Burke's book in relation to one or two other writers and in a large modern intellectual framework. Burke hardly needs to be explicated in the old way any more, as if no one could understand what he was doing or manage his sometimes crabbed prose; and he does not need to be defended, as he once was, for being "worth doing." Of course he is worth doing: his work is serious, large, and coherent. A systematic assessment of his total achievement needs to be undertaken, and someone needs to examine parts of his system in relation to similar undertakings by Burke's contemporaries. Joseph Frank does some of this in a limited but significant way.

◇◇

2 Communication in Society

BY Hugh Dalziel Duncan

THE fragmentation of consciousness in modern society has been described in various ways. In social theory much has been made of Durkheim's *anomie,* Tonnies' *gemeinschaft* and *gesellschaft,* Weber's rationalization of the world, Sorokin's sensate culture, and Cooley's primary and secondary contacts. The "death of the gods" has been lamented in literature, philosophy, music, and art. Many books have been written (before and after Durkheim) to show how man suffers from his estrangement from gods or forces which, as both cause and effect of human consciousness, can be known through symbols but are not subject to symbolic laws. These (we are asked to believe) are derived from some supernatural source whose laws can at best only be dimly perceived by man, for, how can the finite mind of man understand the infinite mind of God, or the other transcendental ultimates of history? It is only through grace (even the Hegelian grace of reason) that man wins his way to salvation, just as it is only through revelation (as earlier, divination) that he can communicate with his gods.

It is still fashionable in social thought to invoke some kind of religious or supernatural order as a paradigm for social order. True, we may, like Weber, call such order "tradition," or, like anthropologists, equate order in society with order in religion, as in their use of ritual as a paradigm for social order. But whatever our terms for the supernatural, once we invoke the supernatural as a source of social order, we find ourself in the midst of paradox. For how can what is "beyond" reason be known through it? We do not avoid paradox by saying that when we use religious moments of experience as our "representative cases" for all moments of consensus we are only creating an abstraction, and that conceptual abstractions are not to be understood as part of the object but as part of our definition of the object. Our concepts determine our hypotheses, as these in turn decide our data, and ultimately the "facts" we experience in our social experience, and the values we attach to them. Thus, if we believe, as did Thomas Jefferson, that authority under rules, as well as under law and God, can determine social consensus, then we can study society as a game. But if we believe that rules are but a crude step on the upward way toward worship of God, then we cannot study society as a game. If we say that art is but a manifestation of the

EDITOR'S NOTE: Reprinted from *Arts in Society*, III, i (1964), 93–101, copyright © 1964 by the Regents of the University of Wisconsin, by permission of the author and publisher.

divine, then obviously we must hurry to the divine for our knowledge of society.

But there are problems, too, in saying that art determines society, or on a more subtle level, that art and society are related in the forms of social consciousness which originate in communication. If we say this, we must show *how* art and consciousness are related. And, whatever our interest in communication as a social event, we must make clear why we have selected one model of art, and not another. Our intellectual heritage in symbolic analysis permits us to distinguish between art, science and religion. It was possible in Weber and Durkheim's day to arrange expressive forms in a hierarchy which ended in religious expression as the representative form of all order in society. Today in the writings of Talcott Parsons and his followers we see purely mechanical models of society, taken from modern science, beginning to supplant religious models of social order. Thus, the widely disparate concepts of "ritual" and "equilibrium" dominate social theorizing, and especially academic theorizing in the United States.

The shortcomings of reducing the social to models taken from religion *or* science (and especially physics), and thus excluding the observable data of sociation as found in art, are becoming obvious to all but the most parochial students of society. It is to Talcott Parsons' credit that he has refused to make ignorance of symbolic analysis a sociological virtue. He admits openly that the future of social theory, as well as the future of symbolic analysis, depends on the development of a social theory of language. We must develop much greater skill in symbolic analysis, not simply so we can talk better as sociologists of art, or as analysts of communication, but as students of society.

The great importance of Kenneth Burke's work is that it is a *methodology*. He does not go on telling us the *what* of communication (namely, that people of a certain age, race, class, caste, sex, education level, etc., read a "message" which urges them to vote for a certain candidate, at a certain time, in a certain place, that this message is distributed in certain ways, that it consists of such and such a percentage of all other messages in the "unit" of communication of which it was part, etc.), but *how* it affects our social relationships. He *begins* where Dewey, Mead, and Cooley *ended* in their concept of symbolization as a kind of "dramatic rehearsal in the imagination" in which the imagined future of the act, or its reconstructed past, is used to order action in a present. Burke pointed out in his articles of the twenties, and in his books of the thirties such as *Permanence and Change, Counter-Statement,* and *Attitudes toward History,* that if we say an act is dramatic, we ought to show what kind of a social drama it is through an analysis of its form and content as a social act. The futures of acts are not locked up in our heads, buried deep in a subjective self, or hidden from the self in the unconscious. They are *public* because they are symbols, *forms* created in the experience of art in their most complex expression, and in speech and all forms of communication in everyday life.

The world of everyday experience, the *empirical* realm of action, is a world of words and expression in which action is determined by communication whose meaning can be known because who is communicating, by what means, in what kind of act, under what conditions, and for what purposes, can be observed directly. But, as Burke stresses in *The Rhetoric of Religion,* there is a realm of words whose meanings extend beyond those used in daily life. This is the supernatural. Even he "who does not believe in the supernatural will recognize that, so far as the purely empirical facts of language are concerned, languages do have *words* for the supernatural." And even if "one assumed it as beyond question that there really *is* a realm of the supernatural, nevertheless our *words* for the discussion of this realm are necessarily borrowed by analogy from our words for the other three orders: the natural, the socio-political, and the verbal (or the symbolical in general, as with the symbol-systems of music, the dance, painting, architecture, the various specialized scientific nomenclatures, etc.)." That is, *all* words for "God" are analogical. When we speak of God's "powerful arm," we use a physical analogy, or of God as the "Father" or "Lord," we use a socio-political analogy, or of God as a "Word," we use a linguistic analogy. For, as Burke says: "The idea of God as a person would be derived from analogy from the sheerly physical insofar as persons have bodies, from the socio-political insofar as persons have status, and from the linguistic insofar as the idea of personality implies such kinds of 'reason' as flower in man's symbol-using prowess (linguistic, artistic, philosophic, scientific, moralistic, pragmatic)."

Burke is *not* saying that religion is to be understood simply as the expression of an anthropomorphic tendency of men to fashion gods after their own image, nor is he saying that man is made in the image of God. His inquiry, he tells us, "stands midway between these two positions, contending merely that, insofar as religious doctrine is verbal, it will necessarily exemplify its nature as verbalization, and insofar as religious doctrine is thorough, its ways of exemplifying verbal principles should be correspondingly thorough." Thus, he holds that if the dramatistic study of language clarifies religious expression, so, too, does the study of religious expression clarify ways in which language affects us. But the point of Burke's work, and the significance of his achievement, is not that he points out that religion and language affect each other, for this has been said before, but that he proceeds to *demonstrate* how this is so by reference to a specific symbolic context. After a discussion "On Words and The Word," he analyses verbal action in St. Augustine's *Confessions.* He then discusses the first three chapters of Genesis, and ends with a brilliant and profound "Prologue in Heaven," an imaginary dialogue between the Lord and Satan in which he proposes that we begin our study of human motives "with complex theories of transcendence," rather than with terminologies developed in the use of simplified laboratory equipment.

In his early writing, Burke was concerned with what he calls the "creative" nature of the word. On page 34 of *The Rhetoric of Religion,* he codifies his previous "speculations" on orientation, transformation, "perspective by incongruity," "exorcism by misnomer" and resimplification (in *Permanence and Change*); on "secular prayer" (in *Attitudes toward History*); on "rebirth" (in both these books and *The Philosophy of Literary Form*); on "god-terms" (in *A Grammar of Motives*); on "glamor," "romance," and "beauty" as purely secular, social analogues of "divinity" (in *A Rhetoric of Motives*); on "pure persuasion" (also in the *Rhetoric*) and on catharsis (in current attempts to decide how poetry "purges" the edified customer).

In the early stages of his search for a model of symbolic action, Burke made much use of anthropological views (particularly those of Malinowski) on communication. Looking back from the vantage point of a finished system, Burke says of this period: "In general, there was a tendency to assume a simple historical development from the 'sacred' to the 'profane,' from the 'spiritual' to the 'secular.' " These efforts "lacked the particular 'logological' reservations as developed in *The Rhetoric of Religion,* and even 'the later ones' (such as *A Grammar of Motives* and *A Rhetoric of Motives*) lacked the specific formulation of this essay (*The Rhetoric of Religion*)." Thus, Burke now feels, after some forty years of search, that he has created a model of the symbolic act which breaks through the rigidities of the "sacred-secular" dichotomy, and at the same time shows us *how* we get from secular to sacred realms of action over the bridge of language.

It would be a complete misreading of *The Rhetoric of Religion* to interpret it as another study in mythic interpretation. Burke carefully distinguishes between "logological" and "mythic" analysis in his essay on Theodore Reik's *Myth and Guilt, The Crime and Punishment of Mankind* (see pages 257–272). Burke argues against current mythic interpretation as a method for explaining human relationships. "The myth-expert's tendency to think by overreliance upon imagery has the further drawback that the *apparent concreteness* of such terms conceals their actual abstractness." (p. 265) The present problem in symbolic analysis is one of avoiding the reduction of human interaction to motion, as in behavioristic theories, or to sheer imagery, as in mythic interpretation. Burke meets this by proposing that we examine a creation myth such as Genesis as a way of propounding "principles of governance" (social order) in terms of narrative rather than as theology, philosophy, metaphysics, or the various social science approaches in economics, political science, psychology, or sociology.

He proposes that we approach terminology from the "standpoint of order (social order) as an empirical problem, compounded of non-verbal materials which the symbol-using animal variously manipulates and to which he is variously related by purposive actions conceived in terms of his symbol-systems." (p. 268) He selects religious expression because theology confronts the problem of social order "in the grand style." Religious systems are *systems of action* based on communication in society. They are great social dramas which are played out on earth before an ultimate audience, God. But where theology confronts the creation of its social drama in the "grand style," that is, as a fully developed cosmological drama with man as its central actor, and the believer studies this drama for its religious *content,* the "logologer" studies religious rituals "solely for their form" insofar as "these forms can be further studied not directly as knowledge but as anecdotes that help reveal for us the quandaries of human governance." (p. 268)

Burke interprets Genesis as an account of the creation interpreted as a statement of "principles of governance." That is, the account of the Creation may be interpreted as saying in effect: "This is, in principle, a statement of what the natural order must be like if it is to be a perfect fit with the conditions of human socio-political order, conditions that come into focus in the idea of a basic covenant backed by a perfect authority." (p. 180) The communication of authority leads from the Biblical idea of authority as based on a Covenant, for as Burke quotes Hobbes: "He is only properly said to reign, that governs his subjects by his word, and by promise of rewards to those that obey it, and by threatening them with punishment that obey it not." The task of the symbol analyst concerned with social order then becomes one of "asking what cluster of ideas is 'tautologically' present in the idea of Order." Burke warns us against the use of rigid formulas. "Such a cycle of terms follows no one sequence. That is, we may say either that the idea of Disorder is implicit in the idea of Order, or that the idea of Order is implicit in the idea of Disorder. Or we might say that the idea of Order implies the idea of Obedience and Disobedience, or that either of them implies the other, or that either or both imply the idea of an Order, etc." (p. 195) Insofar as order is related to action among men in society, it involves the idea of a command, and its proper response, "obey." Thus, "Order is to Disorder as Obedience is to Disobedience."

But we must not think of disorder as simply an absence of order. There are two kinds of disorder. In the first there is a "tendency towards failure to obey completely always," and in the second "an out-and-out enrollment in the ranks of a rival force." (p. 195) Or as we say in contemporary political life, disagreement with authority may be interpreted "either as temperamental deviation from the prevailing orthodoxy or as sinister, secret adherence to an organized enemy alien power." (p. 195) Those who oppose our principles of order may be considered as misguided sinners who have fallen from grace (yet who, in their fall, do not deny our principles of order); or as villains who must be overcome by the hero who personifies a principle of social order; or as heretics, who must be hunted down and destroyed because they personify a principle of disorder; or finally, as the secular variant of the heretic, the traitor who must be captured and put to death because only in his death are we purged of threats to our principles of order.

Thus, disobedience is "cured" through some kind of sacrifice, and since, in matters of governance, man is a socio-political being, the kind of community in which he lives and the roles he can play in it will determine the kind of sacrifice he thinks proper. When our opposition becomes an evil power in its own right, we must find some kind of public victim whose suffering and death can be witnessed by the community as a demonstration of the triumph of good over evil. For the act of sacrifice is both a dramatization of our power to worldly audiences whom we must move to our purposes, and at the same time a plea to supernatural audiences to accept our sacrifice as a sign of our obedience to their authority. As Hitler said in *Mein Kampf,* the common people do not understand arguments about power, arbitrations which end in a handshake, adjudication of differences by umpires, mutual subordination by contesting parties to rules, or calling in others, such as police, to keep order in public ceremonies. Only the dramatization of power, the show of force, moves them. Hence, a "good German" beating a poor Jew to his knees was a powerful communication of authority, and to all Germans a sure indication that the Nazis were powerful authorities who must be obeyed. As the drama of Hitler's Germany unfolded, we saw authoritarianism "perfected" through the dramatization of its power of "perfect" sacrificial victims.

There is private victimage, too, as when we punish ourselves in penance for our sins. The self we punish is punished before an audience, an inner self who stands as audience to the self we punish. Between the public and private mortification of the self stand sacred bodies such as elite guards in any army, or the priests of a church, who practice both private and public acts of mortification which fit them for their special office and thus enable them to dramatize the strength of their faith. Thus, insofar as sacrifice is related to temporal power, it is a purgation of weakness. From the view of those in power, the weaknesses we must destroy in ourselves arise in conflict between our duty to the transcendent principles of order as personified in the sacred body of guardians (such as priests) designated by our rulers, and our duty to family, loved ones, friends, or institutions which authority assures us are but "local" manifestations of some great universal principle of power. Authorities ask us to sacrifice our families to the state in time of war, as our family in turn asks us as individuals to sacrifice a loved one to the family principles of honor, and as God asked Abraham to offer his beloved son, Isaac, in sacrifice because (we are told) in such sacrifice we pass from the satisfaction of a "lower" need to a "higher." As Luther said, Abraham was asked to violate a law of nature (love of family) to uphold a law of God. In this view, suffering becomes a sign of God's grace, and calamities visited upon the community or the individual are a communication from God who warns and chastens us so we will be saved from disobedience, and thus eternal damnation.

In the section on "Principles of Governance Stated Narratively" (pp. 201–208), Burke begins by pointing out the difference between a narrative or dramatic communication and a philosophical or logical communication such as we make when we classify principles of order. A narrative or dramatic statement involves temporal sequence, while classificatory terms for order simply "cluster about one another, variously implying one another, but in no one fixed sequence." Or, in another image, in classificatory discourse, principles of social order are expressed like a chord struck in music, while dramatic statements are like the notes of the chord spun out in arpeggio form. The notes are the same, but the temporal disposition of them is very different. And, further, a fully developed narrative style personalizes the principle of classification, as we see in Genesis where God's creative fiat infuses nature, man, and society with the principle of holy communication. "In the beginning was the Word, and the Word was with God, and the Word was God." (John, 1) Thus, at the very beginning of creation, the principle of communication and the means whereby we communicate (the word) is made sacred. The creation of the world by God is a communicative act, and all order in nature and society must rest upon successful communication between God and Man. As we see in Luther, God's Word does not speak *about,* but *in* the relation of God to man.

Relationship *arises* with the Word, and continues to exist with the Word, by God's speaking it.

Burke argues that the idea of mortification is integral to the idea of dominion, for "the scrupulous subject must seek to 'slay' within himself whatever impulses run counter to the authoritative demands of sovereignty." The ultimate expression of mortification is death. Authorities who seek absolute power over us must link disobedience with sin, and sin, in turn, with death. We must be made to feel guilty when we disobey the commandments of our masters, and we must regard sin as the great threat to social order. This is done by linking death, not simply with the natural condition of man, as a mortal animal, but with the moral order of the universe. The Biblical account of the Creation and Fall tell us that whereas other animals die naturally, men die, not because of their biological nature, but because the first man, Adam, sinned. Thus, when death is viewed in personal terms colored by the conditions of governance as expressed in the moral order, death "is conceived not just as a natural process, but as a kind of 'capital punishment.' " For, if Order gives rise to a sense of guilt, and we seek to obey the laws by policing our impulses from within, we must kill within the self whatever threatens order in the world without.

Burke stresses the fact that dominion, guilt and sacrifice mutually imply one another. For if those in power make us equate disobedience with sin, and teach us to feel guilt over impulses within us which lead to disobedience, they must also provide us with means for expiation of sin, and yet see to it that expiation is carried out in ways which do not threaten their power. This is done in the Bible by the development of the idea of sacrifice. In Genesis, the Noachian Covenant introduces the idea of sacrifice, as when Noah "took of every clean beast, and every clean fowl, and offered burnt-offerings on the altar." (8:20) From here on, says Burke, "more and more clearly, comes the emergence of the turn from mere sacrifice to the idea of outright redemption by victimage." (p. 216) Burke distinguishes here between the *lex talionis* as "the principle of human justice, conceived after the nature of the scales, and grounded in the idea of an ultimate authority," and redemption through sacrifice. Redemptive sacrifice must be more than a payment for sin, and thus a kind of ransom, but a purgation of sin, or a cleansing of the individual and the community in which the sin occurred. It must become, in short, a *symbolic* act of cleansing. The sacrificial agent, as such, is but a vessel of communication with the supernatural power, and his suffering and death must become the death, not merely of his own sin, but of all the members of his community, and eventually of all men. The redemptive act thus becomes a symbolic act of atonement because in such an act the individual acts not for himself alone but for his community. That is, he acts to uphold a principle of order. In religious ritual, the individual may be subordinated to the belief that the world is governed by an eternal cycle of birth and death and that to obey God means to resign to the rule of this circular movement. In this view, life has no intrinsic value because its purpose is fulfilled in submergence in the harmony of the eternal circular return.

As Burke points out, sacrifice is a social drama, an action in life, which is related to temporal rule as well as the "eternal" principles of birth and death. In the cosmologies of the "eternal return" as expressed in religious ritual, "the terms of order . . . go round and round like the wheel seen by Ezekiel, endlessly implicating one another . . ." (p. 217) But when terms for social order are formed into social drama, a significant change takes place. "A drama has a beginning, a middle and an end; it is, in short, an action in which men break out of the eternal cycle to act here and now in a world which exists because of their actions as well as because of the actions of a supernatural power. As narrative or drama, social depictions of authority translate the eternal principles of authority into an irreversible linear progression which promises us some kind of achievement in the world." "But with principle of authority personalized as God, the principle of disobedience as Adam (the 'old Adam in all of us'), the principle of temptation as an Aesopian serpent, Eve as mediator in the bad sense of the word, and the idea of temptation reduced imagistically to terms of eating (the perfect image of a 'first' appetite, or essential temptation, beginning as it does with the infantile, yet surviving in the adult), such reduction of the tautological cycle to narrative linear progression makes possible the notion of an *outcome*." (p. 217)

In further analysis of Genesis as a drama of authority, Burke points out that Adam and Eve's consciousness of nakedness has been interpreted too simply, "without reference to the major stress upon the matter of *a Covenant*." Social order may be based on ultimate powers such as God, in whose eyes all will be equal on the Day of Judgment, but authority in the world is expressed through differentiation of rank and power, or what we call hierarchy. From this standpoint, Genesis must be interpreted as a status, as well as a sexual, drama. "Social order leads to differentiations of status, which are indicated by differences in *clothing*. Thus, the same socio-political conditions that go with a Covenant would also go with clothing, thereby making one conscious of nakedness. The Biblical narrative itself makes clear that, under the conditions of Governance, sexual differentiation was primarily a matter of relative status. In a situation where man is to woman as master to servant, and where the differences between the sexes were attested by clothes, nakedness would be too equalitarian."

Burke here proposes that we think of Adam's original transgression, not as essentially sexual, but as social, for as he says: ". . . after sexual differentiation by clothing had been continued for a sufficient length of time, people began to assume a far greater difference between 'social' and 'sexual' motives than actually exists, and this is true also of modern psychoanalysis – until now we'd need a kind of ironic dissociation such as Marx proposed in connection with the 'fetishism of commodities,' before we could come even remotely near to realizing the extent of the social motives hidden in our ideas of sheerly 'physical' sexuality. However, this marvelously accurate image of nakedness as interpreted from the standpoint of the estrangements resulting from Order in the sense of divergent rank, has been interpreted so greatly in purely sexual terms that often people seem even to think of Adam's original transgression as essentially sexual." Adam and Eve's Fall, Burke argues, is a fall from brotherhood and equality under God. "Insofar as clothes imply social estrangements or differentiation by status, they are by the same token a kind of 'fall.' In themselves they are at odds with the natural order; yet nakedness is at odds with the order of our 'second nature.'" (pp. 220–221)

Thus, in a dramatic or narrative depiction of creation, as contrasted with purely neutral description of creation in the impersonal pragmatic science of the laboratory, the idea of purpose, and its personification in the struggle between the hero and the villain, is derived from the idea of a struggle between principles of social order and disorder. *The Schofield Reference Bible* points out that both the Noachic and the Adamic Covenants deal with the problem of social order. The "changed state of woman" is proclaimed in Genesis, 3:16; the "headship of the man" is discussed as the "entrance of sin, which is disorder, makes necessary a headship . . . vested in man." Burke suggests that "the idea of *purpose,* so essential to the narrative principle of *personality,* is here ingrained in the idea of Order, as being identified with the 'good,' whereby all things, by their mere act of being, contained in themselves the aim of their being."

But, as Burke hastens to point out in the following chapter ("Final Comparing of Cyclical and Rectilinear Styles"), temptation is "intrinsic to the tautological cycle of terms implicit in the idea of Order." Thus, every religion has some kind of "original" as well as "actual" sin. Original sin is the kind of guiltiness "that, as translated into terms of temporal sequence, we 'inherit' from our 'first' ancestor in the male line, as a result of his 'first' disobedience to the 'first' thou-shall-not imposed upon him by the first and foremost authority (to whom he was subject, but from whom he inherited dominion over all created things, including his woman)." Such, as least, is the way we depict the "principle of sin" in narrative terms. What comes first determines what comes second, while the second determines what comes third, until finally an outcome or end of the act is reached. Thus, narrative or dramatic depiction of action has (as Dewey, Mead, and Burke stress) a moment of finality or consummation which brings action to a close and thus reduces the endless circle of birth and death in which the individual becomes merely the manifestation of a process over which he has no control, and which he can (at best) know but cannot change.

The outcome or end of a drama of social order is achieved through a promise of ultimate redemption. Both the first step of original sin and the final moment of redemption are reached through substitution, "The 'old Adam' having sinned for us, and a corresponding Redeemer or Mediator of some sort being required to intercede for us." (p. 223) Thus, while disorder, arising out of the original sin of disobedience, is intrinsic to the idea of order, we are promised atonement for our primal sin through the intervention of a divine mediator who makes it possible for us to break through the endless cycle of terms implicit in the idea of worldly order — "forever circling back upon itself, thus forever 'guilty,' and thus forever demanding 'redemption' . . ." And here "arise the modes of sacrifice that express themselves either 'suicidally,' as mortification, or 'homicidially,' in the slaying of scapegoats more or less clearly identified with the traits of human personality." In such acts, the sacrificial victim serves as a communication, the Son of God is a messenger from God, a "manifestation" of his desire to save us, while in the ascension of the smoke from the burnt offering of the sacrificial victim, men ask their gods to hear their prayers. For, if our communications do not ascend to heaven, and the communication of the gods in turn do not descend to earth, we are lost. Perhaps this explains why there is continual search for curative victims. "For it seems that, even if one believes in the idea of a perfect, supernatural, superpersonal victim, by identification with whose voluntary sacrifice one can be eternally saved, there is still the goad to look for victims here on earth as well who should be punished for their part, real or imaginary, in blocking the believer's path to felicity, or perhaps in threatening to send him on his heavenly way too soon." (p. 223)

With the introduction of the idea of redemption, and its personification in the image of the victim as the divine mediator, and the consequent formation of a specialized body of religious functionaries such as priests through whom we atone for our sins of disobedience, we come upon the fourth element in Burke's analysis of the enactment of social order. This is hierarchy, or the distribution of authority among ranks. For, although communication with God is open to anyone, certain persons are supposed to possess greater knowledge and power in securing proper results. Many people think themselves unable to communicate directly with their gods. Acknowledging their inferiority in this respect, they regard the priests as the only mediators between them and the supreme powers. The priests are their only protectors; without them they could not reach the gods whose response is necessary to salvation. The priest serves as a mediator between man and his gods; it is his principal duty to administer and regulate the communication of men and their gods. Such communication, it should be noted, is twofold; the people speak to their gods through their priests, but at the same time the gods speak to their people through their priests. Thus the power of a priesthood lies in the belief that the priests are able to put themselves into communication with the gods whenever they like.

The paradox in the priestly role, Burke points out, is that the priestly mediator "not only proposes progressively to 'absolve' from guilt; [but he] also serves circularly to intensify the very sense of guiltiness (or 'conscience') for which [he] provides the solution." And even without the priestly intensification of guilt, there is cause enough in the socio-political conditions of life to keep men in fear and anxiety. Such fear must be met by those who would rule us, for men cannot live long in fear and trembling. In such times, ruler and ruled alike turn to those who can mediate with the gods. Political and social troubles, and all the disorder of life, easily lead to dread when they are taken as a sign that "God has hidden His face from men." It is not God's will which visits suffering upon men but estrangement from God which leads to ignorance of his purpose. As Genesis teaches us in the story of the Tower of Babel, and in Eve's disobedience of God's commandment not to eat of the Tree of Knowledge, the people of Israel forfeited Divine favor because they no longer lived in fellowship with God.

As political troubles increased and gloom mounted into dread, the people came to believe that God was not pleased with them. He was displeased because they had disobeyed his commandments and in such disobedience brought disorder in the world. To absolve sin, new sacrifices were required, and a new and more powerful priesthood was selected and trained. The earlier Hebrew sacrifice which was done in joy and confidence of fellowship with God was not enough. An increasing conviction of sinfulness over disobedience of God's commandments deepened the desire to be brought close to God once again. This was done through sacrificial offerings such as the peace offering, the common meal which was an expression of fellowship with God; the Burnt Offering, the burning of a whole carcass, which was an expression of self-surrender and self-dedication; the Trespass Offering, a varied ceremony which was intended to recompense a wrong; and finally, the Sin Offering, the blood put upon the horns of the altar, which was an atonement for sin. Thus, as Schofield informs us, the atonement of Christ, as interpreted by the types of sacrifice in the Old Testament, is substitutionary since the offering takes the offerer's place in death. The sacrificial death "was an execution of the law," and the sinlessness of him who bore our sins is expressed in every animal sacrifice since the animal selected for the sacrifice "must be without blemish." And as we read in Leviticus, Chapter 16, "The Day of Atonement," the high priest Aaron cast lots upon two goats, one for the Lord and the other "for the scapegoat." Then we are told that "Aaron shall bring the goat upon which the Lord's lot fell, and offer him for an sin-offering. (v. 9) But for the goat, on which the lot fell to be the scapegoat, shall be presented alive before the Lord, to make an atonement with him, and to let him go for a scapegoat into the wilderness." (v. 10)

In view of religious uses of hierarchy as a way toward God, and in view of God's absolute sovereignty over nature, man, and society, Burke admonishes us to watch for status scales ranging variously from sovereignty to servitude. We begin, as befits the empirical nature of "logological inquiry," with the natural and socio-political orders of experience. "In the natural order, man is properly defined as a species of animal." In the socio-political order he develops forms of governance which soon inject social classification into a world of natural classification. "This state of affairs can give rise to a vision of 'moral grandeur' when the principle of social rule is extended to the natural realm — and man is seen as a 'ruler' *over all nature*. The socio-political design of governance is thus made absolute; the perspective of socio-political order is felt to infuse the natural order; all nature is seen as being out there for man's use; in sum, nature is man's servant, and man is nature's sovereign."

But, Burke argues, we do not simply pass from the socio-political to the natural. "An intermediate step is needed before the design can take form. The design must be 'mythically' duplicated by the postulating of an analogous arrangement whereby there is a supernatural (or super-socio-political) order, with its corresponding hierarchy. This formal 'perfecting' of the design, ideally duplicating the human socio-political order in 'higher' terms, was 'prior,' was 'there from the start,' to the extent that it sums up all the *principles* felt to have been guiding the socio-political order."

Religious vision says in effect: "Only if the socio-political order is on such-and-such relations with the principles of all order, can the order be reasonable." It is in this way that the "perfecting myth" becomes "like the *originator* of the order it perfects." Once this is done, the final step of the leap into the supernatural is easy enough. The powers of nature, of man, of the sovereigns of the world are in servitude to the principles or laws of social order by which the world is implicitly guided. Even the gods themselves end in servitude to the laws of the universe which they have created and upheld. In this final step, the ruler and his humblest share in submission to the principles of social order. Once such mythic perfection can be imagined, a corresponding design in nature can be imagined. "And the reversal, whereby the man who was ruler becomes himself an underling, removes the imperfections that might otherwise spoil the symmetry of the scheme. That is, insofar as natural calamities defy man's governance, these can be explained as the acts of the higher authority." This does not do away with the problem of the truth or falsity of a myth, it simply "explains the verbal mechanisms by which such myths can arise, regardless of whether they are true or false." (p. 241)

◇◇

See the notes on pages 260 and 357.

THIS is the last and longest of the reviews of *The Rhetoric of Religion* that I know of. The reception of this book marks some sort of nadir in the larger reception of Burke which is hard to explain save in the way that I have done earlier. That a man who had tried and achieved so much should have a major work received so disgracefully – i.e., hardly noticed at all by any element of the American intelligentsia – is a sad indictment of American culture. The reception of Edmund Wilson during the sixties makes an interesting contrast. Each man's achievement is formidable in different ways; that Wilson's should make such a powerful appeal at all levels of the intellectual life of this country is as difficult to understand as what happened to Burke.

As usual, Hugh Duncan's review treats Burke in a sociological context and examines, as few others have done, the role of literature in society. Mr. Duncan is concerned here, as in the earlier selection, with the problem of models or paradigms and with the way in which Burke can be made to function in sociological study. Also, as usual, Hugh Duncan provides one with reliable exposition of Burke's development and system.

◇◇

z Guilt and History

BY Alvin C. Kibel

FOR some time now Kenneth Burke has been extrapolating a theory of literature into a comprehensive view of human nature and society, even while producing it. The enterprise may be compared, perhaps, to the way in which a literary work like *Hamlet* or *Don Quixote* establishes relations to experience that, in turn, influence future readings of it, until the work becomes what philosophers term a "self-fulfilling prophecy" that brings about the conditions of its own truth; only in Burke's case, the work is a critical system still incomplete and the experience is of all the various symbolic activities that comprise human culture. Burke's intention, I think, is to provide a philosophic basis for the practice of "cultural studies" – that form of criticism which takes the understanding of imaginative literature as paradigmatic for the understanding of culture generally. One requisite of this daunting activity is to make abrupt forays from literature into psychology, philosophy and social theory, testing the synoptic power of a critical vocabulary during the process of evolving it. The reader approaching Burke for the first time may, in consequence, experience some difficulty in knowing where to pick up the thread of argument; and Mr. Hyman [who edited *Perspectives by Incongruity* and *Terms for Order*] has done this reader service in separating the wider-ranging excursions from the more straightforward work and offering a representative selection from each.

The continuity of Burke's theoretical development can be made clear by the following, quite early passage.

> The experiences of maturity are revisions and amplifications of . . . childhood patterns. An adult, for instance, may turn his thoughts from a father to a father-government; yet even in later life, should he take an axe and fell a great tree, we need not be surprised to find a strange misgiving permeate him as the noble symbol of shelter comes crashing to the earth. For however neutral his act, though the tree has been felled to satisfy the simple utilitarian needs of firewood, there may also be lurking here a kind of symbolic parricide. Not only firewood, but a parent-symbol, may be brought down in the crash.

Burke's was not the psychoanalytic point that we must all wrestle with demons engendered during early childhood; the Freudian vocabulary

EDITOR'S NOTE: Reprinted from *The American Scholar*, XXXIV (Spring 1965), 303–306, copyright © 1965 by the United Chapters of Phi Beta Kappa, by permission of the author and publisher.

simply gave him a convenient handle for grasping a bulkier theory. Like Freud, Burke looks forward to a modification in our experience of guilt. Unlike Freud, however, he does not trace the origins of suppressed guilt-feelings to events in prehistory, recapitulated during the first few years of life; nor does he look upon religion precisely as a mass-neurosis, no better at promoting an ideal inner strength than the individual neuroses of secular men. For Burke, on the contrary, guilt is endemic to *any* human condition: it is virtually identical with the unacknowledged self-hatred that must accompany man's conflict with himself, nature, his fellowmen (trees being, after all, private property). Man's life comprises not only physical motion but also symbolical action; one can quarrel with one's father or, like Hume, write a book denying the real, substantial power of antecedent causes. Burke doesn't mean to challenge the autonomy of philosophic effort by such interpretations; he means rather to argue the presence of poetic motives in metaphysical thought—means, that is, to underwrite poetry as the archetype of symbolic action generally, because it offers not only symbolical experiences but also appropriate symbolical expiations.

To begin with, Burke's concern was with the competitive paradigms of modern industrial society, which seemed increasingly to demand the commission of symbolical outrages at the very moment that man had lost the memory of communal techniques (religious practices, ancestral customs, traditional pieties) for the propitiating of inner guilt; lately he has been occupied in tracing the guilt-producing mechanisms inherent in the use of language itself. Like Eliot and the New Critics, Burke looks back to an imagined age of communal piety; unlike them, however, he doesn't take poetry as a mere symptom of some higher sensibility, integral or dissociated, as the case may be. For Burke the evacuation of specifically religious feelings signaled an improvement in the psychic economy, and poetry (an acknowledged touch of I. A. Richards here) offers the efficient, humane substitute—both as ritual preparation for life and as a kind of limiting case against which other symbolical activities can be measured. It is the old romantic dream, refurbished out of Freud and Cassirer—"knowledge not purchased by the loss of power."

This account is much too summary to suggest the full range of Burke's ideas; it skimps, for example, his primary emphasis upon poetry as cognition. In some ways, the fault is Mr. Hyman's, whose selections in this double volume reflect his own interest in mythic and ritual *motifs*. (To use a Burkean notation-by-italics, Mr. Hyman is basically concerned with poetry as *symbolic* action, Burke himself with poetry as symbolic *action*.) But in some ways, Burke lends his system to just this summary judgment. To be sure, the notion that symbolic guilt is the by-product of all specifically human activity leads to the kind of literary study that avoids the reduction of art to "salvation" archetypes (in this manner of much New Criticism) and skirts the dangers of Freudian reduction to archetypes of neurosis. Yet one cannot say that Burke has identified guilt as our primary humane emotion with any proficiency: it is simply the *given* of his system, and the result, I think, is a loss in genuine historical perspective. In some ways, Burke is the most diligent of our modern critics. His orientation leads him to take the intricate functioning of a poem as one thing for the poet, another for his readers, and both as important coordinates for critical interpretation. But Burke's theory can do scant justice to the modifications that the changing organization of communal life has worked upon the experience of subliminal guilt. In his critical universe, every *is* projects an *ought,* every assertion of being, however neutral, implies the infringing of secret prohibitions. This sounds like an induction not from literary experience, but from modern literary experience, which frequently dramatizes the obscuring of connections between efficient (hence "reasonable") social activity and the workings of conscience – an obscuring characteristic of modern technological civilization. Burke's literary analyses, then, leave one with the feeling that every work has somehow been made over into an uneasy anticipation of Kafka. This collection represents the two books Burke has been in the course of writing all his life, neither quite successful. Both immensely repay study.

◇◇

ALVIN C. KIBEL was born in 1933. He was educated at Columbia University and has taught English at the City College of New York, Wesleyan, and at the Massachusetts Institute of Technology. He has published articles and reviews in many journals, including *The American Scholar, The Kenyon Review,* and *Partisan Review.* He is currently at work on a study of modern literary criticism.

The early sixties were lean and disappointing years for Burke, who wouldn't or couldn't finish *A Symbolic of Motives,* and for Burkeans, who were waiting for it. *The Rhetoric of Religion* passed almost unnoticed and the various second editions were never reviewed in any significant way. It was not until the publication of this two-volume, all purpose selection from Burke by Stanley Edgar Hyman and Barbara Karmiller that the reception of Burke was revived. This two-volume sampler was, as they say, well received and was followed shortly after by a spate of other books by Burke and the promise of many more to come in short order. Burke's reception has always followed his development very closely. After 1965 and especially after Burke got settled with a new publisher — the University of California Press — that suited him, new books and the promise of more kept coming.

This brief and perceptive review is an indication of how a much younger generation takes Burke. They have come to or on him at a time when his system was nearly complete and through teachers who grew up on him. And they have often been trained on very sophisticated kinds of verbal analysis so that what Burke is doing is not new to them and they are ready to assess him for what he is worth to them almost at once. It is too soon to say how this generation will take or take to Burke. Their needs change so rapidly and so many of them are so antithetical to systems of any kind that one hesitates to make any kind of prediction.

◇◇

Notes on the Reception of Kenneth Burke in Europe

BY Armin Paul Frank

IN ORDER to assess the reception of Kenneth Burke in Europe, it is not sufficient to appraise the pertinent views and opinions of European scholars and critics. An article by, say, René Wellek, who is European both in training and in basic outlook, published in an American quarterly would even be irrelevant from this point of view. Rather, the emphasis in this survey must be rhetorical in the Burkean sense, i.e. audience-oriented. As a consequence, all comments on, and critiques of, Burke's work written specifically for the reading public in European countries will be dealt with here. Such publications have shaped the attitude of Europeans toward Mr. Burke probably more than his own work, particularly since not a single one of his books has so far been translated in its entirety.

The method of presentation in this survey is chronological, and an effort is made to be fair both to his critics and to Mr. Burke.

As early as 1926, when he had only published one book, Kenneth Burke was brought to the attention of at least a part of the European reading public. Indeed, "In and About the Workshop of Kenneth Burke," which *The Calendar*, a London literary review, carried in its

EDITOR'S NOTE: Written for this volume in 1966 (revised 1968).

July issue of that year,[1] was the first long article dealing with both his imaginative and his critical work published up to that time. The author of the essay is an American writer and editor who later professed that his indebtedness to Burke, as far as aesthetic theory is concerned, dated back to 1922–23 when the two men temporarily worked together on the editorial board of the short-lived little *tendenz* magazine *Secession*.[2]

In his article, Gorham B. Munson finds much to praise in Burke's stories, among which he singles out "Olympians" (1922), "The Book of Yul" (1922), and "Prince Llan" (1924) as representative stages of Burke's purposive development as a creative writer. He does, however, reinterpret the author's analysis of his own development and the corresponding arrangement of the stories in the book in which they were collected in 1924, *The White Oxen*. Whereas Burke presents this sequence as a "gradual shifting of stress away from the realistically convincing and true to life" to the "more rhetorical properties of letters,"[3] Munson discerns the "abstract," i.e. nonrepresentative, as the end of this progression: a "cool and moving design" which has almost no relationship with "human problems and behaviour at large." As proof he adduces a somewhat superficial analogy to Aristotle's quantitative parts in terms of beginning, sheer progression, and end, which he uses to support a possible "abstract" reading of "The Book of Yul"; he also draws upon a letter (no date given) in which Burke discusses the possibilities of "abstract" writing in terms of a sequence of beginning, relationships between the parts, end, and coda.

In the light of such an analysis of "Yul" it is not surprising that Munson should emphasize the aspect of "pure aestheticism" as he proceeds to a discussion of Burke's criticism then extant. Mainly relying on the two seminal essays "The Poetic Process" (1925) and "Psychology and Form" (1925) and the Flaubert paper (1922),[4] Munson sums up Burke's critical position at that time in five statements: the function of art is to control waking dreams of the audience; its essence is eloquence; the poetic process is an individuation of basic forms of the mind; the artist's personal process is the turning of means into ends in themselves; and "the good life" is "the multiplication of those satisfying emotional experiences." This summary of several tightly reasoned essays which are based on highly sensitive aesthetic observations is as correct as such summaries usually are.

[1] G. B. Munson, *The Calendar*, III, 2 (July 1926), 129–141; reprinted in *Destinations: A Canvas of American Literature* (New York: J. H. Sears, 1928), pp. 136–159.

[2] Cf. "The Fledgling Years, 1916–1924," *The Sewanee Review*, XL, 1 (January–March 1932), 24–54; esp. 35, 40.

[3] *The White Oxen and Other Stories* (New York: A. and C. Boni, 1924), p. ix.

[4] All three reprinted in *Counter-Statement* (New York: Harcourt, Brace, 1931).

Munson goes on to argue that the Romantic aestheticism of this position is only a half-truth, and he maintains that such a formalistic monism must be complemented by a striving for "objectivity and consciousness" with regard to subject matter, too. "Prince Llan" he sees as a preliminary exercise in, and tentative step toward, some such position, although he rejects the particular kind of harmonious "dualism of mutual completion" which he regards as the epiphany of "Prince Llan"; in a way which is suggestive of his neo-humanist sympathies, he proclaims the necessity of a controlled dualism of coercion. In his judgment, Kenneth Burke is an excellent prosateur, a writer of modern artistic fiction, and a "fine resilient type of critic"; but, taking away with the one hand what he has given with the other, he maintains that Burke, caught between his aestheticism and the saving alternative of neoclassicism, is "too intelligent to remain an aesthete." Yet how could Burke have written the kind of fiction Munson praises and not be the "aesthete" he then was?

To be sure, Kenneth Burke was to develop and elaborate his critical theory, although not along the lines Munson had tried to lay out for him. As his system of thought gradually unfolded to become "Dramatism," it did so not by any radical breaks with previously held views but rather, discarding nothing, by encompassing new points of view and areas of knowledge and speculation, each new phase, as it were, growing out of, but never outgrowing, modifying, but never destroying, what had already been established. But this "rounding out" of the system failed to come to the attention of European observers for quite some time, at least as far as the records tell.

It is, of course, not surprising that many foreign cultural and intellectual events of the later thirties and the forties should have gone unnoticed by Europeans; but even after the aggressive provincialism of Nazi Germany had burned itself up, devastating major parts of other countries in the process, even at a time when material, cultural, and intellectual goods poured into, and were eagerly absorbed by, the wasteland that Europe then was, there is hardly any evidence of a Burkeian influence. American literature and literary criticism made a strong impact. Hemingway, Steinbeck, Wilder, Williams, Frost, Cummings — a random listing — found a ready audience; the "New Criticism," primarily the variation that came to be known as "Yale formalism," influenced the teaching of English literature at many universities in Europe. Such works as Wellek and Warren's *Theory of Literature*, Brooks and Warren's *Understanding Poetry*, and C. Brooks' *The Well-Wrought Urn* became basic texts of many English departments, especially in Germany, and were translated for popular editions;[5] their influence is also evident in many textbooks specifically written for German high school and university students.[6] Scholarly studies in this field abound; there will be occasion to refer to several of them later on.

But in this high-tide influx of American literary ideas even the material basis for a wider reception of Kenneth Burke is very small. Only four translations of essays have come to the present writer's notice.[7] The German version of the title essay from *The Philosophy of Literary Form* (1941), *Dichtung als symbolische Handlung* (1966), certainly could contribute substantially to an understanding of Burke; but though it appeared in a popular series, its publication is too recent to permit an assessment of the impact. The same is true of another translation of Burke's work in this same German series, his contribution to the 1965 Texas Formalist Symposium, "Formalist Criticism: Its Principles and Limitations," a concise and witty summary of his critical position. "The Seven Offices" (1958), which simultaneously appeared in French as "Les Motifs d'action," is characteristic of Burke's thought, but extremely difficult if read in isolation. "Antony in Behalf of the Play" (1935), translated as "Marcus Antonius spricht zum Publikum" (1953), is also a fine, characteristic piece, but perhaps not the best choice as an introduction either, particularly since some of the central points of the rhetorical analysis do not come off so well in German.

Such language difficulties do not beset the English. What is more, one at least of Burke's books has seen a United Kingdom edition, *A Grammar of Motives*;[8] but this occasion was seized by *Scrutiny* to publish a large-scale attack by Marius Bewley, a United States citizen

[5] Wellek and Warren's *Theory of Literature* has been widely translated; among other languages it has appeared in Spanish (1953), Italian (1956), and German (1959). Other influential books of American criticism translated into German are C. Brooks' *The Well-Wrought Urn* (a selection published as *Paradoxie im Gedicht*, Frankfurt: Suhrkamp, 1965) and R. P. Warren's *Selected Essays* (*Ausgewählte Essays*, Gütersloh: Mohn, 1961).

[6] W. Hüllen *et al.*, *Zeitgenössische amerikanische Dichtung: Eine Einführung in die amerikanische Literaturbetrachtung mit Texten und Interpretationen* (Frankfurt: Hirschgrabenverlag, 1960); J. Hagopian *et al.*, *Insight*, 2 vols. (Frankfurt: Hirschgrabenverlag, 1962, 1964).

[7] "Marcus Antonius spricht zum Publikum," *Perspektiven*, No. 5 (November 1953), 137–150; "Les Motifs d'action," *Diogène*, No. 21 (Winter 1958), 82–103 (there is a parallel South American edition, in Spanish); *Dichtung als symbolische Handlung: Eine Theorie der Literatur* (Frankfurt: Suhrkamp, 1966); "Formalistische Literaturkritik: ihre Prinzipien und Grenzen," in Elder Olson *et al.*, *Über Formalismus: Diskussion eines ästhetischen Begriffs* (Frankfurt: Suhrkamp, 1966), pp. 55–93.

[8] London: D. Dobson, 1947. Only two of Burke's essays appeared in British publications: "Trial Translation (From Twelfth Night)," *The New English Weekly*, II, 16 (2 February 1933), 273–274; "Thanatopsis for Critics," *Essays in Criticism*, II, 4 (October 1952), 369–375.

who was then closely associated with F. R. Leavis and his group.[9] Once before Burke had received some incidental rough treatment in the pages of the same review when H. B. Parkes, in an article on "The American Cultural Scene" – so different in tone and assessment from his previous deliberative review of *Attitudes toward History*[10] – referred to Burke's "very rich, though . . . very perverse mind," and described him as an unorthodox Marxist who supported the Communist party and had become – of all things – a "historian rather than a critic of literature."[11] This time *Scrutiny*'s mission was an all-out debunking of Burke's work.

In his essay "Kenneth Burke as Literary Critic," Bewley, quite in keeping with his critical orientation, flatly rejects the psychological, autocathartic foundation of Burke's theory of the Symbolic Act, and the socialist leanings of his criticism. Tentatively describing Burke as the "High Priest of a new critical liturgicism," Bewley nevertheless finds that there is "little that is radically new in Burke." His contribution, Bewley feels, is but one of formulation, of developing a vocabulary that "insulates its user against the shock of the work of art itself" and that provides disciples with a methodology which they will be able to use as a machine to "speed away from any very exacting evaluation of a work of art." But it seems to me that some critics do not even need a "machine" of this type to perform marvels of such "speeding," not only in interpretation but even at the more pedestrian level of plain reading. Thus, for instance, when Bewley calls Burke's grouping of *The Waste Land,* the *U.S.A.* trilogy, and *The Grapes of Wrath* under the heading of drought imagery "irrelevant," he suppresses the immediate context in which Burke strongly asserts the necessity of introducing *differentiae*: "It would be absurd, on noting the imagery of drought in common to Eliot's poem and Steinbeck's novel to conclude: '*The Grapes of Wrath* is just *The Waste Land* over again.'"[12] To be fair to Bewley it must be added that, apart from such overt admonitions, this kind of differentiation is only dealt with *implicitly* in Burke's criticism.

Bewley is especially opposed to Burke's "gruesome substitution of the word 'statistical' for 'symbolic'" and describes the analysis of a poem in terms of Symbolic Action as "something similar to Caroline

[9] "Kenneth Burke as Literary Critic," *Scrutiny*, XV, 4 (December 1948), 254–277; reprinted in *The Complex Fate* (London: Chatto and Windus, 1952), pp. 211–243.

[10] "Kenneth Burke (A Review of *Attitudes toward History*)" (1938), *The Pragmatic Test: Essays on the History of Ideas* (San Francisco: The Colt Press, 1941), pp. 202–220.

[11] *Scrutiny*, VIII, 1 (June 1939), 7–8.

[12] *The Philosophy of Literary Form: Studies in Symbolic Action*, 2nd ed. (Baton Rouge: Louisiana State University Press, 1967), pp. 36–37.

Spurgeon's indexing of images," a "counting of image clusters and psycho-analysing them." Now it is true that Burke's use of the term 'statistical' is not an altogether felicitous strategy because *terminologically* it does imply a "numerical principle of the individuation of a poem" (Bewley). But the reason for Bewley's failure to follow through with his refutation of such a view lies in the fact that *methodologically* the Burkeian analysis of a poem is only partly a statistical procedure, a "counting of image clusters" in a given work spread out before the analyst; it involves the essentially dramatic phase of discovering the agonistic alignment of the various clusters, and the dynamic phase of determining the nature of the progressive transformation of images – a phase which definitely takes this method beyond statistics as Bewley uses the term. Also, the psychoanalytic part of the analysis of the Symbolic Act is not simply a reduction of a given work to the "psychological urgencies behind the composition." The importance of the "literariness" of a work, the part played by the medium and its conventions, was emphatically asserted in the formative phase of Burke's criticism [13] and was, indeed, never jettisoned as the system developed.[14]

Bewley's central reservation against Burke's literary criticism (which can certainly be discovered behind each single objection) can be isolated when one examines such curious statements as the one in which he asserts that Burke's ideas, although frequently stimulating if taken separately, are "something of a plague" when they occur as closely packed as they do in Burke's writing. Now, on reading such a queer formulation, a facetious remark of the type Bewley himself is fond of making may easily come to mind. But a serious critical problem is involved in this curiously phrased observation. Kenneth Burke is indeed more interested in the theory of literature than in a limited analysis of texts in epistemological isolation, although even adverse critics of his work from time to time concede his skill in confronting the poetical text; [15] furthermore, he recognizes the close connection between literary activity and human action in general. In this sense, he is in the mainstream of the tradition of Pragmatic aesthetics. Bewley

[13] Cf. for instance Burke's stressing of "technical form," of "virtues" which are not part of the original expressive act of the poet in "The Poetic Process," *Counter-Statement*, pp. 57–78; also, his emphasis on the *verbalization* of experience (*ibid.*, p. 7) and his concept of eloquence as the essence of art (*ibid.*, pp. 40–41), which is the key concept of *Counter-Statement*.

[14] One striking instance is the discussion of the relationship between the Nazi mentality and the literary context in the work of Thomas Mann; cf. *Philosophy of Literary Form*, p. 49.

[15] Thus B. Placido singles out the essay on Keats' "Urn" as a "happy instance" of Burke's practical criticism; see "La Critica americana contemporanea," *Studi americani*, VIII (1962), 324.

recognizes such a view with approval; but he feels that the use Burke makes of this idea in his criticism restricts his method to a purely extrinsic approach. Burke's method, he says, is an *abstraction* of the Symbolic Act from the work proper; a "perspective by incongruity," it might be added, which defines literature in terms of what it is *not*. Bewley is particularly opposed to the minimizing or debunking mode of this perspective which, he feels, is but a flexible instrument of Marxist criticism.

What Bewley overlooks is the fact that it is absolutely inevitable for a commenting or interpreting critic of any affiliation whatever to use some sort of a "perspective by incongruity." Thus, for instance, William Empson – surely a textual critic if there ever was one – explains poems in terms of what they are not, namely the dictionary; [16] Bewley himself has attempted to elucidate some of Wallace Stevens' *early* poems in terms of his *later* poetry [17] – no doubt a most interesting "perspective." Such is the dilemma of the commenting or interpreting critic: however firmly he focuses his attention on the text, the very nature of his endeavor will cause him to resort to terms and operations other than those of the text, if only because in discussing his object – the poem – he also implicitly or explicitly refers to his sensibility, method, experience, etc. Eliot's repeated warning to shun any kind of interpretative criticism is very much to the point. If criticism is thus restricted to the furnishing of information about the work which the reader cannot reasonably be assumed to possess, interpretation is singled out as an act of experience concomitant with each individual reading of the poem. It does not follow, however, that one must not communicate one's personal act of interpretation; he who chooses to do so should, of course, be aware that a certain level of abstraction, and hence of theory, and the introduction of a perspective by incongruity of some kind are necessary conditions of such a procedure. It is, therefore, quite possible to accept Bewley's term "translation" to describe Burke's Dramatistic analysis of a poem; all that one would have to add is the recognition that "translation" in this sense is the *sine qua non* of any kind of critical analysis and that therefore *in principle* this term cannot be used – as by Bewley – to imply a censure. Bewley, for instance, finds

[16] "Apparently he [Empson] reasons that, since poetry is language highly charged with meaning, the poetic word must invariably stagger under the full weight of its dictionary significances." Elder Olson, "William Empson, Contemporary Criticism, and Poetic Diction," *Critics and Criticism, Ancient and Modern*, ed. R. S. Crane (Chicago: University of Chicago Press, 1952), p. 48. Olson points out many instances where Empson's analyses so clutter a line with "meaning" that it actually becomes meaningless.

[17] "The Poetry of Wallace Stevens," *The Complex Fate*, pp. 150–170.

Burke's analysis of Keats' "Urn" totally unsatisfactory because it also relies on material relating to Keats the man – not only the poet – and because he feels that there is too little contact between the interpretation and the "words themselves"; he even resorts to a kind of statistics which culminates in the observation that "out of three and a half pages devoted to the first two stanzas, only a page and a half is concerned with the actual text."

This last, purely external censure is definitely not much to the point, but neither are many of Bewley's more argumentative objections because in almost every instance they fail to take fully into consideration the explicit or implicit meaning and the argumentative context of the specific passages of Burke's texts they criticize. What is more, a thoroughly convincing rebuttal of a given critical approach, apart from a theoretical refutation, cannot do without the establishment of a rival approach which reveals its superiority *in performance*, by giving a richer reading of the poetic text than the one that is objected to; yet Bewley fails thus to balance the theoretical by the practical.

"The only serviceable argument for another calculus [i.e. critical method] would be its explicit proclamation and the illustrating of its scope of concrete application." This statement from *The Philosophy of Literary Form* [18] may be taken as the implied motto of an article by Sven Linnér, which appeared in the Swedish literary magazine *Samlaren* in the same year in which Bewley's *Scrutiny* essay was republished in *The Complex Fate*.[19] Linnér, who describes Burke's as the most stimulating critical theory he has so far studied, applies the Dramatistic analysis of symbolic action to a poem by Pär Lagerkvist, "Det är vackrast när det skymmer." Quite correctly he defines "'symbolic action" as a principle of order and unity of the poem which is, however, not at all identical with it – a perspective by incongruity, then, which, he feels, is capable of "infusing new life into a poem."

The main tool for analyzing this structure, according to Linnér, is the pentad as developed in *A Grammar of Motives*: scene, act, agent, agency, and purpose. The one reservation he has, however, concerns the fifth term, purpose, which he interprets as a principle of activity; yet he asks whether an agent, such as the lyrical ego of Lagerkvist's poem, might not experience a state of complete passivity, hence absolute purposelessness. From the example given by Linnér it is evident that

[18] *Loc. cit.*, p. 124.

[19] "Kenneth Burke's teori om 'symbolic action' tillämpad på en Lagerkvistdikt" (Burke's Theory of "Symbolic Action" Applied to a Poem by Lagerkvist), *Samlaren*, XXXIII (1952), 44–53; the present author is indebted to Mrs. H. Clerwall-Halbe of the J. W. Goethe-Universität, Frankfurt, for the translation of this article.

he relates "purpose" to the "I" as a *character in the poem.* But this is not "purpose" as a Dramatistic concept. Perhaps a reference back to the inception of Burke's critical theory in *Counter-Statement* will serve to make it completely clear that the "psychology of the hero (the subject)" never amounted to much in Burke's criticism;[20] "chart," the realistic dimension of art, was always slighted. The main concern was either with "audience psychology" – i.e. the rhetorical dimension, the poem as controlling audience responses – or with "author psychology" – i.e. the symbolic dimension, "what the poem does for its author."[21] "Purpose" in the Dramatistic sense relates to this "creative act," to the lyrical ego as the *personal principle controlling the whole poem.* Linnér, to be sure, is analyzing exactly this "purpose" of what he calls the "character of the poem as an act of experience" when he employs the scene-agent ratio for a sensitive sounding of the shift of attitude accomplished by the second stanza of the poem, and when he concludes that the motive of the poem is "fearlessly to accept death." His method is indeed more Burkeian than he seems to be aware of.

The year 1953 could have been decisive as far as the reception of Kenneth Burke's work is concerned. It was the year of the reissue of *Counter-Statement,* the first of the early books of criticism to see a new edition. Most of these early books were among the rarities in European libraries; the new editions helped to fill gaps. But their impact was not immediately felt in Europe. For several years yet, scholarly surveys of contemporary criticism in the United States, doctoral dissertations in the field, and studies of related special subjects continued to ignore

[20] Cf. *Counter-Statement,* p. 42.

[21] This functional conception of the symbolic, based on the author-cathartic aspect of a literary work, is central to *The Philosophy of Literary Form.* Burke later widened the meaning of the term symbolic to include man's linguistic behavior in general, thereby deflecting the emphasis from author-catharsis to the properties of language as such. This shift is in keeping with the first clause of his "Definition of Man" (*The Hudson Review,* XVI, 4, Winter 1963–64, 491–514), i.e., "man is the symbol-using animal" (cf. *The Rhetoric of Religion,* Boston: Beacon Press, 1962, pp. 40–42). An important step in this development is marked by the essay "Terministic Screens" (*Proceedings of the American Catholic Philosophical Association,* Washington, D.C.: Catholic University of America Press, 1965, pp. 87–102). Burke takes a final terminological step in this development of his thought by coining the slight neologism "symbolicity" to denote this dimension of human behavior (cf. "Formalist Criticism: Its Principles and Limitations," *The Texas Quarterly,* IX, 1, Spring 1966, 242–268). In this sense, the title of Burke's most recent collection of essays, *Language as Symbolic Action: Essays on Life, Literature, and Method* (Berkeley and Los Angeles: University of California Press, 1966 – the book contains the essays just mentioned together with 21 others), covers a different and wider range of meaning than the subtitle of the collection of 25 years ago, *The Philosophy of Literary Form: Studies in Symbolic Action.*

Burke's work, or to devote only one or two nondescript sentences to it; or they communicated errors, partly because of lack of information, partly because of adverse bias. A particularly striking example of this kind occurred in 1954 when the *Times Literary Supplement* devoted a special issue to "American Writing Today." The author of "Literary Criticism: The Minds behind the Written Word"[22] feels that only such recent works as Randall Jarrell's *Poetry and the Age* are in the salubrious tradition of Henry James and his "delicate and specific personal perceptions," whereas most of the other critics, adulterated by the "Roman atmosphere of the United States," tend to follow Poe, and "cry constantly for an ideal method or set of water-tight categories." Among the earlier twentieth-century critics Spingarn is given some condescending praise for his good intention of focusing critical scrutiny on the text itself, and More and Babbitt are singled out for what they have in common with Eliot – standards of judgment set above the critic's as well as the poet's temperament. Blackmur, finally, is presented as the most outstanding critic who is "a perfect illustration of what Spingarn had in mind," one who is even better than many of the English impressionistic critics because he sticks to the text and always makes intelligent judgments, "unlike some other American textual critics." His criticism is "not only an act of illumination but a work of art in itself."

Kenneth Burke, by contrast, is anathema; by comparison with Blackmur the reader is given to understand that he is esoteric, has neither common nor extraordinary sense, parades his knowledge, and uses literature for extra-literary purposes. The reviewer, who is apparently completely unaware that Kenneth Burke has also written some fine fiction, and poetry too, goes on to single out unrelated items from Burke's books of criticism which, wrenched from the context as they are, seem to support his view that Burke is a Pavlovian experimenter with the artist's personality and is interested solely in literature's prose meanings and the Freudian connotations of words. This atrocious misrepresentation is only possible because the reviewer seems to be unwilling to follow any one of Burke's arguments coherently. This method would make it easy to put anyone down as a representative specimen of the American "jargon critic" who, corrupted by Freud, had better leave literature alone; such is the reviewer's opinion of Burke. Yvor Winters used a similar method in his discussion of Eliot.[23] All that is achieved in either case is the parading of a certain acrimonious bias.

[22] *Times Literary Supplement*, Special Issue, 17 September 1954, pp. viii, x.

[23] Cf. *In Defense of Reason*, 3rd ed. (Denver: Alan Swallow, n.d.), pp. 460–501.

The most comprehensive and ambitious European study of Kenneth Burke's work to appear so far was published in Italy in 1957. In his essay "Kenneth Burke e la critica americana,"[24] Luciano Gallino sets out to read and comprehend, not to praise or outlaw, Burke's work in terms of philosophy, and he ends up by writing one of the most scathing condemnations so far — one that amounts to a wholesale dismissal of practically all American criticism because Burke is given representational value.

According to Gallino, who supports this part of his argument mainly by references to *Permanence and Change,* there are two typically American elements at the basis of Burke's philosophy: transcendental biologism ("metabiology") and neo-stoicism. Both are typically American in the sense that they are rooted in nineteenth-century Romantic thought, and Burke reveals in his reliance on them that he is unaware of more recent intellectual developments. As far as metabiology is concerned, Gallino says, the antecedents are even more remote, namely Kantian. According to Gallino, Burke, like Kant, realizes that human action cannot be justified without a firm grounding in a moral imperative; moreover, he recognizes the impossibility of determining rationally the nature of this moral basis. Instead, he asserts the ethical nature of the *bios* itself, which places him in the tradition of American speculative biology, of Stanhope and Agassiz, and later of the post-Darwinian "conciliators" of biological evolutionism and ethics, Chauncy Wright and John Fiske. Unlike Romantic thinkers such as Emerson and Whitman, however, the twentieth-century American conciliators of this type (Burke, Tate, Cowley, and Wilson, according to Gallino) had to accommodate even more heterogenous material, namely — apart from Darwinism — Marxism, psychoanalysis, analytical psychology, behaviorism, etc.; these centrifugal forces proved too strong, and the result was twentieth-century neo-stoicism, the doctrine of sustained tension. (At this point, it may be noted, the certainty with which Gallino pins down this development as typically American becomes dubious when one remembers that an openly documented source of Burke's practice of sustaining opposite viewpoints is the concept of *Ironie* as propounded by Thomas Mann, who can hardly be put down as an American or as a Romantic.)

However, even though difficult to reach, such an absolute, universal transcendent philosophical foundation, skeptically grounded, is the objective of Burke's intellectual quest. On this point and some subsequent ones, agreement with Gallino is possible, although one would like to dissociate oneself from his invective. Gallino, for his part, is

[24] *Studi americani,* III (1957), 315–346.

quite outspoken on this point: "At the very moment when Burke's thought wins through to the highest insight – the recognition of life as the manifestation of the cosmos – it is already on the point of falling back into the most extreme stupidity: the negation of life as realized in the historical process."[25] The turning point, according to Gallino, is the closing paragraph of *Permanence and Change*, where Burke "abandons" thought for myth. The really aggravating error of Burke, particularly evident in *A Grammar of Motives*, is seen in the fact that "his system pretends to be a general dialectic of human discourse – an intention which could only be executed by *differentiating* the temporal from the a-temporal, by keeping in mind the fact that what is historically immanent becomes real only in so far as it is *different from* the transcendent, whereas it becomes inane if one intends to reduce the multiplicity of the former to the unity of the 'substance' of the latter. Thus, the dialectical foundation of 'Dramatism' turns into a negation of dialectics."

Gallino's main objection to Burke's criticism is that the concept of "chart," i.e. the realistic aspect of a poem, is altogether neglected by Burke in the sense that he never copes with *differentiae*, although he recognizes the necessity of so doing. Thus Burke's criticism, totally deductive and extensive at the same time, is only concerned with *genus* and abandons the first task of criticism, *krinein*, to discern. Moreover, Gallino feels that the failure of Burke to account for *differentiae* is not only an oversight, which could be amended by a further elaboration of his theory, but a categorical shortcoming implied in its very structure. The case, Gallino says, is irreparable because of Burke's definition of form as audience psychology and/or author psychology: "In both instances Burke's concept of form is derived from 'basic psychological generalities' and is only in a most superficial way related to those historically determined elements of a given work which do not reside in the psychic traumas of the author nor in the audience's 'demands' which inevitably are psychic, too." According to Gallino, all that Burke's criticism can do is translate a work, give a completely inadequate description: "Founded on the concept of the *noumenon*, Burke's criticism tries to describe the *phenomenon*, i.e. the historical accident which is the literary work. Consequently, Burke's concept of form is inane in the sense that the historically determined elements which are conjoined in the work do not correspond to it; because of this insufficiency, it [the form] can never tilt over into content [i.e. has no intrinsic relation

[25] *Ibid.*, p. 331. Indebtedness for philological advice on the translation of this article to Dott. Alessandro Cavalli of the Università L. Bocconi, Milano, Italy, is gratefully acknowledged.

to its content] . . . hence it cannot contribute to the description of the given fact (of the literary work) which, in order to be grasped as a beingness [*esseità*] autonomous from its content, must primarily be regarded in terms of heterogenous content, i.e. as negation of the independence of form." Another way of putting this objection is to say that Burke's criticism fails because its particular version of the "gesture" concept of language disregards the intuitive-expressive nucleus or communicative content without which a speech act is downright impossible.

Now it is true that Gallino locates some weak spots in Burke's literary theory: it does not recognize the historical dimension, and it does to an extent discount the realistic element. To accommodate the historical perspective is not necessarily to relapse into naive chronicling. On the other hand, to look at things *sub specie aeternitatis* also implies the historical perspective because there is no way to discount the historical standpoint of the observer, and a theory which does not rationalize this *conditio sine qua non* of its existence will suffer from this neglect almost like a person who fails to come to terms with his particular form of the *condition humaine*. But it is just as true that Gallino, because of his particular form of left-wing Hegelian bias, pushes his criticism farther than is justified. In the first place, Burke's psychologistic definition of form is not at all as inane as Gallino thinks it is: subject matter is not the only type of realistic detail that makes a work concrete. Not only the "topic" but both the attitudes of the author which are somehow expressed and the attitudes of the audience upon which the work plays are part of the material that is artistically transformed; and both are just as historically grounded as the topic. Burke is aware of this, notably in his Keats essay, in "Antony in Behalf of the Play," and in "Othello."[26] Gallino is not; hence his objection that Burke's concept of form is incapable of participating in the dialectical process of aesthetic form and content is unfounded.

What is more, there is something wrong with Gallino's own concept of a dialectical aesthetics. His continued emphasis on *content* reveals that it suffers from the same shortcoming affecting Hegel's own aesthetics: in both cases, the dialectic was not fully developed. The key sentence of Hegel's *Aesthetics* which defines beauty as the sensuous shining forth of the idea may easily slacken and fall back into an undialectical, ideological *aesthetics of content*: the work of art may—and

[26] "Symbolic Action in a Poem by Keats," *Accent*, IV, 1 (Autumn 1943), 30–42; "Antony in Behalf of the Play," *The Southern Review*, I, 2 (Autumn 1935), 308–319; "Othello: An Essay to Illustrate a Method," *The Hudson Review*, IV, 2 (Summer 1951), 165–203.

for Gallino, does — appear as a sensually appealing statement of (historical) truth. The pun on "shining forth" (German *Schein*), which means both "appearance" and "resplendence," does not go far toward saving dialectic here, although it must be noted that elsewhere (notably in the *Logics*) Hegel developed his dialectical aesthetics more fully. In his essay, Gallino shows no awareness of this fact; not only does he fail to see those dialectical elements that are really there in Burke's theory, he also falls short of a fully developed dialectic himself. What he does is point out some actual shortcomings in Burke's theory; but he advances no proof whatever that they cannot be repaired. Thus, for instance, it is true that Burke's criticism frequently slights the historical dimension; but it is never totally absent. And Gallino is certainly wrong in assuming that criticism must be *exclusively* historical. Perhaps a useful way of defining criticism is to say that it must be fully historical without abandoning itself to historicism; fully formal without giving itself over to formalism; fully psychological without losing itself in psychology; fully sociological without becoming a mere adjunct of sociology; and so forth. Burke's criticism goes a long way toward this ideal.

Finally, concerning the extent to which Burke is a representative American critic, Gallino rests his argument on his claim that in disregarding concrete content Burke disregards all that is historically significant in a work of art. The focus is no longer on man and his world. Gallino regards this loss of humanism — a stock Marxist indictment of "capitalist" art and criticism[27] — as the characteristic mark of recent American literature in the sense that it has become "post-political," i.e. no longer actively concerned with political and sociological commentary. This change, he says, is both reflected and caused by that kind of criticism of which Burke's is the type, one that is concerned with language as an inane gesture, not as an epistemological instrument, and thus betrays the great tradition of Pragmatism. To refute Gallino's view it is only necessary to recall the fallacy of his aesthetics of content; furthermore, it would be difficult for him to take account of such influential critics as Ransom and Tate, who explicitly define poetry as a type of knowledge. Besides, after all that Burke has written, it is an odd indictment to call his criticism post-political. Post-Marxist is perhaps what Gallino means to say.

[27] A representative example is R. Weimann's *"New Criticism" und die Entwicklung der bürgerlichen Literaturwissenschaft: Geschichte und Kritik neuer Interpretationsmethoden* ("The "New Criticism" and the Development of Bourgeois Criticism: A History and Critique of New Methods of Interpretation; Halle: M. Niemeyer, 1962).

More recent discussions of Burke's criticism published in Europe are of the incidental type. The most systematic is in René Wellek's article "Literaturkritik und Literaturwissenschaft" in *Lexikon der Weltliteratur.*[28] Burke is presented as the most advanced critic of the syncretic type of the New Criticism who more often than not uses literature only by way of an illustration in a wider context (any theorist of literature does!) so that his writings — with the possible exception of *Counter-Statement* — are "not literary criticism in the narrow sense of the word." Wellek's views are more fully expressed in "Philosophy and Postwar American Criticism" and "The Main Trends in Twentieth Century Criticism."[29] A short notice, mainly consisting of a comparison of Burke's different concepts of form with Yvor Winters' seven types of structure, can be found in Johan Fjord Jensen's book *Den ny kritik,*[30] which otherwise, as far as Burke's criticism is concerned, does not make any significant contributions (this statement is not to be taken as implying a judgment on the book as a whole). Beniamino Placido, finally, devotes some pages to Burke's criticism in his survey "La critica americana contemporanea."[31] He takes Burke to be representative of one of the three main trends of contemporary American criticism, "symbolical exploration," the other two, "textual analysis" and "historico-biographical recomposition," being represented by C. Brooks and Wilson respectively. Placido does not add much to a critical understanding of Burke but mostly echoes Wellek's, Bewley's, and Gallino's views.

An interesting light is thrown on Burke's reception in Europe by a negative instance: In his comprehensive and important study of the New Criticism in its ideological, political, and sociological context — a study which, however, fails to be completely convincing because many of its conclusions are based on an antiquated form of Marxism — Robert Weimann does not refer to Burke except in a footnote.[32] As he later kindly explained in a letter to the present writer, he feels that Burke in his later works, like Blackmur and Frye, has developed an idiosyncratic private idiom and constructed an ideographic superstructure which takes him beyond literary criticism, beyond the New Criticism.

The European reactions to Kenneth Burke's work — comparatively scarce as they are — have so far been characterized by an increasing

[28] *Lexikon der Weltliteratur im 20.Jahrhundert* (Freiburg: Herder, 1961), Vol. II, columns 178–261.

[29] Cf. *Concepts of Criticism,* ed. S. G. Nichols, Jr. (New Haven and London: Yale University Press, 1963), pp. 316–364; "Main Trends" is also available in a Danish translation in *Vindrosen,* IX (1962), 567–582.

[30] Copenhagen: Berlingske Forlag, 1962, esp. pp. 118–119.

[31] Cf. above, note 15.

[32] Cf. above, note 27.

hostility. What yet remains to be done in this review is to offer some speculations on the possible causes of this adverse trend.[33]

The material basis for a wider reception of any author abroad is the availability of his work in translation. The virtual nonexistence of translations, in the case of Burke, is more than incidental: It indicates a fundamental opposition between his critical position and the dominant literary orientation in Europe; another clear indication of this rift is the fact that European critics are extremely reluctant to experiment with his approach. The ease with which doctrines of the work-centered strand of contemporary American criticism (what is loosely called "formalistic" criticism in current critical jargon; Ransom's "ontological" criticism, Wellek and Warren's "intrinsic" approach) have been absorbed by European scholars is also telling. There is a marked "selective affinity" between this type of criticism and the "climate of literary ideas" in Europe; it corresponds to dominant trends of indigenous literary thought. If one agrees with Eliot's view that "the more distinguished critics of to-day, however widely they differ from each other, all differ in some significant way from the critics of a previous generation"[34] – a vaguely precise definition which has caught on with various historians and systematizers of criticism[35] – one can also easily agree that this definition can be rendered more precise by recognizing that the "significant way" which distinguishes modern critics is the renewed rather than "new" emphasis on the study of the literary texts themselves. The view that the basic tenets of this approach have essentially been derived from the common core of the literary opinions of T. E. Hulme, E. Pound, T. S. Eliot, and I. A. Richards (minus his psychological slant) can hardly be called unorthodox. What is less frequently remembered is the fact that this kind of criticism in the United

[33] The following essays and books may also be relevant but were unavailable to the present reviewer: Kristian Smidt, "Hva er nytt i 'Den nye litteraturkritikken'?" (What Is New in the "New Criticism"?), *Vinduet* (a Norwegian journal), VII (1953), 60–69; Smidt, *James Joyce and the Cultic Use of Fiction* (Oslo, 1955);Smidt, "Den 'nye' og nyere kritikken" (The "New" and Newer Criticism), *Amerika och Norden*, ed. by Lars Åhnebrink (Uppsala, 1964); Harry Järv, *Kritik av den nya kritiken* (A Critique of the New Criticism; Borga, 1953); and L. M. Zemlyanova, *Sovremennaya Zstetika v SSA* (Modern Aesthetics in the U.S.A.; Moscow, 1962). For bibliographical and scholarly advice on this and related matters the author is obliged to Eric Jacobsen, University of Copenhagen; Renata Mayenova, Polish Academy, Warsaw; A. Nikoljukin, Gorky Institute of World Literature, Moscow; Maren-Sofie Røstvig, University of Oslo; and Margaret Schlauch, University of Warsaw.

[34] "The Frontiers of Criticism," *On Poetry and Poets* (London: Faber and Faber, 1957), pp. 103–104.

[35] Cf. R. Stamm, *Englische Literatur* (Bern, 1957), p. 10; N. Frye, "Criticism, Visible and Invisible," *College English*, XXVI, 1 (Summer 1964), 5.

States forms but a part of the twentieth-century critical movement which has developed in interrelated branches in many countries. Among the most important ones are French *explication de textes,* German *werkimmanente Interpretation* and stylistics, the close reading of the British *Scrutiny* group, Russian formalism, and Prague structuralism. Such a key concept as Brooks' "irony" in the sense of a structural principle, not a form of merely verbal indirection,[36] has a close resemblance to Richards' concept of synaesthesis as the harmony of conflicting impulses and to Thomas Mann's *Ironie* in the sense of the "sympathy with the abyss," the artistic merging of moral contraries, and has been traced back to the German Romantic critic Karl Wilhelm Ferdinand Solger and his concept of *Ironie*.[37] Preceding and parallel developments of an analogous idea are evident in Blake's concept of "experience," Coleridge's "virtue," and Keats' "negative capability." Kenneth Burke obviously derived his own concept of "perspective by incongruity" from the same tradition (with an admixture of de Gourmont's, Gide's, and Bergson's ideas). Characteristically he preferred the more precise but less popular way of coining a technical neologism to stretching a conventional term beyond its original meaning. It is equally characteristic of Burke that, in so doing, he extended a primarily literary concept beyond its original sphere, thus transforming it into a speculative instrument.[38]

These tendencies – his preference for a special, sometimes even an idiosyncratic terminology and his bent for subtle, at times highly subjective speculations transcending the realm of literary criticism in the conventional sense of the word, together with his interest in all aspects of the psychological dimensions of literature – seem to be the factors that account for the reserve which so far has characterized his reception in Europe and elsewhere. Even more than Richards he is, in fact, the most representative critic of that branch of the New Criticism in which the consideration of the psychological and the semantic aspect of a work has come to its own. By adopting this occupation and preoccupation Burke has, however, maneuvered himself into a strategically disadvantageous position in relation to the mainstream of modern critical thought.

[36] For the most concise statement of this principle see Brooks, "Irony as a Principle of Structure," *Literary Opinion in America*, ed. M. D. Zabel (New York: Harper, 1951), pp. 729–741.

[37] Cf. E. Lohner, "Die Theorien des 'New Criticism,'" *Neue deutsche Hefte*, V (1958–59), 32.

[38] Cf. *Permanence and Change: An Anatomy of Purpose* (New York: New Republic, 1935), esp. pp. 118–127; *Attitudes toward History* (New York: New Republic, 1937), esp. Vol. II, pp. 201–208.

Thus, on the one hand, Burke is rejected by many modern critics in Europe because he "does something which is not done"; Bewley's and Wellek's criticisms are typical examples of this kind of objection. On the other hand, he is denounced exactly because he "does something which is very much in vogue in Europe" – only in different terms. For Burke's "Dramatism" is in many ways tantamount to a "translation" of Hegelian "dialectics," as he has frequently pointed out – and "dialectical aesthetics" is the second of the dominant trends in European criticism.[39] Now Burke's "translation" is a most valuable endeavor if one considers the extremely problematical nature of a verbatim translation of Hegel's work; but, as has been noted, Burke also transforms dialectics in important ways and adds some elements taken from the American tradition and from his own speculations.[40] Thus it is humanly understandable that many European critics, when confronted with "Burkology," tend to say: "But we have got all this – only so much better." Gallino's objections boil down to this.

There is a great deal of prejudice in such a view; but how to overcome such an intellectual pride? Perhaps it cannot be overcome in one who is so prejudiced. But it can be forestalled in others by making the philosophical or critical or other work in question widely available, by letting it speak in its own terms, by letting it stand on its own merits. To be well received, to exert a substantial influence, does not, of course, only mean to bring other critics under the dominance of one's thought. To be influenced by Burke does not necessarily mean to accept his answers; it does mean one confronts the same questions and studies the answers he gives, without dismissing them prematurely.

In this sense, the recent publication of two of his key essays in a (German) translation is a promising event.[41] Others will follow. The ice may yet be broken.

POSTSCRIPT 1968

Since the above was written about two years ago, some new developments have taken place in "Burkology." The most important was the appearance of Burke's newest collection of critical essays, *Language as Symbolic Action* (1966), and the republication of two earlier books:

[39] *Geistesgeschichte*, i.e. the discussion of literary works in terms of intellectual history, is still very strong in Germany: in France, existentialist and metaphysical concerns characterize much of the contemporary critical scene; in Italy, the after-effects of the Crocean type of impressionist-expressionist criticism may still be felt.

[40] Cf. F. Fergusson, "Kenneth Burke's *Grammar of Motives*" (1946), reprinted in *The Human Image in Dramatic Literature* (Garden City, N.Y.: Doubleday, 1957), pp. 193–204, for a concise comparison and confrontation of dialectics with Dramatism.

[41] Cf. above, note 7.

The unabridged edition of *The Philosophy of Literary Form* was at last made available again in 1967, just as in the previous year the University of California Press ventured a new edition of *Towards a Better Life,* Burke's beautifully written anti-novel of 1932, which had fallen into undeserved oblivion. *The Collected Poems 1915–1967* is being released by the same press, and a new collected edition of Burke's stories, *The Complete White Oxen,* has been announced for the near future.

There is little danger that the pattern of the fifties will be repeated, that this series of Burke's publications will go virtually unnoticed in Europe. Certainly not in England, where the impact of one of the reissued Burke books has been immediately registered by Denis Donoghue in an expertly written article in *Encounter,* and where even the *Times Literary Supplement* has opened its pages to an enthusiastic but precise assessment of Burke's total work based on a skillful comparison with, and apt differentiation from, that of Burke's closest friend, Malcolm Cowley.[42] Probably not in Germany either, where the list of Burke translations has recently been enlarged by a selection of five additional essays from *The Philosophy of Literary Form*: *Die Rhetorik in Hitler's "Mein Kampf" und andere Essays zur Strategie der Überredung.*[43] It may prove to be a provocative book, because the title essay is the earliest document in which a close rhetorical analysis reveals that Nazism was not an inevitable catastrophe which caught the Germans of the thirties like a natural force, but a pseudo-magical system of psycho-rhetorical coercion. If it is not overlooked, it may stir up a lively discussion. It may still be misunderstood, like the previous translation of the title essay from *The Philosophy of Literary Form,* about which many reviewers in Germany and Switzerland – almost predictably – complained that Burke's conception of the "symbolic" did not correspond to accepted literary terminology, though the critical reaction was, on the whole, favorable.[44]

[42] D. Donoghue, "Kenneth Burke's Dangling Novel," *Encounter,* XXIX, 4 (October 1967), 78–84; "The American Jitters," *Times Literary Supplement,* 8 June 1967, 3.

[43] Frankfurt: Suhrkamp, 1967.

[44] One more example of misunderstanding of Burke's criticism occurs in a recent study of Imagist poetics. W. Iser interprets Burke's conception of synecdoche as the basic figure of speech in the light of his own idea that the Imagist poem presents only a fragment, a *part* of reality, and does so in such a way as to require a supplementation by the reader; the *totality* is formed only in the reader's mind (cf. *Immanente Ästhetik: Ästhetische Reflexion: Lyrik als Paradigma der Moderne,* ed. W. Iser, Munich: W. Fink, 1966, p. 370). But Burke's concept of synecdoche is never concerned with a totality *beyond* the literary work; it is strictly an *internal* category. Burke draws on it to support his view that an outstanding *part* of a given work, an image-cluster, may be representative of the *total work.* On the other hand, another young German scholar, K. P. S. Jochum, uses Burke's concept of the dialectics of

But then, misunderstanding is something to which Kenneth Burke is accustomed. As his work now becomes more and more widely known, the topicality of the thought of this "thirty-minded" critic may reveal itself more and more clearly. After a long period of an oversimplified polarization of world politics and a single-minded pursuit of security and stability within the two blocs, the alignment of forces is becoming more and more intricate and flexible; politics in Europe — and not only there — is now characterized by an increasingly extreme factionalization within the various states; and political agitation, violent demonstrations, and extra-parliamentary opposition are again becoming the rule in public life. Because of this, the bewildered citizen will perhaps turn to the work of Kenneth Burke who, like no other critic, has devoted his thought to the study of the mechanisms of factionalization, of the strategies of persuasion, of the style of ingratiation; who has explored the psycho-rhetorical principles of party controversy; and who has dedicated his Dramatistic quest for skeptically grounded certainties to the only humane purpose worthy of unreserved human endeavor and engagement — *ad bellum purificandum.*

◇◇

ARMIN PAUL FRANK was born in Brno, Czechoslovakia, in 1935. Educated in Germany, France, and America, he is currently a research and teaching fellow at the American Studies Institute, University of Frankfurt, Germany. He has published a comparative study (in German) of the radio play in England, France, Germany, and America entitled *Das Hörspiel* (1963); he has completed a study of Kenneth Burke which will be published in the Twayne United States Authors Series; and he is presently working on a study of T. S. Eliot's criticism. With his wife (Mechthild Frank, who was born in Frankfurt, Germany, in 1940 and collaborated with him in preparing the checklist of Burke's writings in this volume), he has translated Burke and other American critics into German. As this article and the definitive checklist testify, he and his wife are devoted to Burke and have contributed to his reception in a meticulous, scholarly, and wonderfully useful way.

Why Burke has been so poorly received in Europe is, as Mr. Frank points out, something of a mystery, especially given the hunger for American works that existed there through much of the modern period.

◇◇

tragedy as the basis of a perspective reading of Yeats' play *At the Hawk's Well*; this interpretation, in turn, is employed to extend Burke's concept ("W. B. Yeats' *At the Hawk's Well* and the Dialectic of Tragedy,' *The Visva-Bharati Quarterly*, XXXI, 1, 1966, 21–28). In referring to this article, the present author actually oversteps the boundaries set by the title of this survey. He does so because he thinks it is interesting to note how devious the ways of possible literary influences may be.

2 *Political Speaking: A Burkeian Approach*

BY Bernard Brock

IN A democratic society political speaking plays a significant role in determining the acceptance or rejection of public policy. Thus, analysis of political speaking becomes necessary as a check upon the power of the politician. It is essential that critics of contemporary political speaking seek more effective tools for criticism – tools which may allow them to gain new perspectives. I suggest that Kenneth Burke's "dramatistic" approach to rhetoric provides a new perspective which would allow the rhetorical critic to gain more functional insights into contemporary political speaking. This essay will attempt to demonstrate the usefulness of Burke's rhetorical approach by setting forth some of his essential principles and by applying them to a contemporary political speech. Preceding this characterization of Burke's principles, the nature of contemporary political speaking will be examined. The political speaker must perform four major tasks. First, he must gain acceptance for himself and his program and rejection of the opposition and its program. Out of this goal of acceptance evolve the other three rhetorical tasks. Second, he must accurately describe man responding to the world around him. Third, the politician must consistently relate his arguments for a policy to a political philosophy. And fourth, he must lead his audience through the stages of his thinking on a given policy. These four major rhetorical tasks face the political speaker, and his skill in gaining these ends to a large extent determines his success as a politician. Furthermore, from these same tasks the role of the critic evolves. He must clearly describe and accurately evaluate the politician's performance in accomplishing his ends. It is to obtain new insights into this process of description and evaluation that I recommend Kenneth Burke's "dramatistic" approach to rhetoric.

The major rhetorical principles which will be characterized are identification, pentad, substance, and the "dramatistic" process.[1] These principles supply the tools which should enable the critic better to describe and evaluate political speaking. First, by employing the concept of identification, the critic may determine the political speaker's strategies for acceptance and rejection. Burke points out that words or

EDITOR'S NOTE: Revised for this volume in 1966 from a speech delivered in 1965.

[1] Quotations from Burke will be documented in the text. The following abbreviation will be used for the single source of all the quotations: GRM, for *A Grammar of Motives and A Rhetoric of Motives* (Cleveland: World Publishing Company, 1962).

verbal symbols carry the attitudes of the speaker who selects them. The speaker will accept some ideas, people, and institutions and reject others, and his audience will variously agree and disagree with him. To the extent that the audience accepts and rejects the same ideas, people, and institutions as does the speaker, identification takes place. The nature of this identification is defined by Burke in *A Rhetoric of Motives.* He states that "A is not identical with his colleague, B. But insofar as their interests are joined, A is identified with B. Or he may identify himself with B even when their interests are not joined, if he assumes that they are, or is persuaded to believe so." (GRM, 544) Burke sees identification as an "acting together" in which division and unity exist simultaneously. There is division because each person remains unique, and there is unity to the extent that there is a locus of motives.

Identification becomes a structural tool for rhetorical criticism as it is applied to speeches to determine the attitudes or stylized answers of the speaker. The critic should ascertain what ideas, people, and institutions the speaker accepts and rejects and then group them into "clusters" which represent the speaker's strategies for identification. In this way, the critic can discover the speaker's strategies for acceptance and rejection.

The second major task which confronts both the political speaker and the critic is to describe accurately man as he responds to the world around him. Burke's concept of the pentad should enable the critic to analyze the politician's description. Burke introduces the pentad in *A Grammar of Motives* by indicating that it answers the questions "What is involved, when we say what people are doing and why they are doing it?" He states that men will disagree about the nature of the terms to be used or about what they represent, but they necessarily must discuss these five areas: "what was done (act), when or where it was done (scene), who did it (agent), how he did it (agency), and why (purpose)." (GRM, 545) Analysis of these five areas should enable the critic to describe the politician's response. However, before the pentad can become a tool for analysis, each term must be understood.

Following from Burke's belief that society is "dramatistic" in nature, the act is the central term in the pentad. In answering the question "What is done?" Burke suggests that the philosophy of realism dominates, and he concludes that realism is not just existence – it is the act of "taking form." The terminology associated with the act suggests an emphasis upon verbs. The second term from the pentad is the scene, and its corresponding philosophy is materialism. The scene, which forms the background or setting for the drama, is generally described in secular terms. Since the scene stands as the background, the speaker easily drifts away from the scene to the act, agent, agency, or purpose. However, this shift in focus has to be slight in order for the philosophy to remain consistent with the materialism characteristic of the scene. The next term, agent, relates to idealism. Burke states that the agent grows out of the spiritualization of the family, and it is dominant whenever important human, economic, or political relations become "idealized" or "spiritualized." The remaining two terms, agency and purpose, draw together in a means-ends relationship. Burke describes this relationship in the following passage from *A Rhetoric of Motives:* "In Aristotle's classification of cause, either a first mover (person, agent) or a last mover (implement, tool, agency) can be classed as an efficient cause. And means are considered in terms of ends. But once you play down the concept of final cause (as modern science does), the distinction between agent and agency becomes sharp. Also, there is a reversal of causal ancestry—and whereas means were treated in terms of ends, ends become treated in terms of means." (GRM, 276) In this means-ends relationship agency or means is associated with pragmatism, while purpose or ends is equated with mysticism. On one hand, pragmatism transcends purpose. This is accomplished in the applied sciences where purpose has been institutionalized into the method or the agency. On the other hand, purpose merges into the "divine essence" and the "creative source." In mysticism the element of oneness is emphasized to the point that distinctions of individuality disappear. This universal purpose becomes a compulsive criterion by which everything else is judged. These five terms form the foundation of Burke's "dramatistic" approach because, as he indicates, they are in accordance with the basic laws of thought and the nature of the world as man experiences it.

In his attempt to describe his view of the world, the political speaker may shift from one term in the pentad to another, as he discusses first the United Nations (agency) and then its goal (purpose), all within the events (act) occurring throughout the world (scene). To follow this movement the critic requires a rhetorical tool which is flexible in nature. Kenneth Burke illustrates the flexibility of the pentad by comparing it to the human hand. "We have likened the terms to the fingers, which in their extremities are distinct from one another but merge in the palm of the hand. If you would go from one finger to another without a leap, you need but trace a new course along another tendon." (GRM, xxiv) This flexibility of operation in the pentad should enable the critic to trace the politician's descriptions of man as he responds to the world around him.

The third area in which both the politician and the critic should be able to apply Burke's principles is the consistent presentation of arguments within a political philosophy. To cope with this task Burke's idea of "substance" is appropriate. Burke turns to Webster's dictionary to describe substance as "The most important element in any existence; the characteristic and essential import, purpose." He concludes that, materially, it is that which stands beneath something. Substance is the scene or the context. It has an intrinsic-extrinsic relationship. This principle, substance, is important in rhetorical criticism, because every speaker must establish a context for the subject of his speech. This context or substance then becomes the political philosophy within which all his arguments must be consistent.

The nature of substance can be understood by returning to the analogy of the pentad and the human hand, wherein the five terms are separate even while they merge into and evolve from a common substance. Similarly, the speaker's attitudes and rhetorical strategies flow from a single substance. Kenneth Burke describes four major types of substance from which the political arguments might flow. They are geometric, familial, directional, and dialectic. Understanding these types of substance should enable the rhetorical critic better to describe the politician's efforts to consistently relate his arguments for a policy to a political philosophy.

Geometric substance places an object in its setting as "existing both in itself and as part of its background" (GRM, 29). This leads to a materialistic notion of determinism which is most consistent with the term "scene" from the pentad. When the term "scene" in the pentad is featured, it signifies a geometric substance. The substance from which the "agent" evolves, when it is featured, is familial substance. "It stresses common ancestry in the strictly biological sense, as lateral descent from maternal or paternal sources" (GRM, 29). Often, this concept of family is "spiritualized" so as to include social and national groups and beliefs. Directional substance, represented by the term agency, is also biologically derived; however, it comes "from a sense of free motion" (GRM, 31). This feeling of movement provides a sense of motivation from within. All generalizations such as "the reasonable man" or "the economic man" would fall in this category. Also, "terminologies that situate the driving force of human action in human passion" (GRM, 32) and treat emotion as motive would be classified as directional substance. Furthermore, "doctrines which reduce mental states to materialistic terms treat motion as Motive," and this encourages sociological speculation in terms of "tendencies" or "trends." The last type of substance is dialectic. It reflects "the ambiguities of substance, since symbolic communication is not a merely external instrument, but also intrinsic to men as agents. Its motivational properties characterize both the 'human situation' and what men are 'in themselves'" (GRM, 33). The ambiguity of external and internal motivation is the concern of dialectical substance. This ambiguity of substance may take many forms, but the central overriding dialectical opposition is found in that key pair, Being and Not-Being. Burke discusses this opposition and suggests how dialectic substance can transcend to the "ultimate abstract Oneness." "The human person, for instance, may be derived from God and a 'super-person.' Or human purpose may be derived from an All-person, or Cosmic Purpose, or Universal Purpose, or Absolute Purpose, or Pure Purpose, or Inner Purpose, etc." (GRM, 35) Clearly, the term central to dialectic substance is "purpose." Understanding Burke's four types of substance should enable the rhetorical critic to describe the politician's efforts to consistently relate his arguments to a political philosophy.

It is important to note that at this point the concepts of identification, pentad, and substance have merged. Identification is necessary in order to decide which of the pentadic terms is highlighted, while the highlighting of a term from the pentad suggests to the critic the type of substance established by the speaker. Just as simultaneous unity and division are essential to Burke's concept of identification, so unity and division exist among all of Burke's rhetorical principles.

The fourth and final task facing the critic of political speaking is tracing the stages the speaker must take the audience through if he is to gain acceptance for his course of action. To accomplish this task, both Burke's concept of "dramatistic" stages and Hultzen's "stock issue" frames will be utilized.

Burke describes man's society as a "dramatistic" process, passing through the stages of guilt, purification, and redemption. Burke indicates that man will either accept or reject his position in the world. Then to the degree that man rejects his place in society he suffers a feeling of guilt. This feeling represents stage one in the "dramatistic" process. Guilt reduces social cohesion and gives man the feeling of being less than whole, so he strives to have this guilt canceled. Stage two in the "dramatistic" process is the act of purification, which is designed to cancel man's guilt and take him into stage three. This is redemption, and it makes man whole again. Guilt, purification, and redemption constitute a balanced psychological process which results from the rejection of the human situation. A particular speaker's attitude of acceptance or rejection may be discovered by locating "clusters" of terms he uses, because these are the terms with which he "identifies." The "dramatistic" process may be used by the critic to explain the stages the politician takes an audience through in order to obtain acceptance or rejection for some policy or action. However, in contemporary speaking the politician often keeps his "dramatistic" process in the background and employs a more formal deliberative structure. For an appropriate analysis of such an approach, one may turn to Lee S. Hultzen's essay "Status in Deliberative Analysis." [2]

Hultzen establishes a stock issue approach to the deliberative method. He discusses four frames in the deliberative process: Ill, Blame, Cure, and Cost. Hultzen phrases each frame into the form of a question which can be applied directly to the analysis of political speeches:

Ill — Is there this ill in the present state of affairs?
Blame — Is this ill curable, caused by a reformable condition?
Cure — Will the proposed remedy actually cure us of this ill?
Cost — Will the cure cost too much?

These frames provide the basis for the analysis of speeches which follow a more formal deliberative process. In this process the Blame causes the Ill, serves as the objective of the Cure, and largely determines whether advantages outweigh disadvantages in the Cost. As a result of these relationships, the Blame interlocks the frames of Ill, Cure, and Cost, thus establishing the sequence for deliberative analysis while the frame of Blame provides a context for the other three.

With this structure for the "stock issues," it is possible to synthesize the frames in the deliberative process and the "dramatistic" stages. Both the rhetorical critic and the political speaker see action as resulting from a series of "stock issues" or psychological stages. The initial frame/ stage is Ill or a feeling of guilt. (Frame/ stage two is Cure or an act of purification.) Frame/ stage three is Cost or the redemption which results from purification. The final frame or stage in the process is Blame or Burke's principles of "substance" which unifies or provides a context for the process. These "stock issue" frames combine with the "dramatistic" stages to form a structure within which the critic can describe the politician's last task, taking his audience through his deliberative process.

It is interesting to note that Hultzen's "stock issue" frames and Burke's "dramatistic" stages represent dialectical counterparts. Hultzen's "stock issue" analysis includes three static frames, Ill, Cure, and Cost, with a dynamic concept, Blame or causation, providing unity. Conversely, Burke's "dramatistic" process is made up of three dynamic stages, guilt, purification, and redemption, with a static concept, substance, as the context. At each point these contrasting systems represent dialectical

[2] Lee Hultzen "Status in Deliberative Analysis," *The Rhetorical Idiom*, ed. Donald C. Bryant (Ithaca, N.Y.: Cornell University Press, 1958), pp. 85–110.

opposites of the same process. In the analysis of most political speeches Hultzen's frames will provide the structure. On the other hand, for some speeches the dynamic stages may provide a more appropriate approach. In any event, either or both of these systems may be used to describe the speaker's deliberative process.

A series of rhetorical tools have been set forth — tools which should enable the critic to more adequately describe and evaluate contemporary political speakers' efforts to accomplish their four major objectives. First, identification should be useful for determining his strategies of acceptance and rejection. Second, the pentad should be helpful as he describes man's response to the world. Third, the concept of substance should be employed in evaluating the politician's consistency. And fourth, the "stock issue" frames and the "dramatistic" stages should provide a structure for the total analysis. By applying these four concepts to political speeches the critic might gain fresh insights into contemporary political speaking. Thus, these rhetorical tools will be applied to one of President Lyndon B. Johnson's speeches in defense of United States foreign policy in Vietnam.

In 1965 and 1966, the most important problem in United States public policy was the war in Vietnam. Amid student protests for peace and in answer to liberal spokesmen who were calling for the administration to justify or change the policy in Vietnam, President Johnson, as he accepted the National Freedom Award in New York on February 23, 1966, chose to defend his Vietnam policies.[3] If Johnson was to gain acceptance for his policies, as a political speaker, he would have to execute successfully the four major rhetorical tasks which have already been described. Thus, this speech will be analyzed as such a rhetorical effort. The ensuing application of Kenneth Burke's rhetorical principles to Johnson's speech should serve as an example for testing whether fresh insights into the process of contemporary political speaking can be obtained.

First, Johnson's strategies for acceptance and rejection will be described by applying the principle of identification. Since a speaker usually makes his major adaptation to the audience in the introduction and the conclusion, these sections will be examined first, and the body of the speech will be analyzed with the other three rhetorical tasks. Johnson opens the speech by recalling for the audience Franklin Roosevelt and his Four Freedoms — freedom of speech and expression, freedom of every person to worship God in his own way, freedom from want, and freedom from fear. These freedoms, Johnson suggests, con-

[3] The following is the source for all the quotations from President Johnson's speech: "Vietnam: The Cause of Human Freedom," *Vital Speeches of the Day*, XXXII (March 1966), 322–325.

stitute the "purpose" of our society, and he quotes Wendell Willkie to indicate that "we must be prepared to extend it [freedom] to everyone." Then Johnson asserts that we have already gained these freedoms for the vast majority of Americans, and we must be willing to extend these freedoms to the "oppressed of this earth." This strategy allows him to relate his "purpose" to Vietnam. Johnson compares "purpose" at home and "purpose" abroad, and he concludes, "We seek to create that climate at home and abroad where unlettered men can learn, where deprived children can grow, where hopeless millions can be inspired to change the terms of their existence for the better." Johnson's "purpose" both at home and abroad is to create a condition in which man (agent) has control over his destiny. His strategy of identification takes the form of unifying "purpose" and "agent."

In his conclusion, Johnson employs the same strategy of identification that he uses in the introduction. He indicates that each night upon retiring he reads the reports that "tell . . . how our men have fared that day in the hills and valleys of Vietnam." Then, after focusing upon "individual acts of heroism, of dedicated men and women," he reads a letter from "an American father" of a dead Army captain. "And this good young American and thousands like him was not on the other side of the world fighting specifically for you or me, Mr. President, he was fighting in perhaps our Oldest American tradition – taking up for people who were being pushed around." At this point in the speech Johnson clearly employs "agent" as a strategy of identification; however, "purpose" is retained for a secondary strategy, evident in Johnson's closing statement, "I ask for your help, for your unceasing sacrifice – the struggle to be free." Johnson's strategy for acceptance is identification with an "agent-purpose" ratio in which "agent" is dominant.

Second, Johnson's response to the war in Vietnam will be described in terms of the entire pentad. Examination of the introduction and conclusion has already revealed a heavy reliance upon "agent" and "purpose." It should be noted that this pattern continues through the entire speech. In fact, when the other terms – scene, act, and agency – are discussed, they are related to "agent" and "purpose." Early in the body of the speech, Johnson describes the "scene" of the war: "Tonight, in Vietnam, more than 200,000 of your Young Americans stand there fighting for your freedom. Tonight our people are determined that these men shall have whatever help they need and that their cause – which is our cause – shall be sustained." His description of the "scene" becomes nothing more than a restatement of the "purpose" for which the "agents" are fighting (act). Likewise, in discussing the "act" Johnson maintains, "We are using that force – and only that force – that is necessary to stop this aggression." He makes it clear that the "act" is under the control of the "agent," so that only the intended "purpose" will be accomplished and no other one. Again, there is a dominance of "agent" and "purpose." Finally, "agency" is reduced to a combination of "agent" and "purpose" when Johnson states that our fighting men will not be denied that help they need: "Our great military establishment has moved 200,000 men across 10,000 miles since last spring. These men have and will have all they need to fight the aggressors. They have already performed miracles in combat. And the men behind them have worked miracles of supply—building new ports, transporting new equipment, opening new roads. The American forces of freedom are strong tonight in South Vietnam, and we plan to keep them so." Actually, only passing references are made to the "agencies" of new ports, equipment, and roads, but the emphasis is upon "the American forces (agent) and freedom (purpose)." Johnson's view of the war does not represent a balanced picture of the pentad. It is portrayed by reducing all elements of the war in Vietnam to "purpose" and "agent."

Third, the concept of substance should be employed in order to understand Johnson's philosophical position on the war. It has already clearly been indicated that Johnson focuses upon "agent" and "purpose" in his discussion of the war. This raises the question of whether one term provides the context for the other. In the conclusion "agent" emerges as the dominant term, as Johnson (agent) read the reports on the men (agents) in Vietnam. Then when Johnson read the letter from the father (agent) of a captain (agent) who died in Vietnam, the appeal became almost entirely personal. In addition to this personal or "familial" appeal at the close of the speech, Johnson's major strategy justifying our presence in Vietnam today was also "familial." In answer to the question "is it worth it . . ." Johnson states that our present policy in Vietnam is keeping the pledge of four Presidents (agents). Franklin D. Roosevelt, Harry S Truman, Dwight D. Eisenhower, and John F. Kennedy were committed to a similar policy in Vietnam. Johnson then provides the logical conclusion to the pledges of these four great Americans, "We will build freedom while we fight, and we will seek peace every day by every honorable means. But we will persevere along the high road of freedom. We are too old to be foolhardy and we are too young to be tired; we're too strong for fear and too determined for retreat." With this transcending statement Johnson terminates the body of the speech by uniting "agent," "act," and "purpose," but this unity maintains a personal identification. Thus, Johnson's personal appeal to "man" throughout the speech suggests an emphasis upon "agent" and a "familial" substance. These two strategies clearly characterize Johnson's philosophical position. His view of the war in Vietnam is that all of the elements in the situation are under the control of the "Master-Agent," President Johnson.

Fourth, the final task in applying these Burkeian concepts to Johnson's speech on Vietnam is to describe how he attempts to lead his audience through the stages of his thinking on the policy. With the aid of Hultzen's "stock issues" and Burke's "dramatistic" process, this should be possible. It is important to note that the stages in the deliberative process, Ill, Blame, Cure, and Cost, are usually handled by a speaker in a systematic manner even though there may be considerable overlapping among the areas. Johnson, in his attempt to gain acceptance for his policy in Vietnam, does not present the frames systematically. In fact, for all practical purposes, he discusses only the frames of Cure and Cost. The frames of Ill and Blame are not discussed directly but are handled indirectly as a part of the introduction and as secondary aspects of the Cure and Cost. This strategy allows Johnson to assume that the United States should participate in the war and to discuss only the degree of participation.

How is Johnson able to employ this strategy without making it apparent that he is begging an important question about U.S. policy? He accomplishes this task in two ways. First, he constructs an extended introduction which indirectly treats the crucial issues. It has been described how Johnson looks to Roosevelt and Willkie to justify carrying the four freedoms to all nations of the world. Thus, he *assumes* that present policy is simply an attempt to carry out this "purpose" in Vietnam. In this case the Ill is the situation in which people are being deprived of the four freedoms, and the Blame is the aggression which is creating this situation. In this manner Johnson disposes of the Ill and Blame by employing his favorite strategy. He does not directly describe the situation in Vietnam which represents the Ill, nor does he demonstrate the cause or Blame for the situation, but he has reduced these elements of the deliberative process to "agent" and "purpose." The second means of bypassing the frames of Ill and Blame is employed in the body of the speech. Instead of discussing the general situation and moving from one frame to another in a systematic development of the speech, Johnson creates an artificial structure for the speech. He does this by suggesting that what is needed is "open free debate in hours of danger . . ." So in the spirit of free debate he sets out to answer the questions that are still being asked. He then selects ten questions and answers them. It is precisely this strategy of posing and answering questions that allows Johnson to handle the frames of Ill and Blame only indirectly. Of the ten questions, seven deal with the

Cure or plan of action and three relate to the Cost of the policy. It should be noted that the strategy for answering the questions is, again, a reduction to "agent" and "purpose." For example, he opens with a question about the objectives of our policy: "First, some ask if this is a war for limited objectives. The answer is plain: The answer is no. Our purpose in Vietnam is to prevent the success of aggression. It is not conquest, it is not empire, it is not foreign bases, it is not domination. It is simply put, just to prevent the forceful conquest of South Vietnam by North Vietnam." In this case Johnson answers the question about the objectives of our policy with a general statement of "purpose" without ever providing a detailed description of the situation (scene) in that country. Finally, in question seven Johnson indirectly touches upon the frames of Ill and Blame. He asks, "who has the right to rule in South Vietnam?" And he answers that the people who have been there for 200 years have this right, "So we will insist for ourselves on what we require from Hanoi: respect for the principle [purpose] of government by the consent of the governed [agent]. We stand for self-determination, for free elections, and we will honor their result." This question and answer define the nature of the Cure in Vietnam, but they indirectly suggest Ill and Blame, since it is assumed that these people are being deprived of the right of self-determination by North Vietnam. However, again Johnson does not attempt to describe the "scene" or to justify this interpretation of Ill and Blame. Each question and answer could be presented, but this would only repeat the Johnson strategy. In his attempt to take his audience through the deliberative process to gain acceptance for his policy, he systematically bypasses the frames of Ill and Blame and reduces the frames of Cure and Cost to "purpose" and "agent."

This brief application of Burkeian concepts to contemporary political speaking should provide a new perspective for analysis of public speaking. Johnson's strategy to gain acceptance from the American public was to identify with an "agent-purpose" ratio. His next strategy was to avoid presenting a balanced picture of the war. He slighted the "scene" or the details of the present state of affairs, and he considered only superficially the "agency" or the instruments necessary for carrying out his policy. Then to the extent that he did discuss the "scene," "agency," and "act," he reduced them to an "agent-purpose" ratio. A fourth strategy appeared when he featured "agent" and established a "familial" substance, which characterized his philosophical position. Johnson's final strategy took the form of only indirectly discussing the frames of Ill and Blame and applying an "agent-purpose" ratio to the frames of Cure and Cost.

Given the use of these strategies, what new insights into Johnson's political speaking have been gained? In this particular speech Johnson has systematically avoided justifying his policy to the American people by *assuming* that it should be the policy to be followed. Also, Johnson's strategy of employing an "agent-purpose" ratio reflects a motive of "consensus." Hugh Duncan in *Communication and Social Order* states that the "agent-purpose" ratio appears "when the act of the leader becomes the purpose of the community."[4] Johnson apparently sees his policy in Vietnam as the "purpose" of the United States, which means that it is above being questioned. Finally, since he avoids "agency" or the instrumental details of his policy, the American people must base their acceptance or rejection solely upon his philosophical position. Each person must decide whether the "Master-Agent" is capable of controlling the necessary variables so that his "purpose" and no other "purpose" is attained in Vietnam.

At a time when politicians rely upon their ability to influence public opinion by reaching the entire nation with a single speech, it is especially important to understand the nature of their appeals. A brief analysis of President Johnson's strategies in seeking acceptance for his policy in Vietnam reveals both the strengths and weaknesses of his position. Thus, the critic may play a significant role in the speaker's acceptance or rejection. Today, the critic needs to aid the public in understanding the conflicting discourse on issues from Medicare to the increasing federal government. This writer feels that the application of Burkeian rhetorical principles to contemporary political speaking does provide a new perspective which will allow critics to gain fresh insights into political speaking and to serve as a check upon the power of the politician.

◇◇

BERNARD BROCK was born in 1932 in Elkhart, Indiana. He has taught a variety of subjects in high school and is presently teaching speech at the University of Minnesota. He studied Burke with Professor Leland Griffin at Northwestern (see below) where there is, thanks to Professor Griffin, a flourishing center for Burke studies. With his mentor, he illustrates one of the genuinely creative and therapeutic ways in which Burke has been studied and absorbed by one generation and then handed down as a legacy to the next and subsequent generations. Professor Brock's essay also illustrates how Burke can be used in the analysis of current political rhetoric and how his work is related to what others — here Lee Hultzen — have done in the same field.

[4] Hugh Dalziel Duncan, *Communication and Social Order* (New York: Bedminster Press, 1962), p. 436.

Leland M. Griffin

An earlier version of this essay was read at a special Burke section of the Midwest Speech Association meeting in Chicago, in 1965. The meeting was organized by Professor Griffin and also included talks by Hugh Duncan and myself. Burke has not been honored in this way often enough.

◇◇

7 *A Dramatistic Theory of the Rhetoric of Movements*

BY Leland M. Griffin

> The relationship between utopia and the existing order turns out to be a dialectical one.
>
> —Karl Mannheim

> The obligations of order hang over us, even if we would revolt against order. Out of such predicaments, ingenious fellows rise up and sing; thus promptly have all our liabilities been by symbol-using converted into assets.
>
> —Kenneth Burke

THE following study in dramatism, the critical perspective of Kenneth Burke, both supplements and complements previous essays by the writer.[1] The attempt here is to develop, for the student of movements, a dramatistic model, or abstraction, of the structure of a movement's rhetoric.[2] The essay involves a synthesis of materials — words, phrases, and concepts — which have been drawn, almost wholly, from the terminology of Burke.[3] The central effort is to identify the dramatistic form of rhetorical movement with the dialectical movement of tragedy, poetic expression in general, and theological or political transformation and transcendence. Taken as a whole, the essay might be regarded as the exegesis of a line from *Towards a Better Life* (which ends, like *The Rhetoric of Religion,* with the key term silence): "speech being a mode of conduct, he converted his faulty living into eloquence."[4]

The essay assumes that all movements are essentially political, concerned with governance or dominion, "the wielding and obeying of authority";[5] that "politics above all is drama";[6] and that "drama requires a conflict."[7] It also assumes that all movements are essentially moral — strivings for salvation, perfection, the "good."[8]

EDITOR'S NOTE: Written for this volume in 1966. Footnotes may be found on pp. 472–478.

The essay employs an imagery of killing — as, according to Burke, "a typical text for today should."[9] And it is frankly speculative. But, as Burke has noted, "this is a time for speculative adventure."[10]

1

Let us begin with a definition of man, and with a paradigm of his history — his "drama," or action. As to the definition,

Man is
the symbol-using (symbol-making, symbol-misusing) animal
inventor of the negative (or moralized by the negative)
separated from his natural condition by instruments of his own making
goaded by the spirit of hierarchy (or moved by the sense of order)
and rotten with perfection.[11]

Man is a being by nature divided, designed for striving, "endowed for struggle" ("if they do not struggle, they rot, which is to say that they struggle in spite of themselves").[12] Man is an *acter*, a maker, a mover; a being who lives by striving, and who "can be expected to err as long as he keeps striving" (*es irrt der Mensch solang' er strebt*).[13] Man is a being who lives by language; who moves and is moved by words; who rises and is redeemed, or fails and falls, through words. Man is a being who lives by purpose or meaning, value and desire; a being who yearns, in this "imperfect world,"[14] for a world of perfection ("the conformity of a reality to its concept").[15] And hence man is a maker of movements; a maker (*poietes*) whose motto might be "By and through language, beyond language. *Per linguam, praeter linguam.*"[16]

As to the paradigm of his history,

Here are the steps
In the Iron Law of History
That welds Order and Sacrifice:
Order leads to Guilt
(for who can keep commandments:)
Guilt needs Redemption
(for who would not be cleansed!)
Order
Through Guilt
To Victimage
(hence: Cult of the Kill). . . .[17]

So man moves through the moments of his drama, which are also the moments of his movements: moves, all told, from Order, Guilt, and the Negative, through Victimage and Mortification, to Catharsis and Redemption.[18] He moves, and is moved, through speech — through the rhetorical power of the word, the persuasive power of language (for rhetoric is the essentially human mode of striving). He is moved by words of meaning, value, and desire; words that draw him *a fronte*, futuristically.[19] And engaged in struggle, in the act of strife, he is cleansed by the dialectical power of the word, the purifying power of language (for dialectic is the essentially human mode of transforming).

And thus the study of a movement implies a study of its rhetoric. And thus the significance of "Order, the Secret, and the Kill": for "to study the nature of rhetoric, the relation between rhetoric and dialectic, and the application of both to human relations in general, is to circulate about these three motives."[20]

2

Because they desire Order (the reign of reason and justice),[21] men build cooperative systems, or orders. All such orders are of necessity hierarchical, involving division, "a ladder of authority that extends from 'lower' to 'higher,' while its *official functions* tend toward a corresponding set of *social ratings*," a set of "different classes" (or "principles," or "*kinds* of beings").[22] Yet though men, in any system, are inevitably divided, "identification is compensatory to division."[23] And through identification with a common condition or "substance," men achieve an understanding (a sense of unity, identity, or "consubstantiality").

Any system that endures implies an "adequate" understanding, a dynamic understanding ("the *understanding* which is active in that it performs the act of unification").[24] It is the understanding essential to the ultimate achievement of integration (ideal unity; "a complete and perfect whole").[25] For it provides the basis for communication; and men must communicate, being by nature symbol-makers. And hence it is the ground, in any system, of "mystery" (the Secret): for "mystery arises at that point where different *kinds* of beings are in communication."[26]

In any "good" system, men accept the "mystery," strive to keep the Secret, preserve the hierarchy. For reason and justice reign. There is a common understanding, an "adequate" understanding. Men agree on meaning, value, and desire; and hence they gladly submit to a code of control, obey the "commandments."[27]

And thus the relations between classes are harmonious, cooperative, symmetrical; and the communication between classes is beneficent and benign, "like the ways of courtship" — a communication that might be likened to the "rhetoric of courtship."[28] It is a rhetoric in the order of love; for it strives for perfect communion, and "the word for perfect communion between *persons* is 'Love!' "[29] It is a rhetoric in the order of peace; for it strives for pure identification, and "in pure identification there would be no strife."[30] And it is a rhetoric energized, and sustained, by the motive of piety ("the yearning to conform with the sources of one's being"; loyalty, or obedience, to one's "natural condition").[31]

And thus a "good" order is one marked by communion and identification, by the practice and persistence of piety. It is an order charged with attitudes of benevolence, and sustained by communication, the relevance of its rhetoric. For because men are pious they avoid error in the use of symbols, strive to use their language with propriety (for piety is also "*the sense of what properly goes with what*"; and "it is pious to exemplify a sense of the appropriate").[32]

And because in a "good" order men are pious, they are "free."[33] And their freedom equals a state of continual movement toward perfection: toward "a complete and perfect whole"; a cooperative system of pure symmetry, perfect harmony, and "*integration*, guided by a scrupulous sense of the appropriate"[34] – an Order marked by perfect communion, pure identification, and absolute communication. For piety is also "a system-builder, a desire to round things out, to fit experiences together into a unified whole":[35] and "if men were wholly and truly of one substance" – *truly integrated, united, in a relation of perfect love* – "absolute communication would be of man's very essence."[36]

But tragically, in this "imperfect world," love is bound to be a taut, potentially frangible relation. For "piety can be painful," a motive difficult to endure;[37] and hence the pious may yield to the temptations of impiety. For men are by nature divided: capable of rising, hence of falling; of accepting, consenting, obeying – hence of rejecting, dissenting, disobeying; capable of loyalty and love, hence of alienation and Victimage, "the *perversions* of love (forms of ill-will towards one's neighbor)"[38] – the malevolent attitudes of pride, envy, wrath, sloth, avarice, gluttony, lust; attitudes, ultimately, in the order of murder. And men are by nature symbol-makers, both users and misusers of symbols: capable of understanding, hence of misunderstanding; of reason, hence of absurdity; of justice, hence of injustice; of courtship, hence of impiety, the *perversion* of courtship – of a rhetoric of abasement, maleficent and malign, like the ways of "rape, seduction, jilting, prostitution, promiscuity . . . sadistic torture or masochistic invitation to mistreatment."[39]

And thus a "good" order may turn faulty; and the symptom of its turning is the growth of verbal corruption – vile error in the use of language, the inappropriate use of symbols. It is an order marked by misunderstanding, the growth of absurdity and injustice, the increasing loss of communion and identification. It is an order strained by impiety, the irrelevance of its rhetoric; an order tending toward Death, the ultimate failure of communication — toward disunity, disintegration, Disorder.

In sum: wherever there is Order there is hierarchy; wherever there is hierarchy there must be communication, and hence "mystery"; and wherever there is "mystery" there must be an understanding — the understanding that makes piety possible. But the maintenance of piety involves the need for obedience — which is to say, the painful need for self-control (self-restraint, self-moderation). And out of this obligation comes the possibility of disobedience: [40] for men are by nature ambitious, Faustian, "rotten with perfection"; and ambition is a disease that ends in pride, "the desire to excel by the abasement of others"; [41] and pride is a fall, the initial perversion of love, the impious yearning that ends in the misuse of symbols — in negation, rejection, "the rebel snapping of the continuity." [42]

As the communication between classes grows ever more malign, men turn from acceptance to rejection of the "mystery," cease to identify with the hierarchy, the prevailing system of authority. And as disloyalty spreads and the bonds of love corrode, the sense of Guilt grows increasingly greater: for in man, the symbol-maker, Guilt is a function of impiety — error, or the yearning to err, in the use of symbols.[43]

Now alienated, divided from the existing order (separated from their "natural condition"), men stand alone, without purpose or desire, hope or direction. They stand in silence, in the hellish state of indecision: stand, until moved to speak. *And speak they will* ("as the gun *will* shoot because it *is* loaded").[44] For men are by nature charged with symbols; and by nature they cannot bear Guilt ("for who would not be cleansed"). And hence, inevitably, they will dream of salvation, the transformation of their condition, a state of Redemption: will envision, consciously or unconsciously (being "rotten with perfection"), an ideal Order — "heaven," paradise, the "good society," Utopia.

And thus, perversely goaded by the spirit of hierarchy, moved by the impious dream of a mythic new Order — inspired with a new purpose, drawn anew by desire — they are moved to act: moved, ingenious men ("inventors of the negative") to rise up and cry *No* to the existing order — and prophesy the coming of the new.

And thus movements begin.

3

To study a movement is to study a striving for salvation, a struggle for perfection, a progress toward the "good." It is a progress that is grounded in Guilt; but "Guilt needs Redemption," and Redemption needs Redeemer – which is to say, a Victim, a scapegoat, a Kill. And thus to study a movement is to study the progress of a killing; which is to say, to study rhetoric. For rhetoric is "in the order of killing, of personal enmity, of factional strife, of invective, polemic, eristic, logomachy"; is "*par excellence* the region of the Scramble, of insult and injury, bickering, squabbling, malice and the lie, cloaked malice and the subsidized lie."[45]

Yet it must not be forgotten that rhetoric, though in the order of killing, is also in the order of love. For it includes communication; and " 'communication' is the most generalized statement of the principle of 'love' " – "the area where love has become so generalized, desexualized, 'technologized,' that only close critical or philosophic scrutiny can discern the vestiges of the original motive."[46]

And it must not be forgotten that rhetoric, at its farthest reach, mounts to the level of "pure persuasion" – "the saying of something, not for an extra-verbal advantage to be got by the saying, but because of a satisfaction intrinsic to the saying."[47] It is rhetoric for the "sheer love of the art," the sheer love of persuasion itself.[48] And it includes, as intrinsic, "a principle of self-interference"[49] (self-restraint, *mortification*, "a scrupulous and deliberate clamping of limitations upon the self").[50]

It must not be forgotten, in sum, that rhetoric, though in the order of Victimage, is also in the order of Mortification; nor that Mortification, at its highest mounting, is in the order of perfect love ("*Greater love hath no man than this, that a man give up his life for his friends*").

4

To study a movement is to study a progress, a rhetorical striving, a becoming. It is a progress from stasis to stasis; for both the origins and "the objectives of a movement are motionless."[51] They begin in the stasis of indecision, and they end in the stasis of "decision persevered in." They begin with Guilt and the dream of salvation. They end with the achievement, and maintenance, of a state of Redemption – of a new identity, a new unity, a new condition or "substance": which is to say, a new *motive* (for " 'substance' and 'motivation' are convertible terms").[52]

Every movement thus has form. It is a progress from *pathema* through *poiema* to *mathema*: from "a suffering, misfortune, passive condition, state of mind," through "a deed, doing, action, act," to "an adequate idea; the thing learned."[53] It is a progress from *auscultation* through *creation* to *revision*: from "the heart-conscious kind of listening, or vigilance, that precedes expression," through "the expression in its unguarded simplicity," to a "modification of the expression in the light of more complicated afterthoughts."[54] It is a progress from *Inferno* through *Purgatorio* to *Paradiso*: from the hell that is indecision, through the purification that is decision, to the heaven that is "the arrival that follows decision persevered in."[55]

To study a movement is to study a drama, an Act of transformation, an Act that ends in transcendence, the achievement of salvation. It is to study the Scenes that bracket the Act, for any movement is a sequence of "moments between the limits of before and after."[56] It is to study the Agents that make the Act; for men are the *acters*, the makers, of movements. It is to study the essentially human Agency that men use in the making of movements; which is to say, to study rhetoric. And the purpose of all such study is to discover the motive, or motives – the ultimate meaning, or Purpose – of the movement.[57]

And hence to study a movement is to study its form: for if movements are acts, acts have form – and form is content,[58] content is meaning, and meaning is motive or Purpose. It is to study the forms, in their particularity and plenitude, within the dramatistic form of rhetorical movement itself: which is dialectical, anagogic, triple-tiered; an organic, progressive, contrapuntal unfoldment, through periods of inception, crisis, and consummation, "through the realms of the damned, the penitent, and the blessed."[59]

5

The inception period of a movement is a time of indecision; of alienation, auscultation, and the innovation of public tensions. It is a time for the identification of destination and devils, the "Mecca" of the movement, and the "evil principles" it opposes.[60] It is a time for the accumulation of individual conversions; for the organization of an opposition; and for the achievement of solidarity, *merger*, in the ranks of the converted.

Movements begin when some pivotal individual or group – suffering attitudes of alienation in a given social system, and drawn (consciously or unconsciously) by the impious dream of a mythic Order – enacts, gives voice to, a *No*.[61] This enactment of the Negative by a Saving Remnant ("prophets," aggressor rhetors, who "see through" the existing order and foretell the coming of the new) will itself be precipitated by some event or attitude, or cluster of events and attitudes, that symbolizes the unacceptable – the manifestation of intolerable pride, the unendurable perversion of reason and justice. The movement's Negative is in essence the announcement of a stand, a "standing together," an *understanding.* It may be called a constitution, manifesto, covenant, program, proclamation, declaration, tract for the times, statement, or counterstatement. It may be expressed in the form of an essay, document, speech, poem, sermon, novel, play, pamphlet or song. Whatever its label or mode of expression, it constitutes the initial act of the movement – the axe raised to its full height, and permitted to fall; or less militantly, the vernal bud from which the movement will unfold into flower.

As the starting point of the movement, the enactment of the Negative may be taken by the student as a "representative anecdote," a moment that embodies, implicitly or explicitly, the key terms and equations of the movement.[62] With these terms and equations the study of a movement begins.[63] They identify *what equals what, what opposes what, what follows what.* They identify the "heaven" of the movement, as well as its "hell"; its gods, or god, as well as its devils ("faulty principles," scapegoats, "vile beasts"). And thus they suggest, however darkly, an answer to the question *why,* the ultimate question of motive. For the key terms prefigure (consciously or unconsciously) the lineaments of the "perfecting myth" that draws the movement futuristically, *a fronte* ("The vision says in effect: 'Only if the socio-political order is on such-and-such relations with the principles of all order, can the order be reasonable.' And thus, the 'perfecting myth' becomes like the originator of the order it perfects").[64]

Arising as it does out of the enactment of a Negative, the rhetoric of the inception period, in its initial phase, is the rhetoric of an *anti* movement, predominantly a rhetoric of negation. Thus the period begins with a rhetoric of dissent and corrosion. It is a rhetoric of dual strategy, designed to produce doubt, and to promote indecision and the sense of division. Its first strategy is to intensify misunderstanding: to permeate the prevailing scene with a sense of the absurdity and injustice of the existing order, the irrelevance of its rhetoric, the failure of its communication. It is a strategy designed to infuse increasing numbers of hearers (the corruptible – the potentially alienable, the uncommitted, the powerless, the "disadvantaged," the "simply curious"),[65] with attitudes of rejection toward the hierarchy – which is to say, with impiety, and with the Guilt that goes with impiety (for "*to flourish in the state of Glory, we must first be sown in Corruption*").[66]

Its second strategy is to provoke conflict. It is a strategy designed to infuse the "priests" of the existing order (the incorruptible – the unalienable, the committed "establishment," the "power structure," the guardian symbols of the prevailing system of authority) with attitudes of rejection and Guilt toward the movement; attitudes that will impel them to the act of opposition — to the organization of a counter-movement, a reactive corps of defendant rhetors that will give salience to the errant symbols ("faulty principles," "vile beasts") of the existing order.

The development of a counter-movement is vital: for "*it is the bad side that produces the movement which makes history, by providing a struggle.*"[67] The counter-movement provides the movement with the potential for crisis, and hence for consummation; for it provides a salient Victim, a scapegoat, a Kill — a rhetorical Vile Beast to be slain. Or put otherwise: it provides a Negation to be negated; and hence the potential for dialectical movement, the purifying struggle of contradictions, the purgative striving that ends in transformation and transcendence.[68]

As the rhetoric of dissent does its work of corrosion, and rhetor and counter-rhetor begin to flower into public notice, the movement enters the second phase of the period of inception — turns to a rhetoric of conversion and catharsis. Its first strategy is to promote decision, to *convert* the estranged; to "turn toward" the movement increasing numbers of the alienated, the undecided; to turn them from their hellish state of indecision and division (passive suffering, *pathema*) toward the movement as a negation of the errant symbols they oppose. It is a strategy designed to convert the impious, to convince them that by attitude they are *of* the movement, and by reason and justice ought to be *in* it; that the movement as the opponent of the counter-movement, which speaks for the state of Corruption, constitutes a Saving Rebellion — a striving for salvation, perfection, the "good."[69]

Its second strategy — since attitudes are but beginnings, mere "*incipient* acts"[70] — is to provoke action. It is a strategy designed to move the converted — through "pity, fear, and the like emotions"[71] — to rise up and cry *No* to the counter-movement (thereby say *Yes* to the movement);[72] to move them to the purgative act (*poiema*) that will purify their "faulty living," enable them to transform their "natural condition," transcend their Guilt — to "shift their coordinates," "acquire a new 'perspective,'" "see around the corner," and hence "prophesy."[73] It is a strategy designed, in brief, to move them to the negation of the counter-Negation; which is to say, to the rhetorical killing of the Kill.

For the killing is rhetorical, whether it is in the order of Victimage or of Mortification. The killing is impious, in the order of murder, when the converted rise up, in the arena of their minds, and negate the contradictions of the counter-movement; when having "suffered," struggled with, the errant symbols of the existing order ("faulty principles," "vile beasts"), they "see through," reject, and thus slay them.[74]

The symbolic rejection of the existing order is a purgative act of transformation and transcendence. It affirms the commitment of the converted to the movement – to the new understanding, which is an "adequate" understanding (for it is a striving for reason and justice). And hence it endows them with a new condition or "substance" – with a new identity, a new unity, a new motive.

And the killing is pious, in the order of Mortification, when the converted negate the negations that they encounter in themselves: when – inevitably tempted to disobey, to deny the "commandments" of the movement – they suffer, "see through," reject, and thus slay the "vile beasts" within.[75] The decision to persevere in their assent to the movement – to say *No* to the errant negatives that rise up in themselves ("in the light of more complicated after-thoughts") – is an act of symbolic self-sacrifice, scrupulous self-restraint (self-control, self-moderation). It is a purgative act of obedience that provides them with a renewed understanding, a "dynamic" understanding ("the *understanding* which is active in that it performs the act of unification").

Yet it must not be forgotten that the killing in a movement may be physical, nonverbal ("beyond language"); and that such killing is also rhetorical. For men may murder, for the sake of terror, in the name of the movement – knowing that their Victims, though silenced, may speak: for Death, though the ultimate failure of communication, is nevertheless, being a mode of conduct, in the realm of speech ("*O eloquent, just, and mighty Death! whom none could advise, thou hast persuaded. . . .*")[76]

And it must not be forgotten, Death being in the realm of speech, that men may die, for the sake of pity, in the name of the movement; nor that of all the modes of dying, none is more eloquent than *martyrdom* – ultimate Mortification, self-Victimage, "a total voluntary self-sacrifice enacted in a grave cause before a perfect (absolute) witness."[77]

Three dangers confront the movement during its period of inception, any of which may cause its abortion. There is always the danger that the counter-movement will triumph; that the movement will be "killed," in the minds of the public, by its opponents. There is the danger that the rhetors of the unfolding movement – confronted by retrograde or recalcitrant factors in the gradually shifting Scene – will fail to revise their strategies, or otherwise err in their efforts to adapt to exigencies unforeseen. And there is the danger that the movement, as its ranks increase, will "splinter" – fail to achieve solidarity, *merger*; that the myth which prefigures the Purpose of the movement, imperfectly conveyed or received (whether consciously or unconsciously) will yield in the minds of a crucial number of converts ("heretics," "sectarians," "extremists") to an impious new vision of Order.

The formal need to circumvent these dangers structures the rhetoric of the final phase of the inception period. It is a rhetoric of profusion and intensity; a rhetoric raised to the level of eloquence. It is a rhetoric charged, to the utmost, with "a frequency of Symbolic and formal effects"; and energized, and sustained, by the pious desire to make utterance "perfect by adapting it in every minute detail to the [natural] appetites" of its hearers. It is a rhetoric marked by a "fullness of preoccupation" with the movement and its myth; by an "exaltation at the correctness," or propriety, of the movement's procedure.[78] It is a rhetoric that achieves and maintains solidarity; that intensifies recruitment and the commitment of the converted; that assures the emergence of triumphant hosts of "prophets" — rhetors united in their identification with the movement, in their conviction that the movement is the way to Redemption. It is a rhetoric that generates, in brief, a moving, mounting, and decisive tide of discourse.

And thus — as the movement succeeds in circumventing the dangers that confront it; as the rhetorical strategies of the inception period, correctly conceived and conveyed and revised to meet the needs of the gradually shifting Scene, begin to touch increasing numbers with the aura of alienation, and to accumulate conversions; as ineffective appeals are abandoned, new modes of argument adopted, available channels of communication subjected to increasingly intensified use, and ever broader publics addressed; as the power of the "priests" wavers and wanes, and the ranks of the aggressor rhetors grow ever greater, maintain solidarity, *merger* — the movement comes to its moment of crisis.

6

The crisis period of a movement is a time of mass decision; of collective catharsis, purgation, the resolution of public tensions.[79] It is the time of the expression ("in its unguarded simplicity") of a determinative public judgment; the time of the death of allegiance to a former system of authority — the time of negation, rejection, "the rebel snapping of the continuity."

Customarily, the crisis period will be a development *gradatim*, the climacteric of a process of cumulative negation; for most movements, as they develop, acquire a complex of issues. Yet even a multi-issue movement, through the calculated or fortuitous intervention of some cataclysmic event, may experience a relatively sudden moment of crisis.

However it comes, the moment of crisis marks the time when a class (or "principle," or *kind* of being) that has represented "the culmination of a society's purposes," gradually arrives "under changing scenic conditions . . . at the point where its act (and therefore its status) is no longer representative of the new conditions in their totality."[80] It is the time when the movement — having spread "by radiation from the few who [were] quickest to sense new factors in their incipient stages"[81] — effects the collective killing of the Kill.[82]

Now the old order dies, the old gods go. And thus the period of crisis is a time of transformation; for "the *killing* of something is the changing of it."[83] And it is a time of creation, *poiema*; for "consubstantiality *is* established by common involvement in a killing,"[84] and the death of the old order is but the birth of the new. And it is also a time of transcendence; for "a genuine 'new order' is a new *social ladder*,"[85] and the birth of the new order is but the birth of a new hierarchy, a new system of authority.

And thus "the obligations of order hang over us," even when we have revolted against order. So the old gods go, the new arrive. The counter-movement yields dominion to the movement. Men are endowed with a new condition or "substance" — with a new identity, a new unity, a new motive.

It is a motive marvelously adequate to the needs of the movement. For if it is the marvel of dialectical movement that "the moment of crisis in transcendence involves a new motive discovered en route"[86] — it is surely the marvel of the rhetoric of movements that, with the transcendence of the moment of crisis, men discover the one motive that will keep them en route. It is the motive that sustains the movement throughout its period of consummation.

7

The period of consummation is a time of decision persevered in. For it is a time of Redemption: men have been purged of absurdity and injustice; and having been purged, they desire to remain so ("for who would not be cleansed"). Reason and justice now reign. Men agree on meaning, value, and desire. And they are charged with attitudes of benevolence — with humility, faith, fortitude, forgiveness, temperance, prudence, and patience; attitudes, ultimately, in the order of self-sacrifice.

So there is a new understanding, an "adequate" understanding; for the order that now exists is essentially "good." And thus the relations between the new classes are harmonious, cooperative, symmetrical; and the new communication between classes is blessed and benign, "like the ways of courtship" — a communication that might be likened, once again, to the "rhetoric of courtship." For it is a rhetoric in the order of love; a rhetoric in the order of peace; and a rhetoric energized, and sustained, by the motive men have discovered — or rediscovered — with the transcendence of the movement's crisis.

For the achievement of transcendence is the achievement of dominion; and with the achievement of dominion men inevitably find, in their totality, that their former act is no longer representative of the new conditions: for now they yearn to conform with the new sources of their being; to be loyal, or obedient, to their new "natural" condition. Or put otherwise: with the transcendence of the movement's crisis, men inevitably find ("under changing scenic conditions") that, having been "prophets," they must now become "priests"; which is to say that they discover, or rediscover, the motive of piety (*mathema*; "the thing learned"). And so they strive to avoid error in the use of language; struggle, without ceasing, to use their language with propriety.

Thus arising as it does out of an attitude of affirmation, the rhetoric of consummation, in the initial phase of the period, is the rhetoric of a *pro* movement, predominantly a rhetoric of assent and allegiance. It is a rhetoric of praise, edification, prayer, petition, courtship; for men accept the new "mystery," the new communication between classes (or "principles," or "*kinds* of beings"). And the rhetoric that they practice is a rhetoric, once again, of dual strategy.

Its first strategy is to arouse, and to gratify, the natural appetite for obedience.[87] Its second is to strive, to the utmost, to actualize the "perfecting myth" of the movement: to achieve the incarnation, or embodiment, in the actualities of the material world ("the realities of a social texture"), of the movement's guiding vision of Order — its dream (conscious or unconscious) of "heaven," paradise, the "good society," Utopia.

They are strategies wholly appropriate to a state of Redemption: strategies designed to infuse the pious with the desire to persevere — to continue, in their obedience, to "exemplify a sense of the appropriate"; and to move them, in their perseverance, to complete the building of the new order — "to round things out, to fit experiences together into a unified whole." They are strategies, put otherwise, wholly rotten with piety; designed to achieve "the conformity of a reality to its concept" — which is to say, a state of perfection: "a complete and perfect whole"; a cooperative system of pure symmetry, perfect harmony, and integration ("guided by a scrupulous sense of the appropriate") — an Order marked by perfect communion, pure identification, and absolute communication.

But tragically, in this "imperfect world," "communication is never an absolute (only angels communicate absolutely)."[88] And while it is true, as "prophets" know, that "insofar as [an opposition] can unite in a new collectivity, progressively affirming its own title to the orthodoxy, tendencies toward the negativistic, satanistic, disintegrative, and 'splintering' fall away" – it is also true, as "priests" learn, that "insofar as [an opposition's] own imaginative possibility requires embodiment in bureaucratic fixities ['the realities of a social texture'], its necessary divergences from Utopia become apparent."[89]

Wherefore Utopia – as an existentially "good" order, the portion of paradise gained, a state which *is* – is inevitably bound, in time, to become an *is not*. And it is a state bound, moreover, while it exists, to stand always "on the verge of being lost":[90] a state of pious men, "huddling together, nervously loquacious, at the edge of an abyss."[91]

For "human beings are not a perfect fit for *any* historic texture";[92] and even in the "heavens" of this earth, the pious remain human. They may gladly submit to a code of control; persevere, strive to obey, struggle to keep the new "commandments" ("if they do not struggle, they rot"). But because they are human, they "can be expected to err" in their striving; which is to say that they can be expected, in time, to disobey – negate, reject, the prevailing system of authority ("for who can keep commandments").

Or put otherwise: while it is true, as "prophets" know, that "man is the only creature who refuses to be what he is"[93] – it is also true, as "priests" learn, that man is inevitably bound to remain what he is: a being by nature divided, ambitious, prone to pride; the symbol-making (symbol-using and misusing) animal, inventor of the negative, goaded by the spirit of hierarchy, ultimately separated from his natural condition by impious dreams of an ideal Order – forever striving, tragically Faustian, wholly "rotten with perfection."

8

"Out of such predicaments, ingenious fellows rise up and sing" – keep the harmony, preserve the symmetry, conserve the cooperative structure: which is to say that they strive, in the time of the new order, to keep the new tension. For the time of the new order, which is the time of a movement in its consummation, is of necessity a time of tension: the tension inherent in a state of harmony, symmetry – a state of solidarity, *merger* ("the comprehension of scattered particulars in one idea").[94] It is the very tension, not to strain for a metaphor, intrinsic to metaphor itself ("the unification of the heterogeneous").[95]

It is a "good" tension, *eutonia*; for it sustains the state of Redemption – which is a state of reason and justice, understanding, love and peace. Yet it is a tension increasingly dependent, as "priests" learn to their pain, on the maintenance of another tension — a private, inner tension — which the pious, being human, may find difficult to endure: the tension of men who must obediently sing *Yes* to the existing order — though they yearn, with mounting anguish, to rise up and cry *No*. It is the tension of men charged with piety, but increasingly ripe with impiety: loyal men who must embody, or make incarnate — in the very texture of their being — the mystic "principle of the oxymoron" ("the co-existence of conflicting orders").[96] For if the state of Redemption is to endure, men must continue their courtship — though they remain by nature divided, "endowed for struggle," prone to pride.

And thus the period of consummation is inevitably a time of revision (self-control, self-restraint, self-moderation). For courtship, which is in the order of love, entails communication ("the most generalized statement of the principle of love"); and communication, in its essence, involves "a principle of self-interference":

> In its essence communication involves the use of verbal symbols for purposes of appeal. Thus, it splits formally into the three elements of speaker, speech, and spoken-to, with the speaker so shaping his speech as to "commune with" the spoken-to. This purely technical pattern is the pre-condition of *all* appeal. And "standoffishness" is necessary to the form, because without it the appeal could not be maintained. For if union is complete, what incentive can there be for appeal? Rhetorically, there can be courtship only insofar as there is division. Hence, only through interference could one court continually, thereby perpetuating genuine "freedom of rhetoric."[97]

And thus the period of consummation, the time of a movement in its ending, is ultimately a time of self-sacrifice, self-Victimage, Mortification. For if men are to continue their courtship, and thus preserve the new hierarchy, they must scrupulously, and deliberately, clamp limitations upon themselves: promptly slay the "vile beasts" that arise in their minds; negate, and thus kill, the errant symbols within.

And thus, by symbol-using ("speech being a mode of conduct"), men convert their liabilities ("faulty living") into assets. Now means become ends. The "rhetoric of courtship" rises to the level of "pure persuasion." Men "take delight in the sheer *forms* of courtship for their own sakes"; "in the process of appeal for itself alone, without ulterior purpose."[98] It is a time of pure praise, edification, prayer, petition; of "pure courtship, homage in general, the ultimate idea of an audience, without thought of advantage, but sheerly through love of the exercise."[99] It is the time of "the rhetorical motive dialectically made ultimate": rhetoric for the sake of rhetoric, courtship for the sake of courtship, harmony for the sake of harmony, symmetry for the sake of symmetry.

And thus it is also a time of eloquence: for what is symmetry but "formal excellence"; and "formal excellence" is eloquence.[100] It is the eloquence of men fully preoccupied with the movement and its myth; men in a state of exaltation at the correctness, or propriety, of their procedure. And it is an eloquence which can be expected, at the farthest reach of the movement, to transcend itself (or "abolish itself") by passing, "beyond language," into the region of Silence.

For it must not be forgotten that Silence, being a mode of conduct, is also, like Death, in the realm of speech. There is the "silence of understanding"[101] — communion so perfect that it transcends the need of words; identification so pure that it promptly fuses contradictions, and thus sustains the continuity, "the co-existence of conflicting orders." And there is the mystic "rhetoric of silence"[102] — the wordless discourse of the "silent inner teacher": the hierarchical god of the movement, the mythic originator of the harmony or symmetry, the "perfect (absolute) witness," "the beloved cynosure and sinecure, the end of all desire" ("though some lovers of such symmetry may insist that their god be named Atheos").[103]

And it must not be forgotten, Silence being in the realm of speech, that man is a maker (*poietes*); nor that "the 'poetic state' is in its essence silent."[104] It is the silence essential to "the heart-conscious kind of listening, or vigilance, that precedes expression" — "the artist's preparatory silence (the silence that must precede the saying, until ripeness is near to rot)."[105] It is "the silence of the quest," the Hunt.[106] And hence it is the silence, *par excellence*, of the impious — the realm of the new Saving Remnant, the proud rhetors of the movement to come.

9

And thus a movement may be said to end in stasis. It is the stasis, in a sense, of Redemption — love achieved, peace attained; the dynamic stasis of "that harmony which is movement so perfect that it is imperceptible, like the movement of a spinning top."[107]

And it is the stasis, in another sense, of pure tension. For because men are pious, they are "free";[108] and their freedom equals a state of continual Mortification — self-restraint, self-control, self-moderation (and "moderation . . . is nothing but pure tension").[109] It is the tension inherent in a state of sheer courtship; the tension intrinsic to the very motive of "pure persuasion": "It is the condition of Santayana's transcendental skepticism, where the pendulum is at rest, not hanging, but poised exactly above the fulcrum . . . Psychologically it is related to a conflict of opposite impulses. Philosophically, it suggests the plight of Buridan's extremely rational ass. . . . Theologically or politically, it would be the state of intolerable indecision just preceding conversion to a new doctrine."

It is a state "uncomfortably like suspended animation." It is "the change of direction, from systole to diastole, made permanent"; "the moment of motionlessness, when the axe has been raised to its full height, and is just about to fall." Or less militantly, "it is the pause at the window, before descending into the street." [110]

10

But no material world, as Burke has noted, could be run on the motive of "pure persuasion." [111] For since men are by nature divided, "every human statement is partial." And if it is true that "there is a point at which rhetoric in its perfection transcends itself or 'abolishes itself' by becoming sheerly dialectical" – it is also true that there is a point at which "even the most 'universal' of dialectical manipulations will disclose partisan motives, willy nilly, whereat we are brought back into the realm of rhetorical partisanship." [112]

So the wheel forever turns. Man's movements, in time, come to an end. And they come to an end in tragedy – for tragedy involves defeat, "the failure of our ends," [113] the ultimate death of the "good."

Yet if his movements are tragic, the fate of man himself is comic – for tragedy also involves triumph, "the beyond of resurrection," [114] an ultimate "prosperous end." [115] And if the wheel forever turns, it is man who does the turning – forever striving, in an "imperfect world," for a world of perfection. And hence man, the rhetorical animal, is saved: for salvation lies in the striving, the struggle itself.

It is the message of the ascending angels in Goethe's *Faust, Part Two*: "whoever strives with all his power, we are allowed to save" (*wer immer strebend sich bemüht, den können wir erlösen*).[116]

It is also the message of Camus: "The struggle itself toward the heights is enough to fill a man's heart. One must imagine Sisyphus happy." [117]

And it is essentially the message, to round things out, of Kenneth Burke – the ultimate meaning, or purpose, of dramatism itself: for ". . . the nearest man will ever get to a state of practical peace among the many persuasions is by theoretical study of the forms in all persuasion." [118]

FOOTNOTES, PAGES 456 TO 472

1. It is intended as supplementary to my "The Rhetoric of Historical Movements," *The Quarterly Journal of Speech*, XXXVIII (April 1952), 184–188; and as complementary to my "The Rhetorical Structure of the 'New Left' Movement, Part One," *The Quarterly Journal of Speech*, L (April 1964), 113–135.

2. ". . . the 'dramatistic' is a critical or essayistic analysis of language, and thence of human relations generally, by the use of terms derived from the contemplation of drama." Kenneth Burke, "Linguistic Approach to Problems of Education," *Modern Philosophies and Education*, Fifty-Fourth Yearbook of the National Society for the Study of Education, Part I, ed. Nelson B. Henry (Chicago, 1955), p. 264.

3. Terms have occasionally been shifted from one context to another, for heuristic purposes, in accordance with Burke's method of "perspective by incongruity." The citations that follow, unless otherwise noted, are from the writings of Burke.

4. *Towards a Better Life* (New York, 1932), p. 211.

5. The definition of politics in "Linguistic Approach to Problems of Education," *op. cit.*, p. 280.

6. *The Philosophy of Literary Form* (Vintage ed., New York, 1957), p. 267.

7. "Catharsis — Second View," *Centennial Review*, V (1961), 130.

8. For Burke on the opening sentence of the *Nicomachean Ethics* see "Towards a Total Conformity: A Metaphysical Fantasy," *The Literary Review*, II (1957–58). 203–207.

9. *A Rhetoric of Motives* (New York, 1953), ix.

10. "Art — and the First Rough Draft of Living," *Modern Age*, VIII (Spring 1964), 162.

11. "Definition of Man," *The Hudson Review*, XVI (Winter 1963–64), 507.

12. *Attitudes toward History* (Beacon ed., Boston, 1961), p. 124.

13. Burke's translation of words spoken by The Lord in the "Prologue in Heaven" of Goethe's *Faust, Part One*. See "The Language of Poetry 'Dramatistically' Considered," *The Chicago Review*, IX (Spring 1955), 42, 46.

14. One of Burke's key terms; e.g., *Attitudes toward History*, pp. 227, 295, 320.

15. The definition is from Martin Foss, *The Idea of Perfection in the Western World* (Princeton, N.J., 1946), p. 8. I take this definition as concise, and harmonious with Burke's concept of perfection as presented in "Definition of Man," *op. cit.*, and in *Permanence and Change* (Hermes ed., Los Altos, Calif., 1954), pp. 292–294.

16. "Linguistic Approach to Problems of Education," *op. cit.*, p. 263.

17. *The Rhetoric of Religion* (Boston, 1961), pp. 4–5.

18. See "On Human Behavior Considered 'Dramatistically.'" *Permanence and Change*, pp. 274–294; and the discussion of "the cycle of terms implicit in the idea of 'order'" in *The Rhetoric of Religion*, pp. 183ff. See also William H. Rueckert, *Kenneth Burke and the Drama of Human Relations* (Minneapolis, 1963), pp. 128–162.

19. Cf. A. J. Ayer, *Man as a Subject for Science*, Auguste Comte Memorial Lecture 6 (University of London, 1964), pp. 12–17.

20. *A Rhetoric of Motives*, p. 265.

21. "The 'social' aspect of language is 'reason.' Reason is a complex technique for 'checking' one's assertions by public reference. . . . Hence, implicit in both language and reason (*logos*, word) there is is a *social* basis of reference affecting the individual. Linked with this is the need to feel the 'reasonableness' of one's society, the reasonableness of its aims and methods. This reasonableness comes to a focus in symbols of authority. . . ." *Attitudes toward History*, pp. 341–342.

"For 'justice' is the logical completion of language, leading one to round the circle by imposing upon oneself the negatives one would impose upon others. . . ." See "Postscripts on the Negative," *The Quarterly Journal of Speech*, XXXIX (April 1953), 211–212.

22. *Attitudes toward History*, p. 374; *A Rhetoric of Motives*, p. 115.

23. *A Rhetoric of Motives*, p. 22.

24. *A Grammar of Motives* (New York, 1945), p. 188.

25. See the definitions for "integrate," "integration," *Webster's New Collegiate Dictionary* (Springfield, Mass., 1953).

26. *A Rhetoric of Motives*, p. 115.

27. "Order by its very nature involves modes of control and self-control that add

up morally to 'mortification.'" "On Catharsis, or Resolution," *The Kenyon Review*, XXI (Summer 1959), 367.

28. Cf. *A Rhetoric of Motives*, p. 115.

29. *The Rhetoric of Religion*, p. 30. ". . . love involves the element of *desire*, a sense of union with something with which one is identified but from which one is divided." *Attitudes toward History*, p. 372. "'Communion' involves the interdependence of people through their common stake in both co-operative and symbolic networks." *Attitudes toward History*, p. 234. ". . . note that communion is a *unification*. Such a feeling of unity implies the transcending of a disunity." *A Grammar of Motives*, p. 297.

30. *A Rhetoric of Motives*, p. 25.

31. *Permanence and Change*, p. 69.

32. *Ibid.*, pp. 74–75.

33. The relation between freedom and piety is discussed in note 108 below.

34. *Permanence and Change*, p. 77.

35. *Ibid.*, p. 74.

36. *A Rhetoric of Motives*, p. 115.

37. *Permanence and Change*, p. 74.

38. "Catharsis – Second View," *op. cit.*, p. 112n.

39. *A Rhetoric of Motives*, p. 115.

40. "Looking into the *act* of Disobedience, we come upon the need for some such term as 'pride,' to name the corresponding *attitude* that precedes the act." *The Rhetoric of Religion*, p. 187. Burke would label his ideal education "Faustological," "since it would center in the study of ambition as a disease." See "Linguistic Approach to Problems of Education," *op. cit.*, p. 272.

41. "Catharsis – Second View," *op. cit.*, p. 112. And see *The Rhetoric of Religion*, p. 184.

42. *A Rhetoric of Motives*, p. 233.

43. Cf. "In failing to abide by the tribal or institutional thou-shalt-not's, or in fearing that one might fail, one piles up a measure of guilt after the analogy of a debt that needs repayment by corresponding sums." "A Dramatistic View of the Origins of Language," *The Quarterly Journal of Speech*, XXXVIII (October 1952), 264.

44. *A Grammar of Motives*, p. 336. I take the phrase as a metaphorical expression of Burke's "principle of perfection" – the notion that "there is a kind of 'terministic compulsion' to carry out the implications of one's terminology." See "Definition of Man," *op. cit.*, pp. 510–511.

45. *A Rhetoric of Motives*, p. 19.

46. *Attitudes toward History*, p. 347; *A Rhetoric of Motives*, p. 19.

47. *A Rhetoric of Motives*, p. 269.

48. *The Rhetoric of Religion*, p. 34n.

49. *A Rhetoric of Motives*, pp. 269, 274.

50. "Thanatopsis for Critics: A Brief Thesaurus of Deaths and Dyings," *Essays in Criticism*, II (October 1952), 372. See also *Permanence and Change*, p. 289; and "Restatement, on Death and Mortification," *The Rhetoric of Religion*, pp. 208–212.

51. *A Rhetoric of Motives*, p. 322.

52. *A Grammar of Motives*, p. 376.

53. For Burke's use of these terms, which he takes to be "at the very center of dialectical motivation," see "Dialectic of Tragedy" and "Actus and Status," in *A Grammar of Motives*, pp. 38–43.

54. Burke's terms for the three stages of artistic production. See *Counter-Statement* (Phoenix ed., Chicago, 1957), pp. 213–214.

55. ". . . we might say Hell is indecision, Purgatory is decision, and Heaven is the arrival that follows decision persevered in." "Catharsis – Second View," *op. cit.*, p. 128.

56. "But 'becoming' itself, in being analyzable as moments between the limits of before and after. . . ." "The Language of Poetry 'Dramatistically' Considered," *op. cit.*, p. 48.

57. See "The Five Master Terms," *Twentieth Century English*, ed. William S. Knickerbocker (New York, 1946), pp. 272–288; and *A Grammar of Motives*, x–xvi.

58. A rhetorical movement is a social act; and "in social acts, form *is* content." Hugh Duncan, *Communication and Social Order* (New York, 1962), p. 320. If a rhetorical movement is an act "contained" by the "psychology of the audience," one might define it as "the creation of an appetite in the mind of the auditor, and the adequate satisfying of that appetite." To do so would be to borrow Burke's definition of "form." *Counter-Statement*, p. 31. The dramatistic approach "through the emphasis upon the act promptly integrates considerations of 'form' and 'content.' " *The Philosophy of Literary Form*, p. 76.

59. The phrase is from "Catharsis — Second View," *op. cit.*, p. 121. For Burke's discussion of two kinds of poetic "unfolding" (the poet's and the reader's), see "Toward a Post-Kantian Verbal Music," *The Kenyon Review*, XX (1958), 543–546.

60. Cf. *The Philosophy of Literary Form*, p. 165; and see Hugh Duncan, *Language and Literature in Society* (Chicago, 1953), p. 121.

61. On the pivotal group, see *Counter-Statement*, p. 71; and Karl Mannheim, *Man and Society in an Age of Reconstruction*, tr. by Edward Shils (London, 1940). On alienation ("that state of affairs wherein a man no longer 'owns' his world because, for one reason or another, it seems basically unreasonable"), see *Attitudes toward History*, pp. 216, 342.

62. Cf. *A Grammar of Motives*, pp. 324ff; and "The Poetic Motive," *The Hudson Review*, XI (Spring 1958), 60.

63. See "Linguistic Approach to Problems of Education," *op. cit.*, pp. 270, 274–278; *Attitudes toward History*, pp. 232–235; *The Philosophy of Literary Form*, pp. 56–86; and "Fact, Inference and Proof in the Analysis of Literary Symbolism," *Symbols and Values: An Initial Study, Thirteenth Symposium of the Conference on Science, Philosophy and Religion*, ed. Lyman Bryson (New York, 1954), pp. 283–306. For an illuminating treatment of Burke's method, see Rueckert, *op. cit.*, pp. 83–111.

64. *The Rhetoric of Religion*, p. 241.

65. *Counter-Statement*, p. 179.

66. Sir Thomas Browne, *The Garden of Cyrus*, *Works*, ed. Geoffrey Keynes, IV (London, 1928), p. 67. Cf. *The Philosophy of Literary Form*, p. 83.

67. Karl Marx, *The Poverty of Philosophy* (International Publishers ed., New York, 1963), p. 121. See James W. Vander Zanden, "Resistance and Social Movements," *Social Forces*, XXXVII (May 1959), 313; and Harvey Seifert, *Conquest by Suffering: The Process and Prospects of Nonviolent Resistance* (Philadelphia, 1965), p. 51.

68. "When approached from a certain point of view, A and B are 'opposites.' We mean by 'transcendence' the adoption of another point of view from which they cease to be opposites." *Attitudes toward History*, p. 336. See also *A Rhetoric of Motives*, p. 53; and Marx, *op. cit.*, pp. 107–108.

69. Conversion is here conceived as involving both attitude and act. Note Burke on the conversion of Augustine, *The Rhetoric of Religion*, pp. 49–117. The form of Augustine's conversion is singularly appropriate for the study of movements; for his turn was from "bad" words to "good," from the teaching of pagan rhetoric to the preaching of the word of God (i.e. "speech being a mode of conduct, he converted his faulty living into eloquence").

70. *A Rhetoric of Motives*, p. 42; *A Grammar of Motives*, pp. 20, 42, 50.

71. "Pity is said to be like a movement towards; and fear (or 'terror') like a movement away-from . . . And we are healed by being enabled to put opposites together in a way that transcends their opposition." "On Catharsis, or Resolution," *op. cit.*, p. 341.

72. Cf. Albert Camus, *The Rebel: An Essay on Man in Revolt*, tr. Anthony Bower (Vintage ed., New York, 1956), p. 13. And see *Attitudes toward History*, p. 21.

73. *Attitudes toward History*, pp. 269–270, 314.

74. The "desire to kill" a certain person "is much more properly analyzable as a desire to *transform the principle* which that person represents." *A Rhetoric of Motives*, p. 13. "Stated broadly the dialectical (agonistic) approach to knowledge is through the *act* of assertion, whereby one 'suffers' the kind of knowledge that is the reciprocal of his act. This is the process embodied in tragedy, where the agent's action involves a corresponding passion, and from the sufferance of the passion there arises an understanding of the act, an understanding that transcends the act. The act, in being an assertion, has called forth a counter-assertion in the elements that compose its context. And when the agent is enabled to see in terms of this counter-assertion, he has transcended the state that characterized him at the start." *A Grammar of Motives*, p. 38.

75. Mortification is "a kind of governance, an extreme form of 'self-control,' the deliberate, disciplinary 'slaying' of any motive that, for 'doctrinal' reasons, one thinks of as unruly . . . it is a systematic way of saying no to Disorder, or obediently saying yes to order." *The Rhetoric of Religion*, p. 190; and see "Thanatopsis for Critics," *op. cit.*, pp. 369–370.

76. Sir Walter Ralegh, *The History of the World* (Edinburgh, 1820), VI, p. 370.

77. *The Rhetoric of Religion*, p. 248.

78. The phrases quoted are from Burke's discussion of "eloquence." See *Counter-Statement*, pp. 165, 41, 170, 37.

79. The period of rhetorical crisis I have previously defined as the time "when one of the opposing groups of rhetoricians . . . succeeds in irrevocably disturbing that balance between the groups which had existed in the mind of the collective audience." See "The Rhetoric of Historical Movements," *op. cit.*, p. 186.

80. *A Grammar of Motives*, p. 420. Cf. "Periods of social crisis occur when an authoritative class, whose purpose and ideals had been generally considered as *representative* of the total society's purposes and ideals, becomes considered as antagonistic." *The Philosophy of Literary Form*, p. 23n.

81. *Counter-Statement*, p. 71.

82. ". . . a shift in allegiance to the symbols of authority equals the symbolic slaying of a parent." *Attitudes toward History*, p. 211. Cf. Ernest Jones, "Evolution and Revolution," *International Journal of Psycho-Analysis*, XXII (1941), 198ff.

83. *A Rhetoric of Motives*, p. 20.

84. *Ibid.*, p. 265.

85. *Ibid.*, p. 264.

86. *A Grammar of Motives*, p. 421.

87. "Obedience to the reigning symbols of authority is in itself natural and wholesome." *Attitudes toward History*, p. 226.

88. *Permanence and Change*, xv.

89. *Attitudes toward History*, pp. 226.

90. The phrase is from Burke's discussion of "pure persuasion." *A Rhetoric of Motives*, p. 285.

91. Cf. *Permanence and Change*, p. 272.

92. *Attitudes toward History*, pp. 225–226.

93. Camus, *The Rebel*, p. 11.

94. *A Grammar of Motives*, p. 403.

95. Philip Wheelwright, *The Burning Fountain: A Study in the Language of Symbolism* (Bloomington, Ind., 1954), pp. 101ff.

96. "Mysticism as a Solution to the Poet's Dilemma," *Spiritual Problems in Contemporary Literature*, ed. Stanley Romaine Hopper (New York, 1952), p. 111.

97. *A Rhetoric of Motives*, p. 271.

98. *The Rhetoric of Religion*, p. 34; *A Rhetoric of Motives*, x.

99. *A Rhetoric of Motives*, pp. 293–294.

100. *Counter-Statement*, p. 37.

101. Cf. Joost Meerloo, *Conversation and Communication* (New York, 1952), p. 115.

102. Cf. Joseph A. Mazzeo, "St. Augustine's Rhetoric of Silence," *Renaissance and Seventeenth-Century Studies* (New York, 1964), pp. 16ff.

103. A conjunction of phrases from *A Rhetoric of Motives*, pp. 333, 291.

104. "Towards a Post-Kantian Verbal Music," *op. cit.*, p. 537.

105. "Thanatopsis for Critics: A Brief Thesaurus of Deaths and Dyings," *op. cit.*, p. 374.

106. "For in the quest one is naturally silent, be it as the animal that stalks its quarry or as the thinker meditating upon an idea." *A Grammar of Motives*, p. 303.

107. The phrase is from Herbert Read's "The Flower of Peace" in *The Forms of Things Unknown* (London, 1960), p. 223.

108. "Freedom" is "self-movement." *A Grammar of Motives*, p. 74. In the final, utopian stage of a movement, men are naturally pious, obedient; and their piety is the essential source of their freedom. Because they are pious they negate their desire to say *No* to the existing order, and hence "court continually, thereby perpetuating genuine 'freedom of rhetoric.'" Cf. note 97.

Because they are pious they are concerned with rhetoric for the sake of rhetoric, *pure form*; and "there is no purer act than pure form"—and "a pure act is by definition pure freedom." *The Rhetoric of Religion*, p. 281. And because they are pious, they praise; and praise "wells up"—"in praise there is the feel of freedom"; "in total admiration, one is wholly free." *Ibid.*, p. 55.

And because they are pious they are necessarily in movement toward a state of perfect symmetry, and hence "free." For they are possessed by the principle of perfection, "the desire to round things out," "the delight in carrying out terministic possibilities 'to their logical conclusion,' in so far as such possibilities are perceived." And "this 'entelechial' motive is the poetic equivalent of what, in the moral realm, is called 'justice.' It is equatable with both necessity and freedom in the sense that the consistent rounding out of a terminology is the very opposite of frustration. Necessary movement toward perfect symmetry is thus free." "The Language of Poetry 'Dramatistically' Considered," *op. cit.*, p. 63.

Put otherwise: the problem of freedom in "utopia" (taken as a metaphor for the ending, or "perfection," of a movement) resolves itself in terms of the Hegelian formula, "freedom is the knowledge of necessity." Yet the freedom that is grounded in man's capacity for the Negative also remains; and hence even in "utopia" men are free to be impious—to negate the negations of the existing order, to say *No* to the prevailing "thou-shalt-nots." Cf. *The Rhetoric of Religion*, p. 222; and the dialog between Satan and The Lord in the "Prologue in Heaven," *ibid.*, pp. 282–283.

109. Camus, *The Rebel*, p. 301.

110. *A Rhetoric of Motives*, p. 294.

111. *Ibid.*

112. "Mysticism as a Solution to the Poet's Dilemma," *op. cit.*, p. 109.

113. Foss, *The Idea of Perfection in the Western World*, p. 63.

114. *Ibid.*

115. "*Comoedia vero inchoat asperitatem alicuius rei, sed eius materia prospere terminatur . . .*" *Dantis Alagherii Epistolae: The Letters of Dante*, ed. Paget Toynbee (Oxford, 1920), pp. 176, 200.

116. *Goethe's Faust*, tr. Walter Kaufmann (New York, 1961), p. 493. On the relation between this passage and its companion ("man can be expected to err as long as he keeps striving"), a relation that epitomizes the tragic attitude toward value, see Henry Alonzo Myers, *Tragedy: A View of Life* (Ithaca, N. Y., 1956), pp. 12–13.

117. *The Myth of Sisyphus*, tr. Justin O'Brien (Vintage ed., New York, 1955), p. 91.

118. "Linguistic Approach to Problems of Education," *op. cit.*, p. 300. Dramatism, Burke's "project directed 'towards the purification of war,'" is conceived as a means

of striving, through study, for a world of peace. The ultimate end is unattainable (or unmaintainable); for in this "imperfect world," where men are by nature divided, one man's "good" may be another's "evil" — and men may always make the Satanic choice, "Evil, be thou my good." Nevertheless, in a world of "many persuasions," dramatistic study in itself offers a measure of salvation. For dramatism would encourage "tolerance by speculation," make "methodical the attitude of patience"; and tolerance and patience are in the order of peace. A world infused with such attitudes would surely be a "better world"; even a world, one must imagine, in which men might be happy.

◇◇

LELAND M. GRIFFIN was born in Kansas City in 1920. He has taught speech at Northwestern University since 1956. His published work consists of long, significant, and brilliant essays on such topics as the edifice metaphor in rhetorical theory, the rhetorical structure of the anti-Masonic movement, and the rhetorical structure of the new-left movement. His endeavors are very Burkeian and tend to derive from the kind of thing Burke did so brilliantly in "The Rhetoric of Hitler's Battle" essay in *The Philosophy of Literary Form.*

Professor Griffin is a long-time student of Burke's work and one of his best "apologists" (for want of a better word). His use of Burke — both in print and in academic life — has always seemed to me exemplary. Professor Brock's essay is one example; those who attended the Burke conference organized by Professor Griffin in 1965 will remember another; and those who have talked with his students will know of still another. The present essay — one of the finest syntheses and applications of Burke I know of — is a final example. Burke is fortunate in having been received in this way in this field by such a person as Professor Griffin.

What Mr. Griffin is trying to do here for the "rhetoric of movements" is what Hugh Duncan did for sociology, what Francis Fergusson did for drama, and what I tried to do for literary criticism: to develop a model or abstraction from Burke for the study of a specific subject. It is difficult to characterize the nature of Professor Griffin's achievement in this essay. One cannot really get Burke in bits and pieces; one must earn him whole, one must have a kind of large synthesizing revelation which allows one to apprehend Burke's inwardness and still remain apart from it and be able to retain one's own identity as an intellect. It is only in this way that Burke can be properly and profoundly used. This is exactly what Professor Griffin has achieved in this essay and why it seems to me a model of how Burke can be received.

◇◇

2 When in Rome, Do as the Greeks

BY Denis Donoghue

IN 1931 Kenneth Burke published a book of critical essays, *Counter-Statement,* and the following year a novel, *Towards a Better Life.* The relation between the criticism and the fiction is peculiarly close, and is not at all undermined by the fact that we meet the principles first and the practice later. Normally, principles are devised to support the practices already delivered; we think of Eliot's early poems and then the early essays, their servants. But in Burke's case we need not worry about the order of things. We think of *Counter-Statement* as an answer to the 'statements' already made by society, by America, by Man. And then we think of Burke translating his counterstatement into corresponding images and rhythms, making his critical universals concrete.

In the Preface to *Towards a Better Life* Burke says that he wanted to write a realistic, objective novel, lively in event and character, with a palpable background in Greenwich Village. But his first efforts in this standard direction were so dismal that he reviewed his terms of reference and concluded that the form, excellent for others, was for him a nuisance; that is, it did not allow him to write as he wanted to write. It struck him, and the lineaments of his talent seemed to agree, that any plot would answer, so long as it allowed him to indulge his favorite modes of expression. These consisted of six procedures: lamentation, rejoicing, beseechment, admonition, sayings, and invective. So his second decision was to move in reverse: to begin with his favorite stylistic gestures and to deduce from these a 'corresponding' assembly of characters and a sequence of events loosely designated as plot. As he said: "*Facit indignatio versus,* which I should at some risk translate: 'An author may devote his entire energies to rage purely through a preference for long sentences.'" Burke would let himself be guided by a sense of style to invent characters and events in which the style would be most becomingly disclosed. It would not be necessary to devise a style for the fiction; the style was already there, waiting in its six resourceful modes. In this preposterous decision Burke cheered himself with the thought that he would at least disown the current standard prose which was apparently designed, like Kleenex, to be used once and thrown away. If the current prose was boisterous in rough statement, the inventions of *Towards a Better Life* would answer back, in counterstatement. In this 'periwig' style the sentences themselves would be internally eventful, contrived with so much stylistic brio that the absence of

EDITOR'S NOTE: Revised for this volume in 1966 from a work in progress.

newsworthy events would pass unnoticed. Hence Burke's prose is exciting as a good sonnet is exciting, by offering a proliferation of verbal events sufficient to engross the most demanding reader. Thus the author hopes to entrance the reader who would otherwise be satisfied only by pictures of war and mayhem, and to send him back to daily life with his lust for excitement somewhat stilled.

To begin with, it was necessary to put the reader in a proper mood for the reception of the book; clearly a condition of critical wakefulness as if he were attending to a song cycle by Bartok. So Burke makes his hero a thoroughly unpleasant character, a twisted creature with whom the reader could not possibly identify himself. The hero's skill in articulation would serve further to place the reader at a safe distance. Listening to John Neal, a self-declared Outsider, the reader would feel no desire to bring him in. So Neal's character was dictated not by observation of Nature but by the decencies of the stylistic occasion. Burke invents an alienated hero by deciding that alienation is the appropriate situation of the reader vis-à-vis the book.

The genesis of the book is therefore in the strictest sense verbal and stylistic. But, once the technique is under way, the possibilities of invention are endless, since there is no known end to the resources of language. By trading on certain incongruities between style and action, Burke can devise exquisitely comic incidents. In the second chapter, for instance, he describes John making an anguished telephone call to his beloved Florence from a public booth: ". . . and while Florence listened to words as desolate as my talent and my predicament could make them, I was grinning into the mouthpiece that the man beyond the glass, waiting to speak here next, might not suspect my condition." So the plot is manipulated to allow for necessary variety in the sentence. It so happens that the demands of the sentence, strictly obeyed, often produce scenes and actions which are wonderfully 'true': true to life, indeed. When John meets Florence, after months of separation, he brings her on a walk to an old ruined house which he has often haunted: "I have gone through the littered rooms, opened musty cupboards, and rummaged among rags with the rung of a broken chair. I have examined this decrepit house, waiting—and into its dismalness I now guided Florence, that her bright curiosity might give it different echoes."

The motto for this is given halfway through the book when John reflects, "If one seeks new metaphors, will he not also find new women?"; a conjunction, by the way, entirely consistent with the magical properties commonly attributed to metaphor by the coolest aestheticians. *Towards a Better Life* is written as a dance is created; where the choreographer designs the movements not, in the first instance, to tell a story, but to give the accomplished bodies an occasion to disclose their resources. Thus the love scene with Florence has "a minuet-like quality." John abuses his friends, urged by the persuasions of his terminology, and by those alone; a gift for words being an imperative to use them in the ways most fitting to the gift. "Yet I could as easily have loved these people," John rightly says. In a fragment at the end of the book we read: ". . . speech being a mode of conduct, he converted his faulty living into eloquence. Then should any like his diction, they would indirectly have sanctioned his habits." The plot itself is guided by principles purely internal to the medium of language, spurred by a sense of the reader's desires. It begins in misery, a condition exacerbated in John's twisted recollection. The misery is appeased; hence a change of scene, Genevieve, John's marriage, children, a move to the country. The appeasement is embodied in an unexpected and joyous meeting with Florence. But this proves, for the moment, a deception, in keeping with the fact that words often run before their deeds. Later the joy is made good. Then John dismisses Florence, as he will later dismiss Genevieve, not for any overt reason in nature but in keeping with the linguistic resource of the Negative; Thou Shalt Not. Finally he dribbles into total isolation, soliloquizing in Hell: hence, silence. This is as much of the plot as we need for the moment.

To give some impression of the dance-like quality of the book it is advisable to quote a fairly long passage. John has been describing a group of people with whom he has been vaguely associated:

> Dare I go further among this uneven lot? No further than to mention briefly a beautiful, and even picturesque woman, a Madame Durant, loved by two men. Through letters, telegrams, sudden visits, and the intervention of relatives, she carried her drama tumultuously across many states. With her arms about Joseph, she would cry out that she loved Josephus and thereupon, misled by a desire for too literal a symmetry, would cross the room to embrace Josephus and protest her love for Joseph. For to be alone with one of them seemed far greater impoverishment than to be with neither, and whichever she lived with, she thought herself conscience-stricken for leaving the other, though in reality suffering most from a drop in the liveliness of her situation. She wept in contentment, insisting that she was degraded — and friends, stopping to rebuke her for her inconstancy, would become her suitors. On one occasion I drank a toast to her elopement, using for the purpose glasses given prematurely as a present for her prospective marriage to the groom now temporarily abandoned though on hand to bid her and his rival farewell — and I left in complex cordiality, loving her, her two men, her dog, and the darkening inhospitable sky which matched my lonesomeness.

We read this prose as if it were verse, perhaps eighteenth-century poetic couplets in which the outside is simple so that the inside may be intricate. It is not fanciful to suggest that every detail in Madame Durant's complicated ménage is contained 'in principle' in the technical resources of language, not forgetting such choice items as rhyme, alliteration, assonance, and the remaining figures of speech and thought. If metaphor suggests a woman, would it not be possible to devise human relationships somehow 'equivalent' to simile, rhyme, oxymoron, as we already say that a certain relationship is paradoxical, and might go on to say that a full stop is a happy marriage, a comma an affair, a semicolon an engagement, a new paragraph a divorce? If speech is a mode of conduct, what is a dictionary?

Meanwhile we ask a prosaic question: what kind of book are we reading? It is certainly not a novel, nor was it meant to be. In ascriptions of this kind we are well advised to consult Northrop Frye's account of the several forms of prose fiction. Then it soon appears that Burke's book is not a freak, a sport of Nature, but an example of a distinguished tradition, the anatomy. It answers in every respect to Frye's description: it deals "less with people as such than with mental attitudes"; its characterization is "stylized rather than naturalistic," presenting people "as mouthpieces of the ideas they represent." The anatomist sees evil and folly "as diseases of the intellect, as a kind of maddened pedantry." The narrative is "loose-jointed." The writing "relies on the free play of intellectual fancy and the kind of humorous observation that produces caricature." The anatomy presents "a vision of the world in terms of single intellectual pattern." The masterpieces of the genre include the *Tale of a Tub*, the *Anatomy of Melancholy*, *Headlong Hall*, and *Brave New World*.[1]

Let us say, then, that *Towards a Better Life* is an anatomy of dissociation. John Neal is detached from Nature as from us: "the weather's metaphysical whisperings" do not sing to him. His human relationships are never more than provisional, the most tentative essays in a doomed genre. Throughout the book he is so conscientious in husbanding grimness that, while buffeted beyond endurance, he is never surprised in principle. He is Nature's victim and therefore our scapegoat. At the end of the book the quality of character has drained away entirely from the people of his experience, collecting itself now only in lampposts, streetcars, and gutters which take on a frightful vitality. John sees these manifestations of his curse as entirely in the nature of things, never a matter of surprise; the last 'event' is a fixation upon a wooden police-

[1] Northrop Frye, *Anatomy of Criticism* (Princeton, N.J.: Princeton University Press, 1957), pp. 308–309.

man outside a cigar shop. This stage in his Gothic tale is conveyed by an unmailed letter to his dead mistress, the style a tissue of quotations from a favorite poet, William Blake. As he sits in his room in New York ("this inexorable city") he says: "Watch the mind, as you would eye a mean dog. Wait. Die as a mangled wasp dies." Thereafter he delivers his testimony in fragments broken from the aphoristic structure. There comes a time, he says, when one must abandon his vocabulary, "for the rigidness of words, by discovering a little, prevents us from discovering more." And this is a time for the roar of silence. The book ends: "Not only not responding, but even refraining from soliloquy—for if we tell no one, the grave burden accumulates within us. Henceforth silence, that the torrent may be heard descending in all its fulness."

It is not enough to say that *Towards a Better Life* is beautifully 'written,' if by this praise we consign the book to an anthology of prose style. However peculiar its origin, it is in fact one of the most moving books in modern literature, as well as one of the purest anatomies. Like John Neal, Burke is skilled in "the hilarious aspects of distress." When modern literature is not comic it is often fretful; the implication is that the hero is right and the world is wrong. It is always the world that is in error, in sin. *Towards a Better Life* divides the malice of things evenly between John and the world: neither has any reason to ascribe to the other a monopoly in ill will. This has the effect of keeping the book's air clear. John never denies the world, or complains of the arbitrary nature of its arrangements. Indeed, if his troubles were of this nature, this would have to be a different life, a different book. He says at one point: "Throughout eternity there is hunger in the fact that the universe *needs to be*, and appeasement in the fact that the universe *is*." This is his idiom. One moment is followed by another, not by a complaint directed against the first. A fragment reads: "Had he found the matter ludicrous, he could have spared himself much indignation." So he spares himself much indignation by finding himself ludicrous. If he is tempted to become a modern mind-man, he knows the answer: "We would not deny the mind; but merely remember that as the corrective of wrong thinking is right thinking, the corrective of all thinking is the body." Meanwhile he walks "boldly through life, head erect and shoulders thrown back in shame." We think of Beckett, Italo Svevo, and the saving spirit of Stoic Comedy.

In the Preface of *Towards a Better Life* Burke pays tribute to Thomas Mann as an author of notable relevance; and we recall a celebrated essay, "Thomas Mann and André Gide," in *Counter-Statement*. The essay is very much to the present point as a brief poetics corresponding to the poem. Burke juxtaposes Mann's irony against Gide's experimentalism. Mann's concern, he notes, is with "serious and lonely fellows, deviations from type, who are overburdened with a feeling of divergency from their neighbours." These Outsiders "watch, they compare themselves with others to their own detriment, they are earnest to the point of self-disgust, and they are weighted with vague responsibilities." Mann has identified art as the problematical sphere of the human: implicit in the artist's work there is "a deliberate entertaining of moral vacillation." This attitude is summed up as irony, "which merges the sympathetic and antipathetic aspects of any subject." Gide, on the other hand, is an adept of curiosity, the question mark. "He views any set code of values with distrust, because it implies the exclusion of other codes." He is on guard, Burke says, "lest the possible be obscured by the real."[2] And the critic quotes a passage from Gide's autobiography which toys with the notion of writing the imaginary history of a nation to prove that the history of man might easily have been different. (It is obvious, by the way, that Burke himself is close to the spirit of Mann's irony.)

At the end of the essay Burke proposes that we disown a too literal interpretation of Gide's 'corruption.' "I should take the specific events in Gide," he says, "as hardly more than symbols: their parallel in life would not be the enacting of similar events, but the exercising of the complex state of mind which arises from the contemplation of such events with sympathy." But this, however genially stated, adds little to the old aesthetic based on therapy and the dramatic imagination; the idea that we are enlarged and improved by contemplating, in the frame of art, actions which we would disavow in practice. Such theorists would emphasize the intransitiveness of the artistic experience, and recommend it as a relief from our all-too-transitive preoccupations. But Burke goes beyond this position. He says: "Irony, novelty, experimentalism, vacillation, the cult of conflict — are not these men trying to make us at home in indecision, are they not trying to humanize the state of doubt?" And later: "Need people be in haste to rebel against the state of doubt, when doubt has not yet permeated the organs of our body, the processes of our metabolism, the desire for food and companionship, the gratification with sun and water?" Burke goes on to say that society might well benefit from "the corrective of a disintegrating art"; which "converts each simplicity into a complexity." An art may be valuable, he says, by "preventing a society from becoming too assertively, too hopelessly, itself." If action could be destroyed by such art as Gide's, this

[2] Kenneth Burke, *Counter-Statement*, 2nd ed. (Los Altos, Calif.: Hermes Publications, 1953), pp. 92–93.

would be disastrous: "but art can at best serve to make action more laboured." And this is good.

The implication is clear. Art is criticism. When society is a mechanistic braggart, the most useful artist is Thersites. In 1931 American society was a braggart; hence in need of all the Gides it could find. The principle is advanced with great rhetorical finesse in *Counter-Statement*: "When in Rome, do as the Greeks." In later books it is often invoked as the theory of the lightning rod, where security is achieved not by avoiding danger but by attracting it in conditions of one's own devising. You may try anything, according to this principle, as long as the experiment is verbal.

I have implied that this Nietzschean notion of art has had peculiar currency in American literature and I shall try to support the implication. But it is hardly possible to devise an aesthetic theory which makes any reference to the position of the artist in modern society without implying that his position is critical. The relation between One and the Many is invariably a critical relation, when seen from the standpoint of the One. When Eliot speaks of the role of the artist in purifying the dialect of the tribe, the several meanings of the verb imply a critical and hygienic force, without which society is too grossly itself. When Richard Blackmur published his choice essays as *The Lion and the Honeycomb*, he added a subtitle *Essays in Solicitude and Critique*, as if to say that critique, carried to one of its limits, was the intimate form of his solicitude. In the same book he gives a classic defense of art in those terms. The function of art, he says, is "to remind the powers that be, simple and corrupt as they are, of the forces they have to control." A modern philosopher has argued that it is essential for people who live in a democratic world to acquire immunity to eloquence. If we bring these sentences together, we see that they are saying the same thing; that the 'statements' of art are counterstatements to the rough-and-burly 'statements' of society, the loud words of the powers that be. It is a commonplace that modern writers have a particular tenderness for complex modes of being, ways of life and feeling which are full of contradiction. The poems of John Crowe Ransom are often concerned with modalities of honor; and when they are not concerned with honor they are concerned with passion. But one of his finest poems, "The Equilibrists," is concerned with a mode of passion which is threatened by honor: the lovers are kept apart by honor, and the imperative seems to wrong the good passion. The poem ends:

> For spin your period out, and draw your breath,
> A kinder saeculum begins with Death.

Would you ascend to Heaven and bodiless dwell?
Or take your bodies honorless to Hell?

In Heaven you have heard no marriage is,
No white flesh tinder to your lecheries,
Your male and female tissue sweetly shaped
Sublimed away, and furious blood escaped.

Great lovers lie in Hell, the stubborn ones
Infatuate of the flesh upon the bones;
Stuprate they rend each other when they kiss,
The pieces kiss again, no end to this.

But still I watched them spinning, orbited nice.
Their flames were not more radiant than their ice.
I dug in the quiet earth and wrought the tomb
And made these lines to memorize their doom: —

EPITAPH

Equilibrists lie here; stranger, tread light;
Close, but untouching in each other's sight;
Mouldered the lips and ashy the tall skull.
Let them lie perilous and beautiful.

It is clear that to this poet the beauty of the lovers depends upon their peril, as the peril depends upon the beauty. Without their contradictions the lovers would be dull things; their beauty pallid, their peril factitious. Society has nothing to say of contradiction, except that in the interest of efficiency it must be abolished. You live by passion or by honor: you cannot have both at once. It is the poet who is particularly concerned with those states of being in which, perhaps to our destruction, we are held by both at once. It is the poet who notes that one radiance has a double source: "Their flames were not more radiant than their ice." So Ransom is struck with the demands made upon these lovers, not by life, or the 'way of the world,' but by their own scruples, their own conscience. The powers that be walk boldly from one place to another, because they are simple and often corrupt. The special people go through life as equilibrists; or they cannot move at all. This is a poem in which solicitude is critique: solicitude for the human spirit is a critique of the large, rough forces which threaten its definition. Ransom would not care so much for lovers who take the easy way. Such people identify themselves with society, and this secures them so completely that they do not need the poet's care. When in that Rome they do as the Romans. They are banal.

I would imply, then, that the poetic imagination in a democratic time tends to be critical and perhaps subversive; or at least that in such poetry there is a special propriety. It would be impossible to ascribe such high powers and qualities to the imagination if it did not live by more exacting laws than those which govern the marketplace. Santayana said of William James that for him philosophy had a Polish constitution: so long as a single vote was cast against the majority opinion, nothing could pass. In poetry, the imagination sets up a Polish constitution. In the marketplace one man has one vote and the majority decides. Not so in the poem. When we speak of the 'world' of the poem, we acknowledge the sense in which the imagination makes its own laws. In modern American literature the imagination is often found exerting pressure upon the governing conventions and public axioms, as Robert Lowell's poem "Children of Light" applies notable pressure to an accepted meaning of American history. Or Richard Wilbur's recent poem "A Miltonic Sonnet for Mr. Johnson, on the Occasion of his Refusal of Peter Hurd's Official Portrait." This is the direct way. But there is another way perhaps even more deeply characteristic of American literature, a transcendental way. This is to criticize the given world by turning away from it, by building "a world elsewhere."

This is the theme of a recent book by Richard Poirier, a work close to my own interests. Mr. Poirier argues that the American tradition in literature is characterized by resistance, within its pages, to the forces of environment that otherwise dominate the world. American writers, he would show, tend to substitute themselves and their imaginations for the world and its thrones and powers, so that their books become rival worlds in which their poor embattled characters can live. Language and style provide the conditions denied in time and place. The function of the book, the fiction, is to give the beleaguered consciousness a home fit to live in. Emerson speaks of the "dream of the self" set off against the "buzz and din." I would not labor the case; it is available. I would only remark that recourse to a "world elsewhere" constitutes the most extreme form of critique. Indeed we cannot describe it in milder terms than subversion. The imagination can go no further in critique than by finding the given world incorrigible in principle, impenetrable in practice. Indeed, there is a certain incongruity in our proposing to 'teach' this literature at all, because the crux of its implication is that the palpable world in which we live and work and teach is beneath salvation, or beneath any salvation worth the candle. And this implication is delivered as a stark, individual gesture. Presumably the only kind of teaching which modern American literature would approve is the kind which is all questions and no answers; tentative, obscure, experimental. When the teaching is backed by public values and shared convictions, modern American literature disowns it, turns aside to its world elsewhere.

Perhaps I digress. But it is clear that the imagination sponsored in modern American literature is extreme in its critique. We normally assume that this is good, that the poetic imagination serves us best when it protects us against our public selves and our shoddy certainties. The trouble is, however, that the deepest visions of alienation and sickness are now packaged for general consumption and sold at cut price. Lionel Trilling has recently complained that those to whom he teaches the masterpieces of modern literature take the great alienated works in their stride. They are not intimidated by Dostoevsky, Conrad, Mann, or Eliot. Indeed the artist who would criticize our society at this moment would probably hold up before its eyes a heroic image, the implication being that we are incapable of rising to it. There is a literature of celebration as well as a literature of direct critique, and both are critical. Indeed, there is a case for sponsoring such a literature now on strictly stylistic grounds, as the persistence of a certain mood in a poem over many stanzas calls for another mood, in relief. This is Burke's own principle, advanced in *Counter-Statement* with great rhetorical force.

But perhaps we need another voice. There is a chapter in Santayana's *Interpretations of Poetry and Religion* in which the philosopher considers the meaning of three words, understanding, imagination, and mysticism. Understanding, he says, is "an applicable fiction, a kind of wit with a practical use." "Those conceptions which, after they have spontaneously arisen, prove serviceable in practice, and capable of verification in sense, we call ideas of the understanding." The public world, we infer, is happy enough with these, and is often rendered happy by less. The imagination is a higher power because it expresses "the universal self" and because it goes far beyond the serviceable. It is inventive and speculative rather than applied. But Santayana warns us that the imagination can be abused. "If the imagination merely alienates us from reality, without giving us either a model for its correction or a glimpse into its structure, it becomes the refuge of poetical selfishness. Such selfishness is barren, and the fancy, feeding only on itself, grows leaner every day." Mysticism, according to Santayana, is the last mode of abstention. "Instead of building a better world, it would undermine the foundations even of the world we have built already." The mystic cannot be satisfied with "anything short of Absolute Nothing." Meanwhile there is the natural world, the given world, such as it is. We cannot do better, Santayana implies, than to live in it, guided by understanding and by the constructive imagination. "When we compare the temple which we call Nature, built of sights and sounds by memory and understanding, with all the wonderful worlds evocable by the magician's wand, may we not prefer the humbler and more lasting edifice, not only as a dwelling, but even as a house of prayer?" This is the voice of one who, living for many years in America, was never at home there; a man, shall we say, of an incorrigibly Mediterranean imagination. What I have been saying is that the imagination in modern American literature tends to be, in Santayana's term, "mystical." But at this point the generalizations must stop. I sometimes think we have raised the idea of the imagination so sublimely in the years since Kant and Coleridge that we have disabled ourselves for the reception of the humbler powers. I have often longed, in recent years, for a literature of the understanding, with little in the way of imaginative pretention. But this is perverse. Perhaps we should settle for Santayana's middle term, the constructive imagination.

But to revert to Burke's novel. I have implied that the energy of this book is turned downward, that it transcends the palpable world by plunging into the sand. But this is inaccurate. In a recent discussion of the book with its author I was admonished to look more closely at the last few pages before thinking of it as an essay in the fiction of mysticism. Burke now reads his book as a ritual of rebirth, an example of a pattern which he finds in many modern novels and poems, the 'sprout-out-of-rot' literature. This description is to account for those works in which the *materia poetica* is unwholesome while the work itself gives an impression of sanity and sanitation. He still thinks of *Towards a Better Life* as "a terror-stricken novel," appropriate to the year of its inception, 1929, but he would now emphasize the intimations of renewal which sprout in its later pages. In this reading John Neal dangles between tragedy and comedy; the tragic grotesque is Burke's name for his hero's place. The squirming of the book is designed to force John from tragedy through the tragic grotesque into comedy. Shall we say, to get kneeling John up from his knees? Towards a better life; that is, towards comedy. The principle reminds me of an aphorism in Lichtenberg: "The healthiest, handsomest, and most regularly built people are the ones who will put up with anything. No sooner has a man an affliction than he has his own view on things."[3] John Neal has so many afflictions that he is himself an affliction, but the aim of the book is to get him to put up with things in the spirit of comedy. This is why he is a fitting scapegoat. As he says near the end: ". . . all I have pondered in malice, some

[3] Quoted in J. P. Stern, *Lichtenberg: A Doctrine of Scattered Occasions* (London: Thames and Hudson, 1963), p. 215: "Die gesundesten und schönsten, regelmässigst gebauten Leute sind die, die sich Alles gefallen lassen. Sobald einer ein Gebrechen hat, so hat er seine eigene Meinung."

one, coming after me, will consider comfortably. What I have learned through being in grave extremities, he will handle with ease."

So there are, Burke would insist, implications of a 'way out' at the end. Even the year 1929 had to come to an end, and 1930 had to begin. In the book the possibility of a 'new life' is both foretold and held in "problematic abeyance." John Neal does not disown his affliction: "let no man discredit your discoveries by pointing to your troubles." His affliction has given him whatever he has, whatever he knows. All one can hope for is a slight but crucial modification in one's stance. "The sword of discovery goes before the couch of laughter. One sneers by the modifying of a snarl; one smiles by the modifying of a sneer. You should have lived twice, and smiled the second time." Burke gives the principle of this sequence in *Attitudes toward History*: "The progress of humane enlightenment can go no further than in picturing people not as *vicious*, but as *mistaken*. When you add that people are *necessarily* mistaken, that *all* people are exposed to situations in which they must act as fools, that *every* insight contains its own special kind of blindness, you complete the comic circle, returning again to the lesson of humility that underlines great tragedy."[4] And certainly, in looking for a way out, one should note the emergence, in the last section, of words like 'vision' and 'promise,' which stand for allegiances hardly possible in contractual terms. One such moment is this: "became bat-blind, that he might have bat-vision." Another recalls the scene in *Jane Eyre*, at the end of Chapter 9, when Helen Burns has died and, fifteen years later, a headstone in the graveyard at Brocklebridge is inscribed with her name and the word 'Resurgam.' In *Towards a Better Life*, two pages from the end, we read, in one of John's last explosions: "*resurgam! resurgam!* I shall rise again! Hail, all hail! Here is a promise: *resurgam*!" The tone at least holds affliction in abeyance, as a storyteller, reciting an interminable tale of woe, might insist that the tale was, at any point, unfinished, and there was no telling yet how it might all turn out. The comedy of Beckett's *Molloy* is in this key, holding its readers sane while threatening to drive them mad.

In Burke the comic proof is style. While John Neal dangles, twists, and squirms, his author maintains his style as the last ditch of possibility, the only way of lifting his depression. There is hope, the book implies, as long as sentences stay true. Faith, hope, and charity are not dead as

[4] Kenneth Burke, *Attitudes toward History* (Los Altos, Calif.: Hermes Publications, 1959), p. 41. I should also cite Burke's Introduction to the second edition of *Towards a Better Life* (Berkeley and Los Angeles: University of California Press, 1966); and his essay "Art—and the First Rough Draft of Living," *Modern Age*, VIII (Spring, 1964), 155–165.

long as grammar, logic, and rhetoric continue to act. This is in keeping with a passage in *The Philosophy of Literary Form* where Burke, posing the question "Style for its own sake?" answers: "Decidedly, not at all. Style solely as the beneath-which-not, as the admonitory and hortatory act, as the example that would prod continually for its completion in all aspects of life, and so, in Eliot's phrase, 'keep something alive,' tiding us over a lean season." [5] It seems a good moment to let the matter rest.

◇◇

DENIS DONOGHUE was born in Tullow, Ireland, in 1928 and is a professor of modern British and American literature at University College, Dublin. He is the author of *The Third Voice, Connoisseurs of Chaos,* and *The Ordinary Universe,* and numerous articles and reviews. He has also taught at Harvard and the University of California, Los Angeles, and has lectured widely in England, Holland, and the United States.

Almost alone among critics writing in Britain, he has received Burke with sympathy and intelligence. He has the distinction of having written one of the few reviews published in England, and, so far as I know, the only favorable one since the twenties, of any book by Burke.

The present essay, which Professor Donoghue kindly rewrote from work in progress so that he could be represented in this volume, is a good example of how, more and more, I think, Burke will be treated: as a modern writer, with the fictional, poetic, and critical works often brought together and discussed in a modern context.

◇◇

[5] Kenneth Burke, *The Philosophy of Literary Form* (New York: Vintage Books, 1957), p. 140.

A CHECKLIST

◇◇

z *The Writings of Kenneth Burke*

BY Armin Paul Frank and Mechthild Frank

IF APPROXIMATE completeness can be claimed for this checklist, it is due to the fact that the ground had been well prepared by the extensive bibliography in William H. Rueckert's *Kenneth Burke and the Drama of Human Relations* (1963). Mr. Rueckert's continued interest and advice are also gratefully acknowledged. Our other, even greater, indebtedness is to the kindness and never-failing patience of Kenneth Burke in answering queries about doubtful material, in providing clues to several altogether obscure sources, and in furnishing a number of entries themselves. We should also like to thank all the librarians, reference librarians, and personal friends who helped to clarify points of detail; all omissions and errors are our own responsibility. The checklist was initially prepared in May 1966 and brought up to date in 1968.

The checklist is divided into the following parts: (1) books, (2) fiction, (3) poetry, (4) essays, (5) music criticism, (6) reviews, (7) commentary, discussions, and miscellaneous, (8) letters and replies, (9) translations, and (10) anthologies containing writings by Mr. Burke. Anthologies which reprint only very short excerpts up to three or four pages are not listed. The order within each section is chronological by the date of first appearance; the items in each section are consecutively numbered.

Cross-references are two-way except in Part 1, where cross-referencing would frequently have amounted to providing complete tables of contents. Tables of contents are, however, given in the case of selective translations of books. Of course, the subsequent inclusion of an item in one of the books is marked under the individual entry in the respective section. The cross-reference style follows accepted bibliographical practice: The number before the period refers to the part, the one after to the individual entry. Thus, [1.6] refers to (1) books, (6) *The Philosophy of Literary Form*. Whenever an item was collected more than once, the references are in strict chronological order, cutting across the categories.

Part 1. Books

1. *The White Oxen and Other Stories*, New York: Albert and Charles Boni, 1924.
2. *Counter-Statement*, New York: Harcourt, Brace and Company, 1931; 2nd ed., Los Altos, Calif.: Hermes Publications, 1953; Phoenix paperback, Chicago: University of Chicago Press, 1957; paperback, Berkeley: University of California Press, 1968.
3. *Towards a Better Life: Being a Series of Epistles, or Declamations*, New York: Harcourt, Brace and Company, 1932; 2nd ed., Berkeley: University of California Press, 1966.
4. *Permanence and Change: An Anatomy of Purpose*, New York: New Republic, 1935; 2nd rev. ed., Los Altos, Calif.: Hermes Publications, 1954; paperback, New York: Bobbs-Merrill, 1965. The 1954 and 1965 editions contain an appendix, "On Human Behavior, Considered 'Dramatistically' "; the 1965 edition, an introduction by Hugh Dalziel Duncan.

5. *Attitudes toward History*, 2 vols., New York: New Republic, Inc., 1937; 2nd rev. ed., Los Altos, Calif.: Hermes Publications, 1959; Beacon paperback, Boston: Beacon Press, 1961.
6. *The Philosophy of Literary Form: Studies in Symbolic Action*, Baton Rouge: Louisiana State University Press, 1941; 2nd ed., 1967; rev. abr. ed., Vintage paperback, New York: Vintage Books, 1957. Translations:
   6a. *Dichtung als symbolische Handlung: Eine Theorie der Literatur*, Frankfurt/Main: Suhrkamp-Verlag, 1966; [4.49].
   6b. *Die Rhetorik in Hitlers "Mein Kampf" und andere Essays zur Strategie der Überredung*, Frankfurt/Main: Suhrkamp-Verlag, 1967; [4.22, 4.39, 4.40, 4.42, 4.43].
7. *A Grammar of Motives*, New York: Prentice-Hall, 1945; London: Dennis Dobson, 1947; 2nd ed., New York: George Braziller, 1955; Meridian paperback, Cleveland and New York: World Publishing Company, 1962 (together with 1.8).
8. *A Rhetoric of Motives*, New York: Prentice-Hall, 1950; 2nd ed., New York: George Braziller, 1955; Meridian paperback, Cleveland and New York: World Publishing Company, 1962 (together with 1.7).
9. *Book of Moments: Poems 1915–1954*, Los Altos, Calif.: Hermes Publications, 1955.
10. *The Rhetoric of Religion: Studies in Logology*, Boston: Beacon Press, 1961.
11. *Perspectives by Incongruity*, ed. Stanley Edgar Hyman, with the assistance of Barbara Karmiller, Midland paperback, Bloomington: Indiana University Press, 1964; a combined clothbound edition of 1.11 and 1.12, Indiana U.P., 1964.
12. *Terms for Order*, ed. Stanley Edgar Hyman, with the assistance of Barbara Karmiller, Midland paperback, Bloomington: Indiana University Press, 1964; a combined clothbound edition of 1.11 and 1.12, Indiana U.P., 1964.

    1.11 and 1.12 contain selections of Mr. Burke's essays, fiction, and poetry, and excerpts from previously published books.
13. *Language as Symbolic Action: Essays on Life, Literature, and Method*, Berkeley: University of California Press, 1966.
14. *Collected Poems, 1915–1967*, Berkeley: University of California Press, 1968; includes 1.9.
15. *The Complete White Oxen: Collected Short Fiction of Kenneth Burke*, Berkeley: University of California Press, 1968; includes 1.1.

Part 2. Fiction

1. "Parabolic Tale, with Invocation," *The Sansculotte*, I (January 1917), 8.
2. "Idylls," *The Smart Set*, LVII (November 1918), 34.
3. "A Man of Forethought," *The Smart Set*, LIX (May 1919), 109–112; [1.15].
4. "Mrs. Maecenas," *The Dial*, LXVIII (March 1920), 346–358; [1.1; 10.36].
5. "The Excursion," *The Dial*, LXIX (July 1920), 27–28; [1.1; 1.11].
6. "The Soul of Kajn Tafha," *The Dial*, LXIX (July 1920), 29–32; [1.15].
7. "David Wassermann," *The Little Review*, VIII (Autumn 1921), 24–37; [1.1].
8. "Olympians," *Manuscripts*, no. 1 (February 1922), 5–7; [1.1].
9. "Scherzando," *Manuscripts*, no. 1 (February 1922), 7–8; [1.1].
10. "Portrait of an Arrived Critic," *The Dial*, LXXII (April 1922), 398–400; [1.1].
11. "The Book of Yul," *Secession*, no. 2 (July 1922), 7–17; [1.1; 1.12].
12. "First Pastoral," *Secession*, no. 3 (August 1922), 18–27; [1.1].
13. "The Death of Tragedy," *The Little Review*, IX (Autumn 1922), 9–17; [1.1].
14. "After Hours," *S4N* (third anniversary issue), November 1922, pages not numbered; [1.1].
15. "In Quest of Olympus," *Secession*, no. 4 (January 1923), 5–18; [1.1; 1.11].
16. "My Dear Mrs. Wurtelbach," *Broom*, IV (January 1923 — misprinted as 1922), 74–78; [1.1].
17. "A Progression," *Secession*, no. 7 (Winter 1923–24), 21–30; [1.1].

18. "Prince Llan: An Ethical Masque in Seven Parts, Including a Prologue and a Coda," *Broom*, VI (January 1924), 12–22; [1.1].
19. "Metamorphoses of Venus," *1924*, no. 4 (1924), 108–118; [1.15].
20. "The White Oxen," only in 1.1, pp. 3–62 and 1.15, pp. 3–41.
21. "A Declamation," *The Dial*, LXXXV (August 1928), 121–125; [1.3].
22. "Second Declamation," *The Dial*, LXXXV (October 1928), 328–332; [1.3].
23. "Third Declamation," *The Dial*, LXXXV (November 1928), 375–379; [1.3].
24. "Fourth Declamation," *The Dial*, LXXXVI (January 1929), 1–5; [1.3].
25. "Fifth Declamation," *The Dial*, LXXXVI (March 1929), 219–223; [1.3].
26. "Sixth Declamation," *The Dial*, LXXXVI (May 1929), 389–393; [1.3].
27. "Seventh Declamation," *Hound & Horn*, III (Fall 1929), 71–77; [1.3].
28. "Eighth Declamation," *Hound & Horn*, III (Winter 1929–30), 204–211; [1.3].
29. "Ninth Declamation," *Hound & Horn*, III (Spring 1930), 376–382; [1.3].
30. "Tenth Declamation," *Pagany*, I (Fall 1930), 19–23; [1.3].
31. "The Anaesthetic Revelation of Herone Liddell," *The Kenyon Review*, XIX (Autumn 1957), 505–559; [1.15].

Part 3. Poetry

1. "Adam's Song, and Mine," *Others*, II (March 1916), 184; [1.14].
2. "Revolt," *The Sansculotte*, I (January 1917), 3; [1.14].
3. "Hokku," *The Sansculotte*, I (January 1917), 4; [1.14].
4. "La Baudelairienne" (prose poem), *The Sansculotte*, I (January 1917), 9; [1.14].
5. "Invocations," *The Sansculotte*, I (January 1917), 11; [1.14].
6. "Spring Song," *Slate*, I (January 1917), 11; [1.14].
7. "The Oftener Trinity," *The Sansculotte*, I (February 1917), 7; [1.14].
8. "Bathos, Youth, and the Antithetical 'Rather,'" *The Sansculotte*, I (February 1917), 7; [1.14].
9. "Nocturne," *The Sansculotte*, I (April 1917), 9; [1.14].
10. "Adam's Song, and Mine" (not identical with 3.1), *The Sansculotte*, I (April 1917), 10; [1.14].
11. "Hymn of Hope," *Slate*, I (April 1917), 80; [1.14].
12. "*Ver Renatus Orbis Est*," *Contact*, no. 4 (1922), 9; [1.9]; [1.14].
13. "Eroticon: As from the Greek Anthology," *Secession*, no. 3 (August 1922), 27 (in 2.12); [1.1; 1.9; 1.11]; [1.14].
14. "Two Portraits," *S4N*, IV (December 1922), pages not numbered; [1.14].
15. "Psalm," *S4N*, IV (May–June 1923), pages not numbered; [1.14].
16. "From Outside," *The Dial*, LXXXVI (February 1929), 91–94; [1.9]; [1.14].
17. "Buildings Should Not Be Tall," *The New Republic*, LXXVIII (April 1934), 271; [1.9]; [1.14].
18. "Lullaby — for Oneself as Adult Male," *The New Republic*, LXXXVII (May 1936), 71; [1.9]; [1.14].
19. "Uneasy Thought of Peace," *The New Republic*, LXXXVII (May 1936), 71; [1.9]; [1.14].
20. "For a Modernist Sermon," *The New Republic*, XCVII (December 1938), 125; [1.9; 1.12; 10.10]; [1.14].
21. "Offering for the Time Capsule," *The New Republic*, XCVII (December 1938), 226; [1.9]; [1.14].
22. "Industrialist's Prayer," *The New Masses*, XXXIII (October 1939), 5; [1.9]; [1.14].
23. "Plea of the People," *The New Masses*, XXXIV (December 1939), 9; [1.9]; [1.14].
24. "In the Margin" (proverbs), *The New Republic*, CI (December 1939), 257; [1.14].
25. "Dialectician's Hymn," *The University Review* (University of Kansas City), VI (December 1939), 133–135; [1.6; 4.113; 1.9 as "Dialectician's Prayer"]; [1.14].
26. "Flowerishes," *The Rocky Mountain Review*, VII (Winter 1943), 7; [1.9]; [1.14].
27. "The Conspirators," *Furioso*, V (Summer 1950), 37; [1.9; 1.11]; [1.14].

28. "Post-Roethkean Translations," *The Hopkins Review*, VI (Winter 1952–53), 6–7; [abbreviated version entitled "Star-Fire," 1.9]; [1.14].
29. "An Old Liberal Looks to the New Year, 1953," *The Nation*, CLXXXI (October 1955), 308; [1.9]; [1.14].
30. "Big Claus and Little Claus," *The Nation*, CLXXXII (April 1956), 331; [1.14].
31. "Case History," *The Nation*, CLXXXIII (July 1956), 21.
32. "A Citizen Looks at the Female Figures on an Ancient Jar," *The Nation*, CLXXXIII (October 1956), 352; [1.14].
33. "Verses from Among Prose," from 2.31 [1.13; 1.14].
34. "A Letter from the Center," *Poetry*, XCIII (October 1958), 14–15; [1.14].
35. "Mother Goose Brought Up to Date" (two poems), *Overture* (special Pittsburgh Bicentennial Festival issue), Spring 1959, 66; [1.14].
36. "Poetic Exercise on the Subject of Disgruntlement," from 4.91; [1.14].
37. "He Was a Sincere, etc.," *The Nation*, CLXXXIX (September 1959), 40; [1.14].
38. "Civil Defense," *The Nation*, CXCI (September 1960), 188; *Bennington College Bulletin*, XXIX (November 1960), 7; [1.14].
39. "The Poet, on His Grand Climacteric," *The Nation*, CXCII (March 1961), 223; [1.14].
40. "Introduction to What," *Location*, I (Spring 1963), 32–37; [1.14].
41. "To the Memory of E. E. Cummings," *Poetry*, CII (April 1963), 31–37; [1.14].
42. "At Yosemite," *Stand*, VI (Fall 1963), 52; [1.14].
43. "Prayer of the Newspaper Editor," from 4.102; [1.13; 1.14].
44. "A Confession, Didactically," *The Journal of General Education*, XV (January 1964), 250; [1.14 as "Didactic Avowal"].
45. "Dawn in Autumn in Vermont," *The Kenyon Collegian* (John Crowe Ransom supplement), XC (February 1964), 25; [1.14].
46. "Lines Anent an Inquiry," *The Nation*, CXCVIII (February 1964), 156; [1.14].
47. "Case History" (not identical with 3.31), *Limbo*, I (March 1964), 63; [1.14].
48. "On Creative Dying — an Exercise" (prose poem), *Limbo*, I (April 1964), 41–48; [1.14].
49. "Here and Now," *Poetry*, CV (December 1964), 188; [1.14].
50. "An Assertion to End on," *Poetry*, CV (December 1964), 189; [1.14].
51. "And Here I Am, Fighting Dandelions," *Poetry*, CVII (March 1966), 363; [1.14].
52. "Heavy, Heavy — What Hangs Over?" *Poetry*, CVII (March 1966), 364; [1.14].
53. "As the Curtain Rises" (a parodistic playlet of the Absurd), *The Centennial Review*, X (Summer 1966), 279–282; [1.14].
54. "Ejaculations Anent a Flaming Catastrophe" [1.13; 1.14].
55. "On Putting Things in Order," *Saturday Review*, LI (May 1968), 37; [1.14].

Part 4. Essays

1. "The Armour of Jules Laforge [*sic*]," *Contact*, probably no. 3 of early series, 1920–23 (not all issues were numbered), 9–10.
2. "Approaches to Remy de Gourmont," *The Dial*, LXX (February 1921), 125–138; [rev. version in "Three Adepts of 'Pure' Literature," 1.2].
3. "The Art of Carl Sprinchorn," *The Arts*, II (December 1921), 158–159.
4. "The Correspondence of Flaubert," *The Dial*, LXXII (February 1922), 147–155; [rev. version in "Three Adepts of 'Pure' Literature," 1.2].
5. "André Gide, Bookman," *The Freeman*, V (April 1922), 155–157.
6. "Last Words on the Ephebe," *The Literary Review* (N.Y. Evening Post), II (August 1922), 897–898.
7. "Chicago and Our National Gesture," *The Bookman*, LVII (July 1923), 497–501.
8. "Notes on Walter Pater," *1924*, no. 2 (1924), 53–58; [rev. version in "Three Adepts of 'Pure' Literature," 1.2].
9. "Dada, Dead or Alive," *Aesthete 1925*, I (the only issue which appeared), February 1925, 23–26.

10. "The Poetic Process," *The Guardian*, II (May–June 1925), 281–294; [1.2; 10.32; 1.11].
11. "Psychology and Form," *The Dial*, LXXIX (July 1925), 34–46; [1.2; 10.12; 10.15; 10.17; 10.33; 1.11; partly reprinted in 10.39; 10.40; 10.47].
12. "William Carlos Williams, The Method of," *The Dial*, LXXXII (February 1927), 94–98.
13. "The Allies of Humanism Abroad," in 10.1, pp. 169–192.
14. "Three Frenchmen's Churches," *The New Republic*, LXIII (May 1930), 10–14.
15. "Thomas Mann and André Gide," *The Bookman*, LXXIII (June 1930), 257–264; [1.2; 10.11; 10.15].
16. "Waste — the Future of Prosperity," *The New Republic*, LXXIII (July 1930), 228–231; *Reader's Digest*, XVII (October 1930), 481–483 (a shortened version); *The New Republic* (anniversary issue), CXXXI (November 1954), 88–89 (shortened version); [10.2; 10.3 (short version); 10.5].
17. "Boring from Within," *The New Republic*, LXV (February 1931), 326–329.
18. "Redefinitions," *The New Republic*, LXVII (July 1931), 286–288; cont. LXVIII (August 1931), 46–47; LXVIII (September 1931), 74–75; [rev. and enl. in "Applica tions of the Terminology," 1.2; 10.14].
19. "Trial Translation (from *Twelfth Night*)," *The New English Weekly* (London), II (February 1933), 373–374; [1.6].
20. "Bankers Arise," *Americana, Satire and Humor*, May 1933, 4.
21. "The Negro's Pattern of Life," *The Saturday Review of Literature*, X (July 1933), 13–14.
22. "War, Response, and Contradiction," *The Symposium*, IV (October 1933), 458–482; [1.6]. Translation: "Krieg, Reaktion und Widerspruch," 1.6b, pp. 68–92.
23. "The Nature of Art under Capitalism," *The Nation*, CXXXVII (December 1933), 675–677; [1.6].
24. "On Interpretation," *The Plowshare*, X (February 1934), 3–79; [rev. version, 1.4].
25. "My Approach to Communism," *The New Masses*, X (March 1934), 16 and 18–20.
26. "The Meaning of C. K. Ogden," *The New Republic*, LXXVIII (May 1934), 328–331.
27. "Caldwell: Maker of Grotesques," *The New Republic*, LXXXII (April 1935), 232–235; [1.6, 1941 edition only; 10.21; 10.42].
28. "Revolutionary Symbolism in America," 10.4, pp. 87–94; [10.30].
29. "Antony in Behalf of the Play," *The Southern Review*, I (Autumn 1935), 308–319; [1.6; 10.22; 10.26; 1.11]. Translation: "Marcus Antonius spricht zum Publikum," *Perspektiven*, no. 5 (November 1953), 137–150.
30. "What Is Americanism" (a symposium on Marxism and the American tradition), *Partisan Review and Anvil*, III (April 1936), 9–11.
31. "The Relation between Literature and Science," 10.6, pp. 158–171.
32. "Foreword" to Harry Slochower, *Three Ways of Modern Man*, New York: International Publishing Company, 1937, 11–16.
33. "Reading While You Run: An Exercise in Translation from English into English," *The New Republic*, XCIII (November 1937), 36–37; [1.6, 1941 edition only].
34. "Acceptance and Rejection," *The Southern Review*, II (Winter 1937), 600–632; [1.5].
35. "Growth among the Ruins" (thoughts on Peter Blume's painting "The Eternal City"), *The New Republic*, XCIII (December 1937), 165–166; [1.6].
36. "Maxims and Anecdotes," *The New Republic*, XCIV (February 1938), 69–70; cont. XCIV (March 1938), 159–160. Taken from 1.5; the author has added titles and made some changes in wording, so that each item might be clear without its context.
37. "Twelve Propositions by Kenneth Burke on the Relation between Economy and Psychology," *Science & Society*, II (Spring 1938), 242–249; [1.6; 10.43].
38. "Literature as Equipment for Living," *Direction*, I (April 1938), 10–13; [1.6; 10.18; partly reprinted in 10.25; 1.11; 10.31; 10.35; 10.43]. Translation: "Literatura jako Ekwipunek Zyciowy," *Tematy*, V (Summer 1966), 39–48.

39. "The Virtues and Limitations of Debunking," *The Southern Review*, III (Spring 1938), 640–656; [1.6]. Translation: "Vom Nutzen und Nachteil des Entlarvens," 1.6b, pp. 93–115.
40. "Semantic and Poetic Meaning," *The Southern Review*, IV (Winter 1938), 501–523; [1.6; 10.41]. Translation: "Semantisches und poetisches Benennen," 1.6b, pp. 116–144.
41. "The Calling of the Tune," *The Kenyon Review*, I (Summer 1939), 272–282; [1.6].
42. "The Rhetoric of Hitler's 'Battle,'" *The Southern Review*, V (Summer 1939), 1–21; [10.7; 1.6; 1.12; 10.44]. Translation: "Die Rhetorik in Hitlers 'Mein Kampf,'" 1.6b, pp. 7–34.
43. "Freud — and the Analysis of Poetry," *The American Journal of Sociology*, XLV (November 1939), 391–417; [1.6, 10.20; 10.28; 10.38]. Translation: "Die Bedeutung der Lehre Freuds für die Literaturkritik," 1.6b, pp. 35–67.
44. "Surrealism," *New Directions in Prose and Poetry*, V (1940), 563–579.
45. "On Musicality in Verse," *Poetry*, LVII (October 1940), 31–40; [1.6; 1.11].
46. "Character of Our Culture," *The Southern Review*, VI (Winter–Spring 1941), 675–694.
47. "Four Master Tropes," *The Kenyon Review*, III (Autumn 1941), 421–438; [1.7, Appendix D].
48. "On Motivation in Yeats," *The Southern Review*, VII (Winter 1941–42), 547–561; [10.13].
49. "The Philosophy of Literary Form," 1.6, pp. 3–117; [partly reprinted in 10.34]. Translation: "Dichtung als symbolische Handlung," 1.6a.
50. "Motives and Motifs in the Poetry of Marianne Moore," *Accent*, II (Spring 1942), 157–169; [1.7; 10.9].
51. "The Study of Symbolic Action," *Chimera*, I (Spring 1942), 7–16.
52. "War and Cultural Life," *The American Journal of Sociology*, XLVIII (November 1942), 404–410.
53. "The Problem of the Intrinsic," *Accent*, III (Winter 1942–43), 80–94; [1.7, Appendix B].
54. "The Five Master Terms, Their Place in a 'Dramatistic' Grammar of Motives," *View*, series III, no. 2 (June 1943), 50–52; [enl. version: 10.8].
55. "The Tactics of Motivation," *Chimera*, I (Spring 1943), 21–33; cont. II (Summer 1943), 37–53.
56. "Symbolic Action in a Poem by Keats," *Accent*, IV (Autumn 1943), 30–42; [1.7; 10.16; 10.19; 10.29; 1.11; 10.35; 10.46; 1.13].
57. "Container and Thing Contained," *The Sewanee Review*, LIII (Winter 1945), 56–78; [1.7, chapter one].
58. "Excerpts from *A Grammar of Motives*," *Accent*, VI (Autumn 1945), 7–12; [1.7].
59. "The Temporizing of Essence," *The Kenyon Review*, VII (Autumn 1945), 616–627; [1.7, final chapter].
60. "The Socratic Transcendence," *The Sewanee Review*, LIII (Autumn 1945), 630–642; [1.7, final chapter].
61. "Kinds of Criticism," *Poetry*, LXVIII (August 1946), 272–282.
62. "Ideology and Myth," *Accent*, VII (Summer 1947), 195–205.
63. "The Imagery of Killing," *The Hudson Review*, I (Summer 1948), 151–167.
64. "The Vegetal Radicalism of Theodore Roethke," *The Sewanee Review*, LVIII (Winter 1950), 68–108; [1.13].
65. "Toward a New Romanticism, Proportion Is Better Than Efficiency," *Films in Review*, I (December 1950), 25–27.
66. "Rhetoric — Old and New," *The Journal of General Education*, V (April 1951), 202–209; [10.49].
67. "Three Definitions," *The Kenyon Review*, XIII (Spring 1951), 173–192; [pp. 183–192 reprinted in 1.11; partly reprinted in 10.40].

68. "Othello: An Essay to Illustrate a Method," *The Hudson Review*, IV (Summer 1951), 165–203; [1.11].
69. "Comments on Eighteen Poems by Howard Nemerov," *The Sewanee Review*, LX (Winter 1951–52), 117–131.
70. "Form and Persecution in the *Oresteia*," *The Sewanee Review*, LX (Summer 1952), 377–396; [1.13].
71. "A 'Dramatistic' View of Imitation," *Accent*, XII (Autumn 1952), 229–241.
72. "Ethan Brand: A Preparatory Investigation," *The Hopkins Review*, V (Winter 1952), 45–65.
73. "Notes on the Lit'ry Life," *Proceedings of the American Academy of Arts and Letters and the National Institute of Arts and Letters*, second series, no. 2 (1952), 39–50.
74. "Thanatopsis for Critics: A Brief Thesaurus of Deaths and Dyings," *Essays in Criticism*, II (October 1952), 369–375.
75. "Mysticism as a Solution to the Poet's Dilemma," *Spiritual Problems in Contemporary Literature: A Series of Addresses and Discussions*, ed. S. R. Hopper, New York: The Institute for Religious and Social Studies, [1952], 105–115.
76. "A Dramatistic View of the Origins of Language," *The Quarterly Journal of Speech*, XXXVIII (October 1952), 251–264; cont. XXXVIII (December 1952), 446–460; and XXXIX (February 1953), 79–92; [1.13].
77. "Postscripts on the Negative," *The Quarterly Journal of Speech*, XXXIX (April 1953), 209–216; [1.13].
78. "Freedom and Authority in the Realm of the Poetic Imagination," *Freedom and Authority in Our Time*, Twelfth Symposium of the Conference on Science, Philosophy and Religion, ed. Lyman Bryson, *et al.*, New York: Published by the Conference and distributed by Harper and Brothers, 1953, 365–375.
79. "Fact, Inference, and Proof in the Analysis of Literary Symbolism," *Symbols and Values: An Initial Study*, Thirteenth Symposium of the Conference on Science, Philosophy, and Religion, ed. Lyman Bryson, *et al.*, New York: Published by the Conference and distributed by Harper and Brothers, 1954, 283–306; [1.12].
80. "The Language of Poetry, 'Dramatistically' Considered," *The Chicago Review*, VIII (Fall 1954), 88–102; cont. IX (Spring 1955), 40–72. [Part II in 1.13].
81. "Policy Made Personal: Whitman's Verse and Prose-Salient Traits," *Leaves of Grass One Hundred Years After*, ed. Milton Hindus, Stanford, Calif.: Stanford University Press, 1955, 74–108; reissue 1966.
82. "Linguistic Approach to Problems of Education," *Modern Philosophies and Education*, Fifty-Fourth Year Book of the National Society for the Study of Education, ed. Nelson B. Henry, Chicago: Published by the Society and distributed by the University of Chicago Press, 1955, LIV, Pt. I, 259–303.
83. "Symbol and Association," *The Hudson Review*, IX (Summer 1956), 212–225.
84. "Recipe for Prosperity. Borrow. Buy. Waste. Want," *The Nation*, CLXXXIII (September 1956), 191–193; *Bennington College Bulletin*, VIII (Winter 1956–57), 3–5; [10.23].
85. "Progress: Promise and Problems," *The Nation*, CLXXXIV (April 1957), 322–324.
86. "Towards a Total Conformity: A Metaphysical Fantasy," *The Literary Review*, I (Winter 1957–58), 203–207.
87. "The Seven Offices," *Diogenes*, no. 21 (Spring 1958), 68–84 (the article also appeared in the French and in the Spanish edition of *Diogenes*); [1.5, 1959 edition only].
88. "The Poetic Motive," *The Hudson Review*, XL (Spring 1958), 54–63.
89. "On the First Three Chapters of Genesis," *Daedalus*, LXXXVII (Summer 1958), 37–64; [10.24; enl. version, 1.10; partly reprinted, 1.12].
90. "Towards a Post-Kantian Verbal Music," *The Kenyon Review*, XX (Autumn 1958), 529–546.
91. "On Catharsis, or Resolution, with a Postscript," *The Kenyon Review*, XXI (Summer 1959), 337–375.

92. "Myth, Poetry and Philosophy," *The Journal of American Folklore*, LXXIII (October–December 1960), 283–306; [1.13].
93. "Motion, Action, Words," *Teachers College Record*, LXII (December 1960), 244–249.
94. "The Brain Beautiful," *Bennington College Bulletin*, XXIX (November 1960), 4–7.
95. "Catharsis — Second View," *Centennial Review of Arts and Science*, V (Spring 1961), 107–132; [10.50].
96. "The Principle of Composition," *Poetry*, XCIX (October 1961), 46–53; [1.12].
97. "A Philosophy of Drama," *University of Chicago Magazine*, October 1961, pp. 7–8, 20.
98. "What Are the Signs of What? A Theory of 'Entitlement,'" *Anthropological Linguistics*, IV (June 1962), 1–23; [1.13].
99. "The Institutions of Art in America," *Arts in Society*, II (Fall–Winter 1962), 57–60.
100. "Terms, Knowledge, Action," *Arts in Society*, II (Spring–Summer 1963), 180–193.
101. "William Carlos Williams, 1883–1963," *The New York Review of Books*, I (special issue of spring and summer books, 1963), 45–47; *Stand*, VI (1964), 15–23; [1.13].
102. "The Thinking of the Body: Comments on the Imagery of Catharsis in Literature," *The Psychoanalytic Review*, L (Fall 1963), 25–68; [1.13].
103. "Commentary on 'Timon of Athens,'" Laurel Shakespeare Edition of *Timon of Athens*, ed. Francis Fergusson, New York: Dell Publishing Company, 1963, 18–30; [1.13].
104. "Definition of Man," *The Hudson Review*, XVI (Winter 1963–64), 491–514; [1.13]. Translation: "Definicja Czlowieka," *Tematy*, IV (Winter 1965), 67–93.
105. "On Form," *The Hudson Review*, XVII (Spring 1964), 103–109.
106. "Shakespearean Persuasion — *Antony and Cleopatra*," *The Antioch Review*, XXIV (Spring 1964), 19–36; [1.13].
107. "Art — and the First Rough Draft of Living," *Modern Age*, VIII (Spring 1964), 155–165.
108. "'Act' as Many-in-One," *Location*, I (Summer 1964), 94–98.
109. "The Unburned Bridges of Poetics, or, How Keep Poetry Pure?" *The Centennial Review*, VIII (Fall 1964), 391–397.
110. "*Somnia Ad Urinandum*, More Thoughts on Motion and Action," *Limbo*, I (February 1965), 30–47; [1.13].
111. Untitled contribution to "R. P. Blackmur: Language as Gesture and Essays by Kenneth Burke, Marianne Moore, Conrad Aiken, John Crowe Ransom and Others," *Nassau Literary Magazine*, May 1965, 4–6.
112. "Faust II — The Ideas behind the Imagery," *The Centennial Review*, IX (Fall 1965), 367–397; [1.13].
113. "Terministic Screens," *Proceedings of the American Catholic Philosophical Association*, Washington, D.C.: Catholic University of America, 1965, 87–102; [1.13].
114. "Version, Con-, Per-, and In- (Thoughts on Djuna Barnes's Novel, *Nightwood*)," *The Southern Review*, n.s., II (Spring 1966), 329–346; [1.13].
115. "Formalist Criticism: Its Principles and Limits," *The Texas Quarterly*, IX (Spring 1966), 242–268; [1.13]. Translation: "Formalistische Kritik: Ihre Prinzipien und Grenzen," in Elder Olson, Kenneth Burke, *et al. Über Formalismus: Diskussion eines ästhetischen Begriffs*, Frankfurt/Main: Suhrkamp-Verlag, 1966.
116. "Kubla Khan: Or, a Vision in a Dream by Samuel Taylor Coleridge," 10.46; pp. 569–582; [as "'Kubla Khan,' Proto-Surrealist Poem," in 1.13].
117. "Dramatic Form — and: Tracking Down Implications," *Tulane Drama Review*, X (Summer 1966), 54–63.
118. "Social and Cosmic Mystery: A Passage to India," *Lugano Review*, I (Summer 1966), 140–155; [1.13].
119. "*Coriolanus* — and the Delights of Faction," *The Hudson Review*, XIX (Summer 1966), 185–202; [1.13].

120. "I, Eye, Ay — Emerson's Early Essay on 'Nature.' Thoughts on the Machinery of Transcendence," *The Sewanee Review*, LXXIV (Fall 1966), 875–895; [1.13; 10.45].
121. "A Theory of Terminology," *Interpretation: The Poetry of Meaning*, eds. Stanley Romain Hopper and David L. Miller, New York: Harcourt, Brace and World, 1967, pp. 83–102.
122. "On Stress, Its Seeking," *Bennington Review*, I (Summer 1967), 32–49; [10.48].
123. "The Responsibilities of National Greatness," *The Nation*, CCV (July 17, 1967), 46–50.
124. "Dramatism," *Communication: Concepts and Perspectives*, ed. Lee Thayer, Washington, D.C.: Spartan Books, 1967, pp. 327–352; also in *International Encyclopedia of the Social Sciences*, New York: Macmillan and Free Press, 1968, Vol. 7, pp. 445–452.

Part 5. Music Criticism

1. "Musical Chronicle," *The Dial*, LXXXIII (December 1927), 535–539.
2. "Musical Chronicle," *The Dial*, LXXXIV (January 1928), 84–88.
3. "Musical Chronicle," *The Dial*, LXXXIV (February 1928), 174–178.
4. "Musical Chronicle," *The Dial*, LXXXIV (March 1928), 265–267.
5. "Musical Chronicle," *The Dial*, LXXXIV (April 1928), 356–358.
6. "Musical Chronicle," *The Dial*, LXXXIV (May 1928), 445–447.
7. "Musical Chronicle," *The Dial*, LXXXIV (June 1928), 536–538.
8. "Musical Chronicle," *The Dial*, LXXXV (July 1928), 85–88.
9. "Musical Chronicle," *The Dial*, LXXXV (December 1928), 529–532.
10. "Musical Chronicle," *The Dial*, LXXXVI (January 1929), 87–89.
11. "Musical Chronicle," *The Dial*, LXXXVI (February 1929), 177–178.
12. "Musical Chronicle," *The Dial*, LXXXVI (March 1929), 242–243.
13. "Musical Chronicle," *The Dial*, LXXXVI (April 1929), 356–358.
14. "Musical Chronicle," *The Dial*, LXXXVI (May 1929), 447–448.
15. "Musical Chronicle," *The Dial*, LXXXVI (June 1929), 538–539.
16. "Schönberg," *The Nation*, CXXXVII (November 1933), 633–643.
17. "Orpheus in New York," *The Nation*, CXXXVIII (January 1934), 52–54.
18. "Two Brands of Piety," *The Nation*, CXXXVIII (February 1934), 256–258.
19. "The End and Origin of a Movement," *The Nation*, CXXXVIII (April 1934), 422–424.
20. "The Most Faustian Art," *The Nation*, CXXXIX (August 1934), 138–140.
21. "Hindemith Does His Part," *The Nation*, CXXXIX (October 1934), 487–488.
22. "A Most Useful Composition," *The Nation*, CXXXIX (December 1934), 719–720.
23. "What Shostakovich Adds," *The Nation*, CXL (February 1935), 230–231.
24. "The 'Problems' of the Ballet," *The Nation*, CXL (March 1935), 343–344.
25. "Recent Records," *The Nation*, CXLI (December 1935), 692–693.
26. "A Bright Evening, with Musicians," *The Nation*, CXLII (January 1936), 27.

Part 6. Reviews

1. "Axiomatics" (John Cournos, *The Mask*), *The Dial*, LXVIII (April 1920), 496–499.
2. "Alcohol in the Eighties" (James Huneker, *Painted Veils*), *The Literary Review* (*New York Evening Post*), I (October 1920), 3.
3. "A Transitional Novel" (Waldo Frank, *The Dark Mother*), *The Literary Review* (*New York Evening Post*), I (November 1920), 6.
4. "Felix Kills His Author" (Floyd Dell, *Moon-Calf*), *The Literary Review* (*New York Evening Post*), I (December 1920), 3.
5. "Puritans Defended" (J. S. Flynn, *The Influence of Puritanism*), *The Literary Review* (*New York Evening Post*), I (February 1921), 2.
6. "The Modern English Novel Plus" (Virginia Woolf, *Night and Day* and *The Voyage Out*), *The Dial*, LXX (May 1921), 572–575.

7. "The Bon Dieu of M. Jammes" (Francis Jammes, *The Romance of the Rabbit*), *The Freeman*, III (May 1921), 211–212.
8. Short, untitled review of Emanuel Morgan, *Pens for Wings*, *The Freeman*, III (June 1921), 286.
9. "The Editing of Oneself" (James Oppenheim, *The Mystic Warrior*), *The Dial*, LXXI (August 1921), 232–235.
10. "Modifying the Eighteenth Century" (Arthur Schnitzler, *Casanova's Homecoming*), *The Dial*, LXXI (December 1921), 707–710.
11. "Chekhov and Three Others" (M. Gorky; A. I. Kuprin; and I. A. Bunin, *Reminiscences of A. Chekhov*), *The New York Times Book Review*, January 1, 1922, 2.
12. "Heroism and Books" (Stefan Zweig, *Romain Roland: The Man and His Work*), *The Dial*, LXXII (January 1922), 92–93.
13. Short, untitled review of Lewis Spence, *An Introduction to Mythology*, *The Freeman*, IV (January 1922), 478.
14. "Heaven's First Law" (William Carlos Williams, *Sour Grapes*), *The Dial*, LXXII (February 1922), 197–200.
15. "*Fides Quaerens Intellectum*" (Paul Elmer More, *The Religion of Plato*), *The Dial*, LXXII (May 1922), 527–530.
16. Short, untitled review of Ernst Buschor, *Greek Vase-Painting*, *The Freeman*, V (May 1922), 238.
17. "Enlarging the Narrow House" (Evelyn Scott, *Narcissus*), *The Dial*, LXXIII (September 1922), 346–348.
18. "The Consequences of Idealism" (Waldo Frank, *Rahab* and *City Block*), *The Dial*, LXXIII (October 1922), 449–452.
19. "The Critic of Dostoevsky" (J. Middleton Murry, *Still Life* and *The Things We Are*), *The Dial*, LXXIII (December 1922), 671–674.
20. "Art and the Hope Chest" (Van Wyck Brooks, *The Ordeal of Mark Twain*), *Vanity Fair*, XIX (December 1922), 59, 102.
21. "Note on *Der Sturm*" (Herwarth Walden, "Kunstdämmerung," *Der Sturm*, 13th year, nos. 7–8), *Secession*, no. 4 (January 1923), 32–33.
22. "Realism and Idealism" (Giovanni Gentile, *The Reform of Education*), *The Dial*, LXXIV (January 1923), 97–99.
23. "Engineering with Words" (Gertrude Stein, *Geography and Plays*), *The Dial*, LXXIV (April 1923), 408–412.
24. "Immersion" (Djuna Barnes, *A Book*), *The Dial*, LXXVI (May 1924), 460–461.
25. "Deposing the Love of the Lord" (Solomon Ibn Gabirol, *Selected Religious Poems of Solomon Ibn Gabirol*), *The Dial*, LXXVII (August 1924), 161–162.
26. "Ethics of the Artist" (Thomas Mann, *Buddenbrooks*), *The Dial*, LXXVII (November 1924), 420–422.
27. "Delight and Tears" (Glenway Wescott, *The Apple of the Eye*), *The Dial*, LXXVII (December 1924), 513–515.
28. "After-Dinner Philosophy" (W. C. Brownell, *The Genius of Style*), *The Dial*, LXXVIII (March 1925), 228–231.
29. "On Re and Dis" (V. F. Calverton, *The Newer Spirit: A Sociological Criticism of Literature*), *The Dial*, LXXIX (August 1925), 165–169.
30. "A New Poetics" (I. A. Richards, *Principles of Literary Criticism*), *The Saturday Review of Literature*, II (September 1925), 154–155.
31. "Codifying Milton" (Denis Saurat, *Milton, Man and Thinker*), *The Dial*, LXXIX (November 1925), 429–430.
32. "Idiom and Uniformity" (Robert Bridges, *The Society's Work*, and Logan Pearsall Smith, *Words and Idioms*), *The Dial*, LXXX (January 1926), 57–60.
33. "Idols of the Future" (essay-review of T. V. Smith, *Notes on the American Doctrine of Equality*), *The Dial*, LXXXI (July 1926), 42–46.
34. "A 'Logic' of History" (Oswald Spengler, *The Decline of the West*), *The Dial*, LXXXI (September 1926), 242–248; [10.36].

35. "Righting an Ethnologic Wrong" (Paul Radin, *Primitive Man as Philosopher*), *The Dial*, LXXXIII (November 1927), 439–440.
36. "Van Wyck Brooks in Transition?" (Van Wyck Brooks, *Emerson and Others*), *The Dial*, LXXXIV (January 1928), 56–59.
37. "Useful Distress" (A. Kreymborg, L. Mumford, and P. Rosenfeld, eds., *The Second American Caravan*), *The New York Herald Tribune Books*, V (October 1928), 5.
38. "A Decade of American Fiction" (an omnibus review), *The Bookman*, LXIX (August 1929), 561–567.
39. "An Urn of Native Soil" (Malcolm Cowley, *Blue Juniata*), *The New York Herald Tribune Books*, V (August 1929), 2.
40. "The Eloquence of Barres" (Maurice Barres, *The Sacred Hill*), *The New York Herald Tribune Books*, VI (November 1929), 4.
41. "Intelligence as a Good" (John Dewey, *The Quest for Certainty*), *The New Republic*, LXIV (September 1930), 77–79; [1.6].
42. "In Quest of the Way" (P. D. Ouspensky, *A New Model of the Universe*), *The New Republic*, LXVIII (September 1931), 104–106.
43. "The Poet and the Passwords" (essay-review of Glenway Wescott, *Fear and Trembling*), *The New Republic*, LXXI (August 1932), 310–313.
44. "Belief and Art" (Joseph W. Krutch, *Experience and Art*), *The Nation*, CXXXV (November 1932), 536–537.
45. "Mainsprings of Character" (Haakon M. Chevalier, *The Ironic Temper: Anatole France and His Time*), *The New Republic*, LXXIII (December 1932), 103–104; [1.6].
46. "Poets All" (C. K. Ogden, *Bentham's Theory of Fiction*), *The Nation*, CXXXVI (January 1933), 70.
47. "The Technique of Listening" (I. A. Richards, *Mencius on the Mind*), *The Nation*, CXXXVI (April 1933), 416.
48. "Hypergelasticism Exposed" (A. M. Ludovici, *The Secret of Laughter*), *Hound & Horn*, VI (July–September 1933), 732–736; [1.6].
49. "Fraught with Freight" (Thomas Mann, *Past Masters*), *The New Republic*, LXXVII (January 1934), 257.
50. "Rugged Portraiture" (author not given, *Rubicon or The Strikebreaker*, a play), *The New Masses*, XI (April 1934), 46.
51. "The Art of Yielding" (John Howard, *Stephen Foster, America's Troubadour*, and Edward B. Marks, *They All Sang; From Tony Pastor to Rudy Vallee*), *The Nation*, CXXXVIII (April 1934), 484–486.
52. "The Esthetic Strain" (John Dewey, *Art as Experience*), *The New Republic*, LXXVIII (April 1934), 315–316.
53. "Permanence and Change" (Thomas Mann, *Joseph and His Brothers*), *The New Republic*, LXXIX (June 1934), 186–187; [1.6].
54. "In Vague Praise of Liberty" (Benedetto Croce, *History of Europe in the Nineteenth Century*), *Hound & Horn*, VII (July–September 1934), 704–707.
55. "Gastronomy of Letters" (Ezra Pound, *ABC of Reading*), *The Nation*, CXXXIX (October 1934), 458–459.
56. "The Universe Alive" (A. N. Whitehead, *Nature and Life*), *The New Republic*, LXXXI (November 1934), 26.
57. "While Waiting" (Edward Dahlberg, *Those Who Perish*), *The New Republic*, LXXXI (November 1934), 53.
58. "Concern about English" (Alexander Laing, *Wine and Physic*), *Poetry*, XLV (February 1935), 294–296.
59. "A Pleasant View of Decay" (Constant Lambert, *Music Ho! A Study of Music in Decline*), *The Nation*, CXL (February 1935), 200–201.
60. "Goethe and the Jews" (Mark Waldman, *Goethe and the Jews*), *The New Masses*, XIV (March 1935), 25.
61. "One Who Wrestled" (Avrahm Yarmolinsky, *Dostoevsky: A Life*), *The New Republic*, LXXXII (March 1935), 192, 194.

62. "Change of Identity" (James T. Farrell, *Judgment Day*), *The New Republic*, LXXXIII (June 1935), 171–172.
63. "Two Kinds of Against" (E. E. Cummings, *No Thanks*, and Kenneth Fearing, *Poems*), *The New Republic*, LXXXIII (June 1935), 198–199.
64. "The Impartial Essence" (Gertrude Stein, *Lectures in America*), *The New Republic*, LXXXIII (July 1935), 227.
65. "Protective Coloration" (Robert Forsythe [Karl S. Crichton], *Redder Than the Rose*), *The New Republic*, LXXXIII (July 1935), 255–256.
66. "The Hope in Tragedy" (Horace Gregory, *Chorus for Survival*), *Poetry*, XLVI (July 1935), 227–230.
67. "Recent Poetry" (an omnibus review), *The Southern Review*, I (July 1935), 164–177.
68. "Renaming Old Directions" (R. G. Tugwell and L. H. Keyserling, eds., *Redirecting Education: I, The United States*), *The Nation*, CXLI (August 1935), 166.
69. "Storm Omens" (Haniel Long, *Pittsburgh Memoranda*), *The New Republic*, LXXXIV (August 1935), 83.
70. "A Radical, but —" (Vardis Fischer, *The Neurotic Nightingale*), *The New Republic*, LXXXIV (October 1935), 221.
71. "Coleridge Rephrased" (I. A. Richards, *On Imagination: Coleridge's Critical Theory*), *Poetry*, XLVII (October 1935), 52–54.
72. "Return after Flight" (Muriel Rukeyser, *Theory of Flight*), *The New Masses*, XVIII (February 1936), 26.
73. "Anatomy of the Mask" (Leonard W. Doob, *Propaganda: Its Psychology and Technique*), *The New Republic*, LXXXV (February 1936), 371–372.
74. "Liberalism's Family Tree" (John Dewey, *Liberalism and Social Action*), *The New Republic*, LXXXVI (March 1936), 115–116; [1.6].
75. "By Ice, Fire or Decay?" (Clifford Odets, *Paradise Lost: A Play in 3 Acts*), *The New Republic*, LXXXVI (April 1936), 283–284; [1.6].
76. "A Sour Note on Literary Criticism" (James T. Farrell, *A Note on Literary Criticism*), *The New Republic*, LXXXVII (June 1936), 211.
77. "Property as an Absolute" (Herbert Agar and Allen Tate, eds., *Who Owns America*), *The New Republic*, LXXXVII (July 1936), 245–246.
78. "Without Benefit of Politics" (Otto Rank, *Truth and Reality* and *Will Therapy*), *The Nation*, CXLIII (July 1936), 78.
79. "Deft Plaintiveness" (James Daly, *One Season Shattered*), *Poetry*, XLVIII (August 1936), 282–285.
80. "Symbolic War" (Granville Hicks, *Proletarian Literature in the United States*), *The Southern Review*, II (Summer 1936), 134–147.
81. "William James: Superlative Master of the Comparative" (Ralph Barton Perry, *The Thought and Character of William James*), *Science & Society*, I (Fall 1936), 122–125. The opening remarks on William James in 1.5 are based on this review.
82. Untitled review of John McMurray, *Reason and Emotion*, *The American Journal of Sociology*, XLII (September 1936), 283.
83. "Cautious Enlightenment" (R. P. Blackmur, *The Double Agent*), *Poetry*, XLIX (October 1936), 52–54.
84. "Methodology of the Scramble" (Harold D. Lasswell, *Politics: Who Gets What, When, How?*), *The New Republic*, LXXXIX (December 1936), 250.
85. "Synthetic Freedom" (Hilaire Belloc, *The Restoration of Property*), *The New Republic*, LXXXIX (January 1937), 365.
86. "The Constants of Social Relativity" (Karl Mannheim, *Ideology and Utopia*), *The Nation*, CXLIV (January 1937), 131; [1.6].
87. "Exceptional Improvisation" (William Empson, *Some Versions of Pastoral*), *Poetry*, XLIX (March 1937), 347–350; [1.6].
88. "The Esthetic Instinct" (Herbert Read, *Art and Society*), *The New Republic*, XC (April 1937), 363–364.

89. "Tentative Proposal" (Allen Tate, *The Mediterranean and Other Poems* and *Reactionary Essays on Poetry and Ideas*), *Poetry*, L (May 1937), 96–100.
90. "A Gist of Gists of Gists" (Edgar Johnson, *One Mighty Torrent: The Drama of Biography*), *The Nation*, CXLIV (May 1937), 622–623.
91. "The Second Study of Middletown" (Robert S. and Helen Merrell Lynd, *Middletown in Transition*), *The New Masses*, XXIII (June 1937), 22, 24; [1.6].
92. "Leave the Leaf Its Springtime" (Frederick Mortimer Clapp, *New Poems*), *Poetry*, L (July 1937), 226–229.
93. "Field Work in Bohemia" (Edmund Wilson, *This Room and This Gin and These Sandwiches*), *The Nation*, CXLV (July 1937), 133–134.
94. "Spender's Left Hand" (Stephen Spender, *Forward from Liberalism*), *The New Republic*, XCII (August 1937), 24–25.
95. "A Recipe for Worship" (Lord Raglan, *The Hero*), *The Nation*, 145 (August 1937), 201–202; [1.6].
96. "Thurber Perfects Mind Cure" (James Thurber, *Let Your Mind Alone!*), *The New Republic*, XCII (September 1937), 220–221.
97. Untitled review of Frank Hyneman Knight, *The Ethics of Competition and Other Essays*, *The American Journal of Sociology*, XLIII (September 1937), 242–244.
98. "The 'Science' of Race-Thinking" (Jacques Barzun, *Race: A Study in Modern Superstition*), *The New Masses*, XXV (October 1937), 22.
99. "Responses to Pressure" (Sir Herbert J. C. Grierson, *Wordsworth and Milton, Poets and Prophets*), *Poetry*, LI (October 1937), 37–42.
100. "A Trail Trails Off" (Mary M. Colum, *From These Roots: The Ideas That Have Made Modern Literature*), *The New Republic*, XCIII (December 1937), 205–206.
101. "Semantics in Demotic" (Stuart Chase, *The Tyranny of Words*), *The New Republic*, XCIII (January 1938), 343–344; [1.6].
102. "Weighted History" (Hilaire Belloc, *The Crisis of Civilization*), *The New Republic*, XCIII (February 1938), 375–376.
103. "Corrosive without Corrective" (Thurman W. Arnold, *The Folklore of Capitalism*), *The New Masses*, XXVI (February 1938), 22–24; [1.6].
104. "Exceptional Book" (William Empson, *English Pastoral Poetry*), *The New Republic*, XCV (May 1938), 81; [1.6].
105. Untitled review of Maurice Duval, *La Poésie et le Principe de Transcendence: Essaie sur la Création Poétique*, *The American Journal of Sociology*, XLIV (July 1938), 167–168.
106. "George Herbert Mead" (Morris, *et al.*, eds., *The Works of George Herbert Mead*), *The New Republic*, XCVII (January 1939), 292–293; [1.6].
107. "Fearing's New Poems" (Kenneth Fearing, *Dead Reckoning*), *The New Masses*, XXX (February 1939), 27–28; [1.6].
108. "Monads — on the Make" (Paul Weiss, *Reality*), *The New Republic*, XCVIII (April 1939), 314–315; [1.6].
109. "The Book of Proverbs" (S. G. Champion, ed., *Racial Proverbs: A Selection of the World's Proverbs Arranged Linguistically*), *The New Republic*, XCIX (June 1939), 230.
110. "Why Coleridge?" (E. K. Chambers, *Samuel Taylor Coleridge*, and Lawrence Hanson, *The Life of S. T. Coleridge*), *The New Republic*, C (September 1939), 163–164.
111. "On Poetry and Poetics" (John Crowe Ransom, *The World's Body: Foundations for Literary Criticism*), *Poetry*, LV (October 1939), 51–54.
112. "Quantity and Quality" (Otto Neurath, *Modern Man in the Making*), *The New Republic*, CI (November 1939), 22–23; [1.6].
113. "The Sources of 'Christabel' " (A. H. Nethercot, *Road to Tryermaine*), *The New Republic*, CII (May 1940), 617.
114. "Key Words for Critics" (Donald Stauffer, ed., *The Intent of the Critic*; John Crowe Ransom, *The New Criticism*; and Allen Tate, *Reason in Madness*), *The Kenyon Review*, IV (Winter 1941–42), 126–132.

115. "Henry Miller, and Harry Levin on James Joyce, New Directions" (remarks on H. Miller, *The Window of the Heart*, and on George Orwell on H. Miller in *New Directions* (1940), and on Harry Levin, *James Joyce*), *Direction*, V (February–March 1942), 18.
116. "The Age of Enterprise" (Thomas C. Cochran and William Miller, *The Age of Enterprise*), *Direction*, VI (Spring 1943), 3–5.
117. "Many Moods" (Olin Downes and Elie Siegmeister, *A Treasury of American Songs*), *The New Republic*, CVIII (June 1943), 869–870.
118. Untitled review of Alfred Kazin, *On Native Grounds*, *Chimera*, II (Autumn 1943), 45–48.
119. "Action as Test" (Arthur E. Murphy, *The Uses of Reason*), *The New Republic*, CX (February 1944), 220–222.
120. "Basic and After" (Frederick Bodmer, *The Loom of Language*), *The New Republic*, CX (April 1944), 566, 568.
121. "Careers without Careerism" (E. Russell Bentley, *A Century of Heroworship*), *The Kenyon Review*, III (Winter 1944–45), 162–166.
122. "The Work of Regeneration" (Marguerite Young, *Angel in the Forest: A Fairy Tale of Two Utopias*), *The Kenyon Review*, VII (Autumn 1945), 696–700.
123. "*Homo Faber, Homo Magus*" (Ernst Cassirer, *The Myth of the State*), *The Nation*, CLXIII (December 1946), 666–668.
124. "Towards Objective Criticism" (S. T. Coleridge, *The Rime of the Ancient Mariner*, ill. by Calder, analyzed by R. P. Warren), *Poetry*, LXX (April 1947), 42–47.
125. "Criticism for the Next Phase" (Rosemond Tuve, *Elizabethan and Metaphysical Imagery*), *Accent*, VIII (Winter 1948), 125–127.
126. "Action, Passion, and Analogy" (Francis Fergusson, *The Idea of a Theater*), *The Kenyon Review*, XII (Summer 1950), 532–537.
127. "On Covery, Re- and Dis-" (essay-review of Rosemond Tuve, *A Reading of George Herbert*), *Accent*, XIII (Autumn 1953), 218–226.
128. "The Dialectics of Imagery" (Charles Feidelson, *Symbolism and American Literature*), *The Kenyon Review*, XV (Autumn 1953), 625–632.
129. "The Criticism of Criticism" (R. P. Blackmur, *The Lion and the Honeycomb*), *Accent*, XV (Autumn 1955), 279–292.
130. "Likings of an Observationist" (Marianne Moore, *Predilections*), *Poetry*, LXXXVII (January 1956), 239–247.
131. "The Carrot and the Stick, or . . ." (William Sargant, *Battle for the Mind*; Vance Packard, *The Hidden Persuaders*; and William H. Whyte, *The Organization Man*), *The Hudson Review*, X (Winter 1957–58), 627–633; [10.27].
132. "The Encyclopaedic, Two Kinds of" (W. K. Wimsatt and C. Brooks, *Literary Criticism: A Short History*; and Northrop Frye, *Anatomy of Criticism: Four Essays*), *Poetry*, XCI (February 1958), 320–328.
133. "The Independent Radical" (Harold Rosenberg, *The Tradition of the New*), *The Hudson Review*, XII (Fall 1959), 465–472.
134. "Democracy of the Sick" (Philip Rieff, *Freud: The Mind of the Moralist*), *The Kenyon Review*, XXI (Autumn 1959), 639–643.
135. "Folktale and Myth" (Joseph Fontenrose, *Python: A Study of the Delphic Myth and Its Origin*), *Journal of American Folklore*, LXXIII (July–September 1960), 270–271.
136. "Invective against the Father" (William Empson, *Milton's God*), *The Nation*, CXCIV (June 1962), 540–541.
137. "Imaginary Lines" (Shirley Jackson, *We Have Always Lived in the Castle*), *The New Leader*, XLV (December 1962), 20–22.
138. "Revival of the Fittest" (Stanley E. Hyman, ed., *Darwin for Today*), *The New Leader*, XLVI (November 1963), 22–24.
139. "Myth, Method, and Tragedy" (Herbert Weisinger, *The Agony and the Triumph*,

Papers on the Use and Abuse of Myth), *The New Leader*, XLVII (November 1964), 21–23.

140. "Prelude to Poetry: Scales and Fugue" (T. S. Eliot, *Knowledge and Experience in the Philosophy of F. H. Bradley*; and Herbert Howarth, *Some Figures behind T. S. Eliot*), *Bookweek*, II (January 1965), 4, 8.

141. "More Dithyrambic Than Athletic" (Norman O. Brown, *Love's Body*), *The Nation*, CCIV (March 27, 1967), 405–407.

Part 7. Commentary, Discussions, and Miscellaneous

1. "For Whom Do You Write?" *The New Quarterly*, I (Summer 1934), 8.
2. "The Writers' Congress," *The Nation*, CXL (May 1935), 571.
3. "Questions for Critics," *Direction*, II (May–June 1939), 12–13.
4. "Embargo," *Direction*, II (November 1939), 2.
5. "What to Do till the Doctor Comes: Thoughts on Conscription," *Direction*, III (November 1940), 7, 24.
6. "Americanism," *Direction*, IV (February 1941), 2, 3.
7. "Where Are We Now?" *Direction*, IV (December 1941), 3–5.
8. "When 'Now' Becomes 'Then,'" *Direction*, V (February–March 1942), 5.
9. "Government in the Making," *Direction*, V (December 1942), 3–4.
10. "The American Way," *Touchstone*, I (December 1947), 3–9.
11. "Human Nature and the Bomb," *University of Chicago Round Table*, no. 622 (19 February, 1950), 1–11. A discussion.
12. "The New Criticism," *The American Scholar*, XX (January 1951), 86–104; cont. XX (April 1951), 218–231. A discussion with W. Barrett, M. Cowley, R. G. Davis, A. Tate, and H. Haydn.
13. "The Threat of the Trivial," *The Nation*, CLXXXII (April 1956), 333. Editorial comment.
14. "NRT Non-Resident Term," *Bennington College Bulletin*, XXVIII (November 1959), 16–17.
15. "What's Good about a Bad First Job," *Mademoiselle*, LIII (June 1961), 70–72, 111.
16. "De Beginnibus," *Bennington College Bulletin*, XXXI (November 1962), 4–10.
17. "A Conversation with Kenneth Burke: On Literature in a Scientific Age," *Riata*, Winter 1963, pp. 45–50. Gordon Mills and Kenneth Burke.
18. "Reflections on the Fate of the Union: Kennedy and After," *The New York Review of Books*, I (December 1963), 10–11.
19. "An *Arion* Questionnaire: The Classics and the Modern Man of Letters," *Arion*, III (Winter 1964), 23–26.
20. "Thirty Years Later: Memories of the First American Writers' Congress," *The American Scholar*, XXXV (Summer 1966), 495–516. A discussion with M. Cowley, G. Hicks, W. Phillips; D. Aaron, moderator.

Part 8. Letters and Replies

1. "The Reader Critic," *The Little Review*, IX (Winter 1922), 45. In reference to "The Death of Tragedy," published in IX (Autumn 1922), and F. W. Pollock's criticism of Mr. Burke's introduction describing smoking on the foredeck and afterdeck of Massachusetts ferries.
2. "Munsoniana," *The New Republic*, LXIX (November 1931), 46.
3. "Counterblasts on 'Counter-Statement,'" *The New Republic*, LXIX (December 9, 1931), 101. An answer to Granville Hicks' review of *Counter-Statement*, "A Defense of Eloquence," in the 2 December 1931 issue, pp. 75–76.
4. "Intuitive or Scientific," *The Nation*, CXLVI (January 1938), 139–140. A letter about Eliseo Vivas' review of *Attitudes toward History*, "Toward an Improved Strategy," in the 25 December 1937 issue, p. 723.
5. "Is Mr. Hook a Socialist?" *Partisan Review*, IV (January 1938), 40–44. The answer

to Hook's review of *Attitudes toward History*, "The Technique of Mystification," in the December 1937 issue, pp. 57–62. Mr. Hook's answer to the letter, "Is Mr. Burke Serious?" follows, pp. 44–47.

6. "A Psychological Approach to the Study of Social Crises," *The American Journal of Sociology*, XLIII (March 1938), 799–803; [1.6]. A letter to the editor in reference to an article by Malamud in the January 1938 issue, pp. 578–592; "Rejoinder" to this letter by I. T. Malamud, March 1938, pp. 803–805.
7. "Comments on Dr. [Wm. Heard] Kilpatrick's Article," *The American Teacher*, XXIV (November 1939), 26–27; [1.6].
8. A letter in the "Your Letters" section, *Direction*, III (November 1940), 21.
9. A letter in the "Communications" section, *The Hopkins Review*, IV (Winter 1950–51), 77–79. A reply to G. A. Smith's review of *Rhetoric of Religion* in the Fall 1950 issue, pp. 54–60.
10. "A Further View," *Four Quarters* (Lassalle College, Philadelphia), V (January 1956), 17.
11. A letter in the "Correspondence" section, *The Sewanee Review*, LXXIII (Winter 1964–65), 484–489. A reply to Joseph Frank's review of *Rhetoric of Religion* in the Summer 1964 issue, 173–175.

Part 9. Translations

1. Alfred Mombert, "Lullaby," *The Sansculotte*, I (January 1917), 4.
2. Thomas Mann, "Loulou," *The Dial*, LXX (April 1921), 428–442.
3. Hans Purrmann, "From the Workshop of Matisse," *The Dial*, LXXIII (July 1922), 32–40.
4. Hugo von Hofmannsthal, "Lucidor: Characters for an Unwritten Comedy," *The Dial*, LXXIII (August 1922), 121–132.
5. Richard Specht, "Arthur Schnitzler," *The Dial*, LXXIII (September 1922), 241–245.
6. Thomas Mann, "Tristan," *The Dial*, LXXIII (December 1922), 593–610; cont. LXXIV (January 1923), 57–76; [9.16]. Translated with Scofield Thayer.
7. Stefan Zweig, "Charles Dickens," *The Dial*, LXXIV (January 1923), 1–24.
8. Julius Maier-Graefe, "German Art after the War," *The Dial*, LXXV (July 1923), 1–12.
9. Arthur Schnitzler, "The Fate of Baron von Leisenbohg," *The Dial*, LXXV (December 1923), 565–582.
10. Heinrich Mann, "Virgins," *The Dial*, LXXVI (February 1924), 123–132.
11. Thomas Mann, "Death in Venice," *The Dial*, LXXVI (March 1924), 213–235; cont. LXXVI (April 1924), 311–333, and LXXVI (May 1924), 423–443.
12. Oswald Spengler, Introduction to *The Downfall of Western Civilization*, *The Dial*, LXXVII (November 1924), 361–378; cont. LXXVII (December 1924), 482–504 and LXXVIII (January 1925), 9–26.
13. Hugo von Hofmannsthal, "Honoré de Balzac," *The Dial*, LXXVIII (May 1925), 357–368.
14. Arthur Schnitzler, "Lieutenant Gustl," *The Dial*, LXXIX (August 1925), 89–117.
15. Arthur Schnitzler, "The New Song," *The Dial*, LXXIX (November 1925), 355–369.
16. Thomas Mann, *Death in Venice*, New York: A. A. Knopf, 1925; reissue 1965. Includes "Tristan" and "Tonio Kröger."
17. Rolf de Maré, "The Swedish Ballet and the Modern Aesthetic," *The Little Review*, XI (Winter 1925–26), 24–28.
18. Marx Loebe, "Georges Papazoff," *The Little Review*, XII (Spring–Summer 1926), 24.
19. Emil Ludwig, *Genius and Character*, New York: Harcourt, Brace and Company, 1927; New York: Blue Ribbon Books, 1932.
20. Thomas Mann, sections from *Pariser Rechenschaft*, *The Dial*, LXXXII (July 1927), 501–510.
21. Émile Baumann, *Saint Paul*, New York: Harcourt, Brace and Company, 1929.

22. Thomas Mann, "Humanism and Europe," *The New Republic*, XC (April 1937), 349.
23. Unsigned translations. Mr. Burke translated most of the German Letters and Vienna Letters in *The Dial* (1921–28), and some items in *Vanity Fair*.
24. Hermann Hesse, "The Early Hour," from 7.18; [1.14].

Part 10. Anthologies Containing Writings by Kenneth Burke

1. Grattan, C. Hartley, ed., *The Critique of Humanism: A Symposium*, New York: Harcourt, Brace and Company, 1930; [4.13].
2. Hankel, Walter S. [pseud.], ed., *Whither, Whither, or After Sex, What? A Symposium to End Symposiums*, New York: Macaulay Co., 1930; [4.16].
3. Thomas, Charles Wright, ed., *Essays in Contemporary Civilization*, New York: Macmillan, 1931; [shorter version of 4.16].
4. Hart, Henry, ed., *American Writers' Congress*, New York: International Publishers, 1935; London: Martin Lawrence, 1935; [4.28].
5. Conklin, Groff, ed., *New Republic Anthology, 1915–1935*, New York: Dodge, 1936; [4.16].
6. Hart, Henry, ed., *The Writer in a Changing World* (Second American Writers' Congress), New York: Equinox Cooperative Press, 1937; [4.31].
7. Anderson, George K., and Eda Lou Walton, eds., *This Generation. A Selection of British and American Literature from 1914 to the Present with Historical and Critical Essays*, New York: Scott, Foresman and Co., 1939; [4.42].
8. Knickerbocker, William S., ed., *Twentieth Century English*, New York: Philosophical Library, 1946; [4.54].
9. Quinn, K., and C. Shattuck, eds., *Accent Anthology*, New York: Harcourt, Brace and Company, 1946; [4.50].
10. Luccock, Halford E., and Frances Brentano, eds., *The Questing Spirit: Religion in the Literature of Our Time*, New York: Coward-McCann, 1947; [3.20].
11. Neider, Charles, ed., *The Stature of Thomas Mann*, New York: New Directions, 1947; [4.15].
12. Stallman, R. W., ed., *Critiques and Essays in Criticism 1920–1948*, New York: Ronald Press Company, 1949; [part of "Lexicon Rhetoricae," 1.2; and 4.11].
13. Hall, James, and Martin Steinmann, eds., *The Permanence of Yeats*, New York: Macmillan Company, 1950; Collier paperback, 1961; [4.48].
14. Glicksberg, Charles I., ed., *American Literary Criticism 1900–1950*, New York: Hendricks House, 1951; [4.18].
15. Zabel, Morton D., ed., *Literary Opinion in America*, New York: Harper and Brothers, 1951; two-vol. paperback, 1962; [4.15 and 4.11].
16. West, Ray B., ed., *Essays in Modern Literary Criticism*, New York and Toronto: Rinehart and Company, 1952; [4.56].
17. Blair, W., T. Hornberger, and R. Stewart, eds., *The Literature of the United States*, vol. II, rev. ed., Chicago: Scott, Foresman and Company, 1953; [4.11].
18. Waite, Harlow O., and B. P. Atkinson, eds., *Literature for Our Time: An Anthology for College Students*, New York: Henry Holt, 1953; rev. ed., 1958; [4.38].
19. Hyman, S. E., ed., *The Critical Performance: An Anthology of American and British Literary Criticism of Our Century*, New York: Vintage Press, 1956; [4.56].
20. Phillips, William, ed., *Art and Psychoanalysis*, New York: Criterion Books, 1957; [4.43].
21. Howe, Irving, ed., *Modern Literary Criticism*, Boston: Beacon Press, 1958; [4.27].
22. Schorer, M., J. Miles, and G. McKenzie, eds., *Criticism*, New York: Harcourt, Brace and Company, rev. ed. 1958; [4.29].
23. Christman, Henry M., ed., *A View of The Nation: An Anthology, 1955–1959*, New York: Grove Press, 1960; [4.84].
24. May, Rollo, ed., *Symbolism in Religion and Literature*, New York: George Braziller, 1960; [4.89].

25. Lane, Lauriat, ed., *Approaches to Walden*, San Francisco: Wadsworth Publishing Company, 1961; [part of 4.38].
26. Markels, Julian, ed., *Shakespeare's Julius Caesar*, New York: Scribner's Sons, 1961; [4.29].
27. Morgan, Frederick, ed., *Hudson Review Anthology*, New York: Vintage Books, 1961; [6.130].
28. Philipson, Morris, ed., *Aesthetics Today*, Cleveland and New York: Meridian Books, 1961; [4.43].
29. Goldberg, G. J., and N. M. Goldberg, eds., *The Modern Critical Spectrum*, Englewood Cliffs, N.J.: Prentice-Hall, 1962; [4.56].
30. Hoffman, Frederick J., ed., *Perspectives on Modern Literature*, Evanston, Ill.: Row, Peterson and Company, 1962; [4.28].
31. Oldsey, Bernard S., and A. O. Lewis, eds., *Visions and Revisions in Modern American Literary Criticism*, New York: Dutton paperback, 1962; [4.38].
32. Scott, Wilbur S., ed., *Five Approaches to Literary Criticism*, New York and London: Macmillan Company, 1962; [4.10].
33. Levich, Marvin, ed., *Aesthetics and the Philosophy of Criticism*, New York: Random House, 1963; [4.11].
34. Linenthal, Mark, ed., *Aspects of Poetry*, Boston: Little, Brown and Company, 1963; [4.49].
35. Sutton, Walter, and Richard Foster, eds., *Modern Criticism: Theory and Practice*, New York: Odyssey Press, 1963; [4.38 and 4.56].
36. Wasserstrom, William, ed., *A Dial Miscellany*, Syracuse, N.Y.: Syracuse University Press, 1963; [6.34 and 2.4].
37. Murphy, Francis, ed., *Discussions of Poetry: Form and Structure*, Boston: D. C. Heath, 1964; [part of "Lexicon Rhetoricae," 1.2].
38. Ruitenbeck, Hendrik M., ed., *Psychoanalysis and Literature*, New York: Dutton paperback, 1964; [4.43].
39. Ellis, H. M., *et al.*, eds., *A College Book of American Literature*, rev. by F. J. Hoffman, 3rd ed. only, New York: American Book Company, 1965; [part of 4.11].
40. Hall, Lawrence S., ed., *A Grammar of Literary Criticism*, New York: Macmillan Company, 1965; [4.11 and part of 4.67].
41. Hayden, Donald E., and E. Paul Alworth, eds., *Classics in Semantics*, New York: Philosophical Library, 1965; [4.40].
42. Malin, Irving, ed., *Psychoanalysis and American Fiction*, New York: Dutton, 1965; [4.27].
43. Perry, John Oliver, ed., *Approaches to the Poem. Modern Essays in the Analysis and Interpretation of Poetry*, San Francisco: Chandler Publishing Company, 1965; [4.38 and 4.37].
44. Winterowd, W. Ross, ed., *Rhetoric and Writing*, Boston: Allyn and Bacon, 1965; [from "Lexicon Rhetoricae," 1.2; and 4.42].
45. Simon, Myron, and Thornton H. Pearsons, eds., *Transcendentalism and Its Legacy*, Ann Arbor, Mich.: University of Michigan Press, 1966; [4.120].
46. Williams, Oscar, ed., *Master Poems of the English Language*, New York: Trident Press, 1966; [4.56 and 4.116].
47. Zitner, S. P., J. Kissane, and M. M. Liberman, eds., *The Practice of Criticism*, Chicago: Scott, Foresman and Company, 1966; [4.11].
48. Klausner, Samuel Z., ed., *Why Man Takes Chances: Studies in Stress-Seeking*, Garden City, N.Y.: Doubleday, 1968; [4.122].
49. Steinmann, Martin, Jr., ed., *New Rhetorics*, New York: Scribner, 1968; [4.66].
50. Grebstein, Norman Sheldon, ed., *Perspectives in Contemporary Criticism*, New York: Harper and Row, 1968; [4.95].

SELECTED BIBLIOGRAPHY

◇◇◇

z Works about Kenneth Burke

BY William H. Rueckert

THIS is a representative and selective bibliography in the sense that I have not made any attempt to be exhaustive and compile a definitive listing. I have deliberately omitted the many short notes, notices, and reviews which have appeared in journals and newspapers — especially between 1945 and the present. If I have failed to list any major pieces on Burke, it is only because I (and my indefatigable helpers, Armin Paul Frank and Mechthild Frank) somehow missed them. In general, and from principle, the bibliography is confined to works directly about Burke. It would have been helpful and interesting to have included here a listing of essays and books — Francis Fergusson's *The Idea of a Theater* is an example — which show the direct or indirect influence of Burke; but it became obvious to me that such a compilation was beyond my knowledge, patience, and talents. For such a listing, I substitute the flat, declarative statement that Burke's influence is massive.

The bibliography is arranged in roughly chronological order for the reasons given in the Preface, with an alphabetical author key on pages 522–523.

1. Munson, Gorham B., "An Amazing Debut" (review of *The White Oxen*), *The Literary Review*, 11 October 1924, p. 3.
2. Anon., "Psychological Drama" (review of *The White Oxen*), *The New York Times Book Review*, 26 October 1924, p. 23.
3. Josephson, Matthew, "Experimental" (review of *The White Oxen*), *The New York Herald Tribune Books*, 16 November 1924, p. 4.
4. Cowley, Malcolm, "Gulliver" (review of *The White Oxen*), *The Dial*, LXXVII (1924), 520–522.
5. Toomer, Jean, "Oxen Cart and Warfare" (review of *The White Oxen*), *The Little Review*, Autumn and Winter 1924–25, pp. 44–48.
6. Bishop, John Peale, "Gulliver on the Subway" (review of *The White Oxen*), *The Saturday Review of Literature*, I (3 January 1925), 427.
7. Munson, Gorham B., "In and About the Workshop of Kenneth Burke," first published in 1926; reprinted in *Destinations: A Canvas of American Literature since 1900*, New York: J. H. Sears and Company, 1928, pp. 139–159.
8. "Announcement," *The Dial*, LXXXVI (1929), 90.
9. Williams, William Carlos, "Kenneth Burke," *The Dial*, LXXXVII (1929), 6–8. This piece was reprinted, without the last five paragraphs, in *Selected Essays of William Carlos Williams*, New York: Random House, 1954; pp. 132–133.
10. Chamberlain, John, "Rhetoric Finds a Champion in Mr. Kenneth Burke" (review of *Counter-Statement*), *The New York Times Book Review*, 25 October 1931, p. 2.
11. Hicks, Granville, "A Defense of Eloquence" (review of *Counter-Statement*), *The New Republic*, LXIX (2 December 1931), 75–76.
12. Schneider, Isidor, "A New View of Rhetoric" (review of *Counter-Statement*), *The New York Herald Tribune Books*, 13 December 1931, p. 4.
13. Hazlitt, Henry, "Two Critics" (review of *Counter-Statement*), *The Nation*, CXXXIV (1932), 77.

14. Chamberlain, John, "Mr. Burke's Experiment in the Novel" (review of *Towards a Better Life*), *The New York Times Book Review*, 31 January 1932, p. 2.
15. Rosenberg, Harold, Review of *Counter-Statement*, *The Symposium*, III (January 1932), 116–122.
16. Gregory, Horace, "The Man on the Park Bench" (review of *Towards a Better Life*), *The New York Herald Tribune Books*, 31 January 1932, p. 2.
17. Cowley, Malcolm, "Unwilling Novelist" (review of *Towards a Better Life*), *The New Republic*, LXX (17 February 1932), 23–24.
18. Cantwell, Robert, "Second Person Singular" (review of *Towards a Better Life*), *The Nation*, CXXXIV (9 March 1932), 289–290.
19. Grattan, C. Hartley, "A Novel Not a Novel" (review of *Towards a Better Life*), *The Saturday Review of Literature*, VII (19 March 1932), 604.
20. Munson, Gorham B. "The Fledgling Years, 1916–1924," *The Sewanee Review*, XL (January–March 1932), 24–54.
21. Schneider, Isidor, Review of *Towards a Better Life*, *The Bookman*, LXXV (April 1932), 101–102.
22. Warren, Austin, "Kenneth Burke: His Mind and Art," *The Sewanee Review*, XLI (1933), 225–236, 344–364.
23. Johnson, Edgar, "The Artist and His World" (commentary on part of *Permanence and Change*), *The New Republic*, LXXX (1934), 109–110.
24. Krutch, Joseph Wood, "Marx as Metaphor" (review of *Permanence and Change*), *The Nation*, CXL (17 April 1935), 453–454.
25. Hazlitt, Henry, "Kenneth Burke's Metaphysics" (review of *Permanence and Change*), *The New York Times Book Review*, 5 May 1935, p. 19.
26. Bates, Ernest Sutherland, "A Spendthrift with Ideas" (review of *Permanence and Change*), *The New York Herald Tribune Books*, 12 May 1935, p. 8.
27. Johnson, Edgar, "Society and the Poetic Mind" (review of *Permanence and Change*), *The Saturday Review of Literature*, XII (26 October 1935), 22.
28. Blackmur, R. P., "A Critic's Job of Work," first published in 1935; reprinted in *Language as Gesture*, New York: Harcourt, Brace and Company, 1952, pp. 391–394.
29. Warren, Austin, "The Sceptic's Progress" (essay-review of *Permanence and Change*), *The American Review*, VI (1935–36), 193–213.
30. Rosenberg, Harold, "Meaning and Communication" (review of *Permanence and Change*), *Poetry*, XLVII (March 1936), 347–349.
31. Tate, Allen, "Mr. Burke and the Historical Environment," *The Southern Review*, II (1936–37), 363–372.
32. Glicksberg, Charles I., "Kenneth Burke: The Critic's Critic," *The South Atlantic Quarterly*, XXXVI (1937), 74–84.
33. DuBois, Arthur E., "Accepting and Rejecting Kenneth Burke" (commentary on part of *Attitudes toward History*), *The Sewanee Review*, XLV (1937), 343–356.
34. Gonklin, Groff, "The Science of Symbology" (review of *Attitudes toward History*), *The New Masses*, XXIV (10 August 1937), 25–26.
35. Brinton, Crane, "What Is History" (review of *Attitudes toward History*), *The Saturday Review of Literature*, XVI (14 August 1937), 3–4, 11.
36. Eliot, T. D., Review of *Permanence and Change*, *American Sociological Review*, II (1937), 114–115.
37. Vivas, Eliseo, "Toward an Improved Strategy" (review of *Attitudes toward History*), *The Nation*, CXLV (25 December 1937), 723.
38. Winters, Yvor, "Primitivism and Decadence: A Study of American Experimental Poetry," first published in 1937; reprinted in *In Defense of Reason*, Denver: Alan Swallow, 1947, pp. 30–89 *passim*.
39. Hook, Sidney, "The Technique of Mystification" (review of *Attitudes toward History*), *Partisan Review*, IV (December 1937), 57–62.
40. Hook, Sidney, "Kenneth Burke and Sidney Hook: An Exchange" (an exchange of letters between Burke and Hook concerning Hook's review), *Partisan Review*, IV (January 1938), 40–47.

41. Wirth, Louis, Review of *Permanence and Change, The American Journal of Sociology*, XLIII (1937–38), 483–486.
42. Schlauch, Margaret, Review of *Attitudes toward History, Science & Society*, II (1937–38), 128–132.
43. Schlauch, Margaret, "A Reply to Kenneth Burke" (commentary on Burke's "Twelve Propositions," which had been written in reply to Miss Schlauch's review), *Science & Society*, II (1937–38), 250–253.
44. McGill, V. J., "Comments on Burke's Propositions" (commentary on the Burke-Schlauch altercation; see numbers 42–43), *Science & Society*, II (1937–38), 253–256.
45. Parkes, Henry Bamford, "Kenneth Burke" (essay-review of *Attitudes toward History*), first published in 1938; reprinted in *The Pragmatic Test: Essays on the History of Ideas*, San Francisco: Colt Press, 1941, pp. 202–220.
46. Smith, Bernard, *Forces in American Criticism: A Study in the History of American Literary Thought*, New York: Harcourt, Brace and Company, 1939, pp. 374, 375, 378, 379, 384, 385.
47. Auden, W. H., "A Grammar of Assent" (review of *The Philosophy of Literary Form*), *The New Republic*, CV (14 July 1941), 59.
48. Guerard, Albert, "Critics Make Us Think" (review of *The Philosophy of Literary Form*), *The New York Herald Tribune Books*, 26 October 1941, p. 25.
49. Buchler, Justus, "Literature as Symbolic Action" (review of *The Philosophy of Literary Form*), *The New York Times Book Review*, 30 November 1941, p. 36.
50. Knickerbocker, William S., "Wam for Maw: Dogma versus Discursiveness in Criticism" (review of *The Philosophy of Literary Form* and J. C. Ransom's *The New Criticism*), *The Sewanee Review*, XLIX (1941), 520–536.
51. Slochower, Harry, "Kenneth Burke's Philosophy of Symbolic Action" (review-essay of *The Philosophy of Literary Form*), *The University Review*, VIII (Winter 1941), 119–123.
52. Smith, Jeffrey, Review of *The Philosophy of Literary Form, The Journal of Philosophy*, XXXIII (1941), 719–720.
53. G[reenberg], C[lement], Review of *The Philosophy of Literary Form, Partisan Review*, VIII (November–December 1941), 515–516.
54. Kuhn, Helmut, Review of *The Philosophy of Literary Form, Philosophy and Phenomenological Research*, II (1941–42), 223–226.
55. Hayakawa, S. I., "The Linguistic Approach to Poetry" (review of *The Philosophy of Literary Form*), *Poetry*, LX (1942), 86–94.
56. Ransom, John Crowe, "An Address to Kenneth Burke" (commentary on *The Philosophy of Literary Form*), *The Kenyon Review*, IV (1942), 219–237.
57. Millet, Fred B., Review of *The Philosophy of Literary Form, American Literature*, XIV (1942–43), 323–325.
58. Blackmur, R. P., "Language as Gesture," first published in 1943; reprinted in *Language as Gesture*, New York: Harcourt, Brace and Company, 1952, pp. 3–4.
59. Hoffman, Frederick J., "The Problem of Influence," *Freudianism and the Literary Mind*, Baton Rouge: Louisiana State University Press, 1945, pp. 102–104.
60. Slochower, Harry, *No Voice Is Wholly Lost: Writers and Thinkers in War and Peace*, New York: Creative Age Press, 1945, see p. vi.
61. Golffing, Francis C., "Kenneth Burke's Dramatistic Criticism" (review of *A Grammar of Motives*), *Poetry*, LXVII (1945–46), 338–341.
62. Ransom, John Crowe, "Mr. Burke's Dialectic" (review of *A Grammar of Motives*), *The New Republic*, CXIV (18 February 1946), 257–258.
63. Guerard, Albert, "Key Terms of Human Conduct" (review of *A Grammar of Motives*), *The New York Herald Tribune Books*, 10 March 1946, p. 20.
64. Tyler, Parker, "Towards a Greater Literary Criticism" (review of *A Grammar of Motives*), *View*, May 1946, pp. 21–22.
65. Freemantle, Anne, Review of *A Grammar of Motives, The Commonweal*, XLIV (17 May 1946), 120–122.

66. Morris, Charles, "The Strategy of Kenneth Burke" (review of *A Grammar of Motives*), *The Nation*, CLXIII (27 July 1946), 106.
67. Black, Max, Review of *A Grammar of Motives, The Philosophical Review*, LV (July 1946), 487–490.
68. Duffey, Bernard, "The Dialectic of Dialectic" (review of *A Grammar of Motives*), *The Rocky Mountain Review*, X (Summer 1946), 225–227.
69. Sargent, S. S., "Of Words and Meaning" (review of *A Grammar of Motives*), *The New York Times Book Review*, 4 August 1946, p. 23.
70. Fergusson, Francis, "Kenneth Burke's *Grammar of Motives*" (essay-review of *A Grammar of Motives*), first published in 1946; reprinted in *The Human Image in Dramatic Literature*, Garden City, N.Y.: Doubleday Anchor Books, 1957, pp. 193–204.
71. Rosenfeld, Isaac, "Dry Watershed" (review of *A Grammar of Motives*), *The Kenyon Review*, VIII (1946), pp. 310–317. Reprinted as "Kenneth Burke's *A Grammar of Motives*" in *An Age of Enormity: Life and Writing in the Forties and Fifties*, Cleveland and New York: World Publishing Company, 1962, pp. 155–164.
72. Stauffer, Donald A., "Salvation through Semantics" (review of *A Grammar of Motives*), *The Virginia Quarterly Review*, XXII (1946), 454–460.
73. Hoffman, Frederick J., Charles Allen, and Carolyn F. Ulrich, *The Little Magazine: A History and a Bibliography*, Princeton, N.J.: Princeton University Press, 1946, *passim* (see the index).
74. Faris, Robert E. L., Review of *A Grammar of Motives, The American Journal of Sociology*, LII (1946–47), 449–450.
75. Kaplan, Abraham, Review of *A Grammar of Motives, Journal of Aesthetics and Art Criticism*, V (March 1947), 233–234.
76. Nemerov, Howard, "The Agon of Will as Idea: A Note on the Terms of Kenneth Burke," *Furioso*, II (Spring 1947), 29–42.
77. Benne, Kenneth D., "Toward a Grammar of Educational Motives" (essay-review of *A Grammar of Motives*), *Educational Forum*, XI (1947), 233–239.
78. Pollock, Thomas Clark, Review of *A Grammar of Motives, American Literature*, XIX (1947–48), 374–376.
79. Elton, William, *A Guide to the New Criticism*, first published in 1948; rev. ed., Chicago: Modern Poetry Association, 1953, *passim*.
80. Hyman, Stanley Edgar, "Kenneth Burke and the Criticism of Symbolic Action," *The Armed Vision: A Study in the Methods of Modern Literary Criticism*, first published in 1948; rev. ed., abridged by the author, New York: Vintage Books, 1955, pp. 327–385 (see also the index; Burke is everywhere in this book).
81. Duffey, Bernard, "Reality as Language: Kenneth Burke's Theory of Poetry," *Western Review*, XII (Spring 1948), 132–145.
82. Bewley, Marius, "Kenneth Burke as Literary Critic," first published in 1948; reprinted in *The Complex Fate*, London: Chatto and Windus, 1952, pp. 211–243.
83. Tate, Allen, "A Note on Autotelism," *The Kenyon Review*, XI (Winter 1949), 13–16.
84. Blackmur, R. P., "The Lion and the Honeycomb," first published in 1950; reprinted in *The Lion and the Honeycomb*, New York: Harcourt, Brace and Company, 1955, pp. 193–195.
85. Cowley, Malcolm, "Prolegomena to Kenneth Burke" (review of *A Rhetoric of Motives*), *The New Republic*, CXXII (5 June 1950), 18–19.
86. Stauffer, Donald A., "The Key Is Substance" (review of *A Rhetoric of Motives*), *The New York Times Book Review*, 11 June 1950, p. 30.
87. Guerard, Albert, "Kenneth Burke and an End to Rhetoric" (review of *A Rhetoric of Motives*), *The New York Herald Tribune Books*, 23 July 1950, p. 8.
88. Chase, Richard, "Rhetoric of Rhetoric" (review of *A Rhetoric of Motives*), *Partisan Review*, XVII (September–October 1950), 736–739.
89. E[hinger], D[ouglas], Review of *A Rhetoric of Motives, The Quarterly Journal of Speech*, XXXVI (1950), 557–558.

90. Copeland, Thomas W., "Critics at Work" (review of *A Rhetoric of Motives* and two other books), *The Yale Review*, XL (1950–51), 167–169.
91. Duncan, Hugh Dalziel, Review of *A Rhetoric of Motives, The American Journal of Sociology*, LVI (1950–51), 592–594.
92. "American Scholar Forum: The New Criticism" (a discussion of the New Criticism by William Barrett, Kenneth Burke, Malcolm Cowley, Robert Gorham Davis, and Hiram Haydn), *The American Scholar*, XX (Winter and Spring 1950–51), 86–104, 218–231.
93. Cowley, Malcolm, *Exile's Return: A Literary Odyssey of the 1920's*, rev. ed., New York: The Viking Press, 1951, *passim* (see the index; Burke is pervasive.)
94. Glicksberg, Charles I., "Kenneth Burke," *American Literary Criticism 1900–1950*, New York: Hendricks House, 1951, pp. 307–309.
95. Sachs, David, "Burke's Rhetoric" (review of *A Rhetoric of Motives*), *Poetry*, LXXVII (February 1951), 295–304.
96. Lansner, Kermit, "Burke, Burke, the Lurk" (essay-review of *A Rhetoric of Motives*), *The Kenyon Review*, XIII (1951), 324–335.
97. Duffey, Bernard, "A Universe of Discourse" (review of *A Rhetoric of Motives*), *Western Review*, XV (Summer 1951), 313–316.
98. Hochmuth [Nichols], Marie, "Kenneth Burke and the 'New Rhetoric,'" *The Quarterly Journal of Speech*, XXXVIII (1952), 133–144.
99. Quinn, J. J., Review of *Counter-Statement*, 2nd ed., *Thought*, XXVIII (1953), 469–470.
100. Holland, L. Virginia, "Rhetorical Criticism: A Burkeian Method," *The Quarterly Journal of Speech*, XXXIX (1953), 444–450.
101. Cowley, Malcolm, "A Critic's First Principles" (review of *Counter-Statement*, 2nd ed.), *The New Republic*, CXXIX (14 December 1953), 16–17.
102. Washburn, Richard Kirk, "Burke on Motives and Rhetoric," *Approach*, No. 9, 1953, pp. 2–6.
103. Duncan, Hugh Dalziel, *Language and Literature in Society*, Chicago: University of Chicago Press, 1953; New York: Bedminster Press, 1961, *passim* (see the index and notes; Burke is everywhere).
104. Blau, Herbert, "Kenneth Burke: Tradition and the Individual Critic," *American Quarterly*, VI (1954), 323–336.
105. Ford, Newell F., "Kenneth Burke and Robert Penn Warren: Criticism by Obsessive Metaphor," *Journal of English and Germanic Philology*, LIII (1954), 172–177.
106. "Literary Criticism: The Minds behind the Written Word," *The Times Literary Supplement*, 17 December 1954, pp. viii, x.
107. Meyer, Gerard Previn, "The Enemy of Bureaucracy," (review of *Book of Moments*), *The Saturday Review*, XXXVIII (3 September 1955), 28–29.
108. Ciardi, John, "The Critic in Love" (review of *Book of Moments*), *The Nation*, CLXXXI (8 October 1955), 307–308.
109. Davie, Donald, Review of *Book of Moments, Shenandoah*, VII (Autumn 1955), 93–95.
110. Holland, L. Virginia, "Kenneth Burke's Dramatistic Approach in Speech Criticism," *The Quarterly Journal of Speech*, XLI (1955), 352–358.
111. Holman, C. Hugh, "The Defense of Art Criticism since 1930," *The Development of American Literary Criticism*, ed. Floyd Stoval, Chapel Hill: University of North Carolina Press, 1955, pp. 231–232, 239, 240.
112. Blum, W. C. "A Poetry of Perspectives" (review of *Book of Moments*), *Poetry*, LXXXVII (March 1956), 362–366.
113. Moore, Marianne, "A Grammarian of Motives" (review of *Book of Moments*), first published in 1956; reprinted in *A Marianne Moore Reader*, New York: The Viking Press, 1961, pp. 233–237.
114. Knox, George, *Critical Moments: Kenneth Burke's Categories and Critiques*, Seattle: University of Washington Press, 1957.

115. Duncan, Hugh Dalziel, "Sociology of Art, Literature and Music: Social Contexts of Symbolic Experience," *Modern Sociological Theory*, ed. Howard Becker and Alvin Boskoff, New York: Dryden Press, 1957, pp. 482–497.
116. Meadows, Paul, "The Semiotic of Kenneth Burke," *Philosophy and Phenomenological Research*, XVIII (1957), 80–87.
117. Adams, Robert M., *Strains of Discord: Studies in Literary Openness*, Ithaca, N.Y.: Cornell University Press, 1958, pp. 7–8, 210.
118. Holland, L. Virginia, *Counterpoint: Kenneth Burke and Aristotle's Theories of Rhetoric*, New York: Philosophical Library, 1959.
119. Fogarty, Daniel, S.J., "Kenneth Burke's Theory" and "Choices and Possibilities for a New Rhetoric," *Roots for a New Rhetoric*, New York: Bureau of Publications, Teachers College, Columbia University, 1959, pp. 56–87, 116–140.
120. Mills, C. Wright, *The Sociological Imagination*, New York: Oxford University Press, 1959, see the Appendix, "On Intellectual Craftsmanship."
121. Fraiberg, Louis, "Kenneth Burke's Terminological Medium of Exchange," *Psychoanalysis and American Literary Criticism*, Detroit: Wayne State University Press, 1960, pp. 183–201.
122. Donohoe, James, Review of *Attitudes toward History*, rev. ed., *Arizona Quarterly*, XVI (1960), 286–287.
123. Day, Dennis G., "Persuasion and the Concept of Identification," *The Quarterly Journal of Speech*, XLVI (1960), 270–273.
124. Kirk, John W., "Kenneth Burke and Identification" (reply to number 122), *The Quarterly Journal of Speech*, XLVII (1961), 414–415.
125. Day, Dennis G., "Kenneth Burke and Identification — A Reply" (reply to number 123), *The Quarterly Journal of Speech*, XLVII (1961), 415–416.
126. Aaron, Daniel, "The Vagaries of Kenneth Burke," *Writers on the Left: Episodes in American Literary Communism*, New York: Harcourt, Brace and World, 1961, pp. 287–290.
127. Rippy, Merrill, Review of *Attitudes toward History* and David Levin's *History as Romantic Art, New Mexico Quarterly*, XXX (1960–61), 104–106.
128. Wellek, René, "The Main Trends of Twentieth-Century Criticism," *The Yale Review*, LI (Autumn 1961), 102–119 (see p. 109 for the specific remarks on Burke).
129. Kaelin, Eugene F., *An Existentialist Aesthetic: The Theories of Sarto and Merleau-Ponty*, Madison: University of Wisconsin Press, 1962, pp. 97–98, 100, 103.
130. Rueckert, William H., "Burke's Verbal Drama" (review of *The Rhetoric of Religion*), *The Nation*, CXCIV (1962), 150.
131. Duncan, Hugh Dalziel, *Communication and Social Order*, New York: Bedminster Press, 1962; Galaxy ed., New York: Oxford University Press, 1968, *passim* (see the index; Duncan has simply absorbed Burke and used him in his own work in sociology — no listing of pages could indicate the extent to which this book is Burkeian).
132. Josephson, Matthew, *Life among the Surrealists: A Memoir*, New York: Holt, Rinehart and Winston, 1962, *passim* (see the index).
133. De Mott, Benjamin, "The Little Red Discount House" (review of *The Rhetoric of Religion* and Stanley Edgar Hyman's very Burkeian book, *The Tangled Bank*), *The Hudson Review*, XV (1962), 551–564.
134. Sutton, Walter, *Modern American Criticism*, Englewood Cliffs, N.J.: Prentice-Hall, 1963, *passim* (see the index).
135. Rueckert, William H., *Kenneth Burke and the Drama of Human Relations*, Minneapolis: University of Minnesota Press, 1963.
136. Gusfield, Joseph R., "A Dramatistic Theory of Status Politics," *Symbolic Crusade: Status Politics and the American Temperance Movement*, Urbana, Ill.: University of Illinois Press, 1963, pp. 165–188.
137. Nichols, Marie Hochmuth, "Kenneth Burke: Rhetorical and Critical Theory," *Rhetoric and Criticism*, Baton Rouge: Louisiana State University Press, 1963, pp. 79–93.

138. Wasserstrom, William, *The Time of the Dial,* Syracuse: Syracuse University Press, 1963, pp. 123–129.
139. Frank, Joseph, "Symbols and Civilization" (review of *The Rhetoric of Religion* and two other books), *The Sewanee Review,* LXXII (1964), 479–489 (only pp. 484–489 are specifically on Burke).
140. Duncan, Hugh Dalziel, "Communication in Society" (review of *The Rhetoric of Religion* and M. McLuhan's *The Gutenberg Galaxy*), *Arts in Society,* III, i (1964), 93–106.
141. Griffin, Leland M., "The Rhetorical Structure of the 'New Left' Movement, Part One," *The Quarterly Journal of Speech,* L (1964), 113–135.
142. Joost, Nicholas, *Scofield Thayer and The Dial,* Carbondale, Ill.: Southern Illinois University Press, 1964, *passim* (see the index).
143. Duncan, Hugh Dalziel, "Introduction," *Permanence and Change: An Anatomy of Purpose,* Library of Liberal Arts Edition, Indianapolis: Bobbs-Merrill Company, 1965, pp. xiii–xiv.
144. Kibel, Alvin C., "Guilt and History" (review of *Perspectives by Incongruity* and *Terms for Order*), *The American Scholar,* XXXIV (Spring 1965), 303–306.
145. Howard, Richard, "Beating His Systems" (review of *Perspectives by Incongruity* and *Terms for Order*), *Book Week,* 16 May 1965, pp. 15, 16.
146. Fraser, G. S., "Technology and Insight" (review of *Perspectives by Incongruity* and *Terms for Order,* and Paul Valery's *Aesthetics*), *Poetry,* CVI (August 1965), 366–368.
147. Fleming, Rudd, Review of *Perspectives by Incongruity* and *Terms for Order, Modern Language Journal,* LXIX (October 1965), 396–397.
148. Lemon, Lee, *The Partial Critics,* New York: Oxford University Press, 1965, pp. 172–177, 188–199.
149. Winterowd, W. Ross, *Rhetoric and Writing,* Boston: Allyn and Bacon, 1965, *passim* (Burke is everywhere in this book).
150. Gomme, Andor, "Strategic Selection: Criticism by Choice of Terms" and "Burke's Method in Action," *Attitudes to Criticism,* Carbondale, Ill.: Southern Illinois Press, 1966, pp. 38–65, 139–144.
151. Frank, Armin Paul, "Notes on the Reception of Kenneth Burke in Europe," *Critical Responses to Kenneth Burke, 1924–1966,* Minneapolis: University of Minnesota Press, 1969, pp. 424–443.
152. Brock, Bernard, "Political Speaking: A Burkeian Approach," *Critical Responses to Kenneth Burke, 1924–1966,* Minneapolis: University of Minnesota Press, 1969, pp. 444–445.
153. Adams, Robert Martin, "Restorations" (review of *Towards a Better Life*), *The New York Review of Books,* VII (20 October 1966), 31–33.
154. Rueckert, William H., "Burke's Other Life" (review of *Towards a Better Life*), *The Nation,* CCIII (12 December 1966), 648–649.
155. Griffin, Leland M., "A Dramatistic Theory of the Rhetoric of Movements," *Critical Responses to Kenneth Burke, 1924–1966,* Minneapolis: University of Minnesota Press, 1969, pp. 456–478.
156. Donoghue, Denis, "When in Rome, Do as the Greeks," *Critical Responses to Kenneth Burke, 1924–1966,* Minneapolis: University of Minnesota Press, 1969, pp. 479–491.
157. "The American Jitters" (review of *Language as Symbolic Action, The Philosophy of Literary Form, Towards a Better Life,* and Malcolm Cowley's *Think Back on Us*), *The Times Literary Supplement,* 8 June 1967, p. 508.
159. Donoghue, Denis, "Kenneth Burke's Dangling Novel" (review of *Towards a Better Life*), *Encounter,* XXIX (October 1967), 78–84.
160. Frank, Armin Paul, and Mechthild Frank, "A Checklist of the Writings of Kenneth

Burke," *Critical Responses to Kenneth Burke, 1924–1966,* Minneapolis: University of Minnesota Press, 1969, pp. 495–512.

161. Brown, Merle E., *Kenneth Burke,* Minneapolis: University of Minnesota Press, 1969.

ALPHABETICAL AUTHOR KEY FOR THE SELECTED BIBLIOGRAPHY